# Psychotropic Drug Directory 2003/04
## *The professionals' pocket handbook and aide memoire*

# Psychotropic Drug Directory 2003/04
## *The professionals' pocket handbook and aide memoire*

**Stephen Bazire**

Fivepin Publishing

Published by Fivepin Publishing Limited.
91 Crane Street, Salisbury, Wilts, SP1 2PU

British Library Cataloguing in Publication Data
A catalogue record for this book is available from the British Library

**ISBN** 0-9544839-0-1

Printed in the UK by The Bath Press, Bath

# CONTENTS

## Chapter 5 — Drug-induced psychiatric disorders     **371**

## Chapter 6 — Miscellaneous information     **401**

## Index and abbreviations     **408**

# FOREWORD

This the second attempt at the 2003/04 edition. I was gearing up for the first in mid-2002 but life, the world and everything conspired to make completion last year impossible and even the future of the whole book looked pretty bleak. Things, however, took a turn for the better early this year and a couple of unexpected factors then created a window of opportunity to attempt to complete the first revision and add the other bits, so I grabbed it with both hands (or at least with four fingers). If you're reading this, I succeeded.

This is the tenth edition of the *Psychotropic Drug Directory*, but I'm not sure if that calls for sympathy, congratulations or a change in my medication. The title (concocted while on a Morris dancing tour in Norwich, with the help of several not entirely sober friends) tries to describe the contents, and how you should use them. The 'directory' part is because the book contains general principles, lists, issues, advice and references to help you make decisions but then directs you where to go to get the further information you might need, since it would be virtually impossible to convey all the subtleties of a research paper, case report or review in a couple of lines. I have, for instance, added well over 1000 new references to the text this year. If I spent a couple of hours thoroughly reading and analysing each and every paper, I'd never be able to finish the book and would have to give up the day job. So, you really should check papers before making important decisions. I would be hugely grateful for any advice or tips about papers that I may have taken at face value and inadvertently missed the errors, hidden bias, multiple publication, etc.

## Before using this book...

It provides a handy reference source and the sections are subsequently arranged in a problem-orientated manner and with a minimum level of knowledge assumed. Information given should be followed up in the appropriate sources when time allows. References, where quoted, are either of good recent review articles or of specific information. Further information can be obtained by referring to the main paper cited and also to the reference section of that main paper. Lists and references are as comprehensive as viable but could never claim to be fully complete, nor could this book ever be as comprehensive as a MedLine or PsychLit search on a chosen topic. The listing of a drug use in this book does not in any way imply that it is licensed or safe for this use and all information is presented in good faith.

Throughout I have tried to be as objective as possible. It must be up to the reader to make up his or her own mind on a topic but I hope the statements and references will have pointed you in the right direction and the time saved in looking papers up will allow more thought. It is inevitable that some papers are from specialist journals but where possible I have always quoted more accessible journals in preference. If the only paper published on the use of a drug is from an obscure or ancient source this may well indicate the status of the paper.

## CHANGES TO THIS EDITION

Major updates have been made to all chapters (especially a revamp of the tables in chapter 2 and sexual side effects, and more drug-drug interactions) and I have continued to include an asterisk to those sections with new data. The new drugs included are memantine plus the new atypicals, which are in the process of being launched in various countries.

## ACKNOWLEDGEMENTS

Writing and continually updating a book such as this is a tremendous challenge and indeed drain on my stamina and enthusiasm. Subsequently, the continued help, encouragement, constructive criticism and advice I have received from colleagues and correspondents throughout the world has always been utterly invaluable and very rewarding. It is wonderful to know that the book has helped improve the pharmaceutical care of many people with mental health needs. I would thus like to thank all the people I have thanked in previous editions (including back to my formative days in Bristol), the many members of the UK Psychiatric Pharmacy Group who have conveyed continued enthusiasm, encouragement and support, and all those people I have met at conferences and talks or who have written to me. Thanks as ever must go to my pharmacy staff at Hellesdon and Colegate for continuing to tolerate and humour me (although their cunning ploy of moving my office to the other end of the department seems to have helped them). I also wish to thank people who have fed back on the contents and/or spotted ambiguities (including Claus Langmaack, Richard Owen, Mohammed Asghar, Richard Gater, Michel Cutait and Kai-uwe Kühn), Prof. David Nutt, Mr Glenn from the N&N (for sorting out my eyes), Birmingham City supporters for being magnanimous in victory last May, Peter Dingle (for reconstructing my PC when it crashed spectacularly last year), Bryan and Michelle Harper; to John Tams, Vaughan Williams, Emmylou Harris, Richard Thompson and John Kirkpatrick for the company; to Paul Woods, Judy and Wendy in the library, to Helen, Vicky, Andy, Lou, Janet, Wendy and Jill for being challenging, my parents and my godmother Kate Baxter for continuing to show interest, and finally Jill, Rosey and Chris for allowing me access to a study now full of incomprehensible bits of paper, although it's not all mine.

Stephen Bazire *BPharm, MRPharmS, DipPsychPharm, MCMHP*
Pharmacy Services Director,
Norfolk Mental Health Care NHS Trust,
Hellesdon Hospital,
Norwich NR6 5BE
England
e-mail: steve.bazire@norfmhc-tr.anglox.nhs.uk
Website for service users: www.nmhct.nhs.uk/pharmacy
UKPPG website: www.ukppg.org.uk
Declaration of interests:
www.ukppg.org.uk/committee.html

April, 2003

# CHAPTER ONE

# DRUG TREATMENT OPTIONS in psychiatric illness

This chapter lists medicines which are indicated for, or have been used in, the conditions listed and the author would welcome suggestions for further inclusions. References should be consulted for fuller details of non-Product Licence uses.

**Drugs are classified as follows:**

**BNF Listed** — are drugs listed in the British National Formulary as indicated in the UK for that condition. See the appropriate section in the BNF or your local equivalent for a review of a drug's role in therapy and its prescribing details. Much information provided here is in addition to that in the standard texts. The current UK SPCs are available on-line by visiting www.emc.vhn.net.

**+ Combinations** — are those which have been used. They carry the risks of additive side-effects and interactions.

● **Unlicensed/Some efficacy** — are drugs of some clinical efficacy, or are strategies which can be employed but where no Product Licence exists in the UK.

○ **Unlicensed/Possible efficacy** — are drugs of minor or unproven importance or efficacy. Again, no Product Licence exists in the UK.

◊ **Others** — includes drugs tried but where no significant data exists since the original reports. The lack of positive follow-up data suggests a lack of efficacy, although if you know otherwise, the author would like to hear.

♦ **No efficacy** — drugs not thought to be of clinical use.

Information in these last three categories is given to provide help once all recognised treatments have been tried. These classifications are to some extent arbitrary and the information is based on data presently available.

**It is the prescribers responsibility to ensure all precautions are taken when prescribing drugs for unlicensed uses.**

## 1.1 ACUTE PSYCHIATRIC EMERGENCY (APE)

Including rapid tranquillisation. See also aggression (*1.2*), mania/hypomania (*1.19*) and psychosis/schizophrenia (*1.26*)

Violent patients (usually either schizophrenic, manic or substance abusers) present a risk to themselves and others. Swift, safe and effective treatment is thus often needed. Rapid tranquillisation (RT) is defined as the procedure for giving varying amounts of antipsychotic medication over brief intervals of time to control agitated, threatening and potentially destructive patients, usually given with benzodiazepines.

**Routes:** IV administration is generally quicker-acting than IM, which is often little quicker than oral drugs (especially if concentrated liquids are used) and allows physical restraint to be removed more quickly. IV drug use does, however, carry additional dangers and the IM route should generally be the preferred choice except in exceptional circumstances. IM absorption will be more rapid in an active patient than a quiet one. Parenteral (IV/IM) doses generally have a higher potency than oral doses, so 'when required' or regular doses prescribed as 'im/po' are entirely inappropriate. All 'when required' doses should be checked daily to ensure maximum doses are not being exceeded. Benzodiazepines are generally safe by (slow) injection, but antipsychotics can be fatal in moderate doses in drug-naive people.

**Doses:** The need for high doses of antipsychotics is unnecessary, as violent patients respond to standard doses and higher doses may in fact be less effective. Use of concomitant benzodiazepines is safer and more effective than using high doses of antipsychotics.

**Time intervals:** There is little published data on optimum times between doses but in the UK, staying within licensed limits usually restricts doses.

**Conditions:** Manic patients may respond well to benzodiazepines, with antipsychotics as adjuncts. Schizophrenic patients usually respond best to antipsychotics, with benzodiazepines as adjuncts. In substance misuse, benzodiazepines and antipsychotics may be effective, but more studies are needed (Dubin, *J Clin Psych* 1988, **49** [Suppl 12], 5–11).

**General principles of the management of acute psychiatric emergency (APE)** (*B J Psych* 1992, **160**, 831)

1. Obtain a drug history and carry out a physical examination if possible. Unless known previous exposure to psychotropics, use doses at lower end of the ranges.
2. Antipsychotics in combination with benzodiazepines are preferred.
3. Parenteral administration is generally quickest and most reliable.
4. No anticholinergics should be used as this may confuse the clinical picture.
5. Swap to oral doses as soon as possible.
6. Check bp and temperature frequently.
7. Although this can be carried out in the community, great care is needed.

**Potential complications of antipsychotics in APE:*** (reviewed by Goldberg *et al* in *Clin Neuropharmacol* 1989, **4**, 233–48).

1. Cardiovascular complications and sudden death – drugs causing QTc prolongation are contraindicated in patients with pre-existing cardiac problems, and care is needed in adrenaline-driven excited patients.
2. Respiratory complications.
3. Extrapyramidal symptoms, especially acute dystonia (may occur in 10–30% of patients within the first 24 hours and later in up to 50% of young males). Akathisia should be considered if agitation occurs or recurs after antipsychotics have achieved adequate behavioural control, as it may be drug-induced and exacerbate the disturbed behaviour.
4. Acute hypotension (minimised if the patient can lie down) – with phenothiazines and in the elderly.
5. Seizures, especially in non-compliant epileptics.
6. Mega-colon (rare), heatstroke and aspiration.
7. Neuroleptic malignant syndrome – see *1.22* for risk factors. Close observation of temperature should be carried out, especially in early stages. Check CPK.
8. Local bruising, pain or extravasation (common, in up to 30% patients).
9. A depot given inadvertently into a vein may be rapidly fatal.
10. Disinhibition with benzodiazepines, especially in people with poor impulse control or impulsivity, high-potency drugs, young or older age, and pre-existing CNS damage (review by Paton, *Psych Bull* 2002, **26**, 460–62) but remains controversial (controlled study showing no effect: Rothschild *et al*, *J Clin Psychopharmacol* 2000, **20**, 7–11).
11. Patient already taking antipsychotics, where additional acute doses reach toxic levels

**Reviews:*** current therapies (McAllister-Williams and Ferrier, *B J Psych* 2001, **179**, 485–89), 'ABC of mental health: Mental health emergencies', Atakan and Davies, *BMJ* 1997, **314**, 1740–42 (causes, safety, RT and aftercare), reappraisal of current options (concludes that parenteral BDZs should now be the mainstay of treatment: McAllister-Williams and Ferrier, *B J Psych* 2001, **179**, 485).

**BNF Listed**

Drugs in this section are licensed for emergency, short-term or adjunct therapy of, eg. acute psychosis, mania, anxiety or exacerbations of chronic psychosis, violent or impulsive behaviour, psychomotor agitation and excitement or violent or dangerously impulsive behaviour (see SPCs for details).

## Antipsychotics:*
### Chlorpromazine
Chlorpromazine injection should be given by deep IM injection only, at 25–50mg every 6–8hrs, with a lower dose (up to 25mg 8 hrly) in the elderly. The IM injection is 2–4 times as potent, on a mg for mg basis, as oral chlorpromazine, and so prescriptions for '100mg po/im' are entirely inappropriate and potentially dangerous. It can cause hypotension, has been associated with sudden death and is not recommended.

### Haloperidol (see also combinations)*
Haloperidol can be used at BNF dose, eg. up to 18mg/d by injection. There have been some concerns about QTc prolongation potential and in the major study (Reilly *et al, Lancet* 2000, **355**, 1048–52) QT prolongation with haloperidol was only just short of significance and there are case reports of *Torsades de Pointes*. The IV route in acutely disturbed patients is thus at best controversial and should be avoided unless essential. Akathisia may exacerbate disturbed behaviour.

### Levomepromazine (methotrimeprazine)
This highly sedative antipsychotic is licensed as an alternative to chlorpromazine, especially when sedation is needed. The injection should be diluted with an equal volume of sodium chloride before use.

### Olanzapine IM *
A number of studies (eg. Wright *et al, Am J Psych* 2001, **158**, 1149–51; n=270, Wright *et al, Schizophr Res* 2001, **49**(Suppl 1), 250–51; n=270, RCT, p/c, d/b, Breier *et al, Arch Gen Psych* 2002, **59**, 441–48) have shown olanzapine IM 10mg to be at least as effective as haloperidol 7.5mg IM in acute agitation in schizophrenia, with a possibly slightly quicker onset of action (eg. at 30 minutes), no QT prolongation and significantly fewer EPS (including dystonia and akathisia). Olanzapine "Velotabs" produce a plasma level profile similar to oral tablets and do not give a rapid release of drug, so are not a suitable rapid onset alternative to injections.

### Risperidone
See combinations.

### Trifluoperazine
This is licensed as an adjunct therapy.

### Zuclopenthixol acetate (Acuphase)
'Clopixol Acuphase' can be given at a dose of 50–150mg stat, then repeated after 2–3 days (maximum every 1–2 days) after the first injection. The maximum cumulative dose is 400mg per 'course', ie. 4 injections or 2 weeks, whichever comes first. The maximum single dose in the elderly is 100mg. While zuclopenthixol acetate appears as effective as haloperidol in APE, sedation at 4 hours may be greater and there is an advantage of the need for fewer injections (McNulty and Pelosi, *EBMH* 1998, **1**, 56). Onset of action is at about 8 hours (peaking at about 36 hours) and so should be used only when initial control has been established with other agents. Several reviews have suggested that more data is needed to prove an advantage over standard therapies (Coutinho *et al, Schizophr Res* 2000, **46**, 111–18; Fenton *et al, CDSR* 2000, 0525). Care is needed with Acuphase® to avoid it being given into a vein of a struggling or over-active patient.

## Benzodiazepines:* (see also combinations)
### Diazepam *
The recommended dose of diazepam is 10mg IV or IM, repeated after not less than 4 hours. IV infusion is possible. IV diazepam is much more consistently absorbed than IM, which in turn is little faster than oral, and slower than the rectal route. If the IV route is used, it is strongly recommended to be into the large vein of the antecubital fossa, with the patient in a supine position, if possible, to minimise the incidence of hypotension. The maximum IV dose is 5mg per minute. Mechanical ventilation and

flumazenil should be available at higher doses in case of respiratory depression as hypoxic drive can be affected. Diazepam has a long half-life and active metabolites and so accumulation and toxic delirium (especially in the elderly or liver-impaired) must be avoided by use of decreased doses later on. A wide safety margin makes diazepam and lorazepam drugs of choice.

**Lorazepam** (see also combinations) *
Lorazepam is usually given by the IV route into a larger vein. IM absorption is as slow as oral administration, but more rapid in an active patient and IM generally carries less risk than IV. Lorazepam injection may be diluted 50:50 with water or normal saline pre-injection. The dose in acute anxiety is 0.025–0.03mg/kg (1.75–2.1mg for a 70kg person), repeated 6-hourly. Many areas use 0.5–2mg po/im every 1–2 hours until symptoms are controlled, missing doses when excessive sedation occurs. This can be a highly effective therapy. Caution is needed in renal and hepatic impairment and in the elderly, where a lower dose may be needed. Lorazepam does not accumulate with repeated doses nor in hepatic impairment, distinct advantages over diazepam. Short-term lorazepam infusion has caused deterioration, possibly due to propylene glycol, a component of lorazepam intravenous formulations (n=1, Cawley, *Pharmacother* 2001, **21**, 1140–44).

---

**+   Combinations**
Combinations of antipsychotics and benzodiazepines are highly effective and generally allow lower doses of both to be used. Patients receiving only a single drug in APE at first are more likely to need second injections (Pilowski *et al*, *B J Psych* 1992, **160**, 831–35). In the only major UK study, a combination of antipsychotic and sedative was favoured by staff as the most effective.

**Antipsychotic + benzodiazepine** *
(see also separate drugs) *
This combination is widely and strongly recommended as the drugs act synergistically, reducing the amount of each drug (but particularly the antipsychotic) required. The effect of the combination is rapid and predictable and the patient less likely to require a second injection. 10mg IM/IV of both **haloperidol** and **diazepam** for a 'drug naive' patient is strongly recommended, with up to 20mg of each for previously antipsychotic-treated patients. **Lorazepam** is a widely used alternative to diazepam, with 2mg IM plus haloperidol IM 5mg being significantly better than lorazepam alone after 60–180 minutes in one APE study (n=98, RCT, Battaglia *et al, Am J Emerg Med* 1997, **15**, 335–40). No serious adverse effects occurred in either treatment group, suggesting superior efficacy for haloperidol/lorazepam over lorazepam alone (n=20, d/b, Bieniek *et al, Pharmacotherapy* 1998, **18**, 57–62). **Risperidone** liquid 2mg plus oral lorazepam 2mg was shown to be as effective in psychotic agitation as haloperidol 5mg IM plus lorazepam 2mg IM, but with less complications (n=30, Currier and Simpson, *J Clin Psych* 2001, **62**, 153–57). The fast-dissolving tablet formulation ("Quicklets") may be of use for ease of administration, although the peak plasma levels occur at 1.4–1.8 hours (the same as tablets).

---

**O   Unlicensed/possible efficacy**
**Amylobarbital/amobarbital sodium**
Great care is needed if used in APE. The IM route should be preferred. If IV must be used, the vial should be diluted and injected *slowly* (maximum 50mg/min) to prevent sudden respiratory depression. It is contraindicated in marked hepatic impairment.

**Clomethiazole (chlormethiazole)**
See SPC for doses for other indications.

**Clonazepam**
Clonazepam is licensed only for status epilepticus in all its clinical forms but

is widely used as an alternative to diazepam and lorazepam. The dose is 1mg (1ml) by slow (1mg per 30 seconds) IV injection, which is strongly recommended to be into the large vein of the antecubital fossa, with the patient in a supine position if possible, to minimise the incidence of hypotension. Care is needed in the elderly and caution in chronic pulmonary insufficiency.

### Midazolam
2.5–10mg IV may be rapidly effective (6–20 minutes) in controlling acute agitation (eg. report by Bond *et al, Am J Psych* 1989, **146**, 925–26). Great care is needed to avoid respiratory depression when given IV.

### Paraldehyde
Infusion should be carried out in specialist centres ONLY, as it needs intensive care facilities.

### Valproate
See entry under mania (*1.20*), where loading doses may be of low risk and highly effective.

---

## 1.2 AGGRESSION

See also acute psychiatric emergency (*1.1*), borderline personality disorder (*1.11*) and self-injurious behaviour (SIB) (*1.29*)

---

Aggression is considered as behaviour with verbal or physical threats which, if carried out, would cause harm to others, self or property. It can include situational (provoked), non-situational (unprovoked), passive, physical or interictal (especially in temporal lobe epilepsy).

Aggression is not a diagnosis in itself, but as well as being potentially drug-induced (through either intoxication or withdrawal), can be considered a symptom of many conditions, including dementia, personality disorders, PTSD, PMS, trauma etc, or as an expression of a variety of emotional or behavioural motivations. Low GABA levels and low serotonin levels in various parts of the brain are associated with aggressive behaviour, and enhanced noradrenaline and dopa-

mine levels in the brain are associated with increased aggression.

### Role of drugs:
Drugs may be useful in helping control some cases where suppression of aggression is considered important on safety grounds.

**Reviews:**[*] pharmacotherapy (Brieden *et al, Pharmacopsychiatry* 2002, **35**, 83–89), general (Hughes, *Psychiatr Serv* 1999, **50**, 1135–37).

---

### BNF Listed
### Lithium *
Most studies have involved aggression in patients with learning disabilities and a two-month trial at 0.6–1.0 mmol/l may be justified in patients unmanageable by environmental factors. Lithium has been shown to reduce aggression and the frequency of episodes in learning disabilities (eg. Langee, *Am J Ment Retard* 1990, **94**, 448–52), reducing impulsive aggression in patients with organic brain damage, brain damaged individuals (Bellus *et al, Brain Inj* 1996, **10**, 849–60) and in two trials in children with aggression or conduct disorder, albeit poorly tolerated (n=50, RCT, d/b, p/c, Campbell *et al, J Am Acad Child Adolesc* Psych 1995, **34**, 445–53; n=86, RCT, d/b, p/c, Malone *et al, Arch Gen Psych* 2000, **57**, 649–54). Lithium may exert an effect via several mechanisms, eg. enhancement of serotonin.

---

### + Combinations
### Fluvoxamine + antipsychotics
An aggressive schizophrenic improved when fluvoxamine 100mg/d was added to risperidone 8mg/d (n=1, Silver and Kushnir, *Am J Psych* 1998, **155**, 1298).

---

### ● Unlicensed/Some efficacy
### Antipsychotics *
Evidence for the efficacy of antipsychotics in aggression is suggestive rather than conclusive as a clinical effect is difficult to quantify. It may be that raised dopamine levels are associated with aggression (Pabis and Stanislav, *Ann Pharmacother* 1996,

**30**, 278–87), in which case dopamine-blocking drugs may have some rationale. Use of higher doses of antipsychotics are generally considered to be effective only via a sedating effect. A number of drugs have been used. **Risperidone** may have some role (De Deyn and Katz, *Int J Ger Psych* 2000, **15**[Suppl 1], S14–22), especially at a lower dose eg. it was effective under several measures for severe, primary aggressive behaviour in adolescents admitted to hospital with disruptive behaviours compounded by sub-average cognitive abilities (n=38, RCT, p/c, 6/52, Buitelaar *et al, J Clin Psych* 2001, **62**, 239–48; review by Young, *EBMH* 2002, **5**, 11). **Zuclopenthixol** appears effective in severe behavioural disturbances in learning disability eg. 2–20mg/d was significantly superior to haloperidol (0.5–5mg/d) at notably modest doses (n=24, d/b, c/o, Malt *et al, B J Psych* 1995, **166**, 374–77) and at 26mg/d in mentally retarded children (n=15, 12/52, Spivak *et al, J Child Adolesc Psychopharmacol* 2001, **11**, 279–84). **Clozapine** reduced seclusion and restraint rates in aggressive, psychotic in-patients over 12 months, with the effect not related to sedation, although the risk-benefit ratio would be important (n=137, Chengappa *et al, Schizophr Res* 2002, **53**, 1–6). Short-term use of clozapine for aggression in an adolescent with autistic disorder has been reported (n=1, Chen *et al, J Clin Psych* 2001, **62**, 479–80).

---

○ **Unlicensed/Possible efficacy**
**Benzodiazepines** *
These are reported to be effective in episodic behavioural disorders by aborting aggression in the prodromal stage. Lorazepam has been used in resistant aggression of dementia, with 1.5–3mg/d effective orally over several years in some patients (*Am J Psych* 1990, **147**, 1250), as has 1–2mg lorazepam IV (Salzman *et al, J Clin Psych* 1991, **52**, 177–80). Use should normally be limited to only a few weeks to minimise the incidence of disinhibition or paradoxical reactions (review by Paton, *Psych Bull* 2002, **26**, 460–62, although the actual incidence may be as low as perhaps <1%) and the problems of dependence/withdrawal, sedation etc.

**Beta-blockers** *
Beta-blockers have been reported to help control aggression in learning disabilities (review, *Am J Mental Retardation* 1990, **95**, 110–19), autism, schizophrenia and in intermittent explosive disorders. Pindolol 40–60mg/d may be effective (n=11, d/b, c/o, 6/52, Greendyke and Kanter, *J Clin Psych* 1986, **47**, 423–26). More robust trials would be needed to confirm these studies, and potential effects on bp and heart-rate will always limit their use (review by Haspel, *Harv Rev Psychiatry* 1995, **2**, 274–81).

**Buspirone**
Several studies (eg. Ratey *et al, J Clin Psych* 1991, **52**, 159–62) and case reports (eg. Quiason *et al, J Am Acad Child Adolesc Psych* 1991, **30**, 1026), have shown some beneficial effect. A three-month trial at 30mg/d seems necessary, and a transient worsening may occur initially (Stanislav *et al, J Clin Psychopharmacol* 1994, **14**, 126–30).

**Carbamazepine**
Data for the use of carbamazepine in aggression is largely anecdotal, based on the proposed association between aggression and TLE or other EEG abnormalities but one trial showed 600mg/d to reduce aggressive behaviour with schizophrenia (RCT, Neepe, *J Clin Psych* 1983, **44**, 326–31). There are case reports of successful use in episodic dyscontrol/aggression (Lewin and Sumners, *B J Psych* 1992, **161**, 722, a link with TLE being considered), violent schizophrenics, paroxysmal behaviour disorder and the elderly demented (n=51, Tariot *et al, Am J Psych* 1998, **155**, 54–61).

## Clonidine
In an open study, 150–400mcg/d reduced aggressiveness in 88% destructive children (n=17, Kemph *et al, J Am Acad Child Adolesc Psych* 1993, **32**, 577–81), who noted some increases in CSF GABA levels.

## Cyproterone
200mg/d over one month has been successful in several cases (*B J Psych* 1991, **159**, 298–99; Thibaut and Colonna, *Am J Psych* 1992, **149**, 411) but the treatment is difficult to use and presents many problems (Byrne *et al, B J Psych* 1992, **160**, 282–83).

## Estrogens (oestrogens)
See dementia (*1.13*).

## Gabapentin *
See dementia (*1.13*). It has also been used in episodic agitation in severely mentally ill patients (n=11, 6/12, Megna *et al, Ann Pharmacother* 2002, **36**, 12–16).

## Lamotrigine
See dementia (*1.13*).

## Phenytoin
An inmate trial showed that 300mg/d phenytoin reduces impulsive aggressive acts but not premeditated attacks (n=60, d/b, p/c, Barratt *et al, J Clin Psychopharmacol* 1997, **17**, 341–49).

## SSRIs *
The use of SSRIs may be rational if low serotonin levels associated with aggression can be corrected. Aggression in learning disabilities may also be associated with unrecognised mood disorders, eg. depression. **Citalopram** may be useful, as 20–60mg/d significantly reduced aggressive incidents with no deterioration nor significant side-effects (n=15, d/b, c/o, 24/52, Vartiainen, *Acta Psych Scand* 1995, **91**, 348–61) and up to 40mg/d reduced impulsive aggression in children and adolescents (n=12, open, 6/52, Armenteros and Lewis, *J Am Acad Child Adolesc Psych* 2002, **41**, 522–29). A similar effect has been suggested with **sertraline** 50–200mg/d (open, Kavoussi *et al, J Clin Psych* 1994, **55**, 137–41; n=1, Campbell and Duffy, *J Clin Psych* 1994, **56**, 123–24). There is a case report and study of uncontrollable aggressive outbursts and anger attacks (secondary to stroke), unresponsive to other antidepressants and antipsychotics, responding rapidly to **fluoxetine** 20mg/d (Weinman and Ruskin, *Am J Psych* 1994, **151**, 1839; Fava *et al, Am J Psych* 1993, **150**, 1158–63). SSRIs have been used successfully for dementia and chronic aggression after head injury (n=3, Kim *et al, Pharmacother* 2001, **21**, 498–501).

## Valproate
Valproate may exert an effect by correcting any abnormally low GABA levels, and a review of 17 studies (none d/b or p/c) indicated valproate has a promising but unproven anti-aggressive effect (n=164, Lindenmayer and Kotsaftis, *J Clin Psych* 2000, **61**, 123–28). Two open studies have shown valproate effective for impulsive aggressive behaviour in people with personality disorders (n=10, open, Kavoussi and Coccaro, *J Clin Psych* 1998, **59**, 676–80) and in adults with learning disabilities (n=28, Ruedrich *et al, J Intellect Disabil Res* 1999, **43**, 105–11). Blood levels above 50mcg/ml seemed most effective.
**Reviews**: management of agitation and aggression in the elderly (Parks-Veal, *Consultant Pharm* 1999, **14**, 557–60).

## Vitamins *
Nutritional supplements (containing vitamins, minerals, and fatty acids) caused dramatic reductions in antisocial behaviour and violent incidents of young offenders within just two weeks (n=231, RCT, p/c, Gesch *et al, B J Psych* 2002, **181**, 22–28).

---

◊ **Others**
Other drugs tried include **dexamfetamine** (Cherek *et al, Psychopharm* 1986, **88**, 381–86), the synthetic progestogen **medroxyprogesterone** (n=3, O'Connor and Baker, *Acta Psych Scand* 1983, **67**, 399–403), **trazodone** (eg. n=1, Mashiko *et al, Psychiatry Clin Neurosci* 1996, **50**, 133–36) and **tricyclics** (mentioned in *Acta Psych Scand* 1988, **78**, 188–90).

# 1.3 AGORAPHOBIA

See also anxiety (*1.6*), panic disorder (*1.24*) and social phobia (*1.33*).

Agoraphobia, an anxiety disorder, is an overwhelming and disabling anxiety provoked by being alone or in public places. Panic attacks may accompany the phobia and depression may be present in up to a half of patients. A connection with serotonin deficiency has been shown.

### Role of drugs:

Drug treatment may be effective in many patients, with psychotherapy an essential component of the treatment package for many. A meta-analysis of 54 published studies has shown that symptoms are improved by tricyclics, and high potency benzodiazepines, and although there may be a short-term deterioration, this usually turns to a longer-term improvement. The best long-term improvement is from exposure therapy, particularly combined with antidepressants, eg. imipramine (Mattick *et al, J Nerv Ment Dis* 1990, **178**, 567–76). There is a weak but significant placebo response to drugs.

**Reviews**: SSRIs in panic and agoraphobia (Bakker *et al, Int Clin Psychopharmacol* 2000, **15**[Suppl 2], S25–30).

---

## BNF Listed
### Citalopram

Citalopram is indicated in the UK for the symptoms of panic disorder, with or without agoraphobia. The dose is 10mg/d for a week, increasing to 20–30mg/d with a maximum of 60mg/d. The maximal effect may take 3 months to develop. See also *1.24*.

### Escitalopram *

Escitalopram is indicated in the UK for the symptoms of panic disorder, with or without agoraphobia. See also *1.24*. The dose is 5mg for the first week, then 10mg/d (maximum 20mg/d). The maximal effect may take 3 months to develop.

### Paroxetine

Paroxetine is licensed in the UK for the symptoms and prevention of relapse of panic disorder, with or without agoraphobia. It may be less likely to produce 'jitteriness' than tricyclics (n=326, naturalistic, Toni *et al, Pharmacopsychiatry* 2000, **33**, 121–31). See also *1.24*.

● **Unlicensed/Some efficacy**
### Benzodiazepines *

Alprazolam (n=69, 3.5yrs, Kilic *et al, Psychother Psychosom* 1997, **66**, 175–78) and diazepam have been used and shown to help, particularly with anxiety symptoms. Clonazepam 1–2mg/d has also shown significant efficacy (n=24, RCT, p/c, 6/52, Valenca *et al, Arq Neuropsiquiatr* 2000, **58**, 1025–29; n=413, RCT, p/c, 16/52, Rosenbaum *et al, J Clin Psychopharmacol* 1997, **17**, 390–400).

### MAOIs

Phenelzine has been studied in agoraphobia with panic attacks and shown to be highly effective at doses of up to 45mg/d (eg. Buigues and Vallejo, *J Clin Psych* 1987, **48**, 55–59).

### Tricyclics

Whilst SSRIs are now first choice, up to 70% may respond to tricyclics, but with 30% dropping out due to side-effects. 20% may worsen, with an increase in panic attacks. Clomipramine, at doses up to 300mg/d, has been shown to be effective (Johnson *et al, Arch Gen Psych* 1988, **45**, 453–59), with a continuous improvement shown over many weeks. Doses as low as 75mg/d may be effective (Gloger *et al, J Clin Psychopharmacol* 1989, **9**, 28–32). A relationship between plasma levels and response has been proposed. See also panic (*1.24*).

---

○ **Unlicensed/Possible efficacy**
### Buspirone

Buspirone has been shown to be well-tolerated and enhance the effect of CBT in panic disorder with agoraphobia (n=41, d/b, 68/52, Cottraux *et al, B J Psych* 1995, **167**, 635–41), although a subsequent naturalistic study was unable to replicate this long-term effect (Bouvard *et al, Psychother Psychsom* 1997, **66**, 27–32).

◊ **Others**
Other drugs tried include **trazodone** at up to 300mg/d (n=11, Mavissakalian *et al, Am J Psych* 1987, **144**, 785–87) and **valproate** (Roy-Byrne *et al, J Clin Psych* 1989, **50**[Suppl], 44–48).

♦ **No efficacy**
**Moclobemide**
The efficacy of moclobemide mono-therapy in panic disorder with agora-phobia was unable to be shown in one study, although the long-term effects of CBT were enhanced with concomitant moclobemide (n=55, RCT, Loerch *et al, B J Psych* 1999, **174**, 205–12).

## 1.4 ALCOHOL DEPENDENCE AND ALCOHOL MISUSE

See also alcohol withdrawal syndrome (*1.5*)

**Symptoms:**
The main diagnostic symptoms of alcohol dependence are of a primacy of drinking over other activities, increased tolerance of alcohol, symptoms of repeated withdrawal, stereotyped pattern of drinking, compulsion to drink and relief drinking.

**Risk factors:** *
Some risk factors for alcohol abuse or being an alcohol-dependent drinker include:
1. Occupation, eg. brewers, reps, doctors, alcohol retailers.
2. Genetics (up to 30–40% influence).
3. Marital/social problems, eg. work.
4. Personality, eg. anxiety.
5. Psychopaths and criminals, eg. taking alcohol before criminal events.
6. Psychiatric illness, eg. depression, anxiety, phobia etc.
7. Use for hypnotic or analgesic purposes.
8. Adverse childhood or adolescent experiences.
9. Parental misuse of alcohol (n=2427, Lieb *et al, Psychol Med* 2002, **32**, 63–78)
10. Sweet taste preference (n=122, Kranzler *et al, Am J Psych* 2001, **158**, 813–15)

The body metabolises one unit of alcohol per hour and peak levels occur one hour after the drink is consumed. One unit gives a man an alcohol blood level of about 15mg/100ml and a woman about 20mg/100ml. Absorption is rapid with low volume drinks, eg. spirits and slower with higher volumes, eg. beer. Alcohol consumption of 7.7–12.9 units per week is associated with the lowest mortality in men (White, *J Clin Epidemiol* 1999, **52**, 967–75, review by Caan, *EBMH* 2000, **3**, 61), a now oft-quoted finding in bars throughout the world.

**Role of drugs:** *
Pharmacological treatment can play its part in an overall plan. Vitamin deficiency occurs and can lead to Wernicke-Korsakoff syndrome, needing initial high dose vitamins by injection (see AWS, *1.5*). Other drugs may be useful to treat associated psychiatric morbidity, such as withdrawal, affective disorders, suicide and hallucinations.

In the longer term, disulfiram, naltrexone and acamprosate may have roles to play. One review concluded that there is good evidence for the efficacy of naltrexone and acamprosate, but not for serotonergic agents or lithium and controlled trials of disulfiram indicate limited efficacy (Garbutt *et al, JAMA* 1999, **281**, 1318–25, 61 refs; reviewed in *EBMH* 2000, **3**, 15). Acamprosate and naltrexone are superior to placebo for relapse prevention in alcoholics, with comparable drop-out rates, with naltrexone having once-daily dosing but more side effects and acamprosate long-term effectiveness but TDS dosing (eg. acamprosate n=3338 vs naltrexone n=200; review of d/b, p/c studies, Hoes, *Clin Drug Invest* 1999, **17**, 211–16; see also Cornish and O'Brien, *Medicine* 1999, **27**, 26–29; n=157, s/b, 1yr, Rubio *et al, Alcohol Alcohol* 2001, **36**, 419–25; Kranzler and Van Kirk, *Alcohol Clin Exp Res* 2001, **25**, 1335–41). There will always be high drop-outs in trials in alcohol dependence and so it will always be difficult to prove an effect from any intervention.

**Reviews:*** pharmacotherapy (Anton, *J Clin Psych* 2001, **62**(Suppl 20), 11–17), management of Korsakoffs (Smith and Hillman, *Adv Psych Treat* 1999, **5**, 271–78), recent advances (Swift, *NEJM* 1999, **340**, 1482–90, 99 refs; Garbutt *et al, JAMA* 1999, **281**, 1318–25), haematological changes in alcohol dependence (Drummond and Ghodse, *Adv Psych Treat* 1999, **5**, 366–75, 30 refs), GP review and options (Feeney and Nutt, *Prescriber* 2000, **11**, 21–30; *Drug & Ther Bull* 2000, **38**, 60–64, 31 refs).

---

## BNF Listed
### Acamprosate *

Acamprosate is licensed in the UK for abstinence maintenance therapy for up to one year in motivated alcohol-dependent patients. It is a GABA analogue and may act to reduce the severity and frequency of relapse by enhancing GABA inhibitory neuro-transmission and antagonising glutamate excitation (glutamate receptors increase in chronic alcohol dependency), reducing intake via reduced reward, possibly restoring normal activity of glutaminergic neurones, which become overexcited by alcohol. It takes about 7 days to reach therapeutic levels and so should be started soon after detoxification (eg. n=296, RCT, d/b, p/c, 26/52, Gual and Legert, *Alcohol Alcohol* 2001, **36**, 413–18). Continued alcohol consumption negates the therapeutic effect, but occasional lapses do not necessarily do this. Many RCTs have shown some clinical effectiveness; eg. a 50% increase in days of continuous abstinence (n=538, Paille *et al, Alcohol and Alcoholism* 1995, **30**, 239–47), a small but significant, improvement in abstinence rates in the first 60 days (67% *vs* 50%) and at 48 weeks (43% *vs* 21%) (n=272, Sass *et al, Arch Gen Psych* 1996, **53**, 673–80) and as a valuable adjunct to psychosocial and behavioural treatment of episodic or chronic alcoholism (n=455, d/b, p/c,

Whitworth *et al, Lancet* 1996, **347**, 1438–42, 29 refs). Overall, acamprosate is well-tolerated, its efficacy may be enhanced by the addition of disulfiram, as an adjunct to psychosocial and behavioural therapies (including counselling) and can be considered a promising first-line pharmacological therapy for the maintenance of abstinence in detoxified alcoholdependent patients. It is certainly not a miracle 'cure' for repeatedly failed detoxification patients and should be combined with continued counselling.

**Reviews:*** general (Anon, *Drugs* 2002, **3**, 13–18; Mason, *J Clin Psych* 2001, **62**(Suppl 20), 42–48; *Form Monograph Serv* 2002, 191–97, 33 refs), mode of action (Littleton, *Addiction* 1995, **90**, 1179–88), extensive review (Wilde and Wagstaff, *Drugs* 1997, **53**, 1038–53, 62 refs), clinical pharmaco-kinetics (Siavin *et al, Clin Pharmacokinet* 1998, **35**, 331–45, 44 refs).

### Disulfiram *

Irreversible inhibition of ALDH (Hepatic Aldehyde-NAD reductase) by disulfiram leads to accumulation of acetaldehyde from incomplete alcohol metabolism (Petersen, *Acta Psych Scand* 1992, Suppl 369, 7–13, see also *4.7.1*). Disulfiram acts as a negative reinforcer for abstinence via the potential for an adversive disulfiram-alcohol interaction, ie. an adversive/conditioning and maintenance therapy in alcoholics. A review of 24 studies published from 1967–1995 implied that while disulfiram can reduce total alcohol consumption, studies are poor, patient selection variable and compliance low. Maximum benefit occurs with supervised treatment (Hughes and Cook, *Addiction* 1997, **92**, 381–95). The BNF tends to underestimate doses needed so it is suggested to start with a loading dose of 400mg/d, with 365mg/d the average dose used. 'Antabuse®' tablets are dispersible and so can be given as a liquid in a supervised setting (eg. with relatives, neighbours, clinics etc, *Alcohol & Alcoholism* 1986, **21**, 385–88). It can also be given as a twice-a-week dose (ie. daily dose x 7 divided by 2) as the enzyme block is irreversible and the clinical effect lasts about 7–10 days.

**Reviews**: general (*Acta Psych Scand* 1992, **86**[Suppl 369], studies (*B J Psych* 1992, **161**, 84–89; *Acta Psych Scand* 1992, **86**[Suppl 369] and compliance improvement, eg. implants, incentives, contracts, patient information etc, *Alcohol Clin Exp Res* 1992, **16**, 1035–41), efficacy (Hughes and Cook, *Addiction* 1997, **92**, 381–95).

### Disulfiram Test Dose

A test dose is now considered less necessary due to the risks involved and that the mode of action is via a conditioning process.

If considered necessary, wait 5 days after commencement of treatment for full enzyme block to occur.

1. Give 10–15ml of 95% alcohol (or 15–25ml spirits).
2. Reaction should start in 5–15 minutes.
3. Repeat in 30 minutes if no reaction. Reaction shows as flushed face, tachy-cardia, nausea, vomiting, fall in blood pressure. (Have crash box plus personnel available). Usual cause of no reaction is too low a dose of disulfiram. Bronchospasm has also been reported (Beri *et al*, *BMJ* 1993, **306**, 396).

### B Vitamins

Vitamin deficiency is due to inadequate diet, impaired absorption, increased metabolic demand and impaired utilisation. Thiamine ($B_1$) is thus primary and priority treatment (but probably under-prescribed) to reverse the mental confusion secondary to thiamine deficiency (Wernicke's syndrome) (*Lancet* 1990, **ii,** 912–13) but only about 5–10mg is absorbed from each oral dose, via a saturable mechanism.

**Review**: Cook and Thomson (*Br J Hosp Med* 1997, **57**, 461–65).

### + Combinations
### Acamprosate + disulfiram

In one study, alcoholics were randomised over one year to placebo or acamprosate, and could request additional disulfiram. Disulfiram improved the effectiveness of acamprosate, but a high dropout did not allow full analysis (n=118, RCT, Besson *et al*, *Alcohol Clin Exp Res* 1998, **22**, 573–79).

### Ondansetron + naltrexone*

A small study indicated the combination was superior to placebo drinking (n=20, RCT, d/b, 8/52, Ait-Daoud *et al*, *Alcohol Clin Exp Res* 2001, **25**, 847–49).

### ● Unlicensed/Some efficacy
### Naltrexone*

Naltrexone has been well studied and may have significant efficacy in alcohol dependence, but the evidence remains contradictory, particularly recently. Many RCTs trials have shown the effectiveness of 50mg/d, eg. less craving, more alcohol-free days and only 23% relapse (eg. n=97, O'Malley *et al*, *Arch Gen Psych* 1992, **49**, 881–89), especially with limited psychosocial treatment (n=111, RCT, p/c, 12/52, Morris *et al*, *Addiction* 2001, **96**, 1565–73) or just medical advice (n=107, RCT, d/b, p/c, 12/52, Latt *et al*, *Med J Aust* 2002, **176**, 530–34). A meta-analysis (1976-Jan 2001) of 7 studies indicated naltrexone reduced alcohol consumption over 12-weeks (Streeton and Whelan, *Alcohol Alcohol* 2001, **36**, 544–52) and Cochrane concludes that naltrexone 50mg/d is effective in the short-term, but longer, combination and low drop-out trials are needed (Srisurapanont and Jarusuraisin, *CDSR* 2002, **2**, 1867). Naltrexone seems to have little effect on reducing alcohol sampling by abstinent alcoholics but has a significant effect on reducing subsequent drinking by somehow breaking the desire for the next drink. This may possibly be through blocking the pleasure (or 'high') caused by alcohol and reducing alcohol-seeking behaviour

(Volpicelli *et al, Am J Psych* 1995, **152**, 613–15) or reduced craving for alcohol (n=43, O'Malley *et al, Am J Psych* 1996, **153**, 281–83). However, some recent studies have been unable to show a significant effect eg. naltrexone 50mg/d did not reduce alcohol use after 13 weeks or one year (n=209, RCT, 12/12, Krystal *et al, NEJM* 2001, **345**, 1734–39; comment by Chick, *EBMH* 2002, **5**, 80), naltrexone was safe but not effective in preventing alcohol relapse (n=171, RCT, d/b, p/c, 12/52, Gastpar *et al, J Clin Psychopharmaol* 2002, **22**, 592–98) and although another trial showed reduced relapse to heavy drinking this was not statistically significant on any other measure of alcohol consumption (n=202, p/c, 12/52, Guardia *et al, Alcohol Clin Exp Res* 2002, **26**, 1381–87). Finally, one trial came to the stunning conclusion that, while naltrexone is only moderately effective in reducing alcohol intake, its efficacy is far greater in people who actually take it (n=97, p/c, Volpicelli *et al, Arch Gen Psych* 1997, **54**, 737–42). Naltrexone 50mg/d has also been shown to augment the effect of CBT in moderate alcohol dependence in socially stable individuals and may be synergistic with CBT. Naltrexone itself was slightly superior to placebo (n=131, RCT, Anton *et al, Am J Psych* 1999, **156**, 1758–64; reviewed by Chick, *EBMH* 2000, **3**, 75).

**Review:**\* editorial (*Prescrire International* 1999, **8**, 9–11, 12 refs), general (Anton, *J Clin Psych* 2001, **62**(Suppl 20), 11–17).

---

○ **Unlicensed/Possible efficacy**
**Benzodiazepines**
Although not recommended in alcoholics for the very real fear of addiction, benzodiazepines have been advocated if they are able to reduce alcohol dependence (as a 'lesser of two evils' strategy). Any use should be well-documented in the patient's notes.
**Buspirone**
Two trials in anxious alcoholics have shown reduced anxiety, alcohol consumption and drinking days (n=61, 12/52, Kranzer *et al, Arch Gen Psych* 1994, **51**, 720–31) and to significantly reduce alcohol craving and consumption in motivated patients (n=50, d/b, p/c, Bruno, *Psychopathology* 1989, **22**[Suppl 1], 49–59), but no effect on drinking nor anxiety has been noted in two other studies (n=66, *Alcohol Clin Exp Res* 1992, **16**, 1007–13; n=156, RCT, Fawcett *et al, Alcohol Clin Exp Res* 2000, **24**, 666–74).

**Carbamazepine**
A significant long-term effect on time to first drink and survival has been shown (n=29, RCT, 12/12, Mueller *et al, Alcohol Clin Exp Res* 1997, **21**, 86–92).

**Nalmefene**
Nalmefene 20mg/d reduced relapse to heavy drinking in alcohol dependence, supporting the view that opioid antagonists are effective (n=105, RCT, Mason *et al, Arch Gen Psych* 1999, **56**, 719–24).

**Ondansetron**
Ondansetron, a 5-HT3 antagonist, at 8mcg/kg/d was superior to placebo in increasing drink-free days, especially for early-onset (pre-25yo) alcoholism (n=271, RCT, Johnson *et al, JAMA* 2000, **284**, 963–71).

**SSRIs** \*
**Citalopram** has produced a modest (16–17%) but significant reduction in alcoholic drink intake and increase in drink-free days in studies of alcoholics (eg. Naranjo *et al, Clin Pharmacol Ther* 1992, **51**, 729–39), possibly by decreasing desire or reducing the reward (see also n=62, d/b, p/c, Tiihonen *et al, Pharmacopsychiatry* 1996, **29**, 27–29). 60mg/d **fluoxetine** reduced alcoholic and total drink intake compared to placebo and to fluoxetine 40mg/d (n=29, Naranjo *et al, Clin Pharmacol & Ther* 1990, **47**, 490–98), as has fluoxetine 20–40mg/d in alcoholics with co-morbid depression (RCT, n=51, Cornelius *et al, Arch Gen Psych* 1997, **54**, 700–5; review by Haslam, *EBMH* 1998, **1**, 41). However, a larger study failed to

reproduce these effects (n=101, RCT, Kranzler *et al, Am J Psych* 1995, **152**, 391–97).
**Review**; Naranjo and Knoke, *J Clin Psych* 2001, **62**(Suppl 20), 18–25)

**Trazodone**

Low dose trazodone decreased craving, depressive and anxious symptoms in detoxified alcohol-dependent patients (open, n=25, Janiri *et al, Alcohol Alcoholism* 1998, **33**, 362–65).

**Valproate** *

A pilot study showed some promise in the treatment of acute alcohol withdrawal and may help some symptoms of protracted abstinence (d/b, p/c, 12/52, Brady *et al, Drug Alcohol Depend* 2002, **67**, 323–30). Valproate may also be a suitable alternative to BDZs in withdrawal due to its lack of abuse potential (n=16, RCT, 6/52, Longo *et al, J Addict Dis* 2002, **21**, 55–64).

◊ **Others**

Other drugs tried include **imipramine** (n=60, *Am J Psych* 1993, **150**, 963–65), **methylphenidate** (*Clin Neuropharmacol* 1986, **9**, 65–70) and **piracetam** (Barnas *et al, Psychopharmacology* 1990, **100**, 361–65).

◆ **No efficacy**

**Amisulpride** *

Low dose amisulpride 50mg/d is ineffective in preventing relapse in primary alcohol dependence (n=71, RCT, d/b, p/c, 6/12, Marra *et al, Alcohol Clin Exp Res* 2002, **26**, 1545–52).

**Donepezil** *

Whilst donepezil was ineffective in reversing Wernicke-Korsakoff's Disease memory changes in one study (n=7, s/b, p/c, c/o, 30/7, Sahin *et al, Clin Neuropharmacol* 2002, **25**, 16–20), high dose donepezil has been reported to help the memory deficits from Korsakoff's psychosis (n=1, Ing *et al, Alcohol Alcohol* 2001, **36**, 553–55, and n=2, Codina *et al, Rev Neurol* 2002, **35**, 341–45).

**Flupenthixol decanoate** *

After detoxification, flupenthixol decanoate 10mg 2/52 actually increased relapses compared to placebo (85% vs 65% for placebo) and so appears to have no role (n=281, RCT, d/b, 12/12, Weisbeck *et al, Alcohol Alcohol* 2001, **36**, 329–34).

**Lithium**

Three trials have shown lack of advantage over placebo (eg. n=22, d/b, 3/12, Olbrich *et al, Nervenarzt* 1991, **62**, 182–86; n=156, RCT, 6/12, Fawcett *et al, Alcohol Clin Exp Res* 2000, **24**, 666–74).

**Lithium + tryptophan**

No effect on alcohol craving, consumption nor mental state cf. placebo (Malec *et al, Lithium* 1994, **5**, 23–27).

## 1.5 ALCOHOL WITHDRAWAL SYNDROME (AWS)

See also alcohol dependence and misuse (*1.4*)

**Symptoms:** *

The presentation of alcohol withdrawal includes psychological symptoms (eg. anxiety and restlessness), psychotic symptoms (eg. hallucinations), tremor, sweating, tachycardia, gastrointestinal symptoms, fits, illusions, clouding of consciousness and delirium tremens (DT), Wernicke's Encephalopathy (Wernicke-Korsakoff syndrome). These last for about 48 hours after the last drink. Fits may first occur within 6–8 hours after cessation of alcohol use and peak at 12–24 hours (chronic alcohol consumption causes adaptation and downregulation of GABA receptors and upregulation of NMDA, so sudden withdrawal leads to hyperexcitability and hence seizures). AWS may be self-limiting or progress to delirium tremens. In DT, fits may occur (either primary or secondary to hypoglycaemia, hypomagnesaemia or hyponatraemia) as may suicidal ideation, gross disorientation, delusions, violence, marked tremor etc. DT peaks on the 3rd or 4th day, and physical complications are common, eg. pulmonary infection and hepatic encephalopathy. Risk factors for alcohol withdrawal delirium include current infection, tachycardia, symptoms of withdrawal with blood levels above 1g/L, and history of epileptic seizures or delirious episodes (n=334, Palmstierna *et al, Psychiatr Serv* 2001, **52**, 820–23).

**Role of drugs: \***
Seizures and psychiatric disturbances are serious problems and treatment of severe AWS is essential. Withdrawal symptoms in hospital may be underestimated and this may lead to undertreatment. A meta-analysis and practice guideline (Chang and Steinberg, *Med Clin North Am* 2001, **85**, 1191–212; Mayo-Smith, *JAMA* 1997, **278**, 144–51, 175 refs; comments in *JAMA* 1997, **278**, 1317–18) concludes that:

- benzodiazepines are suitable agents for alcohol withdrawal
- dosage should be individualised according to withdrawal severity, comorbidity and history of withdrawal seizures
- beta-blockers, clonidine, carbamazepine ameliorate withdrawal severity but evidence of their effect on delirium and seizures is lacking
- phenothiazines ameliorate withdrawal but are less effective than benzodiazepines in reducing delirium or seizures
- thiamine (IM or IV) should be an additional first-line treatment.

**Reviews:\*** management of Korsakoff syndrome (Smith and Hillman, *Adv Psych Treat* 1999, **5**, 271–78), management of acute AWS (Williams and McBridie, *Alcohol Alcohol* 1998, **33**, 103–15; Holbrook *et al, Can Med Ass J* 1999, **160**, 675–80, 42 refs; Claassen and Adinoff, *CNS Drugs* 1999, **12**, 279–91), anticonvulsants in AWS (Malcolm *et al, Am J Addict* 2001, **10**(Suppl), 16–23), alcohol-related seizures (Ahmed *et al, Hosp Med* 2000, **61**, 793–96) and in the elderly (Kraemer *et al, Drugs & Aging* 1999, **14**, 409–25).

---

**BNF Listed**
**Benzodiazepines \***
Benzodiazepines are the drugs of choice for treating acute alcohol withdrawal (meta-analysis of 11 RCTs, n=1286, Holbrook *et al, Can Med Ass J* 1999, **160**, 649–55). **Chlordiazepoxide** (and **diazepam**) are the established treatments in the UK. Lorazepam is also used, as it has an intermediate half-life and no active metabolites, both particularly useful in the elderly or those with hepatic damage. **Lorazepam** 2mg IV was more effective than placebo (3% lorazepam *vs* 24% placebo recurrence) in the prevention of recurrent generalised, alcohol-related seizures (n=186, p/c, D'Onofrio *et al, NEJM* 1999, 340, 915–19; reviewed in *EBMH* 1999, **2**, 107; plus correspondence from Sosis, Matz, D'Onofrio *et al, NEJM* 1999, **341**, 609–10). Doses may also be adjusted in a more refined, symptom-triggered way, with adequate monitoring of symptoms, in patients with particular needs (Saitz *et al, JAMA* 1994, **272**, 519–23 plus editorial 557–58; see also symptom-triggered out-patient detoxification with variable dose chlordiazepoxide, n=108, Wiseman *et al, J Clin Psych* 1998, **59**, 289–93; and oxazepam, n=117, RCT, Daeppen *et al, Arch Int Med* 2002, **162**, 1117–21). Withdrawal symptoms may be underestimated and hence undertreated. Beware of an extended metabolism in liver damage (see *3.6*) and of respiratory depression.

**Reviews**: chlordiazepoxide withdrawal regimens (Chick, *Adv Psych Treat* 1996, **2**, 249–57), chlordiazepoxide *vs* clomethiazole (Duncan and Taylor, *Psych Bull* 1996, **20**, 601–3), general (Peppers, *Pharmacotherapy* 1996, **16**, 49–58).

**Clomethiazole (chlormethiazole)**
Regarded as safe and effective treatment of AWS at up to 16 capsules/d, reducing over 5 to 9 days, it has a low addictive potential (Schied *et al, Acta Psych Scand* 1986, **73**[Suppl 329], 136–39) but dependence (mainly psychological) can be seen in some patients on longer-term therapy (*BMJ* 1987, **294**, 592). The dangers of toxicity may have been exaggerated.

**Reviews**: clomethiazole home detoxification schedules and counter to the argument that clomethiazole is highly toxic (Sowerby and Hunter, *J Substance Misuse* 1997, **2**, 62–63, 114–17), general (Duncan and Taylor, *Psych Bull* 1996, **20**, 601–3; Morgan, *Alcohol Alcohol* 1995, **30**, 771–74).

## Vitamin B supplementation *

Classic signs of vitamin deficiency may only occur in extreme depletion and so are easily missed. B vitamins act as co-enzymes for essential carbohydrate metabolism. Deficiency of nicotinamide, riboflavine ($B_2$) and pyridoxine ($B_6$) can cause neuropathies. Thiamine ($B_1$) must be primary and priority treatment to reverse the mental confusion secondary to thiamine deficiency (Wernicke's Encephalopathy) (Anon, *Lancet* 1990, **ii**, 912–13). Oral thiamine has a saturable absorption mechanism which allows only about 5–10mg/d to be absorbed. Large oral doses are thus ineffective and adequate parenteral therapy should be routine and is essential to treat or prevent Wernicke-Korsakoff syndrome (review, Thompson, *Alcohol Alcohol* 2000, **35**(Suppl 1), 2–7). High-dose (250mg/d) oral thiamine may be effective but not as quickly as parenteral (n=25, RCT, Baines *et al, Alcohol Alcohol* 1988, **23**, 49–52). A reasonable strategy on the use of Pabrinex (IV, HP), is 2 ampoule pairs tds for 2 days, then one pair daily until oral thiamine can be tolerated (Chataway and Hardman *Postgrad Med J* 1995, **71**, 249). It may be necessary to administer glucose *after* thiamine when administering thiamine to prevent Wernicke Encephalopathy (Chataway and Hardman, *Postgrad Med J* 1995, **71**, 249–53).

● **Unlicensed/Some efficacy**
## Alcohol IV

IV alcohol can be used if aggressive therapy is needed (Anon, *Drug Intell Clin Pharm* 1990, **24**, 1120–22).

## Carbamazepine *

An effective and useful treatment, carbamazepine is probably active via an anti-kindling effect. It is non-addictive and its metabolism is generally little affected by liver dysfunction but may be inhibited by higher doses of alcohol. Higher blood levels would thus occur in the same person than if abstinent, so beware of enhanced side-effects (Sternebring *et al, Eur J Clin Pharmacol* 1992, **43**, 393–97). It can be useful also for outpatient detoxifications due to its safety and lack of abuse potential (Ballard *et al, B J Psych* 1991, **158**, 133), supported by a retrospective study (Franz *et al, Eur Arch Psych Clin Neurosci* 2001, **251**, 185–92).

○ **Unlicensed/Possible efficacy**
## Antipsychotics

Decreased dopamine activity may occur in DT (*Postgrad Med J* 1990, **66**, 1005–9) so care is needed with anti-dopaminergic drugs, as this may aggravate symptoms and lower the seizure threshold. NMS may also occur and not be recognised. Temperature regulation and liver function pose further difficulties (*Postgrad Med J* 1990, **66**, 1005–9).

## Beta-blockers

Beta-blockers such as atenolol and propranolol may be useful in treating some symptoms of mild to moderate AWS, eg. tachycardia and tremor, as adjuncts (Guthrie, *Pharmacotherapy* 1989, **9**, 131–43) and to reduce craving (n=180, RCT, d/b, 2/52, Horwitz *et al, Arch Int Med* 1989, **149**, 1089–93) but are not recommended by all (Neff and McQueen, *Drug Intell Clin Pharm* 1991, **25**, 31–32). The variable kinetics of propranolol in cirrhosis and portal hypertension must be considered (Cales *et al, B J Clin Pharmacol* 1989, **27**, 763–70; comparison with diazepam, Worner, *Am J Drug Alcohol Abuse* 1994, **20**, 115–24).

## Gabapentin *

A gabapentin reduction regimen has been used in out-patient detoxications, with minimal abuse potential and lack of cognitive impairment (n=6, 5/7, Myrick *et al, Am J Psych* 1998, **155**, 1632; n=3, 3/7, Bozikas *et* *al, Prog Neuropsychopharmacol Biol Psych* 2002, **26**, 197–99) and as add-on to clomethiazole (n=4, Bonnet *et al, Pharmacopsychiatry* 1999, **32**, 107–9).

### Lofexidine *
Several studies have shown lofexidine (eg. 0.4mg qds for 2–3 days) to be superior to placebo in controlling withdrawal symptoms (eg. n=23, Cushman and Sowers, *Alcohol: Clin Exp Res* 1989, **13**, 361–64) but in a recent RCT lofexidine appeared detrimental as an adjunct to chlordiazepoxide in alcohol detox, with more withdrawal, hypotension and adverse effects and poorer retention with the combination compared to chlordiazepoxide alone (n=72, RCT, Keaney *et al, Alcohol Alcohol* 2001, **36**, 426–30).

### Phenobarbital (phenobarbitone)
Phenobarbital is an anticonvulsant and may help reduce withdrawal tremors (*NEJM* 1988, **319**, 715–16; see also Rodgers and Crouch, *Am J Health-Sys Pharm* 1999, **56**, 175–78).

### Propofol
Benzodiazepine treatment-refractory AWS has been successfully treated with propofol infusion (n=4, McCowan and Marik, *Critical Care Med* 2000, **28**, 1781–84).

### Valproate *
Adjunctive valproate (500mg tds) may be able to reduce the doses of benzodiazepines in AWS, particularly with more severe withdrawal symptoms (n=36, RCT, 7/7, Reoux *et al, Alcohol Clin Exp Res* 2001, **25**, 1324–29) and has been used successfully as monotherapy for AWS (n=1, Longo. *J Clin Psych* 2000, **61**, 947–48).

### Tiapride *
A retrospective study concluded that tiapride and carbamazepine have potential efficacy in AWS (retrospective, Franz *et al, Eur Arch Psych Clin Neurosci* 2001, **251**, 185–92).

### ◊ Others *
Other drugs tried include **buprenorphine** (for abrupt withdrawal; Fudala *et al, Clin Pharmacol & Ther* 1990, **47**,

525–34), **clonidine** (for tremor, tachycardia and hypertension; *J Stud Alcohol* 1987, **48**, 356–70), **dexamethasone** (as 4mg injections; n=110, *Arch Int Med* 1991, **114**, 705–6), **flumazenil** (for AWS; n=20, RCT, s/b, Gerra *et al, Curr Ther Res* 1991, **50**, 62–66), **hydroxyzine** (100mg IM every six hours; Dilts *et al, Am J Psych* 1977, **134**, 92), **lithium** (for withdrawal symptoms but not seizures; n=12, Sellers *et al, Clin Pharmacol Ther* 1976, **19**, 199), **magnesium sulphate** (*Ann Pharmacother* 1992, **26**, 650–52), **nitrous oxide** (rapid relief of AWS; n=104, *B J Psych* 1991, **159**, 672–75) and **phenytoin** (as a prophylactic anticonvulsant in patients with pre-existing epilepsy; *NEJM* 1988, **319**, 715–16).

---

### ◆ No efficacy
### Fluvoxamine
A trial of fluvoxamine in alcoholic Korsakoff syndrome showed no therapeutic role and included 2 apparently fluvoxamine-induced episodes of depression (n=8, O'Carroll *et al, Psychopharmacol* 1994, **116**, 85–88).

### ALZHEIMER'S DISEASE
See Dementia (*1.13*).

### ANOREXIA AND BULIMIA NERVOSA
See Eating disorders (*1.16*).

### 1.6 ANXIETY DISORDER (generalised)
Generalised Anxiety Disorder (GAD) includes also panic disorder (*1.24*) with or without agoraphobia (*1.3*), OCD (*1.23*), social phobia (*1.32*), PTSD (*1.25*).

**Symptoms: ***
There are numerous symptoms of generalised anxiety disorder (although anxiety can in itself be a symptom of many conditions) but can be classified into two main groups:
**Psychological symptoms** include fearful anticipation, irritability, poor concentration, restlessness, sensitivity to noise, disturbed sleep (lying awake worrying, waking intermittently,

unpleasant dreams, but not usually early morning waking) and poor memory (due to poor concentration).

**Physical symptoms** are mainly due to overactivity of the sympathetic system or increased muscle tension, eg. gastrointestinal (dry mouth, difficulty swallowing, wind, loose motions etc), CNS (tinnitus, blurred vision, dizziness), respiratory (constricted chest, difficulty inhaling, overbreathing), cardiovascular (palpitations, heart pain, missed beats, neck throbbing), genitourinary (increased micturition, lack of libido and impotence), muscular tension (tension headache, tremor) and panic attacks (sudden episodes of extreme anxiety or apprehension).

Anxiety must be differentiated from depression, early schizophrenia, dementia, drugs/alcohol abuse including withdrawal and physical illness eg. thyroid dysfunction (n=169, Simon *et al, J Affect Disord* 2002, **69**, 209–17).

**Role of drugs:**
Anxiolytics used as a 'first-aid' measure are quite rational but it is difficult to assess the longer-term effectiveness of these drugs as anxiety tends to vary for reasons other than pharmacotherapy. The decision for longer-term treatment must be considered on an individual basis, with the risk:benefit analysis varying with the disability caused by the symptoms, age of the person etc. Psychological interventions include explanations, reassurance, support and, in more persistent conditions, cognitive and behavioural therapy (Hoehn-Saric, *CNS Drugs* 1998, **9**, 85–98).

**Reviews:*** general (Gale and Oakley-Browne, *BMJ* 2000, **321**, 1204–7, 26 refs; Hallström, *Hosp Med* 2000, **61**, 8–9; Bell and Wilson, *Prescriber* 2000, **11**, 46–48), practical advice on diagnosis and treatment (Birtwistle and Baldwin, *Prescriber* 2001, **12**, 89–101), anxiety in the elderly (Krasucki, *Prescriber* 1998, **9**, 21–31), use of antidepressants (Scott *et al, Adv Psych Treat* 2001, **7**, 275–82), in primary care (Livingstone and Jarvie, *Prescriber* 2002, **13**, 17–28) and in children

(Coyle, *NEJM* 2001, **344**, 1326–27; *NEJM* 2001, **344**, 1279–85).

---

**BNF Listed**
**Benzodiazepines\***
Benzodiazepines may be extremely useful for chronic anxiety and should not be overlooked (rational defence of BDZ prescribing: Williams and McBride, *B J Psych* 1998, **173**, 361–62). Use of benzodiazepines can be restricted to short-term (up to 4-weeks) or intermittent courses. Prior benzodiazepine exposure does not predispose patients to more severe discontinuation symptoms in subsequent courses (review, Rickels and Freeman, *J Clin Psych* 2000, **61**, 409–13).

Although the benzodiazepines have a relative lack of toxicity in overdose, there is some difference between different drugs, eg. temazepam (with rapid absorption and high sedative effect) and possibly flurazepam have a greater toxicity in overdose than other benzodiazepines, eg. diazepam, clonazepam, nitrazepam and oxazepam (303 overdose study by Buckley *et al, BMJ* 1995, **310**, 219–21). All are capable of being fatal in overdose (especially combined with alcohol) and should not be prescribed for patients at high risk of overdose. Users of benzodiazepines are also at greater risk of road-traffic accidents, especially if combined with alcohol (involved in accidents, n=19,386 over 3 years, Barbone *et al, Lancet* 1998, **352**, 1331–36). A retrospective review of hip fractures indicated that doses of >3mg/d diazepam (or equivalent) increased risk of hip fracture by 50%, especially after initiation and after more than a month of treatment. Shorter half-life drugs did not appear to reduce the risk (n=1222+4888, Wang *et al, Am J Psych* 2001, **158**, 892–98).

**Reviews:** avoidance of dependence (Marriot and Tyrer, *Drug Safety* 1993, **9**, 93–103), guidelines for the clinical use of benzodiazepines (Nelson and Chouinard, *Can J Clin Pharmacol* 1999, **6**, 69–83), advantages and disadvantages, mode of action (Lader, *Eur*

*Neuropsychopharmacol* 1999, **9**[Suppl 6], S399–405; Argyropoulos and Nutt, *Prescriber* 2001, 12, 21–28), CSM warning about driving (*Curr Prob Pharmacovig* 1999, **25**, 17).

> Benzodiazepines are indicated for short-term relief of severe anxiety. Other treatment methods should then be started, eg. relaxation, psychotherapy, treating any underlying depression etc. The BNF (*Sec 4.1.2*) sets out cautious advice for the use of benzodiazepines, eg. for short-term use, not used in depression or personality disorder etc.

## Alprazolam
A benzodiazepine once claimed to have some antidepressant activity, probably due to inadequate trial design (*JAMA* 1983, **251**, 215; review by Greenblatt and Wright, *Clin Pharmacokinetics* 1993, **24**, 453–71).

## Bromazepam
UK black-listed benzodiazepine.

## Chlordiazepoxide
Chlordiazepoxide has a slower onset of action and many active metabolites.

## Clobazam
See entry under epilepsy (*1.17.1*).

## Clorazepate (dipotassium clorazepate)
Pro-drug to desmethyldiazepam, there is little to distinguish it from other benzodiazepines.

## Diazepam
Diazepam is the standard longer-acting benzodiazepine, with sedative, anxiolytic and muscle relaxant properties (amongst others). It has a long half-life and many active metabolites.

## Lorazepam
A shorter-acting benzodiazepine with potent receptor-binding properties. Dependence seems to have been a particular problem with this drug and it has received a bad press because of this.

## Oxazepam
A shorter-acting benzodiazepine (the ultimate metabolite of diazepam and some other benzodiazepines) with no active metabolites.

## Non-benzodiazepines
### Beta-blockers
Propranolol, oxprenolol etc at 20–60mg/d may be useful for somatic anxiety symptoms such as tachycardia, sweating, tremor etc and for short-term problems. Studies have shown propranolol less effective than diazepam (n=26, d/b, p/c, c/o, Hallström *et al, B J Psych* 1981, **139**, 417–21) and more effective than placebo (n=57, p/c, Hudson, *B J Clin Pract* 1988, **42**, 419–26). 80–120mg/d may be too high a dose in many patients and can lead to cardiac symptoms. The best response appears to be in doses sufficient to reduce resting pulse by 7bpm (Hallström *et al, B J Psych* 1981, **139**, 417–21) and in patients presenting with autonomic complaints, eg. palpitations, shortness of breath, sweating, rapid ventilation etc.

### Buspirone *
Buspirone is a non-benzodiazepine anxiolytic with negligible sedative, hypnotic, anticonvulsant and muscle relaxant properties. In general, it is considered as effective as the benzodiazepines in GAD, with a lower incidence of dependence, a better side-effect profile and less memory and cognitive impairment (Pecknold, *Drug Safety* 1997, **16**, 118–32), although it has been noted that the efficacy studies were not performed in patients diagnosed with GAD using current criteria (review, Roerig, *J Am Pharm Ass* 1999, **39**, 811–21). It has a slow onset of action and may be underused as it needs four weeks at 10mg TDS for optimum efficacy. Buspirone possibly acts on 5-HT$_{1A}$ receptors and has no effect on withdrawal in benzodiazepine-dependent persons. Indeed, patients with GAD who have recently discontinued BDZs may suffer more ADRs and respond slower to buspirone than those who have neither had BDZs or discontinued more than a month before (n=735, DeMartinis *et al, J Clin Psych* 2000, **61**, 91–94). It has a low 'peak' effect

and so the abuse potential is low and abrupt withdrawal has not been shown to produce withdrawal symptoms.

**Reviews:** general (Pecknold, *Drug Safety* 1997, **16**, 118–32, 241 refs; Apter and Allen, *J Clin Psychopharmacol* 1999, **19**, 86–93), clinical pharmacology and therapeutic applications (Fulton and Brogden, *CNS Drugs* 1997, **7**, 68–88), pharmacokinetics (Mahmood and Sahajwalla, *Clin Pharmacokinet* 1999, **36**, 277–87, 48 refs; Salazar *et al, J Clin Pharmacol* 2001, **41**, 1351–58).

## Hydroxyzine

A poorly studied antihistamine related to the phenothiazines which may be mildly useful in some cases.

## Paroxetine *

Paroxetine is licensed in the UK for GAD. One study showed 20–50mg/d to be rapidly effective in GAD (n=324, RCT, p/c, Pollack *et al, J Clin Psych* 2001, **62**, 350–57) and a second that 20mg/d was effective on many measures of anxiety (n=384, RCT, d/b, p/c, Leibowitz *et al, J Clin Psych* 2002, **63**, 66–74).

## Venlafaxine *

Venlafaxine (as Efexor XL) is licensed for GAD, but should be discontinued after 8/52 if there is no evidence of clinical response. 75mg/d is considered to be the optimum dose (Melichar *et al, J Psychopharmcol* 2001, **15**, 9–12), and for long-term treatment of anxiety 75mg and 150mg/d (but not 37.5mg/d) have both been shown to be superior to placebo for GAD, showing a sustained effect (n=541, p/c, d/b, 24/52, Allgulander *et al, B J Psych* 2001, **179**, 15–22, Wyeth study; see also n=377, RCT, 8/52, Rickels *et al, Am J Psych* 2000, **157**, 968–74; and Feighner *et al, J Aff Dis* 1998, **47**, 55–52). It is also effective for depression with anxiety eg. 75–225mg/d was slightly more effective than fluoxetine (20–60mg/d) in 92 patients with co-morbid GAD and MDD (n=368, 12/52, Silverstone and Salinas, *J Clin Psych* 2001, **62**, 523–29; see also n=359, RCT, Silver-

stone and Ravindran, *J Clin Psych* 1999, **60**, 22–28). Higher doses can be used eg. venlafaxine up to 225mg/day was superior to placebo in non-depressed outpatients with generalized anxiety disorder (n=251, RCT, 6/52, Gelenberg *et al, JAMA* 2000, **283**, 3082–88). In a Wyeth pooled analysis of the 5 RCTs, venlafaxine was found to be as well tolerated and effective in older adults for anxiety as in younger adults (n=1839, Katz *et al, J Am Geriatr Soc* 2002, **50**, 18–25).

**Reviews:** general (*Prescrire Internat* 2001, **10**, 131–34)

---

## ● Unlicensed/Some efficacy

## Antipsychotics *

All have low proven efficacy and marked side-effects. Some atypicals have been used but the evidence for this currently makes it a costly strategy. The use of PRN antipsychotics makes assessment of the underlying causes of agitation more difficult. Such doses should be used carefully and only for infrequent, sustained agitation (Druckenbrod *et al, Ann Pharmacother* 1993, **27**, 645–48). Thioridazine was formerly widely used but is now only licensed for schizophrenia.

## Mirtazapine

Mirtazapine (15–45mg/d) has been shown to be effective within a week for the symptoms of GAD with comorbid depression (n=10, open, 8/52, Goodnick *et al, J Clin Psych* 1999, **60**, 446–48). 15mg/d may be as effective as diazepam 10mg/d in reducing insomnia and anxiety when given the night before surgery (Sorensen *et al, Acta Psych Scand* 1985, **71**, 339–46; see also an outpatient study (n=40, d/b, p/c, Sitsen and Moors, *Drug Invest* 1994, **8**, 339–44)

## SSRIs (see also paroxetine) *

SSRIs have some efficacy in anxiety, with paroxetine licensed. Lower doses may be needed initially, as drugs such as **fluoxetine** (UK SPC includes depression with anxiety), may increase symptoms over the first 1–2 weeks of treatment. **Citalopram** (mean dose 33mg/d) was effective in 85% patients with GAD, including some who had failed with other SSRIs (n=13, 12/52, Varia and Rauscher, *Int Clin Psychopharmacol* 2002, **17**, 103–7) and also in children (n=17, open, Prince *et al, Psychopharmacol Bull* 2002, **36**, 100–7). **Fluvoxamine** may be mildly effective for anxiety in children and adolescents (n=128, RCT, 8/52, RUPPAS, *NEJM* 2001, **344**, 1279–85; critique by Hazell, *EBMH* 2001, **4**, 116). **Sertraline** 50mg/d may be safe and effective in children and adolescents with GAD (n=22, aged 5–17yrs, RCT, d/b, 9/52, Rynn *et al, Am J Psych* 2001, **158**, 2008–14).

### Trazodone

Trazodone has been claimed to be equipotent with some benzodiazepines, eg. a trial showed trazodone to be at least as effective as diazepam and imipramine in generalised anxiety, although the antidepressants had more side-effects (n=230, d/b, p/c, 8/52, Rickels *et al, Arch Gen Psych* 1993, **50**, 884–95).

### Tricyclic antidepressants

Tricyclics may be useful for persistent or disabling anxiety not part of an adjustment/stress reaction. They may take several weeks to act but may be very potent eg. imipramine may be at least as effective as diazepam and trazodone in generalised anxiety, although the antidepressants had more side-effects such as akathisia (n=230, d/b, p/c, 8/52, Rickels *et al, Arch Gen Psych* 1993, **50**, 884–95).

○ **Unlicensed/Possible efficacy**

### Gabapentin *

In patients with a history of alcohol dependency or abuse, gabapentin 100–900mg/d may produce sustained clinical improvement in symptoms of anxiety (n=4, Pollack *et al, Am J Psych* 1998, **155**, 992–93; review by Norton and Quarles, *Hosp Pharm* 2001, **36**, 843–45, 12 refs).

### Passionflower *

Passionflower has an anxiolytic effect, with a low incidence of drowsiness compared to oxazepam (n=36, RCT, d/b, Akhondzadeh *et al, J Clin Pharm Therapeut* 2001, **26**, 363–67).

### Testosterone *

Undiagnosed hypogonadism presenting as GAD has been treated successfully with testosterone injections (n=1, Cooper and Ritchie, *Am J Psych* 2000, **157**, 1884).

### Valproate

There has been some speculation that valproate may have anxiolytic actions (*Am J Psych* 1990, **147**, 950–51) via an effect of enhancing GABA.

◊ **Others**

Other drugs tried include **barbiturates** (such as **amylobarbital**), **mianserin** (n=106, d/b, 6/52, Bjertnaes *et al, Acta Psych Scand* 1982, **66**, 199–207; Murphy, *B J Clin Pharmacol* 1978, **5**, 81S–85S), **nabilone** (n=5, open, Fabre *et al, Curr Ther Res* 1978, **24**, 161–69; n=8, RCT, Glass *et al, J Clin Pharmacol* 1981, **21**[Suppl 8–9], 383S–96S), **nefazodone** (n=21, open, 8/52, Fawcett *et al, Psychopharmacol Bull* 1997, **33**, 521; abstract) and **St. John's wort** (n=100, d/b, 2/52, Panijel, *Therapiewoche* 1985, **41**, 4659–68).

◆ **No efficacy**

### Caffeine

Caffeine consumption should be calculated (see caffeinism *1.35*) in anxiety as higher intakes can cause nervousness, anxiety, restlessness, irritability, palpitations etc, probably by an abnormal sensitivity to caffeine (Bruce *et al, Arch Gen Psych* 1992, **49**, 867–69) via antagonism of adenosine receptors (*Arch Gen Psych* 1985, **42**, 233–43). One study, however, of chronic schizophrenic in-patients showed no change in anxiety when caffeine was removed from the diet (n=26, Mayo *et al, B J Psych* 1993, **162**, 543–45).

**Review**: anxiogenic effects of caffeine (Bruce, *Postgrad Med J* 1990, **66**[Suppl 2], S18–24).

### Ondansetron

One study showed 4mg/d to be no better than placebo, although placebo response was high (n=97, RCT,

Romach *et al, J Clin Psychopharmacol* 1998, **18**, 121–31).

**Yohimbine***

Yohimbine increases self-rated anxiety in anxiety-prone children (n=32, Sallee *et al, Am J Psych* 2000, **157**, 1236–42).

## 1.7 ATTENTION DEFICIT HYPERACTIVITY DISORDER (ADHD) — including hyperkinetic disorder

**Symptoms:**

Attention deficit hyperactivity disorder (ADHD) is characterised by a developmentally inappropriate degree of gross motor activity, impulsivity, inattention and temper outbursts. Children with ADHD have extreme and persistent restlessness, sustained and prolonged motor activity and difficulty in maintaining attention. They are impulsive, reckless, prone to accidents, have learning difficulties (partly due to poor concentration) and often have antisocial behaviour and a fluctuating mood. Onset is before 7 years of age. Symptoms usually fade out by puberty but learning and concentration difficulties and antisocial behaviour may persist into adult life and may, but not always, lead to poor achievement (views on ADHD in *JAMA* 1992, **268**, 1004–7; *JAMA* 1993, **269**, 2368). A variety of transmitter dysfunctions have been proposed, eg. 5-HT, GABA etc. D4 receptor gene and dopamine transporter abnormalities have been implicated, so dopaminergic drugs may be useful (Spencer *et al, J Am Acad Chil Adolesc Psych* 1996, **35**, 409–32).

**Role of drugs:***

Pharmacotherapy is useful for the treatment of severe hyperkinesis or in those resistant to non-drug measures as part of a treatment package. A recent robust study of medication and/or behavioural therapy in children (7–10yrs) with ADHD indicated strongly that careful medication management was effective in reducing core ADHD symptoms, was superior to behavioural therapy and with some limited evidence that the combination was more effective than either alone on some indirect outcome measures (n=579, NTA-CG, *Arch Gen Psych* 2000, **56**, 1073–86; review by Sawyer and Graetz, *EBMH* 2000, **3**, 82). A review of 25 studies of the pharmacotherapy of ADHD in adults concluded that stimulants are the most effective agents, and these drugs remain the treatment of choice (Wilens *et al, CNS Drugs* 1998, **9**, 347–56).

Methylphenidate is clearly the first-line treatment and a meta-analysis of 62 RCTs (n=2897) shows short-acting methylphenidate is effective in under 18's (but unproven beyond that: Schachter *et al, CMAJ* 2001, **165**, 1475–88; review by Connor, *EBMH* 2002, **5**, 50). Stimulants have an immediate effect, with delayed effect from noradrenergic agents eg. pemoline and antidepressants (Wilens *et al, J Atten Disord* 2002, **5**, 189–202). Lack of response to one stimulant does not necessarily predict lack of response to a different one (eg. Elia *et al, Psychiatry Res* 1991, **36**, 141–55).

There is a natural reluctance by many prescribers to use stimulants in younger children and so mild symptoms should be treated with environmental changes. Moderate to severe symptoms may require drug therapy. Dietary restrictions have been reported to help a small number of children (*Ann Pharmacother* 1992, **26**, 565–66) but additive-free diets (eg. the Feingold diet) have not been shown to be effective.

**Reviews:*** extensive overviews (meta-analysis, Klassen *et al, Can J Psych* 1999, **44**, 1007–16; various, *J Clin Psych* 1998 [Suppl 7], 3–79), general (Williams *et al, B J Gen Pract* 1999, **49**, 563–71, 167 refs; McNicholas and Gringras, *Prescriber* 2000, **5**, 19–29), ADHD in adults (Gadow and Weiss, *Arch Gen Psych* 2001, **58**, 784–85), problems in the management of ADHD (Zametkin and Ernst, *NEJM* 1999, **340**, 40–47, 39 refs).

**NB**. Drug trials need to be interpreted carefully as different diagnostic criteria have been used in different studies.

---

**BNF listed**

**Dexamfetamine (dexamphetamine)** *

Amfetamine is clearly superior to placebo on a variety of key measures, remaining effective over the 15 months in one trial (n=62, RCT, Gillberg *et al, Arch Gen Psych* 1997, **54**, 857–64; review by Hall, *EBMH* 1998, **1**, 86). The "Adderall" amphetamine preparation (see *6.2*) produced an 89% positive response, with good tolerability, in one trial (n=154, RCT, d/b, p/c, c/o, Ahmann *et al, Pediatrics* 2001, **107**, e10). Exacerbation of chronic tic disorder by methylphenidate or dexamfetamine has not been shown over at least 1 year (n=19, d/b, p/c, Nolan *et al, Pediatrics* 1999, **103**, 730–37). A trial of dexamfetamine in adults with ADHD showed a significant effect in the short-term, with more data needed to justify long-term therapy (n=68, RCT, Paterson *et al, Aus NZ J Psych* 1999, **33**, 494–502).

**Methylphenidate** *

At appropriate doses of methylphenidate (10–80mg/d), a large proportion of children (and adults: Spencer *et al, Arch Gen Psych* 1995, **52**, 434–43) with ADHD obtain remission of symptoms. Predictors of a positive response include younger age, demonstrable inattention, normal or near normal IQ, low anxiety (Buitelaar *et al, J Am Acad Child Adolesc Psych* 1995, **34**, 1025–32), high levels of hyperactivity at school and relatively low age (n=36, RCT, Zeiner *et al, Acta Paediatr* 1999, **88**, 298–303). Methylphenidate (along with psychosocial treatment) may improve daily academic performance, by 17% in one study (n=45, RCT, p/c, 6/52, Evans *et al, Exp Clin Psychopharmacol* 2001, **9**, 163–75). The effect may not be dose-related, with 60% responding to 10mg/d, and some deteriorating if the dose was increased to 30mg/d. An additional 10mg dose at 4pm may markedly improve late afternoon/evening behaviour without delaying sleep onset or reducing sleep quality (n=12, Kent *et al, Pediatrics* 1995, **96**, 320–25). The new SR preparations (eg. Concerta XL®) seem to obviate the need for this dose structure, with only anorexia occurring at a greater rate than placebo (n=321, RCT, d/b, p/c, Greenhill *et al, ADHD Study Group, Pediatrics* 2002, **109**, e39; OROS system equivalent to TDS: n=282, RCT, Wolraich *et al (Concerta Study Group), Pediatrics* 2001, **108**, 883–92). The response to methylphenidate in ADHD does not appear to be moderated by co-morbid anxiety (n=91, RCT, 4/12, Diamond *et al, J Am Acad Chold Adolesc Psych* 1999, **38**, 402–9; reviewed in *EBMH* 1999, **2**, 108). Side effects are well documented but may in fact be perceived by parents to be inversely proportional to the level of functioning, rather than dose per se (n=65, RCT, d/b, p/c, c/o, Rappaport *et al, J Atten Disord* 2002, **6**, 15–24). Although some tics are significantly worse with methylphenidate, this is generally not to the extent of contraindicating a trial (Gadow *et al, Arch Gen Psych* 1995, **52**, 444–55) and another study showed that in children with ADHD, normal doses of methylphenidate did not cause nor exacerbate tics (n=91, p/c, d/b, Law and Schachar, *J Am Acad Child Adolesc Psych* 1999, **38**, 944–51; reviewed in *EBMH* 2000, **3**, 31). Methylphenidate's mode of action may be blockade of central dopamine transporters (Volkow *et al, Am J Psych* 1998, **155**, 1325–31).

**Review:*** pharmacokinetics and efficacy (Kimko *et al, Clin Pharmacokinet* 1999, **37**, 457–70, 75 refs), side effects (review, Rappaport and Moffitt, *Clin Psychol Rev* 2002, **22**, 1107–31), NICE guidance (*Tech App Guid* Oct 2000, **13**, 1–13).

**Pemoline**

In the UK, pemoline is available on a named-patient basis only due to serious hepatic toxicity (*Curr Prob* 1997, **23**, 10; Wilens *et al, J Clin Psychopharmacol* 1999, **19**, 257–64).

● **Unlicensed/Some efficacy**
**Bupropion** *

Bupropion (mean 3.3mg/kg/d) and methylphenidate (mean 0.7mg/kg/d) were equipotent in children with ADHD in one trial (n=15, RCT, 6/52, Barrickman *et al, J Am Acad Child Adolesc Psych* 1995, **34**, 649–57), and in adolescents with substance misuse disorders (n=13, open, 5/52, Riggs *et al, J Am Acad Child Adolesc Psych* 1998, **37**, 1271–78) and thus provides a pharmacological alternative to stimulants in ADHD (review, Popper, *Child Adolesc Psychiatr Clin N Am* 2000, **9**, 605–46). Use in adult ADHD has also been investigated. Bupropion and methylphenidate were superior (but not statistically) to placebo in adult ADHD (n=30, RCT, d/b, p/c, 7/52, Kuperman *et al, Ann Clin Psychiatry* 2001, **13**, 129–34) and bupropion up to 400mg/d was clinically and significantly superior (76% improved) to placebo (37% improved) and although the exclusion criteria were unclear, further trials are warranted (n=40, RCT, 6/52, Wilens *et al, Am J Psych* 2001, **158**, 282–88; reviewed by Ferre and Nutt, *EBMH* 2001, **4**, 92).

**Clonidine**

Clonidine is widely used for ADHD. A thorough meta-analysis of 11 studies indicates that clonidine 0.1–0.3mg/d has a moderate effect in reducing core ADHD symptoms (better in those without comorbid disorders), which is less than with stimulants, and associated with many side-effects. Parents' efficacy ratings correlated negatively with sedation caused by clonidine (n=150, Connor *et al, J Am Acad Child Adolesc Psych* 1999, **38**, 1551–59; reviewed by Greenhill, *EBMH* 2000, **3**, 74). Other limited studies have shown clonidine (orally or as a patch, which is usually better tolerated) as a viable alternative to stimulants but without stimulant side-effects (full review in *Ann Pharmacother* 1992, **26**, 37–39). Most studies are small and a large RCT is needed to identify its role (review, Chafin

*et al, J Ped Pharm Pract* 1999, **4**, 308–15, 32 refs).

**MAOIs**

MAOIs are not considered generally as effective as stimulants but may help some non-responders, eg. tranylcypromine has been considered as effective as stimulants but the dietary restrictions proved too difficult to manage.

**Tricyclics**

Tricyclics are considered useful in patients non-responsive or intolerant of stimulants. Imipramine, clomipramine, nortriptyline and desipramine have been used, in doses of 10–150mg/d (mean 80mg). In a retrospective, naturalistic study, tricyclics were shown to be effective at antidepressant doses (n=37, Wilens *et al, J Nerv Ment Dis* 1995, **183**, 48–49), although other authors have suggested that lower doses (eg. 25–50mg/d) are effective (Ratey *et al, J Child Adolesc Psychopharmacol* 1992, **2**, 267–75). They produce drowsiness, sadness and irritability, but are less likely to cause insomnia than stimulants. Sudden death, including cardiac arrest, has been reported with relatively low plasma levels (*J Am Acad Child Adolesc Psych* 1991, **30**, 104–8) and so close monitoring is warranted.

○ **Unlicensed/Possible efficacy**
**Antipsychotics**

Some antipsychotics have been used for uncontrollable and explosive behaviour but their side-effect profile makes them unsatisfactory and potentially dangerous. This potential for long-term side-effects and worsening cognitive learning function usually outweighs their potential advantages. Some ADHD patients were included in a study by Hardan *et al* (*J Am Acad Child Adolesc Psych* 1996, **35**, 1551–56) on the use of risperidone.

**Fluoxetine**

Serotonin function may be abnormal in ADHD (Fargason and Ford, *South Med J* 1994, **87**, 302–9) and fluoxetine 20–60mg/d may produce some statistical improvements in some rating scales (n=22, open, Barrickman *et al, J Am Acad Child Adolesc Psych* 1991, **30**, 762–67).

### Gabapentin *

A number of case reports exist eg. aggression, temper and violence responded almost completely ('a miracle') to gabapentin 900mg/d in a 15-year-old boy with ADHD (among other diagnoses) resistant to other therapies (n=1, Ryback and Ryback, *Am J Psych* 1995, **152**, 1399). There is a report of rapid and marked improvement with 200mg/d as an adjunct to methylphenidate (n=1, Hamrin and Bailey, *J Child Adolesc Psychopharmacol* 2001, **11**, 301–9).

### Guanfacine *

Guanfacine has been shown to be superior to placebo in children with ADHD and tic disorder (d/b, n=34, 8/52, Scahill *et al, Am J Psych* 2001, **158**, 1067–74).

### Lithium *

In adult ADHD, lithium (up to 1200mg/d) was equivalent to methylphenidate (up to 40mg/d) on most outcome measures (RCT, d/b, c/o, 16/52, Dorrego *et al, J Neuropsych Clin Neurosci* 2002, **14**, 289–95).

### Nicotine *

Daily transdermal nicotine reduced hyperactivity and learning problems in one pilot study, but was poorly tolerated so other methods of nicotinic receptor modulation may be worth investigating (n=10, RCT, d/b, p/c, 2/52, Shytle *et al, World J Biol Psych* 2002, **3**, 150–55).

### Venlafaxine

There has been a trial (n=10, open, Findling *et al, J Clin Psych* 1996, **57**, 184–89) and case reports (Peak and Gormly, Willens *et al, Am J Psych* 1995, **152**, 1099–100) of response to 56.25–300mg/d.

---

### ◇ Others

Other drugs tried include **levodopa/ carbidopa** (*Pediatr Ann* 1985, **14**, 383–400) and **thyroid** (n=1, *NEJM* 1993, **328**, 997–1001.

### ◆ No efficacy

### Barbiturates

These have been tried but excitation and agitation may result in a negative effect.

### Benzodiazepines

As for barbiturates.

### Caffeine

Caffeine has not proven effective as a minor stimulant (Dulcan, *Pediatr Ann* 1985, **14**, 383–400).

---

## 1.8 AUTISTIC DISORDER

### Symptoms: *

Autism is a neurodevelopmental disorder, characterised by an excessive or morbid dislike of others or society, not responding with normal human emotions towards other people, a morbid self-centred attitude and with major impairments or abnormalities in language, communication, social interactions, imagination and behaviour. The main features include 'autistic aloneness', poor speech and language disorder development, an obsessive desire for sameness, bizarre behaviour or mannerisms, a restricted repertoire of activities and interests, rituals and compulsive behaviour. Onset is not later than 3 years of age, the incidence 4 in 10,000, or up to 20 in 10,000 if including associated conditions (Gillberg and Wing, *Acta Psych Scand* 1999, **99**, 399–406). Up to 25% develop seizures in adolescence, 75% have an IQ in the retarded range and 60 + % need long-term residential care. There is growing evidence that dietary gluten could be implicated in autism, and that a gluten-free diet may ameliorate symptoms, particularly if implemented at a very early stage (review by Shattock and Whiteley, *Pharm J* 2001, **267**, 17–19). A connection with OCD has been made (Gross-Isseroff *et al, World J Biol Psych* 2001, **2**, 193–97).

### Role of drugs: *

Drugs may be of limited use in treating some of the more severe behavioural symptoms. SIB is common (see *1.30*) and may be helped by low dose antipsychotics, to which autistic individuals seem very sensitive and so lower doses may be needed. A therapeutic window may exist with higher doses counter-productive. Family support, education, skills training, behavioural therapy and social support can be significant aspects of the overall management.

**Reviews:*** general (*Drugs & Therapy Perspectives* 1998, **12**, 5–8), drug therapy (King, *J Autism Dev Disord* 2000, **30**, 439–45; Posey and McDougle, *Expert Opin Pharmacother* 2001, **2**, 587–600), ADHD in autism (Aman and Langworthy, *J Autism Dev Disord* 2000, **30**, 451–59).

---

● **Unlicensed/Some efficacy
Antipsychotics *** 
Low-dose antipsychotics have a role to play. Haloperidol was the standard drug with a good evidence base, where 0.5–3mg/d may reduce behavioural symptoms (eg. aggression and SIB) and improve learning. It may be effective over six months, even if non-continuous therapy is used (n=60, 6/12, Perry *et al, J Am Acad Child Adoles Psych* 1989, **28**, 87–92) and was considered powerfully effective in one controlled study (n=45, p/c, d/b, Anderson *et al, J Autism Dev Dis* 1989, **19**, 227–39). As adverse reactions can be significant, a 'start low and go slow' routine is recommended, although other antipsychotics are usually preferred the treatment of the marked tension and agitation which often occurs in autism (mentioned in *B J Hosp Med* 1990, **43**, 448–52). Recent RCTs with **risperidone** have shown an effective and well-tolerated effect eg. 0.5–3.5mg/d for tantrums, aggression and SIB in autism over two months, with 70% of the risperidone-treated children, compared with 12% of the placebo-treated children, achieving a "positive response" (n=101, RCT, d/b, p/c, 8/52, McCracken *et al, NEJM* 2002, **347**, 314–21). It has also been used in explosive aggressive autism (n=11, Horrigan and Barnhill, *J Autism Dev Disorder* 1997, **27**, 313–23). A review

of 19 studies of atypicals concluded that risperidone (n=133, s=13) may be effective in reducing hyperactivity, aggression and repetitive behaviour (with low EPS), olanzapine (n=11, s=3) and clozapine (open, n=3, Zuddas *et al, Am J Psych* 1996, **153**, 738) may also be effective but there is little evidence that amisulpride (RCT, n=9) nor quetiapine (open, n=6) are useful in this population (Barnard *et al, J Psychopharmacol* 2002, **16**, 93–101). Olanzapine 5–10mg/d (mean 8mg) may be an alternative (n=12, RCT, open, 6/52, Malone *et al, J Am Acad Child Adolesc Psych* 2001, **40**, 887–94).

---

○ **Unlicensed/Possible efficacy
Antidepressants *** 
Serotonin reuptake inhibitors may have a role to play, particularly in adults with strong behavioural rigidity. Children and adolescents may be more sensitive to SSRIs and so once again 'start low and go slow' is the advice. Clomipramine may be superior to placebo and desipramine in autistic symptoms, anger and ritualism (n=12, d/b, c/o, 10/52, *Arch Gen Psych* 1993, **50**, 441–47), reduce compulsions and adventitious movements (n=5, open, Brasic *et al, Neurology* 1994, **44**, 1309–12) and an alternative to haloperidol for some symptoms (RCT, n=36, p/c, 7/52, Remington *et al, J Clin Psychopharmacol* 2001, **21**, 440–44). Fluvoxamine has been shown superior to placebo (n=30, d/b, p/c, 12/52, McDougle *et al, Arch Gen Psych* 1996, **53**, 1001–8). There are two cases of dramatic response of OCD–like behavioural symptoms in autistic adults to fluoxetine 20mg/d (Koshes, *Am J Psych* 1997, **154**, 578).

**Levetiracetam *** 
Levetiracetam may improve some symptoms (n=10, Rugino and Samsock, *J Dev Behav Pediatr* 2002, **23**, 225–30).

**Methylphenidate**
The considerable negative effects on tantrums and moods may sometimes be outweighed by the positive effects

on attention and stereotype behaviour. Two studies have shown a significant reduction in hyperactivity in autism from 10–50mg/d (n=10, d/b, p/c, c/o, Quintana *et al, J Autism Dev Disord* 1995, **25**, 283–94; n=13, d/b, p/c, c/o, Handen *et al, J Autism Dev Disord* 2000, **30**, 245–55).

**Mirtazapine***

Mirtazapine was only modestly effective in treating some autism-related symptoms (n=26, open, Posey *et al, J Child Adolesc Psychopharmacol* 2001, **11**, 267–77).

**Naltrexone**

Three controlled studies have shown disappointing results (eg. n=13, d/b, p/c, c/o, Kolmen *et al, J Am Acad Child Adolesc Psych* 1995, 34, 223–31; n=23, d/b, p/c, c/o, 4/52, Willemsen-Swinkels *et al, Biol Psych* 1996, **39**, 1023–31). Although 1mg/kg/d may reduce withdrawal, hyperactivity and SIB, with sedation the only major side-effect (*J Am Acad Child Adoles Psych* 1989, **28**, 200–6), most other measures do not improve. There may be a therapeutic window with doses of 10–25mg/d optimal in some people.

**Valproate***

Two open trials have suggested some improvement in behavioural symptoms associated with autism eg. 91% who completed a trial showed sustained improvement in autistic spectrum symptoms eg. aggression and impulsivity, particularly if an EEG abnormality or seizure history was present (n=14, open pilot, Hollander *et al, J Clin Psych* 2001, **62**, 530–34; see also open, Plioplys, *Arch Pediatr Adolesc Med* 1994, **148**, 220–22).

---

◊ **Others**

Other drugs tried include **buspirone** (eg. n=14, open, Ratey *et al, J Clin Psych* 1989, **50**, 382–84; n=4, Realmuto *et al, J Clin Psychopharmacol* 1989, **9**, 122–25), **carbamazepine** (eg. Gillberg, *J Autism Dev Disord* 1991, **21**, 61–77), **clonidine** (n=9, d/b, p/c, Fankhauser *et al, J Clin Psych* 1992, **53**, 77–82; n=8, p/c, d/b, c/o, Jaselskis *et al, J Clin Psychopharmacol* 1992, **12**, 322–27), **lithium** (eg. n=2, Kerbe-shian *et al, J Clin Psychopharmacol* 1987, **7**, 401–5) and high dose **pyridoxine**.

---

♦ **No efficacy**

**Lamotrigine***

Lamotrigine was ineffective on all measures (n=28, RCT, p/c, 18/52, Belsito *et al, J Autism Dev Disord* 2001, **31**, 175–81).

**Secretin***

Despite much interest, a complete lack of significant effect has been demonstrated (eg. n=95, RCT, Dunn-Geier *et al, Dev Med Child Neurol* 2000, **42**, 796–802; n=20, RCT, Owley *et al, MedGenMed* 1999, **6**, E2; n=56, open, Chez *et al, J Autism Dev Disord* 2000, **30**, 87–94; Roberts *et al, Pediatrics* 2001, **107**, E71; reviewed by Levy, *EBMH* 2002, **5**, 22; n=56, RCT, p/c, 4/52, Owley *et al, J Am Acad Child Adolesc Psych* 2001, **40**, 1293–99; multiple doses showing no symptomatic improvement n=6, d/b, p/c, c/o, Sponheim *et al, Acta Paediatrica* 2002, **91**, 540–45). It thus remains an almost completely unproven therapy (review by Patel *et al, Pharmacotherapy* 2002, **22**, 905–14).

---

# 1.9 BENZODIAZEPINE DEPENDENCE and WITHDRAWAL

Although short-term benzodiazepine use at standard doses is usually without substantial risk of toxicity and dependence, higher dose and longer-term use is not some without risk. Lorazepam, diazepam and flunitrazepam may be more liable to abuse than chlordiazepoxide, nitrazepam and oxazepam (*J Clin Psychopharmacol* 1990, **10**, 237–43), probably due to the more rapid absorption and higher receptor potency. The SDS (Severity of Dependence Scale) can be used to accurately detect BDZ dependence (de la Cuevas *et al, Addiction* 2000, **95**, 245–50; reviewed by Law, *EBMH* 2000, **3**, 119).

**Reviews**: withdrawal syndrome (Petursson, *Addiction* 1994, **89**, 11455–59), general (Hallström, *Int J Psych Clin Pract* 1998, **2**, 31–34; Ferguson,

*Prescriber* 1999, **10**, 118–21; Rickels *et al, J Clin Psychopharmacol* 1999, **19**[Suppl 2], 12S–6S), abuse (history, nature and extent, Robertson and Treasure, *CNS Drugs* 1996, **5**, 137–46, 59 refs), techniques and outcomes of BDZ detoxifications (n=82, Charney *et al, J Clin Psych* 2000, **61**, 190–95).

**Patients where withdrawal should not be attempted:**

Elderly maintained symptom-free by low and unchanging doses
Chronic physical disorders controlled by BDZs (eg. epilepsy)
Where quality of life is so improved by BDZs that long-term use, preferably with intermitten/variable doses, is justified (eg. chronic or severe anxiety or insomnia and an inadequate personality, people who relapse to alcohol and other more dangerous substances when BDZ-free)

**Characteristics of benzodiazepine users:**

**1. Older medically ill or with spasticity or epilepsy:**
Benzodiazepine usually prescribed by a non-psychiatrist. Seldom abused, doses non-escalated, effective long-term. Care with subtle cognitive changes which can occur.

**2. Psychiatric patients with panic or agoraphobic disorders:**
Seldom abused, doses not escalated, necessary long-term.

**3. Psychiatric patients with recurrent dysphoria:**
Long-term indications for use less clear. Abuse of other drugs often occurs.

**4. Chronic sleep disordered patients:**
Drug may be active or preventing a rebound syndrome.

**How to minimise the risk of dependence:**
(*Postgrad Med J* 1984, **60**[Suppl 2], 41–6, Darke *et al, Addiction* 1994, **89**, 1683–90)

Carefully select patients (eg. avoid especially dependence prone, lower education, multiple drug users, criminal background)
Keep the dose low
Stop where possible eg. use shorter courses
Use intermittent or variable doses
Use antidepressants if depression mixed with anxiety is present

**BNF Listed**
**Antidepressants**
The BNF recommends the use of antidepressants if clinical depression is present, although many antidepressants may be anxiolytic in their own right.

**Benzodiazepines** *
Transferring from the current benzodiazepine to diazepam (if necessary) is a common strategy, as diazepam is a longer-acting benzodiazepine and possibly easier from which to withdraw. Addition of an SSRI seems of limited value (n=230, d/b, p/c, Zitman and Couvée, *B J Psych* 2001, **178**, 317–24). If withdrawing chronic BDZs from geriatric in-patients, short-term (one week) substitution

**Withdrawal symptoms in the dependent patient:**
(*Med Tox* 1988, **3**, 324–33)

1° **Psychological**: Tension (to above pre-treatment levels), restlessness, agitation, panic attacks
**Physical** — Dry mouth, sweating, tremor, sleep disturbance, lethargy, headache, nausea, palpitations
**Mental** — Impaired memory and concentration, confusion
2° **Moderate** — Perceptual changes (ie. hypersensitivy to light/sound), dysphoria, flu-like symptoms, anorexia, sore eyes, depersonalisation, depression, abnormal sensations of movement, rebound insomnia
**Severe** (rare)
Convulsions, psychoses (eg. visual hallucinations, paranoia), delusions

**Risk factors for poor withdrawal (need to seek specialist advice):**

Previously severe withdrawal (including history of seizures) or post-withdrawal reaction
Lack of adequate social support
Elderly or infirm
History of abuse of alcohol/other drugs (*J Psychoact Drug* 1983, **18**, 85–96)
Concomitant severe medical or psychiatric illness (including personality problems)
High dose/longer-term use (eg. >30mg/d diazepam equiv. >1yr)

with a low-dose BDZ (eg. lormetaze-pam 1mg/d) at night to help sleep may be effective (RCT, d/b, p/c, Petrovic *et al, Eur J Clin Pharmacol* 2002, **57**, 759–64). Clonazepam may be a useful alternative.

---

● **Unlicensed/Some efficacy**

**Buspirone** *

The BNF cautions against use as it may aggravate withdrawal symptoms (see also buspirone, section *1.6*). However, one study showed buspirone 15mg/d relieved lorazepam withdrawal symptoms and had no rebound anxiety on withdrawal (n=44, RCT, Delle Chiaie *et al, J Clin Psychopharmacol* 1995, **15**, 12–19). Buspirone (38mg/d) and imipramine (180mg/d) have been used successfully in patients with GAD discontinuing long-term BDZs, introduced before a tapered discontinuation (n=107, d/b, Rickels *et al, Am J Psych* 2000, **157**, 1973–79), so the best strategy is to instigate adequate anxiolytic therapy before withdrawing benzodiazepines.

**Carbamazepine**

Carbamazepine is thought to block the development of drug-induced kindling and hence block the development of withdrawal symptoms. Kindling is the term for prior intermittent low intensity electrical or chemical stimulation which lowers the threshold of response to future low-intensity stimulation (Gorelick, *Curr Opin Psych* 1992, **5**, 430–35). 600–800mg/d has been shown to be effective in benzodiazepine withdrawal in several studies (eg. Ries *et al, J Psychoactive Drugs* 1991, **23**, 73–76), including high dose (up to 300mg/d) diazepam (Neppe and Sindorf, *J Nerv Ment Dis* 1991, **179**, 234–35) and in people with panic disorder (Klein *et al, Am J Psych* 1994, **151**, 1760–66). Up to 800mg/d also reduces the chance of withdrawal convulsions and can minimise withdrawal symptoms (eg. emotional lability), especially if withdrawal is abrupt. It may also reduce the inci-

dence of relapse (n=40, RCT, 12/52, Schweizer *et al, Arch Gen Psych* 1991, **48**, 448–52).

**Clonidine**

This may be a helpful adjunct in withdrawal, especially at relatively high dose.

**Valproate**

150–1200mg/d may reduce the intensity of symptoms in protracted withdrawal (eg. n=4, Apelt and Emrich, *Am J Psych* 1994, **147**, 1990), as well as acting as an anticonvulsant (Apelt and Emrich, *Am J Psych* 1990, **147**, 950–51).

---

○ **Unlicensed/Possible Efficacy**

**Antihistamines**

These may be useful as non-benzodiazepine hypnotics where insomnia is a problem.

**Dothiepin (dosulepin)**

Up to 150mg/d of dothiepin may slightly reduced benzodiazepine withdrawal symptoms but did not aid drug withdrawal overall and so appears to have limited use (n=87, d/b, Tyrer *et al, B J Psych* 1996, **168**, 457–61).

**Melatonin**

Controlled-release melatonin has been successfully used to facilitate discontinuation of benzodiazepines (n=34, d/b, 6/52, Garfinkel *et al, Arch Inter Med* 1999, **159**, 2456–60).

---

◇ **Others**

Other drugs tried include **phenobarbital** (*J Psychoact Drugs* 1983, **15**, 85–95, 99–104) and **propranolol** (*Postgrad Med J* 1988, **64**[Suppl], 40–44).

◆ **No efficacy**

**Antipsychotics**

Low dose anxiolytic use may be useful but may make withdrawal symptoms worse (*Lancet* 1987, **i**, 78–79).

**Flumazenil**

Flumazenil may be useful only in overdose where respiratory depression occurs (*Lancet* 1987, **ii**, 463). The BNF states caution in BDZ dependence.

## 1.10 BIPOLAR MOOD DISORDER (prophylaxis thereof)

See also depression (with section on bipolar depression, see *1.14*) and mania (*1.19*) for treatment of a particular episode, plus rapid-cycling mood disorder (*1.28*)

Bipolar mood disorder is a fluctuating, chronic illness with a variety of presentations and sub-divisions. DSM-IV divides the condition into bipolar I (one or more manic or mixed episodes, wide mood swings), bipolar II (the most common form, one or more episodes of depression with at least one hypomanic but no manic episode) and bipolar III (pseudobipolar, often triggered by antidepressants, and which may present as a mixed state).

**Diagnosis:*** Bipolar disorder is often unrecognised, misdiagnosed and inadequately treated: One investigator showed that 23% of bipolars consult a professional within 6 months of the symptom onset, but 48% consult 3 or more professionals before receiving an accurate diagnosis (10% saw 7 or more) and 34% wait 10 or more years for diagnosis (Lish *et al, J Aff Dis* 1994, **31**, 281–94). The average time from the onset of symptoms to starting maintenance therapy is 8.3 years (Baldessarini *et al, Am J Psych* 1999, **156**, 811), and may be even longer with women (n=360, Viguera *et al, Bipolar Disord* 2001, **3**, 245–52). Sadly, many suicide attempts are made during this latency period before lithium is started, the only proven anti-suicide drug. Excess mortality has been shown in bipolar (n=15386) and unipolar (n=39182) disorder in Sweden, both in terms of suicides and from natural causes (population study, Osby *et al, Arch Gen Psych* 2001, **58**, 844–50), but suicide rates are significantly reduced by long-term medication with an antidepressant, neuroleptic, or lithium, or combinations thereof (n=406, 22-yrs, Angst *et al, J Aff Dis* 2002, **68**, 167–81).

There is an overlap with personality disorder, eg. labile affect, irritability, mood instability, stress, low mood/ dysphoria, so some have warned of over-diagnosing BPD and under-diagnosing bipolar disorder. Poor outcome is associated with anxiety (n=124, Feske *et al, Am J Psych* 2000, **157**, 956–62) and concurrent personality disorders (n=59, Dunayevich *et al, J Clin Psych* 2000, **61**, 134–39).

It is also clear that well-being and functioning is inversely proportional to the number of bipolar episodes and so strategies to reduce relapse must be rigorously followed, especially minimising difficult-to-treat bipolar depression (n=64, retrospective, MacQueen *et al, Acta Psych Scand* 2000, **101**, 374–81). Impaired verbal learning and memory in bipolar could also passively limit treatment adherence (n=40, Cavanagh *et al, B J Psych* 2002, **180**, 293–95, 320–26).

### Role of drugs:*

The optimum outcomes in bipolar occur with the appropriate and consistent prescribing of mood stabilisers, training for the person to cope with stresses and risk factors, and family support. Lithium, valproate and carbamazepine are widely used for the prophylaxis of bipolar disorder, although the evidence for carbamazepine and perhaps valproate is not robust. Mood stabilisers still appear underused in bipolar and a large US survey concluded that "In general, the pharmacological treatment of bipolar disorder still departs substantially from the management principles outlined by published guidelines, suggesting that this may be an important area for quality improvement" (Blanco *et al, Am J Psych* 2002, **159**, 1005–10). CBT can significantly help to reduce risk factors for relapse and produce better outcomes in combination with mood stabilisers (review of combination approaches, Rothbaum and Astin, *J Clin Psych* 2000, **61**[Suppl 9], 68–75).

**Reviews:*** bipolar disorder (Müller-Oerlinghausen *et al, Lancet* 2002, **359**, 241–47, 75 refs), bipolar depression, (Haddad and Dursun, *Acta Psych Scand* 2002, **105**, 401–3), reviews of mood stabilisers for bipolar, schizo-affective, depression, mania etc (various authors, *J Clin Psych* 1999, **60**[Suppl 5], 3–52; Bowden, *J Clin Psych* 2000, **61**[Suppl 9], 35–40), diagnosis and treatment in children and adolescents (Silva *et al, CNS Drugs* 1999, **12**, 437– 50), genetics (Potash and DePaolo, *Bipolar Disord* 2000, **2**, 8–26), suicide and bipolar (Jamison, *J Clin Psych* 2000, **61**[Suppl 9], 47–51), longitudinal course (Suppes *et al, J Clin Psych* 2000, **61**[Suppl 9], 23–30, 134 refs), ADRs (McIntyre, *J Clin Psych* 2002, **63**(Suppl 3), 15–20), alternatives to lithium (*Drugs & Ther Perspect* 2002, **18**, 20–23).

## BNF Listed *

Active comparisons between mood stabilisers are rare eg. valproate was superior to placebo and lithium in the only RCT (n=372, RCT, Bowden *et al, Arch Gen Psych* 2000, **57**, 481–89) and lithium outdoes carbamazepine in clinical response in bipolar patients based on inter-episodic morbidity, dropout rate, and rehospitalisation, with 2.5 times higher drop-out rate with CBZ (n=171, 2.5yrs, Kleindienst and Greil, *Psychol Med* 2002, **32**, 493–501). A substantial proportion of patients still do not receive adequate TDM (no tests for 12 months in 37% lithium users, n=718, Marcus *et al, Am J Psych* 1999, **156**, 1014–18). Unfortunately, inappropriate use of antidepressants in undiagnosed bipolar may lead to cycle worsening in many (n=85, naturalistic, Ghaemi *et al, J Clin Psych* 2000, **61**, 804–8).

## Carbamazepine *

Long-term therapy in affective disorders is well-established, either as an alternative to lithium or used in combination in treatment-resistant cases. However, six studies of maintenance carbamazepine in bipolar disorder show equivocal results, eg. incomplete protection, and some uncertainty remains (reviewed by Keck *et al, J Clin Psych* 1998, **59**[Suppl 6], 74–81, 114 refs). Indeed one study showed that only 18% of carbamazepine-trea-

ted bipolars remained stable for 3–4 years and another showed a 50% relapse rate (n=24, open, 4-yrs, Post *et al, J Clin Psychopharmacol* 1990, **10**, 318–27). Carbamazepine is reported to be better for early onset illness and with an alternating pattern of mood. A comparison of 10 studies of carbamazepine against lithium shows a roughly similar efficacy (n=572, table in Davis *et al, Acta Psych Scand* 1999, **100**, 406–17). A thorough review of the available trials implies that trough carbamazepine levels of 7mg/l or above are strongly associated with therapeutic response in bipolar patients (Taylor and Duncan, *Psych Bull* 1997, **21**, 221–23) and thus may require higher doses (eg. 600mg/d) than are currently recommended. Various studies have shown that low dose carbamazepine (15–25 micromol/l) is as effective as high dose carbamazepine (28–40 micromols/l) and lithium (0.6–0.8micromol/l) in bipolar patients, but in unipolar patients, low dose was less effective than the other two (n=58, Simhandl *et al, J Aff Dis* 1993, **28**, 221–31). There is little evidence yet for a rebound mania on discontinuation (eg. n=6, Macritchie and Hunt, *J Psychopharmacol* 2000, **14**, 266–68). It has been suggested that best thing you can do with carbamazepine in bipolar is stop it and allow other drugs to reach therapeutic levels.

## Lithium *

The use of lithium in bipolar was first published by Cade (*Med J Aust* 1949, 349) and is now widely used for the treatment and prophylaxis of bipolar illnesses and with care can be successful and safe. It is effective in Bipolar I and II, by reducing relapses and increasing interepisode intervals (eg. Tondo *et al, Am J Psych* 1998, **155**, 638–45).

**Efficacy**: Although the nine major placebo-controlled trials of lithium as prophylaxis of bipolar disorder have methodological flaws (eg. most used an abrupt lithium-withdrawal control group, which Baldessarini has now shown increases relapse in its own right, detailed discussion of these short-comings by Moncrieff, *B J Psych* 1995, **167**, 569–74), their findings, however, are of great importance (reply to Moncrieff by Goodwin, *B J Psych* 1995, **167**, 573–74). One might also ask of the doubters that if lithium doesn't work, how come there's a known dose-response curve, and withdrawal of something that doesn't work produces relapse? (n=865, 19 RCTs, Davis *et al, Acta Psych Scand* 1999, **100**, 406–17). Cochrane concludes that lithium is more effective than placebo for preventing all relapses in people with bipolar disorder (61% with placebo, 33% with lithium), but not significantly more effective than placebo in unipolar depression (n=825, 9 studies, Burgess *et al, CDRS* 2001, 3013; reviewed by Kennedy and Jones, *EBMH* 2002, **5**, 10). Response may be a familial trait (n=146, Grof *et al, J Clin Psych* 2002, **63**, 942–47). A recent meta-analysis showed a non-significant trend towards better responses to lithium in recent times (Baldessarini and Tondo, *Arch Gen Psych* 2000, **57**, 187–90), so despite the lack of any commercial promotion of lithium, it still apparently works.

**Prophylaxis:*** Lithium appears highly effective as prophylactic therapy, provided it is taken regularly, monitored regularly and the dose and therapy reviewed regularly to minimise side-effects, especially those of weight gain and cognitive dulling. Commencing lithium within the first ten years of illness predicts better preventative outcomes than beginning prophylaxis later, both in major depression, recurrent and bipolar patients (n=270, Franchini *et al, Eur Arch Psychiatry Clin Neurosci* 1999, **249**, 227–30). The prophylactic efficacy is probably maintained for at least ten years (n=86, mean 8.2yrs, Berghofer *et al, Acta Psych Scand* 1996, **93**, 349–54). Data is accumulating that long-term lithium markedly reduces the excess mortality of people with recurrent affective disorders (retrospective study, n=273, Müller-Oerlinghausen *et al, Acta Psych Scand* 1996, **94**, 344–47), probably, at least in part, by (see next section) reducing suicide (Gershon and Soares, *Arch Gen Psych* 1997, **54**, 16–20). Lithium maintenance yields striking long-term reductions of depressive as well as manic morbidity in both bipolar disorder subtypes, with greater overall benefits in Bipolar II patients and with earlier treatment (n=317, retrospective, Tondo *et al, Am J Psych* 1998, **155**, 638–45). Regular lithium use over 5 years has been shown to produce a drastic reduction in time in hospital as 'almost the rule', but irregular use leads to a much poorer outcome (n=402, Maj *et al, Am J Psych* 1998, **155**, 30–35). Adjunctive CBT may enhance the effectiveness of lithium in long-term bipolar prophylaxis (n=15, Fava *et al, J Clin Psych* 2001, **62**, 556–59)

The main problems appear to be when therapy is given to carelessly selected patients given insufficient support (see compliance), education and supervision, illustrated by naturalistic studies, which show a poorer outcome than controlled trials. Goodwin argues strongly that treatment with lithium should be for at least two years (and more probably three years at the minimum) and that up to two years it may have at best no beneficial effect (premature stopping resulting in premature recurrence of mania).

**Suicide reduction:*** Reduced suicide rates have been strongly suggested by studies, something unique in bipolar to lithium (Baldessarini and Jamison, *J Clin Psych* 1999, **60**[Suppl 2], 117–22). An analysis of 22 studies on lithium maintenance showed that suicide was 82% less frequent during lithium treatment, not accounted for by discontinuation (22 studies, meta-analysis, n=5647, Tondo *et al, Acta Psych Scand* 2001, **104**, 163–72), although this has been disputed in one retrospective study of selected suicides (Coryell *et al, Acta Psych Scand* 2001,

**104**, 193–97, editorial comment by Gelenberg, *Acta Psych Scand* 2001, **104**, 161–62; review by Burgess, *EBMH* 2002, **5**, 52). It may be further enhanced by psychotherapy (2yr, Rucci *et al, Am J Psych* 2002, **159**, 1160–64). Although suicide protection may be incomplete, it is 7-fold lower than in non-lithium treated patients (meta-analysis by Müller-Oerlinghausen, *Eur Arch Psych Clin Neurosci* 2001, **251**(Suppl 2), 72-75). It should be noted that excess mortality has also been reported with lithium (n=133, retrospective over 16 years, Brodersen *et al, B J Psych* 2000, **176**, 429–33).

**Mode of action:*** Lithium may exert its effect via many mechanisms eg. inositol monophosphatase enzyme inhibition, decreasing inositol concentrations, inhibiting secondary messenger systems, inhibition of Protein Kinase C activity (which may stabilise aberrant neuronal signals in critical areas of the brain, an action shared with valproate and tamoxifen; Manji *et al, J Clin Psych* 1996, **57**[Suppl 13], 34–46), neuroprotection, Glycogen synthase kinase 3-beta inhibition (GSK-3b regulates gene expression, and inhibiting it increases expression of neuroprotective agents, such as heat shock protein), increased human brain grey matter (Moore *et al, Lancet* 2000, **356**, 1241-42), up-regulation of Bcl-2 (major neuroprotective protein, with speculated rebound reduction in Bcl-2 production on withdrawal: Manji *et al, J Clin Psych* 2000, **61**[Suppl 9], 82–96), protection from glutamate apoptosis (programmed cell death) and serotonin regulation (although acute tryptophan depletion does not reverse the effect on mood and suicidality in bipolar I: n=19, RCT, Hughes *et al, B J Psych* 2000, **177**, 447–51). Some of the long-term benefits of lithium may be mediated by neurotrophic effects.

**Review:*** Mode of action (Shaldubina *et al, Prog Neuropsychopharmacol Biol Psych* 2001, **25**, 855–66).

**Dosing**: Once-daily lithium reduces side-effects, simplifies dosage requirements and reduces renal damage. Alternate daily lithium is not recommended (n=50, d/b, Jensen *et al, J Aff Dis* 1996, **36**, 89–93; Andrade, *Acta Psych Scand* 1996, **94**, 281; Jensen *et al, Acta Psych Scand* 1996, **94**, 281–82).

**Plasma levels:*** Plasma levels of 0.4–0.8mmol/L are generally considered safe and effective as prophylaxis, but below 0.4–0.6mEq/L may be less protective against relapse (eg. n=94, RCT, d/b, Gelenberg *et al, NEJM* 1989, **321**, 1489–93). There was no difference in the protection against affective disorder relapse between high (0.8–1.0mmol/L) and low (0.5–0.8mmol/L) serum lithium levels (naturalistic, n=91, Vestergaard *et al, Acta Psych Scand* 1998, **98**, 310–15), but only a third completed two years lithium prophylaxis successfully, and alcohol or other medication abuse was associated with poor outcome. In acute mania, 1.3–1.5mmol/l, with care, may be appropriate (Thau *et al, Lithium* 1993, **4**, 149–59). In the elderly, a third to half less lithium may be needed due to reduced clearance (n=9, Hardy *et al, J Clin Psychopharmacol* 1987, **7**, 153–58). Plasma monitoring is often poor, but even distribution of clinical guidelines in Aberdeen in 1996 resulted in only transient improved renal and thyroid monitoring and of plasma levels (Eagles *et al, Acta Psych Scand* 2000, **101**, 349–53). Lithium plasma levels may need to be higher in children and adolescents as the brain-to-serum concentration ratio appears correlated positively with age (n=27, Moore *et al, Am J Psych* 2002, **159**, 1240–42).

Predictive methods of estimating the final lithium dose in hospitalised manic in-patients may allow therapeutic levels to be reached quicker and lengths of stay can be reduced (Marken *et al, Ann Pharmacother* 1994, **28**, 1148–52). The brain:plasma ratio is usually considered a relatively constant 1:1 but can vary widely (reported cases of 100:1), which may explain why some people get side-effects on low doses and also means that plasma levels have to be interpreted carefully.

**Compliance or concordance**: The main reason for lithium failure is non-compliance (either complete or erratic) and the patient (and any partner or carer) needs to be aware of the long-term commitment needed. Specialised care, eg. via lithium or mood clinics, may improve patient and professional compliance with lithium use (Guscott and Taylor, *B J Psych* 1994, **164**, 741–46).

Future compliance to lithium after discharge from hospital (and hence likelihood of readmission within one year) has been predicted by measuring pre-and post-leave levels, the so-called lithium level-to-dose ratio (LDR) (Terao and Terao, *Lithium* 1994, **5**, 115–16). For a general review of strategies to improve compliance, see Schou (*Acta Psych Scand* 1997, **95**, 361–63).

**Discontinuation:*** Early (particularly manic) relapse in bipolar illness following lithium discontinuation is now well accepted. Two important studies have shown a significant risk from rapid discontinuation. If stopped in under 14 days, the risk of relapse is much higher (median 50% risk of relapse within 4 months, 100% over 3.5 years) than with slower (15–30 days) withdrawal, with a significant excess over the first six months (Baldessarini *et al*, *J Clin Psych* 1996, **57**, 441–48; Baldessarini *et al*, *Am J Psych* 1997, **154**, 551–53). Since lithium has been shown to reduce mortality, discontinuation is also likely to be associated with increased mortality.

**Abrupt decrease** in lithium levels, either through erratic compliance or major change in dose, is also a powerful predictor of relapse (n=94, Perlis *et al*, *Am J Psych* 2002, **159**, 1155–59). Indeed, the original paper that claims that >0.8mmol/L is superior to lower levels (Gelenberg *et al*, *NEJM* 1989,

**321**, 1489–93) notes that many in the lower level group had rapid reductions in levels which may have induced relapse.

**Lithium refractoriness:*** lithium discontinuation in stable patients, despite adequate lithium levels, has been reported to induce a refractory state (eg. Bauer, *Am J Psych* 1994, **151**, 1522). However, two studies of lithium maintenance treatment periods (mean 4 years) were unable to show this (n=86, Tondo *et al*, *Am J Psych* 1997, **154**, 548–50; n=28, Coryell *et al*, *Am J Psych* 1998, **155**, 895–98), although the latter study has been criticised as being underpowered (Maj, *Am J Psych* 1999, **156**, 1130; plus reply). In a longitudinal study of clinic-attending bipolars compliant with lithium for at least a year, and without co-morbid substance misuse, whilst retreatment showed slightly reduced efficacy, there was no tendency for lesser responses later in treatment (n=360, longitudinal, Tondo *et al*, *B J Psych* 2001, **178**(Suppl 41), S184–S190). A short-term withdrawal syndrome may occur on abrupt discontinuation but a distinct withdrawal syndrome is not established (reviewed in detail by Goodwin, *B J Psych* 1994, **164**, 149–52). See also discontinuation above for discussion of relapse.

**Reviews**: general (*Drug and Ther Bull* 1999, **37**, 22–24; Baldessarini *et al*, *Harv Rev Psych* 2002, **10**, 59–75; Friedrich, *JAMA* 1999, **281**, 2271–73; Schou *et al*, *Bipolar Disord* 1999, **1**, 5–16; Dinan, *BMJ* 2002, **324**, 989–90), plasma monitoring (Aronson and Reynolds, *BMJ* 1992, **305**, 1273), review of good practice (Watson and Young, *Curr Opin Psych* 2001, **14**, 57–63), neurobiology and mode of action (Lenox and Hahn, *J Clin Psych* 2000, **61**[Suppl 9], 5–15, 123 refs), historical perspectives (Soares and Gershon, *J Clin Psych* 2000, **61**[Suppl 9], 16–22, Nemeroff, *J Clin Psych* 2000, **61**[Suppl 9], 3–4), pharmacokinetics and pharmacodynamics (Kilts, *J Clin Psych* 2000, **61**[Suppl 9], 41–46), prophylaxis (editorial review, Vestergaard, *Acta Psych Scand* 2000, **101**, 341–42) and adverse effects (Geisler and Schou, *Adv Drug React Bull* 2001, **206**, 787–90).

### + Combinations

There has been an increased use of polypharmacy in refractory bipolar over recent decades (n=178, Frye *et al*, *J Clin Psych* 2000, **61**, 9–15; review of mood stabiliser combinations, Freeman and Stoll, *Am J Psych* 1998, **155**, 12–21).

### Lithium + antipsychotics

Lithium is frequently used with antipsychotics in maintenance therapy, although only two controlled studies exist. One showed improved efficacy in mania compared to lithium monotherapy, although poorly tolerated (n=33, 8/52, Small *et al*, *Psychopharmacol Bull* 1995, **31**, 265–72; n=11, d/b, c/o, Esparon *et al*, *B J Psych* 1986, **148**, 723–25). Anecdotal reports indicate an additive effect, eg. with clozapine, risperidone, olanzapine etc (reviewed by Freeman and Stoll, *Am J Psych* 1998, **155**, 12–21). See also some efficacy.

### Lithium+calcium-channel blockers

Although there are some reports of efficacy, potential drug interactions make this combination hazardous (reviewed by Freeman and Stoll, *Am J Psych* 1998, **155**, 12–21).

### Lithium + carbamazepine

This combination is widely used, and seems safe and effective, especially for rapid-cycling. A variety of retrospective and prospective studies have shown a well-tolerated and improved prophylactic effect compared to lithium monotherapy (eg. n=33, Small *et al*, *Psychopharmacol Bull* 1995, **31**, 265–72). Occasional neurotoxic reactions have been reported, but mostly in patients with pre-existing brain damage (Shukla *et al*, *Am J Psych* 1984, **141**, 1604–6). An additive anti-thyroid effect may occur, lowering T4 and free T4 levels (*Am J Psych* 1990, **147**, 615–20) although the addition of carbamaze-

pine to lithium has also been claimed help to counteract lithium-induced sub-clinical hypothyroidism, possibly improving efficacy (Bocchetta *et al*, *Acta Psych Scand* 1996, **94**, 45–48).

### Lithium + fluoxetine

Fluoxetine-augmentation of lithium in bipolar mood disorder can help prevent breakthrough depression (n=26, open, 3-year, Tondo *et al*, *Int J Psych Clin Pract* 1997, **1**, 203–6).

### Lithium + lamotrigine

Case reports indicate this may be a useful combination (eg. Calabrese *et al*, *Am J Psych* 1996, **153**, 1236).

### Lithium + valproate

This combination appears useful in resistant bipolar disorder. A one-year pilot study showed that bipolar I patients taking divalproex plus lithium were significantly less likely to relapse than those taking lithium monotherapy (n=12, Solomon *et al*, *J Clin Psych* 1997, **58**, 95–99), although side-effects were more common. Other case reports suggest a synergistic effect.

### Valproate + antipsychotics

Many combinations are used, although there is little data to show a proven efficacy. Reports of valproate used effectively with clozapine and risperidone have appeared (reviewed by Freeman and Stoll, *Am J Psych* 1998, **155**, 12–21). See also some efficacy.

### Valproate + carbamazepine

There have been several reports of efficacy, eg. when valproate was added to carbamazepine non-responders, 69% responded (n=29, Schaff *et al*, *J Clin Psych* 1993, **54**, 380–84), and a case report in rapid-cycling (Ketter *et al*, *J Clin Psychopharmacol* 1992, **12**, 276–81). Plasma level monitoring is needed as both drugs can interact (see *4.5.1*).

### Valproate + lamotrigine

An open study has indicated some efficacy (reviewed by Freeman and Stoll, *Am J Psych* 1998, **155**, 12–21), although the incidence of rash appears higher and valproate increases lamotrigine levels (see *4.5.4*).

● **Unlicensed/Some efficacy
Antipsychotics***

The main roles of antipsychotics in bipolar disorder are:

1. Adjunctive to mood stabilisers for management of acute mania or psychotic depression.
2. Adjunctive maintenance in treatment-resistance.

There is no compelling evidence that antipsychotics as such are effective as mood stabilisers alone in bipolar disorder. There are no RCTs comparing antipsychotics with established mood stabilisers in bipolar disorder, although they are prescribed for up to 84% of bipolars (review; Tohen and Zarate, *J Clin Psych* 1998, **59**[Suppl 1], 38–49; 39%, n=88, open, 6/12, Soares *et al*, *J Aff Dis* 1999, **56**, 1–8), and six months after an acute episode, up to 95% may still be taking them (n=40, Sernyak *et al*, *Am J Psych* 1994, **151**, 133–35). Most patients (even treatment-resistant) can, and should, be stabilised without the need for chronic antipsychotics (n=133, retrospective, Brotman *et al*, *J Clin Psych* 2000, **61**, 68–72). It has been shown that in antipsychotic-naive or antipsychotic-free (for 6 months) psychotic bipolars, there is an increase in $D_2$ receptor density (Pearlson *et al*, *Arch Gen Psych* 1995, **52**, 471–77) and so dopamine-blocking drugs may have some rationale. Depot antipsychotics may be useful in some patients as prophylaxis of bipolar mood disorder, by reducing relapses and time in hospital (18 O/P audit and review by Littlejohn *et al*, *B J Psych* 1995, **166**, 827–29), although flupentixol depot appeared to have no prophylactic effect as lithium augmentation (n=11, d/b, c/o, Esparon *et al*, *B J Psych* 1986, **148**, 723–25).

There is considerable interest in the atypicals. Clozapine, risperidone and olanzapine may be of equivalent efficacy as adjuncts to mood stabilisers in bipolar disorder (retrospective, n=42, Guille *et al*, *J Clin Psych* 2000, **61**, 638–42). Several studies have shown **risperidone** to be useful in mania and bipolar disorder (eg. n=14, open, o/p, 64% improved, Ghaemi *et al*, *Can J Psych* 1997, **42**, 196–99; n=12, open, Ghaemi and Sachs, *Int Clin Psychopharmacol* 1997, **12**, 333–38). A one-year trial of **clozapine** in treatment-resistant bipolar or schizoeffective patients showed clozapine to have significant mood-stabilising properties as add-on therapy compared to placebo (n=38, RCT, Suppes *et al*, *Am J Psych* 1999, **156**, 1164–69; see also n=193, Banov *et al*, *J Clin Psych* 1994, **55**, 295–300; n=34/91, open, Ciapparelli *et al*, *J Clin Psych* 2000, **61**, 329–34). **Quetiapine** may have some applications as an alternative or adjunct in bipolar or schizoaffective disorders (n=145, open, Zarate *et al*, *J Clin Psych* 2000, **61**, 185–89) and a pilot study in bipolar or schizoaffective patients poorly responsive to mood stabilisers, suggested that quetiapine (50–400mg/d) may have some potential (n=20, open, 12/52, Sajatovic *et al*, *J Clin Psych* 2001, **62**, 728–32). **Olanzapine** has attracted much interest in bipolar through extrapolation of its antimanic effect. An extensive review concluding that olanzapine is equivalent to haloperidol and thus an option in the short-term management of mania in Bipolar I, with or without psychotic features (Bhana and Perry, *CNS Drugs* 2001, **15**, 871–904). An open-label continuation study in bipolar has shown some on-going improvements in symptoms (n=139, open, 49/52, Sanger *et al*, *J Clin Psych* 2001, **62**, 273–81). In a longer-term study, however, a sustained mood stabilising effect was evident in only 26% (7/27) of those taking olanzapine as an add-on (n=125, 15/12, Narendran *et al*, *J Clin Psych* 2001, **62**, 509–16). Adjunctive therapy in resistant bipolar (average dose 8.1mg/d) shows some promise (n=23, open, Vieta *et al*, *J Clin Psychopharmacol* 2001, **21**, 469–73).

**Review:*** atypicals in bipolar and schizoaffective disorders (Ghaemi and Goodwin, *J Clin Psychopharmacol* 1999, **19**, 354–61), olanzapine in

Bipolar I (Bhana and Perry, *CNS Drugs* 2001, **15**, 871–904, 110 refs).

## Valproate semisodium

Whilst valproate semisodium is now licensed for mania, valproate is not yet actually licensed as a mood stabiliser (and is unlikely ever to be), albeit widely used for this (review, Davis *et al, Acta Psych Scand* 1999, **100**, 406–17). The one-year study comparing divalproex, lithium and placebo (2:1:1) just failed to show divalproex to be superior to lithium or placebo in the time to any mood episode, but there was a noticeable trend for divalproex (40/52) over placebo (28/52) and lithium (24/52), and it was superior to placebo on nearly all secondary measures (n=372, RCT, Bowden *et al, Arch Gen Psych* 2000, **57**, 481–89). Case studies and open trials (eg. Calabrese *et al, J Clin Psychopharmacol* 1992, **12**[Suppl 1], 53S–56S) suggest a therapeutic effect, particularly in prevention of mania or mixed episodes. Valproate may be highly effective in some bipolar patients refractory to lithium and carbamazepine (n=24, Denicoff *et al, Am J Psych* 1997, **154**, 1456–58).

A thorough review of the available trials implies that trough valproate levels of 50mg/l are strongly associated with therapeutic response in bipolar and manic patients (Taylor and Duncan, *Psych Bull* 1997, **21**, 221–23) and thus, may require higher doses (eg. 1000mg/d) than currently recommended. There is also some data that valproate may allow reduction in the doses of antipsychotics needed in bipolar disorder with psychosis, or even replace them (Reutens and Castle, *B J Psych* 1997, **170**, 484–85). See also entry under mania/hypomania (*1.19*).

---

○ **Unlicensed/Possible efficacy**

## Calcium-channel blockers

Verapamil 120–450mg/d has shown promise as a mood stabiliser (*Biol Psych* 1989, **25**, 128–40), even in the elderly (*Int J Ger Psych* 1992, **7**, 913–15). Nimodipine has been effective in

some trials (eg. Pazzaglia *et al, Psychiatr Res* 1993, **49**, 257–72; Goodnick, *J Clin Psych* 1995, **56**, 330) and is highly lipophilic, allowing adequate CNS concentrations and minimal peripheral effects, an advantage over verapamil. Diltiazem has also been suggested as effective (n=8, open, 12/12, Silverstone and Birkett, *J Psychiatry Neurosci* 2000, **25**, 276–80) They may have some role as add-on therapy in resistant cases.

## Gabapentin *

Whilst gabapentin has no efficacy in mania (see *1.19*), a naturalistic study of resistant bipolar illness produced 18 positive responses with gabapentin (average 539mg/d, range 33–2700mg/d, n=28, Schaffer and Schaffer, *Am J Psych* 1997, **154**, 291–92) and gabapentin was considered moderately to markedly effective in 30% patients with bipolar or unipolar depression mood disorders (n=50, retrospective, open, Ghaemi *et al, J Clin Psych* 1998, **59**, 426–29). Gabapentin augmentation was effective and well tolerated in mild-to-moderate bipolar depression (n=22, open pilot, 12/52, Wang *et al, Bipolar Dis* 2002, **4**, 296–301). In a trial against lamotrigine, gabapentin was no better than placebo (n=45, RCT, p/c, d/b, c/o, 6/52, Obrocea *et al, Biol Psych* 2002, **51**, 253–60).

**Reviews:*** Letterman and Markowitz, *Pharmacotherapy* 1999, **19**, 565–72; Maidment, *Ann Pharmacother* 2001, **35**, 1264–69.

## Lamotrigine *

More RCTs are awaited but there is growing evidence of efficacy, and a US license for long term management of bipolar disorder to delay relapse or recurrence of depressive episodes has been applied for. Lamotrigine 50–200mg/d monotherapy was significantly more effective than placebo in bipolar I depression, the effect being seen as early as the third week (n=195, RCT, Calabrese *et al, J Clin Psych* 1999, **60**, 79–88). This follows an earlier open study of monotherapy and adjunctive in treatment-resistant bipolar (n=75, open, 48/52, Calabrese *et al, Am J Psych* 1999, **156**, 1019–23). It may be more effective in male bipolar patients with fewer prior medication trials (n=45, Obrocea *et al, Biol Psych* 2002, **51**, 253–60). A comparison with a mood stabiliser or antidepressant would now be appropriate (review by Haslam, EBMH 1999, **2**, 75). **Reviews**: general (Keck *et al, J Clin Psych* 1998, **59**[Suppl 6], 74–81, 114 refs; Zerjav-Lacombe and Tabarsi, *Can J Psych* 2001, **46**, 328–33; Engle and Heck, *Ann Pharmacother* 2000, **34**, 258–62, 28 refs).

### Methylphenidate

Methylphenidate was effective and tolerable in 78% depressed bipolars (n=14, open, 12/52, El-Mallakh, *Bipolar Disord* 2000, **2**, 56–59).

### Omega-3 fatty acids

In a not very stringent 4-month trial, omega-3 fatty acids produced a significantly longer remission than placebo, as well as scoring higher on most other outcome measures (n=30, d/b, Stoll *et al, Arch Gen Psych* 1999, **56**, 407–12; general review by Greener, *Prog Neurol Psych* 1999, **3**, 26–27).

### Oxcarbazepine * (see also carbamazepine)

There are case reports of success in bipolar II with co-morbid substance abuse (n=4, Nasr, *Am J Psych* 2002, **159**, 1793).

### Pramipexole

There are reports of treatment-resistant bipolar depression, where the D3 agonist pramipexole augmentation produced improvement (n=2 Goldberg *et al, Am J Psych* 1999, **156**, 798).

### Tamoxifen

There is some interest in tamoxifen as mood stabiliser, as it shares some intra-cellular properties with lithium (see lithium in this section).

### Tiagabine *

Tiagabine 4mg/d was successful as adjunctive therapy in multiple drug-resistant bipolar disorder, continuing to be effective over several months (n=2, Schaffer and Schaffer, *Am J Psych* 1999, **156**, 2014–15) although it was at best only modestly effective in refractory bipolar, with several ADRs in a small trial (n=13, open, Suppes *et al, Bipolar Disorder* 2002, **4**, 283–89).

### Topiramate *

In one study, mild improvement was seen in 47% and marked-to-moderate in 13% bipolars treated with topiramate, (mean 180mg/d), with a dose-related response and weight loss, as well as significant side effects (n=76, open, Ghaemi *et al, Ann Clin Psych* 2001, **13**, 185–89) and there is a report of success in recurrent mania in bipolar I (n=1, Letmaier *et al, Int Clin Psychopharmacol* 2001, **16**, 295–98).

### Vitamins and minerals *

A trial of 36 dietary nutrients produced a 55–66% reduction in bipolar symptoms and a reduction in medication levels, leading to suggestions that bipolar disorder is an inborn error of metabolism, although the mechanism is unknown (n=11, 6/12, Kaplan *et al, J Clin Psych* 2001, **62**, 936–44).

## 1.11 BORDERLINE PERSONALITY DISORDER

See also aggression (*1.2*)

There are a large number of personality disorders, of which borderline personality disorder is but one. Treating personality disorders (and hence personality itself) is obviously somewhat controversial. Patients with BPD more often present for treatment than schizoid, paranoid and avoidant personality types. Research is now often directed towards treating symptom clusters rather than the underlying personality disorder, eg. anxiety, aggression, impulsiveness, etc.

**Symptoms:**
The main symptoms of BPD are of a deeply ingrained maladaptive pattern of behaviour, recognisable from adolescence and continuing through most of adult life. Such people show continued boredom, anger, unstable relationships, impulsive self-harmful behaviour (eg. gambling, stealing, binge-eating, or drinking), variable moods, recurrent suicide threats or behaviour and uncertainty about their personal identity.

**Role of drugs:***
BPD may account for up to 7.5% of psychiatric admissions, with a raised incidence of psychiatric morbidity, mortality users of a wide range of medication (n=664, Bender *et al, Am J Psych* 2001, **158**, 295–302). Pharmacotherapy will not alter ingrained character traits or the effects of abuse, but they may produce modest benefits, with the occasional striking result and be more effective if combined with psychotherapy. Drug therapy, however, is fraught with problems. Side-effects may be grossly exaggerated to avoid treatment and patients may be actively antimedication. Therapeutic alliances (eg. giving a drug a 'trial'), and not abandoning the patient if the drugs work, may help. Care in patients with suicidal tendencies is necessary.

In a critical review of this topic, Tyrer concludes that 'the null hypothesis that drug treatment of personality disorder is inappropriate has not yet been disproved', and that 'our current drug treatment of personality disorder is like following a badly marked track through a dense fog — you can see only a very short distance ahead but are grateful for any guidance going' (Tyrer, *Psych Bull* 1998, **22**, 242–44, 25 refs).

**Reviews**:* general (Various, *Am J Psych* 2001, **158** (Oct Suppl), 25–43; Hori, *Psychiatry Clin Neurosci* 1998, **52**, 13–19; Soloff, *Psychiatr Clin North Am* 2000, **23**, 169–92), classification, epidemiology, diagnosis and assessment, intervention and management (Marlowe and Sugarman, *BMJ* 1997, **315**, 176–79).

---

● **Unlicensed/Some potency**
**Antipsychotics** *
It has been generally accepted that patients with DSM-IV borderline or schizotypical personality disorders may gain significant benefit from psychotherapy and small doses of antipsychotics. Low dose **risperidone** may be effective but better tolerated eg. risperidone (mean 3.27mg/d) helped as an add-on to existing therapies to

improve BPD symptomatology especially aggression and overall functioning (n=15, open, 8/52, Rocca *et al, J Clin Psych* 2002, **63**, 241–44). **Olanzapine** was effective against a range of psychopathological symptoms in females with BPD, with weight gain the only significant side effect (n=28, d/b, p/c, 6/12, Zanarini and Frankenburg, *J Clin Psych* 2001, **62**, 849–54). Two small open trials of **clozapine** (25–100mg/d) in severe BPD patients produced a general improvement in symptoms in one (n=12, Benedetti *et al, J Clin Psych* 1998, **59**, 13–107) and significantly reduced SIB, aggression, seclusion and violence in the other (n=7, Chengappa *et al, J Clin Psych* 1999, **60**, 477–84). **Haloperidol** and **trifluoperazine** may improve anger, hostility and behavioural symptoms, but have been largely superseded, especially as two studies showed haloperidol no better than placebo (Soloff *et al, Arch Gen Psych* 1993, **150**, 377–85) and poor tolerability (n=54, 16/52, Cornelius *et al, Am J Psych* 1993, **150**, 1843–48). Generally, high-potency drugs in low dose were preferred by patients (due to lack of the abhorred sedative effects).

---

○ **Unlicensed/Possible efficacy**
**Antidepressants**
Some symptoms of BPD are shared with depression, eg. self-condemnation, emptiness, hopelessness, boredom and somatic complaints (Rogers *et al, Am J Psych* 1995, **152**, 268–70) and so the use of antidepressants may have some logic. See tricyclics, SSRIs, MAOIs etc in this section.

**Benzodiazepines**
Benzodiazepines are generally considered as contraindicated in BPD due to the tendency to disinhibit and induce rage reactions and dependence, eg. alprazolam was shown to be significantly worse than placebo for behavioural control (n=16, d/b, p/c, c/o, 6/52, Cowdry and Gardner, *Arch Gen Psych* 1988, **45**, 111–19) and the only double-blind study showed alprazolam to be no better than placebo in

children with anxious or avoidant disorders (Simeon *et al, J Am Acad Adolesc Psych* 1993, **13**, 29–33). The use of rapidly absorbed short-acting drugs (eg. lorazepam) may have some limited use in patients with intermittent explosive disorders, where intermittent use can help abort episodes of dyscontrol.

## Carbamazepine

Carbamazepine may be useful for aggression and episodic dyscontrol and although the latter is not epileptic, there are some common precipitating factors (eg. prodromal symptoms, severe disturbance and postepisode relief of tension). Carbamazepine was superior to placebo for behaviour control, but not for dysphoria, in one study of prison inmates, anecdotally producing a state of 'reflective delay' (n=16, d/b, p/c, c/o, 6/52, Cowdry and Gardner, *Arch Gen Psych* 1988, **45**, 111–19, see also lithium) and with 600mg/d, aggressive outbursts were dramatically reduced (in intensity and frequency) compared to placebo (n=14, Gardner and Cowdry, *Am J Psych* 1986, **143**, 519–22). However, an RCT failed to show any effects (n=20, RCT, 30/7, de la Fuente and Lotstra, *Eur Neuropsychopharmacol* 1994, **4**, 479–86).

## Lithium

Lithium has been reported to be useful for episodic dyscontrol and aggression, affective disorder in BPD, emotionally unstable adolescents and in alcoholics with a PD. Anecdotally, it produced a state of 'reflective delay' ('Now I can think whether to hit him or not' as one inmate was reported to say).

## MAOIs

There was some evidence that MAOIs are effective in depression associated with BPD, eg. tranylcypromine (Cowdry and Gardner, *Arch Gen Psych* 1988, **45**, 111–19) and phenelzine. However, two studies have shown phenelzine at 60mg/d to be no better than placebo except for a minor effect on hostility and anger (Soloff *et al,*

*Arch Gen Psych* 1993, **150**, 377–85) and in a 16-week 90mg/d follow-up of phenelzine responders found it to be poorly tolerated and having only a mild effect on irritability and depressive symptoms (Cornelius *et al, Am J Psych* 1993, **150**, 1843–48).

## Methylphenidate

There is one case where methylphenidate was thought to have been effective in a patient with both ADHD and BPD (Van Reekum and Links, *Can J Psych* 1994, **39**, 186–87), although this is open to debate (see amfetamines in this section).

## SSRIs

Some studies indicate that SSRIs may have a role, eg. irritability and aggression improved in the 44% completers in a trial of 50–200mg/d sertraline (n=16, 8/52, Kavoussi *et al, J Clin Psych* 1994, **55**, 137–41). Another study showed that 20–60mg/d fluoxetine significantly reduced anger and distress, with a significant placebo effect also being detectable (n=22, p/c, Selzman *et al, J Clin Psychopharmacol* 1995, **15**, 23–29). Fluoxetine was partially effective in reduced impulsive aggressive behaviour in another study, but with high drop-out rates (n=40, RCT, Coccaro and Kavoussi, *Arch Gen Psych* 1997, **54**, 1081–88, review by Hawton, *EBMH* 1998, **1**, 79). Careful dose titration is needed to minimise agitation.

## Tricyclics

Generally tricyclics are considered ineffective (or even detrimental) in depression associated with BPD, although they may help, particularly in females and those with a history of depression, hypersomnia, with unstable or drug abusing males more likely to be non-responders (Akiskal *et al Arch Gen Psych* 1980, **37**, 777–83).

## Valproate *

Divalproex significantly reduced irritability and anger, impulsivenesss and relationship tempestuousness in women with co-morbid bipolar II and BPD and was well tolerated (n=20, RCT, p/c, d/b, 6/12, Frankenburg and Zanarini, *J Clin Psych* 2002, **63**, 442–46), supporting a previous study in impulsive aggression in SSRIs non-responders (n=10, open, Kavoussi and Coccaro, *J Clin Psych* 1998, **59**, 676–80).

### ◆ No efficacy
**Amfetamines**

Dexamfetamine has been used but with the exception of the occasional patient has proved ineffective. It may be possible to test for amfetamine responsiveness (reviewed by Stein in *B J Psych* 1992, **161**, 167–84).

**Phenytoin**

Two ancient studies showed an often negative effect (eg. Rosenblatt *et al, Curr Ther Res* 1976, **19**, 332–36).

### 1.12 CATATONIA

See also schizophrenia (*1.26*)

**Symptoms:**

Catatonia is usually a rare and potentially lethal type of schizophrenia, dominated by psychosis, stupor, negativism, resistant rigidity, hyperpyrexia, excitement or posturing. It has been linked with Neuroleptic Malignant Syndrome (*1.22*), (eg. Fink, *Biol Psych* 1996, **39**, 1–4).

**Role of drugs:**

ECT is generally considered the treatment of choice for various forms of catatonia eg. organic, lethal, schizophrenic etc. organic catatonia often responds to treatment of the underlying cause, eg. withdrawal of the offending drug etc. Antipsychotic-induced catatonia is also potentially fatal and must be treated symptomatically. A careful history may elicit a drug-symptom association and the potentially offending drug(s) stopped. Antipsychotics are generally unhelpful.

**Reviews**: general (Fink, *Biol Psych* 1994, **36**, 431–33; Singerman and Raheja, *Ann Clin Psychiatry* 1994, **6**, 259–66; Philbrick and Rummans, *J Neuropsychiatry Clin Neurosci* 1994, **6**, 1–13), clinical features, diagnosis, management and prognosis (Clark and Rickards, *Hosp Med* 1999, **60**, 740–43 and 812–15)

### + Combinations
**Lorazepam + dexamfetamine**

See separate drugs/groups.
**Lorazepam + ECT**

Concurrent or sequential use may be successful (n=5, Petrides *et al, Biol Psych* 1997, **42**, 375–81).

**Thyroid hormone + reserpine**

There is a case report of the combination successfully abolishing periodic catatonia (n=1, Komori *et al, Acta Psych Scand* 1997, **96**, 155–56).

### ● Unlicensed/Some efficacy
**Benzodiazepines**

There are many reports of successful benzodiazepine use in catatonia. 1.5–2mg IV **lorazepam** improved 4 patients with antipsychotic-induced catatonia (*J Clin Psychopharmacol* 1983, **3**, 338–42). In an open study comparing lorazepam and ECT, 76% responded to lorazepam (IV and/or oral) within five days and most who failed responded promptly to ECT. A positive response to initial parenteral challenge with lorazepam predicted a positive outcome (n=28, Bush *et al, Acta Psych Scand* 1996, **93**, 137–43). In another open study, short-term benzodiazepine administration (oral lorazepam 2mg or diazepam 10mg IM followed, if needed, by 2–18mg oral lorazepam over 48 hours) was successful in 88% showing catatonic symptoms (n=18, open, Ungvari *et al, Acta Psych Scand* 1994, **89**, 285–88), although the effect may only be short-term (n=18, RCT, Ungvari *et al, Psychopharmacology* [*Berl*] 1999, **142**, 393–98). **Clonazepam** at 2.5mg/d orally or 1mg IV (n=3, *Am J Psych* 1989, **146**, 1230; n=1, Kumar, *Aust NZJ Psych* 2001, **35**, 391) and 10mg of **diazepam** IV (n=2, *Am J Psych* 1984, **141**, 284–85) and **midazolam** (mentioned in *Am J Psych* 1991, **148**, 809) have been used.

**Zolpidem**

There have been a number of reports of dramatic improvement in catatonia with zolpidem (eg. Mastain *et al, Rev Neurol* 1995, **151**, 52–56). Zolpidem has been used as a diagnostic tool for catatonia, eg. by inducing resolution in people thought to have schizophrenia and allowing interviews to take place (cases by Thomas *et al, Lancet* 1997, **349**, 702, and Zaw and Bates, *Lancet* 1997, **349**, 1914).

○ **Unlicensed/Possible efficacy**
**Antipsychotics**
These have been used (referred to in *Am J Psych* 1992, **149**, 144–45) but are generally considered unhelpful (see also below).
**Carbamazepine** *
Carbamazepine was a useful alternative in lorazepam-resistant patients (n=9, Kritzinger and Jordaan, *Int J Neuropsychopharmacol* 2001, **4**, 251–57).
**Olanzapine** *
High dose olanzapine 30mg/d has been used successfully to treat lethal catatonia (n=1, Cassidy *et al, J Psychopharmacol* 2001, **15**, 302–4).
**Risperidone** *
Risperidone-responsive catatonia has been reported (n=2, Valevski *et al, Clin Neuropharmacol* 2001, **24**, 228–31; n=1, Cook *et al, Arch Gen Psych* 1996, **53**, 82–83).

◊ **Others**
Other drugs tried include **barbiturates** (thiopental and amobarbital; referred to in *Am J Psych* 1992, **149**, 144–45), **bromocriptine** (n=1, Mahmood, *B J Psych* 1991, **158**, 437–38), IV **dantrolene** (n=2, Pennati, *Am J Psych* 1991, **148**, 268), **dexamfetamine** (n=1, Smith and Lebegue, *Am J Psych* 1991, **148**, 1265) and **lithium** (n=1, Pheterson *et al, J Am Acad Child Psych* 1985, **24**, 235–37).

**1.13 DEMENTIA** including Alzheimer's, Lewy Body Dementia etc

**Symptoms:**
**Dementia** is an acquired progressive and irreversible reduction in the level of previously attained intellectual, memory and personality/emotional functioning. The main clinical features include disturbed behaviour (disorganised, inappropriate, distracted, restless, antisocial behaviour), lack of insight, impaired thinking (slow, impoverished, incoherent, rigid), poverty of speech, low mood, poor cognitive function (forgetfulness, poor attention, disorientation in time and later place), and impaired memory. Some dementias can be treated, eg. vitamin depletion (eg. $B_{12}$, folic acid, thiamine), infections (encephalitis, neurosyphilis) and drug toxicity.

**Alzheimer's disease** is a form of dementia characterised by senile plaques and neurofibrillary tangles, with reduced levels of acetylcholine and other transmitters in the brain. The degree of dementia is clearly associated more with the degree of neurofibrillary pathology than with the amyloid plaque burden. It usually presents as a steady deterioration. The main features of its insidious onset are forgetfulness, lack of spontaneity, disorientation, depressed mood, decline in self-care, poor sleep (waking disorientated and perplexed) and intellectual impairment (dysphasia, dyspraxia, language decline).

**Lewy Body dementia** is a variant of Alzheimer's disease, more common in men. The key features include early onset, persistent, well-formed, visual hallucinations and motor features of Parkinsonism. Patients may be extremely sensitive to antipsychotics which may result in a sudden onset of EPSEs, profound confusion and deterioration, and can lead to death (McKeith *et al, BMJ* 1992, **305**, 673–78; CSM warning in *Curr Problems* 1994, **20**, 6).

**Role of drugs:** *
Although drugs acting via transmitters do not affect the basic neurological decline, loss of cholinergic function is still the most consistent change (Francis *et al, J Neurol Neurosurg and Psych* 1999, **66**, 137–47). Well-controlled trials have shown more encouraging results for behaviour disturbances. Drug trials have many exclusions and extrapolation to a general population is open to question, but even if delaying admission to a nursing home by one month would pay for a years drug. Using published data, all 3 anticholi-

nesterases have low NNTs (donepezil 4, rivastigmine 7, galantamine 3; Bullock, *B J Psych* 2002, **180**, 135–39) and are rapidly becoming standard treatment. The main issue to be resolved is a point at which treatment should be discontinued.

**Reviews:*** general (Cummings and Cole, *JAMA* 2002, **287**, 2335–38; Fairbairn, *Prescribers' J* 2000, **40**, 77–85; Hughes and Livingstone, *Prescriber* 2000, 85–95; Dooley and Lamb, *Drugs & Aging* 2000, **16**, 199–226), anticholinesterases (Holden and Kelly, *Adv Psych Treat* 2002, **8**, 89–96), newer drug treatments (Gauthier, *Can Med Ass J* 2002, **166**, 616–23, 36 refs; Bullock, *B J Psych* 2002, **180**, 135–39), guidelines for the appropriate use of cholinesterase inhibitors (Van Den Berg *et al, Drugs & Aging* 2000, **16**, 123–38), selectivity of cholinesterase inhibition (Weinstock, *CNS Drugs* 1999, **12**, 307–23), role of atypical antipsychotics (Madhusoodanan *et al, CNS Drugs* 1999, **12**, 135–50), biochemistry of Alzheimer's disease (Stege and Bosman, *Drugs & Aging* 1999, **14**, 437–46), Lewy Body dementia (Zesiewicz *et al, Curr Treat Options Neurol* 2001, **3**, 507–18; McKeith, *B J Psych* 2002, **180**, 144–47; Campbell *et al, Drugs & Aging* 2001, **18**, 397–407; Swanberg and Cummings, *Drug Safety* 2002, **25**, 511–23, 112 refs), use of mood stabilisers (Tariot *et al, Adv Drug Deliv Rev* 2002, **54**, 1567–77).

---

**BNF Listed**
**Acetylcholinesterase Inhibitors ***
There are slight differences between the available drugs. Donepezil inhibits AChE, rivastigmine inhibits AChE and BuChE (which gives more side effects initially but may have advantages in later illness) and galantamine both inhibits AChE and enhances ACh's action on nicotinic receptors (review by Stahl, *J Clin Psych* 2000, **10**, 710–11). In an active comparison, donepezil was as effective as rivastigmine, but better tolerated and with fewer drop-outs (n=111, RCT,

open, Wilkinson *et al, Int J Clin Pract* 2002, **56**, 441–46).

**Reviews:*** Comparison (Bullock, *B J Psych* 2002, **180**, 135–39), cost-effectiveness (Clegg *et al, Int J Technol Assess Health Care* 2002, **18**, 497–507), kinetics and dynamics (Jann *et al, Clin Pharmacokinet* 2002, **41**, 719–39).

### Donepezil *

Donepezil is a piperidine-based reversible selective acetylcholinesterase inhibitor licensed for the symptomatic treatment of mild or moderate Alzheimer's disease. Results from many trials now show that the response is dose-related (10mg/d > 5mg/d) with all measured scales improving (n=818, p/c, 30/52, Burns *et al, Demen & Ger Cog Dis* 1999, **10**, 237–44), including cognitive function and global functioning (RCT, 24/52, Rogers *et al, Neurology* 1998, **50**, 136–45; review by Warner, *EBMH* 1998, **1**, 88). The course of the disease was unchanged as both groups were indistinguishable after a 6-week washout at the study end. Donepezil may also help emotional and behavioural symptoms in AD (n=25, open, Weiner *et al, J Clin Psych* 2000, **61**, 487–92; n=28, open, Paleacu *et al, Clin Neuropharmacol* 2002, **25**, 313–17). Donepezil seems well tolerated and maintained effectiveness over one year (n=286, RCT, p/c, 1yr, Winblad *et al, Neurology* 2001, **57**, 489–95; n=431, p/c, Mohs *et al, Neurology* 2001, **57**, 481–88; n=25, open, 12/12, Rocca *et al, PNBP* 2002, **26**, 369–73; n=423, Doody *et al, Dement Ger Cog Disord* 2001, **12**, 295–300), and even over 2 years in open-labelled extentions, although even after this time the benefits are lost within 6 weeks of stopping (n=763, open, 2yrs, Doody *et al, Arch Neurol* 2001, **58**, 427–33). Donepezil may also be effective in more advanced stages (MMSE 5–17) of Alzheimer's disease (n=290, RCT, p/c, d/b, 24/52, Feldman *et al, Neurology* 2001, **57**, 613–20) and in dementia with Lewy bodies (Rojas-Fernandez, *Ann Pharmacother* 2001, **35**, 202–5). It may also have beneficial effects on training retention in non-demented older adults, so I'm looking forward to a cheap generic brand in a few decades time (n=18, RCT, d/b, p/c, Yesavage *et al, Neurology* 2002, **59**, 123–25). No withdrawal effects have been seen, probably as its half-life is 70 hours. Cochrane concludes that donepezil produces modest improvements in cognitive function (Birks *et al, CDSR* 2000, 1190).

**Reviews**:* general (Dooley and Lamb, *Drugs Aging* 2000, **16**, 199–2 26; Shigeta and Homma, *CNS Drug Rev* 2001, **7**, 353–68; *Drugs Ther Perspect* 2001, **17**, 1–6).

## Galantamine *

Galantamine is a reversible competitive acetylcholinesterase inhibitor, but also stimulates pre- and post-synaptic nicotinic receptors and is indicated for mild to moderate Alzheimer's disease. Doses should be twice a day, preferably with morning and evening meals to minimise cholinergic side-effects. Gradual introduction is recommended, starting at 4mg bd for 4/52, then 8mg bd for 4/52, increasing to 12mg bd if appropriate. A range of studies have shown effectiveness. Galantamine 16–24mg/d was significantly superior to placebo (n=978, RCT, 5/12, Tariot *et al, Neurology* 2000, **54**, 2269–76), with the benefit sustained over 12 months with the 24mg/d dose (n=636, RCT, 6/12 plus 6/12 extension, Raskind *et al, Neurology* 2000, **54**, 2261–68). Galantamine 24–32mg/d was superior to placebo on basic and ADL scores, but not behaviour, with an 82% completion rate at the higher dose (n=386, RCT, d/b, p/c, 3/12, Rockwood *et al, J Neurol Neurosurg Psychiatry* 2001, **71**, 589–95). Another study showed improvement in core symptoms of Alzheimers (n=285, RCT, d/b, p/c, 3/12, Wilkinson and Murray, *Int J Ger Psych* 2001, **16**, 852–57). A review of 5 RCT phase III trials showed galantamine to be significantly superior to placebo (n=3,000, Lilienfeld and Parys, *Dement Geriatr Cogn Disord* 2000, **11** [Suppl 1], 19–27). Galan-

tamine appears to also be effective for patients with vascular dementia or Alzheimer's disease combined with cerebrovascular disease (n=396 + 196 controls, 6/12, Erkinjuntti *et al, Lancet* 2002, **359**, 1283–90; JC study). There appears to be no rebound from abrupt discontinuation. Cochrane concludes that it is effective at doses of 16–32mg/d, with a consistent effect at 3–6 months (7 trials, Olin and Schneider, *CDSR* 2002, **4**, 1747, reviewed by Hirsch, *EBMH* 2001, **4**, 85).

**Reviews**: general (Mann and Jones, *Prescriber* 2001, **12**, 69–74; Scott and Goa, *Drugs* 2000, **60**, 1095–1122; Blesa, *Dement Geriatr Cogn Disord* 2000, **11**[Suppl 1], 28–34; Lilienfeld, *CNS Drug Rev* 2002, **8**, 159–76; Mann and Jones, *Prescriber* 2001, **12**, 69–74; Tariot, *Expert Opin Pharmacother* 2001, **2**, 2027–24; *Formulary Monograph Service* 2001, 181–89, 19 refs), use in vascular dementia (Erkinjuntti, *J Neurol Sci* 2002, **15**, 125–130).

## Rivastigmine *

Rivastigmine is a carbamate-derived "pseudoirreversible" acetylcholinesterase (preferentially the G1 subtype) and butylcholinesterase inhibitor licensed for the treatment of mild to moderately severe Alzheimer's disease. The dose must be titrated at weekly intervals to reduce side-effects. A number of trials have shown some efficacy. Rivastigmine improved global functioning and cognition, particularly in daily living activities (n=725, RCT, 26/52, Rosler *et al, BMJ* 1999, **318**, 633–38). Low-dose rivastigmine (1–4mg/d), high-dose rivastigmine (6–12mg/d) and placebo showed a dose-dependent clinically and statistically significant improvement in cognitive and global assessments, and in activities of daily living (n=725, RCT, Rosler *et al, B303 Exelon Study Group, BMJ* 1999, **318**, 633–40; see also editorial by Flicker, *BMJ* 1999, **318**, 515–16 editorial, who concluded the effect appears modest, but may be more prominent in some patients than others, possibly those with more rapidly progressive disease n=187, open extension, 26/52, Farlow *et al, Arch Neurol* 2001, **58**, 417–22). Rivastigmine may have some use in Lewy body dementia, with a return to pretreatment levels of function 3/52 after discontinuation (n=92 completers, RCT, d/b, p/c, 23/52, Wesnes *et al, Dement & Ger Cog Disord* 2002, **13**, 183–92; n=8, open, Maclean *et al, Int Psychogeriatr* 2001, **13**, 277–88; 98/52, Grace *et al, Int Psychogariatr* 2001, **13**, 199–205). Cochrane concludes from 7 trials that rivastigmine was beneficial at 6–12mg/d in mild to moderate Alzheimer's (n=3370, Birks *et al, CDSR* 2000, 1191; review in *EBMH* 2000, **3**, 10).

**Reviews**: general (Jann, *Pharmacotherapy* 2000, **20**, 1–12, 50 refs; Gottwald and Rozanski, *Expert Opin Investig Drugs* 1999, **8**, 1673–82), pharmacoeconomics (Lamb and Goa, *PharmacoEconomics* 2001, **19**, 303–18), kinetics (Gobburu *et al, J Clin Pharmacol* 2001, **41**, 1082–90).

## Tacrine

Tacrine is licensed in the UK, but not marketed. It is a longer-acting, competitive, reversible cholineresterase inhibitor that produces moderate symptomatic benefit in some people with Alzheimer's Disease. About 15% can tolerate and benefit from the drug and a further 15% will tolerate the drug and show no worsening of cognitive symptoms, although the overall course of the disease is not detectably altered. A review of 49 trials (inc. 21 RCTs), showed modest efficacy in some patients with mild to moderate AD, but the long-term effects are unknown (Arrieta and Artalejo, *Age & Ageing* 1998, **27**[Suppl1], 161–79). Cochrane concludes that the evidence for tacrine is unconvincing and sparse (Qizilbash *et al, CDSR* 2000, 0202). Raised liver enzymes are the major problem.

## Non-anticholinesterases
## Co-dergocrine ('Hydergine'®) *

The Cochrane review of the 19 adequate trials suggests that co-dergocrine shows significant benefits on most rating scales but that the data is limited (Olin *et al, CDSR* 2001, **2**, 0359; see also Bullock, *EBMH* 1999, **2**, 15).

## Memantine *

Memantine is licensed in the UK for moderately severe to severe Alzheimer's disease, a unique indication. Memantine has also, uniquely, been shown to reduce deterioration in moderate-to-severe Alzheimer's Disease (MMSE 3-14, mean 7.9) compared to placebo, based on CIBIC-plus and ADCS-ADLsev, and with low drop-outs (n=252, RCT, p/c, 28/52, Reisberg *et al, NEJM* 2003, **348**, 1333–41). The dose is 5mg/d for the first week, adding 5mg/d each week up to a maximum of 20mg/d as divided doses. Memantine is a NMDA antagonist. It replaces the magnesium ion that blocks NMDA receptors, so acts as a voltage-dependent, non-competitive NMDA-antagonist, blocking the effect of excess glutamate release, thought to be responsible for many symptoms and for disease progression. It appears to have a neuroprotective action (review, Jann, *Expert Opin Investig Drugs* 2000, **9**, 1397–406). Memantine may be used for mild, moderate (n=531, Ruther *et al, Pharmacopsychiatry* 2000, **33**, 103–8) and severe dementia (n=166, RCT, Winblad and Poritis, *Int J Ger Psych* 1999, **14**, 135–46). In mild-to-moderate vascular dementia memantine improved cognition and was well tolerated and safe (n=579, RCT, d/b, p/c, 28/52, Wilcock *et al, Int Clin Psychopharmacol* 2002, **17**, 297–305). Side effects seem low compared to placebo but include hallucinations, confusion, dizziness, headache and tiredness.

**Review**: *Drugs of the Future* 2001, **26**, 908–9.

### + Combinations
**Donepezil + gabapentin**

Behavioural control from gabapentin may augment the cognitive improvement from donepezil (n=2, Dallocchio *et al, J Clin Psych* 2000, **61**, 64).

---

### ● Unlicensed/Some efficacy
**Antipsychotics\***

Antipsychotics are widely used as symptomatic treatments of aggressive, agitated behaviour and as sedatives. With the availability of newer agents, the use of traditional agents such as phenothiazines may be unnecessary clinically, although not without significant financial implications. Antipsychotics should not be used as substitutes for poor standards of care, must be adjuncts to other interventions, must be monitored and reviewed regularly. They increase the rates of falls, sedation, EPSEs and rate of decline in cognitive function, irrespective of initial severity. An indepth review of clinical data concluded that conventional antipsychotics appear to be only modestly effective for behavioural problems associated with dementia, and their short-term benefit is outweighed by the dramatically increased risk of TD among the elderly (Pollock *et al, Consultant Pharm* 1999, **14**, 1251–58).

Of the newer agents, **risperidone** seems effective at an optimum dose of 1mg/d, eg. for aggression and behavioural disturbances (n=344, d/b, 13/52, De Deyn *et al, Neurology* 1999, **53**, 946–55) and in 82% patients with behavioral and psychological symptoms associated with dementia, without impairing cognitive performance (n=34, open, 8/52, Rainer *et al, J Clin Psych* 2001, **62**, 894–900). Maximum benefit may occur after 7–10 days with minimal sedation (n=5, Jeanblanc and Davis, *Am J Psych* 1995, **152**, 1239). 1mg/d was shown to be the optimum dose of risperidone for improving psychotic and aggressive behaviour in institutionalised elderly patients with severe dementia (n=625, RCT, Katz *et al, J Clin Psych* 1999,

60, 107–15). In patients with Lewy Body dementia, psychotic and behavioural symptoms may respond well to low dose risperidone (n=3, Allen *et al, Lancet* 1995, **346**, 185), although even then severe EPSEs (especially rigidity) have occurred at 1mg/d (n=3, McKeith *et al, Lancet* 1995, **346**, 699). In an open-label study extension, patients with dementia receiving risperidone (optimal range 0.75–1.5mg/d) had a very low incidence of TD compared to that expected with typical antipsychotics (n=330, open, Jeste *et al, Am J Psych* 2000, **157**, 1150–55). It appears as effective as olanzapine (n=19, s/b, Ellingrod *et al, Pharmacother* 2002, **22**, 1–5). Starting at very low doses (eg. 0.25mg/d) using the syrup formulation improves tolerability. There are now many trials with **olanzapine** eg. low-dose (5–10mg/d, but not 15mg/d) was superior to placebo in treating agitation, aggression and psychosis in patients with Alzheimer's Disease (n=206, RCT, d/b, p/c, 6/52, Street *et al, Arch Gen Psych* 2000, **57**, 968–76). In a sub-group analysis, olanzapine had some effect in reducing the emergence of psychosis in people with Alzheimer's Disease who didn't have psychosis when they started treatment, if that makes sense (n=165, RCT, Clark *et al, J Clin Psych* 2001, **62**, 34–40, Lilly). It has also been used in Lewy Body Dementia eg. decreased psychotic symptoms but no exacerbation of EPS (n=29, RCT, Cummings *et al, Dement Geriatr Cogn Disord* 2002, **13**, 67–73, sub-analysis), although only 2 tolerated 2.5–7.5mg/d with clear improvement, and 5 could not tolerate it or gained no benefit (n=8, open, Walker *et al, Int J Ger Psych* 1999, **14**, 459–66). **Quetiapine** 50–150mg/d may reduce aggression and behaviour in Alzheimer's with no worsening of cognitive function (open, 12/52, Scharre and Chang, *Alz Dis Assoc Disord* 2002, **16**, 128–30).

**Reviews**: general plus algorithm (Defilippi and Crismon, *Pharmacotherapy* 2000, **20**, 23–33, 43 refs).

## Ginkgo biloba *

Ginkgo biloba 120mg/d stabilised, and in some patients improved, cognitive function for 6–12 months in mild-to-moderate Alzheimer's and multi-infarct dementia (n=155) compared to placebo (n=154), (RCT, Le Bars *et al, JAMA* 1997, **278**, 1327–32). It must be given for 1–3 months before the full therapeutic effect is seen (review in *Medical Letter* 1998, **40**, 63–64). In a trial of mild to severe Alzheimer's, the placebo group showed a significant decline in all measures (ADAS-cog, GERRI and CGI) whilst the GB group were considered to have at least slightly improved on some scales (n=309,
d/b, p/c, 26/52, Le Bars *et al, Dement & Ger Cog Disord* 2000, **11**, 230–37). A rigorous meta-analysis by Oken *et al* (*Arch Neurol* 1998, **55**, 1409–15, reviewed by Bernabei, *EBMH* 1999, **2**, 82), concluded that GB was effective in mild-to-moderate Alzheimer's, and only slightly inferior to donepezil and rivastigmine. However, it fails to boost memory in healthy older adults (n=230, p/c, 6/52, Solomon *et al, JAMA* 2002, **288**, 835–40).

**Reviews:*** Barnes, *Pharm J* 2002, **269**, 160–62; Maidment, *Psych Bull* 2001, **25**, 353–56.

## NSAIDs*

There is growing evidence that NSAIDs might prevent or delay the onset of Alzheimer's and Pick's diseases. Most recently, NSAIDs at any time and aspirin for more than 2 years were shown to be associated with a 55% less chance of developing Alzheimer's disease (n=3227, Breitner *et al, Neurology* 2002, **59**, 880–86) and long-term (at least two years) use of NSAIDs appeared to lower the risk of AD by 80% (but not vascular dementia) with a greater reduction with increasing number of NSAID-taking years, provided these were started before the early signs of the disease (n=6,989, prospective, mean 7 yr follow-up, Stricker *et al, NEJM* 2001, **345**, 1515–21). These are large trials to be taken seriously. However,

a trial of diclofenac/misoprostol in Alzheimer's disease showed no significant differences, but with a trend towards the NSAID having some positive effects (n=41, RCT, 25/52, Scharf *et al, Neurology* 1999, **53**, 197–201). A 5-year case-control study of post-mortem brain tissue showed no significant differences in the amount of inflammatory glia, plaques, or tangles in either diagnostic group, and so whilst long-term NSAIDs in people with Alzheimer's disease may enhanced cognitive performance they may not alleviate the progression of the pathological changes (n=22, Halliday *et al, Arch Neurol* 2000, **57**, 831–36; see also postmortem study, Mackenzie, *Neurology* 2000, **54**, 732–35).

**Reviews**: general (Lucca, *CNS Drugs* 1999, **11**, 207–24 and 372; Flynn and Theesen, *Ann Pharmacother* 1999, **33**, 840–49).

## SSRIs *

Some studies have shown a potential effect with **citalopram** eg. improved confusion, mood, restlessness and irritability in Alzheimer's, but not vascular dementia (n=98, RCT, d/b, 4/52, Nyth and Gottfries, *B J Psych* 1990, **157**, 894–901), improved cognition and emotional functioning (eg. Nyth *et al, Acta Psych Scand* 1992, **86**, 138–45; review by Pollock *et al, Consultant Pharm* 1999, **14**, 1251–58) and superiority over placebo (favourably with perphenazine) for behavioural disturbances associated with dementia (n=85, RCT, d/b, 17/7, Pollock *et al, Am J Psych* 2002, **159**, 460–65). A trial showed slight improvement in confusion/anxiety with **fluvoxamine**, but not cognition or behaviour (n=46, RCT, d/b, p/c, Olafsson *et al, Acta Psych Scand* 1992, **85**, 453–56) and fluvoxamine augmentation of perphenazine may be effective in reducing psychosis in Alzheimer's patients (n=20, d/b, p/c, Levkovitz *et al, J Nerv Ment Dis* 2001, **189**, 126–29). **Sertraline** has been shown to be effective in depression in people with Alzheimer's Disease (n=22, RCT, 12/52, Lyketsos *et al*, *Am J Psych* 2000, **157**, 1686–89).

○ **Unlicensed/Possible efficacy**
**Antihypertensives** *
Cognition appears preserved in elderly patients taking long-term anti-hypertensives (55% reduction in risk of dementia cf placebo, Forette *et al*, *Arch Intern Med* 2002, **162**, 2046–52; n=1900, Murray *et al*, *Arch Intern Med* 2002, **162**, 2090–96).

**Aromatherapy** *
Melissa, an essential balm oil, may reduce agitation in severe dementia (n=71, d/b, p/c, Ballard *et al, J Clin Psych* 2002, **63**, 553–58) and lavender oil (2 hours a day) produced a modest but significant reduction in agitation in dementia in a cunningly placebo-controlled trial (n=15, p/c, *Int J Ger Psych* 2002, **17**, 305–8).

**Buspirone**
There have been reports of vocal grunts, rocking, difficult behaviour and choreoathetoid movements improving with buspirone (eg. n=1, *Lancet* 1988, **i**, 1169; n=1, Hamner *et al, J Clin Psychopharmacol* 1996, **16**, 261–62).

**Carbamazepine** *
Carbamazepine proved useful in one trial for hostility and aggression in demented patients who had not responded to antipsychotics (n=21, RCT, 6/52, Olin *et al, Am J Ger Psych* 2001, **9**, 400–5) and in another for nursing home patients with agitation and dementia, where it showed showed significant short-term efficacy with generally good safety and toler-ability (6/52, 51 sites, RCT, Tariot *et al, Am J Psych* 1998, **155**, 54–61).

**Cycloserine**
Cycloserine 5–50mg/d (a partial ago-nist acting at the NMDA glycine receptor complex) has been shown to enhance implicit memory in Alzheimer patients, supporting the development of NMDA receptor-mediated glutamatergic interventions for the treatment of Alzheimer-related memory disorders (n=108, p/c, d/b, 10/52, Schwartz *et al, Neur-*

*ology* 1996, **46**, 420–24). 100mg/d cycloserine produced a significant improvement in cognitive scores in a short trial (n=17, RCT, Tsai *et al, Am J Psych* 1999, **156**, 467–69).

**Estrogen (oestrogen)** *
Estrogen is a potent factor that pre-vents vascular disease and improves blood flow in diseased vessels, includ-ing blood flow in regions of the brain affected by AD. Estrogen also has direct effects on neuronal function that may play an important role not only in the preservation of neurons, but in the repair of neurons damaged by disease processes. Endogenous estrogen levels may decline in post-menopausal women in whom Alzhei-mer's disease develops (n=143, Manly *et al, Neurology* 2000, **54**, 833–38). A number of trials have shown a poten-tial effect in reducing the risk of devel-oping dementia in postmenopausal women (meta-analysis by Yaffe *et al, JAMA* 1998, **279**, 688–95; review by Whalley, *EBMH* 1998, **1**, 119). Long-term HRT may slow mental decline in older women, especially those over 85 (n=2000, Carlson *et al, Neurology* 2001, **57**, 2210–16) and high-dose transdermal 17-beta-oes-tradiol improved cognition in women with AD (n=20, RCT, p/c, 8/52, Asthana *et al, Neurology* 2001, **57**, 605–12). Estrogen HRT (oral or transdermal) enhanced verbal mem-ory and performance in non-demen-ted cognitively intact older women receiving (n=184, Maki *et al, Am J Psych* 2001, **158**, 227–33). However, some recent trials have failed to show a protective effect from eg. conjugated estrogens (n=120, RCT, 12/12, Mul-nard *et al, JAMA* 2000, **283**, 1007–15; Shaywitz and Shaywitz, *JAMA* 2000, **283**, 1055–56; editorial, review by Hogervorst and McShane, *EBMH* 2000, **3**, 83; n=50, d/b, 12/52, Wang *et al, Neurology* 2000, **54**, 2061–66) and short-term estrogen (n=42 women, RCT, 16/52, Henderson *et al, Neurol-ogy* 2000, **54**, 295–302). Estrogen replacement therapy (ERT) did not appear to slow the decline in cognitive

functioning in postmenopausal women (n=2859, Alves de Moraes *et al, Am J Epidemiol* 2001, **154**, 733–39) or reduce the risk of developing AD (n=112481 + 108925, case-control, Seshadri *et al, Arch Neurol* 2001, **58**, 435–40). Indeed, short-term estrogen may increase disturbed and aggressive behaviour in dementia in the elderly (n=16, RCT, d/b, p/c, 4/52, Kyomen *et al, Am J Psych* 2002, **159**, 1225–7).

**Reviews**: use in elderly men (review and n=2, Shelton and Brooks, *Ann Pharmacother* 1999, **33**, 808–12), general (Monk and Brodaty, *Demen & Ger Cog Disord* 2000, **11**, 1–10; Shepherd, *J Am Pharm Ass* 2001, **41**, 221–28).

## Gabapentin *

Gabapentin has been used for behavioural agitation in Alzheimer's, and in aggressive and agitated demented elderly patients, where 70% were much or greatly improved (n=24, case series, Hawkins *et al, Am J Ger Psych* 2000, **8**, 221–25; review by Miller, *Ann Pharmacother* 2001, **35**, 427–31, 28 refs).

## Insulin

Elevating insulin levels (with or without hyperglycaemia) improves memory in people with Alzheimer's (n=23 + 14 controls, Craft *et al, Arch Gen Psych* 1999, **56**, 1135–40).

## Lamotrigine

There is a case of frontal lobe dementia responding well to lamotrigine up to 100mg/d, but not to other treatments (n=1, 6/12, Devarajan *et al, Am J Psych* 2000, **157**, 1178, letter).

## Methylphenidate *

Methylphenidate 10mg/d has been used successfully for chronic apathy in dementia (n=2, RCT, d/b, c/o, Jansen *et al, J Am Ger Soc* 2001, **49**, 474–76).

## Naftidrofuryl

This is a cerebral vasodilator with some limited effect on cognitive and global functioning (eg. n=84, RCT, Emeriau *et al, Clin Ther* 2000, **22**, 834–44; Goldline, *Clin Ther* 2000, **22**, 1251–52).

## Nicotine

Studies have shown reduced nicotinic cholinergic receptors in the frontal cortex. Nicotine may stimulate the release of acetylcholine in this area. Nicotine is known to improve attention, memory, vigilance and information processing in (so far) healthy humans, but transdermal nicotine (up to 21mg/d) had no significant effect on cognitive functions in patients with Alzheimer's Disease (n=18, p/c, d/b, c/o, Snaedal *et al, Dementia* 1996, **7**, 47–52). Cochrane concludes that there is no reliable evidence for a beneficial effect (Lopez-Arrieta *et al, CDSR* 2000, 0149).

## Piracetam *

Piracetam stimulates ACh release. Mild effects may occur when used alone or with an ACh precursor, although Cochrane concludes that the evidence is not robust enough to prove an effect (Flicker *et al, CDSR* 2001, **2**, 1011).

## Statins *

The use of statins (lovastatin and pravastatin but not simvastatin) may substantially lower the risk of developing dementias (n=1364, Jick *et al, Lancet* 2000, **356**, 1627–31; n=60,000, Josefson, *BMJ* 2000, **321**, 1040).

## Testosterone

Testosterone supplements have been reported to reduce Alzheimer's Disease in both men and women (Anon, *Pharm J* 2000, **264**, 205).

## Trazodone *

Modest reductions in agitation in AD, with fewer side effects in placebo have been shown (comparisons with haloperidol, n=28, RCT, *Am J Geriatr Psychiatry* 1997, **5**, 60–69; n=149, RCT, 16/52, Teri *et al, Neurology* 2000, **55**, 1247–48).

## Valproate *

The only RCT was unable to show an advantage for valproate over placebo in aggressive behaviour in people with dementia (n=42, RCT, d/b, p/c, c/o, 3/52 per arm, Sival *et al, Int J Ger Psych* 2002, **17**, 579–85). However, in a prospective study in 16 patients (68–

95yr) unresponsive to other pharmacotherapy, divalproex 750–2500mg/d for 5 to 34 weeks was generally well tolerated and was moderately effective in decreasing physical agitation and aggression (n=16, open, Herrmann, *Can J Psych* 1998, **43**, 69–72) and divalproex (n=12) was more effective than placebo (n=4) for global symptoms, functioning and aggression in a small trial (n=16, d/b, 10/52, Hollander *et al, J Clin Psych* 2001, **62**, 199–203).

### Vitamins *
Alzheimer's disease has been linked to low levels of B12 or folate, with twice the risk of developing the disease if deficient (n=370, *Neurology* 2001, **56**, 1188) and a study in Hawaii suggested that vitamin E and C supplements may protect against vascular dementia and may improve cognitive function in later life in men (n=3385, Masaki *et al, Neurology* 2000, **54**, 1265–72). Two recent large studies have shown that high dietary intake of vitamin C and vitamin E may lower the risk of AD (n=5395, 6-yrs, Engelhart *et al, JAMA* 2002, **287**, 3223–29) and that vitamin E from food (but not other antioxidants or supplements) may lower the risk of Alzheimer disease (n=815, Morris *et al, JAMA* 2002, **287**, 3230–37).

### Zolpidem
This has been used for dementia-related insomnia and night-time wandering (Shelton and Hocking, *Ann Pharmacother* 1997, **31**, 319–22).

### ◇ Others
Other drugs tried include **amantadine** (n=33, Jibiki *et al, Acta Therapeutica* 1993, **19**, 389–96) and **naltrexone** and **naloxone** (review in *Ann Pharmacother* 1993, **27**, 447–80).

### ◆ No efficacy
### Prednisone
Prednisone 10–20mg/d has been shown to be ineffective (n=138, RCT, 56/52, Aisen *et al, Neurology* 2000, **54**, 588–93), despite initial enthusiasm from a pilot study, where 20mg/d showed some short-term effect in suppressing acute phase proteins, which have a role in plaque formation (n=20, open, Aisen *et al, Dementia* 1996, **7**, 201–6).

### Selegiline *
Selegiline may improve MMSE scores, but with no apparent effect on brain lesions or degenerative changes in brain tissue (n=17, Alafuzoff *et al, Eur J Clin Pharmacol* 2000, **55**, 815–19), although one trial (with questionable methodology) of 10mg/d indicated some slowing of the disease (n=341, RCT, Sano *et al, NEJM* 1997, **336**, 1216–22). Cochrane concluded that the evidence is promising but not yet conclusive to recommend routine use (Birks and Flicker, *CDSR* 2000, 0442) as did another review of available studies (n=1073) which indicated only small short-term improvement in cognition and ADL in Alzheimer's, which disappeared after 4–6 weeks (Wilcock *et al, Int J Ger Psych* 2002, **17**, 175–83).

## 1.14 DEPRESSION

See also bipolar mood disorder (*1.10*), dysthymia (*1.15*), rapid cycling mood disorder (*1.27*) and mania/hypomania (*1.19*)

Depression is a common illness, affecting 3% of the population per year, but remains under-diagnosed, under-treated (especially in men and under 30s) and antidepressants appear under-represented in suicides (n=5281 suicides, Isacsson *et al, B J Psych* 1999, **174**, 259–65), although detection in primary care may be better than perceived by some (n=18,414, Thompson *et al, B J Psych* 2001, **179**, 317–23). The overall cost of depression (eg. work, family, other illnesses) is very high for an eminently treatable condition.

### Symptoms: *
Depression presents with a mixture of biological symptoms (insomnia or hypersomnia, diurnal variation in mood, low appetite, fatigue or loss of energy, constipation, loss of libido, weight loss or gain) and psychiatric

symptoms (depressed mood, loss of interest or pleasure, poor memory, psychomotor agitation or retardation, recurrent thoughts of death or suicide, anxiety, feelings of worthlessness or guilt, including delusions etc). Depression does not include the normal reaction to the death of a loved one. Atypical depression includes the symptoms of depression, plus two from hypersomnia, hyperphagia, rejection sensitivity and severe lethargy (n=579, Posternak and Zimmerman, *Arch Gen Psych* 2002, **59**, 70–76).

**Causes:**
Precipitating factors can include drugs and drug abuse, physical illness and stress, eg. bereavement, loss of job, birth of child, break-up of relationship, work stress, poor social background, time of year, following English cricket etc.

**Role of drugs:**
Although most depressions will resolve with time, antidepressants have a major role in hastening this recovery and reducing suffering. Antidepressants are effective, not addictive and do not generally lose efficacy with prolonged use. Adequate doses (see later) are needed for clinical effect, and continuation for an appropriate period (see later) will minimise relapse. Inadequate treatment and the use of toxic drugs is difficult to defend other than on acquisition cost grounds. Sadly, there still appears to be much sub-therapeutic dosing and duration in the UK, with paroxetine and fluoxetine most likely to be prescribed for a therapeutic period (151 GP practice study, Lawrenson *et al*, *J Aff Dis* 2000, **59**, 149–57). Drugs may also be effective in reducing medically unexplained physical symptoms, eg. headache, tinnitus etc in depression (review, O'Malley *et al*, *J Fam Pract* 1999, **48**, 980–90; reviewed by Price, *EBMH* 2000, **3**, 84).
A viable option is combining medicines with long-term maintenance CBT (Blackburn and Moore, *B J Psych* 1997, **171**, 328–34) or IPT (n=187, RCT, elderly, Reynolds *et al*,

*JAMA* 1999, **281**, 39–45), where a combination is generally more effective than either individually (meta-analysis, DeRubeis *et al*, *Am J Psych* 1999, **156**, 1007–13; disputed by Taylor *et al*, *Am J Psych* 2000, **157**, 1025–26), including where CBT may reduce relapse rates in people on maintenance antidepressants with residual depressive symptoms (Paykel *et al*, *Arch Gen Psych* 1999, **56**, 829–35; review by McGinn, *EBMH* 2000, **3**, 48). In patients either randomised to counselling or antidepressants, or were allowed to choose for themselves between drugs and counselling, no differences were found either in the initial characteristics or in the outcomes and both were equally effective at 8 weeks, so expressing a preference had no apparent effect or benefit on outcomes (n=323, Bedi *et al*, *B J Psych* 2000, **177**, 312–18).

**Treatment of depression:***
The general principles of treatment of depression (with antidepressants) can be summed up by the six D's: diagnosis, drug-related, drug, dose, duration and discontinuation:
1. **Diagnosis** – making, or being able to make, a diagnosis helps.
2. **Drug-related causes eliminated,** eg. excessive caffeine intake, other drugs liable to cause depression (see 5.5), physical (eg. low folate levels) and environmental causes etc.
3. **Drug and Dose**
   **Acute therapy:** Antidepressants must be increased to therapeutic doses, eg. standard dose SSRI, 125–150mg/d tricyclic, and maintained for an adequate duration. If depression remains completely unchanged at 4 weeks of therapeutic dosing, an alternate drug should be tried. Minimal improvement within the first 4 weeks should indicate a further 2-week trial, then change to an alternate drug if there is no further response (n=593, Quitkin *et al*, *Arch Gen Psych* 1996, **53**, 785–92). These times should probably be doubled in the elderly and chronic depression (Gelenberg and Chesen,

*J Clin Psych* 2000, **61**, 712–21). Among responders, the onset of improvement occurs in more than 70% of cases within the first 3 weeks of treatment with little evidence of a pronounced increase in improvement rates beyond this time point, with early improvement highly predictive of better long-term outcomes (Stassen and Angst, *CNS Drugs* 1998, **9**, 177–84). The therapeutic range of the newer antidepressants has been established through dose-finding studies but is less clear for the tricyclics (see TCAs for discussion). There is some data that mirtazapine and venlafaxine may act slightly quicker, especially if more aggressive dosing strategies are used (review by Nierenberg, *J Clin Psych* 2001, **62**(Suppl 15), 22–25). Once-daily dosing is as effective as multiple daily doses, regardless of drug half-life (meta-analysis of 22 studies by the Scrabble players favourite Yýldýz, and Sachs, *J Aff Dis* 2001, **66**, 199–206; review by Barbui, *EBMH* 2002, **5**, 57). Incomplete recovery is more common than generally recognised (Judd, *Acta Psych Scand* 2001, **104**, 81–83).

For advice on switching antidepressants, see *2.2.2*.

4. **Duration:** *

A. **Continuation therapy**: Proper treatment of depression requires relief not just of acute symptoms but continued treatment while the person remains vulnerable. Inadequate or no treatment for six months postresponse in controlled trials has resulted in relapse rates as high as 50% (cf. 20% with adequate treatment, although compliance was not certain in these cases). If depression remits in 12 weeks, continued treatment for 6 months minimises the risk of relapse, but longer therapy confers little additional benefit, except in people with additional relapse risk factors (n=395, RCT, 52/52, Reimherr *et al*, *Am J Psych* 1998, **155**, 1247–53). People

who continue with their initial antidepressant (rather than need to switch or just discontinue) also have lower relapse/recurrence rates over two years (retrospective study, n=4052, Melfi *et al*, *Arch Gen Psych* 1998, **55**, 1128–32). Consistent antidepressant use (eg. 4/12 continuous therapy with an SSRI) is associated with lowest risk of relapse or recurrence (Claxton *et al*, *B J Psych* 2000, **177**, 163–68). Continuation doses should be the **same or close to the therapeutic dose** (*J Aff Dis* 1993, **27**, 139–45). In the elderly, therapy for up to two years after recovery may be needed (*Int J Ger Psych* 1992, **7**, 617–19; *B J Psych* 1993, **162**, 175–82). Patients should also be advised that antidepressants are not 'addictive' as such. If stopped prematurely (less than 13 weeks), antidepressants are still likely to be effective if reintroduced on relapse (n=501, Fava *et al*, *Psychother Psychosom* 2002, **71**, 195–99).

B. **Prophylactic therapy:** * Long-term antidepressant treatment in depressed people is often "strikingly inadequate", even in previous suicide attempters (Oquendo *et al*, *Am J Psych* 2002, **159**, 1746–51). Long-term management benefits depressed patients by increasing long-term compliance and hence prolonging remission (n=211, RCT, Rost *et al*, *BMJ* 2002, **325**, 934–37), since 75% have a further episode, usually within 2 to 3 years, if untreated. Those likely to benefit from maintenance (Kasper and Eder in Winkler *et al*, *Curr Opin Psych* 2002, **15**, 63–68), include those with chronic depression, three episodes or two episodes with risk factors (late or early onset, short interval between episodes, rapid onset, dysthymia, positive family history, co-morbidity, incomplete response, low work adjustment). Other risk factors include being female, unemployed, severe illness and melancholia (n=7076, Spijker *et al*, *Acta Psych Scand* 2001, **103**,

122–30). In a 10-year prospective study of multiple recurrences of major depression, the risk of recurrence increased by 16% with each successive episode, but the risk of recurrence progressively decreased as duration of recovery increased (n=318, Solomon *et al, Am J Psych* 2000, **157**, 229–33). Most antidepressants have been shown to be effective for continuation or maintenance therapy of unipolar depression (review by Winkler *et al, Curr Opin Psych* 2002, **15**, 63–68), and mood stabilisers should be considered as well. Doses should be at full therapeutic levels, not reduced.

**General minimum treatment: duration recommendations:**

First episode — 6 months post-recovery (see 3 above)

Second episode — 2–3 years

Third episode — 5 years or longer.

**Review:*** Maintenance (WFSBP Guidelines, Bauer *et al, World J Biol Psych* 2002, **3**, 69–86).

5. **Discontinuation:** When discontinuing therapy is considered appropriate, slowly reduce doses over a minimum of four weeks. Discontinuation syndromes have been reported for nearly all antidepressants, but particularly paroxetine and venlafaxine. Discontinuation symptoms usually appear within 1–3 days of stopping treatment and improve within a week, while recurrence of depression begins after 3 weeks and continues to worsen. See switching antidepressants in *2.2.2* for a further review, eg. symptoms and management.

**Treatment-resistant depression:**

True 'treatment-resistant' depression often needs a systematic approach to solve. Remember also that resistant depression may also be undiagnosed bipolar (see next section):

1. **Escalate doses for an adequate duration,** an appropriate action for drugs with a dose-response curve, eg. up to 300mg/d or more of a tricyclic or other drug (eg. venlafax-

ine), or to tolerance (monitoring plasma levels carefully), remembering that a few people have multiple copies of, eg. *CYP2D6* and may rapidly metabolise tricyclics. Treatment for up to 9–17 weeks may also be needed (review; Greenhouse *et al, J Aff Dis* 1987, **13**, 259–66). SSRIs tend to have a flat dose-response curve, so switching is probably the best ploy (review; Corruble and Guelfi, *Acta Psych Scand* 2000, **101**, 343–48).

2. **Check blood levels** – levels of 300–400mcg/l of tricyclics have been used by some in true refractory cases (see Hodgkiss *et al, Hum Psychopharmacol* 1995, **10**, 407–15). Dothiepin, amitriptyline and clomipramine have been the tricyclics preferred for high dose therapy. This also detects possible ultra-rapid 2D6 metabolisers.

3. **Switch drugs** – ensure all drug classes have been tried optimally, eg. SSRIs, tricyclics, venlafaxine, mirtazapine, moclobemide (at much higher doses than are currently recommended, eg. over 600mg/d), MAOIs (although high dose moclobemide may be a suitable and safer alternative) etc.

4. **Augment or combine** – use logical combinations of antidepressants, (see later in this section), eg. mirtazapine (n=20, open, Carpenter, *J Clin Psych* 1999, **80**, 45–49), lithium, carbamazepine (but not with tricyclics, where it reduces plasma levels, see *4.5.1*), valproate, lithium/clomipramine/tryptophan, phenelzine/lithium/tryptophan and tricyclic/MAOI. SSRIs should not routinely be used with tricyclics, unless with regular blood level testing, or at all with MAOIs or tryptophan (see *4.3.4*). Use of logical augmentation is also possible, eg. levothyroxine, liothyronine, buspirone, pindolol, mirtazapine etc.

5. **Assure compliance**, eg. by plasma levels etc.

6. Check folate levels (see adjunctive therapy)
**Reviews**: algorithm, the role of psychosurgery and ECT, and extensive review (Bridges *et al, B J Hosp Med* 1995, **54**, 501–6), drug treatments (O'Reardon *et al, Curr Opin Psych* 2000, **13**, 93–98).

**Bipolar depression: \***
Bipolar depression is frequent, longer-lasting than unipolar depression (up to 50% may still be depressed at one year, Hlastala *et al, Depress Anxiety* 1997, **5**, 73–83), often characterised by psychomotor-retarded melancholic symptoms, atypical features and psychosis (39 + 39, Mitchell *et al, J Clin Psych* 2001, **62**, 212–16), a major cause of inter-episode impairment, can be potentiated by substance and alcohol misuse and is much more difficult to treat. The general principles of management include:

1. **Avoid mixed states** in bipolar III, where the risk of self-harm is high.
2. **Avoid sudden dose changes** or switches
3. **Antidepressants** are effective (eg. n=2032, Möller *et al, J Aff Dis* 2001, **67**, 141–46) with care, starting with lowest switch risk drugs, eg. SSRIs, mirtazapine, bupropion but avoiding TCAs if possible. Lamotrigine has a growing reputation as a specific measure for bipolar depression. Addition of an antidepressant is probably more effective than adding a second mood stabiliser (paroxetine vs lithium or valproate; n=27, RCT, d/b, 6/52, Young *et al, Am J Psych* 2000, **157**, 124–26), particularly in people unable to tolerate higher lithium doses (n=117, d/b, p/c, 10/52, Nemeroff *et al, Am J Psych* 2001, **158**, 906–12).
4. **Use mood stabilisers** in the initial acute stage, eg. lithium and valproate show good responses in open trials of bipolar depression (discussion by Sachs *et al, Psychiatr Clin North Am* 1996, **19**, 215–36), as does carbamazepine (open, Dilsaver *et al, Biol Psych* 1996, **40**, 935–37).

5. **Minimise antidepressant exposure** by attempting gradual taper after a continuation phase, provided the patient is genuinely euthymic. Consider however that premature discontinuing antidepressants within the first 3–6/12 of an episode (n=25) has an up to 3 times higher relapse rate than those continuing for at least 8/12 (n=19), with no increase in mania in the latter group (n=44, retrospective, 1-yr, Altshuler *et al, J Clin Psych* 2001, **62**, 612–16).
6. **Offer ECT** for patients at immediate risk of self-harm or unable to tolerate antidepressants. ECT may be better in older people.
7. **Check thyroid function** — poor response in bipolar depression may be related to low FTI and high TSH levels, even if in the alleged therapeutic range (n=65, Cole *et al, Am J Psych* 2002, **159**, 116–21).

The risk of switching to mania with antidepressants in bipolar depression varies from 31–70%. It usually occurs within the first 12 weeks, is lower if used with a mood stabiliser and, if it develops, the best plan is to reduce the antidepressant dose immediately and allow the mood to settle for a month or so. The switch rates in double-blind trials have been reported to be imipramine 9.5%, placebo 7% and fluoxetine 0–16% (n=89, d/b, Cohn *et al, Int Clin Psychopharmacol* 1989, **4**, 313–22), and tranylcypromine 24% and imipramine 28% (n=56, RCT, Himmelhoch *et al, Am J Psych* 1991, **148**, 910–16).

**Reviews\***: general (Haddad and Dursun, *Acta Psych Scand* 2002, **105**, 401–3; Ghaemi *et al, J Clin Psych* 2001, **62**, 565–69), WFSBP Guidelines (Grunze *et al, World J Biol Psych* 2002, **3**, 115–124).

**Loss of antidepressant efficacy:**
This has been reported during long-term maintenance treatment (dubbed 'poop-out') in 9–33% patients with many drugs, eg. fluoxetine, sertraline, amoxapine, tricyclics, MAOIs etc. Explanations may include non-compliance, loss of initial placebo response,

loss of true drug effect, pharmacological tolerance, accumulation of detrimental metabolites, change in illness pathology, unrecognised rapid cycling and a genuine lack of prophylactic efficacy. Strategies to overcome this include:

1. **Increase** the dose (logical, and works with, eg. fluoxetine, ie. Fava *et al, Am J Psych* 1994, **151**, 1372–74).
2. **Decrease** the dose (this may work if the dose has exceeded any 'therapeutic window', but this is poorly supported by published data).
3. **Addition** of dopamine antagonists, eg. bromocriptine (reviewed by Byrne and Rothschild, see below).
4. **Augment** with mood stabilisers, anticonvulsants, thyroid, another antidepressant etc.
5. **Drug holiday** (poorly supported by the literature).
6. **Switch** to a different drug or another similar drug.
7. **Ensure compliance**.

**Reviews**: study and review (Byrne and Rothschild, *J Clin Psych* 1998, **59**, 279–88), short section within review by Sechter and Lane (*J Serotonin Res*, 1997, 30–33).

**Choice of drugs:**
All the main antidepressants appear to have broadly similar efficacy and so antidepressant choice will be based upon the features of depression, suicide risk, concomitant therapy, concurrent illness, side-effect tolerability, time to reach therapeutic dose, cost and special considerations, eg. cognitive impairment, driving etc. As non-compliance or inadequate dosage are the main causes of drug failure, choice of drug should consider these factors. Nearly all antidepressants can be given once a day. Deaths from overdose are mostly from TCAs (predominantly dothiepin and amitriptyline) and most often in deprived areas (Shah *et al, Psychol Med* 2001, **31**, 1203–10). Women may respond better to SSRIs and men to tricyclics (sertraline vs imipramine comparison, n=635, RCT, d/b, 12/12, Kornstein *et al, Am J Psych*

2000, **157**, 1445–52, Pfizer study; critique by Young, *EBMH* 2001, **4**, 114). A meta-analysis of 102 trials (n=10706) of SSRIs vs TCAs, concluded that SSRIs are as effective as TCAs, but better tolerated and with fewer drop-outs, although TCAs may be more effective in in-patient studies (Anderson, *J Aff Dis* 2000, **58**, 19–36; review by Nolert, *EBMH* 2000, **3**, 106).

**Suicidality:** *
The risk of suicide appears to be the same with tricyclics as with the newer drugs, but the rates of death are higher with tricyclics (Jick *et al, BMJ* 1995, **310**, 215–18). The SSRIs and other newer agents have low toxicity in overdose. Antidepressants have been alleged to be associated with the emergence of suicidal tendencies but in fact, fluoxetine shows a slight *reduction* in suicidal behaviour, rather than an increase (n=185, Leon *et al, Am J Psych* 1999, **156**, 195–201). In Sweden, a study of 5281 suicides from 1992–94 showed that antidepressants were detectable in only 12.4% of men and 26.2% of women but overdose by antidepressant was the probable cause of death in only 2.1% of men and 7.9% of women, indicating that underuse of antidepressants was perhaps more relevant than absolute toxicity (n=5281, Isacsson *et al, B J Psych* 1999, **174**, 259–65). Another review showed no convincing evidence that SSRIs cause aggression, violence or suicide (Walsh and Dinan, *Acta Psych Scand* 2001, **104**, 84–91).

**Reviews:** * evidence-based guidelines for pharmacotherapy (BAP Guidelines; Anderson *et al, J Psychopharmacol* 2000, **14**, 3–20) and introduction thereof (Simon, *Curr Opin Psych* 2002, **15**, 77–82), relapse prevention (Forshall and Nutt, *Psych Bull* 1999, **23**, 370–73), depression in old age (Anderson, *Age & Ageing* 2001, **30**, 13–17; Snowdon, *Aust Pres* 2001, **24**, 65–66; Solai *et al, Drugs & Aging* 2001, **18**, 355–68; 98 refs), emergency treatment of depression (Porter and Ferrier, *Adv Psych Treat* 1999, **5**, 3–10), TDM of antidepressants (Burke and Preskorn, *Clin Pharmacokinet* 1999, **37**, 147–65, 87 refs), in primary care (Mulrow *et al*, *Am J Med* 2000, **108**, 54–64; Rao, *Prescriber* 2001, **12**, 29–40), in children and adolescents (Emslie and Mayes, *CNS Drugs* 1999, **11**, 181–89), in women (Desai and Jann, *J Am Pharm Assoc* 2000, **40**, 525–37), atypicals in treatment-resistance (Thase, *J Clin Psych* 2002, **63**, 95–103), atypical depression (n=591, Angst *et al*, *J Aff Dis* 2002, **72**, 125–38), genetics of this familial disorder (Sullivan *et al*, *Am J Psych* 2000, **157**, 1552–62), rapid-onset strategies (Blier, *J Clin Psych* 2001, **62** (Suppl 15), 12–17).

**Types of antidepressants:**
There are many classifications of antidepressants. It is important to remember that reuptake inhibition by antidepressants is just the start of a cascade of events involving changes in the sensitivities of receptors at (somatodendritic) sites, eg. $5HT_{1A}$ receptors, at pre- and post-synaptic sites, as well as changes in neuronal signal transduction beyond the receptor. All neurotransmitter systems seem interdependent. On a transmitter/probable mechanism basis, the following may, however, be useful:

1. Noradrenaline and serotonin reuptake inhibition, eg. tricyclics, venlafaxine (above 150mg/d)
2. Serotonin reuptake inhibition, eg. SSRIs, venlafaxine (lower dose)
3. Noradrenaline reuptake inhibition, eg. reboxetine
4. $5\text{-}HT_2$ blockade plus serotonin reuptake inhibition, eg. trazodone
5. Monoamine oxidase inhibition, eg. moclobemide, MAOIs
6. Pre-synaptic alpha-2-autoreceptor and heteroceptor blockade, eg. mirtazapine
7. Serotonin precursor, eg. tryptophan
8. Dopamine reuptake blockers, eg. bupropion (only licensed in UK for smoking cessation).

---

**BNF Listed**
## Selective Serotonin Reuptake Inhibitors (SSRIs)*
The SSRIs are now first choice drugs in depression in most patients due to their safety in overdose and heart disease and better side-effect profile (eg. lacking anticholinergic, sedation and weight gain effects).

Although chemically distinct, the SSRIs are essentially more similar than different and are all effective antidepressants but their ADR profiles and potential for interactions may help identify clinical differences. Discontinuation rates with SSRIs are probably lower than with the older TCAs (10% overall, 25% due to side-effects), but not *that* great (Anderson and Tomenson, *BMJ* 1995, **310**, 1433–38) and not significantly lower than with the newer tricyclics eg. lofepramine (meta-analysis and investigation of heterogenicity, Hotopf *et al*, *B J Psych* 1997, **170**, 120–27).

**Reviews**: differences in their pharmacological and clinical profiles (de Jonghe and Swinkels, *CNS Drugs* 1997, **7**, 452–67; Anderson and Edwards, *Adv Psych Treat* 2001, **7**, 170–80)

### Citalopram *
Citalopram is well-established across Europe and USA and has been shown to be effective and well-tolerated in studies against standard antidepressants. A review of 30 RCTs showed citalopram to be superior to placebo, of equivalent efficacy to other antidepressants and well tolerated from 20–60mg/d, with linear pharmacokinetics and minimal drug interactions (Keller, *J Clin Psych* 2000, **61**, 896–908, 81 refs; reviewed by Silva de Lima, *EBMH* 2001, **4**, 80), with a particularly robust effect in melancholic depression seen at 40–60mg/d (n=650, RCT, Feighner and Overø *J Clin Psych* 1999, **60**, 824–30). It has been shown to be highly effective in bipolar I or II depression, with a robust and sustained response rate and low ADRs (n=45, open, 8/52, Kupfer *et al*, *Clin Psych* 2001, **62**,

985–90). Relapse prevention has been shown over 15 months in adults (n=427, RCT, 44–77/52, Hochstrasser *et al*, *B J Psych* 2001, **178**, 304–10) and in the elderly (n=121, RCT, 48/52, Klysner *et al*, *B J Psych* 2002, **181**, 29–35). In patients who had responded to citalopram 40mg/d for four months, halving the dose to 20mg/d for a maintenance phase (2-yrs) resulted in a 50% relapse rate, reinforcing the view that full-dose maintenance therapy is required (n=50, Franchini *et al*, *J Clin Psych* 1999, **60**, 861–65; comment by Somawalla, *J Clin Psych* 2001, **62**, 993). It has a very low incidence of interactions *(4.3.2.1)*. The green and yellow 20mg pack in the UK has recently been dispensed with pride by football supporters in the author's home city of Norwich.

**Reviews**: general (Pollock, *Expert Opin Pharmacother* 2001, **2**, 681–98; Parker and Brown, *Ann Pharmacother* 2000, **34** 761–71, 60 refs; Bezchlibnyk-Butler *et al*, *J Psychiatry Neurol* 2000, **25**, 241–54; Joubert *et al*, *Hum Psychopharmacol* 2000, **15**, 439–510).

### Escitalopram *

Escitalopram is the pharmacologically active enantiomer of citalopram (a mix of R- and S-citalopram) and twice as potent on a mg for mg basis (eg, n=380, RCT, d/b, 8/52, Wade *et al*, *Int Clin Psychopharmacol* 2002, **17**, 95–102). The recommended dose for depression is 10mg/d increasing to a maximum 20mg/d. In a comparison with citalopram, escitalopram 10mg/d was at least as effective as citalopram 40mg/d at the study endpoint with few other differences (n=491, RCT, d/b, p/c, 8/52, Burke *et al*, *J Clin Psych* 2002, **63**, 331–36). A pooled analysis of the 3 RCTs (n=1321, Gorman *et al*, *CNS Spectrums* 2002, **7** (suppl 1), 40–44) also showed escitalopram as effective and well tolerated as citalopram, with a slightly increased response at one week and a very low drop-out rate. A poster (n=288, RCT, 8/52, Montgomery *et al*, *ECNP* 2002) has suggested escitalopram (mean 12.5mg/d) at least equivalent response over venlafaxine (mean 95mg/d), although the response rates were high for both treatment arms. The half-life is 27–32hrs and with negligible effects on P450 enzymes. Relapse prevention over 36 weeks has been shown.

**Reviews**: Burke, *Expert Opin Investig Drug* 2002, **11**, 1477–86; Baldwin, *Hosp Med* 2002, **63**, 668–71; McRae, *Curr Opin Invest Drugs* 2002, **3**, 1225–29.

### Fluoxetine *

Fluoxetine is licensed in the UK for depression, with or without anxiety. It has been shown to be clearly superior to placebo and slightly superior to tricyclics with significantly fewer dropouts (rigorous meta-analysis, 30 trials, n=4120, Bech *et al*, *B J Psych* 2000, **176**, 421–28), with 20mg as the most effective dose (n=417, meta-analysis by Beasley *et al*, *J Clin Psych* 2000, **61**, 722–28) and evidence of relapse prevention (n=140, RCT, 48/52, Gilaberte *et al*, *J Clin Psychopharmacol* 2001, **21**, 417–24, Lilly study). Although 20mg/d is the standard dose, some resistant depressions may respond to 60–80mg/d (n=15, open, 4/52, Fava *et al*, *J Aff Dis* 1992, **25**, 229–34) and 40–60mg/d fluoxetine was as effective as low-dose fluoxetine plus lithium, or desipramine for resistant depression (n=101, 4/52, Fava *et al*, *J Clin Psychopharm* 2002, **22**, 379–87). Claims of suicidal ideation (n=6, Teicher *et al*, *Am J Psych* 1990, **147**, 207–10) have been disproven (n=10614, Tollefson *et al*, *Ann Clin Psych* 1993, **5**, 209–24). Fluoxetine shows a slight *reduction* in suicidal behaviour, rather than an *increase* (n=185, Leon *et al*, *Am J Psych* 1999, **156** 195–201). A long half-life may prove a problem in the elderly, although missed doses become less important in continuation and prophylactic therapy and discontinuation symptoms are rare. Twice-weekly dosing (Megna and Devitt, *Ann Pharmacother* 2001, **35**, 45–47) and a weekly tablet (see *6.2*) have been used.

## Fluvoxamine

Fluvoxamine has been compared with, and shown to be as effective as, many standard tricyclics. One trial showed it to also be effective as monotherapy in delusional depression (n=59, Gatti *et al, Am J Psych* 1996, **153**, 414–16). It may have a higher incidence of nausea and vomiting than other SSRIs. Most adverse effects occur in the first month and neuro-psychiatric symptoms are the most common, with headache (3.8%) and dizziness (3.3%) (Edwards *et al, B J Psych* 1994, **164**, 387–95).

## Paroxetine*

Paroxetine is licensed in the UK for depression, including that accompanied by anxiety. Several short-term trials comparing it with standard tricyclics have been published. Well-tolerated long-term relapse prevention (n=53) has been shown (n=108, d/b, 4/12, Baldwin *et al, J Psychopharmacol* 2001, **15**, 161–65). It has a flat dose-response curve, with 20mg/d optimum and no significant advantage for escalating dosage to 40mg/d (n=544, RCT, Benkert *et al, Acta Psych Scand* 1997, **95**, 288–96). Paroxetine's half-life increases from 10 to 21 hours on chronic dosing, but reduces when this is stopped, which may in part explain the many reports of discontinuation effects (see 2.2.2), and which have received much media publicity in recent years.

**Reviews**: general (Wagstaff *et al, Drugs* 2002, **62**, 655–703; Bourin *et al, CNS Drug Rev* 2001, **7**, 25–47).

## Sertraline*

The pharmacological profile of sertraline is similar to fluoxetine, but with a shorter half-life. The standard dose is 50mg/d although 100mg/d is routinely used. The response to the higher dose may be quicker than 50mg/d (n=44, 10/52, Suri *et al, J Clin Psych* 2000, **61**, 942–46). Sertraline may be effective also in delusional depression (comparison *vs* paroxetine, n=46, d/b, Zanardi *et al, Am J Psych* 1996, **153**, 1631–33) and in the elderly (n=210, over 60yo, RCT, 12/52, Bon-dareff *et al, Am J Psych* 2000, **157**, 729–36). Efficacy in chronic major depression has been shown (n=635, RCT, Keller *et al, J Clin Psych* 1998, **59**, 598–607). After a 3-month acute phase, relapse prevention has been shown (n=161, RCT, 4/12, Keller *et al, JAMA* 1998, **280**, 1665–72; see also Baldessarini *et al, JAMA* 1999, **282**, 323–24). Patients in a community nursing home stabilised on sertraline once-daily for 12 or more weeks were successfully changed to equivalent doses of sertraline three times a week (n=44, Karki *et al, J Pharm Technol* 2000, **16**, 43–46). Sertraline has a favourable drug interaction profile (*4.3.2.5*). There is no relationship between plasma levels and response (n=21, Mauri *et al, PNBP* 2002, **26**, 597–601).

**Reviews**: general (Perry and Benfield, *CNS Drugs* 1997, **7**, 480–500, 123 refs), pharmacokinetic profile (DeVane *et al, Clin Pharmacokinet* 2002, **41**, 1247–66).

## Tricyclics*

Doses of 125–150mg/d of tricyclics are effective in depression and clearly superior to placebo. A recent meta-analysis has concluded that low-dose tricyclics (ie. less than 125mg/d) are also superior to placebo, and that higher doses may be more effective than low-dose (Furukama *et al, BMJ* 2002, **325**, 991). Many of the studies include people potentially responsive co-morbid medical conditions, the 5% of people with low CYP2D6 activity (who will have high plasma levels from low doses) and some tricyclics may improve sleep (see bmj.com/cgi/content/full/325/7371/991 for an enlightening correspondence on this paper). The meta-analysis by Bollini *et al* (*B J Psych* 1999, **174**, 297–303), concluding that 'sub-therapeutic' antidepressant doses are effective is only justified if considering fluoxetine 30mg/d as sub-therapeutic, which it isn't (for a good review of the use of sub-therapeutic doses of TCAs, see Donoghue (*Acta Psych Scand* 1998, **98**, 429–31).

# Table of the rationale and risks for combinations of antidepressants

| | Citalopram/escitalopram | Fluoxetine | Fluvoxamine | Paroxetine | Sertraline | Tricyclics | MAOIs | Venlafaxine | Mirtazapine | Reboxetine | Trazodone | Nefazodone | Moclobemide | Flupentixol |
|---|---|---|---|---|---|---|---|---|---|---|---|---|---|---|
| **Fluoxetine** | SS LR-HR | | | | | | | | | | | | | |
| **Fluvoxamine** | SS LR-HR | SS LR-HR | | | | | | | | | | | | |
| **Paroxetine** | SS LR-HR | SS-C4/5/5 LR-HR | SS LR-HR | | | | | | | | | | | |
| **Sertraline** | SS LR-HR | SS-C4/5 LR-HR | SS LR-HR | SS LR-HR | | | | | | | | | | |
| **Tricyclics** | SS-C4/5 LR-HR-C1 | SS-C4/5 LR-HR-C1 SM-LDT | SS-C4/5 LR-HR-C1 SM-LDT | SS-C4/5 LR-HR-C1 SM-LDT | SS-C4/5 LR-LR-C1 | | | | | | | | | |
| **MAOIs** | (SS)-C4/5 SR-HR | (SS)-C4/5 SR-HR | (SS)-C4/5 SR-HR | (SS)-C4/5 SR-HR | (SS) SR-HR-C1 | (SS) SR-HR-C1 | | | | | | | | |
| **Venlafaxine** | SS LR-HR | SS LR-HR | SS LR-HR | SS MR-HR-C1 | SS LR-HR | SS LR-HR | SSU C4/5 SR-HR | | | | | | | |
| **Mirtazapine** | SSU LR-UR | SSU LR-UR | SSU LR-UR | SSU LR-UR | SSU LR-UR | SSU C4/5 LR-UR | SSU C4/5 LR-HR | SSU LR-UR | | | | | | |
| **Reboxetine** | SSU SR-UR VM | SSU SR-UR VM | SSU SR-UR VM | SSU SR-UR VM | SSU SR-UR VM | SSU C4/5 LR-MR | SSU C4/5 LR-HR | SSU LR-UR | SSU SR-UR VM | | | | | |
| **Trazodone** | SS LR-UR | SS LR-UR | SS LR-UR | SS LR-UR | SS LR-UR | (SS) SR-MR | (SS)-C4/5 SR-HR | SS LR-HR | SSU SR-UR | SSU SR-UR VM | | | | |
| **Nefazodone** | SS LR-HR | SS LR-HR | SS LR-HR | SS LR-HR | SS LR-HR | (SS)-C4/5 SR-LR | (SS)-C4/5 SR-HR | (SS) LR-HR | SSU SR-UR | SSU SR-UR | SS LR-HR | | | |
| **Moclobemide** | (SS)-C4/5 SR-MR | (SS)-C4/5 SR-MR | (SS) SR-MR | (SS) SR-MR | (SS) SR-MR | (SS)-C4/5 UR-MR | (SS)-C4/5 SR-HR | (SS)-C4/5 SR-HR | SSU SR-UR | SSU SR-UR | (SS) SR-UR | (SS) SR-UR | | |
| **Flupentixol** | SSU LR-UR | SSU LR-UR | SSU LR-UR | SSU LR-UR | SSU LR-UR | SSU LR-UR | SSU LR-UR | SSU LR-UR | SSU LR-UR | SSU LR-UR | SSU LR-UR | SSU LR-UR | SSU LR-UR | |
| **Tryptophan** | (SS)-C4/5 UR-MR | (SS)-C4/5 UR-MR | (SS)-C4/5 UR-MR | (SS)-C4/5 UR-MR | (SS)-C4/5 UR-MR | (SS)-C4/5 UR-MR | (SS)-C4/5 UR-MR | (SS) UR-MR | SSU UR-LR | SSU UR-LR | (SS) UR-MR | (SS) UR-MR | SSU UR-MR | SSU UR-LR |

SS = serotonin syndrome very possible
(SS) = serotonin syndrome possible or rarely reported
SSU = serotonin syndrome unlikely

LR = low rationale
SR = some rationale
UR = unknown rationale

LH = relatively low hazard or risk known or predicted
MH = medium hazard or risk either known or predicted
HH = high hazard or risk of problems known or predicted so specialist monitoring required
UH = unknown or undocumented hazard

SM-LDT = specialist monitoring required and limit dose of tricyclic
VM = consider venlafaxine ($>$ 200mg/d) or mirtazapine instead for combined 5-HT and NA/NE reuptake blockade

C1 = see chapter 1 for data on positive use of combination
C4/5 = see chapters 4 or 5 for data on risk of interaction or adverse consequences

In England and Wales, deaths (1993–1997) from overdose have risen, with 20% antidepressant-related, 95% from TCAs (predominantly dosulepin and amitriptyline) and most often in deprived areas (n=2503, Shah *et al*, *Psychol Med* 2001, **31**, 1203–10). Patients taking tricyclics are 5 times more likely to have road traffic accidents than untreated controls (Edwards, editorial in *BMJ* 1995, **311**, 887–88).

## Amitriptyline *

A widely-used tricyclic with potent anticholinergic, sedative, weight gaining properties and a long half-life (meta-analysis of amitriptyline vs the rest: Barbui and Hotopf, *B J Psych* 2001, **178**, 129–44; reply by Thompson, *B J Psych* 2001, **178**, 99–100).

## Amoxapine

Amoxapine is structurally similar to maprotiline. The once claimed faster onset of action is probably due to the sedative and anxiolytic effects of its metabolites (eg. loxapine) which have mild antipsychotic/sedative effects. It has a high incidence of seizures (up to 36% in overdose) as well as renal failure, endocrine and EPSEs.

## Clomipramine

A potent tricyclic with an active metabolite, with a possible added advantage in treating depression with an obsessional component. On one measure, clomipramine has been shown to have superior efficacy to imipramine and citalopram (two trial comparison by Fuglum *et al*, *Acta Psych Scand* 1996, **94**, 18–25). Clomipramine doses of 25, 50, 75, 125 and 200mg/d all show improvement, with 125 and 200mg/d showing the greatest improvement, although there was no placebo control group (n=151, d/b, 6/52, DUAG, *Clin Pharmacol & Therapeut* 1999, **66**, 152–65). Once daily dosage can be appropriate.

## Desipramine

Desipramine has a low sedative effect and is suitable for once daily administration. It was discontinued in UK in 2001.

## Dosulepin (dothiepin)

Dosulepin is an established tricyclic in the UK although severe toxicity in over-dose (n=320, Buckley *et al*, *Lancet* 1994, **343**, 159–62) and standard side-effect profile makes its UK popularity slightly surprising. It has significant sedative effects and impairment of concentration and memory and has been shown to be more toxic than other tricyclics, particularly due to its proconvulsive and cardiac arrhythmic effects (*Lancet* 1994, **343**, 159) so should thus not be used in someone actively suicidal. It is frequently prescribed in the community at subtherapeutic antidepressant doses (eg. 75mg/d) which must be a major cause of treatment failure.

## Doxepin

A standard tricyclic with moderate sedation, which may have fewer anticholinergic and cardiac effects than older tricyclics. It has an active metabolite and is suitable for once or twice daily dosing.

## Imipramine *

An established standard tricyclic suitable for once daily administration. Psychotic depression shows high response rate to imipramine (n=52, Bruijn *et al*, *J Aff Dis* 2001, **66**, 165–74). Stimulant side-effects may be trouble-some as may the anticholinergic effects, especially in the elderly and it may provoke fragmentation of motor activity during sleep (n=52, Volkers *et al*, *Eur Neuropsychopharm* 2002, **12**, 273–78).

## Lofepramine

This established UK tricyclic may have relatively fewer side-effects than other tricyclics, eg. it has minimal sedative effects and impairment of concentration and memory compared with dothiepin (Allen *et al J Psychopharmacol* 1993, **7**, 33–38). It is surprisingly safe in overdose, with lofepramine seeming to block the cardiotoxic effects of the main metabolite, desipramine (full review in *Drugs* 1989, **37**, 123–40).

## Maprotiline

Although claimed to be a tetracyclic, maprotiline is more a tricyclic and should be considered such. Cardiac effects are similar to the older tricyclics. It has the greatest incidence of seizures in overdose (and even at standard doses), compounded by its unusually long half-life. Use should be restricted to patients where these risks are absolutely minimal.

## Nortriptyline *

A mildly sedative tricyclic with low cardiotoxic side-effects and suitable for once daily administration. A study of melancholic depression in elderly patients, it was shown to be significantly more effective than fluoxetine (n=22, Roose *et al*, *Am J Psych* 1994, **151**, 1735–39). It is as effective as paroxetine but less well tolerated (n=116, RCT, 12/52, Mulsant *et al*, *Am J Ger Psych* 2001, **9**, 406–14; n=59, RCT, 18/12, Bump *et al*, *Depress Anxiety* 2001, **13**, 38–44). A therapeutic window of 50– 170mg/ml has been identified (eg. APATF, *Am J Psych* 1985, **142**, 155–62).

## Trimipramine

Structurally related to methotrimeprazine/levomepromazine, trimipramine has significant sedative properties, which can be useful for hypnotic and anxiolytic purposes.

| SWITCHING OR DISCONTINUING ANTIDEPRESSANTS |
|---|
| For a table on switching antidepressants and the gaps needed, or advice on the problems of discontinuing, see *Chapter 2.2.5* |

## Other antidepressants
## Mirtazapine *

Mirtazapine is described as a NaSSA (Noradrenergic and Specific Serotonergic Antidepressant). It blocks presynaptic alpha-2 adreno-receptors (increasing noradrenaline transmission) and indirectly enhances serotoninergic transmission, with additional $5-HT_2$ and $5-HT_3$ receptor blockade minimising the incidence of serotoninergic side-effects, eg. nausea, headache and sexual dysfunction. The dose range is 15–45mg/d and recent data shows the optimum starting dose of 30mg/d is well-tolerated. In a number of double-blind trials, mirtazapine has been shown to be as effective over six weeks as amitriptyline (meta-analysis of eight RCTs, n=161 treated, n=132 placebo, p/c, Fawcett and Barkin, *J Clin Psych* 1998, **59** 123–27), and as well-tolerated as fluoxetine but significantly more effective at 3 and 4 weeks of therapy (n=135, RCT, Wheatley *et al*, *J Clin Psych* 1998, **59**, 306–12). Mirtazapine may also be well-tolerated and very effective as an adjunctive in antidepressant-resistant persistent MDD (n=26, RCT, d/b, p/c, 4/52, Carpenter *et al*, *Biol Psych* 2002, **51**, 183–88) and for estrogen-resistant depression in menopausal women (n=22, open, Joffe *et al*, *J Womens Health Gend Based Med* 2001, **10**, 999–1004). A meta-analysis of all 3 completed comparative studies of mirtazapine versus SSRIs (fluoxetine, paroxetine and citalopram) showed a similar AD profile, but hinted at superior efficacy and a robust faster onset of action, statistically significant in all three studies in the first few weeks (reviewed by Thompson, *J Clin Psych* 1999, **60** [Suppl 17], 18–22; discussion 46–48; n=298 + 285 from 3 studies, Quitkin *et al*, *J Clin Psych* 2001, **62**, 358–61). In a comparison with venlafaxine, mirtazapine was as effective (62% vs 52% response) for melancholic depression, evident from week 4 and with lower drop-outs in mirtazapine group (n=157, RCT, 8/52, Guelfi *et al*, *J Clin Psychopharmacol* 2001, **21**, 425–31). An earlier onset of action is related to better overall outcomes. Relapse prevention has been shown to be significantly superior to placebo (n=156, RCT, d/b, 40/52, Thase *et al*, *J Clin Psych* 2001, **62**, 782–88).

**Reviews:*** general (Nutt, *Hum Psychopharmacol* 2002, **17** (Suppl 1), S37–41; Anttila and Leinonen, *CNS Drug Rev* 2001, **7**, 249–64; *J Clin Psych* 2001, **61**, 609–16; Anon, *Drug & Therapeut Bull* 1999, **37**, 1–3), kinetics (Timmer *et al*, *Clin Pharmacokinet* 2000, **38**,

461–74, 56 refs), in the elderly (case reports, Raji and Brady, *Ann Pharmacother* 2001, **35**, 1024–27).

## Mianserin

Mianserin is a tetracyclic with prominent $5HT_{2A}$ and $5HT_{2C}$ antagonist properties, a good safety profile in overdose, low cardiotoxicity and marked sedative properties. Mianserin has been shown to be effective at 20–60mg/d in prophylaxis of recurrent depression (n=22, 18/12, Kishimoto *et al*, *Acta Psych Scand* 1994, **89**, 46–51).

## Moclobemide *

Moclobemide (a reversible inhibitor of monoamine oxidase-A) inhibits only MAO-A and not MAO-B, so an excess of tyramine in the body will displace moclobemide from MAO-A, allowing tyramine metabolism to occur, MOA-B remaining free. This results in a 'cheese-reaction' usually only at amounts above 100–150mg of tyramine (see *4.3.3.3*), unlikely under normal} conditions. A meta-analysis of 38 double-blind and 2 single-blind trials with moclobemide (n=2416) showed it to be about equipotent with imipramine or sedative tricyclic antidepressants in agitated-anxious depressive patients, and all were clearly superior to placebo (Delini-Stula *et al*, *J Aff Dis* 1995, **35**, 21–30). A review of studies indicates that moclobemide may be useful in typical severe depression with melancholia (Paykel, *Acta Psych Scand* 1995, **91** [Suppl 386], 22–27) and 450–750mg/d may be as effective as imipramine (150–250mg/d) in bipolar depression, with less side effects and less switches to mania (2 vs 6) indicating a useful potential role (n=156, RCT, 8/52, Silverstone *et al*, *Acta Psych Scand* 2001, **104**, 104–9).

**Reviews**: Norman and Burrows, *Drug Safety* 1995, **12**, 46–51, 40 refs; Bonnet, *CNS Drug Rev* 2002, 8, 283–30.

## Nefazodone *

Nefazodone has a dual action on serotonin, ie. relatively weak 5-HT reuptake inhibition and powerful $5-HT_2$ blockade, with improved sleep well-known (n=40, RCT, 8/52, Hicks *et al*, *B J Psych* 2002, **189**, 528–35). The optimum dose has not been established but meta-analysis of dose-finding studies suggests 300–600mg/d (Zajecka *et al*, *J Clin Psych* 2002, **63**, 42–47). Relapse prevention has been shown (n=131, RCT, d/b, 36/52 follow on to 16/52 acute, Feiger *et al*, *Int Clin Psychopharmacol* 1999, **14**, 19–28). Due to reports of rare but serious liver failure (some fatal, others requiring transplantation) the drug was withdrawn in 2003 in Europe, but not the rest of the world. See chapter 2 for switching strategies.

**Reviews:** * general (De Vane *et al*, *J Clin Psych* 2002, **63**, 10–17).

## Reboxetine *

Reboxetine is a selective noradrenaline reuptake inhibitor with no dopamine, histamine, adrenergic nor serotonin effects at 8mg/d, but a weak anticholinergic action. In short-term studies it appears as effective as fluoxetine 20–40mg/d (n=381, RCT, d/b, p/c, 8/52, Andreoli *et al*, *J Clin Psychopharmacol* 2002, **22**, 393–99), with possibly greater efficacy in severe depression and in terms of social functioning in those that responded (n=168, RCT, 8/52, Massana *et al*, *Int Clin Psychopharmacol* 1999, **14**, 73–80). A higher level of social functioning has been shown with reboxetine, using a validated scale (SASS) although comparison of nortriptyline and fluoxetine failed to show any difference in SAS scores, suggesting that noradrenergic drive enhancement was not essential for improved social functioning (n=188, open, 13/52, Luty *et al*, *J Psychopharmacol* 2001, **15**, 257–64). Well tolerated relapse prevention has been shown against placebo (n=283, d/b, 46/52, Versiani *et al*, *J Clin Psych* 1999, **60**, 400–6), with reboxetine being well tolerated. Reboxetine has also been used successfully to treat multi-drug resistant depression in Parkinson's Disease (n=1, Lemke, *J Clin Psych* 2000, **61**, 872; n=16, open, 4/52, Lemke *et al*, *J Clin Psych* 2002, **63**, 300–4). There is no effect on reaction time (Hind-marsh, *Eur Neuropsychopharmacol* 1997 [Suppl 1], S17–S21). Interest in use as an SSRI adjunct must be tempered by the lack of safety data.

**Reviews\***: general (Holm and Spencer, *CNS Drugs* 1999, **12**, 65–83; Anon, *Formulary Monograph Service* 1999, 315–21, 29 refs; Scates and Doraiswamy, *Ann Pharmacother* 2000, **34**, 1302–12; Schatzberg, *J Clin Psych* 2000, **61** [Suppl 10], 31–38; Scates and Murali Doraiswamy, *Ann Pharmacother* 2000, **34**, 1302–12), noradrenaline in depression (Various, *J Clin Psych* 2000, **61**, 686–96).

## Trazodone

Trazodone increases NA and 5-HT turnover with low cardiotoxicity and anti-cholinergic side-effects but a higher incidence of drowsiness and nausea, so it makes a good hypnotic as well. It is best taken with food to reduce peak blood levels.

## Venlafaxine \*

Venlafaxine is described as an SNRI (combined 5-HT and NA reuptake blocker), with minimal effects on other transmitters (except dopamine, where it has a not insignificant effect at higher doses). There is evidence for a dose-response relationship (eg. n=147, RCT, Mehtonen *et al*, *J Clin Psych* 2000, **61**, 95–100), with 5-HT reuptake inhibition across the dosage range, NA reuptake inhibition becoming significant around the 150mg/d dose (n=32, Harvey *et al*, *Arch Gen Psych* 2000, **57**, 503–9) and dopamine reuptake inhibition above 225mg/d. A systematic review and meta-analysis has provided some indication that venlafaxine may be more effective at higher doses than SSRIs, with comparable tolerability (32 trials, Smith *et al*, *B J Psych* 2002, **180**, 396–404; Stahl *et al*, *Biol Psych* 2002, **52**, 1166–74). Furthermore, a meta-analysis of 8 comparable d/b studies in MDD indicated that *remission* (as opposed to response) rates with venlafaxine were significantly (10%) higher and earlier than with an SSRI (fluoxetine), with doses of >150mg/d necessary for remission (Thase *et al*, *B J Psych* 2001, **178**, 234–41, Wyeth study). There is some evidence that venlafaxine may be useful in non-chronic treatment-resistant depression, eg. it was shown to be slightly superior at 200–300mg/d to paroxetine 30–40mg/d in such a population (n=122, RCT, Poirier and Boyer, *B J Psych* 1999, **175**, 12–16; discussion of weaknesses in *B J Psych* 2000, **176**, 398; review by Martin, *EBMH* 2000, **3**, 51). The sustained release preparation (Efexor XL) probably gives a reduced incidence of initial nausea and has a once a day dosage. It may have a relatively high fatal toxicity index (Buckley and McManus, *BMJ* 2002, **325**, 1332–33) and discontinuation effects may be significant (see *2.2.5*).

**Reviews**: general (Kienke and Rosenbaum, *Depress Anxiety* 2000, **12** [Suppl 1], 50–54).

> **SWITCHING OR DISCONTINUING ANTIDEPRESSANTS**
>
> For a table on switching antidepressants and the gaps needed, or advice on the problems of discontinuing, see *Chapter 2.2.5*

## Mono-amine oxidase inhibitors (MAOIs)

### Isocarboxazid

A hydrazine derivative which irreversibly blocks the MAO enzyme (editorial by Shader and Greenblatt, *J Clin Psychopharmacol* 1999, **19**, 105).

### Phenelzine

A hydrazine derivative which irreversibly blocks the MAO enzyme. Patients with chronic atypical depression are at high risk of relapse if phenelzine is withdrawn 6 months after the initial response (n=60, RCT, p/c, Stewart *et al*, *Am J Psych* 1997, **154**, 31–36). Phenelzine is as effective as CBT in atypical depression (n=108, RCT, 10/52, Jarrett *et al*, *Arch Gen Psych* 1999, **56**, 431–37).

### Tranylcypromine

A non-hydrazine amfetamine-related MAOI with stimulant effects and a greater incidence of adverse drug interactions. It has been shown to be effective in tricyclic-resistant and anergic bipolar depression in one study (n=16, RCT, d/b, c/o, Thase *et al*, *Am J Psych* 1992, **149**, 195–98).

## Other antidepressants
### Flupentixol
In low dose flupentixol can have some mild antidepressant properties and in some double-blind studies it has proved superior to placebo and amitriptyline. Its efficacy has been queried (*J Psychopharmacol* 1990, **4**, 152–67) as the speed of action is more in line with an anxiolytic effect and a similar case can be put forward for other antipsychotics at low dose.

### Lithium *
Use of lithium as monotherapy in the treatment and prophylaxis of unipolar (as well as bipolar) depression has been well established and has been associated with low mortality (n=827, mean 81/12, Müller-Oerlinghausen *et al*, *Acta Psych Scand* 1992, **86**, 218–22). It has also been shown to be highly significantly effective as an adjunct to other antidepressants (eg. in the elderly with unipolar MDD, a major protective effect: n=50, 2-yrs, Wilkinson *et al*, *Int J Ger Psych* 2002, **17**, 619–22, see also combinations later). If used as augmentation, doses of at least 750mg may be needed for clinical response, with 250mg/d leading to relapse (n=34, d/b, p/c, 9/52, Stein and Bernadt, *B J Psych* 1993, **162**, 634–40). A meta-analysis of placebo-controlled studies has shown that lithium augmentation (600–800mg/d) increases response in depression refractory to tricyclics (8 studies) or SSRIs (one study) (n=234, RCT=9, Bauer and Dopfmer, *J Clin Psychopharmacol* 1999, **19**, 427–34; review by Lam, *EBMH* 2000, **3**, 44; *Bandolier* 2000, **7**, 4–5). Much antidepressant response to lithium is probably mood stabilisation in depressed (but undiagnosed) bipolars and so sudden withdrawal of lithium would be outright dangerous (Faedda *et al*, *Am J Psych* 2001, **158**, 1337–38).

**Reviews**: lithium augmentation in refractory depression (Heit and Nemeroff, *J Clin Psych* 1998, **59** [Suppl 6], 28–33, 36 refs), general review (Rouillon and Gorwood, *J Clin Psych* 1998, **59** [Suppl 5], 32–41; Bauer and Dopfmer, *J Clin Psychopharmacol* 1999, **19**, 427–34). See main entry under bipolar mood disorder (*1.10*) and bipolar depression (introduction).

### Tryptophan *
A naturally occurring amino acid and precursor to serotonin, tryptophan is usually used in combination with tricyclic or other antidepressants. Tryptophan deficiency results in a rapid lowering of mood (review by Bell *et al*, *B J Psych* 2001, **178**, 399–405) and tryptophan depletion reverses antidepressant-induced remission, so tryptophan might help if low tryptophan levels have occurred. Cochrane concludes that the trial data is limited and unreliable but suggests tryptophan may be superior to placebo (Shaw *et al*, CDSR 2002, 3198).

Due to a previous association with eosinophilia-myalgia syndrome (EMS), it is now only licensed in the UK for resistant depression, by hospital specialists, in patients with severe depression continuously for more than two years, after adequate trials of standard drug treatments and as an adjunct to other treatments, harsh restrictions for the low risk involved and possible benefits. Close monitoring of eosinophil levels is necessary and to the signs and symptoms of EMS (eg. muscle or joint pain, fever and rash). The doctor and patient must be registered with OPTICS (Optimax Information and Clinical Support), with progress reported at 3 and 6 months, then 6-monthly. For a review of therapeutic uses, see Smith, *Pharm J* 1998, **261**, 819–21, 40 refs.

**Augmentation strategies** (drugs with no intrinsic antidepressant activity)
**Reviews**: general (*Drugs & Ther Perspect* 2001, **17**, 6–9, Fava, *J Clin Psych* 2001, **62** (Suppl 18), 4–11), risk of

adverse events with the use of augmentation therapy (reviewed by Schweitzer and Tuckwell, *Drug Safety* 1998, **19**, 455–64), anxiolytic antidepressant augmentation (Sussman, *J Clin Psych* 1998, **59** [Suppl 5], 42–50), anticonvulsants as augmentation (Dietrich and Emrich, *J Clin Psych* 1998, **59** [Suppl 5], 51–59).

### Folate (+ SAMe) *

Folate 15mg/d has significantly improved clinical response and recovery from acute psychiatric disorders (review by Reynolds, *BMJ* 2002, **324**, 1512–15, 32 refs) as low folate levels have been associated with melancholic depression and non-response to antidepressants eg. fluoxetine (n=127, RCT, p/c, 10/52, Coppen and Bailey, *J Aff Dis* 2000, **60**, 121–30; comment by Goodwin, *EBMH* 2001, **4**, 41). Folate levels should be included in the assessment of treatment-resistant depressives and perhaps a routine part of clinical assessment of all depressed people (McLaughlin and McMahon, *B J Psych* 1993, **162**, 572). SAMe (S-Adenosyl-methionine) is a closely related active form and has been used to enhance the onset of TCAs (n=40, RCT, p/c, 2/52, Berlanga *et al*, *Psych Res* 1992, **44**, 257–62). Leucovorin (metabolised to methylfolate) has a modest effect in SSRI non-response (n=22, 8/52, Alpert *et al*, *Ann Clin Psych* 2002, **14**, 33–38).

### Levothyroxine (thyroxine) *

Subclinical hypothyroidism may well predispose to depression (Haggerty *et al*, *Am J Psych* 1993, **150**, 508–10). Augmentation with high-dose 150–300mg/d thyroxine proved to have an antidepressant effect in more than 50% of the previously treatment-resistant patients with chronic depression and/or dysthymia (n=9, open, 8/52, Rudas *et al*, *Biol Psychiatry* 1999, **15**, 45, 229–33; review by Joffe, *J Clin Psych* 1998, **59** [Suppl 5], 26–31). Thyroid supplementation may accelerate the onset of tricyclic response in non-refractory depression (5/6 studies found T3 significantly superior to placebo, especially in women: meta-analysis, Altshuler *et al*, *Am J Psych* 2001, **158**, 1617–22).

### Liothyronine

A meta-analysis of the 8 controlled studies showed liothyronine augmentation to produce twice as many responses in refractory depression compared to controls, with moderately large improvements, although one RCT showed negative results (n=292, 8 study meta-analysis, Aronson *et al*, *Arch Gen Psych* 1996, **53**, 842–48). Sub-therapeutic doses of $T_3$ triiodothyronine 25–50 mcg/d (*Am J Psych* 1990, **147**, 255) or $T_4$ levothyroxine up to 0.1mg/d have been used as augmentation to tricyclics etc (n=50, RCT, d/b, p/c, 2/52, Joffe *et al*, *Arch Gen Psych* 1993, **50**, 387–93). This may be effective particularly in rapid-cycling disorder (*1.27*).

### Modafinil *

Augmentation in antidepressant partial or non-responders by modafinil 100–200mg/d produced a remarkable response over 1–2 weeks in all 7 patients (case series, Menza *et al*, *J Clin Psych* 2000, **61**, 378–81) and up to 400mg/d has been used (see Fava, *J Clin Psych* 2001, **62** (Suppl 18), 4–11; Kaufman *et al*, *Eur Psych* 2002, **17**, 167–69).

### Pindolol *

Antidepressants, eg. SSRIs may act by inhibiting the 5-HT reuptake pump, increasing 5-HT availability at postsynaptic receptors. However, this also includes enhancing 5-HT at 5-$HT_{1A}$ receptors situated on the cell body which operate a feedback loop. The initial net outcome is that these cancel each other out. Over a period of weeks, however, the pre-synaptic 5-$HT_{1A}$ receptors become desensitised and the system corrects itself, which may explain the delay in antidepressant action from antidepressants. Pindolol selectively blocks 5-$HT_{1A}$ receptors, and inhibits this feedback loop to increase the speed of onset of action (although not everyone agrees with this: Cremers *et al*, *Biol Psych* 2001, **50**, 13–21). Some trials have shown a clinically important effect eg.

pindolol in combination with SSRIs (eg. Tome *et al, J Aff Dis* 1997, **44**, 101–9; n=11, RCT, Perez *et al, Lancet* 1997, **349**, 1594–97) suggest a faster onset of action, higher response rates and better long-term outcomes (n=3,485, 3-yrs, Rasanen *et al, J Clin Psychopharmacol* 1999, **19**, 297–302). Other trials have failed to reproduce this (eg. fluoxetine, Perez *et al, Arch Gen Psych* 1999, **56**, 375–79), possibly through too low doses (eg. 15mg/d probably needed: n=8, Rabiner *et al, Am J Psych* 2001, **158**, 2080–82) or use of a racemic mix (Isaac and Tome, *Am J Psych* 1997, **154**, 1790–91).

**Reviews**: McAskill *et al, B J Psych* 1998, **173**, 203–8, concluding that larger trials are needed to confirm the effect (discussion by McAllister-Williams and Young, *B J Psych* 1998, **173**, 536–39).

---

### +   Combinations

There is some evidence that combined NA and 5-HT reuptake blocking drugs can produce a quicker antidepressant effect, although it could be that combined drug use produces higher success rates by treating different depressive subgroups.

### Antipsychotics + antidepressants*

There is some evidence accumulating that atypicals may have some role in augmentation of antidepressants, perhaps via $5HT_{2A/2C}$ antagonism (review by Thase, *J Clin Psych* 2002, **63**, 95–103), as well as anxiolytic and anti-irritability effects. Addition of low-dose risperidone to fluvoxamine from the start of treatment has enhanced onset (n=36, open, 6/52, Hirose and Ashby, *J Clin Psych* 2002, **63**, 733–36), and olanzapine and fluoxetine was superior to either agent alone in resistant depression (n=28, d/b, 8/52, Shelton *et al, Am J Psych* 2001, **158**, 131–34). In another study, the addition of a moderate dose of perphenazine to a tricyclic did not improve efficacy in late-life psychotic depression (n=36, RCT, d/b, 4/52, Mulsant *et al, J Clin Psych* 2001, **62**, 597–604), although I personally hope

soon to object to late-life being defined as people aged 50 or older.

### Benzodiazepines + SSRIs *

Cochrane concludes that the 9 studies (n=679) indicate that BDZ augmentation of antidepressants leads to fewer drop-outs and less depression severity at 1–4 weeks, but disappearing at 6–8 weeks, indicating that short-term use may be successful, possibly by minimising initial SSRI (anxiety) side effects, improving sleep or a direct action (comment by Gijsman, *EBMH* 2001, **4**, 45) eg. clonazepam (up to 1mg/d) improved the speed of onset of fluoxetine (cf fluoxetine alone), possibly partly by suppressing SSRI side-effects (n=80, RCT, 3/52, Smith *et al, Am J Psych* 1998, **155**, 1339–45). However, the literature on benzodiazepine augmentation is confusing, with studies showing variable effects (discussion by Furukawa, *Am J Psych* 1999, **156**, 1840).

### Bupropion + tranylcypromine

The cautious use of this combination has been successful in resolving multi-drug resistant depression (n=1, Pierre and Gitlin, *J Clin Psych* 2000, **61**, 450–51).

### Bupropion + venlafaxine/SSRIs *

Bupropion 200–300mg/d may be useful eg. 56% of venlafaxine/SSRI-resistant depressed patients responded when bupropion was added (n=25, Spier *et al, Depress Anxiety* 1998, **7**, 73–75), and in multi-drug resistant depression, bupropion 300mg/d successfully augmented venlafaxine 450mg/d (n=1, Fatemi *et al, Ann Pharmacother* 1999, **33**, 701–3). It may also counteract SSRI or venlafaxine-induced sexual function (n=18, open, 8/52, Kennedy *et al, J Clin Psych* 2002, **63**, 181–86).

### Buspirone + SSRIs *

Buspirone augmentation of SSRIs may produce marked improvement in resistant depressed patients (n=30, 5/52, Dimitriou and Dimitriou, *J Clin Psychopharmacol* 1998, **18**, 465–69) and in SSRI non-responders, addition of 20–60mg/d buspirone produced significant reductions in MADRS scores at the end of week one compared to placebo, but both groups were equivalent at six weeks (n=102, RCT, p/c, d/b, 6/52, Appelberg *et al, J Clin Psych* 2001, **62**, 448–52). Buspirone shares some pharmacodynamic properties with pindolol. However, an RCT failed to show any advantage of adding buspirone to an SSRI in treatment-resistant depression (n=119, Landen *et al, J Clin Psych* 1998, **59**, 664–68), although both the placebo (47%) and buspirone (51%) response rates were high, and an open label extension produced a higher (70%) response rate.

### Carbamazepine + SSRIs *
Carbamazepine augmentation may be useful in SSRI non-responders (n=6, Steinacher *et al, Eur Neuropsychopharmacol* 2002, **12**, 255–60).

### Hydrocortisone + metyrapone
Hydrocortisone 30mg/d plus metyrapone showed a significant effect in depression (n=8, p/c, s/b, c/o, 2/52, O'Dwyer *et al, J Aff Dis* 1995, **33**, 123–28).

### Lithium + antidepressants *
There are eleven double-blind controlled trials of augmentation of tricyclics, sertraline, citalopram, venlafaxine etc (review by Zullion and Baumann, *Pharmacopsychiatry* 2001, **34**, 119–27), with 10 reporting response rates averaging 52% (review by Fava, *J Clin Psych* 2001, **62**(Suppl 18), 4–11). For SSRI augmentation, there is little evidence of a rapid effect but there is for a substantial effect after 1–6 weeks (Zullino and Baumann, *Pharmacopsychiatry* 2001, **34**, 119–27), maintained for 6/12 (n=30, RCT, d/b, p/c, 6/52, open 4/12 extension, Bauer *et al. Am J Psych* 2000, **157**, 1429–35). Adequate lithium levels (0.4mmol/l or more) seem necessary. There is a view that all resistant depressions are unrecognised bipolars and, hence, the use of lithium is logical (see also BNF section).

### Lithium + antidepressants (eg. clomipramine, SSRI or phenelzine) + tryptophan *
Variously known as Triple Therapy or the MRC, Newcastle or London Cocktail, there have been reports of 55% remission rates in severe depression, eg. from:
Clomipramine (to 150mg/d or to tolerance eg. 300–400mg/d)
+ Tryptophan (2–4g/d)
+ Lithium (standard levels)
Alternatives to clomipramine include phenelzine and the SSRIs (n=20, RCT, Barker *et al, Int Clin Psychopharmacol* 1987, **2**, 261–72). Tryptophan enhances the action of clomipramine on 5-HT sites and improves 5-HT absorption. Lithium also affects 5-HT and is an antidepressant in its own right. The combination is effective in severe resistant depression. (Conte, *B J Psych* 1988, **152**, 720 using imipramine, case studies in *Lancet* 1990, **336**, 380).

### Lithium + valproate
A study of refractory depression indicated that sodium valproate (750–1500mg/d) augmentation of lithium (900–1500mg/d) was effective in the 8 patients who did not respond to lithium alone (n=10, Sharma *et al, Lithium* 1994, **5**, 99–103).

### Methylphenidate + SSRIs *
Findings from the first 9 patients in a discontinued RCT showed there to be no advantage in adding methylphenidate to sertraline, in terms of quicker or better response (Postolache *et al, J Clin Psych* 1999, **60**, 123–24). However, augmentation of citalopram in elderly depressed patients may be rapidly successful and well-tolerated (n=10, open, Lavretsky and Kumar, *Am J Ger Psych* 2001, **9**, 298–303; n=5, open, Stoll *et al, J Clin Psych* 1996, **57**, 72–76).

### Mianserin + fluoxetine *
Mianserin 30mg/d has shortening the latency of onset of fluoxetine in MMD and treatment-resistant depression (n=31, RCT, Maes *et al, J Clin Psychopharmacol* 1999, **19**, 177–82)

and adding 60mg/d to fluoxetine 20mg/d non-responders was superior to switching to mianserin or continuing fluoxetine (n=104, d/b, 6/52, Ferreri *et al, Acta Psych Scand* 2001, **103**, 66–72).

### Mirtazapine + venlafaxine/SSRIs *

In persistent MDD, addition of mirtazapine 30mg to existing therapy produced response rate of 64% cf 20% with placebo (n=26, RCT, d/b, p/c, 4/52, Carpenter *et al, Biol Psych* 2002, **51**, 183–88; short review in Fava, *J Clin Psych* 2001, **62**(Suppl 18), 4–11). Mirtazapine has also been used with high-dose venlafaxine, the rationale being to block 5HT2 and 5HT3 receptors, reducing sexual and anxiety side effects and allowing higher doses to be tolerated.

### Nefazodone + SSRIs *

Anecdotal reports suggest some efficacy, although serotonin syndrome and increased anxiety is possible (review in Fava, *J Clin Psych* 2001, **62**(Suppl 18), 4–11).

### Reboxetine + SSRIs

This logical combination has been used successfully with eg. citalopram in resistant depression (Devarajan and Dursun, *Can J Psych* 2000, **45**, 489–90).

### SSRIs + SSRIs

Although there are anecdotal reports (eg. Bondolfi *et al, Psychopharmacol (Berl)* 1996, **128**, 421–25), the combination cannot be recommended and risks serotonin syndrome.

### Tricyclics + MAOIs

Although the BNF urges extreme caution, this combination is known to be effective in some resistant depressions eg. combined isocarboxazid and amitriptyline treatment-resistant depression showed a 50% response, and most remained in remission for up to three years (n=25, open, Berlanga and Ortega-Soto, *J Aff Dis* 1995, **34**, 187–92). Tranylcypromine plus clomipramine is known to be dangerous (two deaths) but other combinations can be used with care in an in-patient setting. Most problems occur when a tricyclic is added to an MAOI. Fewer adverse events have been reported with the reverse. The main adverse events include hyperthermia, delirium, seizures, agitation etc. rather than hypertension. It is best to take great care, eg. separate the doses (eg. MAOI in the morning, tricyclic in the evening), add one to the other in low dose and build up slowly or stop all antidepressants, wait a week, and then start both together at low dose and build up again. The last mentioned seems to be the most widely favoured strategy.

### Tricyclic + SSRIs

Fluoxetine and a tricyclic were effective in a retrospective study of patients not responsive to either agent alone and for whom standard protocols had for some reason not been followed (n=30, open, Weilberg *et al, J Clin Psych* 1989, **50**, 447–49) and fluoxetine 20mg/d and desipramine produced a rapid and effective response in depression in an open study (n=14, Nelson *et al, Arch Gen Psych* 1991, **48**, 303–7). The report by Seth *et al* (*B J Psych* 1992, **161**, 562–5) was so remarkable its findings were contested (Cowen and Power, *B J Psych* 1993, **162**, 266–67). The only double-blind prospective study on the subject showed that high dose fluoxetine (60mg/d) was in fact more effective in partial or non-responders to 20mg/d than a fluoxetine/desipramine combination (Fava *et al, Am J Psych* 1994, **151**, 1372–74). The improved outcome with the combination in people who did not respond to either alone is, in most people, likely to be due to raised TCA levels (n=13, Levitt *et al, J Clin Psych* 1999, **60**, 613; critical review of the therapeutic combination by Taylor, *B J Psych* 1995, **167**, 575–80). The combination should generally be avoided due to the high risk of an adverse interaction (*4.3.2*).

● **Unlicensed/Some efficacy**
### Bupropion (amfebutamone) *

Bupropion is approved in USA for the treatment of depression. In studies in acute depression, bupropion has shown an average response rate of 55%, compared to 29% for placebo. A relapse prevention effect has been shown (n=423, RCT, d/b, p/c, 44/52, Weihs *et al, Biol Psych* 2002, **51**, 753–61). It may be modestly effective as an adjunct in depressed people trying to give up smoking (n=25, 9/52, Chengappa *et al, J Clin Psych* 2001, **62**, 503-8), as an adjunct in resistant, bipolar depression (n=13, open, Erfurth *et al, Neuropsychobiology* 2001, **45** (Suppl 1), 33–36), and the elderly (although 12 weeks may be needed for optimum response: n=31, open, 12/52, Steffens *et al, Int J Ger Psychiatry* 2001, **16**, 862–65). A review of the limited data indicated that bupropion has similar efficacy to SSRIs but less nausea, diarrhoea, somnolence and sexual dysfunction (Nieuwstraten and Dolovich, *Ann Pharmacother* 2001, **35**, 1608–13), but higher cardiovascular, proconvulsive (at doses up to 450mg/d: Pesola and Avasarala, *J Emerg Med* 2002, **22**, 235–39, especially in patients with eating disorders who have lower body weights) and overdose toxicity. The most likely mechanism of action is weak dopamine reuptake blockade. The maximum dosage of 450mg/d should be adhered to since the risk of seizures is dose related (see *3.2*).

## Carbamazepine

Evidence for use as a pure antidepressant is poor but use with lithium or as prophylaxis in bipolar disorder is better established (*Psychological Med* 1989, **19**, 591–604). In one study, 44% of patients with resistant depression showed moderate or marked improvement with carbamazepine (*J Clin Psych* 1991, **52**, 472–76). See main entry under bipolar mood disorder (*1.10*).

## Estradiol/estrogen *

Estrogen receptors occur in the CNS and loss of estrogen has been shown to reduce serotonergic and other functioning (Stahl, *J Clin Psych* 2001, **62**, 317–18; Stahl, *Arch Gen Psych* 2001, **58**, 537–38), and estrogen supplementation of SSRIs may enhance effectiveness in e.g. postnatal depression (where sublingual estradiol produced clinical recovery in 83% at two weeks: n=23, open, Ahokas *et al, J Clin Psych* 2001, **62**, 332–36) and the menopause (n=145, Miller *et al, J Am Geriatr Soc* 2002, **50**, 1826–30). Estradiol skin patches showed a striking improvement in two trials in severe **postnatal depression**. The first showed at 1 month and 3 months (n=37, d/b, p/c, Henderson *et al, Lancet* 1991, **338**, 816–17) and the second showed a sustained improvement over five months with 200mcg/d transdermal estrogen (n=61, d/b, p/c, Gregoire *et al, Lancet* 1996, **347**, 930, further support by Lopez-Jaramillo *et al, Lancet* 1996, **348**, 135–36). The sublingual (n=2, Ahokas *et al, Lancet* 1998, **351**, 109, letter) and transdermal routes (effective in 68% women cf 20% with placebo: n=50, RCT, 12/52, Soares *et al, Arch Gen Psych* 2001, **58**, 529–34) can be used. Although estrogen and progesterone levels are associated with the development of postpartum mood disorders (n=8, Bloch *et al, Am J Psych* 2000, **157**, 924–30), progestogens do not seem to help PND, and may even be detrimental (Lawrie *et al*, Cochrane review 1999, reviewed in *EBMH* 2000, **3**, 19).

**Reviews:**\* general (Stahl, *J Clin Psych* 2001, **62**, 404-5; Schmidt *et al, Am J Obstet Gynecol* 2000, **183**, 414–20).

## Lamotrigine *

Although its primary action is on voltage-sensitive sodium channels, inhibiting pathological release of glutamate, lamotrigine may also have an antidepressant effect, particularly in bipolar depression. Lamotrigine 50–200mg/d monotherapy was significantly more effective than placebo in bipolar I depression, the effect being seen as early as the third week (n=195, RCT, Calabrese *et al, J Clin Psych* 1999, **60**, 79–88). Lamotrigine may also be useful as an adjunct for refractory major depression (n=2, Maltese, *Am J Psych* 1999, **156**, 1833;

n=37, retrospective, Barbee and Jamhour, *J Clin Psych* 2002, **63**, 737–41) and at 200mg/d enhanced the onset of paroxetine in unipolar depression, but not HAM-D scores at the study endpoint (n=40, p/c, d/b, 9/52, Normann *et al, J Clin Psych* 2002, **63**, 337–44).

### Levothyroxine (thyroxine)
See combinations.

### Liothyronine
See combinations.

### Methylphenidate
Methylphenidate can be used in depression (Klein and Wender, *Arch Gen Psych* 1995, **52**, 429–33), as it has a major advantage of a rapid action, often within 48 hours although the effect tends to be transient and it may worsen anxiety and insomnia. It may be effective as augmentation where antidepressants do not work fully, and in the elderly where apathy and withdrawal (but not hopelessness) are prominent features (mentioned by Salzman, *Curr Affective Illness* 1995, **14**, 5–13) and, as such, may help where depression is preventing the rehabilitation processes. It is also useful in medically-ill depressed patients, eg. those with cancer (McDaniel *et al, Arch Gen Psych* 1995, **52**, 89–99; Fawzy *et al, Arch Gen Psych* 1995, **52**, 100–13). 59% showed marked or moderate improvement in a trial of elderly depressed patients (n=29, *J Clin Psych* 1991, **52**, 263–67).

**Reviews**: extensive (Emptage and Semla, *Ann Pharmacother* 1996, **30**, 151–57, 43 refs) and for depression in elderly, medically ill patients (Frye, *Am J Health-Sys Pharm* 1997, **54**, 2510–11).

### Selegiline *
Transdermal selegiline (20mg/d) was surprisingly effective and well-tolerated in MDD (n=177, RCT, p/c, 6/52, Bodkin and Amsterdam, *Am J Psych* 2002, **159**, 1869–75).

### St. John's wort*
SJW is available over-the-counter in most European countries in a variety of preparations. The mode of action is not certain, but might include serotonin or noradrenaline reuptake inhibition (Neary and Bu, *Brain Res* 1999, **816**, 358–63), MAO-A and B inhibition and sigma receptor activity (neuropharmacology reviewed by Bennett *et al, Ann Pharmacother* 1998, **32**, 1201–8). There are many trials showing efficacy in mild to moderate depression (eg. n=375, RCT, d/b, p/c, 6/52, Lecrubier *et al, Am J Psych* 2002, **159**, 1361–66) and equivalent to fluoxetine (n=70, RCT, d/b, Behnke *et al, Adv Ther* 2002, **19**, 43–52; n=149, RCT, 6/52, Harrer *et al, Arzneimittelforschung* 1999, **49**, 289–96). High dose SJW was as effective in the short-term as lower-dose imipramine (up to 100mg/d) and more effective than placebo in moderate depression (n=263, RCT, 8/52, Philipp *et al, BMJ* 1999, **319**, 1534–39; critically reviewed by Morriss, *EBMH* 2000, **3**, 85) and as effective as 150mg/d imipramine (n=320, RCT, Woelk, *BMJ* 2000, **321**, 536–39; enthusiastic review by Hotopf, *EBMH* 2001, **4**, 56). Some caution has been necessary as some early trials included a variety of different *hypericum* preparations, and one trial was published five times with two different first authors (*Bandolier* 1996, **3**, 1–2). Just to confuse matters, a major rigorous trial failed to show a significant antidepressant or anxiolytic effect in major depression (n=200, RCT, p/c, 8/52, Shelton *et al, JAMA* 2001, **285**, 1978–86; review by Hawley and Dale, *EBMH* 2002, **5**, 24), and in a second neither sertraline nor SJW (generously dosed) were effective in moderately severe depression (n=340, RCT, d/b, p/c, 8/52, Davidson *et al, JAMA* 2002, **287**, 1807–14; review by Swann, *EBMH* 2002, **5**, 111; vigorous discussion by Jonas *et al, JAMA* 2002, **288**, 446–49), meaning that endorsement of SJW must be tempered. Most studies are short-term (up to 6/52), and many have high (up to 50%) drop-out rates, indicating that transient mild depression may be common in studies. Care is needed in adjunctive therapy (particularly if purchased OTC – see *4.3.9*).

**Reviews:**\* general (Kelly, *Hosp Med* 2001, **62**, 274–76; Josey and Tackett, *Int J Clin Pharmacol Ther* 1999, **37**, 111–19; Maidment, *Psych Bull* 2000, **24**, 232–34), in the elderly (Vorbach *et al, Drugs & Aging* 2000, **16**, 189–97), safety (Ernst, *Lancet* 1999, **354**, 2014–16) and systematic review of 8 studies (Gaster and Holroyd, *Arch Int Med* 2000, **160**, 152–56).

○ **Unlicensed/Possible efficacy**

**Amisulpride** \*
Amisulpride 50mg/d has been shown to have an antidepressant activity comparable with fluoxetine 20mg/d, with similar incidences of side-effects (n=281, d/b, Smeraldi, *J Aff Dis* 1998, **48**, 47–56) and not inferior to paroxetine 20mg/d for MDD (n=272, RCT, d/b, 56/7, Cassano *et al, Int Clin Psychopharmacol* 2002, **17**, 27–32).

**Buspirone (see also combinations)**
A meta-analysis of studies showed a minor but statistically significant effect at up to 90mg/d in depressed patients (review in *J Psychopharmacol* 1993,**7**, 283–89). One study showed buspirone to be more effective than placebo but less effective than imipramine in major depression in elderly patients (n=177, RCT, Schweizer *et al, J Clin Psych* 1998, **59**, 175–83).

**Clozapine**
Use in refractory psychotic depression has been reported (n=1, Dassa *et al, B J Psych* 1993, **163**, 822–24).

**Dexamethasone**
A number of studies have shown a marked improvement within a week when given 3–8mg IV (n=5, 7/7, Arana, *Am J Psych* 1991, **148**, 1401–2; n=37, 4/7, Arana *et al, Am J Psych* 1995, **152**, 265–67), to 8mg IV twice, 4 days apart (n=7, Beale and Arana, *Am J Psych* 1995, **152**, 959–60) and to 3mg/d for 4 days (n=10, Dinan *et al, Acta Psych Scand* 1997, **95**, 58–61), although other reports indicate that only a minority of patients respond (letter by Wolkowitz *et al, Am J Psych* 1996, **153**, 1112–13). This interesting effect may be via upregulation of glu-cocorticoid receptors, something the SSRIs also do.

**Dexamfetamine**
Dexamfetamine may be rapidly effective for depression and fatigue, with one successful trial in men with HIV (n=23, RCT, 2/52, Wagner and Rabkin, *J Clin Psych* 2000, **61**, 436–40).

**Dehydroepiandrosterone (DHEA)** \*
DHEA up to 90mg/d was successful in 45% treatment-resistant depressives cf. nil for placebo. Larger-scale trials may be warranted (n=22, RCT, d/b, p/c, 6/52, Wolkowitz *et al, Am J Psych* 1999, **156**, 646–49).

**Donepezil** \*
Donepezil may reduce REM latency in depressed patients (n=16, c/o, Perlis *et al, Biol Psych* 2002, **51**, 457–62).

**Hydrocortisone** \*
IV hydrocortisone produced a significantly greater and robust improvement in HAM-D scores than ovine CRH or placebo (n=22, RCT, d/b, p/c, 2/7, DeBattista *et al, Am J Psych* 2000, **157**, 1334–37; comment by Watson and Young, *Am J Psych* 2001, **158**, 1536–37).

**Inositol** \*
Inositol is a precursor of an intracellular secondary messenger system for numerous neurotransmitters. The most recent major trial showed no significant effect in SSRI augmentation (n=27, RCT, p/c, Levine *et al, Biol Psych* 1999, **45**, 270–73) and 12g/d had no effect in SSRI failures (RCT, d/b, Nemets *et al, J Neural Transm* 1999, **106**, 795–98). Previous work had led to some enthusiasm (eg. n=28, p/c, Levine *et al, Am J Psych* 1995, **152**, 792–94; Levine *et al, Israel J Psych Related Sci* 1995, **32**, 14–21). Inositol may, however, be useful in bipolar depression (as well as unipolar), as shown in a trial where 50% responded to 12g/d inositol (cf 30% on placebo) (n=24, RCT, 6/52, Chengappa *et al, Bipolar Disord* 2000, **2**, 47–55).

**Ketoconazole** \*
Ketoconazole inhibits cortisol secretion, lowering cortisol levels. It may have a slow-onset antidepressant

effect (n=17, study by Murphy *et al, Can J Psychiatry* 1998, **43**, 279–86), particularly in hypercortisolemic (but not normal) patients (n=20, RCT, Wolkowitz *et al, Biol Psych* 1999, **45**, 1070–74) and at 400mg/d as add-on therapy in resistant bipolar depression, with no increase in manic symptoms (n=6, open, Brown *et al, Bipolar Disorders* 2001, **3**. 23–29). Limited efficacy in treatment refractory major depression has been noted (n=16, RCT, Malison *et al, J Clin Psychopharmacol* 1999, **19**, 466–70).

## Mifepristone *

Short-term use of 600–1200mg/d of mifepristone (a glucocorticosteroid receptor antagonist) appears to be an option in treating psychotic major depression (PMD), following the theory that "the psychosis in PMD is caused by excessive activation of the hypothalamic-pituitary-adrenal axis" (n=30, open, 7/7, Belanoff *et al, Biol Psych* 2002, **52**, 386–92).

## Olanzapine

Olanzapine 5–20mg/d may have a role as antidepressant augmentation in psychotic depression (n=2, Malhi and Checkley, *B J Psych* 1999, **174**, 460) and a retrospective study indicated olanzapine 10mg/d may have efficacy in psychotic depression, as monotherapy (n=30, open, Rothschild, *J Clin Psych* 1999, **60**, 116–18).

## Opiates

Some anecdotal cases suggest that oxycodone or oxymorphone may produce a sustained effect in refractory and chronic depression, as well as reducing psychogenic pain and distress (n=3, Stoll and Reuter, *Am J Psych* 1999, **156**, 2017), with some efficacy from buprenorphine in refractory, unipolar depression, with a striking response in four (n=10, open, 6/52, Bodkin *et al, J Clin Psychopharmacol* 1995,**15**, 49–57; see also Callaway, *Biol Psych* 1996, **39**, 989–90). The potential for abuse limits their use.

## Pergolide *

Pergolide (a dopamine agonist) has been tried with moderate success as an adjuvant to tricyclics and MAOIs, eg. 55% showed improvement within 7 days, with doses of 0.5–1mg/d (n=20, open, Bouckoms and Mangini, *Psychopharmacol Bull* 1993, **29**, 207–11) and to tricyclics (n=20, open, Izumi *et al, J Aff Dis* 2000, **61**, 127–32).

## Pramipexole *

Pramipexole has been used with some success (n=22, case series, Ostow, *Am J Psych* 2002, **159**, 320–21; n=174, RCT, p/c, 8/52, Corrigan *et al, Depress Anxiety* 2000, **11**, 58–65).

## Protirelin (Thyrotropin-Releasing Hormone, TRH)

Five of eight depressed patients given 500mcg of protirelin intrathecally responded robustly and rapidly (mood and suicidality) but the effect was shortlived (Marangell *et al, Arch Gen Psych* 1997, **54**, 214–22). TRH may thus be involved in mood regulation.

## Omega-3 fatty acids (PUFAs) *

There is some evidence for an association between PUFAs (polyunsaturated fatty acids) and depression, and studies so far have seen some beneficial effect from ethyl-EPA (review by Peet, *Adv Psych Treat* 2002, **8**, 223–29) eg. rapid response to adjunctive use with paroxetine (n=1, Puri *et al, Arch Gen Psych* 2002, **59**, 91–92) with maintenance antidepressants (n=20, d/b, 4/52, Nemets *et al, Am J Psych* 2002, **159**, 477–79), and 1g/d added to current medication appeared effective in treatment-resistant depression (n=70, RCT, d/b, p/c,12/52, Peet and Horrobin, *Arch Gen Psych* 2002, **59**, 913–19).

## Risperidone

Addition of low dose risperidone (0.5–2mg/d) to existing SSRI therapy produced rapid responses in SSRI resistant patients (n=8, open, Ostroff and Nelson, *J Clin Psych* 1999, **60**, 256–59), and in psychotic depression unresponsive to antidepressants responded to risperidone 4mg/d (n=1, Land and Chang, *J Clin Psych* 1998, **59**, 624).

## Sulpiride

Sulpiride (mean dose 181mg/d) may be effective and well-tolerated in mild to moderate depression (n=177, RCT, 6/52, Ruther *et al, Pharmacopsychiatry* 1999, **32**, 127–35).

## Tetracycline antibiotics

Minocycline and demeclocycline have been reported in case studies to have a detectable antidepressant effect (Levine *et al, Am J Psych* 1996, **153**, 582).

## Topiramate *

Adjunctive topiramate may be beneficial for some obese depressed females (n=16, open, Carpenter *et al, J Aff Dis* 2002, **69**, 251–55).

## Tramadol *

Response of refractory MDD to tramadol (structurally similar to venlafaxine) 300–400mg/d prescribed for pain has been reported (n=1, Shapira *et al, J Clin Psych* 2001, **62**, 205–6).

## Valproate

Valproate can be used to augment tricyclics but is probably only of minimum to moderate potency (*Am J Psych* 1990, **147**, 431–34) although response in resistant unipolar depression or dysthymia has been reported (n=1, Kemp, *B J Psych* 1992, **160**, 121–23).

## Verapamil

Dramatic response in an elderly lady has been reported (n=1, *B J Psych* 1991, **158**, 124–25) but disputed (*B J Psych* 1991, **159**, 584–85). See also bipolar (*1.10*).

◊ **Others: ***
Other drugs tried include **ascorbic acid**, **captopril** 50–100mg/d (n=9, open, *J Clin Psychopharmacol* 1991, **11**, 395–96), **bromocriptine** 10–60mg/d (McGrath *et al, J Clin Psychopharmacol* 1995, **15**, 289–91), **cyproheptadine** (n=6, RCT, Greenway *et al, Pharmacotherapy* 1995, **15**, 357–60), **levodopa** (*J Psychopharmacol* 1990, **4**, 152–67), **primidone** (n=1, Brown *et al, Lancet* 1993, **342**, 925) **progabide** (n=1, Thaker *et al, Arch*

*Gen Psych* 1990, **47**, 287–78) and **zotepine** (n=2, Konig and Wolfersdorf, *Tw Neurol Psych* 1994, **8**, 460–63).

◆ **No efficacy**
## Benzodiazepines

There have been some suggestions that alprazolam (*J Aff Dis* 1990, **18**, 67–73) and diazepam (*B J Psych* 1989, **155**, 483–89) have antidepressant activity but some depression rating scales include measures of anxiety and probably explain the alleged effect. The BNF states that they should not be used to treat depression. Discontinuing drugs such as clonazepam prescribed for panic/anxiety control can often lead to improvement of depression (see *5.5*). Short-term adjunctive use may have some role (see combinations).

## Caffeine

Some depressed people may have increased sensitivity to caffeine (Lee *et al, Am J Psych* 1988, **145**, 632–35).

## Testosterone *

The antidepressant effects of IM testosterone in hypogonadal men with major depression were equivalent to placebo (n=30, RCT, d/b, p/c, 6/52, Seidmen *et al, J Clin Psych* 2001, **62**, 406–12).

## 1.15 DYSTHYMIA

See also depression (*1.14*)

**Symptoms: ***
Dysthymia (literally 'ill-humoured') is a low-grade chronic melancholic depression (often with anxiety) of insidious onset, chronic course (lasting at least two years with permanent or intermittent symptoms) and high risk of relapse. It has few of the physical symptoms of depression and is compatible with stable social functioning. Almost all eventually develop superimposed major depression (n=86, 3yr follow-up, Klein *et al, Am J Psych* 2000, **157**, 931–39). The life-time prevalence rate may be around 3–6%, and higher in the elderly. Dysthymia has been associated with low testosterone levels in men and hence a link made with HPG axis dysfunction (n=220,

open, Seidman *et al, Am J Psych* 2002, **159**, 456–59). It has been considered by some to be similar to depressive personality disorder or anxiety and by others as a way of medicalising (and hence ignoring) social problems or as a way of giving someone a medical diagnosis to allow insurance claims.

### Role of drugs:
It is clear that antidepressants are effective in dysthymia, with no proven significant differences between classes, but should form part of an overall treatment strategy including also, eg. IPT and marital therapy. A greater sensitivity to side-effects has been noted in dysthymics, with tricyclics the biggest culprits. SSRIs, moclobemide and MAOIs appear favoured. If one class does not work, switching to another may convey a 40–60% chance of response (Thase, *Curr Opin Psych* 1998, **11**, 77–83, 35 refs). Treatment for several months may be necessary for full response (Lima and Moncrieff, *CDSR* 2000, 1130; review by Thase, *EBMH* 1998, **1**, 111). A low (10–20%) placebo response is seen (Frances *et al, Int Clin Psychopharmacol* 1993, **7**, 197–200).

**Reviews**: meta-analysis (Lima *et al, Psychol Med* 1999, **29**, 1273–89), diagnosis and treatment (Rihmer, *Curr Opin Psych* 1999, **12**, 69–75, 48 refs), in the elderly (Bellino *et al, Drugs & Aging* 2000, **16**, 107–21).

---

● **Unlicensed/Some efficacy**
### Bupropion *
Bupropion SR up to 400mg/d was effective in 71% patients in one trial, with those with a history of substance misuse *less* likely to respond (n=21, open, 8/52, Hellerstein *et al, J Clin Psychopharmacol* 2001, **21**, 325–29).

### MAOIs
Phenelzine at 50–75mg/d and tranylcypromine have both been shown to be as effective as tricyclics, the latter over a two year period (mentioned in *B J Psych* 1995, **166**, 174–83).

### Moclobemide
Moclobemide (mean 675mg/d) has been shown to be significantly more

effective for dysthymia than imipramine (mean 220mg/d) and placebo, with fewer side-effects (n=315, RCT, Versiani *et al, Int Clin Psychopharmacol* 1997, **12**, 183–93), confirming previous studies (review by Petursson, *Acta Psych Scand* 1995, **91**[Suppl 386], 36–39).

### SSRIs *
In dysthymia without major depression, **sertraline** up to 200mg/d may be more effective than placebo over a wide range of efficacy and quality of life measures (n=310, RCT, 12/52, Ravindran *et al, J Clin Psych* 2000, **61**, 821–27) and may improve behaviour and personality in dysthymia (n=410, RCT, d/b, p/c, Hellerstein *et al, Am J Psych* 2000, **157**, 1436–44). It has also been effective in out-patients eg. as effective as imipramine (50–300mg/d), but better tolerated (n=416, RCT, 12/52, Kocsis *et al, Am J Psych* 1997, **154**, 390; n=310, d/b, 12/52, Ravindran *et al, J Clin Psych* 2000, **61**, 821–27). There is some evidence that pre-treatment with a tricyclic may improve subsequent response to sertraline (Thase, *Curr Opin Psych* 1998, **11**, 77–83). Fluoxetine may produce a significant improvement in dysthymic symptoms (n=35, RCT, p/c, 8/52, Hellerstein *et al, Am J Psych* 1993, **150**, 1169–75) and 20mg/d may be more effective than placebo, with 50% of the non-responders at 3 months improving with a dose increase to 40mg/d (n=140, RCT, Vanelle *et al, B J Psych* 1997, **170**, 345–50). **Paroxetine** was superior to psychotherapy and placebo in older dysthymics (n=415, RCT, 11/52, Williams *et al, JAMA* 2000, **284**, 1519–26).

### St John's wort
SJW seems effective in mild to moderate depression, including dysthymia (Laakmann *et al, Pharmacopsychiatry* 1998, **31**[Suppl], 54–59; Volz, *Pharmacopsychiatry* 1997, **30**[Suppl], 72–76).

### Tricyclics *
Amitriptyline and desipramine (n=42, open, 8/52, Marin *et al, Am J*

*Psych* 1994, **151**, 1079–80) have both been studied over 6–12 weeks and found at doses of 150–300mg/d to be 2–3 times more effective than placebo. 50–300mg/d imipramine has been shown to be as effective (but with more drop-outs) as sertraline in long-standing dysthymia, and both were significantly better than placebo (n=416, RCT, 12/52, Kocsis *et al, Am J Psych* 1997, **154**, 390). Desipramine has been shown to be effective for maintenance (n=27, p/c, 2-yrs, Miller *et al, J Aff Dis* 2001, **64**, 231–37).

○ **Unlicensed/Possible efficacy**
**Amisulpride** *

A number of studies have shown amisulpride to have some efficacy in dysthymia, eg. 50mg/d was as effective as sertraline 50–100mg/d, with a significantly faster onset of action (n=313, RCT, d/b, 12/52, Amore *et al, Int Clin Psychopharmacol* 2001, **16**, 317–24), effective for short-term treatment (n=100, RCT, open, 8/52, Rocca *et al, J Affect Disord* 2002, **70**, 313–17) and 50mg/d more effective than increasing paroxetine dose to 40mg/d in SSRI-resistant dysthymia (n=60, open, 3/12, Rocca *et al, Psych Res* 2002, **112**, 145–52). Some dopaminergic side-effects are seen with amisulpride.

**Review:*** substituted benzamides in dysthymia (Pani and Gessa, *Mol Psychiatry* 2002, **7**, 247–53).

**Chromium**

Chromium (as the picolinate) provided a dramatic and complete resolution of dysthymia in a small trial (n=5, s/b, McLeod *et al, J Clin Psych* 1999, **60**, 237).

**Fluvoxamine**

Fluvoxamine may be well tolerated and effective in dysthymic adolescents (n=21, open, Rabe-Jablonska, *J Child Adolesc Psychopharmacol* 2000, **10**, 9–18).

**Mirtazapine**

Mirtazapine 15–45mg/d was effective in 73% of patients with dysthymia, 4 discontinuing because of sedation

(n=15, open, 10/52, *Depress Anxiety* 1999, **10**, 68–72).

**Venlafaxine**

An open study showed venlafaxine (up to 225mg/d) effective in 10 of the 14 patients who completed a 9-week trial (seven quickly to low dose, three only to high dose, n=17, Dunner *et al, J Clin Psych* 1997, **58**, 528–31). Although adverse effects were a problem in another trial, venlafaxine 100–250mg/d was effective (n=22, open, Hellerstein *et al, J Clin Psych* 1999, **60**, 845–49).

◊ **Others**
Other drugs tried include **lithium** (eg. Akiskal *et al, Arch Gen Psych* 1980, **37**, 777–83) and **valproate** (n=1, Kemp, *B J Psych* 1992, **160**, 121–23).

## 1.16 EATING DISORDERS

DSM-IV includes three eating disorders; anorexia nervosa (AN), bulimia nervosa (BN) and eating disorders, not otherwise specified (EDNOS), this latter including binge eating disorder. Remission is more likely in BN than AN.

**Review:** drug treatment of adolescent eating disorders (Kruger and Kennedy, *J Psychiatry Neurosci* 2000, **25**, 497–508), general and primary care (Mehler, *Ann Int Med* 2001, **134**, 1048–59; Cooper, *Prescriber* 2001, 46–48; Becker *et al, NEJM* 1999, **340**, 1092–98, 69 refs; Maddox and Long, *JAMA* 1999, **39**, 378–87; Kaye *et al, Ann Rev Med* 2000, **51**, 299–313), brain, bones and exercise (Bryant-Waugh and Lask, *Hosp Med* 1999, **60**, 472–73, editorial).

### 1.16.1 ANOREXIA NERVOSA

**Symptoms:**
The main diagnostic symptoms of anorexia nervosa are:
1. Amenorrhoea in females (absence of three consecutive menstrual cycles).
2. Refusal to maintain body weight over minimum normal for age and height.
3. Intense fear of becoming obese.
4. Disturbance in body perception, eg. feeling fat even when emaciated.

Anorexia usually starts in the late teens, with distorted body image and relentless dieting. Patients may avoid carbohydrates, induce vomiting, abuse laxatives, take excess exercise, binge eat and suffer depression and social withdrawal. It may occur in up to 2% of schoolgirls and up to 4 in 100,000 of the general population.

### Role of drugs:

Drug therapy is generally most useful as a supportive measure to treat any concurrent conditions. In severely emaciated patients, enteral feeding or even TPN may be necessary.

**Reviews:** overall management (Dalle Grave *et al*, *Eat Weight Disord* 2001, **6**, 81–89; Kruger and Kennedy, *J Psych Neurosci* 2000, **25**, 497–508), in teen-agers (Serpell and Treasure, *Prescriber* 1996, **7**[22], 19–25), SSRIs in anorexia (Ferguson *et al*, *Int J Eat Disord* 1999, **25**, 11–17) and general (Pike, *Clin Psychol Rev* 1998, **18**, 447–75; Marcus and Levine, *Curr Opin Psych* 1998, **11**, 159–63).

---

● **Unlicensed/Some efficacy**
### Nutritional feeding *

TPN may be necessary in severely anorexic patients (review by Jeejeebhoy, *Semin Gastrointest Dis* 1998, **9**, 183–88), where a life-threatening weight loss has occurred, particularly if accompanied by low potassium levels and where conventional therapies have failed. Weight gain can be significant in a relatively short period and TPN can help avert permanent damage or death. Great care is needed where patients are likely to interfere with the IV line with the possibility of infection in a compromised patient and of embolism. Supervised oral feeding with nutritional supplements can also be an effective acute treatment.

### Treatment of any PMS

This may help any premenstrual exacerbations (see *1.26*).

### Tricyclic antidepressants

The main role of the tricyclics may be in maintenance therapy. Doses of 150mg/d or more for 4–6 weeks may be needed.

---

○ **Unlicensed/Possible efficacy**
### Antipsychotics *

OCD and anorexia have responded to **olanzapine** 5mg/d, with reduced fixed body perceptions, no weight loss and improved insight (n=3, Jensen and Mejlhede, *B J Psych* 2000, **177**, 87; n=2, La Vie *et al*, *Int J Eat Disord* 2000, **27**, 363–66), and a pilot study suggested weight gain was likely in anorexia (but 20% lost weight), although changes in psychopathology were not assessed (n=20, open, 10/52, Powers *et al*, *Int J Eat Disord* 2002, **32**, 146–54). **Risperidone** has been used (Newman-Toker, *J Am Acad Child Adolesc Psych* 2000, **39**, 941–42).

### Citalopram *

20mg/d has been used successfully (n=6, Calandra *et al*, *Eat Weight Disord* 1999, **4**, 207–10) and a pilot study suggested some symptom improvement (n=52, RCT, Fassino *et al*, *Eur Neuropsychopharmacol* 2002, **12**, 453–59).

### Fluoxetine

Fluoxetine 60mg/d may not add significant benefit to in-patient treatment of anorexia (n=31, RCT, Attia *et al*, *Am J Psych* 1998, **155**, 548–51), but there is some evidence that it may be of use in preventing relapse in weight restored anorexics (Marcus and Levine, *Curr Opin Psych* 1998, **11**, 159–63).

### Sertraline

A case has been reported of complete response to sertraline at 50mg/d in a woman only partly responsive to fluoxetine (Roberts and Lydiard, *Am J Psych* 1993, **150**, 1753).

### Tramadol *

Tramadol, which has significant MAOI activity and mu opiate antagonism, has been successful at 225mg/d to treat anorexia nervosa (n=1, Mendelson, *Am J Psych* 2001, **158**, 963–94).

## Zinc

Zinc has virtually no side-effects and a 4-week trial may help some people (eg. *Acta Psych Scand* 1990, **82**, 14–17) and 100mg/d produced an increase in BMI twice that of placebo (n=35, RCT, Birmingham *et al*, *Int J Eat Disord* 1994, **15**, 251–55).

◊ **Others**

Other drugs tried include **cyprohepta-dine** (n=72, RCT, Halmi *et al*, *Arch Gen Psych* 1986, **43**, 177–81) and **lithium** (n=16, d/b, 16/52, Gross, *J Clin Psychopharmacol* 1981, **1**, 376–81; Stein *et al*, *B J Psych* 1982, **140**, 526–28).

## 1.16.2 BULIMIA NERVOSA

**Symptoms:**

The main diagnostic symptoms of bulimia nervosa are:

1. Recurrent binge eating.
2. An urge to overeat (including lack of control over eating during binges).
3. Regular self-induced vomiting/laxative abuse/strict dieting/fasting etc.
4. Persistent over-concern with body shape and weight.

There must be a minimum of two binge episodes per week for at least 3 months. Weight and menses are normal.

**Role of drugs:** *

A meta-analysis of antidepressants vs placebo in bulimia showed that short-term remission was more likely with antidepressants, equivalent drop-outs, but with no drug class better than any other (16 RCTs, n=1300, Bacaltchuk *et al*, *Aust N Z J Psych* 2000, **34**, 310–17). Cochrane concludes that all anti-depressants appear equally effective compared to placebo but with a high drop-out rate (Bacaltchuk and Hay, *CDSR* 2001, **4**, 3391) but do not work as antidepressants. Adequate doses are needed, eg. at least 150mg/d equivalent of a tricyclic for adequate duration, eg. at least four weeks. Side-effects (especially anticholinergic) can be severe and result in non-compliance. Drugs should be part of an individualised programme with nutrition and CBT the most effective interventions. CBT and pharmacotherapy may be effective together (review by Mitchell *et al*, *Psychiatr Clin North Am* 2001, **24**, 315–23).

**Reviews:** * general (Brambilla, *CNS Drugs* 2001, **15**, 119–36, 99 refs; Kruger and Kennedy, *J Psych Neurosci* 2000, **25**, 497–508), systematic review (Bacaltchuk *et al*, *Aust NZ J Psych* 2000, **34**, 310–17) and binge eating disorder (Dingemans *et al*, *Intl J Obes* 2002, **26**, 299–307).

**BNF Listed**
**Fluoxetine** *

60mg/d has a significant effect on binge eating and purging, eating attitudes, behaviour and food craving, being also safe and effective in longer-term treatment of bulimia, recent trials confirming this effect where psychological treatments have been inadequate eg. fluoxetine was superior to placebo as maintenance therapy, albeit with a high drop-out rate (n=150, RCT, 16 centres, 12/12, Romano *et al*, *Am J Psych* 2002, **159**, 96–102; review by Palmer, *EBMH* 2002, **120**, 120; see also n=22, RCT, 8/52, Walsh *et al*, *Am J Psych* 2000, **157**, 1332–34). It does not work purely as an antidepressant as the improvement is independent of depression scores and uses higher doses, although any depression may also improve. Its long half-life may help with missed doses.

● **Combinations**
**Naltrexone + fluoxetine**

After a partial response to 60mg/d fluoxetine, addition of 100mg/d naltrexone produced a 'robust' reduction in binge frequency and amount (n=1, Neumeister *et al*, *Am J Psych* 1999, **156**, 797).

● **Unlicensed/Some efficacy**
**MAOIs**

MAOIs can be successful drugs if the dietary restrictions can be overcome.

## PMS treatments

Pyridoxine and progesterones in particular may help to minimise the effects of premenstrual relapses.

## SSRIs (see also fluoxetine above)

**Citalopram** 20mg/d has been used successfully (n=12, Calandra *et al, Eat Weight Disord* 1999, **4**, 207–10). One trial showed **fluvoxamine** to have a significant effect on reducing bulimic behaviour (n=72, d/b, p/c, Fichter, *J Clin Psychopharmacol* 1996, **16**, 9–18), and in binge-eating disorder, with 50–300mg/d effective in most outcome measures in acute treatment (n=85, RCT, 9/52, Hudson *et al, Am J Psych* 1998, **155**, 1756–62). **Paroxetine** has been reputed to have no beneficial effect in an unpublished study. **Sertraline** was significantly superior to placebo in most measures in a short study (n=34, RCT, d/b, 6/52, McElroy *et al, Am J Psych* 2000, **157**, 1004–6).

---

○ **Unlicensed/Possible efficacy**
**Flutamide**

The testosterone receptor antagonist flutamide (250–500mg/d) produced a rapid and marked improvement in bulimic behaviour in two women (Bergman and Eriksson, *Acta Psych Scand* 1996, **94**, 137–39).

## Ondansetron *

Ondansetron was reported to be effective in three small short-term trials by one group of investigators, and may be an option after failure of traditional therapies (reviews by Fung and Ferrill, *Ann Pharmacother* 2001, **35**, 1270–73; Generali and Cada, *Hosp Pharm* 2001, **36**, 547–52, 572). Decreased binge-eating and vomiting has been shown with ondansetron 24mg/d, possibly due to pharmacological decrease in vagal neurotransmission (n=28, RCT, Faris *et al, Lancet* 2000, **355**, 792–97; editorial by Kiss, *Lancet* 2000, **355**, 769–70).

## Reboxetine

Successful use of reboxetine has been reported (n=7, open, El-Giamal *et al, Int Clin Psychopharmacol* 2000, **15**, 351–56).

## Sibutramine *

A preliminary trial showed sibutramine 15mg/d to be markedly effective and well-tolerated for obese patients with binge-eating disorder, with 7 showing a complete resolution of symptoms (n=10, open, 12/52, Appolinario *et al, J Clin Psych* 2002, **63**, 28–30).

## Topiramate *

There is growing interest in topiramate in bulimia. In obese binge-eaters, topiramate produced a total response in 50% and marked improvement in 25% (n=8, open, 16/52, Appolinario *et al, Can J Psych* 2002, **47**, 271–73) and 70% women with binge-eating disorder showed a moderate or good response to topiramate, maintained for up to 30 months (case series, n=13, mean 18/12, Shapira *et al, J Clin Psych* 2000, **61**, 368–72). There have also been several published cases of dramatic response (eg. drug-resistant bulimia. topiramate 150mg/d, n=1, Knable, *Am J Psych* 2001, **158**, 322–23; n=1, Appolinario *et al, Am J Psych* 2001, **158**, 967–68; n=1, Felstrom and Blackshaw, *Am J Psych* 2002, **159**, 1246–47).

## Tricyclics

Many tricyclics eg. amitriptyline (*J Clin Psychopharmacol* 1984, **4**, 186–93) have been used but are of arguable potency. Poor relapse rates suggest serious limitations with longterm efficacy (RCT, d/b, p/c, 6/12, Walsh *et al, Am J Psych* 1991,**148**, 1206–12).

---

◇ **Others: ***

Other drugs tried include **naltrexone** (n=19, RCT, Marrazzi *et al, Int Clin Psychopharmacol* 1995, **10**, 163–72), **trazodone** (n=42, RCT, Pope *et al, J Clin Psychopharmacol* 1989, **9**, 254–59), **valproate** (n=1, *J Clin Pharmacol* 1985, **5**, 229–30) and **zinc** (*Arch Int Med* 1984, **100**, 317–18).

◆ **No efficacy**
**Carbamazepine**

No effect on bulimia was seen in one study (n=6, *Am J Psych* 1983, **140** 1225–26).

## Clozapine

There is a single case of bulimia acutely worsening on clozapine 350mg/d (*Am J Psych* 1992, **149**, 1408).

## Cyproheptadine

Although potentially useful in anorexia it appears to be detrimental in bulimia (*Arch Gen Psych* 1986, **43**, 177–81).

## Lithium

Despite early enthusiasm, lithium is no more effective than placebo (n=91, Hsu *et al*, *J Nerv Mental Dis* 1991, **179**, 351–55).

## Mianserin

No effect was seen at 60mg/d (n=50, 8/52, *B J Clin Pharmacol* 1983, **15**, 195S–202S).

## Moclobemide *

Moclobemide 600mg/d was found to be safe but ineffective in treating bulimia (n=52, RCT, 6/52, Carruba *et al*, *Int Clin Psychopharmacol* 2001, **16**, 27–32).

## 1.17 EPILEPSY

See also status epilepticus (*1.17.1*)

The annual incidence of epilepsy is 50–70 cases per 100 000 (excluding febrile seizure), with a point prevalence of 5–10 per 1000. The lifetime prevalence is 2–5% of the population. Of those people with epilepsy, up to 30–40% have seizures at unacceptably high rates or have additional problems (see Epilepsy Needs document, Brown *et al*, *Seizure* 1993, **2**, 91–103).

## DISCONTINUING ANTICONVULSANTS *

Since all anticonvulsants have side-effects, especially when taken for long periods and even when optimum ranges are adhered to, they should be discontinued when no longer needed. Little advice is given to adults on anticonvulsant discontinuation, with many stopping on their own initiative.

A concentration of fits during or in the first few months after withdrawal suggest that at least some are provoked by drug withdrawal. Other withdrawal effects such as anxiety, agitation and insomnia are a problem but only occur with the barbiturates and benzodiazepines (reviews in *Lancet* 1991, **337**, 1175–80; Kristmann *et al*, *Lancet* 1991, **338**, 53).

Although around 30% children will have a seizure after anticonvulsant withdrawal, the prognosis is still good if a further course of anticonvulsants is taken (n=40, 12-yr follow-up, Bouma *et al*, *J Neurol Neurosurg Psych* 2002, **72**, 507–10).

**Reviews**: withdrawing anticonvulsants (in seizure-free patients, Rosenberg *et al* (*Neurology* 1996, **47**, 600–2; Lhatoo and Sander, *Curr Pharm Des* 2000, **6**, 861–63; Buna, *Pharmacotherapy* 1998, **18**, 235–41), comparative study (n=1013, Chadwick, *Brain* 1999, **122**, 441–48), practical guide (Schmidt and Gram, *Drugs* 1996, **52**, 870–74).

A prognostic index for recurrence of seizures, either on continued treatment or discontinuation, has been advised by the MRC Antiepileptic Drug Withdrawal Study Group (Chadwick *et al*, *BMJ* 1993, **306**, 1374–78), based on a 4-year study of 1021 patients from six European countries, testing the potential for 26 possible risk factors. This is the only major study of withdrawal in patients in remission:

| Starting score (all patients) | −175 |
|---|---|
| Age 16 yrs or older | +45 |
| Taking >1 anticonvulsant | +50 |
| Seizures after starting anticonvulsants | +35 |
| History of 1° or 2° GTC seizures | +35 |
| History of myoclonic seizures | +50 |
| EEG in past year | |
| — not available | +15 |
| — abnormal | +20 |
| Period free from seizures (in years) | +200/t |
| Total scores= | =T |
| Then divide the total score by 100 and expontiate (e$^x$): | $z=e^{t/100}$ |
| Thus the probability of recurrence of seizures is: | |
| Continued treatment: | |
| — by one year | $1-0.89^z$ |
| — by two years | $1-0.79^z$ |
| Slow withdrawal: | |
| — by one year | $1-0.69^z$ |
| — by two years | $1-0.60^z$ |

| Seizures — types, symptoms and treatment | | | | | |
|---|---|---|---|---|---|
| **International Classification** | **Other names** | **Manifestation** | **Age of onset** | **Duration** | **Recovery** |
| Generalised Tonic-Clonic (G.T.C.) | Major motor Grand mal | Sudden loss of consciousness, intense (tonic) muscle spasms, then intermittent seizures. Also flushing & incontinence | Any | 1–5 minutes | Varies up to 1 hr |
| Absence (typical or atypical) | Petit mal | Sudden cessation of activity. Eyes rolling. Unresponsive. Immediate recovery, no awareness | 3–15 Years limit | Seconds | Immediate |
| Myoclonic or Partial seizures with motor symptoms | Minor motor Infantile spasms Myoclonic jerks | Sudden jerk of limbs, May be followed by G.T.C. or atonic seizures | During 1st yr of life (3–9 mo) | Seconds to Minutes | Varies |
| Atonic | Akinetic Astatic 'Drop attacks' | Sudden loss of consciousness | 2+ yrs (3–7 most common) | Minutes | Varies |
| Simple Partial (Partial seizures with simple symptomatology) | Focal (localised) | Spasmodic convulsions. Hallucinations of flashing lights. Numbness, paraesthesia dysphagia & visual phenomena. No loss of consciousness | Any | Minutes | Varies |
| Complex Partial (Partial seizures with complex symptomatology) | Temporal lobe Psychomotor | Unconscious behaviour (chewing, lip smacking, walking), acts of violence, hallucinations of taste, smell or hearing. Unreal feelings. Memory disturbance. Time disturbance. Fear, anxiety, distorted perception, Impaired consciousness | Adolescent and adult | Minutes to hours | Immediate. No awareness |

Generalised epilepsy usually has genetic influence (eg. low threshold). Focal and partial epilepsy is probably due to a damaged brain area.
For further information on the International on the Classification of Epileptic Seizupres (ICES), refer to *Epilepsia* 1981, **22**, 489–501.

## Therapeutic drug monitoring

| Drug | Plasma levels 'Optimum' | Plasma levels Toxic | Half-life | Time to steady state | Peak plasma concs | Sample | Sample frequency | Other checks | Comments |
|---|---|---|---|---|---|---|---|---|---|
| PHENYTOIN *TDM essential | 40–80 micromol/L (10–20 mg/l) upper end for parital seizures. <20 mmol unlikely to work | >80 micromol/L | 20–40 hours (up to 140 at higher levels) | 5 days minimum. 1–5 weeks possibly (variable, dose dependent) | 3–12 hrs dependent on total daily dose | Aim for trough unless confirmation of toxicity required | Every 3–12 months for well stabilised patients | Folate, calcium (both with phenytoin) | Non-linear kinetics, so missed doses, changes in absorption, tablet or capsule brand can markedly affect plasma levels |
| PHENOBARBITAL *TDM useful | 60–180 micromol/L (10–30 mg/l) dependent upon response | >180 micromol/L ↑ chance of stupor | 50–160 hrs, with age | Adults: 10–25 days Children: 8–15 days | 2–6 hrs | Long t½, so time not vital. Best to be consistent each time | Every 6/12 for well-stabilised patients | Folate 6/12 | Blood levels can also be useful as a measure of long-term compliance |
| CARBAMAZEPINE *TDM fairly useful | 20–50 micromol/L (4–12 mg/l). 20–40 for GTC + poly-therapy, 30–50 for monotherapy | >50 micromol/L | 5–38 hrs | 1–4 weeks (enzyme induction). Changes stabilise in about a week | 2.5–24 hrs (mean 6 h)—less if taken with food | Aim for trough level unless side-effects suspected | Every six months for well-stabilised patients | FBC in initial stages of treatment. Thyroid? Serum sodium | Plasma levels only of real use for anticonvulsant action. Are of limited use (eg. toxicity) in affective disorders |
| SODIUM VALPROATE/ VALPROIC ACID TDM unproven | 300–700 mmol/L (50–100 mg/L) proposed. Care in elderly | >700 mmol/L—but few side-effects or correlation proved | 6–20 hrs. longer in liver disease + polytherapy | 30–85 hrs | E/C tabs 2–4 hrs. Sol tabs + syrup: 1–3 hrs | Short t½ so need great care interpreting. Only serial levels are accurate | On request | LFT for 6/12 + plasma amylase if in abdomial pain | Levels may be useful where control is poor or if toxicity suspected. Hepatotoxicity may be dose related |

Unbound levels of phenytoin and valproate may be useful (*Neurology* 1992, **42**, 988–90)    ANTICONVULSANTS –overuse of levels–*Br Med J*, 1987, **294**, 723

This important and accessible paper should be consulted in order to use this predictive model to its optimum. It should prove useful in counselling patients in the community who wish to withdraw from anticonvulsants. Further validation is being carried out.

**Additional risk factors on discontinuing anticonvulsants:**

- Polypharmacy (4 or more anticonvulsants)
- Active epilepsy
- Age (50 years or older)
- 5 weeks or less between reductions
- Longer duration of treatment or illness (more than 30 months is a higher risk)
- Number of seizures before fits controlled (higher risk of relapse if more than 100 fits occur before control)
- Interval seizure less than one month at onset of illness
- Type of seizure: Complex partial seizures, tonic-clonic or combinations of seizures are more likely to relapse than simple partial seizures
- Number of drugs required before seizure control (ie. time taken to control fits)
- Abnormal EEG: 'Class 4'/epileptiform are the highest risk
- Adult/late onset seizures (after 10 to 12 years of age)
- Underlying cerebral disorder
- Withdrawal in less than 6 months

**References**: n=161, RCT, Peters *et al, Neurology* 1998, **50**, 724–30; n=226, Caviedes and Herranz, *Seizure* 1998, **7**, 107–14; n=409, RCT, Chadwick *et al, Epilepsia* 1996, **37**, 1043–50.

**Favourable factors for discontinuing anticonvulsants:**

- Primary generalised seizures
- Childhood onset (after the age of one, better >5yrs)
- Short duration of epilepsy
- No cerebral disorder
- Normal IQ
- Normal EEG (or no gross abnormalities, underlying neurological disorder or learning disability), before and after discontinuation
- Few seizures documented, especially juvenile myoclonic epilepsy
- History of non-compliance/concordance without relapse (in which case withdrawal should be encouraged)
- Medication below quoted therapeutic levels at time of discontinuation
- More than two years since last seizure, especially in children

**Role of drugs:**

Drug therapy is probably the single most important aspect in managing seizures. One study of 392 patients showed that treatment after a first fit reduced the recurrence rate at 24 months from 51% (untreated) to 26% (treated with first line anticonvulsant) (First Seizure Trial Group, *Neurology* 1993, **43**, 478–83). In a systematic review, the NNTs for new anticonvulsants as add-on therapy for refractory epilepsy were topiramate (1000mg/d= 2.9, 600mg/d=3.0), vigabatrin (300mg/d=3.3), tiagabine (32mg/d= 6.5), lamotrigine (500mg/d=7.2) and gabapentin (1200mg/d=7.4) (Marson *et al, Epilepsia* 1997, **38**, 859–80; comment in *Bandolier* 1998, **5**, 4–5).

Plasma level monitoring for anticonvulsants is often over-used and should be restricted to:

1. Patients on phenytoin or polypharmacy where dosage adjustment is necessary due to poor control or dose-related toxicity.
2. People with learning disabilities, where assessing toxicity is difficult.
3. Patients with renal or hepatic disease.
4. Pregnant women.
5. Where poor compliance is suspected

**Reviews:** general (Feely, *BMJ* 1999, **318**, 106–9; Hart, *Prescriber* 2000, 45–60), managing severe epilepsy in the community (Motterhead, *Prescriber* 2002, **13**, 67–88), AED efficacy according to seizure type (Mattson, *Neurology* 1998, **51** [Suppl 4], S15–S20, 28 refs), TDM of AEDs (Nelson and Gray, *Psych Bull* 2001, **25**, 356–58), modes of action (Rho and Sankar, *Epilepsia* 1999, **40**, 1471–83), Lennox-Gastaut Syndrome (Schmidt and Bourgeois, *Drug Safety* 2000, **22**, 467–77, 51 refs), refractory seizures (Devinsky, *NEJM* 1999, **340**, 1565–70, 43 refs), managing epilepsy in children (Crawford, *Prescriber* 2001, **12**, 77–80), teenagers (McLellan and Cross, *Prescriber* 2002, **13**, 24–37) and the elderly (Stephen and Brodie, *Lancet* 2000, **355**, 1441–46, 50 refs).

## BNF Listed

### First-line/monotherapy drugs *

A number of trials and reviews have concluded that carbamazepine, phenobarbital and phenytoin are equipotent (Tudur *et al*, *CDSR* 2002, **2**, 1911; Tudur *et al*, *CDSR* 2002, **2**, 1904), but carbamazepine is better tolerated and there may be some sub-types that respond preferentially to one drug. Carbamazepine may be preferable to valproate for partial-onset seizures (Marson *et al*, *Epilepsia* 2002, **43**, 505–13).

### Carbamazepine *

Carbamazepine is a broad spectrum anticonvulsant, licensed in the UK for adjunctive or first-line therapy in partial or generalised epilepsy (excluding absence and myoclonus). It has been compared with valproate in complex partial and secondary GTC in a large adult study, where they were considered of similar efficacy but with carbamazepine better for complex partial seizures (Mattson *et al*, *NEJM* 1992, **327**, 765–71; comments in *NEJM* 1993, **328**, 207–9) for partial-onset seizures (n=1265, 5 studies, Marson *et al*, *Epilepsia* 2002, **43**, 505–13) and with fewer long-term side-effects. The sustained release tablets can be used as a once-a-day dosage, with careful monitoring if seizures continue, although lower trough concentrations mean some patients may need twice daily dosing. Sudden withdrawal may increase cardiac sympathetic activity in sleep which could lead to seizure-

induced hypoxia, and predispose to sudden unexpected death in epilepsy (n=12, Hennessy *et al*, *Neurology* 2001, **57**, 1650–54).

**Reviews:*** pharmacokinetics (Graves *et al* (*Pharmacotherapy* 1998, **18**, 273–81), mode of action (Ambrosio *et al*, *Neurochem Res* 2002, **27**, 121–30).

### Lamotrigine *

Lamotrigine is indicated for adjunctive or monotherapy in partial or generalised epilepsy, Lennox-Gastaut and juvenile myoclonic epilepsy. It is thought to stabilise pre-synaptic neuronal membranes by blockade of voltage-dependent sodium channels, with this secondarily inhibiting the release of excessive excitatory glutamate and aspartate. It may only be fully effective when rapid firing occurs, ie. before and during a seizure, and it may also reduce neuronal death (Leach *et al*, *Epilepsia* 1991, **32**, 4–8). It is well tolerated as monotherapy in adults with newly diagnosed epilepsy (review of published RCTs, Mullens, *Clinical Drug Investigation* 1998, **16**, 125–33), at up to 500mg/d as monotherapy in adults with partial seizures (n=156, d/b, Gilliam *et al*, *Neurology* 1998, **51**, 1018–25) and in the elderly (n=208, 13 trials, Giorgi *et al*, *Drugs & Aging* 2001, **18**, 621–30). It may produce significantly fewer untoward cognitive and behavioural effects than carbamazepine (n=25, RCT, d/b, c/o, 10 + 10/52, Meador *et al*, *Neurology* 2001, **56**, 1177–82). Cochrane concludes that it is effective in drug-resistant partial epilepsy (n=1243, s=11, Ramaratnam *et al*, *CDSR* 2001, **3**, 1909). Lamotrigine has a good pharmacokinetic profile, eg. long half-life, low protein binding and few interactions. The 2–5% risk of rashes can be reduced in adults with a starting dose of 25mg/d for two weeks, then 50mg/d for two weeks, then increasing every 1–2 weeks, halved if added to valproate (where rash is also more likely to occur, Gilman, *Ann Pharmacother* 1995, **29**, 144–51) or allergic to trimethoprim, and doubled if combined with concurrent enzyme inducing drugs, eg. phenytoin, carbamazepine etc.

**Reviews**:* general (Arzimanoglou *et al, Rev Neurol (Paris)* 2001, **157**, 525–36), safety review of 68 trials, with particular emphasis on rash (Messenheimer *et al, Drug Safety* 1998, **18**, 281–96, 28 refs), use in children (Messenheimer *et al, Drug Safety* 2000, **22**, 303–12, 35 refs), saliva and serum monitoring (Tsiropoulos *et al, Ther Drug Monit* 2000, **22**, 517–21).

## Oxcarbazepine *

Oxcarbazepine exerts its action primarily through its metabolite (the monohydroxy derivative, MHD). It is related to carbamazepine but may be better tolerated, and may be useful in patients unable to tolerate carbamazepine due to adverse or allergic reactions and in those receiving concomitant medications with a high potential to interact with carbamazepin (*Formulary Monograph Service* 2000, 143–50, 34 refs). If necessary, abrupt switch from CBZ to oxcarbazepine on a 1:1.5 basis (or 1:1 for doses of CBZ >800mg/d followed by titration to tolerance if necessary), may be effective and well-tolerated (n=51, retrospective, Homberg *et al, Nervenarzt* 2001, **72**, 918–23). A consensus view suggested starting at 150mg/d, and increasing by 150mg/d alternate days to 900–1200mg/d (Schmidt *et al, Acta Neurol Scand* 2001, **104**, 167–70). It is indicated for partial seizures with or without secondary GTC seizures (eg. n=79, RCT, Beydoun *et al, Neurology* 2000, **54**, 2245–51), as monotherapy (where 2400mg/d is well tolerated and efficacious: n=96, RCT, d/b, Sachdeo *et al, Neurology* 2001, **57**, 864–71) or adjunctive therapy in adults and children, with an average maintenance dose of 2,400mg/day. It is less likely to induce enzymes than carbamazepine, and probably has minimal autoinduction. About 25–30% of patients who have experienced hypersensitivity to carbamazepine may experience such reactions with oxcarbazepine, in which case oxcarbazepine should be withdrawn immediately. Hyponatraemia can occur, and so regular sodium levels are advisable.

**Reviews**:* general (Glauser, *Pharmacother* 2001, **21**, 904–19, 105 refs; Wellington and Goa, *CNS Drugs* 2001, **15**, 137–63; Shorvon, *Seizure* 2000, **9**, 75–79; Castillo *et al, CDSR* 2000, **3**, 2028), TDM (Chong and Dupuis, *Ann Pharmacother* 2002, **36**, 917–20), side effects (Wellington and Goa, *CNS Drugs* 2001, **15**, 137–63), safety and efficacy (Beydoun, *Pharmacotherapy* 2000, **20**, 152S–58S), use in affective and schizoaffective disorders (Dietrich *et al, Pharmacopsychiatry* 2001, **34**, 242–50).

## Phenytoin *

Phenytoin is a broad spectrum anticonvulsant licensed for adjunctive or first-line therapy in partial or generalised epilepsy (excluding absence and myoclonus) and status epilepticus, and is believed to stabilise seizure threshold. Phenytoin is not now routinely recommended for use in children as it can cause permanent learning difficulties. A wide range of side-effects and non-linear kinetics make it a difficult drug to use (review of optimising phenytoin by Valodia *et al, J Clin Pharm & Therap* 1999, **24**, 381). A study of 45 patients aimed at establishing dosing rules to minimise toxic effects with phenytoin produced the following:

1. Increase dose by 100mg/d if the steady state plasma level is less than 7mcg/ml.
2. Increase dose by 50mg/d if the steady state plasma level is 7 or more but less than 12mcg/ml.
3. Increase dose by 30mg/d when initial plasma levels are 12mcg/ml or more.

NB the "optimal" range is only a guide and higher plasma levels may be needed (n=1, Kozer *et al, Ther Drug Monit* 2002, **24**, 386–89), as interpatient and intrapatient variability in phenytoin protein binding mean serum concentration monitoring is unreliable (n=48, 163 samples, Linh Banh *et al, Ther Drug Monit* 2002, **24**, 379–85).

## Topiramate *

Topiramate is now licensed in the UK as monotherapy for partial and generalised seizures, with or without secondary generalisation. The target dose is 100mg/d, with the optimal dose around 200–400mg/d in many patients. Twice daily dosing is appropriate and the recommended starting dose is now 25mg/d for the first week, increased by 25–50mg/d every 1–2 weeks to 200–400mg/d. There is a multiple mode of action, including sodium channel blockade, GABA enhancement, glutamate inhibition and weak carbonic anhydrase inhibition, which may explain its effect in resistant epilepsy and severity of side-effects, eg. ataxia, dizziness and somnolence. These can be minimised by slower dose titration. Topiramate may have a role in refractory partial epilepsy, with 600mg/d as effective as 800mg/d as add-on therapy in refractory partial epilepsy (n=190, RCT, Privitera *et al*, *Neurology* 1996, **46**, 1678–83), in Lennox-Gastaut syndrome, (n=98, RCT, p/c, 11/52, Sachdeo *et al*, *Neurology* 1999, **52**, 1882–88; n=97, open extension to RCT, Glauser *et al*, *Epilepsia* 2000, **41**[Suppl1], S86–S90) in West syndrome (n=11, Glauser *et al*, *Epilepsia* 2000, **41**[Suppl 1], S91–S94), and in children (n=51, Mohamed, *Seizure* 2000, **9**, 137–41). In a pooled analysis of topiramate as add-on therapy, seizures were reduced by more than 50% in 43% of topiramate-treated and 12% of placebo-treated patients (n=743, 6 d/b, p/c trials, Reife *et al*, *Epilepsia* 2000, **41**[Suppl 1], S66–S71). Cochrane concludes that topiramate has efficacy as add-on in partial epilepsy, but long-term and monotherapy were unproven (n=1049, RCT, s=9, Jette *et al*, *CDSR* 2002, **3**, 1417), but longer trials are needed. Although plasma level monitoring is not required, plasma concentrations correlate with CSF levels (n=14, Christensen *et al*, *Ther Drug Monit* 2001, **23**, 529–35) and may be of use in older people or with interacting drugs

(n=344, May *et al*, *Ther Drug Monit* 2002, **24**, 366–74) as levels may be two-fold lower with valproate or lamotrigine (n=116, Contin *et al*, *Ther Drug Monit* 2002, **24**, 332–37).

**Reviews:** * general (Biton *et al*, *Ann Pharmacother* 2001, **35**, 173–79; Kellett *et al*, *J Neurol, Neurosurg & Psych* 1999, **66**, 759–63), in children (Ormrod and McClellan, *Paediatric Drugs* 2001, **3**, 293–319, 95 refs), pharmacokinetics and interactions (Johannessen, *Epilepsia* 1997, **38**[S1], S18–S23; Langtry *et al*, *Drugs* 1997, **54**, 752–73, 104 refs), pharmacology (Shank *et al*, *Epilepsia* 2000, **41**[Suppl 1], S3–9).

## Valproate

This established drug is licensed for adjunctive or first-line therapy in partial or generalised epilepsy (excluding absence and myoclonus), Lennox-Gastaut syndrome and juvenile myoclonic epilepsy. The sustained release preparations overcome the short plasma half-life. There is little correlation between blood levels and therapeutic effect and so routine blood level monitoring is of limited use, although saturation protein binding may occur above 100mg/l, requiring great care. Serious toxicity is rare and careful supervision initially will guard against major problems, eg. liver toxicity.

## Benzodiazepines

Benzodiazepines are excellent anticonvulsant drugs in the short-term but tolerance limits long-term use. They may be useful for 'rescue' or special events, eg. holidays, family events etc. (review by Henriksen, *Epilepsia* 1998, **39**[Suppl 1], S2–S6).

## Clobazam *

Clobazam is licensed as adjunctive therapy in partial or generalised epilepsy and as intermittent therapy. Tolerance can develop and so low doses (eg. 10–20mg/d) and intermittent administration help minimise this. Sustained response is more likely in patients with a shorter duration of epilepsy, a known etiology and higher clobazam (but not n-desmethylclobazam) plasma levels (n=173, Singh *et al*, *Epilepsia* 1995, **36**, 798–803). It may be especially effective for stimulus-provoked attacks, catamenial epilepsy if given for one week in four and in intractable childhood epilepsy (n=63, Sheth *et al*, *J Child Neurol* 1995, **10**, 205–8), add-on in refractory epilepsy (n=97, open, Montenegro *et al*, *Epilepsia* 2001, **42**, 539–42) and in children with intractable epilepsy (n=31, Jan and Shaabat, *Saudi Med J* 2000, **21**, 622–24).

**Reviews**: Shorvon, *Epilepsia* 1998, **39**[Suppl 1], S15–S23; Fisher and Blum, *Epilepsia* 1995, **36**[Suppl 2], S105–14.

## Clonazepam

Clonazepam is licensed for adjunctive therapy in partial or generalised epilepsy (including absence and myoclonus), infantile spasms, status and Lennox-Gastaut syndrome. It has marked anticonvulsant properties but its usefulness is limited by tolerance (which may possibly be reversed with flumazenil 1.5mg IV) and sedation. Review by Tassinari *et al*, *Epilepsia* 1998, **39**[Suppl 1], S7–S14.

## Diazepam

Diazepam is occasionally useful orally as an adjunct and in short-term therapy, although studies on it are limited. Use in status epilepticus is well established (see below). Review by Tassinari *et al*, *Epilepsia* 1998, **39**[Suppl 1], S7–S14.

## Barbiturates
### Phenobarbital (phenobarbitone) *

Phenobarbital is licensed as adjunctive or first-line therapy in partial or generalised epilepsy (excluding absence and myoclonus). Concerns about cognitive and psychomotor impairment and dependence have rightly limited its use (Cohrane review: Taylor *et al*, *CDSR* 2001, **4**, 002217).

## Primidone *

A barbiturate metabolised mainly to phenobarbital but also to phenylethylmalonamide. It is being discontinued in UK during 2003.

## Add-on or adjunct therapy/others
### Acetazolamide *

Although this carbonic anhydrase inhibitor is a potent anticonvulsant, used for absence and other seizures, rapid tolerance and long-term side-effects render it of limited use (review by Reiss and Oles, *Ann Pharmacother* 1996, **30**, 512–19, 68 refs). It has been used at 10–20mg/kg as an adjunct in refractory localised epilepsies, with no evidence of renal calculi (n=37, open, Katayama *et al*, *Brain Dev* 2002, **24**, 150–54) and in catamenial epilepsy (n=20, survey, Lim *et al*, *Epilepsia* 2001, **42**, 746–49).

### Ethosuximide

Ethosuximide is licensed as first-line or adjunctive therapy in generalised absence seizures but is poorly studied and due to its side-effects, eg. gastric upset, has largely now been replaced by valproate.

### Gabapentin *

Gabapentin is licensed in the UK as adjunctive therapy in refractory partial and secondarily generalised epilepsy (with a reduction of 50% or more in partial seizures in 25–33% patients but few become seizure-free). There is a strong dose:response relationship, with much interpatient variability (requiring individual optimisation), with 1200mg/d probably the minimum effective maintenance dose, although 600, 1200 and 2400mg/d have been shown to be equipotent in refractory complex partial or secondarily generalized seizures (n=275, RCT, 6/12, Beydoun *et al*, *Neurology* 1997, **49**, 746–52). Gabapentin may be effective as add-on therapy in children with refractory partial seizures (n=247, RCT, 12/52, Appleton *et al*, *Epilepsia* 1999, **40**, 1147–54) and as affective as lamotrigine in newly diagnosed epilepsy (n=309, RCT, d/b, 30/52, Brodie *et al*, *Epilepsia* 2002, **43**, 993–1000). The mode of action is not established (review by Kelly, *Neuropsychobiology* 1998, **38**, 139–44). It has a low order of toxicity, uncomplicated kinetics, no clinically important interactions and plasma levels are not necessary. A TDS dosage is recommended, with no more than 12hrs between doses. A rapid discontinuation withdrawal syndrome has been reported (n=3, Norton, *Clin Neuropharmacol* 2001, **24**, 245–46). Cochrane concludes that gabapentin has efficacy as an add-on in drug-resistant epilepsy, but trials are short-term, with long-term efficacy and monotherapy unproven (Marson *et al*, *CDSR* 2000, 1415).

**Reviews:\*** general (n=3100, PMSS, Wilton and Shakir, *Epilepsia* 2002, **43**, 983–92; *Prescrire International* 2000, **9**, 40–42; Morris, *Epilepsy* 1999, **40**[Suppl 5], S63–70), as monotherapy (Beydoun, *Epilepsia* 1999, **40**[Suppl 6], S13–16).

### Levetiracetam *

Levetiracetam is licensed as adjunctive therapy for partial seizures with or without secondary generalisations. Although structurally related to piracetam, it has a distinct pharmacological profile (Genton and Van Vleymen, *Epileptic Disord* 2000, **2**, 99–105) and the mode of action is unclear. It has good bioavailability, rapidly achieves steady-state concentrations, has linear kinetics, minimal protein binding, and minimal metabolism. It needs to be given twice a day. It has been investigated at 1–3g/d for resistant partial seizures, where it has been effective and well tolerated (n=294, RCT, Cereghino *et al*, *Neurology* 2000, **55**, 236–42; n=286, d/b, p/c, Ben-Menachem and Falter, *Epilepsia* 2000, **41**, 1276–83; n=324, RCT, Boon *et al*, *Epilepsy Res* 2002, **48**, 77–89), at 1–2g BD as add-on in refractory epilepsy (n=119, RCT, 24/52, Betts *et al*, *Seizure* 2000, **9**, 80–87) and in children with partial seizures (n=24, open, Glauser *et al*, *Epilepsia* 2002, **43**, 518–24). 31% of patients had a greater than 50% reduction in seizures when used as add-on in another study in refractory partial seizures (n=324, RCT, 12/52, Shorvon *et al*, *Epilepsia* 2000, **41**, 1179–86). 4g/d may be the upper limit of efficacy in many patients (n=29,

p/c, Grant and Shorvon, *Epilepsy Res* 2000, **42**, 89–95). It is well-tolerated long-term (n=1422, up to 5-yrs, Krakow *et al*, *Neurology* 2001, **56**, 1772–74), the main side effect being somnolence, which can be minimised by starting at a lower dose. A positive impact on epilepsy-related quality of life has been reported (Cramer *et al*, *Epilepsia* 2000, **41**, 868–74). Cochrane concludes that levetiracetam is effective as add-on in localised partial epilepsy (n=1023, s=4, ≤24/52, Chaisewikul *et al*, *CDSR* 2001, **1**, 1901) but that more data is needed.

**Reviews:\*** pharmacokinetic profile (Patsalos, *Pharmacol Ther* 2000, **85**, 77–85), general (Dooley and Plosker, *Drugs* 2000, **60**, 871–93; Betts, *Prescriber* 2001, **12**, 39–44).

### Piracetam

Piracetam is a GABA derivative, licensed in the UK for cerebral myoclonus, especially of cortical origin (Brown *et al*, *Mov Disorder* 1993, **8**, 63–68; n=20, RCT, Koskiniemi *et al*, *J Neurol Neurosurg Psychiatry* 1998, **64**, 344–48) and up to 70% may become seizure-free if they can swallow enough of it.

### Tiagabine *

Tiagabine is licensed in the UK as adjunctive therapy for partial seizures, with or without secondary generalisation. It is a potent GABA reuptake inhibitor in neuronal and glial cells, increasing GABA-mediated inhibition of the brain. Several studies have shown an effect in refractory partial seizures (14% achieving a 50% or greater increase in seizure-free days, n=154, d/b, p/c, Kalviainen *et al*, *Epilepsy Res* 1998, **30**, 31–40) and refractory complex partial seizures (up to 29% had a >50% reduction in seizures, n=297, RCT, Uthman *et al*, *Arch Neurol* 1998, **55**, 56–62). Data on monotherapy is limited. Tiagabine has linear kinetics, a short half-life (requiring bd to qds dosage), an inducable metabolism and a number of drug interactions (see *4.5.9*). Cochrane concludes that tiagabine is effective as adjunctive therapy but is associated with many ADRs (Pereira *et al*, *CDSR* 2002, **3**, 1908).

**Reviews:*** general (Schachter, *Expert Opin Pharmacother* 2001, **2**, 179–87; Stephen and Brodie, *Prescriber* 1999, **10**, 19–24; *Drug & Ther Bull* 2000, **38**, 47–48, 17 refs), pharmacokinetics (Samara *et al*, *Epilepsia* 1998, **39**, 868–73), extensive (pharmacodynamics, therapeutic potential, Adkins and Noble, *Drugs* 1998, **55**, 437–60, 89 refs).

### Vigabatrin *

Vigabatrin is licensed as adjunctive therapy in refractory partial and secondary generalised epilepsy, Lennox-Gastaut and infantile spasms and as monotherapy for West Syndrome. Use is now limited by ocular changes (eg. impaired contrast sensitivity and usually irreversible loss of field: n=100, Newman *et al*, *Eye* 2002, **16**, 567–71) in up to 50% patients (n=24, Gross-Tsur *et al*, *Ann Neurol* 2000, **48**, 60–64) and should not now be initiated as monotherapy (*Cur Prob Pharmacovig* 1999, **25**, 13) although it retains a role in childhood epilepsy (n=73, survey, Prasad *et al*, *Epilepsia* 2001, **42**, 54–61). Total vigabatrin exposure is the most significant factor in predicting visual field loss (n=92, Hardus *et al*, *Epilepsia* 2001, **42**, 262–67). It should only be used when there is no alternative, accompanied by a baseline and six-monthly peripheral field examination (Hardus *et al*, *Epilepsia* 2001, **42**, 262–67; n=17, Paul *et al*, *Epilepsia* 2001, **42**, 525–30).

**Reviews:*** general (Gidal *et al*, *Ann Pharmacother* 1999, **33**, 1277–86, 115 refs), use in children (*BMJ* 2000, **320**, 1404), ocular problems (Newman *et al*, *Eye* 2002, **16**, 567–71; Spence and Sankar, *Drug Safety* 2001, **24**, 385–404, 33 refs).

---

### + Combinations
### Valproate + lamotrigine *

The combination of valproate and lamotrigine may have some advantage over the drugs individually in refractory complex partial seizures, as well as being well tolerated if used with care (n=20, open, c/o, Pisani *et al*, *Epilepsia* 1999, **40**, 1141–46; Morris *et al*, *Ther Drug Monit* 2000, **22**, 656–60). See also lamotrigine.

### ● Unlicensed/Some efficacy
### Clomethiazole (chlormethiazole)

Use in refractory cases, particularly children, can be successful (*Arch Dis Childhood* 1982, **57**, 242).

### Nitrazepam

Nitrazepam has been used successfully for infantile spasms and myoclonic seizures. Although side-effects such as motor and cognitive impairment exist, it can still be useful in refractory cases (review by Shorvon, *Epilepsia* 1998, **39**[Suppl 1], S15–S23).

### ○ Unlicensed/Possible efficacy
### Calcium-channel blockers *

Cochrane concludes that flunarizine (in refractory childhood fits: n=14, open, Hoppu *et al*, *Pediatr Neurol* 1995, **13**, 143–47, but is difficult to use: n=93, RCT, Pledger *et al*, *Neurology* 1994, **44**, 1830–36) may have a weak effect and the evidence for nifedipine and nimodipine is not convincing (Chaisewikul *et al*, *CDSR* 2001, **4**, 2750).

### Carnitine

Intractable epilepsy in a child who was found to have carnitine deficiency, was treated successfully with L-carnitine 100mg tds and valproate (n=1, Shuper *et al*, *Lancet* 1999, **353**, 1238).

### Fluoxetine

In patients with complex partial seizures, addition of fluoxetine resulted in disappearance of seizures in six and a 30% reduction occurred in the other eleven (n=17, open, Favale *et al*, *Neurology* 1995, **45**, 1926–27).

### Goserelin

Reduction in the number of attacks in catamenial epilepsy has been shown, although long-term treatment would have problems (*Lancet* 1992, **339**, 253).

## Midazolam

Acute childhood seizures have been managed with intranasal midazolam (n=20, *Lancet* 1998, **352**, 620).

◊ **Others:** *

Other drugs used include **aromatherapy** (ylang ylang, camomile and lavender: Anon, *Pharm J* 1993, **251**, 798), **buspirone** (in progressive myoclonus epilepsy: Pranzatelli *et al*, *J Neurol Neurosurg Psych* 1993, **56**, 114–15), **clomiphene** (n=1, *Arch Neurology* 1988, **45**, 209–10), **magnesium** (Walker *et al*, *Anaesthesia* 1995, **50**; 130–35 plus discussion in *Anaesthesia* 1995, **50**, 824–25), **medroxyprogesterone** (in women: *Epilepsia* 1985, **26**, S40–51), **progesterone** (especially in women with catamenial exacerbations: n=25, open, Herzog, *Neurology* 1995, **45**, 1660–62), **propranolol** (synergistic with carbamazepine: n=1, *Am J Psych* 1990, **147**, 1687–88) and **vitamin E** (300mg/d as add-on: n=10, *DICP Ann Pharmacother* 1991, **25**, 362–63).

### 1.17.1 STATUS EPILEPTICUS

Status epilepticus is a state where multiple seizures occur without complete recovery between seizures. There are a number of different definition of status epilepticus, but usually refers to seizures longer than 5 minutes or two seizures without regaining consciousness. Mortality can be high, but a rapid and aggressive treatment reduces this, and any permanent neuronal damage.

**Role of drugs:** *

To prevent permanent brain damage, first line therapy must be to support with oxygen and a glucose drip if possible.

First-line drugs eg. benzodiazepines are usually successful to abort status epilepticus. Refractory seizures are frequently caused by acute neurological problems, eg. encephalitis, CVA or trauma. Hypoxia and ischaemia can add to brain disruption and respiratory depression and hypotension are side-effects of the drugs used. Transfer to an ITU may be appropriate. In a

5-year comparison of four treatments (diazepam 0.15mg/kg followed by phenytoin 18mg/kg, lorazepam 0.1mg/kg, phenobarbital 15mg/kg and phenytoin 18mg/kg) for generalized convulsive status epilepticus, lorazepam appears more effective than phenytoin, and easier to use than phenobarbital or diazepam plus phenytoin (n=384, RCT, Treiman *et al*, *NEJM* 1998, **339**, 792–98). A systematic review concluded that pentobarbital, propofol and midazolam were all were effective for refractory status epilepticus (n=193, s=28, Classen *et al*, *Epilepsia* 2002, **43**, 146–53).

**Reviews:** * general (Misra and Singh, *J Indian Med Assoc* 2002, **100**, 299–303; Hirsch and Claassen, *Curr Neurol Neurosci Rep* 2002, **2**, 345–56; Rosenow *et al*, *Epileptic Disord* 2002, **4**(Suppl 2), 41–51; Silver and Cockerell, *Prescriber* 2002, **13**, 17–25; Fountain, *Epilepsia* 2000, **41**[Suppl 2], S23–30; Bleck, *Epilepsia* 1999, **40**[Suppl 1], S59–63), benzodiazepine routes (Rey *et al*, *Clin Pharmacokin* 1999, **36**, 409–24, 98 refs) and in the elderly (Waterhouse and DeLorenzo, *Drugs & Aging* 2001, **18**, 133–42, 94 refs).

**BNF Listed**

## Amylobarbital (sodium)

See the SPC for injection details, vital for this potentially toxic drug.

## Clonazepam

0.5–1.5mg by slow IV injection (possibly followed by an infusion) may be useful in refractory cases not responsive to diazepam. A prolonged effect may be seen. It is comparable with lorazepam and probably has the lowest respiratory depressant effect of the benzodiazepines (*Pharmacy World & Science* 1993, **15**, 17–28).

## Diazepam *

0.15–0.25mg/kg (ie. around 10–30mg) given as a slow IV injection over 5 minutes or rectal administration (eg. rectal tubes) is first choice treatment in the UK. Rates above 5mg/min IV are associated with respiratory depression. A diazepam infusion at 3mg/kg in 24 hours can be tried for maintenance (case in *Ann Pharmacother* 1993, **27**, 298–301). The speed of rectal absorption is second only to IV absorption (*Int J Pharmaceutics* 1980, **5**, 127). It is also safe and effective when administered by paramedics in out-of-hospital situations (n=205, RCT, p/c, Alldredge *et al*, *NEJM* 2001, **345**, 631–37).

## Fosphenytoin *

Fosphenytoin is a water soluble parenteral pro-drug converted to phenytoin, is rapidly absorbed (therapeutic levels in 5–20 mins) and licensed for status and as a substitute for oral phenytoin. It is better tolerated at injection sites, well-tolerated (open, Pryor *et al*, *Epilepsia* 2001, **42**, 245–50) and with complete IM absorption. It can be given up to three times more rapidly IV and can be given IM, where cardiac monitoring is not necessary. Conversion to phenytoin takes about 15 minutes and so fosphenytoin is less appropriate for the sole initial treatment of status epilepticus. Although more expensive, fosphenytoin may be cost neutral due to reduced side-effects (Armstrong *et al*, *Pharmacotherapy* 1999, **19**, 844–53, 39 refs), although this has been disputed (editorial by Labiner, *Arch Int Med* 1999, **159**, 2631–32, 12 refs; review by DeToledo and Ramsay, *Drug Safety* 2000, **22**, 459–66, 58 refs) and overuse suggested (n=55, Johnson and Wrenn, *Am J Emerg Med* 2001, **19**, 293–94).

**Reviews**: general (Browne, *Clin Neuropharmacol* 1997, **20**, 1–12), IV use (Ramsay and Detoledo, *Neurology* 1996, **46**[S1], S17–S19; Marchetti *et al*, *Clin Therapeutics* 1996, **18**, 953–66).

## Lorazepam *

Lorazepam may be preferable to diazepam, due to a longer duration of action (about 2 hours), shorter elimination half-life, no active metabolites and possibly less respiratory depression. Lorazepam appears more effective than phenytoin, and easier to use than phenobarbital or diazepam plus phenytoin (n=384, RCT, Treiman *et al*, *NEJM* 1998, **339**, 792–98). In con-

vulsive status epilepticus (CSE) lorazepam 4mg IV was equivalent to diazepam 10mg IV but superior in terms of fewer recurrences (Cock and Schapira, *QJM* 2002, **95**, 225–31). It is also safe and effective when administered by paramedics in out-of-hospital situations (n=205, RCT, p/c, Alldredge *et al*, *NEJM* 2001, **345**, 631–37).

## Paraldehyde *

Given by IM injection (up to 5 ml per muscle site, glass syringe needed) or rectally (50/50 mixture with arachis oil, 2:1 in oil or cottonseed oil or mixed with 0.9% sodium chloride), paraldehyde can be rapidly effective, especially in infants and children where venous access is limited but is painful at the site of injection. It is also active, albeit unpleasantly, by mouth and also by IV infusion (4–8% infusion in sodium chloride 0.9% — *Pharmacy World & Science* 1993, **15**, 17–28). It may have a role in on-going pervasive and resistant seizures (Armstrong and Battin, *J Child Neurol* 2001, **16**, 915–17; Thulasimani and Ramaswamy, *Anaethesia* 2002, **57**, 99–100).

**Reviews**: toxicology (von Burg and Stout, *J Appl Toxicol* 1991, **11**, 379–81) and kinetics (Ramsay, *Epilepsia* 1989, **30**[Suppl 2], S1–S3).

## Phenytoin

Phenytoin (or fosphenytoin) is a useful second-line to the benzodiazepines, used as 10–20mg/kg intravenously over 15 minutes (not exceeding 50mg/minute) in 0.9% saline for recurrent or persistent seizures. It is effective from 20–30 minutes after injection but is not effective intramuscularly. It is not an easy drug to use due to the risk of hypotension and cardiac dysrhythmias.

---

## ● Unlicensed/Some efficacy
## Midazolam *

Continuous IV infusion can be used for status (n=20, case series, Koul *et al*, *Arch Dis Childhood* 1997, **76**, 445) with 1–3mg/hr rapidly successful in many patients (*Arch Emerg Med*

1987, **4**, 169–72). It has a sudden onset of action (30–90 seconds) but care is needed with this acute onset and the potentially fatal respiratory depression as midazolam half-life prolongs significantly after sustained infusion (n=2, Naritoku and Sinha, *Neurology* 2000, **54**, 1366–68). Continuous midazolam infusion has been reported as effective as diazepam, although in one study recurrence and mortality were higher than with diazepam infusion (n=40, RCT, open, Singhi *et al*, *J Child Neurol* 2002, **17**, 106–10). The IM (Towne and DeLorenzo, *J Emerg Med* 1999, **17**, 323–28), buccal liquid (n=42, RCT, Scott *et al*, *Lancet* 1999, **353**, 623–26, editorial, *ibid*, 608–9) and intranasal routes (n=47, RCT, *BMJ* 2000, **321**, 83) may be safe, effective, more socially acceptable and convenient alternatives to IV and rectal diazepam.

**Reviews**: general (Shorvon, *Epilepsia* 1998, **39**[Suppl 1], S15–S23; Denzel *et al*, *Ann Pharmacother* 1996, **30**, 1481–83, 90 refs; Fountain and Adams, *Clin Neuropharmacol* 1999, **22**, 261–67; Molmes and Riviello, *Pediatr Neurol* 1999, **20**, 259–64).

**Propofol** *
Propofol has been used (review by Carley and Crawford, *Emerg Med J* 2002, **19**, 143–44; see also Claassen *et al*, *Epilepsia* 2002, **43**, 146–53).

**Phenobarbital (phenobarbitone)**
A parenteral loading dose of 10–20mg/kg (*Am J Hosp Pharm* 1993, **50**[Suppl 5), S5–S16) with a maintenance dose of 5–7mg/kg/day can be used, although some feel that this bolus dose too high and phenobarbital should not be given at a dose greater than 100mg/min (Zeisler and Beck, *Am J Hosp Pharm* 1994, **51**, 1578). It has a slow onset and causes cardiac and respiratory depression (reviews in *Pharmacy World & Science* 1993, **15**, 17–28).

**Thiopental (sodium thiopentone)**
Induction of anaesthesia with a 2.5% solution (4–8mg/kg) can be effective, continued with an infusion of 0.2% solution until seizure-free for 24

hours. Phenobarbital should be substituted once fitting stops, as thiopentone accumulates in fat and effects the myocardium.

**Thiamine**
The use of thiamine may be indicated and prevent serious complications when glucose IV is given as supportive therapy in status (Efawgse, *JAMA* 1994, **270**, 854–59; Slovis and Wrenn, *JAMA* 1994, **271**, 980–81).

**Valproate** *
Valproate has been used IV (n=3 and review, Morton and Quarles, *Pharmacotherapy* 2000, **20**, 88–92; n=3, Hovinga *et al*, *Ann Pharmacother* 1999, **33**, 579–84), including rectally and in patients with hypotension (n=13, Sinha and Naritoku, *Neurology* 2000, **55**, 722–24), although one review considered it too early to recommend first line use (Hodges and Mazur, *Ann Pharmacother* 2001, **35**, 1465–70).

---

○ **Unlicensed/Possible efficacy**
**Chloral**
Doses of up to 30mg/kg at four hourly intervals given orally or rectally may be effective in resistant status, although onset may be delayed (review in *Ann Emerg Med* 1990, **19**, 674–77).

**Etomidate**
This non-barbiturate induction agent has some anticonvulsant activity. Doses of 0.2–0.3mg/kg IV repeated after 20 minutes have been successful, as has infusion at 25mg/kg/min. Care would be needed as etomidate may cause involuntary muscle contractions and epileptiform seizures during prolonged IV infusion.

**Flumazenil**
IV doses may be effective as an anticonvulsant (*Lancet* 1991, **337**, 744, 133–37). In intractable epilepsy, flumazenil may be superior to diazepam, without sedation (n=12, d/b, c/o, Sharief *et al*, *Epilepsy Research* 1993, **15**, 53–60), although it may induce seizures (n=67, Schulze-Bonhage and Elger, *Epilepsia* 2000, **41**, 186–92). Review by Reisner-Keller and Pham

in *Ann Pharmacother* 1995, **29**, 530–32.

## Lidocaine (lignocaine)

A 1% solution given as a 2–3mg/kg bolus over 2 minutes can be rapidly effective (ie. within minutes) in cases refractory to other drugs (De Giorgio *et al*, *Epilepsia* 1992, **33**, 913–16). The effect lasts about 30 minutes but due to the relatively short duration, a second dose is needed in about 50% of cases (Pascual *et al*, *J Neurol Neurosurg Psychiatry* 1992, **55**, 49–51). If successful, IV infusion at 4mg/kg/hour may be considered. Enhanced seizure activity after high doses and cardiac arrhythmias are potential problems and so it should be used only with caution if any form of heart block or sinus bradycardia exists as it may induce ventricular arrhythmia or complete heart block.

## Propofol *

Propofol has established anticonvulsant activities. There have been a number of reports of successful use by IV infusion (n=1, Begemann *et al*, *Epilepsia* 2000, **41**, 105–09). Propofol has been compared with barbiturates (n=16) in refractory status epilepticus and a protocol for use proposed (Stecker *et al*, *Epilepsia* 1998, **39**, 18–26). A retrospective chart analysis suggested propofol and midazolam were of similar efficacy in refractory status epilepticus (n=14, Prasad *et al*, *Epilepsia* 2001, **42**, 380–86).

## GILLES DE LA TOURETTE

See Tourette's Syndrome *(1.33)*.

## 1.18 INSOMNIA

Insomnia, ie. difficulty in initiating or maintaining sleep, is a symptom of an illness, not an illness itself and should always be treated as such. It can be caused by a variety of external (eg. environment) and internal (eg. psychiatric illness, stress, physical illness, drugs, see *5.14* etc) stimuli, and can be transient, chronic, initial or early morning wakening. The causes, where possible, should be determined and treated, as well as emphasis on sleep hygiene.

**Principles of sleep hygiene:**

1. Avoid excessive use of caffeine (particularly within 3–4 hours of going to bed), alcohol or nicotine. A hot milky drink at bedtime may promote sleep.
2. Do not stay in bed for prolonged periods if not asleep. Go to another dimly lit room – watching TV can have an alerting effect.
3. Avoid daytime naps or long periods of inactivity.
4. A warm bath or exercise a few hours before bedtime may promote sleep.
5. Avoid engaging in strenuous exercise or mental activity near bedtime.
6. Make sure that the bed and bedroom are comfortable and avoid extremes of noise, temperature and humidity.
7. Establish a regular bedtime routine, eg. going to bed at the same time and rising at the same time every morning, regardless of sleep duration.
8. Diet – carbohydrate (eg. pasta etc) helps sleep, but not eating a big meal within about 2 hours of going to bed. Sugar may inhibit sleep, as may some vitamin supplements.

**Role of drugs: ***

Assuming sleep hygiene is good, any hypnotics should always be used on a PRN basis, as tolerance may develop to the sedative effects within 2–3 weeks (especially with the benzodiazepines). Short-term use for short-term reasons is usually without problem and can be very useful and comforting for the patient. Longer-term use needs the risk:benefit analysis considered carefully. The principles of sleep hygiene should be discussed and any problems corrected before prescribing hypnotics. A meta-analysis of 22 RCTs of BDZs or zolpidem showed consistent superiority over placebo up to 5 weeks but the evidence beyond 5 weeks is unclear (Nowell *et al*, *JAMA* 1997,

**278**, 2170–77, 86 refs). CBT (Smith *et al, Am J Psych* 2002, **159**, 5–11; n=75, 6/52, Edinger, *JAMA* 2001, **285**, 1856–64), temazepam or both, have been shown to improve short-term outcomes for older people with persistent insomnia (Morin *et al, JAMA* 1999, **17**, 991–99, reviewed in *EBMH* 1999, **2**, 117) and in persistent insomnia. Guidelines for management of chronic insomnia are difficult to formulate.

**Reviews**:* comprehensive (Wilson and Nutt, *Adv Psych Treat* 1999, **5**, 11–18; Nishino and Mignot, *Clin Pharmacokinet* 1999, **37**, 305–30, 91 refs), general (Hallström, *Prescriber* 2002, **13**, 65–76; *Drugs & Ther Perspect* 2000, **15**, 5–9), sleep disorders in elderly (Jagus and Benbow, *Adv Psych Treat* 1999, **5**, 30–38; Ancoli-Israel, *Sleep* 2000, **23**[Suppl 1], S23–30) and children (Stores, *Prescriber* 2001, **12**, 29–39), benzodiazepines and zolpidem (Nowell *et al, JAMA* 1997, **278**, 2170–77; reviewed by van Bemmel, *EBMH* 1998, **1**, 117), withdrawal (*Drugs & Ther Perspect* 1999, **14**, 12–14), non-drug methods of managing insomnia (Yang and Spielman, *Dis Manage & Health Outcomes* 1999, **5**, 209–24).

**Predicting hypnotic dependence risk** (*BMJ* 1993, **306**, 706)

| Factor | Score |
|---|---|
| Benzodiazepine hypnotic used | 3 |
| High mean dose | 2 |
| Duration of treatment >3months | 2 |
| Dependent personality | 2 |
| Short elimination half-life drug | 2 |
| Tolerance or dose escalation | 2 |
| TOTAL | |
| Dose higher than BNF mean No dependence, abrupt withdrawal | =0 |
| Some dependence risk, withdraw over two weeks recommend | =1–4 |
| Strong dependence risk, withdraw over 4–12 weeks | =5–8 |
| High risk of dependence, withdraw gradually plus support programme | =8–13 |

## BNF Listed

### Benzodiazepines

Benzodiazepines may be extremely useful in the short-term for insomnia, helping to facilitate essential high-quality sleep (rational defence of BDZ prescribing, Williams and McBride, *B J Psych* 1998, **173**, 361–62). A meta-analysis of 45 RCTs indicated benzodiazepines are effective in improving sleep latency and duration but ADRs (drowsiness, dizziness etc.) are common, although methodologically these studies are flawed (meta-analysis, n=2672, Holbrook *et al, CMAJ* 2000, **162**, 225–33; reviewed by Furukawa, *EBMH* 2000, **3**, 81). Users of benzodiazepines and zopiclone are also at greater risk of road-traffic accidents, especially if combined with alcohol (involved in accidents, n=19, 386 over 3 years, Barbone *et al, Lancet* 1998, **352**, 1331–36).

**Review**: rational use (Ashton, *Drugs* 1994, **48**, 25–40).

### Flunitrazepam *

This longer-acting benzodiazepine may have an abuse potential (reviewed by Woods and Winger, *J Clin Psychopharmacol* 1997, **17**[3 Suppl 2], 1S–57S; reviewed by Druid *et al, Forensic Sci Int* 2001, **122**, 136–41), including in combination with other drugs, and is probably underrated in this respect, especially in forensic settings (Daderman and Edman, *Psych Res* 2001, **103**, 27–42).

### Flurazepam

A benzodiazepine with a short half-life but with longer-acting metabolites.

### Loprazolam

An intermediate-acting benzodiazepine, with a half-life of 7–15 hours.

### Lormetazepam *

An intermediate acting benzodiazepine marketed in the UK as a hypnotic. Short-term use has no effect on daytime vigilance nor motor task performance (n=12, RCT, d/b, c/o, Iudice *et al, Int J Clin Pharmacol Ther* 2002, **40**, 304–9).

## Nitrazepam

A longer-acting benzodiazepine similar to diazepam, which has active metabolites. Stable plasma levels can be attained in 5 days so avoid in the elderly.

## Temazepam

A shorter-acting benzodiazepine, whose abuse potential has been well recognised.

---

## The Z hypnotics
### Zaleplon *

Zaleplon is a pyrazolopyrimidine hypnotic, a selective full agonist at the omega-1 benzodiazepine receptor (Noguchi et al, Eur J Pharmacol 2002, **434**, 21–28). It can be taken at bedtime or after the person has failed to go to sleep, because peak plasma levels occur after 1 hour and it has a short half-life (1 hour). 5mg (elderly) and 10mg (adults) has been shown to be an effective hypnotic, with a significant reduction in sleep latency, comparable to zolpidem, but no rebound insomnia over four weeks nor withdrawal, unlike zolpidem (n=615, RCT, Elie et al, J Clin Psych 1999, **60**, 536–44). Several studies have shown a lack of residual effects the next day even with 10mg zaleplon was taken 2 hours before waking, while residual effects from zolpidem were detectable 5 hours after a dose (n=36, Danjou et al, Br J Clin Pharmacol 1999, **48**, 367–74; n=13, d/b, p/c, c/o, Stone et al, B J Clin Pharmacol 2002, **53**, 196–202; n=30, p/c, c/o, Verster et al, J Clin Psychopharmacol 2002, **22**, 576–83). Indeed one study showed zaleplon 10mg to have no or minimal residual effects even when taken as little as an hour before waking, with 20mg only having residual effects 3 hours before waking, an advantage compared to zolpidem 10mg (n=40, RCT, d/b, p/c, c/o, Hindmarch et al, Hum Psychopharmacol 2001, **16**, 159–67) and zopiclone (n=30, RCT, s/b, p/c, c/o, Vermeeren et al, Sleep 2002, **25**, 224–31). Lack of both long-term tolerance and rebound insomnia has been suggested (Dooley and Plosker, Drugs

2000, **60**, 413–45). Use in the elderly also appears safe and effective (RCT, 2/52, Hedner et al, Int J Geriatr Psych 2000, **15**, 704–12) as well as, anecdotally, for jet-lag.

**Reviews**: general (Richardson et al, MedGenMed 2002, **14**, 9; Israel and Kramer, Ann Pharmacother 2002, **36**, 852–59; Anon, Am J Health-Sys Pharm 2000, **57**, 430–31; Wilson and Nutt, Prescriber 2000, **11**, 85–93 and 49–56; Patat et al, Hum Psychopharmacol 2001, **16**, 369–92; Anon, Formulary Monograph Service 1999, 75–80, ibid 395–402, 43 refs; Maidment, J Pharm Tech 2001, **17**, 39–43; Hurst and Noble, CNS Drugs 1999, **11**, 387–92), extensive (Weitzel et al, Clin Ther 2000, **22**, 1254–67; Dooley and Plosker, Drugs 2000, **60**, 413–45), kinetics (Greenblatt et al, Clin Pharmacol Ther 1998, **64**, 553–61), in the elderly (Walsh et al, Clin Drug Investig 2000, **20**, 143–49) and pharmacology (Rush et al, Psychopharmacology [Berl] 1999, **145**, 39–51; Heydorn, Expert Opin Investig Drugs 2000, **9**, 841–58).

### Zolpidem *

Zolpidem is a imidazopyridine hypnotic which binds preferentially to the omega-1 benzodiazepine receptor. It decreases time to sleep and increases total sleep time and efficiency but does not affect sleep architecture. It has a rapid onset of action and a short (6–8 hrs) duration. It has been shown in several studies to be equivalent to flunitrazepam but with few significant residual effects (eg. n=245, RCT, d/b, p/c, Allain et al, Clin Drug Investigat 2001, **21**, 391–400) and at least as effective as zopiclone, with less rebound on discontinuation and better tolerated eg. no metallic taste (n=479, d/b, 14/7, Tsutsui et al, J Int Med Res 2001, **29**, 163–77). Indeed, lack of residual psychomotor effects in one study led to suggestions the drug be considered for use in navy fighter and other pilots (n=12, Sicard et al, Aviat Space Environ Med 1993, **64**, 371–75). Chronic abuse of zolpidem, at up to 600mg/d has been reported (n=1, Gericke and Ludolph,

*JAMA* 1994, **272**, 1721–72; n=1, Aragona, *Clin Neuropharmacol* 2000, **23**, 281–83).

**Reviews:**\* extensive (Israel and Kramer, *Ann Pharmacother* 2002, **36**, 852–59; Holm and Goa, *Drugs* 2000, **59**, 865–89, 191 refs; Darcourt *et al*, *J Psychopharmacol* 1999, **13**, 81–93), clinical pharmacokinetics (Salva and Costa, *Clin Pharmacokinetics* 1995, **29**, 142–53).

## Zopiclone

This non-benzodiazepine preferentially binds to two of the three benzodiazepine receptor subtypes. Treatment duration is recommended for up to 28 days. Zopiclone is equivalent, but not superior, to BDZs (n=2672, meta-analysis, Holbrook *et al*, *CMAJ* 2000, **162**, 225–33; reviewed by Furukawa, *EBMH* 2000, **3**, 81). Misuse and dependence has been reported (eg. Clee *et al*, *Addiction* 1996, **91**, 1389–90) and may be greater in those with dependent personalities (letters by Sikdar, Ayonrinde and Sampson, *BMJ* 1998, **317**, 146). It has a low incidence of side-effects and hangover effect compared to temazepam.

**Reviews:** extensive (Noble *et al*, *Drugs* 1998, **55**, 277–302; Hajak, *Drug Saf* 1999, **21**, 457–69), kinetics (Fernandez *et al*, *Clin Pharmacokinet* 1995, **29**, 431–41), abuse potential/ dependence (Lader, *J Neurol* 1997, **244**[4 Suppl 1], S18–S22).

## Other hypnotics
### Antihistamines \*

Antihistamines may be effective. Promethazine has a relatively long half-life but low abuse potential. Diphenhydramine may have an abuse potential (de Nesnera, *J Clin Psych* 1996, **57**, 136–37) and has been strongly linked to cognitive impairment and decline in older hospitalised patients and is best avoided in this patient group (n=426, Agoustini *et al*, *Arch Intern Med* 2001, **161**, 2091–97).

### Barbiturates

Barbiturates should only be used for severe and intractable insomnia where there are compelling reasons and only in patients already taking barbiturates (CSM warning in *Curr Problems* 1996, **22**, 7), where toxicity in overdose (probably incorrectly blamed for the death of people such as Marilyn Monroe) can be high.

### Chloral \*

Chloral has properties similar to the barbiturates and is relatively safe in the elderly as the half-life is not significantly lengthened. An abuse potential exists and it can be toxic in overdose (n=1, Frankland and Robinson, *Can J Psych* 2001, **46**, 763–64).

### Clomethiazole (chlormethiazole)

A thiamine derivative with sedative-hypnotic and anticonvulsant properties. It has a rapid onset of action and short half-life, even in the elderly, although they may be more sensitive to it. Dependence and abuse has been reported but is not considered too important if the patient is not dependence prone (*Lancet* 1979, **ii**, 953–54). It is unsafe in overdose.

### Triclofos

A chloral-related drug with similar actions to chloral but with less gastric irritation and a more palatable taste. Only available as a liquid in the UK.

● **Unlicensed/Some efficacy**
### Other sedative drugs at night \*

Other sedative drugs the patient may already be taking, especially antipsychotics and antidepressants, may be prescribed as a single dose at night. In longer-term therapy most can be given this way. It is also important to avoid the use of 'stimulating' drugs at night, eg. anticholinergics, MAOIs etc. Trazodone may be particularly useful if the insomnia is secondary to, eg. SSRIs. Low-dose doxepin (25–50mg) has been shown to produce mild to moderate but significant rapid and sustained improvement in insomnia compared to placebo, although rebound insomnia and side effects were noted (n=47, p/c, Hajak *et al*, *J Clin Psych* 2001, **62**, 453–63). Many sedative antidepressants are toxic in overdose and may disrupt REM sleep.

## Mirtazapine *

Insomnia is reported by 90% depressed patients, but stimulation of 5-HT$_2$ receptors is thought to underlie insomnia and the changes in sleep architecture seen with SSRIs/SNRIs. Mirtazapine blocks 5-HT$_2$ receptors and may improve sleep eg. 30mg increased sleep efficiency and decreased wakenings and their duration but with no effect on REM (n=20, RCT, d/b, p/c, 3/7, Aslan *et al, Sleep* 2002, **25**, 677–79). It may in fact help normalise abnormal REM sleep (n=32, Schittecatte *et al, Psych Res* 2002, **109**, 1-8). In depressed patients, mirtazapine produces a significant shortening of sleep-onset latency, increases a total sleep time, and leads to a marked improvement in sleep efficiency (Thase, *J Clin Psych* 1999, **60** [Suppl 17], 28–31; discussion 46–48).

## Phenothiazines

Promazine at 25–100mg can be fairly sedative with a low abuse potential, but a significant side-effect profile.

---

### ○ Unlicensed/Possible efficacy
## Alcohol

Alcohol causes sedation, increases slow wave sleep, reduces and disrupts REM sleep, the diuretic effect is counter-productive and overdose can have serious consequences. Rebound arousal can occur with higher doses when blood concentrations reach zero, leading to awakening (Stradling, *BMJ* 1993, **306**, 573–75). Alcohol is thus not recommended for routine medical use. Having said that, it is used widely as self-medication and, unlike chloral, is available in a number of highly palatable formulations (eg. Adnams, Woodfordes, Smiles), and in lager.

## Lavender oil

Ambient lavender oil odour may improve sleep duration in the elderly (understandably open study, n=4, Hardy *et al, Lancet* 1995, **346**, 701).

## Nicotine

Low concentrations of nicotine can cause mild sedation and relaxation and so a cigarette could help sleep in an anxious person. Higher levels cause arousal and agitation (Stradling, *BMJ* 1993, **306**, 573–75).

## Melatonin *

Not yet licensed in the UK, slow-release melatonin may be effective. It improved sleep *in* major depression, but had no effect *on* depression (n=24, open, Dolberg *et al, Am J Psych* 1998, **155**, 1119–21) and 2mg significantly improved sleep efficiency in chronic schizophrenics with poor sleep, but not in those with better sleep efficiency (n=19, RCT, Shamir *et al, J Clin Psych* 2000, **61**, 373–77). Melotonin (mean dose 5.4mg) has also been shown to be effective for inital insomnia in medically-ill patients (n=33, RCT, d/b, p/c, 16/7, Andrade *et al, J Clin Psych* 2001, **62**, 41–45). Review by Pepping (*Am J Health-Sys Pharm* 1999, **56**, 2520, 2523–24, 2527).

## Paroxetine

Paroxetine 20mg/d may be an effective treatment for primary insomnia (n=15, open, Nowell *et al, J Clin Psych* 1999, **60**, 89–95) although this might be a placebo response (Musa, *J Clin Psych* 1999, **60**, 795).

## Tryptophan

Tryptophan at 1–2g may facilitate going off to sleep, reducing latency time and increasing total sleep time (*JAMA* 1989, **29**, 274–78).

---

### ◆ No efficacy
## Caffeine

Caffeine competes with the inhibitory neurotransmitter adenosine, causing cortical arousal and decreased sleep. 150mg of caffeine before retiring has a marked effect on sleep latency, reduces sleep efficacy and REM periods. Its half-life of 5 hours means any ingested near bedtime will effect sleep latency (Stradling, *BMJ* 1993, **306**, 573–75). See caffeinism (*1.35*).

## 1.19 MANIA AND HYPOMANIA

See also bipolar mood disorder (*1.10*), rapid-cycling disorder (*1.27*) and acute psychiatric emergency (*1.1*).

### Symptoms:

Hypomania, the more common and milder form of mania, is defined as an abnormal elation of mood, alternating with irritability, great energy, inability to concentrate, flight of ideas (rapid changing of the subject with some connections), insomnia etc. Obsessive preoccupation with some idea, activity or desire may occur. The main presenting symptoms are a euphoric and labile mood (irritable, angry, grandiose), bright or untidy appearance, low sleep requirement, increased drive and energy, reduced insight, pressure of speech, flight of ideas, expansive thought, and an overactive and intrusive manner.

### Role of drugs:

Hypomania or mania represents a particular phase of a bipolar (or rarely a unipolar) illness. Both usually require specific long-term mood-stabiliser drug treatment for the bipolar component (ie. lithium, valproate, carbamazepine etc) and non-specific shorter-term treatments (eg. antipsychotics, benzodiazepines) for the insomnia, agitation, hyperactivity, etc. to calm the patient and prevent exhaustion and harm. A night of sleep deprivation is likely to escalate any manic patient to a higher degree of mania and so hypnotic/sedative use should be considered appropriate (n=67, Wehr *et al, Arch Gen Psych* 1982, **39**, 559–65). Any co-morbid substance misuse should be tackled at the same time, as recovery from mania is poorer in people with a history of substance abuse (retrospective review, n=204, Goldberg *et al, J Clin Psych* 1999, **60**, 733–40).

Antipsychotics are potent antimanic agents, but generally should not be continued into the maintenance phase, although this frequently occurs. Lithium remains the best established mood-stabiliser, especially in hypomania. Evidence for an antimanic effect for valproate (particularly in mixed states) is better than carbamazepine. It may be that patients who have had more than about 10 previous manic episodes may respond less well to lithium than previously (n=154, Swann *et al, Am J Psych* 1999, **156**, 1264–66). This effect may not be true with valproate. See bipolar mood disorder (*1.10*) for maintenance strategies.

Treatment goals for mania should be:
1. Discontinue any 'manicogenic' agents (see *5.7* for lists).
2. Stabilise any medical conditions.
3. Start non-specific calming medications, eg. BDZs, antipsychotics.
4. Start specific mood-stabilisers, eg. lithium, valproate and carbamazepine – preferably when the patient is able to consent to longer-term therapy.

**Reviews:**\* treatment of acute mania and resistant mania (Keck and McElroy, *Psychopharmacol Bull* 2001, **35**, 130–48; Tohen and Grundy, *J Clin Psych* 1999, **60**[Suppl 5], 31–36), concise (Daly, *Lancet* 1997, **349**, 1157–60, 74 refs), comprehensive (Licht, *Acta Psych Scand* 1998, **97**, 387–97, 89 refs), loading strategies for lithium, valproate and CBZ (Keck *et al, Bipolar Disord* 2000, **2**, 42–46, 37 refs) and review of RCTs in acute mania (Keck *et al, J Aff Dis* 2000, **59**[Suppl 1], S31–37).

### BNF Listed
### Antipsychotics (see also olanzapine) \*

Some older antipsychotics have broad indications that may include mania. See unlicensed section and olanzapine.

### Carbamazepine

The 5 RCTs of carbamazepine in acute mania show a response rate equivalent to lithium and chlorpromazine (review by Keck *et al, J Clin Psych* 1998, **59**[Suppl 6], 74–81, 114 refs). It may be more effective in rapid cycling, early age of onset and predominant mania (n=215, retrospective, Okuma, *Neuropsycho-biology* 1993, **27**, 138–45). Other trials have used combination therapy, eg. with lithium. Doses of up to 1600mg/d or more have been used in resistant patients (Ballenger, *J Clin Psych* 1988, **49**[Suppl 1], 13–19), but no loading dose strategies have been published in bipolar (see Keck *et al, Bipolar Disord* 2000, **2**, 42–46). See also bipolar mood disorder (*1.10*).

## Lithium *

Lithium may be effective in acute mania/ hypomania although the onset of action may be delayed for 5–7 days or longer. A systematic overview of lithium concluded that it should remain first line in acute mania (n=658, 12 trials, Poolsup *et al, J Clin Pharm Ther* 2000, **25**, 139–56). Serum levels of 0.9–1.4mmol/l may be necessary in the short-term for a therapeutic effect and should be reduced once mood is normalised. Loading with lithium in mania is surprisingly little studied but has been tried with rapid success, many responding within 48 hours. The only recent study available showed that in 15 manic in-patients given 20mg/kg/d for up to 10 days, only 5 completed (although 7 dropouts improved sufficiently to allow discharge and only 2 had ADRs). All had levels >0.6mmol/l after the first day, which was generally well tolerated and showed a rapid improvement, although this needs confirming in a full study (n=15, open, Keck *et al, Bipolar Disord* 2001, **3**, 68–72). At least four previous depressive or 12 previous manic episodes are associated with reduced antimanic response to lithium (Swann *et al, Acta Psych Scand* 2000, **101**, 444–51).

**Review**: efficacy and side-effects in mania (Bowden, *J Clin Psych* 2000, **61**[Suppl 9], 35–40). See also bipolar mood disorder (*1.10*).

## Olanzapine *

Olanzapine is licensed in the UK for moderate to severe manic episodes (although the SPC states that "olanzapine has not been demonstrated to prevent recurrence of manic or depressive episodes"). The starting dose is 15mg/d as monotherapy and 10mg/d in combination. Several Lilly studies have shown some efficacy eg. in acute mania, response to olanzapine (49%) was better than placebo (24%) (n=139, RCT, 3/52, Tohen *et al, Am J Psych* 1999, **156**, 702–9). Olanzapine (mean 17mg/d) produced a significantly greater mean improvement in mania scores and protocol-defined remission in acute mania than valproate (mean 1400mg/d), with more weight gain, somnolence, dry mouth and increased appetite, but less nausea (n=248, RCT, d/b, 3/52, Tohen *et al, Am J Psych* 2002, **159**, 1011–17). Olanzapine was superior to placebo as add-on to valproate or lithium in manic and mixed bipolar episodes, although weight gain with olanzapine was significant and, since short-term treatment often becomes long-term, data from the 18-month follow-up will be needed to quantify this problem (n=344, RCT, d/b, 6/52, Tohen *et al, Arch Gen Psych* 2002, **59**, 62–69; comment by Gardner, *EBMH* 2002, **5**, 89). Two other studies showed olanzapine as effective as lithium in acute mania on most measures (n=30, RCT, d/b, 4/52, Berk *et al, Int Clin Psychopharmacol* 1999, **14**, 339–43) and in manic or mixed bipolar disorder, 5–20mg/d was superior to placebo and generally well tolerated (n=115, RCT, 4/52, Tohen *et al, Arch Gen Psych* 2000, **57**, 841–49). Some caution and monitoring may be prudent due to a reported and potentially conflicting mood elevating effect.

**Reviews:** * short-term management of Bipolar I mania (Bhana and Perry, *CNS Drugs* 2001, **15**, 871–904).

## Valproate semisodium *

Valproate semisodium is licensed in the UK for mania and hypomania. It may be more effective than lithium in mania with depressive symptoms (n=179, RCT, d/b, Swann *et al, Arch Gen Psych* 1997, **54**, 37–42), rapid cycling and mania with co-morbid substance abuse, but less effective in severe mania or co-morbid BPD (review by Keck *et al, J Clin Psych* 1998, **59**[Suppl 6], 74–81, 114 refs). It is also a very effective adjunct to neuroleptics (see combinations). More rapid control of mania is likely if loading doses are used to achieve plasma concentrations earlier. Divalproex loading doses of 20mg/kg/d have been shown to give a rapid response (often within 3 days) to manic and psychotic symptoms (McElroy *et al, J Clin Psych* 1996, **57**, 142–46). Oral loading doses of divalproex (30mg/kg/d on days 1 and 2, then 20mg/kg/d days 3–10) may produce more rapid therapeutic levels in acute mania, with no adverse effects (n=59, RCT, Hirschfeld *et al, J Clin Psych* 1999, **60**, 815–18). Valproate infusion (initially 125mg over 1 hour) may be rapidly effective (n=1, Herbert and Nelson, *Am J Psych* 2000, **157**, 1023–24). Compared to younger adults, valproate may have a lower therapeutic window (65–90mcg/mL) in the elderly (n=59, retrospective, Chen *et al, J Clin Psych* 1999, **60**, 181–86). A realistic study under realistic conditions, including more severely ill patients, suggests that prompt rapid stabilisation with valproate may allow transition to maintenance without neuroleptics (n=136, RCT, d/b, p/c, 21/7, Müller-Oerlinghausen *et al, J Clin Psychopharmacol* 2000, **20**, 195–203; review by Swann, *EBMH* 2000, **3**, 113).

**Reviews**: general (*Prescrire Internat* 2001, **10**, 113–15; *Prescriber* 2001, 27–34), loading dose strategies (Keck *et al, Bipolar Disord* 2000, **2**, 42–46).

---

### + Combinations
#### Lithium + antipsychotics *
A review of this combination concluded that the slow onset of action of lithium/valproate means they are more adjuncts to antipsychotics initially, rather than vice versa (Cookson, *B J Psych* 2001, **178**(Suppl 41), S148-S156). See also antipsychotics.

#### Lithium + carbamazepine
Carbamazepine can be used in resistant cases in combination with lithium (Kramlinger and Post, *Arch Gen Psych* 1989, **46**, 794–800, review of literature in *Comprehensive Psych* 1990, **31**, 261–65). See *4.4* for neurotoxicity warning.

#### Lithium + clonazepam
See zuclopenthixol + clonazepam.

#### Nifedipine + antipsychotics
Combination use in acute mania and schizoaffective disorders has been reported (Beaurepaire, *Am J Psych* 1992, **149**, 1614–15).

#### Valproate + lithium
Divalproex successfully augmented lithium in resistant rapid-cycling mania in elderly patients (n=4, Schneider and Wilcox, *J Aff Dis* 1998, **47**, 201–5).

#### Valproate + antipsychotics
See valproate above.

#### Zuclopenthixol + clonazepam
In a comparison of two drug combinations (zuclopenthixol plus clonazepam versus lithium plus clonazepam) in acute mania, approximately two thirds improved fully or partially on both combinations, with no statistical differences between the two (n=28, s/b, Gouliaev *et al, Acta Psych Scand* 1996, **93**, 119–24).

---

● **Unlicensed/Some efficacy**
**Antipsychotics** (see also olanzapine)*
There is some evidence that hypomania has a hyper-dopaminergic component (eg. Pearlson *et al, Arch Gen Psych* 1995, **52**, 471–77) and so treatment with dopamine-blocking drugs may be rational (n=528, Chou *et al, Ann Pharmacother* 1996, **30**, 1396–98). Antipsychotics are certainly routinely and widely used, although the majority of even refractory bipolars can be stabilised without long-term neuroleptics (n=133, Brotman *et al, J Clin Psych* 2000, **61**, 68–72). A review of 15 RCTs showed that antipsychotics produce a more rapid antimanic effect than lithium (predictably) but lithium is superior at 3

weeks (Keck *et al, J Clin Psych* 1998, **59**[Suppl 6],74–81). Several studies have suggested **risperidone** to be useful in bipolar disorder (eg. n=14, open, O/P, 8/52, 64% improved, Ghaemi *et al, Can J Psych* 1997, **42**, 196–99; n=12, open, Ghaemi and Sachs, *Int Clin Psychopharmacol* 1997, **12**, 333–38) and in conjunction with mood stabilisers eg. risperidone plus a mood stabiliser was as effective as haloperidol plus mood stabiliser or mood stabiliser alone in acute mania (n=156, RCT, d/b, p/c, 3/52, Sachs *et al, Am J Psych* 2002, **159**, 1146–54). **Quetiapine** 450mg/d augmentation of valproate is more effective in adolescent mania than valproate alone (n=30, RCT, d/b, p/c, 6/52, Delbello *et al, J Am Acad Child Adolesc Psych* 2002, **41**, 1216–23). Although problematic, **clozapine** (mean 500mg/d) may be effective in 72% treatment-resistant manics or schizoaffectives (n=25, open, Calabrese *et al, Am J Psych* 1996, **153**, 759–64). Another study showed significant improvement relative to treatment as usual in bipolar (n=38, RCT, 1yr, Suppes *et al, Am J Psych* 1999, **156**, 1164–69) and up to 550mg/d was effective in treatment-refractory psychotic mania (n=22, open, 12/52, Green *et al, Am J Psych* 2000, **157**, 982–86).

### Benzodiazepines
Short-term medium or high doses of benzodiazepines can be used alone or as adjuvants to other therapies in acute phases of hypomania, eg. diazepam by itself, lorazepam (Salzman *et al, Psychosomatics* 1986, **27**, 17–21) or clonazepam at 4–16mg/d (n=12, RCT, d/b, c/o, Chouinard *et al, Biol Psych* 1983, **18**, 451–66). For acute symptoms they have a rapid onset, are highly sedative and are well tolerated, with a low EPSE side-effect risk. Their role in longer-term therapy should be restricted to PRN use.

### Clomethiazole (chlormethiazole)
See benzodiazepines above for use of sedatives in controlling acute mania.

### Lamotrigine
Lamotrigine may have mood stabilising and mood elevating effects. Its primary action is on voltage-sensitive sodium channels, which stabilises neuronal membranes, inhibiting pathological release of glutamate. A case series with lamotrigine 50–250mg/d (mean of responders 141mg) in refractory bipolars showed a 50% response rate at 5 weeks (n=16, Sporn and Sachs, *J Clin Psychopharmacol* 1997, **17**, 185–89).

### Verapamil *
120–450mg/d has shown promise as a mood stabiliser (*Biol Psych* 1989, **25**, 128–40), even in the elderly (*Int J Ger Psych* 1992, **7**, 913–15). A study showed that up to 320mg/d was as effective in acute mania as lithium (n=20, *Am J Psych* 1992, **149**, 121–2). However, a short random-assignment, parallel-group in-patient trial found no benefit for verapamil over placebo (n=32, RCT, 3/52, Janicak *et al, Am J Psych* 1998, **155**, 972–73), and so longer trials may be necessary. A naturalistic study in bipolar women suggested that verapamil was effective in mania with a response rate comparable to other mood stabilisers but that an RCT would be needed to confirm this (n=37 women, open, Wisner *et al, Biol Psychiatry* 2002, **5**, 745–52).

○  **Unlicensed/Possible efficacy**
### Omega-3 fatty acids
Fish oils may have some application (reviewed by Maidment, *Acta Psych Scand* 2000, **102**, 3–11, 40 refs).

### Levetiracetam *
There is a well-documented case of acute mania responding to levetiracetam up to 2500mg/d (n=1, Goldberg and Burdick, *Am J Psych* 2002, **159**, 148).

### Oxcarbazepine
See carbamazepine. Oxcarbazepine has been used successfully in acute mania at 2400mg/d compared with haloperidol 42mg/d, where it had a slower onset of action but fewer side effects (n=42, Emrich, *Int Clin Psychopharmacol* 1990, **5**[Suppl 1],

83–88). In a comparison with lithium in acute mania, oxcarbazepine was equally effective, but with a slower onset and less well tolerated (n=58, d/b, mentioned by Grant and Faulds, *Drugs* 1992, **43**, 873–88). Another comparison with lithium showed no clear oxcarbazepine responders, although the study design was flawed (n=18, allegedly RCT, 3yr, Wilde-grube, *Int Clin Psychopharmacol* 1990, **5**[Suppl 1], 89–94).

### Phenytoin

Phenytoin augmentation of haloperi-dol in acute mania was more effective than haloperidol, and may indicate that blockade of voltage-activated sodium channels is a common thera-peutic mechanism for anticonvulsants in acute mania (n=39, RCT, 5/52, Mishory *et al, Am J Psych* 2000, **157**, 463–65).

### Topiramate *

Open trials have suggested modest efficacy for topiramate in mania (n=14, open, 4/52, Bozikas *et al, Prog Neuropsychopharmacol Biol Psych* 2002, **26**, 1203-6; 50% response, n=10, open, 28/7, Calabrese *et al, J Clin Psychopharmacol* 2001, **21**, 340–42) and as an adjunct in resistant bipolar depression and mania (n=34, open, Vieta *et al, J Clin Psychophar-macol* 2002, **22**, 431–35). Two short exposures (with a gap) to topiramate as an add-on to existing mood stabili-sers both showed improvement in manic symptoms, indicating that response was linked to the addition of topiramate (n=11, Grunze *et al, J Clin Psych* 2001, **62**, 464–68; although the number of authors [9] almost out-numbers the number patients). It is difficult to rapidly load in mania due to ADRs although it may be useful in obese bipolars.

**Review:*** use in mood disorders, (Chengappa *et al, Bipolar Disord* 2001, **3**, 215–32, 98 refs).

### ◊ Others *

Other drugs tried include **dexamfeta-mine** (Clower, *Psychopharmacol Bull* 1988 **24**, 168), **clonidine** (in antipsy-chotic-resistant mania; Jouvent *et al, B J Psych* 1988, **152**, 293), **doxepin** 100mg/d (n=1, Kaye, *Am J Psych* 1992, **146**, 802–3), **levothyroxine** (0.3–0.5mg/d for rapid or 48hr cycling mania; n=7, Stancer and Persad, *Arch Gen Psych* 1982, **39**, 311–12), **methy-lene blue** (to reduce pathotoxic vana-dium ion concentrations; n=31, d/b, c/o, 2yrs, Naylor *et al, Biol Psych* 1986, **21**, 915–20; Moody *et al, Biol Psych* 1989, **26**, 850–52) and **spirono-lactone** (n=1, Gillman and Lichtig-feld, *BMJ* 1986, **292**, 661–62).

---

### ◆ No efficacy

### Antidepressants *

A retrospective study of patients dis-charged from hospital with bipolar I depression or mania showed a rela-tively high use of antidepressants in bipolar mania (either alone or in com-bination) and although this included some trazodone for insomnia, the rest wasn't for insomnia, a worrying finding (n=1864, Lim *et al, Bipolar Disord* 2001, **3**, 165–73).

### Caffeine

High caffeine intake will risk reducing sleep and exacerbating mania.

### Gabapentin *

The only two double-blind placebo-controlled studies have failed to show any advantage over placebo in mania (eg. n=117, Pande, gabapentin study group, *Bipolar Disorders* 1999, **1**[Suppl 1], 17; Pande *et al, J Clin Psy-chopharmacol* 1999, **19**, 341–48). However, a number of case reports (eg. Stanton *et al, Am J Psych* 1997, **154**, 287) and open studies (n=25, up to 1440mg/d, Cabras *et al, J Clin Psych* 1999, **60**, 245–48) had suggested a potential effect in mania in some people, a good advert for evidence-based approaches to treatment.

### Tiagabine

Tiagabine has no detectable anti-manic activity as mono- or adjunc-tive therapy compared to stand-ard treatments (n=8, open, 14/7, Grunze *et al, J Clin Psych* 1999, **60**, 759–62).

## 1.20 MOVEMENT DISORDERS
### (Drug-induced, dopamine-related)

Akathisia, pseudoparkinsonism, dyskinesias and dystonias have all been associated with antipsychotics and other drugs (see *5.8*). All can occur acutely or chronically.

**Reviews**: extensive (Ebadi & Srinivasan, *Pharmacological Reviews* 1995, **47**, 575–604, 433 refs), role of atypicals in management (Fernandez and Friedman, *CNS Drugs* 1999, **11**, 467–83).

### 1.20.1 AKATHISIA *

Akathisia consists of subjective (unpleasant feelings of inner restlessness and the urge to move) and objective components (rocking while standing or sitting, lifting feet as if marching on the spot and crossing and uncrossing legs while sitting). Its prevalence may be high in schizophrenics treated with older antipsychotics eg. mild akathisia (41%), moderate-to-severe akathisia (21%) (Sachdev & Kruk, *Arch Gen Psych* 1994, **51**, 963–74), and chronic akathisia in up to 24% of in-patients (Halstead *et al, B J Psych* 1994, **164**, 177–83), a higher incidence than usually noticed. Antipsychotic-induced akathisia, which has been connected wth suicidal behaviour (review of 83 reports, Hansen, *Hum Psychopharmacol* 2001, **16**, 495–505) is classified according to the time of onset from start of antipsychotic treatment (acute, tardive, withdrawal or chronic akathisia). The cause is probably an imbalance of cortical and nigrostriatal dopaminergic innervation.

**Role of drugs:**
Antipsychotic-induced akathisia may be confused with agitation or psychosis, and can result in an inappropriate increase in antipsychotic dose. Standardised titration and the use of novel antipsychotics are successful measures of prevention. Propranolol or other lipophilic beta-blockers seem to be the most consistent therapies for acute akathisia, with addition of benzodiazepines a sensible next choice. Cyproheptadine, anticholinergics or benzodiazepines can be tried. Dose reduction is vital.

**Reviews:** * editorial (Bakheit, *Postgrad Med J* 1997, **73**, 529–30), general (Miller and Fleischhacker, *Drug Safety* 2000, **22**, 73–81, 71 refs), effect on clinical outcome (n=34, Luthra *et al, Gen Hosp Psych* 2000, **22**, 276–80), use of serotonin based drugs (Poyurovsky and Weizman, *B J Psych* 2001, **179**, 4–8, including an algorithm).

● **Unlicensed/Some efficacy**
**Reduce dose or switch drugs** *
Recognising akathisia as drug-related will allow consideration of reducing doses or switching to another agent.

**Anticholinergics** *
These may be useful if the akathisia forms part of an extra-pyramidal side-effect profile but are generally considered less useful. There may be a specific Parkinsonian-related subtype of akathisia responsive to anticholinergics (Barnes and McPhillips, *B J Psych* 1999, **174** (Suppl 38), 34–43). 5mg iv biperiden has been shown to be rapidly effective (within 10 minutes) for severe akathisia (n=23, open, Hirose and Ashby, *Int J Psychiatry Med* 2000, **30**, 185–94). Cochrane concludes that there is no reliable evidence to support or refute the use of anticholinergics for neuroleptic-induced acute akathisia (Lima *et al, CDSR* 2002, **3**, 3727).

**Benzodiazepines** *
Clonazepam 0.5–3mg/d (average 1.7mg/d) has been used for antipsychotic-induced akathisia and tardive akathisia (*Hum Psychopharmacol* 1991, **6**, 39–42). 81% patients in a study improved, with the effect prominent in two days (n=21, open, *Acta Psych Scand* 1989, **80**, 106–7). Diazepam 10–17mg IV (at 5mg/30s) has provided rapid relief of acute neuroleptic-induced akathisia (n=18, open, Hirose and Ashby, *J Clin Psych* 2002, **63**, 524–27).

**Beta-blockers**
30–80mg/d of propranolol can produce a dramatic and persistent

improvement, particularly if the akathisia is not connected with Parkinsonian side-effects, but it may take up to three months to act in chronic cases (d/b, p/c, Kramer *et al, Biol Psych* 1988, **24**, 823–27). Propranolol seems equipotent with the other lipophilic beta-blockers metoprolol (*Biol Psych* 1990, **27**, 673–75) and betaxolol (*Am J Psych* 1992, **149**, 647–50) and has been used for fluoxetine (*Biol Psych* 1991, **30**, 531–32) and olanzapine-induced akathisia (n=1, Kurzthaler *et al, Am J Psych* 1997, **154**, 1316). Nadolol (ineffective, n=20, d/b, *J Clin Psych* 1991, **29**, 1215–19), sotalol and atenolol are less effective.

### Cyproheptadine *
Cyproheptadine is a potent $5HT_{2A/2C}$ antagonist with antihistaminic and anticholinergic properties. In a short trial of 16mg/d, NIA markedly improved in 15 and partly in 2, any psychosis or depression remained unchanged, and the improvement was reversed on withdrawal (n=17, open, 4/7, Weiss *et al, B J Psych* 1995, **167**, 483–86) and this has been supported by a more robust trial (n=30, RCT, d/b, 7/7, Fischel *et al, J Clin Psychopharmacol* 2001, **21**, 612–15).

---

### ○ Unlicensed/Possible efficacy
### Apomorphine
In a study of tardive akathisia, low dose apomorphine reduced objective (movement) effects but not subjective distress (Karstaedt and Pincus, *Neurology* 1993, **43**, 611–13).

### Buspirone *
Although a partial agonist at $5HT_{1A}$ receptors, it appears to only have a minor effect in NIA with only 20% getting any effect (n=10, Poyurovsky and Weizman, *Int Clin Psychopharmacol* 1997, **12**, 263–68).

### Iron supplements
There is a disputed similarity with Ekbom's syndrome (*Biol Psych* 1991, **29**, 411–13) although no relationship between plasma iron and chronic akathisia has been found (Barnes *et al, B J Psych* 1992, **161**, 791–96).

### Mianserin
Mianserin, a potent $5HT_{2A/2C}$ antagonist, at 15mg/d has been shown to produce a significant improvement in NIA and dysphoria (n=15, RCT, 5/7, Poyurovsky *et al, B J Psych* 1999, **174**, 238–42).

### Mirtazapine *
Mirtazapine may be useful for NIA, probably via $5HT_{2A/2C}$ antagonism (n=1, 5/7, Poyurovsky and Weizman, *Am J Psych* 2001, **158**, 819).

---

### ◇ Others *
Other drugs tried include **amantadine** (n=4, Zubenko *et al, J Clin Psychopharmacol* 1984, **4**, 218–20), **tryptophan** (n=6, open, *Biol Psych* 1990, **27**, 671–72), **moclobemide** (n=1, Ebert and Demling, *Pharmacopsychiatry* 1991, **24**, 229–31), **ritanserin** (Miller *et al, NPBP* 1992, **16**, 247–51) and **clonidine** (*Am J Psych* 1987, **144**, 235–36).

---

### ◆ No efficacy
### Granisetron *
5HT3 antagonists seem to have no efficacy in NIA, as a study with granistron showed no effect (n=10, 4/7, Poyurovsky and Weizman *Int Clin Psychopharmacol* 1999, **14**, 357–60).

---

## 1.20.2 PSEUDOPARKINSONISM or PARKINSONIAN SIDE-EFFECTS

Symptoms include akinesia, rigidity, bradykinesia and coarse tremor at rest (but not pill rolling), can take a few weeks to occur and may remit spontaneously. EPSEs can occur even in untreated schizophrenics (Chatterjee *et al, Am J Psych* 1995,**152**, 1724–29).

### BNF Listed
### Anticholinergics (antimuscarinics)
*The case for anticholinergics:*
1. Lack of use of anticholinergics in antipsychotic-treated schizophrenia is associated with *reduced* survival (n=88, 10-year prospective study, Waddington *et al, B J Psych* 1998, **173**, 325–29).
2. They may improve compliance with antipsychotics (McClelland, *B J Psych* 1974, **124**, 151–59).

3. PRN or low-dose regular use probably has a low potential for adverse impact.
4. Anticholinergics may partly help negative symptoms in acutely psychotic schizophrenics (eg. Mahaptra *et al, Biol Psych* 1993, **33**, 95) and so may only be detrimental to positive symptoms during *acute* phases (when excess dopaminergic activity is thought to occur) but not during stable phases (Tandon and Dequardo, *Am J Psych* 1995, **152**, 814–15, plus discussion by Goff).

*The case against anticholinergics:*

1. Anticholinergics have been shown to adversely effect memory (especially visual) in schizophrenics and in the elderly, probably a result of their effect on the cholinergic system.
2. They may exacerbate tardive dyskinesia.
3. Abrupt withdrawal can produce rebound EPSEs, cholinergic rebound, myalgia, depression, anxiety, insomnia, headaches, g/i distress, vomiting, nightmares, rebound pesudoparkinsonism and malaise (n=110, Marken *et al, CNS Drugs* 1996, **5**, 190–99), so a slow taper over 2-weeks is necessary.
4. There is an abuse potential (eg. 6% in a cohort of n=214, Zemishlany *et al, Int Clin Psychopharmacol* 1996, **11**, 199–202), possibly due to an alleged euphorant effect, although this may be more of an attempt to self-medicate than to treat EPSEs. True abusers tend to be those who frequently 'lose' medication or request unnecessary dose increases.
5. Some studies have shown that anticholinergics significantly worsen positive symptoms in acutely psychotic schizophrenics (eg. Mahaptra *et al, Biol Psych* 1993, **33**, 95).

*How to use:*

1. Conventional wisdom is that when used for antipsychotic-induced side-effects, few patients need them regularly long-term, 'when required' being preferable, eg. often only for a couple of days after a typical depot to match peak blood levels. They are probably best prescribed only for overt symptoms and then discontinued gradually after three months, reinstated only if symptoms reappear. An attempt should be made to reduce the dose or discontinue any anticholinergic every three to six months, as up to 95% of patients may be able to continue without them (Tarrier *et al, B J Psych* 1989, **154**, 625–28). The standard recommendation of discontinuing after 3 months where EPSEs are under reasonable control is supported by a consensus statement from the WHO (WHO, *B J Psych* 1990, **156**, 412), although unless there is clear evidence of abuse, anticholinergics should not be denied if the patient requests them, in moderate doses for EPSEs.
2. There is little, if any, clinically significant difference between the agents in this group.

**Reviews**: managing antipsychotic-induced parkinsonism (Mamo *et al, Drug Saf* 1999, **20**, 269–75, 49 refs; Holloman and Marder, *Am J Health-Sys Pharm* 1997, **54**, 2461–77), role of anticholinergic drugs (Barnes and McPhillips, *CNS Drugs* 1996, **6**, 315–30), anticholinergic abuse and misuse (Marken *et al, CNS Drugs* 1996, **5**, 190–99).

The drugs in this class are:

### Benzhexol (trihyphenidyl)

This is an anticholinergic with some smooth muscle effects. Abuse has been reported, with doses of up to 100mg/d (Deutsch and Eyma, *Am J Psych* 1992, **149**, 574–75).

### Benzatropine

This is an anticholinergic agent with antihistaminic properties. It has a long half-life (up to 24 hours) and a prolonged action . It was withdrawn in the UK in 2003.

### Biperiden

This drug is similar to benzhexol but with more potent antinicotinic effects.

## Methixene

This drug is similar to atropine, with antimuscarinic, antihistaminic and direct antispasmodic properties. It is claimed to be a more potent anti-tremor agent than the others.

## Orphenadrine

Orphenadrine is related to the anti-histamine diphenhydramine and is similar to benzhexol. Overdose is associated with greater death rates than with other anticholinergics, and also of overuse (SløRdal and Gjerden, *B J Psych* 1999, **174**, 275–76; Buckley and McManus, *B J Psych* 1998, **172**, 461–64), so avoid if possible.

## Procyclidine

An anticholinergic similar to benz-hexol. Abuse has been reported (*B J Psych* 1982, **141**, 81–4) but another study was unable to show a euphor-ant effect (*Acta Psych Scand* 1986, **74**, 519–23).

---

● **Unlicensed/Some efficacy**

Dose reduction of any antipsychotic, or switch to an antipsychotic with lower EPSE eg. an atypical.

---

○ **Unlicensed/Possible efficacy**

## Amantadine

Amantadine is not usually recom-mended for drug-induced EPSEs (BNF) but has been found to be as effective as biperiden, with no worsen-ing of any TD (d/b, c/o, Silver *et al, J Clin Psych* 1995, **56**, 167–70) although no comparison of cognitive function was made. Amantadine may be a better tolerated in elderly patients, with similar efficacy to the anticholinergics (review by Mamo *et al, Drug Saf* 1999, **20**, 269–75).

## Diphenhydramine

Oral or parenteral (25–50mg) diphen-hydramine has been reported to pro-duce rapid (within minutes) reversal of symptoms. Maintenance doses of 25–50mg tds have also been used widely.

## Estrogen (oestrogen)

High levels of estrogen have been reported to reduce hyperkinetic symp-toms in women with psychosis (n=25, Thompson *et al, Acta Psych Scand* 2000, **101**, 130–34).

## Zolpidem *

Zolpidem 5mg qds has been used suc-cessfully to treat persistent and un-responsive EPSE (n=1, Farver and Khan, *Ann Pharmacother* 2001, **35**, 435–37).

◊ **Others**

Other drugs tried include **quinine** (*Am J Psych* 1989, **146**, 801) and **oral cal-cium** (*B J Psych* 1988, **152**, 722–23).

---

♦ **No efficacy**

## Bromocriptine

This is not recommended for drug induced extrapyramidal side-effects (BNF).

## Calcium-channel blockers

Verapamil, nifedipine and diltiazem showed no effect on EPSEs in one study (*B J Psych* 1989, **146**, 269).

---

### 1.20.3 TARDIVE DYSKINESIA

**Symptoms:**

Tardive dyskinesia (TD) is an involun-tary hyperkinesia, which increases with anxiety, goes away during sleep and in some cases may be irreversible. Symptoms include choreas, tics, dysto-nias, orolingual dyskinesias etc but not tremor. It is generally seen as repeti-tive, involuntary and purposeless movements of, eg. the tongue, neck and jaw. TD can be consciously sup-pressed by the sufferer for limited peri-ods but reappears when distracted and worsens during periods of stress. The incidence may be up to 30–40% in long-term patients although figures of 10–20% seem more likely.

**Causes: ***

There is growing evidence from treated and untreated schizophrenic popula-tions that TD rates in both are roughly the same, implying that TD may be a late symptom of schizophrenia, and that antipsychotics might bring for-ward (rather than cause) such symp-toms. Spontaneous dyskinesias and parkinsonism fluctuate with time, and are an integral part of the schizophrenic process (n=37, McCreadie*et al, B J Psych* 2002, **181**, 135–37), and brain structural differences in treated and never-treated patients show similar patterns (McCreadie *et al, Arch Gen Psych* 2002, **59**, 332–36). TD was apparent in 4–11% drug-naïve first episode schizophrenics, suggesting it is a symptom of schizophrenia (Puri *et al, J Neurol Neurosurg Psychiatry* 1999, **66**, 76–78). Whilst there is a clear association between antipsychotic drug use and TD, there is no established relationship with the length of treatment, dose nor actual drug used.

The main neurotransmitter theories are 'denervation super-sensitivity' caused by increased numbers of post-synaptic $D_2$ receptors occurring in response to chronic dopamine blockade, resulting in GABA transmission irregularities in the Substantia Nigra Pars Reticulate, or possibly a GABA defect. Impaired neuroleptic metabolism may be important (n=18, Bates *et al, Acta Psych Scand* 1999, **99**, 294–99).

## Risk factors: *

These include length of exposure to antipsychotics in the elderly (n=741, Sweet *et al, Arch Gen Psych* 1995, **52**, 478–86), alcohol consumption (Duke *et al, B J Psych* 1995, **164**, 630–36), advancing age (n=162, 5yrs, Yassa *et al, Am J Psych* 1992,**149**, 1206–11), being male (n=48, Joseph, *Acta Psych Scand* 1990, **81**, 530–33; especially in elderly, n=706 chronic psychotics, van Os *et al, Acta Psych Scand* 1999, **99**, 288–93), having negative symptoms of schizophrenia (Liddle *et al, B J Psych* 1993, **163**, 776–80), previous head injury, presence of organic brain disease (eg. retardation, epilepsy) structural brain damage, earlier drug-induced Parkinsonism, akathisia or dystonias, lithium (Ghadirian *et al, J Clin Psych* 1996, **57**, 22–28), non-right-handedness (n=48, Joseph, *Acta Psych Scand* 1990, **81**, 530–33), being diabetic (50% increase – Woerner *et al, Am J Psych* 1993, **150**, 96–98), and concurrent affective or negative symptoms.

## Treatment strategies:

1. **Slowly withdraw or reduce the dose of the antipsychotic** – if the drug was exacerbating the condition, the TD may improve. Psychosis may relapse, and this is an unproven and hazardous strategy (McGrath and Soares, *CDSR* 2000, 0459). Ensuring that the original diagnosis is correct and valid is important. It may be possible to reintroduce the antipsychotic again in the short-term or at reduced doses. Drug 'holidays' seem detrimental. Some predictors of improvement have been identified (n=49, Glazer *et al, B J Psych* 1990, **157**, 585–92) but the risk of relapse (even in long-term patients without proper diagnosis) was noted to be high. Dose reduction may help.

2. **Withdraw or reduce any anticholinergic drugs** if possible – these can provoke or exacerbate TD, although not a risk factor as such

3. **Keep antipsychotic drug use down in the long-term to minimum effective doses**. Reducing individual doses has little influence but overall the lower doses tend to lead to improvement (n=44, 10yrs, Yassa and Nair, *Acta Psych Scand* 1992, **86**, 262–66)

4. **Avoid increasing the dose or adding another antipsychotic** – this does **not** work in the long-term as it blocks any excess dopamine activity initially, but the condition will then worsen, but may be used in the short-term and for special occasions.

5. **Consider an alternative antipsychotic, eg. quetiapine, olanzapine** (n=1714, RCT, Glazer, *J Clin Psych* 2000, **61**[Suppl 4], 21–26) **or risperidone** if an antipsychotic is needed. **Clozapine** also has a virtually clear record and some patients with severe TD make a clinically remarkable improvement on clozapine (see next page).

6. **Consider other adjuncts** eg. **tetrabenazine**, benzodiazepines, buspirone, calcium antagonists or beta-blockers. ECT is also an option.

7. **\*GABA agonist treatment** — see GABA agonists/enhancers.

**Reviews**: general (*Maudsley Prescribing Guidelines* 2001; Tarsy, *Curr Treat Options Neurol* 2000, **2**, 205–14; Sachdev, *Aust NZ J Psych* 2000, **34**, 355–69; Simpson, *J Clin Psych* 2000, **61**[Suppl 4], 39–44), 'miscellaneous' treatments (McGrath and Soares, *CDSR* 2000, 0208).

---

**BNF listed**
**Tetrabenazine \***
Tetrabenazine is licensed in the UK, with a starting dose of 12.5mg, titrated to 25–75mg/d (maximum 200mg/d). TD is often a fluctuating condition and so short-term and rescue use is appropriate. Patients with refractory TD receiving tetrabenazine (mean 58mg/d) had significantly improved AIMS scores over 20 weeks, as judged by 'blind videotape raters', a good trick if you can do it (n=20, Ondo *et al, Am J Psych* 1999, **156**, 1279–81). Informal follow-up of 400 patients with movement disorders, suggested a noticeable benefit from tetrabenazine in those (n=94) with TD (n=526, Jankovic and Beach, *Neurology* 1997, **48**, 358–62).

---

● **Unlicensed/Some efficacy**
**Calcium-channel blockers**
Nifedipine has been used, with higher doses seemingly more effective, with the elderly and people with more severe TD respond better (review by Cates *et al, Ann Pharmacother* 1993, **27**, 191–96, 14 refs). Verapamil (Obad and Ovsiew, *B J Psych* 1993, **162**, 554–56) and diltiazem may also be useful.

---

○ **Unlicensed/Possible efficacy**
**Amantadine**
Amantadine was superior to placebo in one study (d/b, c/o, 18/52, Angus *et al, J Clin Psychopharmacol* 1997, **17**, 88–91).
**Baclofen**
See GABA agonists.

**Benzodiazepines**
Cochrane concludes that benzodiazepines had no proven advantage over placebo (McGrath and Soares, *CDSR* 2000, 0205), although there have been reports of clonazepam decreasing dystonic symptoms (n=19, RCT, Thacker *et al, Am J Psych* 1990, **147**, 445–51).
**Buspirone**
Buspirone (up to 180mg/d) may be useful (n=8, open, 12/52, Moss *et al, J Clin Psychopharmacol* 1993, **13**, 204–9) and even in severe TD at up to 240mg/d (n=1, Neppe, *Lancet* 1989, **2**, 1458).
**Clozapine**
In approximately 43% of cases of TD, especially with dystonic features, improvement (ie. >50% reduction in symptoms) has been seen when the current antipsychotic was replaced with clozapine (n=30, Lieberman *et al, B J Psych* 1991, **158**, 503–10; see also n=7, open, Bassitt *et al, Eur Arch Psych Clin Neurosci* 1998, **248**, 209–11).
**Cyproheptadine**
In a study of patients with TD taking haloperidol, significant improvement in symptoms occurred when cyproheptadine 8–24mg/d was added (n=10, open, Lee *et al, J Serotonin Res* 1994, **1**, 91–95).
**Donepezil \***
A pilot study indicated that donepezil 5–10mg/d might suppress symptoms of antipsychotic-induced TD (n=10, open, 8/52, Caroff *et al, J Clin Psych* 2001, **62**, 772–75).
**GABA agonists/enhancers**
Valproate, baclofen (n=31. RCT, d/b, Glazer *et al, Psychopharmacol (Berl)* 1985, **87**, 480–83) and progabide have been suggested but Cochrane concludes from the 8 small, short-term studies that the evidence is inconclusive and unconvincing (Soares *et al, CDSR* 2001, **2**, 0203).
**Gabapentin**
Some suggestion of efficacy has been made (n=16, open, case series,

Hardoy *et al, J Aff Dis* 1999, **54**, 315–17).

## Insulin
Low-dose insulin has been suggested as superior to placebo (see McGrath and Soares, *CDSR* 2000, 0208).

## Melatonin *
Melatonin 10mg/d has been shown to decrease AIMS scores in TD (n=22, d/b, p/c, c/o, 6/52, Shamir *et al, Arch Gen Psych* 2001, **58**, 1049–52).

## Olanzapine *
There are several cases of a marked reduction in pre-existing symptoms of TD when treated with olanzapine (n=4, Littrell, *Arch Gen Psych* 1998, **55**, 279–80; n=2; Soutullo *et al, J Clin Psychopharmacol* 1999, **19**, 100–1; n=2, Agarwal and Kumar, *J Clin Psych* 2001, **62**, 298–99).

## Ondansetron *
Ondansetron (a 5-HT3 antagonist) 12mg/d produced a significant reduction in neuroleptic-induced TD and in psychotic symptoms (n=12, open, 12/52, Sirota *et al, Am J Psych* 2000, **157**, 287–89; although this could have been an interaction).

## Piracetam *
Piracetam has been used to treat TD and akathisia (n=1, Fehr *et al, J Clin Psychopharmacol* 2001, **21**, 248–49).

## Pyridoxine
There are several case reports of pyridoxine 200mg/d producing a rapid and sustained reduction in TD symptoms (eg. n=1, Lerner and Liberman, *J Clin Psych* 1998, **59**, 623–24).

## Quetiapine *
TD in schizophrenics may improve with a switch to quetiapine (n=3, Alptekin and Kivircik, *Int Clin Psychopharmacol* 2002, **17**, 263–64).

## Risperidone *
There are a number of case reports of remission of TD (eg. Santone *et al, Clin Drug Invest* 1997, **14**, 502–6; Rangwani *et al, Ann Clin Psych* 1996, **8**, 27–29) and 55% schizophrenics with TD showed response of TD symptoms when risperidone (mean 6.7mg/d) was used to replace existing typical antipsychotics (n=9, open, 52/

52, Chen *et al, Am J Psych* 2001, **158**, 1931–32).

## Valproate
See GABA agonists.

---

◊ **Others:** *
Other drugs tried include **beta-blockers** (eg. propranolol: *Biol Psych* 1983, **18**, 391–94), **botulinum toxin** (*B J Psych* 1992, **161**, 867–68), **bromocriptine** (*Arch Gen Psych* 1989, **46**, 908–13; *Integr Psych* 1989, **6**, 171–79) and **piracetam** (Chaturvedi, *J Clin Psych* 1987, **48**, 255).

---

◆ **No efficacy**
## Anticholinergics
Discontinuing may result in improvement in TD (n=10, d/b, p/c, p/c, Griel *et al, B J Psych* 1984, **145**, 304–10) although the evidence for any effect is poor (Soares and McGrath, *CDSR* 2000, 0204), and it may be that they just exacerbate the movement disorder.

## Citalopram
One study showed citalopram had no effect on the symptoms of TD (n=13, Korsgaard *et al, Clin Neuropharmacol* 1986, **9**, 52–57).

## Lithium
One study showed lithium to have no consistent effect on the symptoms of TD (n=11, d/b, c/o, Mackay *et al, Psychol Med* 1980, **10**, 583–87), supported since by other studies (Yassa *et al, Can J Psych* 1984, **29**, 36–37). Lithium may even exacerbate TD (see 5.8.4).

## Vitamin E *
Two RCTs have failed to find any significant effect from Vitamin E (up to 1600iu/d) in long-term tardive dyskinesia (n=40, RCT, 20/52, Dorevitch *et al, Biol Psych* 1997, **41**, 114; n=158, RCT, up to 2 years, Adler *et al, Arch Gen Psych* 1999, **56**, 836–41). Vitamin E may be effective in a subgroup of patients with TD (18 trial review, Boomershine *et al, Ann Pharmacother* 1999, **33**, 1195–1202). Cochrane concludes that Vitamin E may have some effect, but that the evidence is inadequate (Soares and McGrath, *CDSR* 2000, **2**, 0209) and

one small but careful study indicated B₆ appeared to reduce TD symptoms in schizophrenia (n=15, RCT, d/b, p/c, 4/52, Lerner *et al, Am J Psych* 2001, **158**, 1511–14).

## 1.20.4   DYSTONIA (tardive or acute) (subtype of TD)

Dystonia is a syndrome of sustained or slow involuntary muscular contractions, resulting in twisting of the neck, limbs, trunk or face. Acute dystonia from antipsychotics is more likely to occur in younger, more severely ill patients, especially antipsychotic-naive schizophrenics with predominantly negative symptoms (Aguilar *et al, Am J Psych* 1994, **151**, 1819–21) and so care should be taken with antipsychotic use in this group. The onset of dystonias may be delayed for several years.

**Reviews**: general (Adityanjee *et al, Biol Psych* 1999, **45**, 715–30), extensive review and algorithm (Raja, *Drug Safety* 1998, **19**, 57–72, 176 refs).

● **Unlicensed/Some efficacy**
### Anticholinergics
These can be effective in acute dystonia but are less useful in chronic dystonia, although some symptoms may partially respond (n=32, Wojcik *et al, Am J Psych* 1991, **148**, 1055– 59). Biperiden has been shown to prevent dystonias from occurring in first-onset psychotic patients treated with haloperidol (Agular *et al, Am J Psych* 1994, **151**, 1819–21).

+ **Combinations**
### Clozapine + clonazepam
There is a case of multiple drug-resistant disabling tardive dystonia responding partly to clozapine and virtually completely when clonazepam was then added (n=1, Shapleske *et al, B J Psych* 1996, **168**, 516–18).

○ **Unlicensed/Possible efficacy**
### Benzodiazeines
See combinations.
### Botulinum toxin
This may relieve the pain and symptoms of strabismus and possibly dys-

tonias. It is a powerful neurotoxin which destroys nerve terminals at the end plates (TTAS-AAN, *Neurology* 1990, **40**, 1332–36) and may help tardive dystonia (n=34, open, Tarsy *et al, Clin Neuropharmacol* 1997, **20**, 90–93).
### Clozapine*
Severe and persistent tardive dystonia showed marked improvement during clozapine therapy, up to 300mg/d (n=1, *J Nerv Ment Dis* 1993, **181**, 137–38; n=1, Sieche and Giedke, *J Clin Psych* 2000, **61**, 949). It is possible that many patients with tardive dystonia improve on clozapine. See also combinations.
### Levodopa
Beneficial effects from combined levodopa and a central anticholinergic have been reported in a patient with severe drug-induced tardive dystonia (Looper and Chouinard, *Can J Psychiatry* 1998, **43**, 646–47, letter).
### Olanzapine*
Olanzapine up to 7.5mg/d may have some role in improving tardive cervical dystonia (n=4, s/b, Lucetti *et al, Clin Neuropharmacol* 2002, **25**, 71–74) and 15mg/d over 7 months reduced symptoms of tardive dystonia in one patient (Jaffe and Simpson, *Am J Psych* 1999, **156**, 2016).

◊ **Others*
Other drugs tried include **baclofen** (Greene, *Clin Neuropharmacol* 1992, **15**, 276–88; mentioned in Narayan, *Drugs* 1991, **41**, 889–926), **bromocriptine** (n=15, d/b, c/o, Newman *et al, Clin Neuropharmacol* 1985, **8**, 328–33; *Arch Gen Psych* 1989, **46**, 908–13), **diphenhydramine** (Leigh *et al, Ann Neurol* 1987, **22**, 13–17) and **tetrabenazine** (Kong *et al, Mov Disorder* 1986, **1**, 193–208).

◆ **No efficacy**
### Carbamazepine
This has been shown to be ineffective (*Psychopharmacol Bull* 1985, **21**, 345–46).

## 1.21 NARCOLEPSY

**Symptoms:**
Narcolepsy is a rare and often mis-diagnosed disabling neurological disorder of excessive daytime sleepiness, sleep paralysis, hypnagogic hallucinations, cataplexy (sudden loss of muscle tone provoked by strong emotions, eg. laughter) and abnormalities in REM sleep, with a strong genetic linkage, and normally starting in the 20s or 30s. The incidence ranges from 1 in 1,000 to 10,000 in Europe, but appears to be a frequently missed diagnosis. About 70% of sufferers also experience cataplexy during the day. Recent theories of its cause have centred around a loss of neurones from the neuropeptide hypocretin system in the hypothalamus.

**Role of drugs:**
The use of stimulants is considered first-line treatment, with some antidepressants useful in some resistant cases, and the risks of pharmacotherapy are usually outweighed by the risks to the patient of vehicle crashes, workplace mishaps etc.
**Reviews:*** drug options (Mitler and Hayduk, *Drug Saf* 2002, **25**, 791–809), general (Krahn *et al, Mayo Clin Proc* 2001, **76**, 185–94; Overeem *et al, J Clin Neurophysiol* 2001, **18**, 78–105; Faccenda, *Scott Med J* 2000, **45**, 68–69; Green and Stillman, *Arch Fam Med* 1998, **7**, 472–78; Gerhardstein *et al, Respir Care Clin N Am* 1999, **5**, 427–46; Stores, *Arch Gen Child* 1999, **81**, 519–24; Bassetti, *Curr Treat Options Neurol* 1999, **1**, 291–98), in children (Guilleminault and Pelayo, *Paediatr Drugs* 2000, **2**, 1-9).

---

**BNF Listed**
**Amphetamines** (dexamphetamine)
5–50mg/d can be highly effective although doses of 40–60mg/d have been shown to be more effective than lower doses (methamfetamine: n=16, RCT, d/b, Mitler *et al, Sleep* 1993, **16**, 306–17). If tolerance develops, drug holidays may be necessary. Although dexamfetamine is not immune from problems of chronic stimulant ingestion, many can take it for decades without apparent adverse consequences. Dexamfetamine acts by enhancing release of noradrenaline, dopamine and serotonin, but the stimulant effect appears to be mainly via dopamine.

**Modafinil\***
Modafinil is a wake-promoting agent chemically and pharmacologically unrelated to methylphenidate, amfetamine or pemoline. Its precise mechanism of action is unknown. Modafinil is indicated for the improvement of wakefulness in patients with excessive daytime sleepiness associated with narcolepsy. It significantly increases daytime sleep latency but does not suppress cataplexy. Modafinil offers advantages because of its lack of rebound phenomena after treatment withdrawal and its low abuse potential. Modafinil 600mg/d appears the maximum tolerated dose (n=32, RCT, Wong *et al, J Clin Pharmacol* 1999, **39**, 30–40), with 200–400mg/d optimum (n=283, RCT, 9/52, Modafinil study group, *Ann Neurol* 1998, **43**, 88–97) and with no tolerance in a 40-week follow-on, nor withdrawal (RCT, 9/52, n=271, Modafinil study group, *Neurology* 2000, **54**, 1166–75). It may also be useful for narcolepsy associated with closed-head brain injury and with sedating psychotropics (n=10, case series, Teitelman, *Am J Psych* 2001, **158**, 970–71). Studies directly comparing it to amfetamines and methylphenidate, currently the preferred therapies for narcolepsy, are not yet available.
**Reviews**: pharmacology and efficacy (McClellan and Spencer, *CNS Drugs* 1998, **9**, 311–24), mode of action (Stahl, *J Clin Psych* 2002, **63**, 467–68), general (Anon, *Formulary Monograph Service* 1999, 93–102, 22 refs; *Prescrire International* 1999, **8**, 5–7).

---

● **Unlicensed/Some efficacy**
**Methylphenidate**
2.5–5mg bd (up to 60mg/d) can be used (see also dexamfetamine above).

In an active comparison, methylphenidate improved performance and waking, pemoline only performance and protriptyline neither, although all three were better than placebo (n=17, p/c, Mitler *et al, Sleep* 1986, **9**, 371–72). Tolerance can be a problem, with drug holidays helpful. It is generally considered as good as dexamfetamine (n=40, open, Zwicker *et al, J Sleep Res* 1995, **4**, 252–55) but with a better side-effects profile (reviewed by Challman and Lipsky, *Mayo Clin Proc* 2000, **75**, 711–21).

**SSRIs**

These are generally considered less effective than tricyclics but some positive results have been reported with eg. fluoxetine (Langdon *et al, Sleep* 1986, **9**, 371–72).

**Tricyclics**

Clomipramine and imipramine can be used for cataplexy and sleep paralysis, particularly in stimulant-resistant or intolerant patients. Clomipramine at 10–25mg/d can be effective and may have the most specific effect on cataplexy (n=21, open, Guilleminault *et al, Acta Neurol Scand* 1976, **54**, 71–87). Side-effects from tricyclics can be considerable and rebound cataplexy can occur with abrupt withdrawal ('Status Cataplecticus').

○ **Unlicensed/Possible efficacy**

**Codeine**

Codeine has a limited efficacy on subjective measures (n=8, RCT, Fry *et al, Sleep* 1986, **9**, 269–74) but it has been dramatically effective (n=1, Benbadis, *Pharmacotherapy* 1996, **16**, 463–65) and as effective as pentazocine (n=1, 8yrs, *Lancet* 1981, **i**, 92).

**MAOIs**

MAOIs may be useful in refractory cases, albeit difficult to use (eg. tranylcypromine; n=1, Gernaat *et al, Pharmacopsychiatry* 1995, **28**, 98–100).

**Pentazocine**

See codeine, above.

**Reboxetine ***

Reboxetine 10mg/d produced a marked and significant stimulant and anticataleptic effect (n=12, open,

2/52, Larrosa *et al, Sleep* 2001, **24**, 282–85).

**Selegiline**

Two trial have shown a potent and dose-related effect, at doses of at least 20mg/d (n=30, RCT, Mayer *et al, Clin Neuropharmacol* 1995, **18**, 306–19; n=17, d/b, c/o, Hublin *et al, Neurology* 1994, **44**, 2095–101), and may be useful in patients who get disturbing side-effects with stimulants.

◇ **Others ***

Other drugs used include benzodiazepines such as **clonazepam** (1–4mg/d; Thompson *et al, Ann Neurol* 1982, **12**, 62–63), **clonidine** 150–300mcg/d (Salin-Pascual *et al, J Clin Psych* 1985, **46**, 528–31), **levodopa** (which may improve vigilance and performance but not capacity to fall asleep rapidly; n=6, Boivin and Montplaisir, *Neurology* 1991, **41**, 1267–69) and **propranolol** (n=48, 18/12, Meier-Ewart *et al, Sleep* 1985, **8**, 95–104; see also n=4, Kales *et al, Ann Int Med* 1979, **91**, 741).

**1.22 NEUROLEPTIC MALIGNANT SYNDROME (NMS)**

**Symptoms:***

This is a rare and potentially fatal idiosyncratic dose-independent adverse drug reaction resulting in a sudden loss in control of body temperature during drug therapy. The main diagnostic symptoms are hyperthermia or fever and severe muscle rigidity, with two or more of: diaphoresis, dysphagia, tremor, incontinence, altered consciousness, tachycardia, altered blood pressure, leucocytosis and raised creatinine phosphokinase concentration (Adityanjee, *B J Psych* 1991, **158**, 706–7). Body temperature rises rapidly and can be fatal in a short time (eg. 24–72 hrs) due to renal and respiratory failure. Clinical features progress over 24–72 hours and subside over 5–10 days (oral drugs) or 10–21 days (depots). The incidence is unknown but it may possibly occur in up to 0.15% (range 0.02–2.44%) of all patients given antipsychotics although this may be reducing due to increased awareness, early intervention and reduction in risk factors (n=2695, 4yrs, Keck *et al, Am J Psych* 1991, **148**, 880–82). Death rates have been reported to be 14% (range 4–30%) for oral antipsychotics and 38% for depots. The cause is thought to be a sudden over-blockade of dopaminergic function, resulting in a disruption to the thermoregulatory centre. Anaesthetists see a similar syndrome as malignant hyperthermia. It has been linked with lethal catatonia (*1.12*) and serotonin syndrome (Carbone, *Emerg Med Clin North Am* 2000, **18**, 317–25).

**Risk factors include:** *
**History** – previous NMS, known cerebral compromise, previous ECT (Sachdev *et al, Am J Psych* 1997, **154**, 1156–58).
**Mental state** – agitation (Sachdev *et al, Am J Psych* 1997, **154**, 1156–58), overactive and/or in need of restraint or seclusion (Sachdev *et al, Am J Psych* 1997, **154**, 1156–58), catatonia, affective disorder (n=25, Sachdev *et al, Am J Psych* 1989, **146**, 914–18).
**Physical state** – dehydration (Sachdev *et al, Am J Psych* 1997, **154**, 1156–58), postpartum (n=4, *Ann Clin Psych* 1999, **11**, 13–15), Parkinson's disease (n=98, Ueda *et al, Neurology* 1999, **52**, 777–82), young, male, high serum creatinine kinase (n=32, Hermesh *et al, J Clin Psychopharmacol* 2002, **22**, 252–56).
**Drugs** – (see *5.9*) high potency antipsychotics, IM therapy (eg. depot fluphenazine, Deng *et al, Am J Psych* 1990, **147**, 1149–55, or haloperidol: n=24, Rosebush *et al, Am J Psych* 1989, **146**, 717–25), high doses over short periods (Sachdev *et al, Am J Psych* 1997, **154**, 1156–58), recent changes, rapid neuroleptisation, concurrent MAOIs.

Symptoms may be modified (eg. absence of fever) in the presence of carbamazepine (n=1, Dalkin *et al, B J Psych* 1990, **157**, 437–38).

**Neuroleptic re-challenge:** *
Re-challenge with antipsychotics may show a high NMS recurrence rate. In one review of 41 re-challenges, 7 were rechallenged with the same drug, 4 were successful and of 27 re-challenges with another drug, 16 were fully successful (Wells *et al, Drug Intell Clin Pharm* 1988, **22**, 475–80). Another study showed that 87% were able to tolerate antipsychotics again if a two-week recovery period was allowed (n=15, Rosebush *et al, J Clin Psych* 1989, **50**, 295–98, 472), and monitored carefully. Rechallenge with clozapine has been successful (Weller and Kornhuber, *B J Psych* 1992, **161**, 855–56). One NMS with typicals was unsuccessfully challenged with quetiapine (n=1, Hatch *et al, Pharmacother* 2001, **21**, 1003–6). Depots are contraindicated.

**Guidelines for the re-introduction of antipsychotics following NMS** (Williams and MacPherson, *Irish J Psych Med* 1997, **14**, 147–48):

1. Review diagnosis of NMS to ensure the key features were present.
2. Review psychiatric diagnosis and need for further antipsychotics.
3. Consider alternative strategies, eg. benzodiazepines for anxiety/agitation, carbamazepine for behaviour, ECT.
4. Leave as long a gap as possible (eg. 5–14 days), considering risk of untreated psychosis.
5. Choose a drug from a different group, particularly any previously used without problem, or a low potency drug. Use a low starting dose and small increments. Contraindicate depots.
6. Perform alternate day CPK, interpreted in the context of the global clinical picture.
7. Perform daily temperature, pulse and muscle tone measures, weekly wbc's and ensure adequate hydration and nutrition.
8. Obtain an informal or formal second opinion, as informed consent may not be possible. Inform family and carers of the decisions and risks (and document).
9. Educate patients and carers of the symptoms of early NMS and of the appropriate action to take, ie. seek

urgent medical advice. Ensure the primary care team is also aware of these symptoms and required actions.

**Role of drugs:**

NMS is potentially life-threatening and treatment should be immediate and intensive. The main treatment strategies are:

1. Withdrawal of antipsychotics, lithium and antidepressants immediately.
2. Correct dehydration and hyperpyrexia, eg. using ice packs, rehydration and sedate with benzodiazepines if necessary.
3. Measure WCC, U&E, LFT and CK.
4. Drug treatment of acute symptoms is usually essential (review of responses to treatment in *Arch Int Med* 1989, **149**, 1927–31). Dantrolene or bromocriptine are probably the most useful. ECT can be used (review, Trollor and Sachdev, *Aust NZ J Psych* 1999, **33**, 650–59).

**Reviews:*** general (Khan and Farver, *SDJ Med* 2000, **53**, 395–400; Andreassen and Pedersen, *Ugeskr Laeger* 2000, **162**, 1366–70; Velamoor, *Drug Safety* 1998, **19**, 73–82; McDonough *et al, Ir Med J* 2000, **93**, 152–54), novel antipsychotics and NMS (n=32, Hasan and Buckley, *Am J Psych* 1998, **155**, 1113–16).

---

○ **Unlicensed/Some efficacy**

**Amantadine**

Amantadine may be third line choice and has been reported to be successful in a number of cases at 100mg bd (Blumlein, *Psychiatr Prax* 1997, **24**, 257–58).

**Bromocriptine**

Bromocriptine is usually used at doses of 7.5–60mg/d and has been shown to reduce the duration and mortality of NMS (Sakkas *et al, Psychopharmacol Bull* 1991, **27**, 381–84). It has, however, been suggested that it might prolong the course of symptoms when compared to supportive therapies (Rosebush *et al, B J Psych* 1991, **148**, 709–12).

**Dantrolene**

IV dantrolene (a skeletal muscle relaxant licensed for malignant hyperthermia; eg. n=21, Tsutsumi *et al, Psych Clin Neurosci* 1998, **52**, 433–38) and is probably the treatment of choice. It has been shown to reduce the duration and mortality of NMS (n=9, Nisijima and Ishiguro, *Biol Psych* 1993, **33**, 45–48). It reduces body temperature in 2–24 hours but muscular rigidity may take 4–16 days (Rosenberg and Green, *Arch Int Med* 1989, **149**, 1927–31). As with bromocriptine it has been suggested that it might prolong the course of symptoms compared to supportive therapy (Rosebush *et al, B J Psych* 1991, **148**, 709–12).

**Lorazepam**

IV lorazepam has been used if dantrolene and bromocriptine have failed (see also diazepam).

---

● **Unlicensed/Possible efficacy**

**Anaesthetics**

Anaesthetics have been used for emergency treatment in a person recovering from NMS (Parke and Wheatley, *Anaesthesia* 1992, **47**, 908–9).

**Anticoagulants**

Since death can be from pulmonary embolism, complete anticoagulation has been suggested as adjunctive therapy (van harten and van Agtmael, *Am J Psych* 1995, **152**, 1103).

**Diazepam**

There may be a benzodiazepine responsive sub-type of NMS, with predominantly catatonic symptoms, rapidly responsive to bolus diazepam, and where continuous IV administration is effective (Miyaoka *et al, Am J Psych* 1997, **153**, 882). Its longer half-life has been reported to complicate recovery (Velamoor, *B J Psych* 1992, **160**, 135–36).

**Levodopa**

Intravenous levodopa has been used as an effective alternative to dantrolene for NMS (Nisijima *et al, Biol Psych* 1997, **41**, 913–14, letter), as has the carbidopa/levodopa combination

(Shoop and Cernek, *Ann Pharmacother* 1997, **31**, 119, letter).

### Nifedipine

25mg s/l has been used (*Psychosomatics* 1994, **35**, 168–70).

## 1.23 OBSESSIVE-COMPULSIVE DISORDER (OCD)

**Symptoms:**
OCD is characterised by recurrent and intrusive thoughts of compulsive, stereo-typed, repetitive behaviour or thoughts, eg. recurrent checking, hand-washing etc. Functioning is impaired by obsessive thoughts and rituals. Resisting these thoughts results in heightened anxiety. OCD probably has a lifetime prevalence of 2.5–3%.

**Role of drugs:** *
There is much evidence for the cause of OCD being related to a dysfunctional serotonin system, and SSRIs and clomipramine have been shown to be effective eg. an SSRI (sertraline) was more effective and tolerable than a noradrenergic agent (desipramine) in concurrent OCD and major depression (n=166, d/b, Hoehn-Saric *et al*, *Arch Gen Psych* 2000, **57**, 76–82).

Several meta-analyses (eg. Ackerman and Greenland, *J Clin Psychopharmacol* 2002, **22**, 309–17) have drawn the same conclusions:

1. Only antidepressants affecting the serotonin system are effective
2. The SSRIs as a class are similarly effective to clomipramine and both are superior to non-serotonergic drugs, with clomipramine perhaps slightly more effective than SSRIs
3. Concomitant depression does not seem necessary for improvement in obsessive-compulsive symptoms.
4. Relapse is common on discontinuation.
5. Dosage usually needs to be high, eg. 250–300mg clomipramine, or 60–80mg fluoxetine. Response is slow and may not occur for several weeks.

Although drugs may only reduce symptomatology by 30–60%, many patients consider this a significant benefit. SSRIs (inc. clomipramine) are likely to be less effective when hoarding obsessions and compulsions are present (n=354, Mataix-Cols *et al, Am J Psych* 1999, **156**, 1409–16). There is, however, some doubt about the long-term outcome and efficacy of SSRIs in OCD (n=60, 1-5yrs, Alonso *et al, J Clin Psych* 2001, **62**, 535–40).

Psychotherapy, behaviour therapy and cognitive therapy are also useful, especially in combination with SSRIs (eg. meta-analysis by van Balkom *et al, Clin Psychol Rev* 1994, **14**, 359–81).

**Reviews:*** general (Fineberg, *Adv Psych Treat* 1999, **5**, 357–65), options and flowchart (*Drugs & Therapy Perspectives* 1998, **11**, 5–8, 13 refs), drug treatment options (McDonough and Kennedy, *Harv Rev Psych* 2002, **10**, 127–37; WFSBP Guidelines, Bandelow *et al, World J Biol Psych* 2002, **3**, 171–99; Hollander *et al, Psychiatr Clin North Am* 2000, **23**, 643–56), algorithms for pharmacotherapy (Albert *et al, Panminerva Med* 2002, **44**, 83–91; *B J Psych* 1998, **173**[Suppl 35], 1–70).

---

### BNF Listed
### Clomipramine

Clomipramine is clearly superior to placebo and non-serotonergic drugs (s=11, d/b, c/o, Piccinelli *et al, B J Psych* 1995, **166**, 424–43), with clomipramine (but not N- desmethylclomipramine, more a NA reuptake inhibitor) levels correlating significantly with positive treatment outcome (Mavissakalian *et al, J Clin Psychopharmacol* 1990, **10**, 261–68). Intravenous clomipramine may be effective in patients intolerant or non-responsive to oral clomipramine (n=54, RCT, Fallon *et al, Arch Gen Psych* 1998, **55**, 918–24; n=15, RCT, Koran *et al, Am J Psych* 1997, **154**, 396–401). See also introduction.

### Fluoxetine *

Fluoxetine has shown a significant clinical effect at 20mg/d, developing over 13 weeks, and continuing to be effective for at least 9 months with few side-effects (eg. n=130, RCT, p/c, 12/12, Romano *et al, J Clin Psychopharmacol* 2001, **21**, 46–52). It may also be effective in children, but takes over 8 weeks to reach full effect (n=43, RCT, p/c, 16/52, Liebowitz *et al, J Am Acad Child Adolesc Psych* 2002, **41**, 1431–38). The response is not related to plasma levels (Koran *et al, Am J Psych* 1996, **153**, 1450–54), although higher doses (eg. 60–80mg/d) may be needed.

**Fluvoxamine \***

Fluvoxamine has been shown to be partially or very effective in several trials (eg. n=38, d/b, p/c, 10/52, Jenike *et al, Am J Psych* 1990, **147**, 1209–15), and as good as clomipramine but better tolerated (n=227, RCT, d/b, 10/52, Mundo *et al, Hum Psychopharmacol* 2001, **16**, 461–68), showing a clinical effect in about 4–6 weeks, although it may not be of any additional benefit in patients non-responsive to fluoxetine or clomipramine, except where side-effects had been limiting (open, Mattes, *Am J Psych* 1994, **151**, 1524). A therapeutic window may occur as increasing the dose above 200mg/d reversed the improvement seen (n=1, *Lancet* 1992, **339**, 689).

**Paroxetine**

Paroxetine is licensed in the UK for the symptoms of OCD at doses of 40–60mg, being more effective than placebo, equipotent to clomipramine, but better tolerated in adults (n=406, RCT, 6/12, Zohar *et al, B J Psych* 1996, **169**, 468–74) and in children with OCD (n=20, open 12/52, Rosenberg *et al, J Am Acad Child Adolesc Psych* 1999, **38**, 1180–85).

**Sertraline \***

Sertraline is licensed for OCD in adults and also in children and adolescents (dose: 6–12yo 25–50mg/d, 13–17yo, adult dose, no dose increases after less than a week, and lower body weight may require lower doses). Sertraline has been shown to be effective in many studies (eg. n=167, RCT, p/c, 12/52, Kronig *et al, J Clin Psychopharmacol* 1999, **19**, 172–76), with a possible dose-response relationship, eg. 50mg/d and 200mg/d were more potent than 100mg/d, but adverse effects were dose-related (n=324, p/c, Greist, *Arch Gen Psych* 1995, **52**, 289–95). It appears slightly more effective than fluoxetine but was as well-tolerated in an extended OCD trial (n=150, RCT, d/b, 6/12, Bergeron *et al, J Clin Psychopharmacol* 2002, **22**, 148–54). Rapid titration of sertraline to 150mg/d over 5 days may give a faster onset of action in OCD relief with similar tolerability to slower (15 days) titration (n=32, s/b, 12/52, Bogetto *et al, Eur Neuropsychopharm* 2002, **12**, 181–86). A relapse prevention effect has been shown in a maintenance study, where the sertraline group had a lower drop-out than placebo (9% vs 24%), with lower acute exacerbations (12% vs 35%), and with lack of prominent discontinuation symptoms after sertraline cessation (n=649, 223 completers, RCT, 6/12, Koran *et al, Am J Psych* 2002, **159**, 88–95; review by Soomro, *EBMH* 2002, **5**, 115). High dose sertraline (300mg/d) may be effective in treatment-resistant OCD (n=1, Byerly *et al, Am J Psych* 1996, **153**, 1232–33). Reviewed by Perry and Benfield (*CNS Drugs* 1997, **7**, 480–500).

---

**+ Combinations**

**Carbamazepine + clomipramine**

Carbamazepine may be useful as augmentation in refractory OCD (n=1, Iwata *et al, J Clin Psych* 2000, **161**, 528–29).

**Citalopram + clomipramine**

Citalopram plus clomipramine was markedly more effective than clomipramine in treatment-resistant OCD (n=16, open, 3/12, Pallanti *et al, Eur Psychiatry* 1999, **14**, 101–6).

**Clomipramine + risperidone**

Risperidone-augmentation of clomipramine-resistant OCD was effective in 50% (n=14, open, Ravizza *et al, Psychopharmacol Bull* 1996, 32, 677–82).

**Inositol + SSRIs**

One trial showed inositol at 18g/d to significantly reduce Y-BOCS rating scale scores (n=13, d/b, c/o, 6/52, Fux *et al, Am J Psych* 1996, **153**, 1219–21).

30% patients responded to inositol augmentation of SSRIs (n=10, open, Seedat and Stein, *Int Clin Psychopharmacol* 1999, **14**, 353–56).

## Lithium + SSRIs
The only study of lithium augmentation of fluvoxamine was unable to show a clinically significant effect (n=30, d/b, p/c, McDougle *et al, J Clin Psychopharmacol* 1991, **11**, 175–84).

## Pindolol + SSRIs
Pindolol 7.5mg/d may improve the respose to paroxetine in multiple SSRI-resistant OCD (n=14, d/b, p/c, 6/52, Dannon *et al, Eur Neuropsychopharmacol* 2000, **10**, 165–69).

## SSRIs + antipsychotics *
**Risperidone** can augment SSRIs in resistant cases (eg. n=70, RCT, McDougle *et al, Arch Gen Psych* 2000, **57**, 794–801; Ramasubbu, *Arch Gen Psych* 2002, **59**, 472–73), with doses of 3mg/d more effective than lower doses (Baker, *J Clin Psych* 1998, **59**, 131–33). Antipsychotics may improve outcomes in fluvoxamine-resistant OCD (eg. *B J Psych* 1990, **157**, 762–65), including risperidone (n=3, McDougle *et al, J Clin Psych* 1995, **56**, 526–28). **Olanzapine** 5mg/d (43% responders, n=23, open, Bogetto *et al, Psychiatry Res* 2000, **96**, 91–98) has been used eg. olanzapine 2.5mg/d augmented fluoxetine 20mg/d (n=1, Marusic and Farmer, *B J Psych* 2000, **157**, 567) and augmented in SSRI partial responders (n=10; 4 complete and 3 partial responses, case series, open, 8/52, Weiss *et al, J Clin Psych* 1999, **60**, 524–27; n=9, 2/3rds responded, open, 6/52, Francobandiera, *Can J Psych* 2001, **46**, 356–58). **Quetiapine** may be useful as an adjunct in SSRI-resistant OCD (n=10, open, 8/52, Denys *et al, J Clin Psych* 2002, **63**, 700-3) and produced significant improvement in 65% compared to none with placebo augmentation (n=27, s/b, 8/52, Atmaca *et al, Int Clin Psychopharmacol* 2002, **17**, 115–19).

## SSRIs + buspirone
A trial of **fluvoxamine** and buspirone was not successful (McDougle, *Am J Psych* 1993, **150**, 647–49, 819–21), but there are case reports with other SSRIs eg. **sertraline** (n=2, Menkes, *B J Psych* 1995, **167**, 823–24; n=1, Veivia *et al, J Pharm Technology* 1995, **11**, 50–52) and **fluoxetine** (Alessi and Bos, *Am J Psych* 1991, **148**, 1605).

## SSRI + reboxetine *
Adding a NARI to an SSRI may help resolve depression in OCD (n=10, Mancini *et al, J Aff Dis* 2002, **68**, 59–65).

## Tricyclics (combined)
Addition of desipramine to clomipramine in SSRI-resistant OCD patients did not enhance its action (Barr *et al, Am J Psych* 1997, **154**, 1293–95), but addition of nortriptyline 50mg/d to clomipramine 150mg/d produced a more rapid onset of action than clomipramine alone (n=30, RCT, Noorbala *et al, J Clin Pharm Ther* 1998, **23**, 155–59).

---

● **Unlicensed/Some efficacy**
## Citalopram *
Citalopram has been shown to be as effective as fluvoxamine and paroxetine (n=30, s/b, Mundo *et al, J Clin Psychopharmacology* 1997, **17**, 267–71; review by Pato, *Int Clin Psychopharmacol* 1999, **14**[Suppl 2], S19–26). Very high dose citalopram (160mg/d) may be effective in severe, resistant OCD (n=1, Bejerot and Bodlund, *Acta Psych Scand* 1998, **98**, 423–24). Predictors of response include longer duration of more severe illness, no previous SSRI and an adequate dose for adequate duration (RCT, Stein *et al, Int Clin Psychopharmacol* 2001, **16**, 357–61).

## Tricyclics (except clomipramine)
Many tricyclics have been studied and some have been shown to be superior to placebo but generally they are not as potent as clomipramine or the SSRIs, eg. imipramine (Volavka *et al, Psych Res* 1985, **14**, 85–93) and amitriptyline. Nortriptyline (Thoren *et al*,

*Arch Gen Psych* 1980, **37**, 1281–85) has been shown to be ineffective.

○ **Unlicensed/Possible efficacy**
**Antipsychotics** (see combinations)
Some atypicals may have a role as adjunctive therapy in treatment resistant cases (see combinations).

**Gabapentin**
Gabapentin up to 3600mg/d may be useful in patients only partially responsive to fluoxetine 30–100mg/d (n=5, open, 6/52, Cora-Locatelli *et al, J Clin Psych* 1998, **59**, 480–81).

**Phenelzine**
75mg/d was shown to be equipotent with clomipramine 225mg/d in a trial (n=30, d/b, Vallejo *et al, B J Psych* 1992, **161**, 665–70) but in a randomised comparison (n=60, RCT, Jenike *et al, Am J Psych* 1997, **154**, 1261–64), phenelzine 60mg/d was shown to be inferior to fluoxetine (80mg/d) except in patients with asymmetry or other atypical obsession, and no preferential response in patients with high anxiety levels was detected.

**Tramadol**
There is a case of rapid reduction in OCD symptoms with 100mg/d tramadol, allowing fluoxetine to be introduced as the long-term treatment (Goldsmith *et al, Am J Psych* 1999, **156**, 660–61).

**Venlafaxine**
One trial showed a slight positive effect for venlafaxine 225mg/d in OCD (n=16, d/b, p/c, 8/52, Yaryura-Tobias and Neziroglu, *Arch Gen Psych* 1996, **53**, 653–55). There are case reports of response in treatment-resistance and rapidly and dramatically to 150–300mg/d (n=3, Ananth *et al, Am J Psych* 1995, **152**, 1832; Grossman and Hollander, *Am J Psych* 1996, **153**, 576–77).

◇ **Others**
Other drugs tried include **buspirone** (Pato *et al, Am J Psych* 1991, **148**, 127–29; extensive review in *Ann Pharmacother* 1992, **26**, 1248–51; see also combinations), **clonazepam** up to

10mg/d (n=28, d/b, c/o, 6/52, Hewlett *et al, J Clin Psychopharmacol* 1992, **12**, 420–30) and **diphenhydramine** up to 250mg/d (n=28, d/b, c/o, 6/52, Hewlett *et al, J Clin Psychopharmacol* 1992, **12**, 420–30).

♦ **No efficacy**
**Clozapine**
An open study was unable to show any effect for clozapine in refractory OCD (n=10, McDougle *et al, Am J Psych* 1995, **152**, 1812–14). There are a number of reported cases of OCD being unmasked or induced by clozapine (Baker *et al, J Clin Psych* 1992, **53**, 439–42).

**Flutamide**
The anti-androgen flutamide was almost completely ineffective in one trial (n=8, Altemus *et al, J Clin Psych* 1999, **60**, 442–45).

**Oxytocin**
Initial enthusiasm was not confirmed in a study of intranasal administration (n=3, Salzberg and Swedo, *Am J Psych* 1992, **149**, 713–14).

**Tricyclics**
See possible efficacy section.

**Trazodone**
A study showed trazodone up to 300mg/d to be equipotent with placebo (n=21, d/b, c/o, 10/52, Pigott *et al, J Clin Psychopharmacol* 1992, **12**, 156–62).

## 1.24 PANIC DISORDER

See also anxiety (*1.6*)

**Symptoms:***
Panic disorder usually presents as sudden attacks of anxiety, where physical symptoms predominate, peak within 10 minutes and with an associated fear of serious consequences, eg. heart attack. These attacks need to include four of the following: palpitations, abdominal distress/nausea, numbness/tingling, inability to breathe or shortness of breath, choking, sweating, chest pains, dizziness, depersonalisation (common), flushes/chills, fear of dying and trembling/shaking (extensive review by Johnson *et al, Drugs* 1995, **49**, 328–44, 150 refs). Lifetime

prevalence is up to 3.5%, with a point prevalence of 1.5% (males) and 2.8% (females). There is frequently a family history.

**Role of drugs:** *

In general, short-term benefits may be gained with drug therapy. SSRIs are as effective as tricylics long-term, but better tolerated and with a slow onset of action and initial worsening (meta-analysis, 34 RCTs, 9 open, n=2367; Bakker *et al, Acta Psych Scand* 2002, **106**, 163–67; although efficacy may have been overestimated: s=12, Otto *et al, Am J Psych* 2001, **158**, 1989–92). Slow dose titration helps with tolerability. Placebo responders tend to show an early and temporary remission but quality of life does not necessarily improve (Rapaport *et al, Am J Psych* 2000, **157**, 1014–16). CBT should be considered if there is no significant improvement within 6–8 weeks (APA, *Am J Psych* 1998, **155**[Suppl:1–3]). Although paroxetine and clomipramine may be superior to CBT and placebo (SB funded, n=131, d/b, 12/52, Bakker *et al, J Clin Psych* 1999, **60**, 831–38), combined therapy is generally better than for either therapy alone in the maintenance phase (CBT vs. imipramine, a poorly tolerated and less serotonergic agent; n=326, RCT, 12/12, Barlow *et al, JAMA* 2000, **283**, 2529–36; Glass, *JAMA* 2000, **283**, 2573–74). Relapse rates at 6–12 months can be as high as 75% on discontinuation, and so continued treatment and support is necessary in most patients over at least a year (Scott *et al, Adv Psych Treat* 2001, **7**, 275–82). Benzodiazepines have a quicker onset but obvious problems eg. dependence potential and tolerance.

**Reviews:** * general (Rapaport and Barrett, *Curr Psychiatry Rep* 2001, **3**, 295–301; Nash and Nutt, *Prescriber* 2002, **13**, 29–41; Pollack and Marzol, *J Psychopharmacol* 2000, **14**(Suppl 1), S25–30), genetics (van den Heuvel *et al, J Clin Psych* 2000, **61**, 756–66), practice guidelines (APA, *Am J Psych* 1998, **155** May Suppl), refractory panic (Mathew *et al, Psychopharmacol Bull*

2001, **35**, 97–110; Slaap and den Boer, *Depress Anxiety* 2001, **14**, 112–22), and the risk-benefit with pharmacotherapy (Bennett *et al, Drug Safety* 1998, **18**, 419–30, 92 refs).

**BNF Listed**

**Benzodiazepines** *

Benzodiazepines are rapidly effective and so are useful in patients needing immediate relief (review by Kasper and Resinger, *Eur Neuropsychopharmacol* 2001, **11**, 307–21), although claims for their effectiveness have been strongly challenged (Marks *et al, Arch Gen Psych* 1989, **46**, 668–70). Many benzodiazepines have been studied eg. **alprazolam** at 2–6mg/d (n=69, open, Kilic *et al, Psychother Psychosom* 1997, **66**, 175–78), which may be no better than placebo for anxiety, better for hostility but produce more aggression in response to provocation (n=23, d/b, p/c, Bond *et al, J Aff Dis* 1995, **35**, 117–23). **Clonazepam** is longer-acting, with 1–2mg/d the best balance between benefit and tolerability (n=413, RCT, p/c, 13/52, Rosenbaum *et al, J Clin Psychopharmacol* 1997, **17**, 390–400). Early coadministration of clonazepam with sertraline may facilitate early improvement in panic symptoms (n=50, RCT, d/b, Goddard *et al, Arch Gen Psych* 2001, **58**, 681–86). **Diazepam** may also be effective (n=241, RCT, p/c, d/b, 8/52, Noyes *et al, J Clin Psych* 1996, **57**, 349–55). The main problems are discontinuation, where relapse may be more common with shorter-acting benzodiazepines, eg. alprazolam (n=50, Noyes *et al, Am J Psych* 1991, **148**, 517–23) and transfer to an SSRI in due course is advised. People with panic disorder may have abnormal benzodiazepine receptors (*Biol Psych* 1989, **26**, 744–48).

**Reviews:** general (Davidson, *J Clin Psych* 1997, **58**[Suppl 2], 26–28).

**Citalopram** *

The starting dose for citalopram in panic disorder is 10mg/d for one week, increasing to 20–30mg/d as the optimum dose (n=475, RCT, p/c, d/b,

8/52, Wade *et al, B J Psych* 1997, **170**, 549–53), to a maximum of 60mg/d. Citalopram may also control phobic symptoms in panic, especially at 20–30mg/d (n=475, RCT, 8/52, Leinonen *et al, J Psychiatry Neurosci* 2000, **25**, 25–32). After an 8-week trial (n=475), an optional continuation phase (n=279) showed 20–60mg/d citalopram to be effective and well tolerated over one year (n=279, RCT, d/b, 8/52, Lepola *et al, J Clin Psych* 1998, **59**, 528–34). It appears quicker acting than paroxetine, but equipotent (n=58, RCT, s/b, 60/7, Perna *et al, Pharmacopsychiatry* 2001, **34**, 85–90).

### Escitalopram *

Escitalopram is licensed in UK for panic disorder, with or without agoraphobia. The initial dose is 5mg/d for the first week, then 10mg/d, increasing to a maximum of 20mg/d.

### Paroxetine *

Paroxetine is licensed for panic disorder and for the prevention of relapse. A 10mg/d starting dose is recommended. Large studies have shown a significant effect, eg. as effective as citalopram (n=58, RCT, s/b, 60/7, Perna *et al, Pharmacopsychiatry* 2001, **34**, 85–90) and as effective as clomipramine but with a more rapid onset of action and less side-effects (eg. n=367, d/b, p/c, 12/52, Lecrubier *et al, Acta Psych Scand* 1997, **95**, 145–52). Continued improvement is maintained with low drop-outs (n=176, RCT, d/b, p/c, 36/52 follow-on, Lecrubier *et al, Acta Psych Scand* 1997, **95**, 153–60) and with an optimum effective dose of 40mg/d (n=278, d/b, p/c, Ballenger *et al, Am J Psych* 1998, **155**, 36–42). In a multicentre RCT, paroxetine plus CBT was significantly more effective than placebo plus cognitive therapy in reducing the number of panic attacks in the study group, as well as being well tolerated (n=120, Oehrberg *et al, B J Psych* 1995, **167**, 374–79).

### Tricyclics *

Tricyclics are established as effective in panic disorder. They may take 4 weeks to start to work and 12 weeks for maximal effect. Initial jitteriness is a common problem and so it is usually necessary to start at a low dose (10–25mg/d) and warn patients that they may feel more jittery and anxious initially (n=81, RCT, p/c, 8/52, Uhlenhuth *et al, J Aff Dis* 1989, **17**, 261–70). **Clomipramine** has been shown to be effective at less than 100mg/d (eg. n=180, d/b, Caillard *et al, Acta Psych Scand* 1999, **99**, 51–58) and with a biphasic response, symptoms worsening over 12 weeks before improving. It is as effective as paroxetine in panic disorder, but with a slower onset of action and more side-effects (n=367, d/b, p/c, 12/52, Lecrubier *et al, Acta Psych Scand* 1997, **95**, 145–52), and with efficacy maintained over 36 weeks (Lecrubier *et al, Acta Psych Scand* 1997, **95**, 153–60). **Imipramine** is effective (*vs* placebo) in all studies using doses above 150mg/d (*B J Psych* 1989, **155**[Suppl 6], 46–52). Long-term maintenance is needed for most patients, especially with a high baseline BDI and who need higher doses to reach remission (n=51, RCT, Lotufo-Neto *et al, J Clin Psychopharmacol* 2001, **15**, 13–17), weight gain was a specific and significant effect, as are dry mouth, sweating and increased heart rate, but sexual dysfunction decreases over time (n=51, RCT, p/c, d/b, 12/12, Mavissakalian *et al, J Clin Psychopharmacol* 2002, **22**, 155–61). A 2-year follow-up shows a continued and substantial prophylactic efficacy (n=18, RCT, Mavissakalian and Perel, *Ann Clin Psych* 2001, **13**, 63–67). Early detection of relapse may be a viable alternative to long-term therapy (n=51, RCT, d/b, 12/12, Mavissakalian and Perel, *J Clin Psychopharmacol* 2002, **22**, 294–99).

---

● **Unlicensed/Some efficacy**

### MAOIs

Phenelzine at 45–90mg/d may be at least as effective as imipramine in patients with panic attacks as part of 'endogenous depression' (n=35, open,

6/12, Buiges and Vallejo, *J Clin Psych* 1987, **48**, 55–59) and in atypical depression with panic attacks (n=119, RCT, d/b, p/c, Liebowitz *et al, Arch Gen Psych* 1988, **45**, 129–37). Generally considered third line for tricyclic-resistant cases.

### SSRIs (except paroxetine, escitalopram and citalopram, which are licensed) *

**Fluoxetine** is effective when initial doses are kept very low (2.5–5 mg/d) then increased, as higher doses produce side-effects as well as anxiety and over-stimulation, possibly due to serotonergic supersensitivity. Fluoxetine 20mg/d is clearly superior to placebo over a range of symptoms in panic disorder (n=243, RCT, Michelson *et al, Am J Psych* 1998, **155**, 1570–77; RCT, p/c, 24/52, Michelson *et al, B J Psych* 1999, **174**, 213–18). If there is no response by 6/52, it may benefit from an increase up to 60mg/d (12/52, RCT, Michelson *et al, B J Psych* 2001, **179**, 514–18). Once weekly fluoxetine dosing (10–60mg/week) has proved successful as maintenance over two years (n=10, open, 24/12, Emmanuel *et al, J Clin Psych* 1999, **60**, 299–301). **Sertraline** has been shown to be superior to placebo in reducing panic attacks, with no advantage of a dose above 50mg/d (n=178, multisite d/b, p/c, Londborg *et al, B J Psych* 1998, **173**, 54–60), well tolerated (eg. n=168, RCT, 10/52, Pohl *et al, Am J Psych* 1998, **155**, 1189–95) and in preventing relapse compared to abrupt withdrawal (n=183, 52+28/52, Rapaport *et al, Acta Psych Scand* 2001, **104**, 289–98). Pooled data indicates that sertraline is an effective treatment for panic disorder, even in people with risk factors for poor response (n=664, s=4, d/b, Pollack *et al, J Clin Psych* 2000, **61**, 922–27), with early response predicting final remission, a useful aid to decision making (n=544, p/c, Pollack *et al, J Psych Res* 2002, **36**, 229–36). **Fluvoxamine** compared favourably with placebo and cognitive therapy (n=55, RCT, p/c, 8/52, Black *et al,*

*Arch Gen Psych* 1993, **50**, 44–50) and is equipotent with clomipramine *Arch Gen Psych* 1990, **47**, 926–32) and cognitive therapy (n=32, RCT, d/b, c/o, Pigott *et al, Arch Gen Psych* 1993, **50**, 44–50), but not all placebo trials have shown efficacy. It may have a biphasic response, with symptoms worsening over 12 weeks before improving, although one study noted a potent anti-panic action with a relatively rapid onset (n=188, RCT, p/c, 8/52, Asnis *et al, Psychiatr Res* 2001, **103**, 1–14).

### Venlafaxine
One trial suggested low-dose (mean 47mg/d) venlafaxine may be highly effective in panic attacks (n=13, open, 10/52, Papp *et al, Psychopharmacol Bull* 1998, **34**, 207–9).

---

### ○ Unlicensed/Possible efficacy

### Inositol *
Inositol 12g/d improved panic symptoms, whereas lorazepam did not (n=25, d/b, p/c, c/o, 4/52, Benjamin *et al, Am J Psych* 1995, **152**, 1084–86) and was superior to fluvoxamine 150mg/d in reducing panic attacks (n=20, RCT, c/o, 8/52, Palatnik *et al, J Clin Psychopharmacol* 2001, **21**, 335–39).

### Moclobemide *
In one study, the long-term effects of CBT were enhanced with concomitant moclobemide 600mg/d (n=55, RCT, 8/52, Loerch *et al, B J Psych* 1999, **174**, 205–12) but moclobemide was ineffective as monotherapy. Comparisons with clomipramine (n=135, RCT, 8/52, Kruger and Dahl, *Eur Arch Psych Clin Neurosci* 1999, **249**(Suppl 1), S7-10) and fluoxetine (RCT, d/b, 8/52, Tiller *et al, Eur Arch Psych Clin Neurosci* 1999, **249**(Suppl 1), S19–24) showed similar efficacy but the comparator drugs may have been at subtherapeutic doses.

### Mirtazapine *
Mirtazapine may be a rapidly effective alternative to SSRIs for panic (n=28, RCT, open, 12/52, Boshuisen *et al, Int Clin Psychopharmacol* 2001,

**16**, 363–68). 60% patients showed a sustained response to mirtazapine at 16 weeks (n=10, open, Carpenter *et al, Ann Clin Psychiatry* 1999, **11**, 81–86) and it may be effective in treatment-intolerant individuals (n=2, Berigan and Harazin, *Primary Psych* 1999, **6**, 36; n=15, open, Carli and Sarchiapone, *Arch Gen Psych* 2002, **59**, 661). Mirtazapine was similar in efficacy and tolerability to fluoxetine in one trial (n=27, RCT, 8/52, Ribeiro *et al, Braz J Med Biol Res* 2001, **34**, 1303–7).

**Nefazodone \***
A small study (n=14, open, 8/52, Demartinis *et al, J Clin Psych* 1996, **57**, 245–48), but it may increase anxiety (Strohle and Ehrenthal, *J Clin Psychopharmacol* 2002, **22**, 95–96).

**Oxcarbazepine**
Increasing an oxcarbazepine dose from 600mg/d to 900mg/d has successfully treated panic disorder (n=1, Windhaber *et al, J Clin Psych* 1997, **58**, 404–5).

**Pindolol \***
Augmentation of SSRIs has been suggested (see Mathew *et al, Psychopharmacol Bull* 2001, **35**, 97–110).

**Pramipexole \***
Successful augmentation of SSRIs with pramipexole up to 1.5mg/d has been reported (n=2, Marazziti *et al, Am J Psych* 2001, **158**, 498–99).

**Reboxetine \***
Reboxetine was well-tolerated and reduced panic attacks and anxiety in a pilot study (n=29, open, 6/52, Dannon *et al, Hum Psychopharmacol* 2002, **17**, 329–33) and 6-8mg/d was effective and well-tolerated for panic (with or without agoraphobia) on most measures (n=82, RCT, d/b, p/c, 8/52, Versiani *et al, J Clin Psych* 2002, **63**, 31–37).

**Valproate**
Valproate 1500mg/d may be useful for resistant panic disorder (eg. cases by Marazziti and Giovanni, *Am J Psych* 1996, **153**, 842–43; Roberts *et al, Am J Psych* 1994, **151**, 1521). Divalproex sodium (300–600mg/d) improved affective symptoms, parti-

cularly panic, in all 10 study completers, in patients with panic disorder and mood instability who have not responded to conventional therapy (n=13, open, 8/52, Baetz and Bowen, *Can J Psychiatry* 1998, **43**, 73–77).

◊ **Others**
Other drugs tried include **carbamazepine** (Tondo *et al, Am J Psych* 1989, **146**, 558–59; review by Keck *et al, J Clin Psychopharmacol* 1992, **12**[Suppl] 36S–41S), **clonidine** (reviewed by Puzantian and Hart, *Ann Pharmacother* 1993,**27**, 1351–53), **ondansetron** (Schneier *et al, Anxiety* 1996, **2**, 199–202), **propranolol** (n=29, RCT, 6/52, Ravatis *et al, J Clin Psychopharmacol* 1991, **11**, 344–50) and **trazodone** (n=74, d/b, 8/52, Charney *et al, J Clin Psych* 1986, **47**, 580–86).

♦ **No efficacy**
**Buspirone**
Buspirone was not superior to placebo in one study (d/b, c/o, *J Clin Psych* 1988, **49**[8, Suppl], 30–36) nor in combination with CBT (n=77, RCT, Bouvard *et al, Psychother Psychosom* 1997, **66**, 27–32).

**Caffeine**
Caffeine is anxiogenic and panic patients seem to be more sensitive to its effects (*Am J Psych* 1988, **145**, 632–35).

**Maprotiline**
This has been shown to be ineffective at doses of up to 150mg/d (*Int Clin Psychopharmacol* 1988, **3**, 59–74).

## 1.25 POST-TRAUMATIC STRESS DISORDER

**Symptoms:**
PTSD is an anxiety disorder resulting from an extreme stressful event, eg. serious threat to life or involvement of a loved one in a catastrophic event, and where a personal vulnerability exists. The person then re-experiences the event recurrently by dreams, feelings etc. PTSD may be quite common yet often unrecognised and may lead to significant morbidity and mortality.

The lifetime prevalence may be 1–9%. A number of sub-types of PTSD have now been recognised (*Curr Opin Psych* 1995, **8**, 98–101). Severe trauma can produce long-lasting neurobiological changes and drugs that affect these changes may thus have a beneficial effect. Interestingly, only drugs with a significant effect on the serotonin system seem to work.

### Role of drugs: *
Drug treatment is still relatively poorly studied but from current data it seems that 'positive' symptoms (eg. nightmares etc) respond better whereas 'negative' symptoms of avoidance (eg. social withdrawal etc) are less responsive to drugs. There is an almost total lack of response to placebo in chronic PTSD. Most drugs shown to be active are also antidepressants, although depression and PTSD are quite distinct entities (eg. Dinan *et al, Biol Psych* 1990, **28**, 665–72). SSRIs, TCAs and phenelzine increase response rates (comment by McCleery, *EBMH* 2001, **4**, 54). Higher doses for longer periods (at least 5 weeks) seem necessary.

**Reviews:*** general (Kilic, *Acta Psych Scand* 2001, **104**, 409–11; Cyr and Farrar, *Ann Pharmacother* 2000, **34**, 366–76, 99 refs; McIvor, *Progress Neurol Psych* 1998, **2**, 18–21; Turner, *Lancet* 1999, **354**, 1404–5, 7 refs; Cyr and Farrar, *Ann Pharmacother* 2000, **34**, 366–76, 99 refs), pharmacotherapy (Pearlstein, *J Clin Psych* 2000, **61**[Suppl 7], 40–43; WFSBP Guidelines, Bandelow *et al, World J Biol Psych* 2002, **3**, 171–99; Davis *et al, Expert Opin Pharmacother* 2001, **2**, 1583–95; Hageman *et al, Acta Psych Scand* 2001, **104**, 411–22).

---

### BNF Listed
### Paroxetine *
Paroxetine is now licensed in the UK for PTSD, with a standard 20mg dose, increasing gradually to 50mg/d if needed. Paroxetine 20mg and 40mg/d has been shown to be effective and well-tolerated in adults (both male and female) with chronic PTSD (n=551, RCT, p/c, 12/52, Marshall *et al, Am J Psych* 2001, **158**, 1982–88) and reduces disability after 12 weeks treatment (n=307, d/b, p/c, 12/52, Tucker *et al, J Clin Psych* 2001, **62**, 960–68). It has also been used successfully for post-traumatic grief (n=15, open, Zygmont *et al, J Clin Psych* 1998, **59**, 241–45) and non-combat-related, chronic PTSD (n=17, open, 12/52, Marshall *et al, J Clin Psychopharmacol* 1998, **18**, 10–18).

### Sertraline *
Sertraline is now licensed in the UK for PTSD, but may only be effective in women. Two main trials in PTSD show sertraline (mean dose 150mg/d) superior to placebo in measures of global and functional outcomes and symptom severity (n=187, RCT, 12/52, Brady *et al, JAMA* 2000, **283**, 1837–44; critical review by Bisson, *EBMH* 2000, **3**, 109) and sertraline 50–200mg/d produced a 60% response rate (cf. 38% with placebo), and was well-tolerated (n=208, RCT, p/c, 12/52, Davidson *et al, Arch Gen Psych* 2001, **58**, 485–92). It seems particularly effective in treating psychological symptoms of PTSD eg. anger, anhedonia, detachment and numbing as opposed to somatic symptoms eg. insomnia, exaggerated startle response etc (n=400, 12/52, Davidson *et al, Psychol Med* 2002, **32**, 661–70). Two open-label continuation studies have shown a prophylactic effect eg. relapse rates with sertraline (5%, mean dose 137 mg/d) were lower than placebo (26%) in those responding to a 12-week acute phase (n=96, open, 24/52, Davidson *et al, Am J Psych* 2001, **158**, 1974–81) and 92% who completed the 12/52 RCT maintained response over the next six months and 54% of the non-responders converted to response (n=128, open 24/52, Londberg *et al, J Clin Psych* 2001, 62, 325–31). **Review**: Schwartz and Rothbaum, *Expert Opin Pharmacother* 2002, **3**, 1489–99.

### ● Unlicensed/Some efficacy
**Fluoxetine**

Fluoxetine (up to 60mg/d) was shown to be superior to placebo in civilians with PTSD (41% response), with a low placebo response rate of 4% (n=53, RCT, p/c, 12/52, Connor *et al, B J Psych* 1999, **175**, 17–22), confirming previous studies (particularly regarding avoidant symptoms, n=64, RCT, 5/52, van der Kolk *et al, J Clin Psych* 1994, **55**, 517–22). Care may be needed initially with use in patients with co-morbid panic attacks, as fluoxetine may increase panic/anxiety (short review of fluoxetine in PTSD by Marshall *et al, Am J Psych* 1995, **152**, 1238–39), so start low and go slow.

**MAOIs\***

Phenelzine exerted a notable effect on intrusive and avoidance symptoms (n=60, RCT, d/b, 8/52, Kosten *et al, J Nerv Ment Dis* 1991, **179**, 366–70). The strong inhibitory effect on REM sleep may be contributory.

**Tricyclics\***

Amitriptyline (Davidson *et al, Arch Gen Psych* 1990, **4**, 259–69) and imipramine (n=60, RCT, p/c, 8/52, Kosten *et al, J Nerv Ment Dis* 1991, **179**, 366–70) have been shown to produce a modest and clinically meaningful effect. The main feature is that doses of 300mg/d for at least 8 weeks are needed.

### ● Unlicensed/Possible efficacy
**Antipsychotics\***

Antipsychotics are generally considered to be poorly effective. Lack of effect from **olanzapine** at up to 20mg/d in PTSD has been shown (n=15, RCT, d/b, p/c, 10/52, Butterfield *et al, Int Clin Psychopharmacol* 2001, **16**, 197–203), although an open study showed some effects in psychotic symptoms of combat-induced PTSD (n=48, open, 8/52, Petty *et al, Int Clin Psychopharmacol* 2001, **16**, 331–37) and in people unresponsive to 12 weeks SSRI at maximum tolerated dose, addition of olanzapine was significantly superior to placebo on

some specific measures but not global response (n=19, d/b, p/c, 8/52, Stein *et al, Am J Psych* 2002, **159**, 1777–79). **Quetiapine** has improved symptoms in resistant PTSD (n=1, Sattar *et al, Ann Pharmacother* 2002, **36**, 1875–78). Adjunctive **risperidone** in combat resistant PTSD was well tolerated and produced a modest improvement (n=40, RCT, d/b, p/c, 5/52, Hamner *et al, Int Clin Psychopharmacol* 2003, **18**, 1–8) and at 1mg/d has been highly effective for hyperarousal, irritable aggression and dyscontrol (n=1, Monnelly and Ciraulo, *J Clin Psychopharmacol* 1999, **19**, 377. **Clozapine** has been used successfully in co-morbid psychosis and PTSD (n=1, Hamner, *Am J Psych* 1996, **153**, 841).

**Benzodiazepines\***

The potential anti-arousal effect could be useful and beneficial effects have been seen with alprazolam (n=16, RCT, d/b, c/o, Braun *et al, J Clin Psych* 1990, **51**, 236–38) and clonazepam at 4–5mg/d (n=13, open, 6/12, Gelpin *et al, J Clin Psych* 1996, **57**, 390–94). Care is needed with possible abuse, induction of depression and the potential for the release of impulsive or antisocial behaviour and severe withdrawal reactions (n=8, Risse *et al, J Clin Psych* 1990, **51**, 206–9). Controlled trials have not been able to substantiate an effect.

**Bupropion\***

In one study, bupropion decreased depressive symptoms and most patients reported global improvement, although PTSD symptoms remained mostly unchanged (n=17, open, Canive *et al, J Clin Psychopharmacol* 1998, **18**, 379–83; expert consensus guidelines in *J Clin Psych* 2000, **61**, 1–76).

**Buspirone\***

Open studies have suggested some efficacy on all symptom clusters (eg. Hamner *et al, Depress Anxiety* 1997, **5**, 137–39), including aggression, and possibly with a rapid onset (n=1, Duffy, *Ann Clin Psych* 1992, **4**, 193–96).

## Carbamazepine*

Some effect on hyperarousal, hostility and intrusive symptoms has been reported (eg. Wolf *et al, Biol Psych* 1988, **23**, 642–44), with a small study (Lipper *et al, Psychosomatics* 1986, **27**, 849–54) and case report (Looff *et al, J Am Acad Child Adolesc Psych* 1995, **34**, 703–4).

## Gabapentin*

Successful use has been reported (n=2, Berigan, *J Clin Psych* 2002, **63**, 744) and there is one case series (n=30, Hamner *et al, Ann Clin Psych* 2001, **13**, 141–46).

## Liothyronine/triiodothyronine*

25mcg/d has been used successfully to significantly augment the effect of ineffective SSRI (fluoxetine or paroxetine 40mg/d) monotherapy (n=5, Agid *et al, J Clin Psych* 2001, **62**, 169–73).

## Mirtazapine*

A number of studies have suggested an effect eg. in a pilot study of 45mg/d, 50% showed a 50% or more improvement (n=6, open, 8/52, Connor *et al, Int Clin Psychopharmacol* 1999, **14**, 29–31), it was effective and well tolerated in PTSD in Korea (n=15, open, 8/52, Bahk *et al, Hum Psychopharmacol* 2002, **17**, 341–44) and in PTSD nightmares, mirtazapine may have some significant effects, perhaps by an effect on sleep (n >300, Lewis, *Am J Psych* 2002, **159**, 1948–49).

## Nefazodone

Some open trials have suggested some efficacy (eg. n=12, open, 12/52, Gillin *et al, J Clin Psych* 2001, **62**, 789–96; n=14, 9/52, Garfield *et al, J Trauma Stress* 2001, **14**, 453–60; n=19, open, Zisook *et al, J Clin Psych* 2000, **61**, 203–8) and where three primary PTSD symptom clusters, sleep and anger improved (n=10, open, 12/52, Hertzberg *et al, J Clin Psych* 1998, **59**, 460–64).

## Prazosin*

Prazosin (mean dose 9.6mg/d) may reduce nightmares in veterans with chronic PTSD if taken for at least 8/52 (n=59, retrospective chart analysis, Raskind *et al, J Clin Psych* 2002, **63**, 565–68).

## SSRIs*

**Citalopram** was partly effective in 2 cases (n=2, Khouzam *et al, Mil Med* 2001, **166**, 921–23). **Fluoxetine** 20–80mg/d was superior to placebo and effective for PTSD at a mean dose of 57mg/d (n=226 + 75, RCT, d/b, p/c, 12/52, Martenyi *et al, J Clin Psych* 2002, **63**, 199–206) and for relapse prevention (n=131, RCT, p/c, d/b, 6/12, Martenyi *et al, B J Psych* 2002, **181**, 315–20). **Fluvoxamine** 100–300mg/d (mean 150mg) appeared to improve combat-related PTSD but not depressive symptoms (n=15, open, 14/52, Escalona *et al, Depress Anxiety* 2002, **15**, 29–33). Dreams linked to the traumatic experience may also respond, although not insomnia (n=21, open, 10/52, Neylan *et al, J Trauma Stress* 2001, **14**, 461–67). An open trial in Vietnam veterans showed an effect at 4–6 weeks, maintained at 10 weeks (Marmar *et al, J Clin Psych* 1996, **57**[Suppl 8], 66–70).

## Topiramate*

A naturalistic review showed a rapid effect on PTSD symptoms for add-on or adjunctive topiramate (n=35, open, Berlant and van Kammen, *J Clin Psych* 2002, **63**, 15–20).

## Trazodone*

A small open study suggested an effect (n=6, Hertzberg *et al, J Clin Psychopharmacol* 1996, **1**, 294–98).

## Valproate

Intrusion, hyperarousal and depressive symptoms may respond to valproate, (n=16, 8/52, Clark *et al, J Trauma Stress* 1999, **12**, 395–401) and use in combat-related PTSD has been reported (Fesler, *J Clin Psych* 1991, **52**, 361–64).

◊ **Others**

Other drugs tried include **propranolol** at 120–160mg/d (mentioned in *B J Psych* 1992, **160**, 309–14), **clonidine** for self-mutilatory behaviour (*J Aff Dis* 1987, **13**, 203–13) and as an adjunct to **imipramine** (Kinkie and

Leung, *J Nerv Ment Dis* 1989, **177**, 546–50), **cyproheptadine** for nightmares (eg. Brophy, *Mil Med* 1991, **156**, 100–1) and **lithium** (Kitchner and Greenstein, *Military Med* 1985, **150**, 378–81).

♦ **No efficacy**

**Flumazenil** *

Two studies have shown no effects (eg. Coupland *et al, Biol Psych* 1997, **41**, 988–90).

**Naltrexone** *

Only non-significant subtle improvements were seen in a small, short trial (n=8, open, 2/52, Lubin *et al, Hum Psychopharmacol* 2002, **17**, 181–85).

---

**PSYCHIATRIC EMERGENCY, ACUTE**

See acute psychiatric emergency (*1.1*).

---

**1.26 PSYCHOSIS AND SCHIZOPHRENIA**

See also catatonia (*1.12*)

---

**Symptoms:**

Schizophrenia can be considered a 'perceptive disorder' and Schneider's 'First rank symptoms' are often quoted as the main diagnostic features. They include hearing thoughts spoken aloud, 'third person' hallucinations, hallucinations in the form of a commentary, somatic hallucinations, thought withdrawal or insertion, thought broadcasting, delusional perceptions and feelings or actions experienced as being made or influenced by external agents.

Schizophrenics most frequently have a lack of insight, auditory hallucinations, ideas of reference, suspiciousness, flatness of affect, voices speaking to them, delusional mood, delusions of persecution and thoughts spoken aloud.

**Possible causes of schizophrenia:**

The dopamine hypothesis, ie. excess dopamine activity in the mesolimbic remains the most widely quoted theory, but is clearly not the whole story and there are many other theories eg. hypofunction of the glutamate sys-

tems, particularly at the NMDA subtype of glutamate receptor, combined dopamine hyperfunction and glutamate hypofunction (*Am J Psych* 2001, **158**, 1393–99; extensive review by Goff and Coyle, *Am J Psych* 2001, **158**, 1367–77, 148 refs) and 5-HT$_2$ hyperfunction. The balance between D$_2$ and 5-HT$_2$ may be important. Abnormal connections between nerves involving amino acid neurotransmitters may be a consequence of developmentally reduced synaptic connectivity (during perinatal and adolescent periods) rather than loss of neuronal or glial cells (McGlashan and Hoffman, *Arch Gen Psych* 2000, **57**, 637–48).

Antipsychotics are thought to exert a significant part of their clinical effect via blockade of mesolimbic (Farrison, *Lancet* 2000, **356**, 958–59) D$_2$ receptors (the 'short' D$_2$ receptors). Although receptor blockade takes hours and the clinical effect takes weeks, it has been noted that homovanillic acid (the principal metabolite of dopamine) levels take several weeks (not hours or days) to decrease. Other theories include thalamic glutamatergic dysfunction.

**Role of drugs in schizophrenia:** *

Antipsychotics have a major role in the treatment of schizophrenic illnesses. Two separate treatment phases can be considered:

**1. Acute phase:** *

Many antipsychotics have an immediate calming effect, which is useful in relieving patient distress in the acute stage, and then reducing the intensity of psychotic experiences, the onset usually being delayed by one or two weeks from the start of full-dose treatment. There is little proven advantage of using higher doses of drugs, eg. above about 12–15mg/d of high-potency antipsychotics (eg. haloperidol) and higher doses give the recipient a bad experience. Naturalistic studies have suggested that patients most at risk of excessive antipsychotic dosing include those on depots, Afro-Americans, with a history of hospitalisations and being more thought disor-

**The Royal College of Psychiatrists 1994: Consensus statement
on 'The Use of High-Dose Antispsychotic Medication'**
(Thompson, *B J Psych* 1994, **164**, 448–58)

The upper end of BNF antipsychotic does ranges is often not clearly established and usually defined by limits of safety and the SPC. The BNF states that doses above these limits should only be used 'with caution and under specialist supervision'. 'Chlorpromazine equivalents' have been used to compare drugs or calculate total doses of multiple drugs but maximum doses vary between drugs and dosage equivalents are of only limited use (see *2.2.1*). BNF maximum doses can also be used. The evidence and scientific rationale for the effectiveness of high doses is limited.

**Main dangers of high dose antipsychotics:**
1. Sudden cardiac-related death — eg. QT prolongation etc.
2. CNS toxicity, eg. CNS and respiratory depression, hypoxia, seizures etc.

**Main uses of antipsychotics above BNF limits:**
1. **Psychiatric Emergency**: See Acute Psychiatric Emergency (Chapter *1.1*).
2. **Acute Treatment**: ie. after the emergency, but before the antipsychotic takes full effect. Doses should be reduced as soon as possible, once the patient has responded. ECT can be a suitable alternative.
3. **Long-term treatment**: eg. in treatment-resistant schizophrenia where residual symptoms impair living or rehabilitation:
   i) **As polypharmacy**: the BNF describes the prescribing of multiple antipsychotics as 'not recommended' as it 'may constitute a hazard' and side-effects are not minimised.
   ii) **Poor resources**: Inadequate resources/environment often result in the need for more medication at higher doses.

**Factors to be considered before prescribing high-dose antipsychotics:**
a. the diagnosis is fully correct
b. plasma levels are therapeutic and drug compliance occurring/assured
c. treatment duration has been fully adequate
d. reduced doses for a trial period have been tried
e. adverse social and psychological factors minimised
f. alternative drug therapies tried, eg. 'atypicals', lithium, antidepressants, carbamazepine, etc

**If exceeding BNF antipsychotic doses, the following should be routine:**
a. multidisciplinary team and patient (or advocate) discussion, obtaining valid consent if possible, making a thorough record of the decision and reasoning, including target signs and symptoms, and outcome evaluation.
b. consideration of any contra-indications, eg. cardiac, age, renal, hepatic, weight, smoker etc., and any interactions, eg. with tricyclics, terfenadine etc.
c. ECG pre-treatment to exclude 'QT' prolongation, repeated every 1–3 months.
d. doses increased only slowly.
e. regular checks carried out on pulse, bp, temperature and hydration
f. Prescription reviewed regularly and reduced after 3 months if no improvement.

See also Jusic and Lader, *B J Psych* 1994, **165**, 789–91. Polypharmacy is still widespread in the UK (Chaplin and McGuigan, *Psych Bull*, 1996, **20**, 452–54) which may in part be a result of the 'Consensus Statement' as prescribers may now use several drugs at lower dose instead of one at higher dose and now partly as a result of non-evidence-based augmentation with atypicals.

| Antipsychotics in early-onset or first-episode schizophrenia/psychosis * | |
|---|---|
| **Aims of treatment** | <ul><li>Minimise harm from illness and side effects from drugs</li><li>Minimise deterioration (user/carers/relatives) by optimising compliance</li><li>Reduce stigma from symptoms aiming for complete, not incomplete, remission</li><li>Increase engagement by minimising adverse experience with medication through use of minimum effective doses</li></ul> |

**Principles of Pharmacological management** (Carpenter, *Am J Psych* 2001, **158**, 1771–73)

| | |
|---|---|
| **Early intervention with effective antipsychotics** | <ul><li>Produces better outcomes (n=53, 13/12 follow-up, Malla *et al, Psychiatr Serv* 2002, **53**, 458–63) and response more likely (review, McGorry *et al, Curr Opin Psych* 2000, **13**, 37–43)</li><li>Delays in diagnosis leads to longer untreated psychosis (n=43, Larsen *et al, Schizophr Bull* 1996, **22**, 241–56). If the DUP (Delay in Untreated Psychosis) is less than 2 yrs, response may be more likely (n=88, Malla *et al, Schizophr Res* 2002, 54, 231–42; McGlashan, *Biol Psych* 1999, **46**, 899–907; n=248 consecutive admissions, Drake *et al, B J Psych* 2000, **157**, 511–15), but some evidence indicates that DUP is not important (n=53, Barnes *et al, Br J Psych* 2000, **177**, 207–11), although there are psychosocial consequences of a long DUP.</li><li>Substance misuse early in the illness has been linked with increased severity of illness, many starting misuse in the month or so before onset of the illness (n=232, Bühler *et al, Schizophr Res* 2002, **54**, 234–51).</li></ul> |
| **Drug dose** | <ul><li>Slow titration needed - both introduction and discontinuation</li><li>Early intervention allows optimum use of low doses (Tauscher and Kapur, *CNS Drugs* 2001, **15**, 671–78)</li></ul> |
| **Patient preference essential** | <ul><li>Consider what patient prefers (weight gain being the most unpopular of side effects and it's impact on the user must not be trivialised)</li><li>Explain that there is no clear way of treating prodromal symptoms without the high risk of treating false positives (Larsen *et al, Acta Psych Scand* 2001, **103**, 323–34)</li></ul> |
| **Duration of treatment** | <ul><li>The relapse rate over 5 years is high (n=104, Robinson *et al, Arch Gen Psych* 1999, **56**, 241–47). On discontinuation up to 78% may experience an exacerbation or relapse within one year and 96% may do so within 2 years (n=53, RCT, open, 18/12, Gitlin *et al, Am J Psych* 2001, **158**, 1835–42). Thus patients should be advised that not taking antipsychotics for several years will almost inevitably lead to relapse and re-hospitalisation.</li></ul> |
| **Drugs choice should consider that:** | <ul><li>Minimal "obvious" ADRs make patient look different, which reduces compliance/engagement (n=42, Amminger *et al, Schizophr Res* 2002, **54**, 223–30)</li><li>Older drugs have high incidence of EPS, raised prolactin and adverse cognitive effects</li><li>Newer drugs have higher incidence of weight gain (which should be dealt with early, not after it has happened) and diabetes</li></ul> |

---

**Choice of antipsychotic in early onset/first episode schizophrenia/psychosis***

The evidence base is limited at the moment but growing, with most evidence for risperidone and olanzapine, although there is no reason to believe that other antipsychotics would not also be effective.

| | |
|---|---|
| **Risperidone** | A mean dose of 2.7mg/d appears effective and safe in first-episode psychosis (n=24, 6/12, Yap *et al, Singapore Med J* 2001, **42**, 170–73), with doses better below 4mg/d, with slow titration highly effective (Williams, *J Clin Psych* 2001, **62**, 282–89; RCT, n=183, 6/52, Emsley, *Schizophr Bull* 1999 **25**, 721–29). Risperidone may be superior to typicals, with a lower relapse rate (n=19×2, Malla *et al, J Clin Psych* 2001, **62**, 179–84), with particular improvements in sustained attention, vigilance, speed of processing (n=17, 8/52, Hong *et al, Schizophr Res* 2002, **53**, 7–16). Even very low dose (1–1.8mg/d) can produce dramatic improvements in prodromal phase or first episode schizophrenia (n=10, open, 12/52, Cannon *et al, Am J Psych* 2002, **159**, 1230–32; n=436, open, 2yrs, Fraile *et al, Actas Esp Psiquiatr* 2002, **30**, 142–52). In a comparison of 2mg/d and 4mg/d in first-episode psychosis, 2mg/d was as effective as 4mg/d with fewer side effects, and although 4mg/d was slightly better at 4/52, the two were similar at 8/52, so it may make little pharmacological sense in dose escallating at an early stage (n=49, d/b, 8/52, Merlo *et al, J Clin Psych* 2002, **63**, 885–91). |
| **Olanzapine** | Low-dose olanzapine may be preferable to haloperidol in first-episode schizophrenia, with superior efficacy and reduced side-effects (n=83, selected sub-analysis of larger n=1996 study; RCT, Sanger *et al, Am J Psych* 1999, **156**, 79–87, Lilly-run), although weight gain is a major issue for patients. |
| **Quetiapine** | Low EPS, weight gain and prolactin effects make quetiapine an ideal drug of choice, but first-episode data is lacking. |

**Reviews**: general (Carpenter, *Am J Psych* 2001, **158**, 1771–73; Kasper, *J Clin Psych* 1999, **60**(Suppl 23), 5–9; Remington *et al, Bt J Psych* Suppl 1998, 172, 66–70), predictors of response (Robinson *et al, Am J Psych* 1999, **156**, 544–49).

---

dered (eg. n=293, Walkup *et al, J Clin Psych* 2000, **61**, 344–48). Most response is likely to occur within 3–4 weeks and if little occurs by 6–8 weeks, raising doses is unlikely to help.

Atypicals are not statistically better than typicals once controlling for comparator dose (23 RCT meta-regression analysis, Geddes *et al, BMJ* 2000, **321**, 1371–76; review by McIntosh, *EBMH* 2001, **4**, 77), but this assumes EPS are "minimal cost". In this analysis, studies were only a median of 6.5/52 duration, so ADRs from longer-term use are not known (low-dose typicals vs atypicals — discussion of both sides of arguements by Taylor [*Psych Bull* 2000, **24**, 465–68] and Oosthuizen *et al,* [*Psych Bull* 2001, **25**, 194]). 'Treatment-resistance' in the acute phase may include true resistance and those with sub-optimal treatment.

**2. Relapse prevention:** *

Relapse of schizophrenia occurs in around 80% of untreated schizophrenics and so maintenance therapy, which reduces relapse rates significantly, is usually indicated. Sadly, it is not yet possible to identify the 20% who do not relapse and thus do not need long-term drug therapy. If antipsychotics are stopped, relapse may be delayed for 2–6 months with the patient often feeling better (due to reduced side-effects) before the relapse. Intermittent therapy (prodrome-based or crisis intervention) has been advocated but generally accepted as ineffective (n=363, RCT, Gaebel *et al, Schizophr Res* 2002, **53**, 145–59). Side-effects, particularly the underrated akathisia, weight gain and dysphoria tend to reduce compliance. Concordance implies an agreement between the prescriber and patient as to the degree of drug taking acceptable to both. In patients, this will balance the positive effects of the drug (eg. symptom suppression) and the negative effects (eg. side-effects). Schizophrenia is very sensitive to psychosocial factors often requiring comprehensive, continuous and individualised therapy. Schizophrenics have better adherence with atypicals over the first six months of therapy (but not at 12/12, using prescription refill records) and so interventions to improve compliance are needed for all patients (n=288, 12/12, Dolder *et al, Am J Psych* 2002, **159**, 103–8). Compliance therapy has been show to improve attitude, concordance and insight on an intensive one-to-one basis (Kemp *et al, BMJ* 1996, **312**, 345–49), although some service users consider this brain-washing.

**Review**:* optimal duration of prophylactic antipsychotics in schizophrenia (Bosveld-van Haandel *et al, Acta Psych Scand* 2001, **103**, 335–46).

### 3. Withdrawal/discontinuation

See *2.2.1.6*.

### Risk factors for relapse *

Medication risk factors include:

- Drug used eg. rehospitalisation rates for schizophrenics discharged on atypicals (olanzapine, n=313 or risperidone, n=268) were similar (31% and 33% respectively) but considerably lower than those (n=458) discharged on conventional antipsychotics (48%) over a two year period (Rabinowitz *et al, Am J Psych* 2001, **158**, 266–69).

- Duration of untreated psychosis (DUP): A retrospective chart analysis indicated that DUP is the best predictor of outcome ie. those with more insidious onset and severe negative symptoms are more likely to have multiple episodes (n=67, 4yrs, Altamura *et al, Schizophr Res* 2001, **52**, 29–36).

- Unmanaged substance misuse: this reduces antipsychotic effects in dual diagnosis, with sooner and longer readmissions especially in those non-compliant with drugs (n=99, 4yrs, Hunt *et al, Schizophr Res* 2002, **54**, 253–64).

- Doses: Some ethnic trends in drug responses and doses may need to be lower in some racial groups (n=192, 6/52, Emsley *et al, J Clin Psych* 2002, **63**, 9–14).

**Reviews**:* acute episodes (Hayashida and Nakane, *Psychiatry Clin Neurosci* 1999, **53**, Suppl, S3-7), general (Launer, *Prescriber* 2001, **12**, 53–60), recent advances (Barnes and Joyce, *Curr Opin Psych* 2001, **14**, 25–37), GP guide (Taylor and Geddes, *Prescriber* 2002, **13**, 31–51; Launer and MacKean, *Prog Neurol Psych* 2000, **4**, 24–27), adolescent schizophrenia (Hollis, *Adv Psych Treat* 2000, **6**, 83–92), atypicals in the elderly (Wynn Owen and Castle, *Drugs & Aging*, 1999, **15**, 81–89) and new *vs* old drugs (Stanniland and Taylor, *Drug Safety* 2000, **22**, 195–214, 86 refs; *Drugs Ther Perspect* 2000, **16**, 7–12, 22 refs), choice of antipsychotics (Tauscher and Kapur, *CNS Drugs* 2001, **15**, 671–78), psychosocial interventions (*Effective Health Care* 2000, **6**, 1–8, 42 refs), genetics (Malhotra, *Curr Opin Psych* 2001, **14**, 3–7).

---

### BNF Listed

---

#### Phenothiazines
#### Chlorpromazine

Chlorpromazine is used for a wide range of psychotic conditions but use in the elderly is problematical. IV use is not recommended unless the injection is diluted and the patient is in a supine position. Cochrane concludes that chlorpromazine reduce relapses and improves global improvement *cf* placebo, but with the (obvious) risk of side-effects (summary, plus comment by Barnes, *EBMH* 1998, **1**, 83).

### Fluphenazine
An oral preparation is available but is usually used as a depot (see depots).

### Levomepromazine (methotrimeprazine)
This phenothiazine, related to promethazine, has significant sedative effects but causes little respiratory depression (study *vs* haloperidol and risperidone, Blin *et al*, *J Clin Psychopharmacol* 1996, **16**, 38–44).

### Pericyazine
A piperidine phenothiazine similar to thioridazine, with marked sedative and hypotensive side-effects. Use has increased with the problems with thioridazine, but little is published about the drug.

### Perphenazine
A piperazine phenothiazine with a relatively short half-life (8–12 hours).

### Prochlorperazine
A piperazine phenothiazine better known for its use as an antiemetic and in Ménières disease.

### Promazine
Promazine is similar to chlorpromazine and retains a minor role as a non-dependence-prone hypnotic, although the potential for side-effects should not be ignored.

### Thioridazine *
Due to concerns about the long-known issue of QT prolongation, thioridazine is now only licensed for resistant schizophrenia, considered inappropriate for patients with a history of cardiac arrhythmias and requires a baseline ECG and serum potassium, plus monitoring throughout treatment. A dose-related increase in risk of lengthened QT-interval has been reported, detectable at doses as low as 10mg/d (n=596, Reilly *et al*, *Lancet* 2000, **355**, 1048–52). A case-control study showed a specific association with sudden unexplained death in psychiatric in-patients, prob-

ably through drug-induced arrythmia (Reilly *et al*, *B J Psych* 2002, **180**, 515–22) and so there is a clear association with sudden death, with a risk of 1 per 1000 bed years (under 65) or 12 per 1000 bed years (over 65) (Reilly *et al*, *Psych Bull* 2002, **26**, 110–12).

### Trifluoperazine
A piperazine phenothiazine widely used as an antipsychotic and sometimes claimed to have 'activating' effects at low doses.

---

### Butyrophenones
### Benperidol *
Benperidol is a potent D2 blocker marketed originally as specific for antisocial forms of sexual behaviour, uncontrolled studies and reports claiming beneficial effects. Cochrane concludes that there is insufficient evidence to assess the drugs effectiveness, with only one poor RCT, where it was inferior to perphenazine (Leucht and Hartung, *CDSR* 2002, 3083). See benperidol under sexual deviancy disorders (*1.31*).

### Haloperidol * (see also depots)
Haloperidol is the prototype butyrophenone, widely used for the treatment of acute and chronic psychosis, both orally and as an injection (aqueous and depot). Although frequently used in the acute situation at relatively high dose, there is no additional antipsychotic advantage from doses higher than 12mg/d in psychosis (eg. n=176, RCT, d/b, 13/52, Volavka *et al*, *Arch Gen Psych* 1992, **49**, 354–61), and in acute mania (n=47, RCT, d/b, Rifkin*et al*, *B J Psych* 1994, **165**, 113–16). Indeed, 4mg/d may be as effective as 10mg/d and 40mg/d in newly-admitted in-patients, mostly schizophrenics (Stone *et al*, *Am J Psych* 1995, **152**, 1210–12) and even ultra-low doses (1–2mg/d) may be effective and well-tolerated in first-episode psychosis (n=35, open, Oosthuizen *et al*, *J Psychopharmacol* 2001, **15**, 251–55) producing 53–74% $D_2$ receptor occupancy, with substantial clinical improvement and minimal side-effects (n=7, Kapur *et al*, *Am J Psych*

1996, **153**, 948–50; n=2, Hirsschowitz *et al, Am J Psych* 1997, **154**, 715–16). Any dose above 20mg/d should thus be the exception rather than the rule. This is illustrated by a 63% dose reduction in chronic treatment-resistant schizophrenics on high-dose haloperidol resulting in improvement of symptoms and side-effects, further improved by intensive behaviour therapy (n=13, open, Liberman *et al, Am J Psych* 1994, **151**, 756–59).

The therapeutic window appears to lie between about 5.6–16.9mcg/L and plasma level monitoring may be indicated in some people (n=552, Ulrich *et al, Clin Pharmacokinet* 1998, **34**, 227–63). The elimination half-life in brain tissue is about 6.8 days, with significant amounts still detectable after 2 weeks. Thus, residual side-effects may continue for many weeks or months after stopping the drug, due to persistence of active CNS levels (Kornhuber *et al, Am J Psych* 1999, **156**, 885–90). Cochrane concludes that haloperidol is superior to placebo, but with substantially increased EPSE (n=2120, RCTs=20, Joy *et al, CDSR* 2001, 3082, reviewed by McGrath, *EBMH* 2001, **4**, 112; Waraich *et al, CDSR* 2002, **3**, 1951). There have been some concerns over a dose-related increase in risk of lengthened QT-interval (n=596, Reilly *et al, Lancet* 2000, **355**, 1048–52), especially if given by the IV, rather than IM route.

**Reviews:**\* Pharmacokinetics (Kudo and Ishizaki, *Clin Pharmacokinetics* 1999, **37**, 435–56, 231 refs).

### Thioxanthenes
**Flupentixol** (see also depots)
An oral preparation is also available.

**Zuclopenthixol** (see also depots)
Longer-term therapy is well tolerated and established (eg. *B J Clin Res* 1991, **2**, 140–56), as an oral preparation and as a shorter- and longer-acting depot. A slow onset and long half-life makes use in acute psychiatric emergencies less useful, where zuclopenthixol acetate ('Acuphase') is preferable.

### Diphenylbutylpiperidines
**Fluspirilene**
See depots.
**Pimozide**
Pimozide is effective against a wide range of positive symptoms (Sultana and McMonagle, *CDSR* 2000, **3**, 1949), but with potential cardiotoxic effects (see *3.2*). A review concluded that pimozide had effects on global functioning and mental state similar to typical antipsychotics (Gray, *EBMH* 2000, **3**, 117) but none of the trials reviewed involved delusional disorders, and so any use in delusional disorders is based almost entirely on case reports.

### Benzamides, substituted
**Amisulpride** *
Low dose amisulpride (related to sulpiride) blocks pre-synaptic D2 and D3 autoreceptors, higher doses blocking post-synaptic receptors, with little effect on other receptors. It is often classified as "atypical" (or even an "atypical" atypical: Lecrubier, *Int Clin Psychopharmacol* 2000, **15**(supppl 4), S21–26). A meta-analysis of 18 amisulpride RCT studies (n=2214) showed some effect at low dose for predominantly negative symptoms and lower use of anticholinergic drugs (Leucht *et al, Am J Psych* 2002, **159**, 180–90; caution expressed by Remington and Kapur, *EBMH* 2002, **5**, 85). Another meta-analysis of 4 studies suggests negative symptoms respond to low-dose amisulpride (when it is an autoreceptor blocker, increasing dopamine turnover), but that the placebo response is high, the response of positive symptoms is lacking, and that at the dose necessary for positive symptom response (when it becomes a D2/D3 blocker), it's effect was essentially that of a typical agent (Storosum *et al, Schizo Bull* 2002, **28**, 193–201).

Amisulpride 50–100mg/d seems optimum for negative symptoms (eg. n=232, d/b, p/c, Danion *et al, Am J*

*Psych* 1999, **156**, 610–16; review by Moller, *Eur Arch Psychiatry Clin Neurosci* 2001, **251**, 217–24). Efficacy has been shown against haloperidol (eg. n=488, RCT, 12/12, Colonna *et al, Int Clin Psychopharmacol* 2000, **15**, 13–22; n=21, RCT, d/b, c/o, 5/7, Ramaekers *et al, J Clin Psychopharmacol* 1999, **19**, 209–21), superior to risperidone for response (n=309, RCT, d/b, 6/12, Sechter *et al, Neuropsychopharmacol* 2002, **27**, 1071–81) and at 200–800mg/d equivalent to olanzapine 5–20mg/d at 2/12, but with less weight gain (n=377, RCT, d/b, 6/12, Martin *et al, Curr Med Res Opin* 2002, **18**, 355–62). 400–800mg/d may improve depressive symptoms in schizophrenia compared to risperidone and haloperidol (n=612, 4/52, Peuskens *et al, Eur Neuropsychopharm* 2002, **12**, 305–10). EPSEs and raised prolactin are generally considered to be dose-dependent. Oral bioavailability is poor. Cochrane concludes that amisulpride has a good general profile, may improve global and negative symptoms and might be more acceptable and more tolerable than high-potency conventional antipsychotics (n=2443, RCTs=19, Mota *et al, CDSR* 2002, **2**, 1357).

**Reviews**: general (Burns and Bale, *J Int Med Res* 2001, **29**, 451–66; Rein *et al, Acta Psych Scand* 2000, **101**, 23–27; Curran and Perry, *Drugs* 2001, **61**, 2123–50; Green, *Curr Med Res Opin* 2002, **18**, 113–17), receptor blockade (Curran and Perry, *CNS Drugs* 2002, **16**, 207–11).

**Sulpiride**

Sulpiride is a specific dopamine ($D_2$, plus some $D_3$ and $D_4$) receptor blocker, well-established in the UK. The incidence of EPSEs is much reduced, making it a useful drug (extensive review by Caley and Weber, *Ann Pharmacother* 1995, **29**, 152–60, 55 refs).

**Atypical or second generation antipsychotics** *

'Atypical' is a widely-used term to describe a wide range of antipsychotics with specific characteristics, eg. minimal EPSEs, lack of sedation, fast dissociation from D2 receptors (Kapur and Seeman, *Am J Psych* 2001, **158**, 360–69; review by Seeman, *Can J Psych* 2002, **47**, 27–38) etc. It may be better to either consider antipsychotics on a spectrum, from typical (eg. chlorpromazine) at one end to atypical (eg. clozapine) at the other, or to base it upon a particular definition of atypical.

**Reviews of atypicals**:* terminology (Fleischacker, *Curr Opin Psych* 2002, **15**, 1–2), general (Worrel, *Am J Health-Sys Pharm* 2000, **57**, 238–58, 155 refs; Pandarakalam, *Hosp Med* 2000, **61**, 10–14; Marder *et al, Curr Opin Psych* 2000, **13**, 11–14; *J Clin Psych* 2000, **61**, 223–32).

**Clozapine** * (see also separate tables)

Clozapine is the prototype atypical antipsychotic, indicated for treatment-resistant schizophrenia and psychotic disorders in Parkinson's Disease. Before starting, patients should have a physical examination and cardiac disease excluded.

Clozapine is probably effective in up to 30–50% of treatment-resistant schizophrenics (n=268, RCT, d/b, p/c, 6/52, Kane *et al, Arch Gen Psych* 1988, **45**, 789–96) and this may rise to 60% if adequate doses are given for up to 12 months. A one-year study of treatment refractory or antipsychotic-intolerant schizophrenics showed that 50% of the former and 76% of the latter groups responded to clozapine over 52 weeks, the peak response occurring at 12–24 weeks (n=84, open, Lieberman *et al, Am J Psych* 1994, **151**, 1744–52). Improvement in BPRS at the end of the first week is more likely to predict later response than those showing little or no improvement at one week (n=40, 5/52, Stern *et al, Am J Psych* 1994, **151**, 1817–18). There is probably little clinical gain in prolonging exposure to clozapine beyond 8 weeks at any particular dose if no response is seen (n=50, open, Conley *et al, Am J Psych*

1997, **154**, 1243–47). Clozapine has been shown to be superior to risperidone in positive symptoms, EPSEs and prolactin, but not on negative symptoms (n=29, d/b, parallel, 6/52, Breier *et al, Am J Psych* 1999, **156**, 294–98). In resistant schizophrenia, clozapine was superior to risperidone on most efficacy measures, although both were well-tolerated (n=273, RCT, d/b, 12/52, Azorin *et al, Am J Psych* 2001, **158**, 1305–13). A meta-analysis of atypicals in treatment-resistant schizophrenia indicated that clozapine has consistent superiority over typicals (efficacy and safety), but that for other atypicals inconclusive (meta-analysis, n=1916, s=12, Chakos *et al, Am J Psych* 2001, **158**, 518–26). In partially responsive outpatients, clozapine offered substantial benefits over haloperidol in a broad range of symptoms except negative ones (n=71, RCT, d/b, 29/52, Kane *et al, Arch Gen Psych* 2001, **58**, 965–72).

Valproate is usually used as prophylaxis of clozapine-induced seizures, but gabapentin may be an alternative (n=1, Usiskin *et al, Am J Psych* 2000, **157**, 482–83). Hyper-salivation (possibly due to an altered swallow reflex) can be managed with hyoscine tablets, or atropine eye drops orally (Antonella and Tessier, *J Psych and Neurosci* 1999, **24**, 250).

**Mode of action**: Clozapine's mode of action is open to some debate, eg. it has a low occupancy of $D_2$ receptors (30–60%) and thus may act via $D_1$, 5-$HT_2$, ACh, 5-$HT_6$ and 5-$HT_7$ receptors and inhibition of pre-synaptic alpha-2 autoreceptors. Some $D_2$ limbic specificity has been detected.

**Blood levels:** These may be useful in optimising therapy if poor response occurs. Plasma clozapine levels of 200–450ng/ml have been shown to be superior to levels of 150ng/ml and below (n=56, VanderZwaag *et al, Am J Psych* 1996, **153**, 1579–84). Levels over 350ng/ml (Kronig *et al, Am J Psych* 1995, **152**, 179–82) should only be reached with extreme care (review by Duncan and Taylor, *Psych Bull* 1995, **19**, 753–55) and blood levels may not necessarily be related to therapeutic efficacy (n=41, Kurz *et al, B J Psych* 1998, **173**, 341–44). Low plasma levels may occur in CYP1A2 rapid metabolisers. Reviewed by Olesen (*Clinical Pharmacokinetics* 1998, **34**, 497–502, 20 refs.).

**Suicide reduction:**[*] Clozapine may reduce suicide rates in schizophrenics, eg. a study showed reduction in both suicides and suicidal ideation (n=88, Meltzer and Okayli, *Am J Psych* 1995, **152**, 183–90), making a contribution to the risk:benefit analysis of clozapine. The InterSePT study (n=980, RCT, d/b, 2yrs, Meltzer *et al, Arch Gen Psych* 2003, **60**, 82–91) has shown a 25% reduction in suicide events compared to olanzapine. The suicide rate for schizophrenia can be as high as 1 in 10, a startling comparison with the risk of 1 in 50 for reversible agranulocytosis. However, another study failed to show a reduced completed suicide rate with clozapine (9.2–10.5% in each group over 4 years), as the reduced rate was entirely due to reduced respiratory disorders (n=1514 plus 2830 matched-controls, 4yrs, Sernyak *et al, Am J Psych* 2001, **158**, 931–37; disputed by Ertugrul and Meltzer, *Am J Psych* 2002, **159**,

---

**CLOZAPINE UK PRESCRIBING AND MONITORING SUMMARY**

Clozapine is indicated in the UK for treatment-resistant schizophrenia and psychosis in Parkinson's Disease, ie. patients 'non-responsive' or 'intolerant' of conventional antipsychotics (*Table 1*). It can be dispensed on a weekly, fortnightly or four-weekly basis (*Table 2*), but only following a satisfactory blood result (*Table 3*). At the time of writing The Clozaril Patient Monitoring Service (CPMS) controls these tests in the UK.

**Table 1. Summary of UK clozapine prescribing restrictions**

| | |
|---|---|
| 'Non-responsive' | Lack of satisfactory clinical improvement despite the use of at least two marketed antipsychotics prescribed at adequate dose for an adequate duration. |
| 'Intolerance' | The impossibility of achieving clinical benefit with conventional antipsychotics because of severe or untreatable neurological or other adverse reactions eg. extrapyramidal or tardive dyskinesia. |
| Patient requirements | Hospital based originally.<br>Normal white cell and differential blood counts.<br>Enrolled with CPMS. |
| Prescriber and dispensing requirements | Consultant must be registered with CPMS.<br>Hospital or nominated community pharmacy must be registered with CPMS. |

**Table 2. Summary of UK clozapine minimum blood test requirements**

| Blood tests | Required frequency | Validity * |
|---|---|---|
| Pre-treatment | Single full blood screen | 10 days, if satisfactory (green) |
| First 18 weeks of treatment<br>First sample at 3 days | Weekly (usually Monday or Tuesday with result on Wednesday or Thursday). | 10 days (not including day of sample, if satisfactory (green) |
| Weeks 19–52 | Every 2 weeks, if blood results have been satisfactory | 21 days (not including day of sample, if satisfactory (green) |
| Weeks 53 onwards | Every 4 weeks, if 'stable haematological profile' | 42 days (not including day of sample, if satisfactory (green) |
| Discontinuation (temporary or permanent) | Weekly (up to 18 weeks) or fortnightly (19 weeks onward) for four weeks after completely stopping clozapine | If test result has not been or does not go red, clozapine may be restarted. See table 4 |

**Table 3. Summary of UK Clozaril Patient Monitoring Service Test Result**

| Result | Meaning | Action |
|---|---|---|
| Green | Satisfactory | Routine tests |
| Amber | wbc or neutrophil counts below accepted levels. | Repeat test twice a week until either red or green |
| Red | wbc below 3000/mm$^3$ and/or absolute neutrophils below 1500/mm$^3$. | Immediate cessation of therapy. Sample blood daily until patient recovered. No further prescribing allowed unless an error has occurred or consultant takes full responsibility. |

**Table 4. Summary of UK CPMS temporary breaks in clozapine therapy advice**

| 1. Dose | | |
|---|---|---|
| Dose on discontinuing | Break | Dose on restart |
| Any | <48 hours | Restart on previous dose |
| Any | >48 hours | Restart at 12.5–25mg and build up gradually to previous dose to minimise dose-related side-effects |
| **2. Sampling frequency** | | |
| Previous monitoring frequency | Break | Monitoring on restart |
| Weekly | <1 week | Weekly, no need to restart 18 week period |
| Weekly | >1 week | Weekly, MUST restart 18 week period |
| After 18 weeks: | | |
| Fortnightly | ≤3 days | Fortnightly |
| Fortnightly | >3 days | Weekly for 6 weeks, then fortnightly |
| 4 weekly | ≤3 days | Four weekly |
| 4 weekly | >3 days | Weekly for 6 weeks, then 4 weekly |
| Fortnightly or 4 weekly | >4 weeks | Weekly for 18 weeks, then resume as previous |

323–25; comment by Reinstein *et al, Clin Drug Investig* 2002, **22**, 341–46).

**Blood dyscrasias**: Clozapine can cause a usually reversible neutropenia in 3-4% of patients which may lead to agranulocytosis in 0.8% of patients over one year, with a non-dose-related higher risk in older people and those with lower base-line wbc counts (Alvir *et al, NEJM* 1993, **329**, 162–67). Onset peaks around 8–10 weeks (range 0.5–24 + weeks) and treatment is thus restricted as per *Table 2*. A recent meta-analysis concluded the incidence of dyscrasias in long-term therapy may be as high as 7%, and that conclusive evidence for clozapine's superior efficacy was lacking (n=2530, Wahlbeck *et al, Am J Psych* 1999, **156**, 990–99). A CPMS database study indicated that agranulocytosis rises 2.4-fold in Asians compared to Caucasians, and there is an age-related increase in risk of 53% per decade, but no dose-relationship (n=12,760, Munro *et al, B J Psych* 1999, **175**, 576–80). Clozapine (and olanzapine) are both able to induce transient granulocytopenia without the usual rise in granulocyte colony stimulating factor (G-CSF) levels. The use of G-CSF in neutropenia is both effective and logical (eg. n=1, Schuld *et al, Acta Psych Scand* 2000, **102**, 153–55; Sperner-Unterweger *et al, B J Psych* 1998, **173**, 82–84). Use in people with a low wbc count due to benign ethnic neutropenia may be allowed with haematologist advice.

**Cost-effectiveness:*** Despite the high acquisition costs of clozapine in the UK, it can still be a very cost-effective treatment for resistant schizophrenia. Savings result almost exclusively from reduced costs of hospitalisation (Meltzer *et al, Am J Psych* 1993, **150**, 1630–38; review in *Lancet* 1993, **306**, 1427–28; UK study n=63, Hayhurst *et al, J Psychopharmacol* 2002, **16**, 169–175) but are partly offset by increased demands on active rehabilitation resources in outpatient care (n=21, Jonsson and Walinder, *Acta Psych Scand* 1995, **92**, 199–201).

**Reviews**: general (*J Clin Psych* 1998, **59**(Suppl 3), 1–48), management of clozapine side-effects (Young *et al, Schizophr Bull* 1998, **24**, 381–90), GP role (Launer, *Prescriber* 2000, **11**, 35–38), predicting response (Hu *et al, CNS Drugs* 1999, **11**, 317–26).

## Olanzapine *

Olanzapine is licensed for the treatment of schizophrenia and for relapse prevention. It blocks a wide variety of receptors, eg. $5\text{-HT}_{2A/C}$, $5\text{-HT}_3$, $5\text{-HT}_6$, $D_{1-5}$, $M_{1-5}$, alpha-one and H1, with some mesolimbic dopamine selectivity. The starting and main therapeutic dose is 10mg/d (range 5–20mg/d, UK mean 15–18mg/d). Many studies have shown a clinical effect, eg. where olanzapine (mean dose 15mg/d) was more effective than haloperidol (10–20mg/d) on negative symptoms (n=335, RCT, 12/12, Tollefson and Sanger, *Am J Psych* 1997, **154**, 466–74), superior to haloperidol for all symptoms of schizophrenia, with fewer side-effects, including EPSEs and prolactin levels (n=1996, d/b, 6/52, Tollefson *et al, Am J Psych* 1997, **154**, 457–65) and superior to risperidone for primary negative symptoms and with less side-effects (Lilly study, n=339, d/b, 28/52, Tran *et al, J Clin Psychopharmacol* 1997, **17**, 407–18; reviewed by Cunningham Owens, *EBMH* 1998, **1**, 55). It may also be effective for secondary negative symptoms, but not necessarily in having a direct beneficial effect on primary negative symptoms (n=39, open, 12/52, Kopelowicz *et al, Am J Psych* 2000, **157**, 987–93). Neuropsychological changes in early phase schizophrenia during 12 months of treatment with olanzapine (5–20mg/d), risperidone (4–10mg/d), or haloperidol (5–20mg/d) showed olanzapine may have some superior cognitive effects (n=65, Purdon *et al, Arch Gen Psych* 2000, **57**, 249–58). Olanzapine was also shown to be superior to haloperidol in schizoaffective disorder, with less drop-outs and fewer EPSEs, but more weight gain (n=300, 12/12, Tran *et al, B J Psych* 1999, **174**, 15–22).

The main side-effects are somnolence and weight gain (which may halt or even reverse with time; n=20, open, 12/12, Rodriguez-Perez *et al, PNBP* 2002, **26**, 1055–62), but with low EPSEs and may have a lower incidence of treatment-emergent tardive dyskinesia than haloperidol (re-analysis of data from three studies, Tollefson *et al, Am J Psych* 1997, **154**, 1248–54; n=1714, RCT, d/b, up to 2.6yrs, Beasley *et al, B J Psych* 1999, **174**, 23–30, Lilly). A transient rise in prolactin levels can occur. Most of the cost-pressures in the community due to olanzapine are the result of off-license use. One (non-Lilly) study in treatment-resistant schizophrenia suggested that switching from an atypical/haloperidol to olanzapine may improve cognitive function but improved psychopathology in only 9% (n=45, Lindenmayer *et al, J Clin Psych* 2002, **63**, 931–35). Olanzapine levels may be useful to optimise doses and assess the of influence of gender, smoking and interactions (n=194, Skogh *et al, Ther Drug Monit* 2002, **24**, 518–26)

**Reviews**: general (Kando *et al, Ann Pharmacother* 1997, **31**, 1325–34); pharmacology and kinetics (Falsett, *Hosp Pharm* 1999, **34**, 423–35, 91 refs; Callaghan *et al, Clin Pharmacokinetics* 1999, **37**, 177–93; Stephenson and Pilowsky, *B J Psych* 1999, **174**[Suppl 38], 52–58).

## Quetiapine *

Quetiapine is structurally related to clozapine but without the need for blood nor ECG monitoring. Doses of 300–450mg/d (range 150–750mg/d) are quoted as the most effective. Doses need to be increased gradually over several days initially, and a starter pack is available in the UK. Many double-blind randomised trials indicate that the drug is as effective in schizophrenia as reference drugs (eg. n=101, Peuskens and Link, *Acta Psych Scand* 1997, **96**, 265–73; n=448, RCT, 6/52, Copolov *et al, Psychol*

*Med* 2000, **30**, 95–105). Quetiapine appears to have limbic selective D2 and D3 blockade, resulting in very low EPSE (n=6, Stephenson *et al, B J Psych* 2000, **177**, 408–15), prolactin elevation and related side-effects (eg. Arvantis and Miller, *Biol Psych* 1997, **42**, 233–46; Small *et al, Arch Gen Psych* 1997, **54**, 549–57). In schizophrenics only partially responsive to typicals, significantly more responded to quetiapine 600mg/d than haloperidol 20mg/d, and quetiapine was better tolerated (n=288, d/b, 8/52, Emsley *et al, Int Clin Psychopharmacol* 2000, **15**, 121–31). Improved cognitive function may occur when switching from haloperidol to quetiapine (n=58, RCT, Velligan *et al, Schizophr Res* 2002, **53**, 239–48). Headache, somnolence and dizziness are common adverse events. Quetiapine shows transiently high D2 occupancy which drops rapidly over 12–14 hours, which may explain the low EPSE and low prolactin elevation (n=12, Kapur *et al, Arch Gen Psych* 2000, **57**, 553–59). Cochrane concludes that although quetiapine is more effective than placebo, no difference could be detected against traditional antipsychotics, drop-outs due to adverse effects were lower with quetiapine, but still high (Srisurapanont *et al, CDSR* 2000, **3**, 0967).

**Reviews:*** general (Hellewell, *Hosp Med* 2002, **63**, 600–3; Kasper and Müller-Spahn, *Exp Opin Pharmacother* 2000, **1**, 783–801, 87 refs; Dev and Raniwalla, *Drug Safety* 2000, **23**, 295–307; Green, *Curr Med Res Opin* 1999, **15**, 145–51), safety (Dev and Raniwalla, *Drug Saf* 2000, **23**, 295–307), pharmacokinetics (DeVane and Nemeroff, *Clin Pharmacokinet* 2001, **40**, 509–22), use in Parkinsons Disease (Matheson and Lamb, *CNS Drugs* 2000, **14**, 157–72; *Drugs & Ther Perspect* 2001, **17**, 1–5).

## Risperidone *

Risperidone is licensed for acute and chronic psychosis. It has $D_2$ and $5-HT_2$ blocking actions and has been shown to be effective against both positive and negative symptoms with few side-effects. It may also improve sleep in schizophrenics (cf. haloperidol, n=109, Yamashita *et al, Psychiat Res* 2002, **109**, 137–42).

**Dose:\*** The optimum dose is around 4–6mg/d with little or no advantage in exceeding this dose (review: Williams, *J Clin Psych* 2001, **62**, 282–89). Titration to 6mg/d over 3 days is recommended, but a slower titration has been recommended (over weeks rather than days, stabilising on 2–4mg/d initially before proceeding to higher doses), particularly in drug-naïve first-episode schizophrenics and the elderly as this markedly reduces the final doses needed, EPSE and the risk of non-compliance (n=17, Kontaxakis *et al, Am J Psych* 2000, **157**, 1178–79), and may lead to better outcomes (retrospective review; n=1056, Love *et al, J Clin Psych* 1999, **60**, 771–75; n=96, McGorry, *J Clin Psych* 1999, **60**, 794). 60% of acutely exacerbated schizophrenics can tolerate and respond well to 6mg/d and, in the remaining 40%, most then tolerate and respond to lower doses (3–4mg/d), with equivalent plasma levels to the higher dose, illustrating the effect of slower metabolism (n=31, open, 6/52, Lane *et al, J Clin Psych* 2000, **61**, 209–14). Even very low dose (1–2mg/d) can produce dramatic improvements in prodromal phase or first episode schizophrenia (n=10, 12/52, open, Cannon *et al, Am J Psych* 2002, **159**, 1230–32). In the acute phase, a rapid dose-loading regimen (1mg every 6–8 hours up to 3mg bd) has been relatively well tolerated and is effective in acute states (n=11, Feifel *et al, J Clin Psych* 2000, **61**, 909–11), and the availability of a quick dissolving tablet (Risperdal Quicklets®) may facilitate this. Risperidone 4mg/d had a more rapid onset of action in psychosis/schizophrenia compared to haloperidol 10mg/d, particularly during the first week (n=227, RCT, Rabinowitz *et al, J Clin Psych* 2001, **62**, 343–46).

**Efficacy:\*** Risperidone has shown efficacy across a wide range of symptoms of psychosis and schizophrenia, eg. against positive and negative symptoms, disorganised thoughts, hostility and affective symptoms and superior at 4 weeks and better tolerated than haloperidol (n=67, d/b, 8/52, Wirshing *et al, Am J Psych* 1999, **156**, 1374–79). Comparisons with olanzapine have been favourable eg. more effective than olanzapine with comparable side-effects (n=42, open, 6/12, Ho *et al, J Clin Psych* 1999, **60**, 658–63) or lower weight gain (n=377, RCT, Conley and Mahmoud, *Am J Psych* 2001, **158**, 765–74) and lower relapse rates over 2 years (n=142, naturalistic retrospective study, Chengappa *et al, J Clin Psych* 1999, **60**, 373–78). Relapse prevention has now been clearly shown by a one year study against haloperidol, where the risperidone group had a greater reduction in psychotic symptoms and EPSE and a lower relapse rate (n=397, average follow-up 1yr, Csernansky *et al, NEJM* 2002, **346**, 16–22; comment by McIntosh, *EBMH* 2002, **5**, 77).

**Refractory schizophrenia:\*** similar efficacy has been claimed for risperidone in treatment-resistant or intolerant schizophrenia against clozapine (n=86, d/b, Bondolfi *et al, Am J Psych* 1998, **155**, 499–504; fiercely criticised by Meltzer and others, *Am J Psych* 1999, **156**, 1126–28), only slightly less effective than clozapine, but with fewer side-effects (n=35, open, 12/52, Lindenmayer *et al, J Clin Psych* 1998, **59**, 521–27) equivalent to clozapine on negative symptoms, but not on positive symptoms (n=29, d/b, parallel, 6/52, Breier *et al, Am J Psych* 1999, **156**, 294–98) and better tolerated and more effective than haloperidol (n=67, d/b, Wirshing *et al, Am J Psych* 1999, **156**, 1374–79). In another study, 25% refractory schizophrenics responded to risperidone (mean 7mg/d) and 58% responded to clozapine (mean 520mg/d), suggesting that risperidone may be worth a try before clozapine (n=24, Sharif *et al, J Clin Psych* 2000, **61**, 498–504).

**Cognitive function:** There is growing evidence for the role of poor cognitive function (especially working memory) in poor outcome of schizophrenia, and risperidone has been shown to produce an improvement in cognitive function (n=25, Rossi *et al, Acta Psych Scand* 1997, **95**, 40–43), including against haloperidol (n=59, Green *et al, Am J Psych* 1997, **154**, 799–804).

**Reviews:** TDM (therapeutic range of 25–150microg/L, n=50, Odou *et al, Clin Drug Investigat* 2000, **19**, 283–92).

**Zotepine** *

Zotepine is a tricyclic dibenzothiepine licensed for schizophrenia. Both zotepine and its active metabolite norzotepine have a high affinity for a range of dopamine and serotonin receptor sub-types, and some NARI activity. To minimise hypotension, the dose should be titrated from 25mg TDS every 4 days to a maximum of 300mg/d (as a TDS dose). It has been compared with haloperidol, low dose chlorpromazine and higher dose chlorpromazine 300–600mg/d (less EPSE and greater improvement in BPRS, n=158, RCT, 8/52, Cooper *et al, Acta Psych Scand* 2000, **101**, 218–25). Relapse prevention has been shown (n=121, d/b, p/c, 6/12, Cooper *et al, Psychopharmacol [Berl]* 2000, **150**, 237–43). Cochrane concludes from 10 studies that zotepine is as effective as typical and atypical antipsychotics and superior to placebos (n=1006, Fenton *et al, CDSR*, 2000, **2**, 1948; reviewed by Remington, *EBMH* 2000, **3**, 78) and a further meta-analysis suggested efficacy over comparator drugs, although nearly all trials were no more than 12/52 duration (15 studies, Butler *et al, Int J Psych Clin Pract* 2000, **4**, 19–27), although it may have low EPS (n=108, open, 42/7, Kasper *et al, Int Clin Psychopharmacol* 2001, **16**, 163–68). The risk of seizures is dose-related and rises above 300mg/d. An ECG is recommended pre-treatment in people with CHD, at risk of hypokalaemia or taking other drugs known to prolong QTc

**Review***: Prakash and Lamb (*CNS Drugs* 1998, **9**, 153–75, 115 refs; Cooper, *Prescriber* 2000, **11**, 35–42).

## Other antipsychotics

### Loxapine *

Loxapine is a dibenzoxazepine antipsychotic. There is some PET evidence that loxapine is an equipotent blocker of 5-HT$_2$ and D$_2$ receptors, and hence might be claimed to be 'atypical' (Kapur *et al, Am J Psych* 1997, **154**, 1525–29), but Cochrane concludes that it is under-researched and had no clear advantages over other typical drugs. It will be discontinued in the UK by 2004.

### Oxypertine *

Oxypertine was discontinued in the UK in March 2002.

### Depot and long-acting injections *

Depot administration of antipsychotics is widely used in Europe. The major advantage is of assured compliance, with associated and proven reduction in relapses, rehospitalisation and severity of relapse, plus reduction in bio-availability problems (some people metabolise antipsychotics extensively via the first-pass effect). By being sure of doses received, depots **should** be able to facilitate better downward titration of doses to reduce the incidence of side-effects. The major disadvantages include the impossibility of altering a dose if side-effects develop (eg. dystonia, NMS), patients seeing depot administration as 'being controlled', having no control over their treatment or, worse still, as being a punishment. Many patients and families/carers are insufficiently educated about the pros and cons of depot administration. Used properly they can lead to reduced relapses, low side-effects and stable therapeutic effects. It should not be enough just to prevent relapse with a depot.

A review (Adams *et al, B J Psych* 2001, **179**, 290–99; reviewed by McGorry, *EBMH* 2002, **5**, 42), concludes that depots are safe and effective and may confer a slight advantage over oral drugs in reducing relapse rates. The **Cochrane** reviews of depots note the lack of decent trials and low patient numbers eg. for **fluspirilene**, the 7 studies have low numbers, no advantage over oral drugs and no outcome data (Quraishi and David, *CDSR* 2000, **2**, 1718). **Haloperidol** decanoate has 2 studies *vs* placebo which show lower drop-outs on depot, but no difference against oral haloperidol (n=22), and the 8 trials *vs* other depots showed no discernable difference (Quraishi and David, *CDSR* 2000, **2**, 1361). **Pipothiazine** has 14 studies, with no advantage over oral (n=166) and no differences against other depots (9 studies, n=455, Quraishi and David, *CDSR* 2001, **3**, 1720). The data for **fluphenazine** decanoate is very limited, the 6 studies showing no difference between depot and oral (Adams and Eisenbruch, *CDSR* 2000, **2**, 0307). **Flupentixol** decanoate has no trials against placebo, no difference against oral (but possibly less EPSE), high dose is no better than low dose, and no advantage over other depots (Quraishi and David, *CDSR* 2000, 1470). Although there are no placebo trials for **zuclopenthixol** decanoate, the 4 trials showed reduced relapse against other depots (but possibly with more side effects) but the data suggests 'real differences' over other depots (Coutinho *et al*, *CDSR* 2000, **2**, 1164).

The incidence of problems and complications (eg. bleeding or haematoma, leakage, inflammatory nodules etc) associated with long-term depot injections have probably been underreported (retrospective study by Hay, *BMJ* 1995, **311**, 421). Depot injections do, of course also hurt, the pain declining over 10 days and has a negative effect on patient attitude towards medication (n=34, Bloch *et al*, *J Clin Psych* 2001, **62**, 855–59), although there is some evidence to the contrary (Walburn *et al*, *B J Psych* 2001, **179**, 300–7). The need for a meticulous (Z-

tracking) injection technique (Belanger-Annable, *Canadian Nurse* 1985, **81**, 1–3) and using the most appropriate preparation and dose for that individual are essential for long-term success (Muldoon, *BMJ* 1995, **311**, 1368).

**Reviews**: overview (Gerlach, *Acta Psych Scand* 1994, **89**[Suppl 382], 28–32; Taylor, *Psych Bull* 1999, **23**, 551–53; Kennedy and Mikhail, *Lancet* 2000, **356**, 594), extensive review of depots place in therapy (Davis *et al*, *Drugs* 1994, **47**, 741–73, 170 refs), optimising the use of depots (Dencker and Axelsson, *CNS Drugs* 1996, **6**, 367–81).

---

### Pharmacokinetics

The graph with each depot shows plasma levels against time for each drug. All are single first-dose profiles. Chronic treatment will show considerably less fluctuation but, surprisingly, there is still evidence of large variations in the plasma levels of haloperidol decanoate and flupenthixol decanoate, although there was no relationship between side-effect ratings and fluctuations in plasma levels (n=30, 3yrs, Tuninger and Levander, *Br J Psych* 1996, **169**, 618–21).

### Flupentixol decanoate ('Deplxol', 'Depixol Conc.', 'Depixol Low Volume')

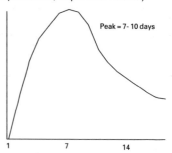

Peak = 7- 10 days

**Flupentixol decanoate** (Depixol ®) is the most widely prescribed depot in the UK. It is a dopamine specific thioxanthene antipsychotic with potentially activating effects at low dose, and has been dubbed a 'partial atypical' (Kuhn *et al*, *Fortschr Neurol Psychiatr* 2000, **68**[Suppl 1], S3841):

- Duration of action=3–4 weeks
- Peak=7–10 days
- Rate limiting half-life=8 days (single dose), 17 days (multiple doses)
- Time to steady state=10–12 weeks.

## Fluphenazine decanoate

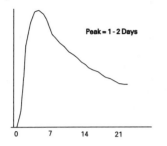

Peak = 1 - 2 Days

**Fluphenazine decanoate** (Modecate ®) is a phenothiazine that can be given up to four-weekly as a depot. Responders have been shown to have greatest improvement with fluphenazine levels above 1.0ng/ml and doses above 0.2–0.25mg/kg/d (Levinson *et al, Am J Psych* 1995,**152**, 765–71; Miller *et al, J Clin Pharm Ther* 1995, **20**, 55–62). 25mg fluphenazine every 6 weeks or every 2 weeks produces similar side-effects, symptom relief and relapse rates, but with reduced drug exposure with the longer dosage interval (n=50, RCT, 54/52, Carpenter *et al, Am J Psych* 1999, **156**, 412–18).
- Duration of action=1–3 weeks
- Peak=6–48 hours
- Rate limiting half-life=6–10 days (single doses), 14–100 days (multiple doses)
- Time to steady state=6–12 weeks (*B J Psych* 1991, **158**, 658–65).

## Fluspirilene ('Redeptin')

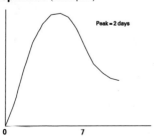

Peak = 2 days

**Fluspirilene** (Redeptin ®) is now only available in the UK as an import from Belgium, as a water-based micro-crystalline injection.
- Duration of action=1.5 weeks
- Peak within 2 days
- Rate limiting half-life=7–9 days
- Time to steady state=5–6 weeks.

## Haloperidol decanoate ('Haldol Decanoate')

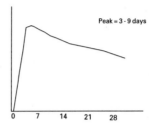

Peak = 3 - 9 days

**Haloperidol decanoate** (Haldol Decanoate ®) is longer-acting and a 4-week interval between injections is possible. It is probably best reserved for chronic relapsing schizophrenics responsive to haloperidol (full review in *Drug Intell Clin Pharm* 1988, **22**, 290–95). The optimum dose has been reported to be 200mg/month, although rates of deterioration with 50–100mg/month were not significantly greater in one study compared to 25mg/month, and ADRs were possibly higher (n=105, RCT, d/b, Kane *et al, Am J Psych* 2002, **4**, 554–60; review by Marois and Roy, *EBMH* 2002, **5**, 113).
- Duration of action=4 weeks
- Peak=3–9 days
- Rate limiting half-life=18–21 days (single + chronic)
- Time to steady state=10–12 weeks at monthly dosing

## Pipothiazine palmitate ('Piportil Depot')

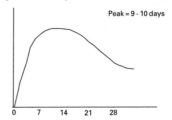

Peak = 9 - 10 days

**Pipothiazine** (Piportil ®) is a piperidine phenothiazine marketed in the UK as the palmitate:
- Duration of action=4 weeks
- Peak=9–10 days
- Rate limiting half-life=14–21 days (chronic)
- Time to steady state=8–12 weeks.

## Risperidone (Risperdal Consta ®)*

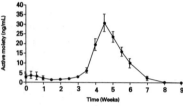

*(Reproduced courtesy of Janssen-Cilag)*

This novel long-acting injection uses risperidone molecules in a synthetic and absorbable polymer microsphere base suspended in water. It is licensed for schizophrenic and other psychoses. The initial dose is 25mg fortnightly (equivalent to oral doses of up to 4mg/d), with a maximum of 50mg every two weeks. From current data, there appears little or no advantage from using doses above 25mg/fortnight. Since there is no significant drug release for 3–4 weeks, with a peak at 4–6 weeks, it is possible that a third fortnightly injection could be given before the full effect of the first is seen. Patients should thus be pretreated with risperidone orally for at least a few days before the injection is commenced to rule out any severe EPSE, hypotension or other idiosyncratic reactions. Oral cover may be needed for the first 3 weeks, then tapered during week four. Dose escalation should occur at no greater intervals than alternate injections. There may be a small release in the first few days from the surface of the granules. Elimination is complete 7–8 weeks after the last injection. The vials must be stored at 2-8°C, although can be kept at <25°C for up to 7 days.

## Zuclopenthixol acetate ('Clopixol-Acuphase')

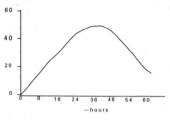

**Zuclopenthixol acetate** is available as 'Clopixol-Acuphase' in the UK. 50–150mg as a single dose provided a rapid and effective reduction in psychotic symptoms in 25 patients (*Curr Med Res Opin* 1990, **12**, 58–65) over about 78 hours. It is a drug of choice in acute psychiatric emergency in many areas. See also acute psychiatric emergencies (*1.1*).
- Duration of action=2–3 days
- Peak=24–40 hrs (*Psychopharmacology*, 1986, **90**, 412–16)
- Rate limiting half-life=32 hrs +/_ 7hrs
- Time to steady state=6 days.

## Zuclopenthixol decanoate ('Clopixol', 'Clopixol Conc')

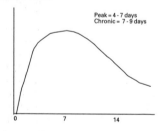

**Zuclupenthixol decanoate** (Clopixol ®) is an established antipsychotic which has also been used in high dose in aggression, particularly in learning disabilities and forensic patients but is not indicated for this.
- Duration of action=2–4 weeks
- Peak=4–9 days
- Rate limiting half-life=17–21 days (multiple doses)
- Time to steady state=10–12 weeks.

## + (Not yet licensed) antipsychotics*

A number of antipsychotics are available in only some countries but may become available in others during the life of this book, and so are included here for information.

### Aripiprazole *

Aripiprazole is a dopamine D2 and $5HT_{1A}$ receptor partial agonist, and a $5HT_{2A}$ receptor antagonist. It stimulates dopamine receptors but to a lower level than dopamine, whilst blocking endogenous dopamine (100% D2 occupancy reduces D2 activity by about 30%). Thus, when dopamine activity is high it reduces this (and hence psychotic symptoms) and if low will slightly increase it. EPSE thus appear unlikely even at high dose. There is only a minimal effect on alpha-1, $H_1$ and $5HT_{2C}$ receptors. Doses of 10–15mg/d seem effective. In the major published trial to date, aripiprazole 15–30mg/d was therapeutically equivalent to haloperidol 10mg/d and superior to placebo, but with no statistical body weight changes, EPS, QTc nor raised prolactin (n=414, RCT, d/b, p/c, 4/52, Kane *et al, J Clin Psych* 2002, **63**, 763–71). Kane concluded that aripiprazole is the first agent that is not a D2 antagonist to demonstrate a rapid onset of action with sustained antipsychotic efficacy over 4 weeks. Short reports of efficacy have been shown compared to risperidone (n=404, 4/52, Saha *et al, J Biol Psych* 2001, **2**(Suppl 1), 305S) and olanzapine (Cornblatt *et al, Int J Neuropsychopharmacol* 2002, **5**(Suppl 1), S185). Overall it seems well tolerated, with no effect on prolactin (Carson *et al, Int J Neuropsychopharmacol* 2002, **5**(Suppl 1), S186).
**Reviews**: *Form Monograph Serv*, Apr 2002, 143–47.

### Sertindole *

Sertindole is available in the UK on a named-patient basis. Patients started in the UK in the first year of re-launch will be entered into post-marketing surveillance, with one open trial and one comparative with another atypical. Sertindole was licensed for schizophrenia in people who are intolerant of at least one other antipsychotic and not in acute emergencies. It has $D_2$, $5HT_2$ and alpha-1 blocking activity, the $D_2$ blockade having a uniquely high limbic specificity leading to EPSEs equivalent to that of placebo at all therapeutic doses (n=497, d/b, p/c, 8/52, Zimbroff *et al, Am J Psych* 1997, **154**, 782–91). Five RCTs involving 1000 patients over 8 weeks have shown clinical effectiveness in both positive and negative symptoms compared to haloperidol (review by Pickar, *Lancet* 1995, **345**, 557–62). To minimise the risk of postural hypotension, the initial dose is 4mg/d, increased at 4mg/d every 4–5 days, to 12–20mg/d (n=16, s/b, Sramek *et al, J Clin Psychopharmacol* 1997, **17**, 419–22). Slight lengthening of QTc has been shown in some patients, although no cases of ventricular arrhythmia have been seen in trials nor post-marketing surveillance. This QTc prolongation has led to highly cautionary monitoring requirements (see SPC for full details). An ECG is required before and during treatment (see *3.2.1* for details), as well as baseline serum potassium and magnesium (corrected if abnormal). Main side effects are nasal congestion, reduced ejaculatory volume, dizziness and dry mouth (probably due to nasal effects than anticholinergic activity).
**Reviews:*** general (Tamminga *et al, Int Clin Psychopharmacol* 1997, **12**(Suppl 1), S29–35; Lee *et al, J Clin Psych* 1997, **58**, 410–16; Hale *et al, Int J Psych Clin Pract* 2000, **4**, 55–62; Wilton *et al, J Psychopharmacol* 2001, **15**, 120–26).

### Ziprasidone *

Ziprasidone is licensed in USA and some European countries for schizophrenia, it is effective in the treatment of positive, negative and depressive symptoms of schizophrenia and schizoaffective disorder. It appears to be well tolerated and to cause few, if any, EPSE or hyperprolactinaemia. Weight gain is uncommon. No serious cardiac adverse events have so far been reported. Its relative efficacy and tolerability compared with established atypicals is unclear at the moment. The main side effects are rash (5%) and orthostatic hypotension. Ziprasidone 5–20mg has been shown effective in acute psychosis, and better tolerated than haloperidol IM (n=132, 3/7, Brook *et al, J Clin Psych* 2000, **61**, 933–41), superior to placebo on PANSS with placbo level EPSE (n=278, RCT, d/b, p/c, 1yr, Arato *et al, Int Clin Psychopharmacol* 2002, **17**, 207–15), in schizoaffective disorder (n=115, RCT, d/b, p/c, 6/52, Keck *et al, J Clin Psychopharmacol* 2001, **21**, 27–35) and effective for relapse prevention (n=301, RCT, d/b, 28/52, Hirsch *et al, J Clin Psych* 2002, **63**, 516–23).

**Reviews**: general (Carnahan *et al, Pharmacotherapy* 2001, **21**, 717–30, 46 refs).

---

**+ Combinations**

Polypharmacy with antipsychotics falls into three main categories:

● same class;
● multiclass (2 drugs at full dose);
● Adjunctive and augmentation (low dose of one with standard dose of another).

Despite widespread use, there is in fact only one RCT of combination antipsychotics in schizophrenia (review, *Drugs & Ther Perspect* 2000, **16**, 9–12, 14 refs).

**Clozapine + olanzapine**

A patient responded to clozapine 100mg/d and olanzapine 10mg/d when individually neither was satisfactory (Rhoads, *J Clin Psych* 2000, **61**, 678–80).

**Clozapine + ondansetron**

Ondansetron (4mg bd) enhanced the action of clozapine in treatment-refractory schizophrenic (n=1, Briskin and Curtis, *Am J Psych* 1997, **154**, 1171). See also unlicensed/possible efficacy.

**Clozapine + risperidone \***

Resistant schizophrenics may respond quickly and noticeably to a combination of clozapine and risperidone (n=2, Morera *et al, Acta Psych Scand* 1999, **99**, 305–7; n=3, Raskin *et al, Acta Psych Scand* 2000, **101**, 334–36), although a moderate (four-fold) rise in prolactin levels can occur (n=40, open, Henderson *et al, J Clin Psych* 2001, **62**, 605–8).

**Clozapine + sulpiride \***

In the only RCT of combined antipsychotics, in treatment-resistant schizophrenia, clozapine and sulpiride produced a substantially greater improvement than clozapine alone (n=24, Shiloh *et al, B J Psych* 1997, **171**, 569–73), although the two study groups had some initial differences. The rationale was additional D2 blockade, enhancing that of clozapine (n=1 and review, Stubbs *et al, Acta Psych Scand* 2000, **102**, 390–94).

**Clozapine + quetiapine**

After 6-months on clozapine (200–800mg/d), randomly selected patients had 25% of the clozapine dose converted to quetiapine (1mg clozapine:2mg quetiapine). The average weight loss was 0.22–10.5kg after one-month, and maintained, with '100% user satisfaction' reported, and improvement in those (n=13) who had developed diabetes (n=65, open, 10/12, Reinstein *et al, Clin Drug Invest* 1999, **18**, 99–104).

**ECT + antipsychotics \***

Combined ECT and antipsychotics may be beneficial for positive (but not negative) symptoms of schizophrenia, with a 55% response rate and a possible role early in an acute exacerbation of chronic schizophrenia (n=93, *Psychiatry Res* 2001, **105**, 107–15).

**Lamotrigine + antipsychotics \***

In treatment-resistant schizophrenia, lamotrigine augmentation of clozapine (n=7) produced a significant reduction of BPRS, but not when augmenting risperidone (n=3), haloperidol (n=3), olanzapine (n=3) or flupentixol (n=1). Topiramate (n=9) had no detectable augmentation effect on these drugs (open, 24/52, Dursun and Deakin, *J Psychopharmacol* 2001, **15**, 297–301), which adds to the theory that glutamate hyperfunction may be involved. A small open study suggested that adjunctive lamotrigine (125–250mg/d) could produce a significant improvement in schizophrenics only partly responding to clozapine (n=6, open, 24/52, Dursun and McIntosh, *Arch Gen Psych* 1999, **56**, 950; see also n=3, Saba *et al, J Neuropsych Clin Neurosci* 2002, **14**, 86), suggesting a differential effect with atypicals.

### Loxapine + cyproheptadine
Loxapine 15mg/d plus cyproheptadine 8mg twice a day, produced a 33% to 43% improvement in BPRS scores in the first two weeks (n=3, open, Kapur and Zipursky, *Arch Gen Psych* 1998, **55**, 666–67).

### Reboxetine + antipsychotics *
Reboxetine has no advantage over placebo as an adjunct to haloperidol in schizophrenia (n=30, RCT, 6/52, Schutz and Berk, *Int Clin Psychopharmacol* 2001, **16**, 275–78).

### Risperidone + olanzapine
This combination has been used, with some success (n=5, open, Lemer *et al, Clin Neuropharmacol* 2000, **23**, 284–86).

### Valproate + antipsychotics *
There is some data that valproate may be able to reduce the doses of antipsychotics needed in schizoaffective disorder, or even replace them (Reutens and Castle, *B J Psych* 1997, **170**, 484–85) eg. early augmentation of haloperidol by valproate produced a faster response, less in-patient days and improved affective state (open, Wassef *et al, J Clin Psychopharmacol* 2001, **21**, 21–26).

---

### ● Unlicensed/Some efficacy
### Benzodiazepines
Benzodiazepines have no antipsychotic effect but short-term use may reduce anxiety, tension and insomnia and high doses may have sympto-matic effects. They may also allow lower doses of antipsychotics to be used, as high doses of antipsychotics are often used for their additional sedative properties eg. in psychotic agitation. For acute psychiatric symptoms they have a rapid onset, are highly sedative, well-tolerated and a low EPSE risk. Diazepam has been shown to be equivalent to fluphenazine and superior to placebo in treating prodromal signs of exacerbation of schizophrenia, either in antipsychotic refusers or as an adjunct to low-dose antipsychotics (n=53, d/b, Carpenter *et al, Am J Psych* 1999, **156**, 299–303). See also Acute Psychiatric Emergency (*1.1*).

### Carbamazepine *
Carbamazepine has been used in addition to antipsychotics to improve behaviour in overactive or aggressive schizophrenics. The effect on 'core' symptoms is likely to be secondary or small (Elphick, *Psycholog Med* 1989, **19**, 591–604) and only in schizophrenics, not schizoaffectives (n=162, d/b, p/c, 4/52, *Acta Psych Scand* 1989, **80**, 250–59). It is ineffective as maintenance (n=27, d/b, c/o, 95/7, Carpenter *et al, Arch Gen Psych* 1991, **48**, 69–72). Based on available RCTs, Cochrane could not recommend carbamazepine for routine use in schizophrenia, either as monotherapy or augmentation (Leucht *et al, CDSR* 2002, **3**, 001258) and a related systematic review and meta-analysis of the 10 RCTs (n=283) of carbamazepine augmentation in schizophrenia failed to show any clinically significant positive effect (n=283, Leucht *et al, J Clin Psych* 2002, **63**, 218–24).

---

### ❍ Unlicensed/Possible efficacy
### Amoxapine *
An open pilot study suggested amoxapine may have "atypical" antipsychotic effects (n=17, open, 6/52, Apiquian *et al, Schizo Res* 2003, **59**, 35–39).

### Anticholinesterases *
There has been some interest in **donepezil**, particularly for negative

symptoms. Whilst moderate improvements in manual dexterity, memory and processing speed have been noted, the general effect is modest and needs elucidating (n=15, open, 6/52, Buchanan *et al, Schizo Res* 2003, **59**, 29–33). However, donepezil at 5–10mg/d as an adjunct to risperidone was unable to produce any significant improvements in cognitive function in schizophrenia (n=36, d/b, p/c, 12/52, Friedman *et al, Biol Psych* 2002, **51**, 349–57) and it produced strong improvements in verbal fluency but not in symptomatology in one schizophrenic (n=1, MacEwan *et al, Acta Psych Scand* 2001, **104**, 469–72) and improved memory in another (n=1, Howard *et al, J Psychopharmacol* 2002, **16**, 267–70). Unlike donepezil, rapid improvement in refractory negative symptoms of schizophrenia has been reported with **galantamine** (n=1, Rosse and Deutsch, *Clin Neuropharmacol* 2002, **25**, 272–75) and addition of galantamine to risperidone has been clinically valuable in clozapine-intolerant chronic schizophrenics (n=2, Allen and McEvoy, *Am J Psych* 2002, **159**, 1244–45).

**Bromocriptine**

It has been speculated that increasing some dopaminergic function may improve negative symptoms of schizophrenia. Bromocriptine (n=6, open, Levi-Minzi *et al, Compr Psych* 1991, **32**, 210–16), and dexamfetamine (mentioned by Breier in *Curr Opin Psych* 1995, **8**, 41–44) may decrease these negative symptoms, at least in some sub-groups of patients.

**Celecoxib \***

Adjunctive Cox-2 inhibitor celecoxib 400mg/d with risperidone 2-6mg/d produced a greater improvement in symptoms in acute exacerbations of schizophrenia compared to placebo (n=50, d/b, 5/52, Müller *et al, Am J Psych* 2002, **159**, 1029–34).

**Cycloserine \***

D-cycloserine is a partial agonist of a glutamate receptor sub-type and addition of D-cycloserine 50mg/d to typical antipsychotics, risperidone and

olanzapine produced a significant reduction in negative symptoms (n=24, d/b, p/c, c/o, 6/52, Heresco-Levy *et al, Am J Psych* 2002, **159**, 480–82; n=9, Goff *et al, Am J Psych* 1995, **152**, 1213–15), supporting the view that glutamate function may be important in schizophrenia. However, in another trial of clozapine-treated patients, successive placebo and increasing cycloserine doses failed to show an improvement in negative symptoms (n=10, Goff *et al, Am J Psych* 1996, **153**, 1628–30). Dietary supplementation with high-dose glycine is a possible adjuvant treatment option.

**Cyproheptadine**

The addition of cyproheptadine 24mg/d to haloperidol 30mg/d significantly reduced negative symptoms (n=30, RCT, Akhondzadeh *et al, J Clin Pharm and Ther* 1999, **24**, 49), supporting an earlier study, where 32mg/d showed a good response in 40%, with two relapsing on withdrawal (n=10, open, Silver *et al, Biol Psych* 1989, **25**, 502–4).

**Dipyridamole**

Combined dipyridamole (75mg/d) and haloperidol (16–20mg/d) was superior to haloperidol alone in schizophrenia, possibly being via an effect on the interaction between the adenosine and dopamine systems (n=30, RCT, Akhondzadeh *et al, J Clin Pharm Ther* 2000, **25**, 131–38).

**Estradiol (oestradiol)**

In 10 women with postpartum psychosis, estradiol reversed symptoms in 100% over two weeks, a remarkable outcome that deserves further study, say the authors (n=10, open, 6/52, Ahokas *et al, J Clin Psych* 2000, **61**, 166–69). There is also a report of daily percutaneous estradiol gel alone abolishing all psychotic symptoms in a woman whose schizoaffective psychosis appeared premenstrually (n=1, Korhonen *et al, Acta Psych Scand* 1995, **92**, 237–38).

**Folate**

15mg/d in addition to psychotropic drugs significantly improved clinical response and recovery from acute psychiatric disorders (n=123, RCT, d/b, p/c, 6/12, Godfrey et al, Lancet 1990, **336**, 392–95; Wing and Lee, B J Psych 1992, **160**, 714–15).

### Ginkgo Biloba *
Ginkgo Biloba used as an adjunct to haloperidol enhanced it's effectiveness and reduced EPS compared to placebo (n=109, RCT, d/b, p/c, 12/52, Zhang et al, J Clin Psych 2001, **62**, 878–83; comment by Knable, EBMH 2002, **5**, 90).

### Glycine *
In two trials of this excitatory amino acid as adjunct therapy, 15g/d produced some responders in chronic treatment-resistant schizophrenics (n=6, J Clin Psychopharmacol 1990, **10**, 71–72) and a reduction in negative and cognitive symptoms (n=11, RCT, Heresco-Levy et al, B J Psych 1996, **169**, 610–17). Best results were in patients with low pre-treatment plasma glycine levels. However, glycine 60g/d had no statistically significant effects when used as augmentation of clozapine in schizophrenia (n=30, d/b, p/c, Evins et al, Am J Psych 2000, **157**, 826–28). Adjunctive high-dose glycine was effective with no increase in antipsychotic levels (n=12, RCT, Javitt et al, Int J Neuropsychopharmacol 2001, **4**, 385–91).

### Lithium *
Lithium-responsive psychosis does occur and may be familial and perhaps genetically distinct from the bulk of schizophrenias (n=24 + families, Sautter et al, J Aff Dis 1990, **20**, 63–69) eg. with few negative symptoms and an absence of a family history of schizophrenia (n=66, Schexnayder et al, Am J Psych 1995, **152**, 1511–13). Generally, use of lithium does not result in symptomatic improvement but may help where affective symptoms are prominent (n=21, d/b, p/c, c/o, Terao et al, Acta Psych Scand 1995, **92**, 220–24; n=5, case series, Martin et al, J Clin Psych 2000, **61**, 948).

### Melatonin
Melatonin 2mg significantly improved sleep efficiency in chronic schizophrenics with poor sleep, but not in those with better sleep efficiency (n=19, RCT, Shamir et al, J Clin Psych 2000, **61**, 373–77).

### Mianserin *
Mianserin 30mg/d as an adjunct to haloperidol or perphenazine produced a significant improvement in BPRS compared to placebo (n=27, d/b, p/c, Shiloh et al, Int Clin Psychopharmacol 2002, **17**, 59–64).

### Ondansetron
Ondansetron may block raised dopamine function without sedating. There is an isolated case report of a good response at 4mg/d in a drug-resistant patient (n=1, Lancet 1991, **i**, 1173). In a study of psychosis in advanced Parkinson's Disease, 94% responded to ondansetron, with reduced hallucinations, paranoid delusions and confusion (n=16, open, 8/52, Zoldan et al, Neurology 1995, **45**, 1304–8). See also combinations.

### Omega-3 Fatty Acids *
There is some evidence for abnormal phospholipid metabolism in schizophrenia, although trials with PUVAs have produced inconsistent but usually favourable findings (review by Peet, Adv Psych Treat 2002, **8**, 223–29). E-EPA (Ethyl Eicosapentaenoic Acid) may be effective as adjunctive therapy for persistant psychotic symptoms (n=40, RCT, 12/52, Emsley et al, Am J Psych 2002, **159**, 1696–98). However, omega-3 fatty acids have been shown to be ineffective in treating residual symptoms of schizophrenia (n=87, RCT, 16/52, Fenton et al, Am J Psych 2001, **158**, 2071–74).

### SSRIs *
There has been some interest in the SSRIs as adjuvant therapy. **Citalopram** has been trialled successfully for the depressive/anxiety symptoms of PANSS (RCT, Taiminen et al, Int Clin Psychopharmacol 1997, **12**, 31–35) and has been shown to improve subjective well-being (n=90, d/b, p/c,

Salokangas *et al, Acta Psych Scand* 1996, **94**, 175–80). **Fluoxetine** 20mg/d significantly improved positive and negative symptoms in conjunction with antipsychotics in two open studies of treatment-resistant schizophrenics (n=9, open, 6/52, Goff *et al, Am J Psych* 1990, **147**, 492–94; Bachr and Ruskin, *Am J Psych* 1991, **148**, 274–75), but may increase the incidence of EPSEs (review: Ciraulo and Shader, *J Clin Psychopharmacol* 1990, **10**, 48–50) and was ineffective in clozapine-treated patients (n=33, open, p/c, 8/52, Buchanan *et al, Am J Psych* 1996, **153**, 1625–7). A small study indicated that adjunctive paroxetine may offer sustained efficacy in treating negative symptoms of chronic schizophrenia (n=8, open, 30/12, Jockers-Scherübl *et al, J Clin Psych* 2001, **62**, 573). **Fluvoxamine** was ineffective in augmentation of risperidone-resistant schizophrenia (n=30, open, 12/52, Takashi *et al, Hum Psychopharmacol* 2002, **17**, 95–98; review of fluvoxamine as an adjunct by Silver, *CNS Drug Rev* 2001, **7**, 283–304), but should only be used with clozapine with extreme care (see *4.2.2*).

### Tetrabenazine

This has been used for the treatment of psychoses and psychoneuroses but the high incidence of side-effects makes this a relatively unsuitable drug.

◊ **Others**

Other drugs that have been tried include **azathioprine** (n=1, Levine, *Lancet* 1994, **344**, 59–60), high dose **beta-blockers** (propranolol: *Lancet* 1980, **ii**, 627–28; nadolol up to 120mg/d: *Clin Pharm* 1989, **8**, 132–35), **clonidine** as augmentation (*B J Psych* 1988, **152**, 293), **calcium-channel blockers** (such as nifedipine: *Am J Psych* 1992, **149**, 1615; and verapamil: *Drug Intell Clin Pharm* 1990, **24**, 838–40), **dexamfetamine** (small trial, van Kammen and Bornow, *Int Clin Psychopharmacol* 1988, **3**, 111–21), **famotidine** (n=1, *Lancet* 1990, **335**, 1312; review by Martinez, *Ann Pharmac-*

*other* 1999, **33**, 742–47, 14 refs), **levodopa** (letter in *Am J Psych* 1988, **145**, 1180), **naltrexone/naloxone** (review by Welch and Thompson, *J Clin Pharm Ther* 1994, **19**, 279–83) and **prednisone** (n=1, Cohen *et al, Lancet* 1996, **347**, 1228).

♦ **No efficacy**

### Buspirone

Buspirone has various receptor activities, eg. $5\text{-HT}_{1A}$ partial antagonism and dopamine antagonism but no improvement was seen at up to 2400mg/d (n=10, 4/52, *Curr Therap Research* 1975, **18**, 701–5), and exacerbation of psychosis has been reported (n=1, Pantelis and Barnes, *J Psychopharmacol* 1993, **7**, 295–300). However, antipsychotic-resistant psychotic symptoms responding to buspirone 10mg/d has been reported (n=1, Medrano and Padierna, *Am J Psych* 1996, **153**, 293).

### Caffeine

Excess caffeine consumption can present as psychosis, increased arousal (eg. n=13, d/b, p/c, Lucas *et al, Biol Psych* 1990, **28**, 35–40) and has a psychotogenic effect (n=2, Zaslove *et al, B J Psych* 1991, **159**, 565–67). However, moderate use of caffeine has probably little effect on anxiety, depression and psychosis (eg. n=26, RCT, d/b, c/o, Mayo *et al, B J Psych* 1993, **162**, 543–45).

### Methylphenidate

Bolus IV methylphenidate has been used to induce an exacerbation of symptoms, in an attempt to predict those people most likely to relapse when antipsychotics are discontinued (mentioned in Klein and Wender, *Arch Gen Psych* 1995, **52**, 429–33).

### Topiramate *

Topiramate had no effect on BPRS when added to clozapine, risperidone, olanzapine or flupentixol (n=9, open, Dursun and Deakin, *J Psychopharmacol* 2001, **15**, 297–301) and a study suggested significant deterioration when added to existing antipsychotics in refractory schizophrenia, and so should not be used with clozapine as anticonvulsant cover (n=5, open, Millson *et al, Am J Psych* 2002, **159**, 675).

## Tricyclics

Tricyclics seem ineffective in treating depressive symptoms during acute psychotic episodes and may even be counterproductive (n=58, RCT, d/b, p/c, 4/52, Kramer *et al, Arch Gen Psych* 1989, **46**, 922–28).

## Vitamin B6 *

No difference in PANSS scores was detectable with $B_6$ supplementation in stable chronic schizophrenics (n=15, d/b, p/c, c/o, 9/52, Lerner *et al, J Clin Psych* 2002, **63**, 54–58).

## 1.27 RAPID-CYCLING BIPOLAR DISORDER

See also bipolar mood disorder (*1.10*), mania/hypomania (*1.19*) and depression (*1.14*)

Rapid-cycling bipolar disorder is a subclass of bipolar mood disorder, where four or more mood episodes occur in one year. Although it is a relatively uncommon (eg. 5–15% of all bipolars seen at mood disorder clinics) and often transient condition, the clinical significance of the sub-group is that it accounts for up to 80% of lithium non-responders, that antidepressant therapy of depressive phases can induce or worsen cycling in some patients (eg. Wehr and Goodwin, *Am J Psych* 1987, **176**, 633–36) and that rapid-cycling is a risk factor for suicide. Some studies suggest rapid-cycling may be associated with an underlying thyroid abnormality (Joffe *et al, Psych Res* 1988, 25, 117–21; Bauer *et al, Arch Gen Psych* 1990, **47**, 427–32). Depression has been stated to be the primary problem in rapid-cycling bipolars.

### Role of drugs:

There will probably always be a lack of robust data on the pharmacotherapy of rapid-cycling as research is complicated by the unpredictable and spontaneously remitting nature of the condition. The initial action must be to immediately stop any antidepressants

or other contributory drugs. Carbamazepine, valproate and lithium (although up to 80% may be lithium non-responders) are the first line monotherapy options. If ineffective, they may then be used in combination. Levothyroxine, nimodipine and clozapine may be effective in some patients not responsive to first line drugs and may be worth a therapeutic trial.

**Reviews:** * definitions (Maj *et al, Am J Psych* 1999, **156**, 1421–24), general (Goodnick *et al, Expert Opin Pharmacother* 2001, **2**, 1963–73; Shelton and Calabrese, *Curr Psych Reports* 2000, **2**, 310–15), use of novel anticonvulsants (Calabrese *et al, J Clin Psych* 2002, **63**(Suppl 3), 5–9).

## BNF listed

### Carbamazepine

Several studies (eg. n=18, open, 6/12, Joyce, *Int Clin Psychopharmacol* 1988, **3**, 123–29) have shown a long-term response rate ranging from 20% to 70%. The original carbamazepine study (Kishimoto *et al, B J Psych* 1983, **143**, 327–31) showed a particular effect in rapid-cycling. Doubt has, however, been raised about long-term efficacy as many people seem to lose the therapeutic response over several years (n=24, open, 4yrs, Post *et al, J Clin Psychopharmacol* 1990, **10**, 318–27).

### Lithium

Although around 80% of rapid-cyclers are lithium non-responsive (as opposed to 41% of non-rapid cyclers), lithium undoubtedly has some effect, probably by reducing the intensity of relapses rather than the actual number (n=107, open, Misra and Burns, *Acta Psych Scand* 1977, **55**, 32–40). Lithium response may be better if the sequence of relapse is mania, depression and then remission rather than depression, then mania and remission (Grof *et al, PNBP* 1987, **11**, 199–203). Poor compliance, particularly if intermittent (eg. frequent abrupt stopping), may complicate treatment by inducing relapse.

### + Combinations
#### Carbamazepine + valproate
Synergy has been reported (n=1 and review: Ketter *et al, J Clin Psychopharmacol* 1992, **12**, 276–81).

#### Lithium + carbamazepine
The combination can be useful in rapid-cyclers non-responsive to the individual drugs (eg. n=16, retrospective, Di Costanzo and Schifano, *Acta Psych Scand* 1991, **83**, 456–59). See interactions for cautions on the use of this combination (*4.5.1*).

#### Lithium + levothyroxine/thyroxine
Low dose levothyroxine added to lithium in a rapid-cycler produced complete euthymia within seven days (n=1, Bernstein, *J Clin Psychopharmacol* 1992, **12**, 443–44).

#### Lithium + valproate
Open studies have included this combination in rapid-cyclers, and reported an additive or potentiating effect, sometimes within a matter of days (mentioned by Sharma and Persad, *Lithium* 1994, **5**, 117–25).

#### Thyroid + tricyclic
Sub-therapeutic doses of $T_3$ tri-iodothyronine 25–50mcg/d (n=1, Cooke, *Am J Psych* 1990, **147**, 255) or $T_4$ levothyroxine up to 0.1mg/d have been used as augmentation to tricyclics and phenelzine (although care is needed with any use of antidepressants in rapid-cycling). This may be effective particularly in rapid-cycling disorder (n=11, open, Bauer and Whybrow, *Arch Gen Psych* 1990, **47**, 435–40) rather than equally in all depressions. See also levothyroxine/liothyronine.

---

### ● Unlicensed/Some efficacy
#### Lamotrigine *
In the largest and only prospective placebo-controlled study in rapid-cycling disorder, lamotrigine was well-tolerated, and may be useful in some rapid-cyclers (n=324, open + n=182, d/b maintenance phase, Calabrese *et al, J Clin Psych* 2000, **61**, 841–50) with survival rates favouring lamotrigine (significantly so in bipolar II patients), with 41% stable without

relapse at 6/12 (cf 26% placebo). Lamotrigine was remarkably effective compared to lithium in a trial in refractory rapid-cycling (n=14, RCT, open, 1yr, Walden *et al, Bipolar Disorder* 2000, **2**, 336–39; n=6, open, Jusumakar and Yatham, *Am J Psych* 1997, **154**, 1171–12). The optimum dose appears to be 50–200mg/d, although doses as high as 500mg/d have been used.

#### Levothyroxine/thyroxine/liothyronine *
Levothyroxine has potential efficacy at 0.3–0.5mg/d (or liothyronine 140–400mcg/d) for rapid or 48-hour cycling mania. 91% patients in one study showed clear-cut improvement of rapid-cycling on levothyroxine, supranormal free levothyroxine levels being necessary for clinical response, with minimal side-effects (n=11, open, Bauer and Whybrow, *Arch Gen Psych* 1990, **47**, 435–40) and significant response was seen in a 2-year study (n=6, open, Afflelou *et al, Encephale* 1997, **23**, 209–17). Levothyroxine 0.25–0.3mg/d, creating a slightly hyperthyroid state, was shown effective (via an unplanned dose reduction) in a lady with long-standing resistant rapid-cycling (n=1, Extein, *Am J Psych* 2000, **157**, 1704–5).

#### Valproate
No controlled studies have been carried out but several open studies have found a significant effect, with up to 83% showing a good response, particularly against manic episodes and perhaps less so with depressive episodes (reviewed by Sharma and Persad, *Lithium* 1994, **5**, 117–25), logical bearing in mind a probable GABA-enhancing mode of action. There are suggestions that the response does not wear off with time, unlike carbamazepine.

**Reviews**: easily digestible reviews (Calabrese *et al, Can J Psych* 1993, **39**[Suppl 2], 57–61; Calabrese *et al, J Clin Psychopharmacol* 1993, **13**, 280–83).

○ **Unlicensed/Possible efficacy**

**Calcium-channel blockers**

There have been reports nimodipine (highly lipophilic, allowing adequate CNS concentrations and minimal peripheral effects) in rapid-cycling with a very marked response in some patients (n=12, RCT, d/b, p/c, Pazzaglia *et al, Psychiatr Res* 1993, **49**, 257–72; Goodnick, *J Clin Psych* 1995, **56**, 330), with 90–180mg/d optimal. Verapamil is poorly lipophilic with a low central effect. See bipolar disorder (*1.10*).

**Clonazepam**

Cases exist of clonazepam being useful as an adjunct to lithium in lithium-refractory bipolars (n=5, open, Aronson *et al, Am J Psych* 1989, **146**, 77–80).

**Clozapine**

A number of case reports indicate clozapine may be effective in treatment-resistant rapid cycling (n=2, Calabrese *et al, J Clin Psychopharmacol* 1991, **11**, 396–97; n=3, Suppes *et al, Biol Psych* 1994, **36**, 338–40).

**Gabapentin\***

Some of the studies of gabapentin in mania included some rapid-cycling patients and moderate efficacy was reported (but see mania) by Shelton and Calabrese (*Curr Psych Reports* 2000, **2**, 310–15).

**Mexiletine**

Mexiletine (200–1200mg/d) may have some role as an adjunct in rapid-cyclers (n=20, open, 6/52, Schaffer *et al, J Aff Dis* 2000, **57**, 249–53).

**Olanzapine \***

Ten rapid-cyclers were classified as responding during dysphoric mania (n=13, open, 4/52, Gonzalez-Pinto *et al, J Clin Psychopharmacol* 2002, **22**, 450–54).

◆ **No efficacy**

**Antidepressants**

Up to 50% of cases of rapid-cycling may be antidepressant-induced and so discontinuation of any such drugs has to be first line treatment (n=51, open, Wehr *et al, Am J Psych* 1988, **145**, 179–84) although this has been challenged by Coryell *et al ( Arch Gen Psych* 1992, **49**, 126–31). If necessary, antidepressants should be used in rapid-cyclers only in severe depression, in low dose and only in the acute stage.

## 1.28 SEASONAL AFFECTIVE DISORDER (SAD) \*

See also depression (*1.14*), mania/hypomania (*1.19*) and bipolar mood disorder (*1.10*).

SAD is a recurrent affective disorder, predominantly major depression, but can include mania or hypomania. It has a characteristic seasonal relationship, usually autumn or winter (20 studies, Magnusson, *Acta Psych Scand* 2000, **101**, 176–84), for at least two or three years, with full remission at a characteristic time of the year and outnumbering any non-seasonal episodes. The incidence may be around 1–10% (2.4% in North Wales) and peaks in winter. Atypical depressive features include hypersomnia, increased appetite and weight and carbohydrate cravings. Theories for the cause include excess melatonin secretion, delayed or reduced amplitude circadian rhythms and serotonergic dysfunction. It is often undiagnosed with about half of sufferers being given other depressive diagnoses and antidepressants (Michalak *et al, B J Psych* 2001, **179**, 31–34). Light therapy is considered first choice for SAD (review and algorithm, *Drugs & Therapy Perspectives* 1998, **12**, 6–9, 14 refs), although it is not without risk, with side-effects including jumpiness (9%), headache (8%), and nausea (16%), despite a beneficial effect on improving bothersome symptoms (n=83, open, Terman and Terman, *J Clin Psych* 1999, **60**, 799–808). It's effects may be dose-related (meta-analysis, Lee and Chan, *Acta Psych Scand* 1999, **99**, 315–23). Bright white light appears no more effective than dim red light (n=57, RCT, Wileman *et al, B J Psych* 2001, **178**, 311–16).

**Role of drugs**: Whilst phototherapy is established, preliminary data from controlled trials indicates that drug treatment may also be effective, with the SSRIs fluoxetine and sertraline, and moclobemide suggested as effective.

**Reviews**: general (Rodin and Thompson, *Adv Psych Treat* 1997, **3**, 352– 59, 27 refs; Jepson *et al, JAMA* 1999, **39**, 822–29; Zulman and Oren, *Curr Opin Psych* 1999, **12**, 81–86, 51 refs), guide to diagnosis and management (Partonen and Lonnqvist, *CNS Drugs* 1998, **9**, 203–12).

---

○ **Unlicensed/Possible efficacy**
**Beta-blockers**
In a trial of up to 60mg/d propranolol administered pre-sunrise (5.30–6am), 73% of those with winter depression responded, and those transferred to placebo showed varying degrees of relapse. The effect may be via short-term, short-acting beta-blocker-induced truncation of nocturnal melatonin secretion early morning but not in the evening (n=33, d/b, p/c, Schlager, *Am J Psych* 1994, **151**, 1383–85). Atenolol appeared less effective in another trial (n=19, d/b, p/c, c/o, Rosenthal *et al, Am J Psych* 1988, **145**, 52–56), but a small group of patients showed a sustained and substantial response.

**Fluoxetine**
Fluoxetine may produce clinically useful improvements in SAD symptoms at 20mg/d (n=10, open, 6/52, Childs *et al, B J Psych* 1995, **166**, 196–98). In an out-patient study, fluoxetine 20mg/d was superior to placebo (59% to 34%), but was not quite statistically significant (n=68, p/c, 5/52, Lam *et al, Am J Psych* 1995, **152**, 1765–70).

**Melatonin**
A small study showed that low dose melatonin taken in the early afternoon reduced depression, possibly by a 'phase shift' mechanism (n=5, Lewy *et al, Psychiatry Res* 1998, **77**, 57–61).

**Mirtazapine**
One study has shown a rapid and well-tolerated effect in SAD (n=8,

open, 4/52, Hesselmann *et al, Hum Psychopharmacol Clin Exp* 1999, **14**, 59–62).

**Moclobemide**
Moclobemide 400mg/d for SAD was superior to placebo in a trial (n=34, RCT, d/b, p/c, 14/52, Lingjaerde *et al, Acta Psych Scand* 1993, **88**, 372–80).

**Reboxetine \***
A pilot study indicated a rapid and significant effect in SAD in 65% patients, including atypical symptoms in the first week (n=16, open, 6/52, Hilger *et al, Eur Neuropsychopharmacol* 2001, **11**, 1-5).

**St. John's wort**
One study showed some effect (s/b, see Kasper, *Pharmacopsychiatry* 1997, **30**[Suppl 2], 89–93).

**Tranylcypromine**
86% responded completely to tranylcypromine (mean dose 30mg/d) in winter depression (n=14, open, Dilsaver and Jaeckle, *J Clin Psych* 1990, **51**, 326–29).

---

♦ **No efficacy**
**Ginkgo biloba**
One study was unable to show an effect from 'Bio-Biloba' in preventing winter depression (n=27, RCT, 10/52, Lingaerde et al, *Acta Psych Scand* 1999, **100**, 62–66).

---

## 1.29 SELF-INJURIOUS BEHAVIOUR (SIB)

SIB is a self-destructive behaviour resulting in significant tissue damage, but without lethal intent. It can occur in learning disabilities (eg. Lesch-Nyhan syndrome), as well as in OCD, sadomasochism, schizophrenia, borderline personality disorder etc. There seems to be a variety of causes, eg. relief of dysphoria, poor impulse control, dissociation etc.

**Role of drugs:**
Opiate antagonists may be useful where a reward mechanism seems to exist. There is some evidence of a serotonergic involvement. Antipsychotics seem to work mainly via a non-specific sedating mechanism.

**Review**: psychopharmacology of severe SIB associated with learning disabilities (Clarke, *B J Psych* 1998, **172**, 389–94).

---

**+ Combinations**
**Clozapine + clomipramine**
This combination was successful in treating compulsive self-mutilation in a drug-resistant mild learning disability patient (n=1, Holzer *et al, Am J Psych* 1996, **153**, 133).

---

**● Unlicensed/Some efficacy**
**Antipsychotics***
Chlorpromazine and haloperidol are frequently prescribed but evidence for their efficacy is suggestive rather than conclusive. **Risperidone** was shown effective for up to 52 months in 75% of developmentally disabled in-patients (retrospective chart analysis, Brahm *et al, Pharmacotherapy* 2001, **21**, 382). Low-dose **olanzapine** (5mg/d) has been used successfully for SIB in BPD (n=2, Hough, *J Clin Psych* 2001, **62**, 296–97). **Clozapine** 200mg/d has been effective in a few cases (n=2, Hammock *et al, J Autism Dev Disord* 2001, **31**, 109–13).

**Buspirone**
In a trial of developmentally disabled individuals with self-injury and anxiety, 64% responded to doses of 20–45mg/d with a maximal response seen more than three weeks later (n=14, open, Ratey *et al, J Clin Psych* 1989, **50**, 382).

**Lithium**
Studies suggest that lithium is effective in both aggression and self-injury. In one study, response was seen in 2–8 weeks with a lithium serum concentration of 0.7–1.0mEq/L (n=42, d/b, p/c, 4/12, Craft *et al, B J Psych* 1987, **150**, 685).

**Naltrexone/naloxone***
There is conflicting data about the efficacy of naltrexone in SIB. Some trials have shown a lack of efficacy eg. mentally retarded and autistic adults failed to respond, and indeed many patients worsened (n=33, d/b, p/c, c/o, Willemsen-Swinkels *et al, Arch Gen Psych* 1995, **52**, 766–73). Although 50–100mg/d showed some improvement in hand-to-head and head-to-object SIB, the 14-day duration in the 2nd trial and variation in behaviour made statistical evaluation invalid (n=8, d/b, Thompson *et al, Am J Mental Retard* 1994, **99**, 85–102). Other studies have, however, shown some efficacy eg. 25–100mg/d orally (n=4, *Am J Mental Retardation* 1990, **95**, 93–102) and some show that SIB may get *worse* over the first few weeks of naltrexone but *then* improves and so short studies could miss the effect. It may be that lower doses (eg. 10–50mg/d) may be more effective and it undoubtedly helps some patients (eg. n=1, 32/52, Griengl *et al, Acta Psych Scand* 2001, **103**, 234–36; n=1 plus review, White and Schultz, *Am J Psych* 2000, **157**, 1574–82, 121 refs). There is some evidence of raised opioid peptide activity in autism, fragile-X syndrome and other mental handicaps, which would explain the effect.

**Propranolol**
Propranolol may decrease SIB and response may be seen with average doses of 120mg/d which may be immediate or gradual over several weeks (review; Ruedrich *et al, Am J Ment Retard* 1990, **95**, 110–19).

---

**○ Unlicensed/Possible efficacy**
**Clomipramine**
Clomipramine 25–125mg/d reduced SIB target symptoms rapidly in many subjects (n=11, open, Garber *et al, J Am Acad Child Adolesc Psych* 1992, **31**, 1157–60).

**Dextromethorphan**
30mg/d successfully controlled SIB and aggression in a man with learning disabilities (*B J Psych* 1992, **161**, 118–20).

**Fluoxetine**
Some benefit (reductions in SIB from 20–85%) has been shown in mentally retarded young adults (Ricketts *et al, J Am Acad Child Adolesc Psych* 1993, **32**, 865–69).

**Topiramate***
Topiramate 200mg/d was observed to produce remission of self-mutilation in a patient with BPD (n=1, Cassano *et al, Bipolar Disorders* 2001, **3**, 161).

## 1.30 SEROTONIN SYNDROME

Serotonin syndrome (SS) is a condition caused by drug-induced serotonin hyperstimulation. It probably goes largely unreported as symptoms are usually mild and difficult to diagnose, although it can be severe, with deaths reported (Sampson and Warner, *Br J Gen Pract* 1999, **49**, 867–68, editorial).

**Sternbach's Diagnostic Criteria:**
1. At least three of the following: mental state changes (esp. confusion), agitation/restlessness, sweating, diarrhoea, fever, hyperreflexia, tachycardia, myoclonus, lack of co-ordination, shivering, tremor.
2. Other causes, eg. infection, metabolic, substance abuse or withdrawal ruled out.
3. No concurrent antipsychotic dose changes prior to symptom onset.

Other symptoms can include nausea, vomiting, tachycardia and myoclonus. Hypertension, convulsions and multiple organ failure have been reported. Onset is usually within a few hours of drug/dose changes and usually resolves in 24 hours. Recurrent mild symptoms may occur for weeks before a full-blown syndrome appears. Severe cases have been confused with NMS (*1.22*).

**Causes:**
SS has been reported with SSRIs, MAOIs (including moclobemide and selegiline), tricyclic and related drugs, dextromethorphan and levodopa, usually in combination but can be with single drugs or in overdose (see *5.13* for sample list). Patients usually present within 24 hours of a medication initiation, overdose or dose change.

**Role of drugs:**
First-line treatment should be to discontinue identifiable serotonergic drugs (including over-the-counter sympathomimetics), then provide symptomatic support, eg. cooling blankets etc. Mild cases can usually be managed with drug discontinuation and benzodiazepines. More severe cases require major supportive measures. No prospective studies are available yet to compare the reported drug treatments for serotonin syndrome.

**Reviews:*** general (Mason *et al*, *Medicine (Baltimore)* 2000, **79**, 201-9; Gillman, *J Psychopharmacol* 1999, **13**, 100-9; Mills, *Crit Care Clin* 1997, **13**, 763–83; LoCurto, *Emerg Med Clin North Am* 1997, **15**, 665–75.

---

● **Unlicensed/Some efficacy**

### Benzodiazepines
Lorazepam (1–2mg by slow IV injection every 30 minutes until excessive sedation occurs) has been recommended as being effective and superior to clonazepam for serotonin toxicity. Clonazepam has a lower affinity for peripheral benzodiazepine receptors than lorazepam and diazepam which may explain its lower efficacy (eg. Nierenberg and Semprebon, *Clin Pharmacol Ther* 1993, **53**, 84–88).

### Chlorpromazine
IM chlorpromazine has been used for its sedative effect (n=1, Graham, *Med J Aust* 1997, **166**, 166–67).

### Cyproheptadine *
Cyproheptadine (a non-specific 5-HT blocker) at 4–8mg orally (but perhaps as high as 10–20mg), repeated every 2–4 hours up to 0.5mg/kg/d maximum (beware of urinary retention) has been claimed to be the best antiserotonergic drug strategy, with case reports of rapid success (Lappin and Auchincloss, *NEJM* 1994, **331**, 1021–22; n=3, McDaniel, *Ann Pharmacother* 2001, **35**, 870–73).

---

○ **Unlicensed/Possible efficacy**

### Mirtazapine
Mirtazapine has been proposed as a possible treatment as it blocks $5-HT_2$ and $5-HT_3$ receptors (Hoes, *Pharmacopsychiatry* 1996, **29**, 81).

### Nitroglycerin
Rapidly successful use of nitroglycerin (2mg/kg/min) in severe SS has been reported (n=1, Brown and Skop, *Ann Pharmacother* 1996, **30**, 191).

## Propranolol

Propranolol (1–3mg every 5 minutes, up to 0.1mg/kg) may be useful as it blocks $5\text{-}HT_{1A}$ and $5\text{-}HT_2$ receptors (Guze and Baxter, *J Clin Psychopharmacol* 1986, **6**, 119–20).

## 1.31 SEXUAL DEVIANCY DISORDERS

Sexual deviancy disorders are abnormalities of a basic biological drive (rather like eating and it's disorders, similarly difficult to treat) and are recognised as psychiatric syndromes, and include exhibitionism, fetishism, sexual masochism or sadism, paedophilia and voyeurism, but not rape (considered a sexual expression of aggression rather than an aggressive expression of sexuality). The main characteristic is of intense, recurrent sexual arousal and fantasies, particularly connected with inanimate objects, children, non-consenting adults or the self.

### Role of drugs: *

Drug therapy may sometimes be a useful adjunct to other therapies, due to the chronic nature of the disease and its high and unpredictable relapse rates, but needs care and is controversial. One review (Bradford, *J Sex Res* 2000, **37**, 248–57) suggested a treatment hierarchy of CBT, SSRIs, low-dose antiandrogen, higher dose antiandrogen, then very high dose antiandrogen. Deviant sexual behaviour is rare in women and so drug therapy is usually aimed at reducing sexual drive in men. The success of any form of treatment is highly dependent on detailed evaluations and diagnosis. Placebo-controlled studies have huge ethical complications.

**Review:*** extensive of pharmacological options (Bradford, *J Sex Res* 2000, **37**, 248–57), sexual functioning (Meston and Frohlich, *Arch Gen Psych* 2000, **57**, 1012–30), treatment protocols for cyproterone, medroxyprogesterone etc (Reilly *et al, Can J Psych* 2000, **45**, 559–63).

### BNF listed
#### Benperidol

Benperidol is a standard and expensive butyrophenone which, although licensed for control of deviant antisocial sexual behaviour, has no proven use other than as an antipsychotic. The only double-blind study published showed a slight reduction in sexual thoughts but not in behaviour (*Drug Ther Bull* 1974, **12**, 2).

#### Cyproterone (acetate) *

Cyproterone is available in many countries to treat severe hypersexuality and sexual deviation in men. It has both antiandrogenic and antigonadotropic actions and probably acts by disrupting the receptors' response to androgens (review: Cooper, *Can J Psych* 1986, **31**, 73–79). It can reduce sexual interest, drive and arousal, as well as deviant fantasies and behaviour and significantly reduce some sexual behaviours in paraphilias and paedophilia (n=19, RCT, d/b, p/c, c/o, Bradford *et al, Arch Sex Behav* 1993, **22**, 383–402). Few proper trials support it's use and there are no adequate double-blind crossover trials in learning disability. Onset of action may be delayed for 2–3 weeks and is reversible within 3–6 weeks of stopping. An adequate trial of 4 months is thus usually recommended. A depot injection is available on a named patient basis and a syrup can be made. Relapse rates may also be reduced (Bradford, *J Sex Res* 2000, **37**, 248–57). Cyproterone 100mg/d rapidly cured a woman of severe sexual obsessions, maintained over two years and after discontinuation (Eriksson, *B J Psych* 1998, **173**, 351) and so may have other applications.

### ● Unlicensed/Some efficacy
#### LHRH antagonists *

Luteinising hormone-releasing hormone (gonadorelin, LHRH) antagonists can produce complete chemical castration and thus have a potent effect on sexual deviancy (Rousseau *et al, Can J Psych* 1990, **35**, 338–41; n=11, 12/12, Briken *et al, J Sex Marital Ther* 2001, **27**, 45–55). Nafarelin has been used for this purpose. Flutamide, a pure antiandrogen similar to cyproterone, has been used in conjunction with nafarelin and in one case resulted in rapid discontinuation in exhibitionism (n=1, Rousseau *et al, Can J Psych* 1990, **35**, 338–41). Leuprolide acetate is an alternative (n=1, Dickey, *Can J Psych* 1992, **37**, 567–69) and a depot leuprolide significant suppressed self-reported deviant sexual interests and behaviour and was well tolerated, although bone demineralisation occurred in 3 (n=12, open, Krueger and Kaplan, *Arch Sex Behav* 2001, **30**, 409–22). Also used has been triptorelin (n=6, Thibaut *et al, Acta Psych Scand* 1993, **87**, 445–50), where 3.75mg/month plus psychotherapy was effective over 3–12 months in all men with severe paraphilia (n=30, open, Rosler and Witztum, *NEJM* 1998, **338**, 416–22) and a depot of triptorelin palmoate reduced episodes of deviant sexual behaviours (n=30, Rösler and Witztum, *NEJM* 1998, **338**, 416–22).

### Medroxyprogesterone (acetate) *

Medroxyprogesterone has indirect antiandrogenic activity by preventing testosterone release from the testicles (Cooper, *Can J Psych* 1986, **31**, 73–79) and increasing the metabolic clearance of testosterone, resulting in suppression of sexual arousal and libido. Adverse effects include weight gain, diabetes and DVTs although feminisation has not been reported. Again, few proper trials have been carried out. Due to a possible central tranquillising effect, care is needed on ethical grounds (Berlin, *Bull Am Acad Psych Law* 1989, **17**, 233–39).

### SSRIs *

Low serotonin has been shown to produce increased sex-drive in animals, and so SSRIs may have a significant effect in reversing this eg. reduced daily frequency and duration of paraphilia and related disorders has been shown (n=26, open case series, Kafka and Hennen, *J Clin Psych* 2000, **61**, 664–70). A similarity between sexual deviancy and OCD has been postulated and there are case reports of the successful use of fluoxetine to decrease the intensity and intrusiveness of sexual fantasies, resulting in more conventional sexual behaviour and impulse control (eg. n=199, Greenberg and Bradford, *Sexual Abuse* 1997, **9**, 525–32). SSRI-induced anorgasmia may be a contributory factor to this effect. Controlled clinical trials are needed to confirm a definite effect.

---

### ○ Unlicensed/Possible efficacy

### Imipramine

Some improvements in paraphilic and nonparaphilic sexual addictions and depressive symptoms were noted in 90% patients treated with imipramine, fluoxetine or lithium (n=10, Kafka, *J Clin Psych* 1991, **52**, 60–65).

### Lithium

See imipramine.

### Methylphenidate

Methylphenidate may be cautiously but effectively used to augment the effect of SSRIs in paraphilias and related disorders (n=26, Kafka and Hennen, *J Clin Psych* 2000, **61**, 664–70).

### Naltrexone *

Compulsive sexual behaviour has been treated with naltrexone and SSRIs (n=2, Raymond *et al, Int Clin Psychopharmacol* 2002, **17**, 201–5).

## 1.32 SOCIAL PHOBIA (social anxiety disorder)

See also anxiety disorder (*1.6*).

Social phobia is the second most common phobia, where the sufferers fear public ridicule, scrutiny and negative evaluation, with fear of making a public mistake, embarrassment or criticism. Situations include public speaking, social gatherings, writing under supervision or eating and drinking in public. Anticipatory anxiety leads to impaired performance. Two sub-divisions include general and specific social phobia. It is a serious and disabling anxiety disorder associated with marked reduction in quality of life (n=829, s=3, RCTs, p/c, Stein and Kean, *Am J Psych* 2000, **157**, 1606–13) but underdiagnosed, with less than 5% receiving a diagnosis (n=3862, Katzelnick *et al, Am J Psych* 2001, **158**, 1999–2007).

**Role of drugs:**\* Drugs and behavioural approaches are commonly used. SSRIs are clearly superior to placebo and are emerging as the gold standard drug therapy, with another SSRI or moclobemide second line and MAOIs and benzodiazepines third. The only predictor of response is length of treatment, which should be at least 12 weeks (Stein *et al, J Clin Psych* 2002, **63**, 152–55). Combined drugs and psychological treatments do not generally provide better results than psychological therapies alone. A placebo response has been found to be moderately large (15 p/c studies, Oosterbaan *et al, J Psychopharmacol* 2001, **15**, 199–203).

**Reviews:**\* general (Van Ameringen *et al, CNS Drugs* 1999, **11**, 307–15; *Drugs & Therapy Perspectives* 2000, **16**, 8–9; Lipsitz and Schneier, *Pharmaco-Economics* 2000, **18**, 23–32; Sareen and Stein, *Drugs* 2000, **59**, 497–509, 66 refs), symptoms, subtypes and severity (Stein *et al, Arch Gen Psych* 2000, **57**, 1046–52), drug options (Blanco *et al, Biol Psych* 2002, **51**, 109–20), BDZs and anticonvulsants (Jefferson, *J Clin Psych* 2001, **62**(Suppl 1), 50–53, 22 refs).

**BNF listed**
**Paroxetine** \*
Several studies show paroxetine to be superior to placebo, eg. at 20–50mg/d reducing symptoms and avoidance (n=187, RCT, p/c, 12/52, Stein *et al, JAMA* 1998, **280**, 708–13), with 40mg/d the optimum dose (n=384, d/b, 12/52, Liebowitz *et al, J Clin Psych* 2002, **63**, 66–74), although with a high drop-out rate, some caution over confidence in the study has been expressed (Dahl, *EBMH* 1999, **2**, 53). Paroxetine 20–50mg/d significantly improved symptoms in another study, with the effect measurable from week 4 onwards (n=290, RCT, 12/52, Baldwin *et al, B J Psych* 1999, **175**, 120–26; review by Wilson, *EBMH* 2000, **3**, 41), another similar design study showing similar results (n=92, RCT, Allgulander, *Acta Psych Scand* 1999, **100**, 193–98). An analysis of 3 trials indicated that lack of response at 8 weeks did not predict long-term lack of response and so a minimum of 12 weeks treatment is necessary (Stein *et al, J Clin Psych* 2002, **63**, 152–55; review by Prakash and Foster, *CNS Drugs* 1999, **12**, 151–69).

○ **Unlicensed/Possible efficacy**
**Benzodiazepines** \*
The BDZs have a rapid onset, good tolerability and flexible dose, but cause sedation, incoordination and long-term use is frowned upon. Diazepam may be ineffective (n=31, d/b, c/o, s/b, James and Savage, *Am Heart J* 1984, **108**, 1150–55), alprazolam (n=65, 12/52, Gelernter *et al, Arch Gen Psych* 1991, **48**, 938–45) was equivalent to other treatments and clonazepam has been widely studied (review by Jefferson, *J Clin Psych* 2001, **62**(Suppl 1), 50–53) and appears safe and effective.

**Bupropion**
Bupropion has been used (n=10, open, 12/52, Emmanuel *et al, Depress Anxiety* 2000, **12**, 111–13).

## Gabapentin

Gabapentin (900–3600mg/d) was well tolerated and significantly reduced symptoms in one trial (eg. n=69, RCT, d/b, p/c, 14/52, Pande *et al, J Clin Psychopharmacol* 1999, **19**, 341–48).

## Moclobemide *

Moclobemide has been compared favourably with phenelzine (n=78, RCT, d/b, 24/52, Versani *et al, B J Psych* 1992, **161**, 353–60), building up to 600mg/d over two weeks and maintaining for twelve weeks to produce a therapeutic effect (Nutt and Bell, *Adv Psych Treat* 1997, **3**, 79–85). Another trial showed some efficacy but the advantage over placebo was relatively small and often not significant (n=77, p/c, Schneier *et al, Br J Psych* 1998, **172**, 70–77), and it was not effective at up to 900mg/d over placebo (n=523, p/c, 12/52, Noyes *et al, J Clin Psychopharmacol* 1997, **17**, 247–54).

## MAOIs/phenelzine *

In a complex trial, phenelzine was slightly superior to Group CBT, and both were superior to placebo (n=133, 12/52, Heimberg *et al, Arch Gen Psych* 1998, **55**, 1113–14; reviewed by Thyer, *EBMH* 1999, **2**, 80). Phenelzine was also effective for social fear, avoidance and performance fear (8/52, Walker and Kjernisted, *J Psychopharmacol* 2000, **14**(Suppl 1), S13–23).

## Mirtazapine *

One pilot study showed 41% responders and warrants full studies (n=14, open, 12/52, van Veen *et al, Int Clin Psychopharmacol* 2002, **17**, 315–17).

## Moclobemide *

Moclobemide was superior to placebo from week 4 in one study of social phobia with or without comorbid anxiety (n=390, RCT, p/c, d/b, 3-9/12, Stein *et al, Int Clin Psychopharmacol* 2002, **17**, 161–70; see also n=71, RCT, s/b, 8/52, Atmaca *et al, Hum Psychopharmacol* 2002, **17**, 401–5).

## Nefazodone

76% improved in one trial (n=23, open, 12/52, Van Ameringen *et al, J Clin Psych* 1999, **60**, 96–100).

## SSRIs *

**Citalopram** 40mg/d appears well-tolerated and as effective (75% response) as moclobemide (n=71, RCT, s/b, 8/52, Atmaca *et al, Hum Psychopharmacol* 2002, **17**, 401–5), supported by additional reports (eg. n=22, open, Bouwer and Stein, *J Aff Dis* 1998, **49**, 79–82; Varia *et al, PNBP* 2002, **26**, 205–8). **Fluvoxamine** may have some role, 200mg/d (average dose) being shown to be superior to placebo (n=92, RCT, Stein *et al, Am J Psych* 1999, **156**, 756–60) and in treating clozapine-induced social phobia (n=12, open, 12/52, Pallanti *et al, J Clin Psych* 1999, **60**, 819–23). **Sertraline** (up to 200mg/d) was more effective than placebo in a well designed flexible-dose trial, although the exclusion criteria were unclear (n=204, RCT, 20/52, van Ameringen *et al, Am J Psych* 2001, **158**, 275–81; review by Pieters, *EBMH* 2001, **4**, 91), and another trial showed some efficacy (n=12, d/b, c/o, Katzelnick *et al, Am J Psych* 1995, **152**, 1368–71). It's efficacy in general practice may be enhanced by combination with exposure therapy (n=387, RCT, d/b, 24/52, Blomhoff *et al, B J Psych* 2001, **179**, 23–30). See also fluoxetine below.

## Tricyclics *

One small open trial showed low response and high drop-out from side effects (n=15, open, 8/52, Simpson *et al, J Clin Psychopharmacol* 1998, **18**, 132–35).

---

## ◆ No efficacy

## Beta-blockers *

There is no evidence for efficacy, except perhaps in people where management of tremor is essential, eg. musicians (eg. nadolol; n=31, d/b, c/o, s/b, James and Savage, *Am Heart J* 1984, **108**, 1150–55). Pindolol 15mg/d was no more effective than placebo in augmenting SSRI treatment of generalised social phobia (n=14, d/b, p/c. c/o, 4/52, Stein *et al*, *Am J Psych* 2001, **158**, 1725–27).

### Fluoxetine*

A large pilot study failed to show that fluoxetine up to 60mg/d was superior to placebo, which itself had an un-usually high response rate (n=60, RCT, d/b, 14/52, Kobak *et al, J Clin Psychopharmacol* 2002, **22**, 257–62).

### Valproate*

A small study showed complete ineffectiveness of valproate up to 1500mg/d (n=16, mentioned by Jefferson, *J Clin Psych* 2001, **62**(Suppl 1), 50–53).

### 1.33 TOURETTE'S SYNDROME (Gilles de la Tourette)

See also OCD (*1.23*) and self-injurious behaviour (1.29).

### Symptoms:

The main diagnostic symptoms of this hereditary multiple tic disorder include multiple tics, vocal tics (grunts, snarls etc. including obscenities), stereotyped movements (jumping and dancing), overactivity, learning difficulties and emotional problems. It occurs in 1–5 per 10,000 of the population and is more common in males. It has an onset at 5–6 years, beginning with respira-tory or vocal tics with grunting or barking noises. Psychiatric co-morbid-ity is common, eg. OCD, anxiety, depression, ADHD etc.

### Role of drugs:

If the disease is affecting the person's ability to function, drug therapy may be useful. Low starting doses, gradual increases and adequate trials are neces-sary. Dysregulation of presynaptic dopamine function has been proposed (Malison *et al, Am J Psych* 1995, **152**, 1359–61), and drugs such as haloperi-dol are often effective.

**Reviews:** general (Kossoff and Singer, *Paediatr Drugs* 2001, **3**, 355–63; Robertson and Stern, *B J Hosp Med* 1997, **58**, 253–55), pharmacological options (Jimenez-Jimenez and Garcia-Ruiz, *Drugs* 2001, **61**, 2207–20).

### BNF Listed
### Haloperidol

0.5–40mg/d is the licensed drug of choice. Side-effects may be limiting and its efficacy has been questioned (n=22, p/c, d/b, Sallee *et al, Am J Psych* 1997, **154**, 1057–62). See also pimozide and nicotine chewing gum.

● **Unlicensed/Some efficacy**
### Clonidine*

Clonidine 0.1–0.6mg/d may be as effective as haloperidol in some patients. In one trial, clonidine was more effective than placebo (n=47, d/b, *Arch Gen Psych* 1991, **48**, 324–28), but in another of clonidine (up to 0.2mg/d) and desipramine (up to 100mg/d) in children with both ADHD and Tourette's syndrome, desipramine was superior to clonidine in reducing ADHD and tic symptoms (n=37, d/b, p/c, c/o, Singer *et al, Pediatrics* 1995, **95**, 74–81). Clonidine or methylphenidate alone and in com-bination are effective for ADHD with comorbid tics (n=16, RCT, p/c, 16/52, TSSG, *Neurology* 2002, **58**, 527–36; review by Goldberg, *EBMH* 2002, **5**, 122).

### Lorazepam

1.5–10mg/d may be useful as adjuvant therapy.

### Pimozide

Two trials have shown pimozide 1–20mg/d to be superior to haloperi-dol, eg. in children with Tourette's and ADHD (n=66, open, Sallee *et al, Acta Psych Scand* 1994, **90**, 4–9; n=22, p/c, d/b, Sallee *et al, Am J Psych* 1997, **154**, 1057–62).

### Risperidone*

There are now a number of studies showing a significant effect. Risperi-done (mean dose 2.5mg/d) was clearly superior to placebo on global assess-ment of Tourette symptoms (n=48, RCT, d/b, p/c, Dion *et al, J Clin Psy-chopharmacol* 2002, **22**, 31–39) and a mean dose of 3.8mg/d was at least as effective as pimozide (mean 2.9mg/d), but was much better tolerated (n=50, d/b, 12/52, Bruggeman *et al, J Clin Psych* 2001, **62**, 50–56). Risperidone may have a similar efficacy to clonidine over a wide range of symptoms (n=21, RCT, d/b, 8/52, Gaffney *et al, J Am Acad Child Adolesc Psych* 2002, **41**, 330–36) and there are cases of response in multiple drug-resistant Tourette's syndrome and OCD responding rapidly to risperidone 6mg/d (Giakas, *Am J Psych* 1995, **152**, 1097–98; Shulman *et al, Neurology* 1995, **45**, 1419) and one open trial (n=38, 4/52, Bruun and Budman, *J Clin Psych* 1996, **57**, 29–31).

### Sulpiride
200–400mg/d has been used, and has been considered by some as a treatment of choice.

---

### + Combinations
### Naltrexone + codeine
Sequential use of naltrexone (100–300mg/d) and codeine phosphate (15–120mg/d) has proved effective (n=2, McConville *et al, Lancet* 1994, **343**, 601). See also naltrexone/opiate antagonists.

---

### ○ Unlicensed/Possible efficacy
### Buspirone
Drug-resistant Tourette's has been treated successfully with buspirone 30mg/d (n=1, Dursun *et al, Lancet* 1995, **345**, 1366–67).

### Cannabinoids
In a survey of people with Tourette's who had tried marijuana, 82% reported a reduction or complete remission in motor and vocal tics, urges and OCD symptoms (n=17, Muller-Vahl *et al, Acta Psych Scand* 1998, **98**, 502–6). A report of effective use of Delta-9-THC has been published (n=1, Muller-Vahl *et al, Am J Psych* 1999, **156**, 495), with RCT's now planned.

### Fluoxetine
81% patients with OCD in Tourette's syndrome had improved symptoms on fluoxetine (n=32, open, *Neurology* 1991, **41**, 872–74). A potential effect for fluoxetine has been suggested in children with OCD symptoms in Tourette's syndrome (n=11, Kyrlan *et al, Clin Neuropharmacol* 1993, **16**, 167–72).

### Methadone
Up to 110mg/d has been used successfully in one treatment-resistant case (Meuldijk and Colon, *Am J Psych* 1992, **149**, 139–40).

### Methylphenidate *
Methylphenidate can aggravate tics or be associated with their appearance (Klein and Wender, *Arch Gen Psych* 1995, **52**, 429–33) but one study has shown that although some tics are significantly worse, generally these are not to the extent of contraindicating a trial, eg. in ADHD with Tourette's (Gadow *et al, Arch Gen Psych* 1995, **52**, 444–55). See also clonidine.

### Nicotine
Nicotine chewing gum enhanced the symptomatic effects of haloperidol when used in combination (n=10, open *Am J Psych* 1991, **148**, 793–94). Transdermal nicotine (7mg/d) was superior to placebo as an adjunct to haloperidol (n=70, 56 completers, d/b, p/c, Silver *et al, J Clin Psych* 2001, **62**, 707–14; n=6, Silver and Sanberg, *Lancet* 1993, **342**, 182). A further open study (n=16, aged 9–15 years) has shown that a single transdermal nicotine patch (7mg/24 hours) shows a significant effect over 1–2 weeks, with considerable individual variation (Silver *et al, J Am Acad Child Adolesc Psychiatry* 1996, **35**, 1631–36). Long-term use has obvious problems, and PRN usage may help minimise this.

### Olanzapine *
There is small study and case reports of response (n=10, open, 8/52, Budman *et al, J Clin Psych* 2001, **62**, 290–94; n=1, Bhadrinath, *B J Psych* 1998, **173**, 366) and it may be as effective but better tolerated than pimozide (n=4, d/b, c/o, 52/52, Onofrj *et al, J Neurol* 2000, **247**, 443–46).

### Paroxetine
Paroxetine may have a role in treatment of episodic rage in Tourette's (n=45, open, 8/52, 75% had reduced or absent rage episodes, Bruun and Budman, *J Clin Psych* 1998, **59**, 581–84).

## Pergolide
Pergolide (up to 300mcg/d) was shown to be safe and effective in children with Tourette's disorder, chronic motor or vocal tic disorder (n=245, RCT, 6/52, Gilbert *et al, Neurology* 2000, **54**, 1310–16).

## Selegiline
Selegiline was just significantly superior to placebo in children with Tourette's syndrome and ADHD (n=24, d/b, p/c, c/o, Feigin *et al, Neurology* 1996, **46**, 965–68).

## Topiramate *
There have been cases of Tourette's syndrome responding to topiramate up to 200mg/d (n=2, Abuzzhab and Brown, *Am J Psych* 2001, **158**, 968).

## ◊ Others *
Other drugs used include **calcium-channel blockers** (verapamil and nifedipine, but diltiazem; n=2, Walsh *et al, Am J Psych* 1986, **143**, 1467–68), **clomiphene** (*Postgrad Med J* 1987, **63**, 510), **nifedipine** (Berg, *Acta Psych Scand* 1985, **72**, 400–1; Goldstein, *J Clin Psych* 1984, **45**, 360), and **pentazocine** (*Clin Pharm* 1985, **4**, 494).

## ♦ No efficacy
## Naltrexone/opiate antagonists
One study of a selective opioid antagonist suggested that Tourette's syndrome does not arise from a primary abnormality of opioid receptor dysfunction (n=6, Weeks *et al, Lancet* 1994, **343**, 1107–8).

## 1.34 TRICHOTILLOMANIA
See also OCD (*1.23*)

### Symptoms:
Trichotillomania presents as impulsive pulling out one's own hair (scalp, eyebrows, and eyelashes as well as pubic, chest etc), resulting in noticeable hair loss. It is associated with obsessive-compulsive behaviour, and can occur in the presence of learning disability, anxiety, depression, schizophrenia and borderline personality disorder and may result in relief of tension. It can be episodic or chronic, is more common in females.

### Role of drugs:
A range of psychological and behaviour therapies are used and may be most effective when combined with drug therapies (Swedo and Leonard, *Psych Clin North Am* 1992, **15**, 777–90). Drug therapy is still unproven and drug trials need to be of at least 8–10 weeks duration to prove or disprove an effect in an individual case. There is evidence that longer-term treatment with SSRIs may be of benefit (Swedo *et al, NEJM* 1993, **329**, 141–42). A retrospective review of treatment outcomes, showed significant benefit from behavioural and pharmacological treatments (n=63, Keuthen *et al, Am J Psych* 1998, **155**, 560–61). One trial showed that CBT was more effective than clomipramine, and both were superior to placebo (n=23, RCT, 9/52, Ninan *et al, J Clin Psych* 2000, **161**, 47–50). Dermatological help is beneficial.

**Reviews:** * treatment options (Christenson and O'Sullivan, *CNS Drugs* 1996, **6**, 23–34), diagnosis (Hanna, *Child Psychiatry Hum Dev* 1997, **27**, 255–68), general (Hautmann *et al, J Am Acad Dermatol* 2002, **46**, 807–21; Walsh and McDougle, *Am J Clin Dermatol* 2001, **2**, 327–33; Diefenbach *et al, Clin Psychol Rev* 2000, **20**, 289–309; Keuthen *et al, Psychother Psychosom* 1998, **67**, 202–13).

## + Combinations
## Olanzapine + SSRI *
Symptom improvement has been reported when olanzapine 10mg/d was added to fluoxetine 40mg/d (n=1, Potenza *et al, Am J Psych* 1998, **155**, 1329–30). Olanzapine 1.25–7.5mg/d has been used with some success as augmentation of citalopram in refractory cases (n=4, Ashton, *Am J Psych* 2001, **158**, 1929–30).

## Risperidone + fluvoxamine *
Resistant trichotillomania has responded to risperidone augmentation of fluvoxamine (n=1, Gabriel, *Can J Psych* 2001, **46**, 285–86).

● **Unlicensed/Some efficacy**
**Clomipramine**
Several studies (eg. Swedo *et al, NEJM* 1989, **321**, 497–501) have shown clomipramine in doses of around 180mg/d to be effective in some patients with trichotillomania. Some patients non-responsive to fluoxetine have then responded to clomipramine (eg. Naylor and Grossman, *J Am Acad Child Adolesc Psych* 1991, **30**, 155–56).

○ **Unlicensed/Possible efficacy**
**Citalopram**
Citalopram may be safe in trichotillomania, with modest but significant improvements (n=14, open, 12/52, Stein *et al, Eur Arch Psychiatry Clin Neurosci* 1997, **247**, 234–36).

**Fluoxetine**
Fluoxetine appears minimally effective, the doses required are high (up to 80mg/d) and if response occurs, relapse is not uncommon. One study failed to show an effect on hair-pulling at up to 80mg/d on any of the measures used (n=23, d/b, c/o, 31/52, Streichenwein and Thornby, *Am J Psych* 1995, **152**, 1192–96) but there are some reports of response (eg. Winchel *et al, J Clin Psych* 1992, **53**, 304–8; n=21, RCT, d/b, c/o, 18/52, Christenson, *Am J Psych* 1991, **148**, 1566–71). It is generally considered second line to clomipramine.

**Fluvoxamine**
Some potential use has been reported in reducing overall distress but not hair pulling (n=21, open, 12/52, Stanley *et al, J Clin Psychopharmacol* 1997, **17**, 278–83).

**Haloperidol** *
Haloperidol has been used successfully as augmentation of SSRIs (n=9, open, Van Ameringen *et al, J Aff Dis* 1999, **56**, 219–26).

**Inositol** *
Inositol, a glucose isomer with notable effects on serotonin, was well tolerated and effective in reducing hair pulling in patients unwilling to take or intolerant of SSRIs (n=3, Seedat *et al, J Clin Psych* 2001, **62**, 60–61).

**Lithium**
80% patients tried on lithium for chronic hair pulling showed reduced hair pulling and some hair re-growth, possibly via an effect on aggressive behaviour (n=10, open, 14/12, Christenson *et al, J Clin Psych* 1991, **52**, 116–20).

◊ **Others** *
Other drugs tried include **paroxetine** (n=1, Reid, *Am J Psych* 1994, **151**, 290), **pimozide** as SSRI augmentation (eg. *J Clin Psych* 1992, **53**, 123–26) and **trazodone** (eg. Sunkureddi and Markovitz, *Am J Psych* 1993, **150**, 523–24).

**Unlicensed/non-UK drugs**

Two UK sources of special, foreign and unlicensed drugs are Durbin, 180 Northolt Road, Mornington Crescent, South Harrow, Middlesex HA2 0LT, www.durbin.co.uk, and *IDIS*, Millbank House, 171-185, Ewell Road, Surbiton, Surrey KT6 6AX, www.idispharma.com.

**1.35–6 OTHER DRUG RELATED TOPICS**

**1.35 CAFFEINISM**

Caffeine consumption at 250–500mg/d is regarded as moderate use. Caffeinism is estimated to start at a consumption of between 600mg and 750mg/d, with above 1000mg/d well into the toxic range. 12mcg/mL is the US Olympic Committee upper limit for caffeine levels (*Am J Hosp Pharm* 1990, **47**, 303). Caffeine dependence displays features of a typical psychoactive substance dependence, ie. withdrawal, continued use despite caffeine-induced problems, tolerance and persistent desire or unsuccessful attempts to cut down or control use (n=16, Strain *et al, JAMA* 1994, **272**, 1043–48). Positive effects of moderate amounts include increased alertness and vigilance and reduced fatigue.

Caffeine withdrawal is a DSM-IV diagnosis and thus should be taken seriously. Sudden withdrawal can produce headaches (52%), rebound drowsiness, fatigue/lethargy and depression (n=62, d/b, 4/7, Silverman et al, *J Psychopharmacol* 1991, **5**, 129–34; *NEJM* 1992, **327**, 1109–14; review by Dews *et al, Food Chem Toxicol* 2002, **40**, 1257–61), with many other effects reported.

**Intake can be calculated thus:**

| Source | caffeine content | |
|---|---|---|
| | per 100ml | per container |
| Brewed coffee | 55–85mg | 140–210mg/mug |
| Instant coffee | 35–45mg | 85–110mg/mug |
| Decaffeinated coffee | 2mg | 5mg/mug |
| Cocoa | 3mg | 7mg/mug |
| Brewed tea | 25–55mg | 55–140mg/mug |
| Coca Cola | 11mg | 36mg/can |
| Pepsi Cola | 7mg | 22mg/can |
| Milk chocolate | | 22mg/100g |
| Hedex Seltzer | | 60mg/sachet |
| Aqua Ban | | 100mg/tablet |
| a mug is taken as being 250ml | | |

## Symptoms of caffeinism (acute or chronic):

**Adverse-effects of low to moderate doses**: Diuresis, increased gastric secretion, fine tremor, increased skeletal muscle stamina, mild anxiety, negative mood, palpitations, nervousness

**Side-effects of high doses**: chronic insomnia, persistent anxiety, restlessness, tension, irritability, agitation, tremulousness, panic, poor concentration, confusion, disorientation, paranoia, delirium, tremor, muscle twitching and tension, convulsions, vertigo, dizziness, tinnitus, auditory and visual hallucinations, facial flushing, hyperthermia, hypertension, nausea, vomiting, abdominal discomfort, headaches, tachypnoea and disturbed sleep.

**Adverse consequences**: There is some contradictory evidence about the effect of caffeine on people with mental health problems. Clearly, high doses can cause significant effects. Acute high doses (10mg/kg) significantly increase arousal and have a psychotogenic effect in schizophrenics (n=13, d/b, Lucas *et al, Biol Psych* 1990, **28**, 35–40). Schizophrenics often have higher caffeine intakes and average intake

should be routinely monitored (Rihs *et al, Eur Arch Psychiatry Clin Neurosci* 1996, **246**, 83–92) as it can exacerbate schizophrenia (n=2, Mikkelsen, *J Clin Psych* 1978, **39**, 732–36). Ward studies have shown that '*chronic caffeine use created clinically significant levels of anxiety and tension that could be reduced by decreasing caffeine consumption*'. Caffeinism can present as anxiety neurosis, precipitate or exacerbate psychosis and make these more resistant (n=2, Zaslove *et al, B J Psych* 1991, **159**, 565–67) to drug treatment, especially antipsychotics. The clinical signs of affective diseases can be modified. 150mg of caffeine at bedtime has been shown to have a marked effect on sleep latency, total sleep time and reduced sleep efficacy and REM periods. Consumption may be influenced by some genetic factors (n=1934 twin study, Kendler and Prescott, *Am J Psych* 1999, **156**, 223–28).

Conversely, there are reports of lack of correlation between caffeine consumption and anxiety and depression, with no changes when a ward moved to decaffeinated products (n=26, d/b, c/o, Mayo *et al, B J Psych* 1993, **162**, 543–45) and little difference in behaviours between caffeinated and decaffeinated periods (Koczapski *et al, Schizophr Bull* 1989, **15**, 339–44). Withdrawal of caffeine from a group of severely retarded and highly disturbed patients produced no improvement in sleep patterns, but reintroduction was accompanied by a highly significant increase in ward disturbances (2/52, Searle, *J Intellect Disabil Res* 1994, **38**, 383–91), which may explain the contradictions in evidence.

**Methods of caffeine reduction**:
1. Recognition of problems of excess (>750mg/d) caffeine and likely benefits of reduction.
2. Identification of all current caffeine sources and pattern of consumption.
3. Gradual reduction, eg. making weaker drinks, taken less often, increasing use of caffeine-free equivalent drinks, particularly at

'usual' drinking times of the day, mixing caffeine and decaffeinated coffee to give a lower strength.

4. Use of analgesia (caffeine-free, of course) for withdrawal headaches.

5. Setting a target for consumption, which will not need to be complete abstinence, eg. caffeine drinks only at set times in the day, eg. on rising etc.

**Causes:**

Patients may drink large quantities of tea and coffee to relieve thirst/dry mouth caused by tricyclic and phenothiazine side-effects, and caffeine is more attractive and less fattening than fruit pastilles or wine gums. In-patient settings, especially in the evening, often build in caffeine consumption.

**Reviews**: general (Smith, *Food Chem Toxicol* 2002, **40**, 1243–55; Glass, *JAMA* 1994, **272**, 1065–66), in psychiatric patients (Kruger, *Psychol Rep* 1996, **78**, 915–23).

## 1.36 ELECTRO-CONVULSIVE THERAPY

ECT was first used in its current form in 1938 (*BMJ* 1988, **297**, 1354–55) and is an established treatment for major depression, especially if marked with melancholia, psychomotor retardation, psychosis or delusions. It is also used in mania (especially manic delirium), more rarely catatonia and drug-resistant Parkinsonism. ECT is probably superior to, or at least as effective as, drugs and tends to be quicker-acting in severely depressed patients, although there remains some dispute about this. Combining maintenance ECT with antidepressants has been suggested as improving outcomes in patients who have responded to acute treatment with ECT, compared to antidepressants only (n=58, retrospective chart review, Gagné *et al, Am J Psych* 2000, **157**, 1960–65).

ECT facilitates monoaminergic transmission by increasing receptor sensitivity and increasing the turnover and release of noradrenaline (Ottosson *et al, Biol Psych* 1985, **20**, 933–46).

**High-risk patients:** These include those with severe cardiovascular disease, arrhythmias, pacemakers, obstructive pulmonary disease, asthma, pregnancy, osteoporosis, cerebral tumours, hydrocephalus and multiple sclerosis. If the patient has hypertension, sublingual nifedipine 20 minutes prior to ECT attenuates the hypertensive response (*Anaesth Intensive Care* 1989, **17**, 31–33).

**Premedication:** Atropine or glycopyrrolate are used as antimuscarinics occasionally, mainly in patients with cardiovascular risks (*Convulsive Therapy* 1989, **5**, 48–55).

**Muscle relaxants:** Suxamethonium is used to prevent fractures that can occur during the procedure secondary to the tonic-clonic muscular contractions (*Anaesthesia* 1988, **43**, 474–76).

**Induction agents:*** **Propofol** is now widely used since methohexital was withdrawn. It is well tolerated and short-acting with quick recovery, but shortens seizure length by up to 25% (*Anaesthesia* 1989, **44**, 168–69). It may effect seizure threshold and may be associated with bradycardia and hypotension. Some small studies indicate that seizure duration does not affect overall efficacy (*J Drug Dev* 1991, **4**[Suppl 3], 117–18; *Aust NZ J Psych* 1991, **25**, 255–61; n=20, d/b, Fear *et al, B J Psych* 1994, **165**, 506–9), although ECT courses may be prolonged. **Etomidate** is short-acting, has a rapid recovery, less hypotension than propofol and may lengthen seizure duration compared to methohexital and propofol (Ilivicky *et al, Am J Psych* 1995, **152**, 957–58). It may perhaps cause convulsions pre-ECT (n=1, Nicoll and Callender, *B J Psych* 2000, **177**, 373), is painful at the injection site, has a high incidence of extraneous muscle movements, and rarely causes adrenocortical dysfunction with repeated doses (a major concern which limits use with longer courses) although it can be successful (n=3, Benbow *et al, Psych Bull* 2002, **26**, 351–53). Sodium **thiopentone** has little documented effect on seizure threshold or duration but the longer duration of action can delay recovery (a particular problem in the elderly). Review by Freeman, *Psych Bull* 1999, **23**, 740–41.

**Maintenance:*** ECT has been used at 2-, 3- and then 4-weekly intervals for six months to prevent relapse (reviews by Andrade and Kurinji, *J ECT* 2002, **18**, 149–58; Gupta, *Am J Psych* 2001, **158**, 1933–34).

**Reviews:** in the elderly (Flint and Gagnon, *Can J Psych* 2002, **47**, 734–41), systematic review (s=115, Wijeratne *et al, Med J Aus* 1999, **171**, 250–54) and running an ECT department (Russell, *Adv Psych Treat* 2001, **7**, 57–64).

---

## Drug considerations
### Antipsychotics
Antipsychotics lower the seizure threshold and would be expected to lead to seizures at lower ECT doses.

### Benzodiazepines
Benzodiazepines may lessen the improvement with unilateral ECT (Abrams, *B J Psych* 1992, **161**, 129–30; Green, 717–18; n=124, Jha and Stein, *Acta Psych Scand* 1996, **94**, 101–4), and reduce the effectiveness, even several months after treatment is stopped, probably by raising seizure threshold, having an effect on seizure duration, number of sub-maximal seizures or increasing the number of treatments needed.

### Bupropion *
Use with ECT has been reported (n=2, Kellner *et al, J Clin Psychopharmacol* 1994, **14**, 215–16) as has prolonged seizures when used with lithium and venlafaxine (n=1, Conway and Nelson, *J ECT* 2001, **17**, 216–18).

### Caffeine *
240mg IV of caffeine has been used to augment seizure duration (reported by the ideally named Coffey *et al, Am J Psych* 1990, **147**, 579–85) or 300–1000mg orally (n=30, Ancill and Carlyle, *Am J Psych* 1992, **149**, 137), as has 125mg IV during treatment (Jaffe and Dubin, *Am J Psych* 1992, **149**, 1610). A small study showed a complex effect which deserves a full

study to determine the optimum dose, timing etc. (Francis *et al, Am J Psych* 1994, **151**, 1524–26). Cases of cardiac dysrhyrhmia have been reported in the elderly, so care is needed (n=3, Jaffe *et al, Convuls Ther* 1990, **6**, 308–13).

### Carbamazepine
Logic would dictate that since carbamazepine is an anticonvulsant it would have an effect on reducing seizures (as benzodiazepines above). A small retrospective study showed that in 7 patients taking either valproate or carbamazepine, seizure durations were slightly shorter but that this appeared to have no dramatic effect on the efficacy nor side-effects of ECT (n=7, Zarate *et al, Ann Clin Psych* 1997, **9**, 19–25).

### Clozapine
Novartis recommend suspending clozapine for 24 hours pre-ECT to reduce the risk of unwanted seizures. A meta-analysis of reported cases (n=36, Kupchik *et al, Clin Neuropharmacol* 2000, **23**, 14–16) indicates that 67% benefit but adverse events occur in 17%, including prolonged seizures (n=1, Bloch *et al, B J Psych* 1996, **169**, 253–54), and supraventricular tachycardia (Beale *et al, Convul Ther* 1994, **10**, 228–31).

### Flumazenil
Effective ECT was only possible in a benzodiazepine-dependent depressed woman when the anticonvulsant effect of clonazepam was reversed by flumazenil 0.1mg (Berigan *et al, Am J Psych* 1995, **152**, 957).

### Ketamine
Enhanced ECT seizure duration has been reported (mentioned in review by Weiner *et al, Psych Clin North Am* 1991, **14**, 857–67).

### Lithium
The use of lithium with ECT has been reported to cause severe memory loss, neurological abnormalities and a reduced antidepressant effect although a retrospective study showed no increase in side-effects nor other problems (n=31, Jha *et al, B J Psych* 1996, **168**, 241–43). It has been sug-

gested that ECT facilitates lithium toxicity, possibly by releasing lithium from cells, producing a pure toxicity. Elderly patients may be more susceptible to this combination. Some sources recommend discontinuing lithium 48 hours before ECT to prevent this neurotoxicity (see Lithium Encyclopaedia for Clinical Practice 1987, 274–83) and not re-started for several days after the last treatment (Ferrier *et al, Adv Psych Treat* 1995, **1**, 102–10). A review of the pros and cons of the use of lithium in ECT (Lippmann and El-Mallakh, *Lithium* 1994, **5**, 205–9) concluded that there must be clear indications for concurrent use of both treatments. However, discontinuing lithium would risk discontinuation effects and be potentially dangerous (see lithium in *1.10*).

### MAOIs

MAOIs are normally contraindicated with surgery as they can interact with opiates but there may be no great problem with the ECT itself (Freese, *Convul Ther* 1985, **1**, 190–94).

### Mirtazapine

An open study indicated that there were no problems with mirtazapine, either started before or during the course of ECT (n=19, Söderström, poster, XI World Congress Psychiatry, August 1999, Germany). There are cases of successful and uneventful use (n=2, Farah, *Convul Ther* 1997, **13**, 116–17).

### Moclobemide

The manufacturers recommend, as a precaution, suspending moclobemide for 24 hrs pre-ECT, although there is no data on its use with ECT.

### Naloxone

Naloxone has no detectable effect (Rasmussen *et al, Convuls Ther* 1997, **13**, 44–46).

### Nefazodone *

A case series showed no unduly prolonged seizures nor other problems (n=10, Ahmed, *Int J Psych Clin Pract* 1999, **3**, 64, letter), although BMS have a few reports of hypotension and prolonged seizures.

### Rivastigmine *

There is one case of a course of 8 being successful with the person taking rivastigmine throughout (n=1, Zink *et al, J ECT* 2002, **18**, 162–64).

### SSRIs

A small study showed a significantly longer seizure duration in patients taking SSRIs compared to other antidepressants (n=13, Potokar *et al Int J Psych Clin Pract* 1997, **1**, 277–80), although an earlier review did not support the theory that **fluoxetine** causes prolonged seizures (n=12, *Convulsive Therapy* 1989, **5**, 344–48). There are reports of prolonged seizures with ECT and **paroxetine** and in a rater-blinded comparison, seizure length was twice as long in those taking paroxetine (n=14, Curran, *Acta Psych Scand* 1995, **92**, 239–40). There are several reports of prolonged seizures with **fluvoxamine** and ECT and Duphar recommend a 4-day interval between stopping fluvoxamine and giving ECT. There is only limited experience with ECT and **sertraline** or **citalopram**.

### Theophylline

Theophylline (related to caffeine) at 100–400mg IV has been reported to facilitate ECT seizures in previously resistant patients (n=7, Leentjens *et al, Convuls Ther* 1996, **12**, 232–37). There are two reports of status epilepticus and increase in seizure duration with concomitant ECT.

### Trazodone

A prolonged seizure duration has been reported (*Am J Psych* 1993, **150**, 525).

### Tricyclics

Combined tricyclic and ECT therapy is often used and would seem to present no routine problems. The use of anaesthetics could enhance the risk of cardiac arrhythmias and hypotension.

### Valproate

A small retrospective study showed that in patients taking either valproate or carbamazepine, seizure durations were slightly shorter but that this appeared to have no dramatic effect on the efficacy nor side-effects of ECT (n=7, Zarate *et al, Ann Clin Psych* 1997, **9**, 19–25).

### Venlafaxine *

When propofol is used as an anaesthetic, venlafaxine seems safe with ECT at doses of up to 300mg/d but at higher doses, the possibility of asystole cannot be excluded (n=13, Gonzalez-Pinto *et al, J Neuropsych Clin Neurosci* 2002, **14,** 206-9). Prolonged recovery and unstable blood pressure has been reported in an elderly woman (Jha and Tomar, *Int J Ger Psych* 2002, **17**, 979–80).

### Zopiclone

Reduced seizure length has been reported with 7.5–15mg of zopiclone the previous night (n=2, *J Psychopharmacol* 1991, **5**, 268–69) and so it is best avoided.

# CHAPTER TWO

# SELECTING DRUGS, DOSES and PREPARATIONS

## Table 2.1.1: Hypnotics — relative effects *

| Gp | Drug | Usual night dose mg/d | Adult max. dose mg/d | Elderly max dose mg/d | Elim half-life (hours) adult | elderly | G/I upset | Hang-over | Depen-dence potent-ial |
|---|---|---|---|---|---|---|---|---|---|
| **Shorter acting Benzodiazepines** | | | | | | | | | |
| 1a | Loprazolam | 1 | 2 | 1 | 7–15 | 20 | ○ | ● | ● |
| 1a | Lormetazepam | 1 | 1.5+ | <Ad | 10 | 14 | ○ | ● | ● |
| 1a | Temazepam | 10–20 | 40 | 20 | 5–11 | 14+ | ○ | ● | ●● |
| **Longer acting Benzodiazepines** | | | | | | | | | |
| 1b | Flunitrazepam | 1 | 2 | 1 | 35 | 35 | ○ | ●● | ● |
| 1b | Flurazepam | 15 | 30 | 15+ | 47–95 | ? | ○ | ●●● | ●● |
| 1b | Nitrazepam | 5 | 10 | 5 | 18–36 | 40+ | ○ | ●●● | ● |
| **Chloral and derivatives** | | | | | | | | | |
| 2 | Chloral betane | 707 | 5 tabs | <Ad? | 7–10 | Same | ●●● | ● | ● |
| 2 | Triclofos | 1 g | 2 g | 1 g | ? | ? | ● | ? | ? |
| **Other hypnotics** | | | | | | | | | |
| 3 | Clomethiazole | N/A# | 2caps# | Same | 4–5 | Same | ○ | ● | ●● |
| 4 | Promethazine | 25 | 50 | – | ? | ? | ○ | ○ | ○ |
| 5 | Zaleplon | 10 | 10 | 5 | 2 | 3 | ○ | ○ | ○ |
| 6 | Zopiclone | 7.5 | 7.5 | <Ad | 3.5–6 | 8 | ● | ● | ● |
| 7 | Zolpidem | 5 | (10) | 10 | 2 (2–5) | Longer | ○ | ○ | ○ |

**Groups**:
1a = Shorter acting or minimally-accumulating benzodiazepines
1b = Longer acting or accumulating benzodiazepines
2 = Chloral and derivative
3 = Clomethiazole (chlormethiazole)
4 = Antihistamine
5 = Pyrazolopyrimidine
6 = Imidazopyridine
7 = Cyclopyrrone

**Side-effects**:
●●● = Marked effect       ○ = Little or nothing reported
●● = Moderate effect      ? = No information available
● = Mild effect

**Other abbreviations**:
Nightly dose = Usual dose for an adult as stated in the UK SPC
Adult max. dose = Maximum adult hypnotic dose as stated in the UK SPC
Eld. max dose = Maximum elderly hypnotic dose as stated in the UK SPC
# = 1 capsule is therapeutically equivalent to 5ml syrup (1 cap = 192mg clomethiazole base, and 5ml syrup = 157mg clomethiazole base). Indicated for severe insomnia in the elderly only.

## Table 2.1.2: Anxiolytics — relative effects*

| Gp | Drug | Average dose mg/day | Adult max. dose mg/d | Elderly max dose mg/d | Half-life (hrs) adult (+range) | elderly | Drowsi-ness | Depen-dence potent-ial |
|---|---|---|---|---|---|---|---|---|
| **Shorter acting Benzodiazepines** | | | | | | | | |
| 1a | Alprazolam | 1 | 3 | 0.75 | 14 (6–20) | L | ●● | ●● |
| 1a | Bromazepam | 9 | 18–60 | <Ad | 16 (9–20) | ? | ●● | ●● |
| 1a | Lorazepam | 4 | 4 | <Ad | 12 (8–25) | Same | ●●● | ●●● |
| 1a | Oxazepam | 30 | 120 | 80 | 8 (5–15) | Same | ●●● | ●● |
| **Longer acting Benzodiazepines** | | | | | | | | |
| 1b | Chlordiazepoxide | 30 | 100 | <50 | 12 (6–30) | L | ●●● | ●● |
| 1b | Clobazam | 30 | 60 | 20 | 18 (9–77) | L | ● | ●● |
| 1b | Clorazepate | 15 | 15? | <Ad | PD | L | ●●● | ●● |
| 1b | Diazepam | 6 | 30 | 15 | 32 (21–50) | L | ●●● | ●● |
| **Beta-blockers** | | | | | | | | |
| 2 | Oxprenolol | 80 | 80 | 80 | 4#(3–6) | Same | ● | ○ |
| 2 | Propranolol | 80 | 120 | – | 2#(1–2) | Smae | ● | ○ |
| **Other Anxiolytics** | | | | | | | | |
| 3 | Buspirone | 30 | 45 | 45 | 7 (2–11) | Same | ○ | ○ |

**Groups**:
1a = Shorter acting or minimally-accumulating benzodiazepines
1b = Longer acting or accumulating benzodiazepines. These also have active metabolites
which enhance their length of action
2 = Beta-blockers
3 = Azapirone (Azaspirodecanedione)

**Side-effects**:
●●● = Marked effect            ○ = Little or nothing reported
●● = Moderate effect           ? = No information available
● = Mild effect

**Other abbreviations**:
Adult max. dose = Maximum adult hypnotic dose as stated in the UK SPC. Most only recommend treat-
ment for up to four weeks at this dose.
Eld. max dose = Maximum elderly hypnotic dose as stated in the UK SPC. Most state that half the adult
dose should be adequate.
PD = Pro-drug metabolised to desmethyldiazepam (t1/248–200hrs)
# = Pharmacological action longer than t1/2 suggests.

The data on the previous and three following pages is based on a large number of papers. Note was taken of
presentation of data, equivalence of doses used etc. When non-comparable papers are excluded, there is a surprisingly
high level of consistency on reported relative side-effects. Individuals response may, of course, vary widely. Many
effects may be dose-related.

**Table 2.1.3: Antidepressants — relative side-effects**

| Group | Drug | Adult oral max. dose mg/d | Eld. oral max. dose mg/d | Relative side-effects (most will be dose-related) | | | | | | |
|---|---|---|---|---|---|---|---|---|---|---|
| | | | | Anti-cholinergic | Cardiac | Nausea | Sedation | Overdose | Pro-con-vulsant | Sexual dysfunction |
| **Tricyclics** | | | | | | | | | | |
| 1a | Amitriptyline | 200 | 75 | ●●● | ●●● | ●● | ●●● | ●●● | ●●● | ●● |
| 1a | Amoxapine | 300 | 150 | ●●● | ●● | ● | ●●● | ●● | ●● | ● |
| 1a | Clomipramine | 250 | 75 | ●●● | ●● | ●● | ●●● | ●● | ●●● | ●●● |
| 1a | Dosulepin (dothiepin) | 150 | 75 | ●● | ●●● | ○ | ●●● | ●●● | ●● | ●● |
| 1a | Doxepin | 300 | 50 | ● | ●●● | ● | ● | ●● | ●● | ● |
| 1a | Imipramine | 300 | <Ad | ●● | ●● | ●● | ● | ●● | ●● | ●● |
| 1a | Lofepramine | 210 | 75 | ●● | ● | ●● | ● | ○ | ○ | ●● |
| 1b | Maprotiline | 150 | 50 | ●● | ●● | ●● | ● | ●● | ●● | ● |
| 1a | Nortriptyline | 150 | <Ad | ●● | ● | ● | ● | ●● | ●● | ●● |
| 1a | Trimipramine | 300 | <Ad | ●●● | ●● | ● | ● | ●● | ● | ●● |
| **SSRIs** | | | | | | | | | | |
| 2a | Citalopram | 60 | 40 | ○ | ○ | ●● | ○ | ○ | ○ | ●● |
| 2a | Escitalopram | 20 | <20 | ○ | ○ | ●●● | ○ | ○ | ○ | ●● |
| 2b | Fluoxetine | (20) | (80) | ○ | ○ | ●● | ○ | ○ | ○ | ● |
| 2c | Fluvoxamine | 300 | 300 | ● | ○ | ●●● | ● | ○ | ○ | ● |
| 2d | Paroxetine | 50 | 40 | ○ | ○ | ●● | ○ | ○ | ○ | ●●● |
| 2e | Sertraline | 200 | 200 | ○ | ○ | ●● | ○ | ○ | ○ | ●● |

**Table 2.1.3:  Antidepressants — relative side-effects (continued)**

| Group | Drug | Adult oral max. dose mg/d | Eld. oral max. dose mg/d | Relative side-effects (most will be dose-related) | | | | | | |
|---|---|---|---|---|---|---|---|---|---|---|
| | | | | Anti-cholinergic | Cardiac | Nausea ‡ | Sedation | Overdose § | Pro-convulsant | Sexual dysfunction |
| **MAOIs** | | | | | | | | | | |
| 3a | Isocarboxazid | 60 | <Ad | •• | •• | •• | O | •• | O | • |
| 3a | Phenelzine | 90 | (90) | •• | • | •• | O | •• | O | • |
| 3b | Tranylcypromine | CA30 | (30) | • | • | •• | • | ••• | O | • |
| **Others** | | | | | | | | | | |
| 4 | Mianserin | 90+ | <Ad | • | O | O | ••• | O | O | • |
| 5 | Mirtazapine | 45 | 45 | O | O | O | •• | O | •• | •• |
| 6 | Moclobemide | 600 | 600 | • | O | • | O | O | ? | • |
| 7 | Flupentixol | 3 | 2 | •• | O | O | • | • | ? | O |
| 8 | (Nefazodone) | (600) | (400) | • | O | • | • | ? | ? | O |
| 9 | Reboxetine | 12 | NR | • | O | • | O | O | O | O |
| 8 | Trazodone | 600 | +300 | • | • | •• | ••• | • | O | •• |
| 10 | Tryptophan | 6 g | 6 g | O | •• | • | •• | • | O | •• |
| 11 | Venlafaxine | 375 | 375 | O | • | • | • | •• | • | •• |
| 12 | Bupropion (U) | – | – | • | O | • | O | •• | •• | O |

**Groups:**

1a = Tricyclic
1b = Tricyclic with a middle ring bridgie
2a = Bicyclic isobenzofuran
2b = Bensenepropanamine
2c = Aminoethyl oximer of aralkyl ketone
2d = Phenylpiperidine
2e = Naphthylamine derivative
3a = Hydrazine MAOI
3b = Non-hydrazine MAOI
4 = Tetracyclic
5 = 'NaSSA'
6 = 'RIMA'
7 = Thioxanthene
8 = Triazolopyridine
9 = 'NARI'
10 = Amino acid
11 = 'SNRI'

**Side-effects:**

••• = Marked effect
•• = Moderate effect
• = Mild effect
O = Little or minimal effect
? = No information or little reported
U = unlicensed in UK for depression

**Other abbreviations:**

‡ = Typical serotonergic side-effect
Adult max. dose = Maximum adult antidepressant dose in UK SPC
Eld. max. dose = Maximum elderly antidepressant dose as stated in UK SPC. Most state that half the adult dose may be sufficient
§Overdose = Based on UK Fatal Toxicity Index (Henry *et al. BMJ* 1995, **310**, 221–24, Henry *et al. Eur J Med* 1992, **1**, 343–48). For review of epidemiology and relative toxicity of antidepressant drugs in overdose see Henry (*Drug Safety* 1997, **16**, 374–90, 92 refs).

**Table 2.1.4: Antidepressants — pharmacokinetics etc**

| Drug | Major active metabolites | Half-life (hrs) | Peak plasma conc (hrs) | 5-HT | NA/NE | DA |
|---|---|---|---|---|---|---|
| **Tricyclics** | | | | | | |
| Amitriptyline | | 8–24 | 6 | +++ | ++++ | + |
| | Nortriptyline | 18–96 | (4–5) | + | ++++ | + |
| Amoxapine | 7-8-hydroxy | 8 | 1–2 | + | +++ | + |
| | | | – | | | |
| Clomipramine | Desmethyl- | 17–28 | 2.5 | +++ | Weak | |
| | | >36 | 4–24 | + | +++ | |
| Dothiepin (dosulepin) | Desmethyl- | 14–40 | 3 | + | + | + |
| | | 22–60 | – | | | |
| Doxepin | Desmethyl- | 8–24 | 4 | + | + | |
| | | 30–72 | | | | |
| Imipramine | Desipramine | 4–18 | 2 | +++ | + | + |
| | | 12–24 | (4–5) | + | ++++ | |
| Lofepramine | Desipramine | 1.6–5 | 1–2 | + | ++++ | |
| | | 12–24 | 4–5 | + | ++++ | |
| Maprotiline | Desmethyl- | 12–108 | 8–24 | + | +++ | |
| Nortriptyline | (Desmethyl-) | 18–96 | (4–5) | + | +++ | |
| Trimipramine | | 7–23 | 3 | + | + | + |
| **Selective Serotonin Reuptake Inhibitors** | | | | | | |
| Citalopram | | 33 | 2–4 | ++++ | | |
| Escitalopram | | 30 | 2–4 | ++++ | | |
| Fluoxetine | Norfluoxetine | 24–140 | 6–8 | ++++ | | + |
| | | 168–216 | – | + | | |
| Fluvoxamine | None | 13–22 | 2–8 | +++ | | |
| Paroxetine | None | 24 | 6 | ++++ | + | |
| Sertraline | Desmethyl- | 25–36 | 4–10 | +++ | | |
| | | 66–109 | 8–12 | + | | |

**Table 2.1.4: Antidepressants — pharmacokinetics etc (continued)**

| Drug | Major active metabolites | Half-life (hrs) | Peak plasma conc (hrs) | Transmitter/receptor profile | | |
|---|---|---|---|---|---|---|
| | | | | 5-HT | NA/NE | DA |
| **Mono-amine oxidase inhibitors** | | | | | | |
| Isocarboxazid | | | | | | |
| Phenelzine | | 1.5 | | | | ↑ |
| Tranylcypromine | | 2.5 | 2.5 | | | ↑ |
| **Others** | | | | | | |
| Mianserin | Desmethyl- 8-hydroxy- | 12–29 | 1–3 | ↑ | ↑ | ↑ |
| Mirtazapine | None | 20–40 | 1–3 | +++ | +++ | + |
| Moclobemide | None | 1–2 | 1 | ↑ | ↑ | ↑ |
| Flupentixol | | 35 | 3–8 | | | |
| Nefazodone | Several | 2–4 | 30min(1–3h) | +++# | | |
| Reboxetine | NK | 13 | 2 | ++# | +++ | |
| Trazodone | mCPP | 3–7 | ½–2 | | | |
| Venlafaxine § | -desmethyl | 1–2<br>1–11 | 5(2–7)<br>10(8–13) | +++§ | +++§ | +§ |

**Abbreviations used:**

++++ = Marked potency  + = Minimal
+++ = Moderate potency  O = Nil or virtually nil
++ = Minor potency   = Not known

**Other abbreviations:**

$ = Dose-dependent reuptake inhibition (see CI)
Desmethyl- = Metabolite is desmethyl-parent drug
A = Potent postsynaptic 5-HT agonist
# = Also potent central 5-HT antagonist
NA/NE = Noradrenaline or norepinephrine
↑ = Cytoplasmic levels increase
5-HT = 5-hydroxytryptamine or serotonin

**Table 2.1.5:  Antipsychotics — relative side-effects***

| Group | Drug | Adult oral max. dose mg/d | Eld oral max dose mg/d | Anticho-linergic | Cardiac | EPSE | Hypo-tension | Sedation | Minor O/D | Weight gain | Prolactin | Pro-convulsant |
|---|---|---|---|---|---|---|---|---|---|---|---|---|
| **Phenothiazines** | | | | | | | | | | | | |
| 1a | Chlorpromazine | 1000 | <Ad | ●●● | ●● | ●● | ●●● | ●●● | ●●● | ●●● | ●●●? | ●●? |
| 1a | Levomepromazine (methotrimeprazine) | 1000 | NR | ●●● | ●● | ●●? | ●●● | ●●● | ●●● | ? | ●●●? | ●●? |
| 1a | Promazine | 800 | <Ad | ●● | ●●● | ● | ●●● | ●● | ●● | ? | ●●●? | ●●●? |
| 1b | Pericyazine | (300) | <Ad | ●● | ●●● | ● | ●●● | ●●● | ●● | ? | ●●●? | ●●●? |
| 1b | Thioridazine | 600?? | <Ad | ●● | ●●● | ● | ●● | ●● | ● | ●● | ●●●? | ●●? |
| 1a | Fluphenazine | CA20 | CA10 | ●● | ●●● | ●●● | ● | ●● | ●● | ● | ●●●? | ●? |
| 1a | Perphenazine | 24 | <Ad | ● | ●● | ●●● | ● | ● | ●● | ●● | ●●●? | ● |
| 1b | Trifluoperazine | – | <Ad | ○ | ●● | ●●● | ● | ● | ●● | ? | ●●●? | ●? |
| **Others** | | | | | | | | | | | | |
| 2 | Benperidol | 1.5 | <Ad | ? | ? | ? | ● | ● | ? | ? | ●●●? | ? |
| 2 | Haloperidol | 30 | 30 | ● | ●● | ●●● | ● | ● | ● | ? | ●●? | ● |
| 3 | Flupentixol | 18 | <Ad | ●● | ○ | ●●● | ● | ● | ● | ● | ●●? | ● |
| 3 | Zuclopenthixol | 150 | <Ad | ● | ● | ●●● | ○ | ● | ● | ? | ●●? | ○? |
| 4 | Pimozide | 20 | <Ad | ○ | ●●● | ●● | ● | ● | ● | ○ | ●●●? | ● |
| 5 | Amisulpride | 1200 | 1200 | ○ | ○ | ● | ○ | ○ | ● | ● | ●●● | ●? |
| 5 | Sulpiride | 2400 | 2400 | ● | ○ | ● | ○ | ● | ○ | ● | ●●? | ○? |
| 6 | Loxapine | 250 | – | ●● | ● | ●● | ● | ●● | ●● | ● | ●●? | ●● |

**Table 2.1.5: Antipsychotics — relative side-effects (continued).***

| Group | Drug | Adult oral max. dose mg/d | Eld oral max dose mg/d | Anticho-linergic | Cardiac | EPSE | Hypo-tension | Sedation | Minor O/D | Weight gain | Prolactin | Pro-convulsant |
|---|---|---|---|---|---|---|---|---|---|---|---|---|
| **Depots ◆** | | | | | | | | | | | | |
| 1a | Fluphenazine decanoate (D) | 100–2 | <Ad | ●● | ●● | ●●● | ● | ●● | | ● | ●●●? | ● |
| 1b | Pipotiazine palmitate (D) | 200–4 | <Ad | ●● | ●● | ●●● | ● | ● | ? | ? | ●●●? | ●●? |
| 2 | Haloperidol decanoate (D) | 300–4 | <Ad | ● | O | ●●● | O | ● | ? | ● | ●●● | ●? |
| 3 | Flupentixol decanoate (D) | 400–1 | <Ad | ●● | ● | ●● | ● | ●● | ● | ? | ●●? | ? |
| 3 | Zuclopentixol decanoate (D) | 600–1 | <Ad | ●● | ● | ●● | ● | ●● | ● | ? | ●●●? | O? |
| 4 | Fluspirilene (D) | 20–1 | <Ad | | | ● | | | ? | ? | ●● | ● |
| 10 | Risperidone (D) | 50–2 | 25–2 | O | O | ● | ● | ●? | | ● | ●● | O |
| **2nd generation** | | | | | | | | | | | | |
| 7 | Clozapine | 900 | (900) | ●●● | ●●● | O | ●● | ●●● | ? | ●●● | O | ●●● |
| 8 | Olanzapine | 20 | 20 | ● | O | O | ● | ●● | O | ●●● | O | ●●● |
| 9 | Quetiapine | 750 | <Ad | ● | ● | O | ●● | ●? | ? | ● | O | ● |
| 10 | Risperidone | (16) | 4 | O | O | ● | ●● | ● | ? | ● | ●●● | O |
| 11 | Zotepine | 300 | 150 | ●● | ●●● | ● | ●● | ●? | ? | ●●●? | ●●●? | ●●● |
| 12 | Sertindole | (20) | (20) | O | ●● | O | ●● | O | O | ●● | O | ● |
| 13 | Ziprasidone (not UK) | – | – | O | ● | O | O | O | ? | O | O | O |
| 14 | Aripiprazole (U) | TBA | TBA | O | O | O | O | O | ? | ● | O | O |

**Groups:**
1a = Phenothiazine — aliphatic side chain
1b = Phenothiazine — piperidine side chain
1c = Phenothiazine — piperazine side chain (also includes prochlorperazine)
2 = Butyrophenones
3 = Thioxanthene
4 = Diphenylbutylpiperidines
5 = Benzamide/orthopramide
6 = Dibenzodiazepine
7 = Dibenzodiazepine

O = Little or nothing
? = No information

**Side-effects:**
●●● = Marked effect
●● = Moderate effect
● = Mild/transient effect

**Other abbreviations:**
Adult max. dose = Maximum adult oral antipsychotic dose as stated in UK SPC. May be smaller for other indications.
Eld. max. dose = Maximum oral antipsychotic dose in the elderly as stated in UK SPC. Most state that a starting dose of half to a quarter of the adult dose should be adequate, with small dose increments.
◆ = 2–200 means 200mg every 2 weeks. 400–1 means 400mg every week etc.
(U) = Unlicensed in UK/Europe at time of writing

**Table 2.1.6: Antipsychotics – A guide to comparative receptor blockade**

| Drug/group | Receptor blockade (5) | | | | | | | | | | 5HT$_{2A}$:D$_2$ affinity ratio | Half-life (hours) | Time to peak (oral) (2) | Main metabolite(s) |
|---|---|---|---|---|---|---|---|---|---|---|---|---|---|---|
| | D$_1$ | D$_2$ | D$_3$ | D$_4$ | 5HT$_{1A}$ | 5HT$_{2A}$ | M$_1$ | $\alpha$-1 | $\alpha$-2 | H$_1$ | | | | |
| **Phenothiazines** | | | | | | | | | | | | | | |
| Chlorpromazine | ++ | + | ++ | + | | +++ | ++ | +++ | + | ++ | 10:1 | 6 (2–119) | 3 (IM 1–4, IV 2–4) | Many |
| Fluphenazine HCl Fluphenazine decanoate | ++ | +++ | +++ | ++ | | ++ | + | ++ | O | + | 1:2 | FHCl 33 FD 14–26/7 | FHCl 3 FD 24 hrs | Some, unclear if active |
| Levomepromazine | ++ | ++ | +++ | ? | | +++ | +++ | +++ | O | +++ | 5:1 | 15–30 | 1–3 | Some, unclear if active |
| Pericyazine (3) | ++? | +? | ++? | +? | | +++? | +++? | +++ | O | ++? | N/K | N/K | N/K | N/K |
| Perphenazine | ++ | ++ | NK | ? | | +++ | + | ++ | ++ | +++ | 2:1 | 10 (8–12) | 4–8 | Some, unclear if active |
| Thioridazine | ++ | + | ++ | + | | +++ | +++ | +++ | + | + | 5:1 | 21–24 | N/K | Mesoridazine |
| Trifluoperazine | ++ | ++ | NK | + | | +++ | + | +++ | + | + | 2:1 | 24 | 2–4 | Several |
| **Others** | | | | | | | | | | | | | | |
| Benperidol | +? | +++ | +? | +? | | +? | O? | +? | +? | ++? | N/K | 8 | 2 | 1% unchanged in urine |
| Haloperidol HCl Haloperidol decanoate | ++ | +++ | +++ | + | + | ++ | + | ++ | O | + | 1:25 | 21 (10–38) 21/7 | 2–6 | Hydroxy-haloperidol |
| Flupentixol HCl Flupentixol decanoate | | | | | | | | | | | | 22–36 D 3–7/7 (1) | FHCl 3–6 FD 3–10/7 | Inactive |
| Zuclopenthixol HCl Zuclopenthixol Decanoate, Zuclopenthixol acetate | ++ | +++ | + | NK | | +++ | ++ | ++ | NK | ++ | 1:3 | 20 | ZHCl 3–4 ZD 5–7/7 ZA 24–48 hrs | Inactive |
| Sulpiride | O | +++ | + | O | | O | O | O | O | O | 1:50 | 6–8 | 2–6 | Nil |
| Amisulpride | O | +++ | +++ | O | | O | O | O | O | O | N/K | 12–17 | 1–4 | Nil |
| Loxapine | ++ | + | NK | O | | +++ | ++ | +++ | O | +++ | 7:1 | 4 (1–14) | 1 | Several. Low potency |
| Pimozide | + | +++ | +++ | + | | +++ | + | +++ | + | O | 1:5 | 53–55 | 6–8 | Some, unclear if active |
| Fluspirilene | NK | NK | NK | NK | | NK | NK | NK | NK | NK | N/K | 32– >300 | 1–48 | Inactive |

**Table 2.1.6:  Antipsychotics — A guide to comparative receptor blockade (continued).**

| Drug/group | Receptor blockade (5) | | | | | | | | | | $5HT_{2A}:D_2$ affinity ratio | Half-life (hours) | Time to peak (oral) (2) | Main metabolite(s) |
|---|---|---|---|---|---|---|---|---|---|---|---|---|---|---|
| | $D_1$ | $D_2$ | $D_3$ | $D_4$ | $5HT_{1A}$ | $5HT_{2A}$ | $M_1$ | $\alpha$-1 | $\alpha$-2 | $H_1$ | | | | |
| **Atypicals** | | | | | | | | | | | | | | |
| Clozapine | ++ | ++4 | ++ | +++ | + | +++ | +++ | +++ | ++ | +++ | 20–30:1 | 4–12 | 2–3 | Norclozapine |
| Olanzapine | ++ | ++4 | + | ++ | + | +++ | +++ | ++ | + | +++ | 50:1 | 30 (21–54) | 3–6 | Inactive |
| Quetiapine | O | ++ | + | NK | ++ | ++ | O | ++ | O | +++ | 1:1 | 6 | 1.5 | 2 major active |
| Risperidone | + | +++ | + | + | ++ | +++ | O | +++ | +++ | ++ | 8–11:1 | 20–30 | 1 (liquid) | Hydroxy-risperidone |
| Zotepine | +++ | +++ | +++ | ++ | ++ | +++ | ++ | +++ | +++ | +++ | 4:1 | 14–24 | 1 and 10–12 | Norzotepine (inactive) |
| Sertindole | + | ++++ | + | + | | +++ | O | +++ | O | + | 100:1 | 55–90 | 10 | Dehydrosertindole |
| Ziprasidone | O | + | + | O | PAg | ++ | O | + | O | O | 3:1 | 7 | 4–5 | Manyl |
| Aripiprazole | O | PAg | O | O | PAg | AAnt | O | O | O | O | N/A | 75 (31–146) | 3–7 | None known |

Receptor binding: +++=High affinity; ++=Moderate; +=Low; O=Very low; NK = Not known; ?= Possible; PAg = Partial agonist; AAnt = Antagonist
Initial ref: Siloh, Nutt and Weizman (2000) *Atlas of Psychiatric Pharmacotherapy*. Martin Duniz, London (very colourful and useful)

1. Flupentixol decanoate half-life longer (up to 17 days) on continuous administration
2. Time to oral peak may vary with food
3. Receptor-binding studies for pericyazine have not been published, but is reported to have some differences to chlorpromazine
4. Sertindole, olanzapine and clozapine appear to have some limbic selectivity.
5. Inclusion of a receptor may give some guide to therapeutic action and adverse effects
6. There is a considerable degree of variation between published sources, depending upon how the results are presented, whether they are single studies or averages, the receptor sources, assay type etc. These figures should be taken only as a guide, eg. there is little or nothing published about fluspirilene.

---

**List of other Abbreviations used in Tables 2.1.1 to 2.1.6**

L=Half-life is longer in elderly.
<Ad=Maximum dose is less than the adult dose
Anticholinergic=Anticholinergic or
antimuscarinic side-effects

Pro-convulsant=Pro-convulsive effect
CA=Care above
EPSE=Extra-pyramidal side-effects
NR=Not recommended

---

## 2.2 SWITCHING OR DISCONTINUING PSYCHOTROPICS

Switching psychotropics can be achieved using a variety of methods, varying in rate, overlap, gap and complexity. These are summarised in the graphs and comments shown. Those remarks specifically relating to anti-psychotics are marked with #.

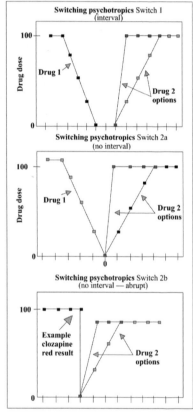

### Switch 1 – drug-free interval

(discontinue first drug, leave drug-free interval, introduce second drug):

**Advantages:**

1. Minimises combined ADRs.
2. Low relapse risk, if the patient is relatively stable and the gap is not prolonged.
3. Minimal interaction potential.
4. Side-effects from the second drug are less likely to be confused with discontinuation effects from first drug
5. Anticholinergic drug doses can be titrated as needed #.
6. Recommended for switches to clozapine to reduce additive myelosuppressive potential #.
7. Low medication error potential.

**Disadvantages:**

1. Takes time, which delays the desired relief of symptoms or side-effects and may extend in-patient stays #.
2. Fear of relapse during gap and changeover (probably rare).
3. Early relapse might be interpreted as lack of efficacy of the second drug.

---

### Switch 2a and 2b: No interval

(stop first drug, start second immediately)

**Advantages:**

1. Straightforward.
2. Low medication error potential.
3. Appropriate for in-patient settings with better supervision.
4. Appropriate where an acute, severe reaction to a drug has occurred, eg. statutory abrupt withdrawal of clozapine due to a blood dyscrasia #.
5. Sometimes acceptable for high-risk switches to clozapine to reduce additive myelosuppressive potential #.

**Disadvantages:**

1. May raise unrealistic expectations from patient and family of a rapid improvement on the second drug.
2. Less suitable for clozapine #.

3. Combined ADRs may occur, albeit short-lived.
4. Potential for drug interactions if the first drug has a long half-life.
5. Rapid discontinuation of the first drug may produce higher relapse rates.
6. Discontinuation effects from the first drug might be interpreted as side-effects of the second.

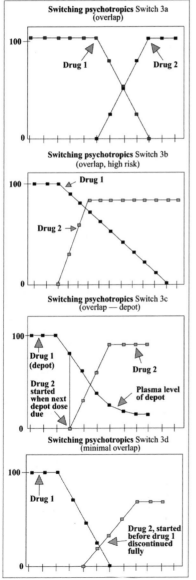

**Switching psychotropics** Switch 3a
(overlap)

Drug 1    Drug 2

**Switching psychotropics** Switch 3b
(overlap, high risk)

Drug 1

Drug 2 →

**Switching psychotropics** Switch 3c
(overlap — depot)

Drug 1
(depot)

Drug 2
started
when next
depot dose
due

Drug 2

Plasma level
of depot

**Switching psychotropics** Switch 3d
(minimal overlap)

Drug 1

Drug 2, started
before drug 1
discontinued
fully

### Switch 3a, 3b, 3c, 3d: Partial overlap

(Add new drug, either at standard dose or quickly titrated upwards, while slowly tapering the first drug)

**Advantages:**

1. Appropriate when side-effect relief is needed but a high relapse risk.
2. No sudden changes occur, which might destabilise the patient.
3. 3c may be appropriate for depot to oral switches, where plasma levels of depot will decline slowly and withdrawal reactions have not been reported #.
4. Useful for high potency anti-psychotics to an atypical, and from a low potency drug where cholinergic rebound may occur. Either way, anticholinergic cover can be retained for several weeks #.

**Disadvantages:**

1. If taper is too quick, two drugs may be given at sub-therapeutic doses.
2. Combined ADRs may occur.
3. Potential for drug interactions, especially with antidepressants.
4. Potential for medication errors if not planned fully in advance – involve carers and patient if patient is at home.
5. High potential for polypharmacy if switch never completed, eg. if discharged and message not passed on, or the patient improves and there is a reluctance to discontinue the first drug and possibly de-stabilise the patient #.

### Switch 4: Full overlap

(add new drug to therapeutic dose and then slowly taper previous drug)

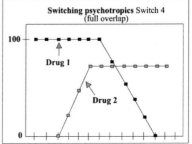

**Switching psychotropics** Switch 4
(full overlap)

Drug 1

Drug 2

**Advantages:**
1. Safest if relapse prevention is of greatest concern.
2. Most appropriate if the patient has recently (eg. <3 months) recovered from acute relapse with the first drug.
3. Low risk of discontinuation effects of the first drug.
4. If depot to oral antipsychotic, this may be lowest risk opportunity to assess compliance with oral drugs #.
5. Slow taper is possible and is better for drugs with high anticholinergic activity.

**Disadvantages:**
1. Combined ADRs may occur (but not necessarily with antipsychotics, Gardner *et al, Can J Psych* 1997, **42**, 430–31).
2. Potential for drug interactions.
3. Potential for medication errors if not planned and completed fully.
4. High potential for polypharmacy if switch never completed, eg. if discharged and message not passed on, or patient improves and there is a reluctance to discontinue the first drug and possibly destabilise the patient #.

## 2.2.1 SWITCHING OR DISCONTINUING ANTIPSYCHOTICS

**Reviews**: switching from typicals to atypicals (Taylor, *CNS Drugs* 1997, **8**, 285–92), general (Weiden *et al, J Clin Psych* 1997, **58**[Suppl 10], 63–72, 60 refs; Amery and Marder, *Int J Psych Clin Pract* 1998, **2**, S43–S49), discontinuing antipsychotics (Tranter and Healy, *J Psychopharmacol* 1998, **12**, 401–6).

### 2.2.1.1 General advice on switching

**Indications for switching antipsychotics** include (Weiden *et al, J Clin Psych* 1997, **58**[Suppl 10], 63–72):
1. Persistent positive (distressing and disruptive) symptoms.
2. Persistent negative (restrictive and burdening) symptoms.
3. Relapse despite compliance.
4. Persistent distressing adverse effects such as EPSEs, akathisia, hyper-prolactinaemia, poor self-image and sexual dysfunction.
5. Oral to depot or other formulation change.

There are as yet no published controlled trials on switching antipsychotics.

**Risks of discontinuing (or switching) antipsychotics** (review and guidance, Keks *et al, CNS Drugs* 1995, **4**, 351–56):
1. Cholinergic rebound (eg. nausea, vomiting, restlessness, anxiety, insomnia, fatigue, malaise, myalgia, diaphoresis, rhinitis, paraesthesia, GI distress, headaches, nightmares). It may occur after discontinuation or if a second drug has less anticholinergic effects or anticholinergic drugs are withdrawn too soon (Luchins *et al, Am J Psych* 1980, **137**, 1395–98). It can be severe but tends to be relatively brief and predictable.
2. Withdrawal dyskinesias, eg. extrapyramidal symptoms, rebound akathisia (which may be confused with anxiety or psychosis, Dufresne and Wagner, *J Clin Psych* 1988, **49**, 435–38), rebound dystonia and worsening tardive dyskinesia (Glazer *et al, Biol Psych* 1989, **26**, 224–33). Withdrawal EPSEs may, in part, be related to cholinergic rebound. These have been reported in mentally healthy people taking metoclopramide as an antiemetic (see Tranter and Healy, *J Psychopharmacol* 1998, **12**, 401–6) and can be minimised by slow tapering (n=81, d/b, p/c, Battegay, *Comp Psych* 1966, **7**, 501–9).
3. Other discontinuation symptoms, eg. NMS (Spivak *et al, Acta Psych Scand* 1990, **81**, 168–69).
4. Relapse or destabilization–this may present an unacceptable risk to the patient. Relapse rates of up to 50% at 6 months after abrupt discontinuation has been reported (n=1210, Viguera *et al, Arch Gen Psych* 1997, **54**, 49–55), gradual discontinuation reducing this risk (reviewed by Tranter and Healy,

*J Psychopharmacol* 1998, **12**, 401–6). True relapses tend to occur from 1–6 months after even abrupt withdrawal of oral drugs (eg. Prien *et al, B J Psych* 1968, **115**, 679–86) and 3–6 months with depots (Wistedt, *Acta Psych Scand* 1981, **64**, 65–84), probably due to persistence of drug at receptor level (Cohen *et al, Arch Gen Psych* 1988, **45**, 879–80). There may be a particular problem with clozapine, where relapse or rebound psychosis can be more severe (eg. Baldessarini *et al, Arch Gen Psych* 1995, **52**, 1071–72, see also *2.2.1.4*).

5. Anxiety or stress from the switch causing symptom flare-up.
6. Medication errors.
7. The replacement drug being less effective than the former, or having different but still unacceptable side-effects, resulting in premature abandonment and an inadequate trial of the new drug.

**General principals for switching antipsychotics:**

1. Ensure a treatment target is set and measured (take care that the key aims of a switch are not easier and less risky to achieve by, eg. dose or timing adjustment of the first drug).
2. Avoid switches coinciding with major life stress events.
3. Avoid switching after a change in treatment team. Allow full assimilation into the new treatment team first.
4. Avoid switching within 3–6 months of recovery from a drug which was successfully used to treat a major relapse.
5. In patients previously non-compliant with oral drugs now stable for under a year on a depot (Weiden *et al, J Clin Psych* 1997, **58**[Suppl 10], 63–72).
6. If possible, slowly taper the first antipsychotic, probably over at least eight weeks, as this reduces the risk of relapse (Wyatt, *Arch Gen Psych* 1995, **52**, 205–8) and emergent extra-pyramidal and psychotic symptoms.

7. Slowly taper any anticholinergic, which may also be allowed to continue for a time after the drug has been discontinued. Reintroduce if necessary for any emergent symptoms.
8. Monitor mental and physical state regularly (particularly during the first month).

**Advice to patients before switching to atypicals:**

1. Warn about possible ADRs, eg. weight gain, short-term sedation, time course and implications of reduced prolactin inhibition.
2. Need for adequate trial and need to complete switch, plus time scale.
3. How to define success.
4. How to measure success and the chances thereof.
5. The new drug isn't perfect.

## 2.2.1.2 Antipsychotic dose equivalents

The antipsychotic dose(s) of each drug within each heading of this section are approximately equivalent to others under the same heading (eg. perphenazine 24mg/d is equivalent to chlorpromazine 300mg/d and to flupentixol 60mg 2/52), based on the references indicated.

There is a genuine lack of agreement about antipsychotic equivalents. This is mainly because the three methods of assessing antipsychotic equivalence (clinical studies, non-clinical/receptor binding studies and manufacturers' information) can produce up to a five-fold difference in the equivalents then recommended (full discussion by Rey *et al, Int Clin Psychopharmacol* 1989, **4**, 95–104), particularly true in the case of high-potency antipsychotics. Ranges quoted here are thus unweighted for individual variation and are valid, but imprecise. For example, antipsychotics (excluding some atypical drugs) displace ligands from dopamine receptors (particularly D2 receptors) at a rate that highly correlates with their antipsychotic potency (eg. Peroutka & Snyder, *Am J Psych* 1980, **137**, 1518–22) and so roughly equivalent antipsychotic doses can be calculated. However, some dose relationships, eg. haloperidol, are unlikely to be linear and sedation and anxiety may not be directly related to dopamine blockade (reviewed by Hilton *et al, Psych Bull* 1996, **20**, 359–62). High-potency drugs, eg. haloperidol, fluphenazine etc have the highest quoted variance, over 1000% in some cases. This may lead to prescribing in higher doses than necessary (Dewan and Koss, *Acta Psych Scand* 1995, **91**, 229–32). Additionally, higher doses of antipsychotics tend to be used to control disruptive behaviour rather than just to control psychotic symptoms (Peralta *et al, Acta Psych Scand* 1994, **90**, 354–57). Using the percentage of the maximum BNF dose has been proposed as an alternative, but is also imprecise, as maximum doses may not be equivalent, eg. is flupentixol decanoate 400mg a week really equivalent to 50mg a week of fluphenazine decanoate?

**Antipsychotic equivalence** is specifically quoted here and the doses are as accurate as data allows but to avoid any confusion you **must** consider the following:

1. Antipsychotic equivalence should not be confused with **sedation**, which in some cases, eg. haloperidol (with a relatively low sedative effect) causes confusion over equivalence. Indeed, there may be no extra antipsychotic effect from haloperidol above 12–20mg/d (see *1.27*).

2. With some drugs there may not be a linear relationship between dose and antipsychotic effect.

3. Dose frequency with depots may be important (*Curr Ther Res* 1982, **31**, 982) as the first pass effect may reduce the effective doses of oral preparations.

4. If using a 'broad-spectrum' drug (eg. the so-called 'dirty' drugs, such

as chlorpromazine) and converting to a D2 receptor selective drug (eg. flupenthixol, sulpiride etc), the use of conversion tables may not thus be appropriate and may result in enhanced side-effects or overdosage.

5. Differing half-lives may complicate the calculations and final dose recommendation.

6. Haloperidol and fluphenazine seems a particular problem.

7. These equivalent doses are not necessarily equivalent in terms of maximum doses in the BNF/SPC.

### Antipsychotic equivalent doses

| | Oral | mg/d (+range) |
|---|---|---|
| 1 | Chlorpromazine | 100mg ($\cong$25–50mg IM[4]or 250mg rectally) |
| | Fluphenazine | 2mg (1.25–5mg) |
| | Levomepromazine | NK |
| | Pericyazine | 24mg |
| | Perphenazine | 8mg (7–15mg) |
| | Prochlorperazine | 15mg (14–25mg) |
| | Promazine | 100mg (50–200mg) |
| | Thioridazine | 100mg (75–104mg) |
| | Trifluoperazine | 5mg (2–8mg) |
| 2 | Benperidol | 2mg |
| | Droperidol | 4mg (Short $t_{\frac{1}{2}}$) or 3mg IM/IV |
| | Haloperidol[6] | 3mg (1–5mg) or 1.5mg IM/IV* for doses up to 20mg/d |
| 3 | Flupentixol | 2mg |
| | Zuclopenthixol | 25mg (25–60mg) up to 150mg/d |
| 4 | Pimozide | 2mg (1–3) (Long $t_{\frac{1}{2}}$) |
| 5 | Remoxipride | 75mg |
| | Amisulpride | 100mg (40–150mg) |
| | Sulpiride | 200mg (200–333mg) |
| 6 | Loxapine | 10mg (6–25mg) |
| 7 | Clozapine | 100mg (30–150mg) |
| | Olanzapine | NK |
| | Quetiapine | NK |
| | Zotepine | NK |
| 8 | Risperidone[3] | 1.5mg (0.5–3mg) |

| | Depot | mg/week |
|---|---|---|
| 1 | Fluphenazine[2] | 5–10mg (1–12.5mg) |
| 1 | Pipothiazine | 10mg (5–12.5mg) |
| 2 | Haloperidol | 15mg (5–25mg) |
| 3 | Flupentixol | 10mg (8–20mg) |
| 3 | Zuclopenthixol | 100mg (40–100mg) |
| 4 | Fluspirilene | 2mg (NE) |

Bioavailability from oral haloperidol is about 50% of IM, with IV approximately equivalent to IM.

**Key:**
NE=Not fully established.
90mg (75–100)=Recommended average dose + ranges quoted in the literature. The wider the range, the greater the uncertainty about the exact equivalent.

---

**The Actual Dose of a new drug required=**

$$\frac{\text{Current total daily (oral) or weekly (depot) drug dose}}{\text{Equivalent dose stated for that drug in that form}} \times \text{equivalent dose of the new drug as stated in that table}$$

8. For 'atypicals', therapeutic doses are better defined and so no equivalent doses are appropriate.

You should always check your answer against the SPC limits to ensure an inappropriately high dose (eg. beyond BNF/SPC limits) is not inadvertently considered (review, Atkins *et al, Psych Bull* 1997, **21**, 224–26).

**Further reading**

1. Peroutka and Synder, *Am J Psych* 1980, **137**, 1518–22
2. Anon, *Am J Psych* 1990, **147**, 258–60 + Refs
3. Remington *et al, Am J Psych* 1998, **155**, 1301–2
4. Dewan and Koss, *Acta Psych Scand* 1995, **91**, 229–32 (excellent review)
5. Schwartz and Brotman, *Drugs* 1992, **44**, 981–92
6. Hilton *et al, Psych Bull* 1996, **20**, 359–62

### 2.2.1.3 Switching antipsychotic doses and/or preparations

**Typical depot switches**

**Oral antipsychotic to typical depot**

Anecdotal evidence shows that the change can usually be made uneventfully (eg. review in *Clin Pharmacokinet* 1985, **10**, 315–33) although there are no formal studies. Converting to the same drug as a depot should present no problems if doses are chosen carefully (eg. 3c, see also *2.2.1.4*)

**Altering the frequency of a typical depot**

Such a change should present no great problems, provided antipsychotic levels do not drop too low or go too high.

**Changing from one typical depot to another typical depot**

No significant problems are usually experienced (Soni *et al, Acta Psych Scand* 1992, **85**, 354–59) and a direct exchange from one depot to another can often be made uneventfully (eg. 3c).

## Combined oral antipsychotic plus depot to depot alone

This can be an unusually difficult procedure and relapses may occur more frequently with this change when compared to other changes. Relapses can occur particularly in the first 3–4 months, when antipsychotic levels can be inadvertently sub-therapeutic (Soni *et al, Acta Psych Scand* 1992, **85**, 354–59). Any change should be done verging on the side of caution, eg. increasing the depot dose, then reducing the oral dose later.

### 2.2.1.4 Specific antipsychotic drug switches (where specific information is available)

NMS has been reported during many antipsychotic switches eg. from haloperidol to risperidone (n=1, Reeves *et al, Ann Pharmacother* 2001, **35**, 698–701).

**Switching from clozapine**

Converting clozapine to other antipsychotics seems particularly problematic (n=30, RCT, Shiovitz *et al, Schizophr Bull* 1996, **22**, 591–95). Relapse after clozapine discontinuation seems to be of a higher incidence, may be more rapid (Shore, *Schizophr Bull* 1995, **21**, 333–37) and withdrawal symptoms may be more severe (n=10, open, 12/52, Still *et al, Psychiatr Serv* 1996, **47**, 1382–84) than with other drugs. For gradual discontinuation of clozapine, it is best to simultaneously introduce and escalate the doses of another antipsychotic.

**Switching to clozapine**

Due to the potential for an increased risk of agranulocytosis, ideally, a previous drug should be completely withdrawn before clozapine is started, including depots (eg. switch 1), but this is not always practical. Clozapine is a very sedative and hypotensive drug, so care is needed with additive effects, so start with gradual dose titration. Pharmacokinetic interactions are unlikely (see *4.2.2*).

**Switching to oral risperidone \***

Risperidone can cause hypotension, so gradual dose titration over at least

3 days to 4–6mg/d is recommended. Slower increases may help some people. Additive hypotension with low potency drugs may occur during a switch. A sudden switch (along with gradual withdrawal of anticholinergics) may be successful in about 60% patients, but a more gradual switch would be preferable (n=36, Kirov *et al, Acta Psych Scand* 1997, **95**, 439–43). A review of switching to risperidone recommended reducing the existing antipsychotic dose, then overlapping risperidone with the existing therapy, rather than making an abrupt switch (Borison *et al, Clin Ther* 1996, **18**, 592–607). Risperidone may be a suitable replacement if introduced before slow clozapine withdrawal, ie. switch 4 (Zimbroff, *Am J Psych* 1995, **152**, 1102).

### Switching to risperidone long-acting injection (Risperdal Consta) *

It is important to understand the release kinetics of the injection before deciding a switch strategy ie. therapeutic levels are not reached until week 4 (ie. just before the 3rd injection) but only reach optimum in weeks 5–6 (ie. after the 3rd injection). Assessment of the response to oral risperidone is strongly recommended before giving the first injection, then giving oral for 3–4 weeks. It should only rarely be necessary to go above the recommended dose of 25mg/d:

### For oral antipsychotics (inc. risperidone) to Risperdal Consta:

Continue for 3 weeks, then discontinue step-wise during week 4 (preferably through time-limited prescriptions to avoid polypharmacy)

### Typical depot to Risperdal Consta:

The manufacturers recommend starting Consta one week *before* the last fortnightly injection, with oral drug available if the risk of relapse is high. Alternatively, switch on the depot due date, supplementing with oral risperidone for 3–4 weeks.

### Switching to olanzapine: *

Additive EPSEs, hypotension and drug interactions are unlikely to occur and so switch 3a is usually suitable with care. In one open study of a clozapine to olanzapine switch by patients wishing to avoid blood monitoring, 8 of 19 successfully completed the switch (using switch 4) and the others required restabilised on clozapine (n=19, Henderson *et al, J Clin Psych* 1998, **59**, 585–88). In a comparison of four different typical/risperidone to olanzapine switches in partially remitted, clinically stable schizophrenic out-patients, the most successful method was starting 10mg olanzapine then gradually discontinuing the original drug (*switch 3b*); next most successful was gradual introduction/gradual discontinuation (*switch 3a*) and probably best for elderly/frail patients; most drop-outs (usually sleep-related) were with abrupt discontinuation (switch 2a/b) and gradual olanzapine introduction (n=209, 82% completed, open, Kinon *et al, J Clin Psych* 2000, **61**, 833–40). Due to a lesser effect on prolactin, unexpected (but in these cases welcome) pregnancies have been reported a couple of months after a switch from typicals to olanzapine, despite no contraceptive use for 4–5 years (n=2, Neumann and Frasch, *Nervenarzt* 2001, **72**, 876–78).

### Switching from oral to depot fluphenazine

If transferring from oral fluphenazine, multiply the total daily oral dose by 1.2 and administer as fluphenazine decanoate IM every one to two weeks. Accumulation occurs and so the dosing interval may be increased to every three weeks or so after four to six weeks of therapy (Ereshefsky *et al, J Clin Psych* 1984, **45**, 50). Concomitant oral therapy should be limited to the initial period or during times of decompensation.

### Switching from oral to depot haloperidol

If transferring from stabilised oral haloperidol to depot, multiply the total daily oral dose by 15–20, to a maximum of 300mg, preferably much lower. Accumulation occurs and so the decanoate dose should be decreased by 25% a month until the minimum effective dose is achieved. The average maintenance dose appears to be about 200mg every four weeks. Elderly patients or those stabilised on less than 10mg/d oral haloperidol should receive haloperidol decanoate in an IM dose that is 10–15 times the oral dose every four weeks. Concomitant oral therapy should be limited to the initial period or during times of decompensation.

### Switching to amisulpride *

For a general review see Peuskens (*Curr Med Res Opin* 2002, **18**(Suppl 3), S23–28).

### 2.2.1.5 Post-switching Issues

(Based on an extensive review by Weiden *et al, J Clin Psych* 1998, **59**[Suppl 19], 36–49)

### A. Assessing response:

1. For all drugs, aim for a minimum of 3 months at full therapeutic dosage.
2. Be cautious of any significant gains (eg. reduced side-effects) within 6/52 of the last drug stopping, as drug concentrations at receptor level may outlast plasma levels (see haloperidol, *1.27*).
3. Even if gains occur, make sure full therapeutic dose is achieved, as discontinuation of the previous drug will lead to a gradual loss of its side-effects (including cognitive impairment), which may be interpreted as improvement.
4. If gains occur, it has been suggested to delay discontinuing any anticholinergic and/or antiakathisia drugs until during the second month.
5. Raised prolactin levels may take over 3/12 to resolve, so women need to be warned about this, and to ensure they have adequate contraceptive cover.
6. If positive changes occur, the patient should be cautioned not to risk relapse by 'over doing it'.

### B. Managing a sub-optimum response to a switch:

1. No improvement by 6/52 – exclude non-compliance with the switch, substance misuse and inadequate dosage. Try to work towards 12/52 at full dose.
2. Some response by 6/52 – don't get too excited, continue to 12/52.
3. Partial response between 6/52 and 12/52 – consider an increase in dose, and try to go for an 6/12 trial.
4. Initial response followed by worsening of positive symptoms – check worsening is not actually improvement (eg. previous positive symptoms hidden by the patient now surfacing), try to restabilise and aim for 12/52 at full dose.

### C. Long-term issues:

1. With improvements in insight, increased psychosocial support and monitoring will be needed to reduce the risk of post-psychotic depression and self-harm.

### Long-term polypharmacy with antipsychotics

The advantages of long-term monotherapy are that one is better able to judge the effectiveness of any given drug accurately and medication regimens are simple and not confused by polypharmacy (extensive review, Weiden *et al, J Clin Psych* 1998, **59**[Suppl 19], 36–49).

**Appropriate justifications** for polypharmacy might include:

1. Clozapine intolerance, as augmentation of a low clozapine dose.
2. Clozapine partial response, as augmentation.
3. When discontinuing a depot poses an unacceptable risk eg. forensic patients.
4. Patients refusing to stop an old drug or refusing to try clozapine.

**Inappropriate reasons** for polypharmacy, however, include:

1. As a substitute for failing to plan and communicate a switch, which is then never fully completed.
2. Where clinical improvement occurs before a switch is completed, and the clinician 'quits while ahead'

rather than risking completing the change.

### 2.2.1.6 Discontinuing Antipsychotics

Withdrawal symptoms (eg. tardive psychosis, dyskinesias etc) have been reported upon abrupt discontinuation (eg. n=1, Alphs and Lec, *J Clin* Psych 1991, **52**, 346–48) eg. cholinergic rebound-headache, restlessness, diarrhoea, nausea and vomiting (Lieberman, *Psychosomatics* 1981, **22**, 253–54). In 1006 schizophrenics withdrawing from antipsychotics abruptly, the risk of relapse reached 25% in 10 weeks and 50% within 30 weeks, with little additional relapse risk up to 3.7 years. With gradual withdrawal, risk of relapse was lower (n=1210, retrospective, Viguera *et al*, *Arch Gen Psych* 1997, **54**, 49–55). For a comprehensive and fascinating review of neuroleptic discontinuation syndrome, see Tranter and Healy (*J Psychopharmacol* 1998, **12**, 401–6).

### 2.2.2 SWITCHING BENZODIAZEPINES

Switching benzodiazepines may be advantageous for a variety of reasons, eg. to a drug with a different half-life pre-discontinuation. Whilst there is broad agreement in the literature about equivalent doses, clonazepam has a wide variety of reported equivalences and particular care is needed with this drug. Inter-patient variability and differing half-lives means the figures can never be exact and should be interpreted using your own pharmaceutical knowledge.

**Benzodiazepines**[1,2,3,4]

| See note in introduction re: half lives | |
|---|---|
| Diazepam | 5mg (oral, im or iv) |
| Alprazolam | 0.5mg |
| Bromazepam | 3mg |
| Chlordiazepoxide | 15mg (10–25mg) |
| Clobazam | 10mg |
| Clonazepam | 0.5mg (0.25–4)[4] |
| Clorazepate | 7.5mg (7.5–10) |
| Flunitrazepam | 0.5mg |
| Flurazepam | 7.5–15mg |
| Loprazolam | 0.5–1mg |
| Lorazepam | [4]0.5–1mg at ≤ 4mg/d 2mg at ≥5mg/d |
| Lormetazepam | 0.5–1mg |
| Nitrazepam | 5mg (2.5–20mg) |
| Oxazepam | 15mg (15–40mg) |
| Temazepam | 10mg |

### 2.2.3 SWITCHING ANTICHOLINERGICS

See *1.20.1* about the overall indications for the use of anticholinergics. Equivalent doses are:

| Benzatropine | 1mg |
|---|---|
| Biperiden | 2mg |
| Orphenadrine | 50mg |
| Procyclidine | 2mg |
| Benzhexol (trihexyphenidyl) | 2mg |

(Saklad, personal communication)

### 2.2.4 SWITCHING DRUGS OF ABUSE OR DEPENDENCE

Switching drugs of abuse/dependence, usually to methadone, is a common treatment strategy. The following table may be of some use, although caution is obviously necessary regarding, eg. the potency of individual samples of street drugs etc. Many dose equivalents are also derived from analgesic equivalents, which may not necessarily be the same as those necessary to prevent withdrawal symptoms.

**NARCOTICS**

| Drug | Qty | Methadone |
|---|---|---|
| Actified Compound | 100ml | 6mg |
| Buprenorphine | 0.3mg | 2.5mg |
| Codeine linctus | 100ml | 20mg |
| Codeine Phosphate | 15mg | 1mg |
| Diamorphine BP | 10mg | 10mg |
| Diamorphine inj[4] | 5mg | 10mg |
| Diconal | 1 tab | 5mg |
| Dihydrocodeine | 30mg | 2.5mg |
| Dr Collis Browns | 100ml | 10mg |
| Gees Linctus | 100ml | 10mg |
| Morphine inj | 10mg | 10mg |
| Morphine oral[4] | 15mg | 10mg |
| MST tablets[2] | 10mg | 3.25mg |
| Palfium | 5mg | 5–10mg |
| Pentazocine | 25mg | 2mg |
| Pethidine tabs/inj | 50mg | 5mg |
| Street Heroin | 1/4g* | 20mg* |
| Street Morphine* | 1/4* | 15mg* |

*This is obviously highly variable depending upon its purity

### References

1. *B J Pharm Pract* 1989, **11**, 106–10.
2. Murphy and Tyrer, *B J Psych* 1991, **158**, 511–16.
3. *Clinical Handbook of Psychotropic Drugs*, 4th edn, Bezchlibnyk-Butler *et al*, Hogrefe and Huber, Toronto.
4. Cowen, *Adv Psych Treat* 1997, **3**, 67.

## 2.2.5 SWITCHING OR STOPPING ANTIDEPRESSANTS

Switching from one antidepressant to another, either for reasons of side-effects or lack of efficacy, can be problematical and present unexpected problems for the unwary. It is often necessary to leave gaps of drug-free days, eg. the 14-day gap after stopping an MAOI before starting another antidepressant is well known. However, other problems may occur and the prescriber must be aware of these to avoid unnecessary adverse events. For a summary of sequential strategies for switching antidepressants, see Thase and Rush, *J Clin Psych* 1997, **58**[Suppl 13], 23–29.

**Factors which must be considered before choosing a switch regimen:**

i. Speed at which the switch is needed, eg. with less urgency a more cautious regimen can be used. Since many drugs are used in combination, faster switches can obviously be made, but additional monitoring is recommended.

ii. Current dose of the first drug.

iii. Individual drugs and their effects, neurotransmitter effects, kinetics etc.

iv. Individuals susceptibility to (additive) side-effects.

**Potential problems:**

i. Cholinergic rebound, eg. headache, rest lessness, diarrhoea, nausea and vomiting (Lieberman, *Psychosomatics* 1981, **22**, 253–54) from withdrawal of drugs affecting ACh, eg. tricyclics.

ii. Antidepressant withdrawal or discontinuation symptoms (see *13*).

iii. Serotonin Syndrome for drugs affecting serotonin (see *1.31*).

iv. Interaction between the two drugs, eg. altered drug levels from altered metabolism (see *4.3*).

v. Discontinuation effects from the first drug being interpreted as side-effects of the second.

**How to use the table overleaf:**

i. Look down the vertical column headed 'from' and find the drug or drug group the patient is currently taking.

ii. Follow that line along until you come to the column of the drug or drug group to which you wish to change.

iii. The details there give the current known information. For further details look up the reference number quoted.

**Example**: Changing from tranylcypromine to a tricyclic requires a 14-day drugfree gap (reference 9) but changing from a tricyclic to tranylcypromine only requires a 7-day drug-free gap (reference 9).

### 1. MAOI-MAOI:

A two-week gap is recommended, especially if the MAOI is changed **to** tranylcypromine. The SPC for tranylcypromine recommends leaving at least a seven-day gap after stopping other antidepressants, then starting tranylcypromine at half the usual dosage for one week. Careful observation is essential. An open study of switching MAOIs with less than a 14-day gap showed that only one patient suffered adverse events, indicative of either tranylcypromine withdrawal or a mild serotonin syndrome. A shorter gap may be feasible with full dietary control, good compliance and close monitoring (n=8, Szuba *et al, J Clin Psych* 1997, **58**, 307–10). However, since deaths have been reported with such a switch (eg. n=1, Bazire, *Drug Intell Clin Pharm* 1986, **20**, 954–56), caution is recommended.

### 2. SSRI-TCA:

Fluoxetine, paroxetine and fluvoxamine (but probably not citalopram, escitalopram and sertraline at standard doses) can double or triple tricyclic levels (particularly of amitriptyline, imipramine, desipramine, nortriptyline and clomipramine), by CYP2D6 inhibition and so care is needed. Prescribing both drugs together over a change-over period is not advised unless the drugs are chosen carefully and specific care is taken.

## Switching antidepressants

| From | | Hydra-zines | Tranyl-cypromine | Tricyclics | Citalopram/escitalopram | Fluvox-amine | Fluox-etine | Sertraline | Parox-etine |
|---|---|---|---|---|---|---|---|---|---|
| **To** → MAOIs | | MAOIs | | | SSRIs | | | | |
| M A O I S | Hydra-zines | 14/7[1] | 14/7[1] | 7–14/7[9] | 14/7[7] | 14/7[7] | 14/7[7] | 14/7[7] | 14/7[7] |
| | Tranyl cypro-mine | 14/7[1] | ■ | 14/7[9] | 14/7[7] | 14/7[7] | 14/7[7] | 14/7[7] | 14/7[7] |
| Tricyclics | | 7/7[9] | 7/7[9] | NSPR[4] | Care[2] | Great Care[2] | Great Care[2] | Care[2] | Great Care[2] |
| Citalopram/ escitalopram | | 7/7[7] | 7/7[7] | Care[2] | ■ | SSP[5] | SSP[5] | SSP[5] | SSP[5] |
| Fluvoxamine | | 4/7[7] | 7–14/7[7] | Great care[2] | SSP[5] | ■ | SSP[5] | SSR[5] | SSR[5] |
| Fluoxetine | | 5/52[7] | 5/52[7] | Great care for 28/7[2] | SSP[5] | SSP[5] | ■ | SSP[5] | SSP[5] |
| Sertraline | | 7/7[7] | 7–14/7[7] | Care[2] | SSP[5] | SSP[5] | SSP[5] | ■ | SSP[5] |
| Paroxetine | | 14/7[7] | 14/7[7] | Great care[2] | SSP[5] | SSP[5] | SSP[5] | SSP[5] | ■ |
| Trazodone Nefazodone | | 7/7[6,7] | 7/7[6,7] | OP[13] | Care[3,6] | Care[3,6] | Care[3,6] | Care[3,6] | Care[3,6] |
| Tryptophan | | 14/7[10] or care | 7–14/7[10] or care | NSPR | Care[11] | Care[11] | Care[11] | Care[11] | Care[11] |
| Moclobemide | | NSPR[7] | NSPR[7] | OP[15] | NSPR[8] | NSPR[8] | 2/52[8] | NSPR[8] | NSPR[8] |
| Venlafaxine | | 7/7[16] | 7/7[16] | NSPR[16] | Care[16] | Care[16] | Care[16] | Care[16] | Care[16] |
| Mirtazapine | | 7/7[7] | 7/7[7] | NSPR[12] | NSPR[12] | NSPR[12] | NSPR[12] | NSPR[12] | NSPR[12] |
| Mianserin | | 14/7[1] | 14/7[1] | NSPR | NSPR | NSPR | NSPR | NSPR | NSPR |
| Reboxetine | | 1/52[17] | 1/52[17] | NSPR[17] | NSPR[17] | NSPR[17] | NSPR[17] | NSPR[17] | NSPR[17] |
| Just plain stopping:[17] | | Over 4/52[17] | Over 4/52[73] | Over 4/52[17] | Over 4/52[17] | Over 4/52[17] | Reduce to 20mg/d, then stop | Over 4/52[17] | Over 4/52[17] or longer |

NSPR= No significant problems reported, careful cross-taper
OP   = Occasional problems
SSP  = Serotonin Syndrome possible (see ref 5)
NB: Patients with bipolar mood disorders should be monitored closely for manic episodes following discontinuation or change of any antidepressant medication (*J Clin Psych* 1985, **5**, 342–3)

| From \ To | Trazodone[16] Nefazodone | Tryptophan | Moclo-bemide | Venla-faxine[16] | Mirtazapine | Mianserin | Reboxetine |
|---|---|---|---|---|---|---|---|
| MAOIS Hydrazines | 14/7[6,7] | 14/7[10] or care | 1/7[7] with care | 14/7[16] | 2/52[7] | 14/7[1] | 2/52[17] |
| MAOIS Tranylcypromine | 14/7[6,7] | 1/7[10] | 7/7[1,7] with care | 14/7[16] | 2/52[7] | 14/7[1] | 2/52[17] |
| Tricyclics | NSPR | NSPR[10] | NSPR[15] | Variable[16] | NSPR[12] | NSPR | NSPR[17] |
| Citalopram/ escitalopram | Care[3,6] | Care[11] | 7/7[14] | Care[16] | NSPR[12] | NSPR | NSPR[17] |
| Fluvoxamine | Care[6] | Care[11] | 4–5/7[14] | Care[16] | NSPR[12] | NSPR | NSPR[17] |
| Fluoxetine | Care[6] | Care[11] | 4–45/7[14] | Care[16] | NSPR[12] | NSPR | NSPR[17] |
| Sertraline | Care[6] | Care[11] | 4–13/7[14] | Care[16] | NSPR[12] | NSPR | NSPR[17] |
| Paroxetine | Care[6] | Care[11] | 4–5/7[14] | Care[16] | NSPR[12] | NSPR | NSPR[17] |
| Trazodone Nefazodone | Care[16] | NSPR | NSPR | Care[16] | NSPR[12] | NSPR | NSPR[17] |
| Tryptophan | NSPR | ■ | NSPR | NSPR | NSPR[12] | NSPR | NSPR[17] |
| Moclobemide | NSPR[6,8] | NSPR | ■ | NSPR | NSPR[12] | NSPR | NSPR[17] |
| Venlafaxine | Care[16] | NSPR[16] | NSPR[16] | ■ | NSPR[16] | NSPR[16] | NSPR[17] |
| Mirtazapine | NSPR[12] | NSPR[12] | NSPR[12] | NSPR[12] | ■ | NSPR[12] | NSPR[17] |
| Mianserin | NSPR | NSPR | NSPR | NSPR | NSPR[12] | ■ | NSPR[17] |
| Reboxetine | NSPR[17] | NSPR[17] | NSPR[17] | NSPR[17] | NSPR[17] | NSPR[17] | ■ |
| Just plain stopping: | Over 4/52[17] | Over 4/52[17] | Over 4/52[17] | Over 4/52[17] or longer | Over 4/52[17] | Over 4/52[17] | Over 4/52[17] |

NSPR = No significant problems reported, careful cross-taper
OP = Occasional problems
SSP = Serotonin Syndrome possible (see ref 5)
NB: Patients with bipolar mood disorders should be monitored closely for manic episodes following discontinuation or change of any antidepressant medication (*J Clin Psych* 1985, **5**, 342–43)

Ideally, 'drop-and-stop' before starting the next drug is recommended.

**Factors to be considered:**

i. **Speed** at which the switch is needed, eg. faster switches can obviously be made, but additional monitoring, eg. tricyclic levels and cardiac status is recommended.

ii. **SSRI dose** – CYP2D6 inhibition is dose-related for some drugs, eg. paroxetine, fluoxetine.

iii. **Tricyclic** – stronger serotonin re-uptake inhibitors are more likely to produce serotonin syndrome (eg. clomipramine), and tertiary tricyclics (eg. imipramine, amitriptyline, clomipramine) are also metabolised by CYP3A3/4 and CYP1A2, inhibited by fluvoxamine.

iv. **P450 status** of the patient.

v. **Individual** susceptibility to tricyclic and SSRI side-effects.

**Main potential problems** (see also introduction for details):

i. Cholinergic rebound.

ii. Tricyclic/SSRI discontinuation symptoms (see ref 13).

iii. Serotonin Syndrome (see *1.31*).

iv. Increased tricyclic levels via CYP2D6 inhibition by SSRIs (see *4.3.1*).

**Suggested switch regimens:**

**Tricyclic → fluoxetine, paroxetine or fluvoxamine:** Taper tricyclic dose to around 25–50mg/d, start SSRI at usual starting dose and discontinue tricyclic over next 5–7 days, with careful observation.

Main potential problems (see above for details): Serotonin syndrome, raised tricyclic levels by P450 inhibition, cholinergic rebound or tricyclic withdrawal.

**Tricyclic → citalopram, escitalopram or sertraline:** As above, but less potential for interaction so problems less likely. A serotonin syndrome has been reported with sertraline and amitriptyline (Alderman *et al, Ann Pharmacother* 1996, **30**, 1499–500).

**Fluoxetine → tricyclic:** Stop fluoxetine, wait several days for peak levels to fall,

then add tricyclic cautiously at low dose and build up slowly. Care is needed for up to four weeks as the interaction potential may be prolonged (see *4.3.2*). An abrupt switch from fluoxetine 20mg/d to amitriptyline 50–100mg/d resulted in 14% dropping out due to adverse reactions, the rest tolerating the switch (Rutten *et al*, MI).

Main potential problems (see above for details): Serotonin syndrome (especially with drugs such as clomipramine) and higher tricyclic levels via CYP2D6 inhibition.

**Paroxetine → tricyclic:** Taper paroxetine dose to about 10mg/d, and introduce tricyclic at low dose. After several days, discontinue paroxetine and increase tricyclic dose to therapeutic levels.

Main potential problems (see above for details): Paroxetine withdrawal (see *17*), serotonin syndrome (especially with drugs such as clomipramine) and higher tricyclic levels via CYP2D6 inhibition.

**Fluvoxamine → tricyclic:** As paroxetine. Main potential problems (see above for details): Fluvoxamine withdrawal (rare, see *17*), serotonin syndrome (especially with drugs such as clomipramine) and higher tricyclic levels via CYP1A2 and 3A3/4 inhibition (especially with tertiary tricyclics).

**Citalopram, escitalopram or sertraline → tricyclic:** If necessary, reduce to minimum doses of citalopram (20mg/d), escitalopram (10mg) or sertraline (50mg/d). Stop SSRI and introduce tricyclic, titrating dose upwards as tolerated. With standard doses of SSRIs, few problems should be seen.

**Main potential problems** (see above for details): SSRI withdrawal (rare, see *17*), serotonin syndrome (especially with eg. clomipramine) and higher tricyclic levels via CYP2D6 inhibition (low risk).

**3. Trazodone-others:**

Trazodone and fluoxetine have been used together but risks enhanced sedation (eg. n=8, Nirenberg *et al, J Clin Psych* 1992, **53**, 83) and serotonin syndrome (n=1, George and Godleski, *Biol Psych* 1996, **39**, 384–85). Fluoxetine can slightly raise trazodone levels (see *4.3.2.2*). A serotonin syndrome with low dose trazodone added to **paroxetine** would indicate the need for similar care (n=1, Reeves and Bullen, *Psychosomatics* 1995, **36**, 159–60). There is no information on changing from trazodone to the other SSRIs at present but a gradual switch, with close observation of the patient would seem sensible for all SSRIs. See also *5*.

**4. TCA-TCA:**
No significant problems reported but a gradual switch is recommended as per normal practice.

**5. SSRI-SSRI:**
Any combination of SSRIs can precipitate a serotonin syndrome (see *1.30*). Thus, careful observation initially and a gentle change-over is recommended. A washout period would further minimise the possibility of problems. An example of potential problems has been shown in a report of a 'therapeutic substitution', where outpatients were abruptly swapped from **fluoxetine to sertraline** (20mg:50mg respectively dose substitution). 63% swapped successfully but 37% failed, including 18% with intolerable adverse effects, (nervousness, jitters, nausea and headache), suggestive of a serotonin-like syndrome (n=54, Stock and Kofoed, *Am J Hosp Pharm* 1994, **51**, 2279–81). One study showed that abrupt switching from **fluoxetine to paroxetine** produced an increased level of side-effects such as insomnia, nausea, dry mouth, nervousness and tremor in the immediate switch group when compared to a two-week washout, which was well tolerated (n=240, d/b, Kreider *et al, J Clin Psych* 1995, **56**, 142–45). However, paroxetine had no effect on the kinetics of fluoxetine and norfluoxetine in a study (n=9, Domin-

guez *et al, J Clin Psychopharmacology* 1996, **16**, 320–23).

**6. Nefazodone-others:**
If **MAOIs** are stopped shortly before **nefazodone** is started, then initial care and a gradual dose introduction is appropriate. No other recommendations are available at the time of writing, but the **SSRI to nefazodone** switch may have problems. SSRIs typically have an antagonistic effect at 5-HT$_{2C}$ receptors, which is lost when discontinued, and mCPP (a major metabolite of nefazodone) has 5-HT$_{2C}$ agonist activity. When switching from an SSRI to nefazodone, this change in 5-HT$_{2C}$ status may produce some central effects, with dysphoria, anxiety and anxiety reported. It is best to taper the SSRI and introduce nefazodone gradually. Use of fluoxetine pre-nefazodone can increase the AUC of mCPP which can increase anxiety in the short-term.

**7. MAOIs-SSRIs:**
The time to wait between stopping an SSRI and starting an MAOI depends upon the respective SSRI. The SPC for tranylcypromine recommends leaving at least a seven-day gap after stopping other antidepressants, then starting tranylcypromine at half the usual dosage for one week. The BNF recommends a two-week gap from the SSRIs before an MAOI is started but this appears only to be strictly correct for paroxetine.

**Fluvoxamine → MAOI:** fluvoxamine has a short half-life and so isocarboxazid/phenelzine may be started 4–5 days after stopping fluvoxamine (4–5×half-life) or 7 days for tranylcypromine.

**Paroxetine → MAOI:** two-week gap (MI).

**Fluoxetine → MAOI:** a serotonin syndrome has been reported when tranylcypromine was started six weeks after fluoxetine was stopped, due to persistence of norfluoxetine (but not fluoxetine) in the blood (letter in *Am J Psych* 1993, **150**, 837). Since several reported interactions exist, it might be better to allow 6 weeks after stopping fluoxetine before starting an MAOI (*Drug & Ther Bull* 1990, **28**, 334, BNF). The isocarboxazid SPC recommends a gap longer than 2 weeks.

**Sertraline → MAOI:** a one-week gap should elapse before starting an MAOI. A serotonergic syndrome has been reported with sertraline and tranylcypromine (see SSRI interactions *4.3.2*). The manufacturer suggests that a two-week gap between sertraline and MAOI therapies would be prudent.

**Trazodone → MAOI:** the SPC recommends a one-week gap. In one study, combined treatment did not show hypertensive reactions but an increase in side-effect severity, eg. sedation, postural hypotension etc occurred (n=13, Nierenberg and Keck, *J Clin Psychopharmacol* 1989, **9**, 42).

**Moclobemide → MAOI:** moclobemide has a half-life of 14 hours and so stopping moclobemide one day and starting another antidepressant the next day is adequate.

**Mirtazapine → MAOI:** a one-week wash-out period is recommended, by the UK manufacturers.

**MAOI → SSRIs:** a two-week gap (*Drug & Ther Bull* 1990, **28**, 33–34, BNF) has been suggested but longer may be safer as a severe serotonin syndrome has been reported with a two-week gap between stopping tranylcypromine and starting fluoxetine (n=1, Ruiz, *Ann Emerg Med* 1994, **24**, 983–85), even although tranylcypromine has a relatively short action (ie. reversible MAO inhibition).

**MAOI → trazodone:** the SPC recommends a two-week gap after stopping trazodone before MAOIs (see also trazodone to MAOI above).

**MAOI → moclobemide:** a gap is not needed between stopping an MAOI and starting moclobemide, provided MAOI dietary restrictions are maintained for 10–14 days.

**MAOI → mirtazapine:** a two-week wash-out period is recommended.

**8. Moclobemide-SSRIs:**
Due to a lack of clinical information, the manufacturers of **fluoxetine** recommend that normal MAOI procedures be observed for **moclobemide**, and so a two-week gap after stopping moclobemide is stated. This would appear over-cautious and Roche recommend that when changing to an SSRI only an 8–12 hour gap is needed.

**9. Tricyclics-MAOIs:**
These have been used together uneventfully (see *1.14*) but have also interacted (see *4.3.4*):

**MAOIs → tricyclic:** a 10–14-day gap is often recommended (isocarboxazid '1–2 weeks') particularly if imipramine, desipramine, clomipramine or tranylcypromine are involved. Using initial low doses of the tricyclic is essential.

**Tricyclic → MAOI:** A one-week gap is recommended (BNF) and is advisable particularly if imipramine, clomipramine or tranylcypromine are involved. Using initial low doses of the MAOI is essential.

**10. Tryptophan-MAOIs:**
Behavioural and neurological toxicity has been reported with concomitant high dose tryptophan and MAOIs and so initial observation and care would seem advisable. See also *1*.

**11. Tryptophan-SSRIs:**
Cases of central toxicity, agitation and nausea have occurred with the combination and are suggested as likely to occur with other SSRIs. It would thus be prudent to observe the patient carefully and consider the possibility of a serotonergic syndrome developing.

**12\*. Mirtazapine-others:**
Mirtazapine has multiple routes of metabolism (2D6, 3A4 and 1A2) so switching problems will be unlikely in terms of P450 inhibition. The only recommendation is for MAOIs (see *7*). Fluoxetine 20–40mg/d has been switched abruptly to mirtazapine 15mg/d, without problems (n=40, Preskorn *et al, Biol Psych* 1997, **41**, 96S), although serotonin syndrome

has been reported during a cross-over switch to venlafaxine (n=1, Dimellis, *World J Biol Psych* 2002, **3**, 167).

### 13.* Trazodone/nefazodone-TCAs:

Two isolated cases exist of hypomania after abrupt change from trazodone to imipramine (n=2, Haggerty and Jackson, *J Clin Psych* 1985, **5**, 342–43) and a serotonin syndrome when low-dose trazodone was added to nefazodone (n=1, Margolese and Chouinard, *Am J Psych* 2000, **157**, 1022) so care with switch.

### 14. SSRIs-moclobemide:

The SPC recommends a gap of 4–5 half-lives after stopping an SSRI before starting moclobemide, as serotonin syndromes have been reported (see *4.3.3.3*). However, in a study where up to 600mg/d moclobemide was added to established fluoxetine therapy, there was no change in the number, intensity, or type of adverse events. Fluoxetine markedly inhibited the metabolism of moclobemide but did not lead to excessive accumulation, and there was no evidence of the development of a 'serotonin syndrome' (n=18, RCT, p/c, Dingemanse *et al, Clin Pharmacol Ther* 1998, **63**, 403–13).

**Citalopram/escitalopram → moclobemide:** a 7-day gap is recommended.

**Fluoxetine → moclobemide:** with fluoxetine's long half-life, the gap should be as much as six weeks if five times the half-life of norfluoxetine is calculated. A gap of three weeks together with careful monitoring would seem a reasonably practical figure. See also above, where no clinically significant problem was apparent and a shorter gap may be appropriate.

**Fluvoxamine → moclobemide:** a 3-day gap is recommended (but see above).

**Paroxetine → moclobemide:** a 5-day gap is recommended (but see above), although paroxetine's half-life can be longer in the elderly.

**Sertraline → moclobemide:** with the long half-life of desmethylsertraline, the gap should be up to 13 days but 5 and 7 days is recommended by Roche

and Pfizer respectively (but see above).

### 15.* Tricyclics-moclobemide:

**Tricyclic → moclobemide:** a gap is recommended if the tricyclic concerned is a 5-HT reuptake inhibitor. Roche only mention clomipramine needing a 7-day gap (study by Laux *et al, Psychopharmacology Berlin*1988, **96** [Suppl], 230) although theoretically amitriptyline (5-day gap) and imipramine (4-day gap) might be included as well. However, healthy volunteers taking either clomipramine 100mg/d or amitriptyline 75mg/d for at least a week, were swapped abruptly to moclobemide (150mg first day, 300mg/d thereafter) or placebo. There was no increase in incidence or severity of side-effects nor any significant pharmacokinetic interaction between the drugs (n=24, d/b, p/c, Dingemanse *et al, J Clin Psychopharmacol* 1995, **15**, 41–48).

**Moclobemide → tricyclic:** abrupt switching from moclobemide to tricyclics appears well tolerated (n=13, open, Becker *et al, Psychiatr Prax* 1989, **16**(Suppl 1), 44–47) but switching to clomipramine may cause some problems (open, Luax *et al, Psychopharmacology* 1988, **Suppl 96**, 230).

### 16. Venlafaxine-others:

**MAOI → venlafaxine:** Wyeth recommend a 14-day gap between stopping an MAOI and starting venlafaxine. This is appropriate as there are a number of reports of interactions, eg. extreme agitation, diaphoresis, rapid respiration and raised CPK after a 37.5mg dose of venlafaxine seven days after phenelzine 45mg/d was stopped (Phillips and Ringo, *Am J Psych* 1995, **152**, 1400–1) and serotonin syndrome (eg. n=4, Diamond *et al, Neurology* 1998, **51**, 274–76). In the first reported case, the reaction did not occur a further seven days later and strongly suggests that a 14-day gap is indeed required.

**Venlafaxine → MAOI:** Wyeth recommend a 7-day gap (see above).

**Tricyclic → venlafaxine:** 5 times the first drugs half-life should be allowed as a wash-out time before starting venlafaxine (MI). For some tricyclics this would require leaving a 2–3-week gap, an unnecessarily extended period. The company, however, have no evidence of any problems.

**Venlafaxine → other drugs:** no information.

**Other drugs → venlafaxine:** no information.

**17*. Withdrawal or discontinuation:**
Adverse discontinuation events have been reported for many antidepressants. Such symptoms are not, however, indicative of dependence, which usually requires **three** of the following:

- Tolerance
- Withdrawal symptoms
- Use greater than needed
- Inability to reduce doses
- Excessive time taken procuring drug
- Primacy of drug taking over other activities
- Continued use despite understanding of adverse effects.

Discontinuation symptoms have a number of characteristics, eg. they usually start within 1–2 days of stopping and resolve within 24hrs of restarting the drug, and are more common with longer courses or higher doses. They can occur with missed doses and about 30% of patients on SSRIs have dosing lapses of 2 or more days, long enough to produce discontinuation symptoms in patients on some short-acting SSRIs (n=82, 3/12, Meijer *et al, B J Psych* 2001, **179**, 519–22), but not fluoxetine (*Curr Prob* 2000, **26**, 11–12). The UK *Drug and Therapeutics Bulletin* (1999, **37**, 49–52) recommends:

- After less than 8 weeks treatment, withdraw over 1–2 weeks
- After 6–8 months treatment, taper over a 6–8 week period
- After long-term maintenance treatment, reduce the dose by 25% every 4–6 weeks.

**Management:**

1. Reduce the dose stepwise every week or so, stabilising between reductions, eg. paroxetine 20mg/d, 10mg/d, 10mg alternate days (but not less frequently). Use of the syrup, gradually diluted, may also be effective

2. Transfer to a long half-life drug, eg. fluoxetine (care with switching), then reduce (clomipramine case, Benazzi, *Am J Psych* 1999, **156**, 661–62; venlafaxine case, Giakas and David, *Psychiatr Ann* 1997, **27**, 85–92)

3. Treat the emerging syndrome symptomatically, eg. nausea, headache and diarrhoea have been managed with ondansetron (n=1, Raby, *J Clin Psych* 1998, **59**, 621–22) and ginger root (Schechter, *J Clin Psych* 1998, **59**, 431–32).

**Reviews:*** recognition, prevention and management of antidepressant withdrawal syndromes (Haddad, *Drug Safety* 2001, **24**, 183–97), general (Haddad, *J Clin Psych* 1998, **59**, 541–48; Healy, *Prescriber* 2002, **13**, 91–99), WHO reporting system (Stahl *et al, Eur J Clin Pharmacol* 1997, **53**, 163–69).

**Main withdrawal symptoms:**

**Tricyclics:** cholinergic rebound, eg. headache, restlessness, diarrhoea, nausea and vomiting (Lieberman, *Psychosomatics* 1981, **22**, 253–54), flu, lethargy, abdominal cramps, sleep disturbance, movement disorders.

**MAOIs:** psychosis, hallucinations, disorientation, catatonia (n=2, Liskin *et al, J Clin Psychopharmacol* 1985, **5**, 46–47), irritability, hypomania (Rothchild, *J Clin Psychopharmacol* 1985, **5**, 340–41), nausea, sweating, palpitations, nightmares, delirium (Liebowitz *et al, Am J Psych* 1978, **135**, 1565–66).

**SSRIs:** dizziness, vertigo/lightheadedness, nausea, fatigue, headache, sensory disturbance, 'electric shocks' in the head, insomnia, abdominal cramps, chills, flu-like symptoms, increased dreaming, anxiety/agitation and volatility, not caused by anything else, eg. physical illness, other drugs etc. (occur if you 'FINISH' treatment, ie. Flu-like symptoms, Insomnia, Imbalance, Sensory disturbance, Hyperarousal; Berber, *J Clin Psych* 1998, **59**, 255).

**Reviews**:* SSRI withdrawal (Healy, *Prescriber* 2002, **13**, 91–9; Zajecka *et al, J Clin Psych* 1997, **58**, 291–97; *J Clin Psych* 1997, **58**[Suppl 7], 5–40).

**Specific drugs:**

**Comparative data:** There have been a number of comparative studies between SSRIs. Interruption for 5–8 days of maintenance therapy produced few discontinuation symptoms with fluoxetine (long half-life), some with sertraline and most with paroxetine (n=242, RCT, d/b, 4/52, Rosenbaum *et al, Biol Psych* 1998, **44**, 77–87, study funded by Lilly). In another study, suddenly discontinuing fluoxetine showed slightly more dizziness and somnolence at weeks 2–4, but no difference at week 6 compared to continuous treatment (n=395, RCT, 12/52, Zajecka *et al, J Clin Psychopharmacol* 1998, **18**, 193–97; review, Kendrick, *EBMH* 1999, **2**, 31). A third study of 5-day interruption showed increased symptoms after a second missed dose with paroxetine, with impaired functional performance at five days, sertraline with less pronounced changes, and fluoxetine with no significant symptoms (n=107, RCT, Michelson *et al, B J Psych* 2000, **174**, 363–68).

**Citalopram***: even rapid discontinuation appears only to produce mild and transient effects (n=225, RCT, d/b, 10/52, Markowitz *et al, Int Clin Psychopharmacol* 2000, **15**, 329–33).

**Escitalopram**: See citalopram.

**Fluoxetine:** has a long half-life and discontinuation problems are rare eg. isolated cases of extreme dizziness 3–14 days after fluoxetine stopped (Einbinder, *Am J Psych* 1995, **152**, 1235), of severe, dull, aching pain in the left arm after abrupt withdrawal, which remitted after reintroduction (n=1, Lauterbach, *Neurology* 1994, **44**, 983–84) and of reversible delirium

(Kasantikul, *J Med Assoc Thailand* 1995, **78**, 53–54).

**Fluvoxamine:** a slow withdrawal may be preferred (Szabadi, *B J Psych* 1992, **160**, 283–84).

**Paroxetine:*** has been associated with more discontinuation reports than other SSRIs (Young *et al, B J Psych* 1997, **170**, 288). Cases reports include fever, severe fatigue, headache, nausea, vomiting and agitation (eg. Debattista and Schatzberg, *Am J Psych* 1995, **152**, 1235–36) and electrical shock-like sensations (Frost and Lal, *Am J Psych* 1995, **152**, 180). It has presented as stroke (n=2, Haddad *et al, J Psychopharmacol* 2001, **15**, 139–41) and confused with dothiepin side effects during a switch (n=1, Haddad and Qureshi, *Acta Psych Scand* 2000, **102**, 466–68). This phenomenon may be more frequent because paroxetine has a short half-life (using French Pharmacovigilance database; Trenque *et al, Pharmacoepidemiol & Drug Safety* 2002, **11**, 281–83) and inhibits its own CYP2D6 metabolism. This dissipates much quicker than fluoxetine and sertraline (n=45, RCT, open, Liston *et al, J Clin Psychopharmacol* 2002, **22**, 169–73) and, as concentrations fall, less inhibition occurs and levels fall quicker, leading to a more rapid drop. Discontinuation symptoms tend to resolve in a few days or on reintroduction of paroxetine. The CSM recommends tapering if withdrawal symptoms occur, ie. stop if problems occur then restart and taper over 12 weeks, with either half-tablet doses or alternate day (but not less frequently) therapy. However, even a four-week gradual dose reduction may not prevent significant symptoms of vertigo, light-headedness and gait instability, so care is needed (n=5, Pacheco *et al, B J Psych* 1996, **169**, 384).

**Sertraline:*** discontinuation reactions are relatively uncommon, eg. fatigue, cramps, insomnia etc, which resolved on restarting and where tapering over about 14 weeks was successful (Louie *et al, Am J Psych* 1994, 151, 450–51), electrical shock-like sensations (Frost and Lal, *Am J Psych* 1995, **152**, 180) and postural hypotension (n=1, Amsden and Georgian, *Pharmacotherapy* 1996, **16**, 684–86). Abrupt sertraline 100mg/d discontinuation has been enhanced by buspirone 15mg/d (n=1, Carrazana *et al, Am J Psych* 2001, **158**, 966–97).

**Nefazodone:** 'electrical sensations down the legs', dizziness and nausea have been reported for 2–3 days after abrupt cessation of nefazodone (final dose 200mg bd, 9/7 course, n=1, Kotlyar *et al, Am J Psych* 1999, **156**, 1117).

**Tryptophan:** many patients had their tryptophan stopped abruptly after it was withdrawn from the market without apparent serious withdrawal problems, other than recurrence of depression.

**Venlafaxine:** if used for more than six weeks, withdrawal over at least a week is recommended by the manufacturers. A 1999 UK SPC change includes withdrawal reactions from abrupt cessation, dose reduction or tapering of venlafaxine, and includes fatigue, headache, nausea, vomiting, dizziness, dry mouth, diarrhoea, insomnia, nervousness, confusion, paraesthesia, sweating and vertigo. Other symptoms include abdominal distension and congested sinuses (n=1, resolving within 12 hours of restarting, Farah and Lauer, *Am J Psych* 1996, **153**, 576), gastrointestinal upset (which responded to reintroduction and then slow reduction over 1–4 weeks, n=3,

Louie *et al, Am J Psych* 1996, **153**, 1652) and classic SSRI-type discontinuation symptoms (eg. confusion, headache, agitation, abdominal distension and sweating) occurring 16 and 20 hours after stopping (n=2, Agelink *et al, Am J Psych* 1997, **154**, 1473–74; review of similarity to SSRI symptoms, n=13, Boyd, *Med J Aus* 1998, **169**, 91–92). An outpatient study showed that 7 of the 9 patients discontinuing sustained-release venlafaxine reported the emergence of adverse reactions, compared to 2 of the 9 stopping placebo (n=9, d/b, p/c, Fava *et al, Am J Psych* 1997, **154**, 1760–62). It may not prevented by maprotiline, but resolved by sertraline (n=1, Luckhaus and Jacob, *Int J Neuropsychopharmacol* 2001, **4**, 43–44).

**Mirtazapine:\*** a withdrawal hypomania is all that has been reported to date (n=1, MacCall and Callender, *B J Psych* 1999, **175**, 390).

**Moclobemide:\*** a discontinuation syndrome may present with influenza-like symptoms. Sertraline may not modify the symptoms, suggesting a different mechanism (n=1, Curtin *et al, J Psychopharmacol* 2002, **16**, 271–72).

**Reboxetine:** no withdrawal or discontinuation syndrome has been observed in studies with reboxetine, with few additional effects on abrupt withdrawal (SPC). There is no data on switching antidepressants, other than a requirement for a gap with MAOIs.

## Table 2.3 — SELECTING DRUGS, DOSES & PREPARATIONS: LIQUIDS & INJECTIONS AVAILABLE IN THE UK *

| Drug | Commercial liquid | Extemporaneous liquid[1] | Injection[2] | Other |
|------|-------------------|---------------------------|--------------|-------|
| **Antidepressants[1,2]** | | | | |
| Amitriptyline | 10mg/5ml SF soln[3] 25mg/5ml[3] syrup 50mg/5ml[3] syrup | Possible[27] | Discontinued s/c possible[28] | Suppositories[22] |
| Amoxapine | - | Possible[34] | N/K | N/K |
| Citalopram | 40mg/ml drops | - | Reported [53] | N/K |
| Clomipramine | - | Syrup possible | Discontinued | N/K |
| Dosulepin (dothiepin) | 25mg/5ml SF syrup[3] 75mg/5ml SF syrup[3] | - | N/K | Suppositories[7] |
| Doxepin | - | Mentioned in USP[25] | N/K | Suppositories[43] |
| Escitalopram | - | - | - | - |
| Fluoxetine | 20mg/5ml liquid | - | N/K | Sub-lingual[50] |
| Flupentixol | - | Import possible[39] | Depot | N/K |
| Fluvoxamine | - | No hard data[40] | N/K | N/K |
| Imipramine | - | - | N/K | Possible [54] |
| Isocarboxazid | - | 1/52 expiry possible | N/K | N/K |
| Lofepramine | 70mg/5ml susp[3] | - | N/K | N/K |
| Maprotiline | - | ? | N/K | N/K |
| Mianserin | - | Yes[19] | N/K | N/K |
| Mirtazapine | 15mg/ml SF soln[3] dispersable tablets[48] | - | IV[48] | - |
| Moclobemide | - | Yes[44] | N/K | N/K |
| Nefazodone | - | N/K | N/K | N/K |
| Nortriptyline | - | Yes[20] | N/K | N/K |
| Paroxetine | 10mg/5ml | - | N/A | N/K |
| Phenelzine | - | Not possible[18] | N/K | N/K |
| Reboxetine | - | N/K | N/K | N/K |
| Sertraline | - | Just possible[29] | N/K | N/K |
| Tranylcypromine | - | 3/12 expiry possible | N/K | N/K |
| Trazodone | 50mg/5ml SF liquid | - | N/A[21] | N/K |
| Tryptophan | - | - | N/K | N/K |
| Venlafaxine | - | Capsule granules? | N/K | N/K |
| **Benzodiazepines and anxiolytics** | | | | |
| Alprazolam | - | Tabs can be crushed | N/K | N/K |
| Bromazepam | - | N/K | N/K | N/K |
| Buspirone | - | N/K | N/K | N/K |
| Chlordiazepoxide | - | Yes[47] | N/K | N/K |
| Clorazepate | - | - | N/K | N/K? |
| Diazepam | 2mg & 5mg/5ml soln 2.5 and 10+mg/5ml susp[3] | - | 5mg/ml IV/IM[8] | Rectal tubules[45] Suppositories |
| Hydroxyzine | - | N/K | N/K | N/K |
| Loprazolam | - | N/K | N/K | N/K |
| Lorazepam | - | N/K | 4mg/ml IV/IM[4] | Rectal, sub-lingual tabs[4] |
| Meprobamate | - | Mentioned in USP | N/K | N/K |
| Midazolam | - | Yes[42] | 2mg/ml[17] 5mg/ml[17] | Intranasal[17] Buccal[17] |
| Nitrazepam | 2.5mg/5ml susp | - | N/K | N/K |
| Oxazepam | - | N/K | N/K | N/K |
| Propranolol | 5, 10 and 50mg/5ml SF soln[3] | - | 1mg/ml | N/K |
| Temazepam | 10mg/5ml syrup[3] | - | N/K | N/K |
| **Antipsychotics** | | | | |
| Benperidol | - | N/K | N/K | N/K |
| Chlorpromazine | 25mg/5ml syrup[3] 50mg/5ml syrup[3] 100mg/5ml syrup[3] 100mg/5ml susp | - | 25mg/ml IM 100mg/ml[5] | Suppositories |
| Clozapine | - | Possible[6] | N/K | N/K |

## Table 2.3 — SELECTING DRUGS, DOSES & PREPARATIONS: LIQUIDS & INJECTIONS AVAILABLE IN THE UK *

| Drug | Commercial liquid | Extemporaneous liquid[1] | Injection[2] | Other |
|---|---|---|---|---|
| Flupentixol | - | Import possible[39] | Depot | N/K |
| Fluphenazine | - | 2/52 expiry possible | Depot | N/K |
| Fluspirilene | - | N/K | Depot | N/K |
| Haloperidol | 1, 5 and 10mg/5ml SF syrup[3] 1 and 2mg/ml liquid | - | 5mg/ml IM/IV 10mg/ml IM/IV Depot | N/K |
| Levomepromazine | - | Yes[32] | 25mg/ml IV/IM/SC | N/K |
| Loxapine | - | Known in USA[35] | Known in USA[35] | Sub-cut known[35] |
| Olanzapine | - | Extemp possible[51] | IM licensed[53] | Velotabs |
| Pericyazine | 10mg/5ml syrup | - | N/K | N/K |
| Perphenazine | 4mg/5ml SF syrup[3] | - | Known[30] | N/K |
| Pimozide | - | N/K | N/K | N/K |
| Prochlorperazine | 5mg/5ml syrup | Effervescent sachets | 12.5mg/ml IV | Suppositories |
| Promazine | 25mg/5ml SF syrup[3] 50mg/5ml SF syrup[3] | - | 50mg/ml IM | N/K |
| Quetiapine | - | N/K | N/K | N/K |
| Risperidone | 1mg/ml | - | Long-acting injection | Quicklets |
| Sulpiride | 200mg/5ml SF syrup[3] | - | N/K | N/K |
| Thioridazine | 10, 25 and 50mg/5ml syrup[3] 25, 100mg/5ml susp | - | N/K | N/K |
| Trifluoperazine | 1mg/5ml syrup 5mg/5ml SF syrup[3] | - | Discontinued | N/K |
| Zuclopenthixol | - | 2/52 expiry extemp[13] plus imports[13] | Depot+Acuphase | N/K |

**Anticonvulsants**

| Drug | Commercial liquid | Extemporaneous liquid[1] | Injection[2] | Other |
|---|---|---|---|---|
| Carbamazepine | 100mg/5ml SF liquid | Chew-tabs | N/K | Rectal[15] |
| Clomethiazole | 250mg/5ml syrup | - | Discontinued | ? |
| Clonazepam | 0.5mg and 2mg/5ml SF soln[3] | - | 1mg/ml | Dispersible tablets in USA |
| Clobazam | - | Any strength[24] | N/K | N/K |
| Diazepam | See benzodiazepines | - | Various | Rectal tubules |
| Ethosuximide | 250mg/5ml syrup | Capsules[46] | N/K | N/K |
| Fosphenytoin | - | - | 75mg/ml IM/IV | - |
| Gabapentin | - | Not advised[26] | N/K | N/K |
| Lamotrigine | - | Dispersable tablets[38] | N/K | Rectal possible[38] |
| Levetiracetam | - | - | - | - |
| Oxcarbazepine | 60mg/ml susp. | - | - | - |
| Paraldehyde | Pure | Various | Pure[16] | Enema[10] |
| Phenobarbital | 15mg/5ml | - | 200mg/ml IM/IV | ? |
| Phenytoin | 30mg/5ml susp 90mg/5ml SF susp[3] | - | 50mg/ml IV | Rectal possible[49] |
| Piracetam | 333.3mg/ml soln | - | - | - |
| Primidone | 250mg/5ml discontinued in UK | - | N/K | N/K |
| Tiagabine | - | - | - | - |
| Topiramate | - | Sprinkle capsules[52] | - | - |
| Valproate | 200mg/5ml syrup 200mg/5ml SF liquid | Others known[33] | 400mg IV | Suppositories[12] |
| Vigabatrin | - | Powder[41] | N/K | N/K |

**Hypnotics**

| Drug | Commercial liquid | Extemporaneous liquid[1] | Injection[2] | Other |
|---|---|---|---|---|
| Benzodiazepines | See benzodiazepines | | | |
| Chloral | 'Welldorm' 500mg/5ml syrup[3] | - | N/K | Rectal possible |
| Clomethiazole | See anticonvulsants | | | |
| Promethazine | 5mg/5ml syrup | - | N/K | N/K |
| Triclofos | 500mg/5ml syrup | - | N/K | N/K |
| Zaleplon | - | N/K | N/K | N/K |
| Zolpidem | - | N/K | N/K | N/K |
| Zopiclone | - | N/K | N/K | N/K |

**Table 2.3 — SELECTING DRUGS, DOSES & PREPARATIONS: LIQUIDS & INJECTIONS AVAILABLE IN THE UK ***

| Drug | Commercial liquid | Extemporaneous liquid[1] | Injection[2] | Other |
|---|---|---|---|---|
| **Anticholinergics** | | | | |
| Benzhexol (trihexyphenidyl) | 2mg/5ml SF soln[3] 5mg/5ml syrup | Yes[31] | N/K | N/K |
| Benzatropine | - | N/K | 1mg/ml IM/IV | N/K |
| Biperidin | - | N/K | N/K | N/K |
| Orphenadrine | 50mg/5ml SF soln[3] 25mg/5ml SF elixir | N/K | N/K | N/K |
| Procyclidine | 2.5mg & 5mg/5ml SF[3] | Injection used [36] | 10mg/2ml[36] | N/K |
| **Miscellaneous** | | | | |
| Cyproterone | - | 3/12 expiry | Named pt basis | N/K |
| Acamprosate | - | - | - | - |
| Bupropion | - | - | - | - |
| Disulfiram | - | Disp. tablets[11] | Implants tried[23] | N/K |
| Naltrexone | - | - | Implants tried[42] | |
| Lithium | 5.4mmol/5ml[3] 10.8mmol/5ml[3] | - | N/K | Vaginal [14] |

N/K=no information known to the UK manufacturers  SF=sugar-free

1.  Extemporaneously prepared antidepressant liquids need care as most tricyclics have marked local anaesthetic actions.
2.  Review of IV antidepressants in *Int Drug Therapy Newsletter* 1981, **16**, 35.
3.  Produced by Rosemont Pharmaceuticals, Leeds (address in BNF). Some are 'specials'.
4.* IM injections of lorazepam must be diluted with an equal quantity of water or saline and used only where oral or IV routes are not possible. A sub-lingual presentation of lorazepam is available in US (Greenblatt *et al, J Pharmaceut Scie* 1982, **71**, 248–52). Rectal use of lorazepam is possible (*Paediatr Neurol* 1987, **3**, 321–26). Intranasal lorazepam is possible (n=11, Wermeling *et al, J Clin Pharmacol* 2001, **41**, 1225–31).
5.  100mg/ml chlorpromazine concentrate is a 'special' from Penn Pharmaceuticals.
6.* A clozapine suspension is possible (Ramuth *et al, Pharm J* 1996, **257**, 190–91), using Guy's Hospital Paediatric base and stable for up to 18 days. Bioavailability may be lower than tablets and so care is needed (n=10, Coker-Adeyemi and Taylor, *Pharm J* 2002, **269**, 650–52).
7.  Various strengths of dothiepin are available as a 'special' from Knoll, whose specials unit have made suppositories to special order and could provide powder if necessary.
8.  Available as diazepam solution ('Valium') and diazepam emulsion ('Diazemuls').
9.  Diazepam 5mg/5ml syrup is available from Lagap Pharmaceuticals.
10. Paraldehyde can be used as an enema, diluted 50:50 either with arachis oil or water (see entry in *1.17.2*).
11. 'Antabuse' tablets are readily dispersible.
12. Valproate suppositories have been used (*Arch Neurol* 1989, **46**, 906–9) and 300mg and 100mg suppositories are available on named-patient basis from Synthelabo.
13. 2mg/5ml and 20mg/5ml syrups of zuclopenthixol are available in parts of Europe. Lundbeck's export department in Copenhagen would be able to advise on availability.
14. Vaginal absorption of lithium appears possible (case report Tente *et al, JAMA* 1994, **272**, 1723–24).
15. A rectal gel of carbamazepine has been used (*Clin Pharm* 1990, **9**, 13–14; Storey and Trimble, *NEJM* 1992, **327**, 1318–19). Carbamazepine suppositories are available in UK, at 125mg and 250mg. 125mg rectally is equivalent to 100mg orally so increase the oral dose by 25% to convert to rectal,with a maximum rectal dose 250mg qds for 7 days.
16. Special from Penn Pharmaceuticals.
17.* Intranasal midazolam is possible (Lahat *et al, Lancet* 1998, **352**, 620 letter), and as effective as IV diazepam in febrile seizures (n=47, RCT, Lahat *et al, BMJ* 2000, **321**, 83–86), more effective than rectal diazepam (n=22, Fisgin *et al, J Child Neurol* 2002, **17**, 123–26), with a rapid onset and high bioavailability shown (n=6, RCT, c/o, Knoester *et al, B J Clin Pharmacol* 2002, **53**, 501–7). An oral syrup has been tried (Marshall *et al, J Clin Pharmacol* 2000, **40**, 578–89; Mehta *et al, Hosp Pharm Pract* 1993, **3**, 224–26) stable for 14 days at 4°C in flavoured liquid gelatin (Bhatt-Mehta, *Am J Hosp Pharm* 1993, **50**, 472–45). Buccal/sublingual absorption of midazolam is possible as an alternative to rectal diazepam for acute seizures in refractory epilepsy (RCT, Scott *et al, Lancet* 1999, **353**, 623–26, comment by Wiebe, *Evidence-Based Med* 2000, **5**, 20, disputed by Ellis *et al, Lancet* 1999, **353**, 1796). For midazolam pharmacokinetics following intravenous and buccal administration, see Schwagmeier *et al (B J Clin Pharmacol* 1998, **46**, 203–6).
18. Phenelzine is too unstable in water for even a short-dated liquid to be made.
19. A solution with a seven-day expiry is possible but the very strong local anaesthetic action of mianserin makes this distinctly unpleasant.
20. A nortriptyline syrup was available in the UK at one time and is available in USA at 10mg/5ml.
21. A trazodone injection was tested some years ago.

22. Amitriptyline is absorbed rectally (*Pharmacotherapy* 1990, **10**, 256) and so suppositories are possible and have been reported to successful (*NEJM* 1982, **306**, 996).
23. Implants of disulfiram can be tried but do not prove to be particularly successful. They are available on a named-patient basis, imported from G Streuli and Co AG (Ltd), Pharmazutika, 8730, Uznach, Switzerland. The 100mg tablets (10 + ) are implanted subcutaneously in the lower abdominal wall.
24. Extemporaneous liquids of clobazam are possible, stable for one month at room temperature (MI).
25. Doxepin has a bitter taste but an extemporaneous preparation has been made (ask Pfizer).
26. Gabapentin capsules can be broken open and the contents swallowed but it has an unpleasant taste. The drug itself is soluble, more particularly in acid solution. Rectal absorption of gabapentin has been shown to be poor (n=2, Kriel *et al, Epilepsia* 1997, **38**, 1242–44).
27. An extemporaneous amitriptyline liquid can be made, which has an eight-week expiry.
28. A small study showed that sub-cutaneous amitriptyline may be possible (*Acta Univ Palacki Olomuc, Fac Med* 1968, **49**, 291–305).
29. Sertraline is poorly soluble and a particularly unpleasant bitter taste. A suspension in methylcellulose suspending base would be needed. No stability data exists so would have to have a very short expiry.
30. A perphenazine injection is made by Schering in the USA.
31. The formula for an extemporaneous benzhexol syrup, stable for 4 weeks, is held by Lederle.
32. A levomepromazine syrup has been used at Bangour Hospital, West Lothian, stable for 7 days in a fridge.
33. Valproate solutions of 200mg/ml and 300mg/ml are available in many countries.
34. There is no theoretical reason why a short-expiry suspension of amoxapine could not be made.
35*. A 25mg/ml oral concentrate of loxapine is available in USA (Lederle). An extemporaneous liquid could be made, but needs to be in an acid solution. A 50mg/ml IM injection is also available in the USA (Lederle) and can be used subcutaneously (Saunder *et al, Am J Health-System Pharm* 1999, **56**, 1259–61).
36. Procyclidine injection in glycerin and orange syrup is possible (7 day expiry) for oral use. The injection is now marketed in UK by Auden McKenzie.
37. Tetrabenazine 10mg/ml syrup using 'Nitoman' tablets has been used. Rosemont used to make this as a special.
38.* Dispersible lamotrigine tablets of 5mg, 25mg and 100mg are available in UK. Rectal absorption of compressed tablets is possible, but is not as quick or complete as when given orally (n=12, RCT, Birnbaum *et al, Epilepsia* 2000, **41**, 850–53; n=12, c/o, Birnbaum *et al, Pharmacotherapy* 2001, **21**, 158–62).
39. Flupentixol drops containing 100mg/ml or 4mg/ml are available in some European countries. Lundbeck's export department in Copenhagen would be able to advise on availability.
40. Fluvoxamine is not available as a syrup. Duphar state that tablets can be crushed to form a suspension of unknown stability, which needs to be prepared freshly each time.
41. Sachets of pure vigabatrin powder are available from Marion Merrell Dow Ltd. which can be added to a drink immediately before use, or through a nasogastric tube if necessary.
42.* Naltrexone implants have been used, including in high-risk pregnant heroin users (n=1, Hulse and O'Neill, *Aust NZJ Obstet Gyn* 2002, **42**, 93–94).
43. Rectal doxepin given as capsules has been mentioned (Storey & Trimble, *NEJM* 1992, **327**, 1318–19)
44. Moclobemide tablets can be dispersed in water and the liquid (including sediment) taken.
45. Available as 'Stesolid' (Dumex) and 'Rectubes' (CP). Absorption from 'Stesolid' rectal solution peaks at 15 minutes (Moolenaar *et al, Int J Pharmaceutics* 1980, **5**, 127–37). An unmarketed diazepam rectal gel (Diastat) displays rapid, consistent absorption and is well tolerated. Alterations in cognition were mild and dissipated within 4hr of drug administration and it may offer an easy, safe and bioavailable method to administer diazepam (Cloyd *et al, Epilepsia* 1998, **39**, 520–26, comparison of rectal diazepam gel and placebo for acute repetitive seizures, Dreifuss *et al, NEJM* 1998, **338**, 1869–75).
46. Warner Lambert state that ethosuximide capsules can be cooled until solid and then cut up and mixed with food. Alternatively, the liquid content of 'Zarontin' capsules can be emptied out and mixed with warm water or other drinks. No stability data exists and so these actions should only be done at the time of each dose.
47. Roche have the formula for a chlordiazepoxide 2mg/ml syrup using 'Librium' capsules, which is stable for one week in a fridge.
48.* An IV injection of mirtazapine is licensed in Germany, and a significantly fast onset of action has been reported with IV mirtazapine 15mg/d (n=27, 14/7, Konstantinidis *et al, Eur Neuropsychopharm* 2002, **12**, 57–60). Dispersible mirtazapine tablets are equivalent to oral tablets (n=40, c/o, van den Heuvel *et al, Clin Drug Investig* 2001, **21**, 437–42).
49. Absorption of 200mg phenytoin from rectal suppositories with polyethylene glycol base is highly variable, unpredictable and not recommended (n=6, open, Burstein *et al, Pharmacother* 2000, **20**, 562–67), although suggested as possible (Chang *et al, Ann Pharmacother* 1999, **33**, 781–86).
50. Fluoxetine can be absorbed sub-lingually from the oral liquid to give therapeutic blood levels (n=2, Pakyurek and Pasol, *Am J Psych* 1999, **156**, 1833–34).
51.* A liquid olanzapine has been prepared (Harvey *et al, Pharm J* 2000, **265**, 275–76). Dispersible tablets are also available. An IM olanzapine injection was licensed in 2000 in many countries.
52. Topiramate 'sprinkle' capsules (50mg) are available in UK (*Pharm J* 2000, **265**, 866).
53.* IV citalopram has been used in resistant OCD (n=39, 3/52, open, Pallanti *et al, J Clin Psych* 2002, **63**, 796–801; review by Kasper and Muller-Spahn, *Eur Arch Psych Clin Neurosci* 2002, **252**, 105–9).
54.* Imipramine syrup was available in UK but withdrawn in 2002.

## 2.4 WEIGHT CHANGES WITH PSYCHOTROPIC DRUGS

### Importance *

Drug-induced weight gain is a potential threat to health, lowers self-esteem and the social embarrassment caused may lead to non-concordance (and hence risks relapse). Patients may eg. become out-of-breath, have to spend money on new clothes (when already short of money), get embarrassed and often won't go out - it's life, Jim, but not as we'd want to know it.

The available data is difficult to compare due to the non-equivalence of collection and presentation. Some body weight gain is common with many psychotropic drugs, and although in most instances the gain is not 'clinically' significant (although it may be significant to the individual), the gain induced by some drugs, such as lithium and atypical antipsychotics, *can* be clinically significant. Risk factors for weight increase have not yet been well characterised, although in general is greatest in individuals with a past and/or family history of obesity (Ackerman and Nolan, *CNS Drugs* 1998, **9**, 135–51, 96 refs). The FDA definition of 'clinically significant' weight gain is 7% or greater increase over baseline weight.

**Review**: body weight changes with psychotropics (mechanisms and management, Pijl and Meinders, *Drug Safety* 1996, **14**, 329–42).

## ANTIPSYCHOTICS *

The table below provides an active comparison between drugs, but does not include all antipsychotics. Weight gain with olanzapine appears to be at least partly reversible by nutritional advice and exercise (n=92, males, retrospective, Wirshing *et al, J Clin Psych* 1999, **60**, 358–63), unlike clozapine, where it is greater than the other atypicals and appears to be sustained despite nutritional advice and exercise. Numerous mechanisms have been proposed, including: *

- Sedation – leading to decreased activity
- Thirst – anticholinergic dry mouth may increase fluid and calorie intake
- Reduced metabolism – fat and carbohydrate oxidation.
- Neurotransmitter-mediated increase in appetite, leading to increased food intake via 5-HT$_{2C}$

**Relative weight gain with antipsychotics**–greatest at top (Allison *et al, Am J Psych* 1999, **156**, 1686–96, 96 refs, review by Fenton, *EBMH* 2000, **3**, 58; n=427, Brecher *et al, Int J Psych Clin Pract* 2000, **4**, 287–91)

| | Long-term change* | 95% CI | Change at 10/52[†] |
|---|---|---|---|
| Perphenazine | 5.8 | 0.4–11.1 | – |
| Clozapine | 5.7 | 4.3–7 | 4 (2.7–5.3) |
| Chlorpromazine | 4.2 | 2.9–5.4 | 2.1 (0.9–3.4) |
| Olanzapine | 4.2 | 3.7–4.6 | 3.5 (3.3–3.7) |
| Sertindole | 2.9 | 2.7–3.2 | 3 (1.8–4.1) |
| Thioridazine | 2.8 | 1.6–4 | 3.4 (1.8–5.2) |
| Quetiapine | 2.5 | <1.5–3.5 | (0?) |
| Risperidone | 1.7 | 1.4–2 | 2 (1.6–2.4) |
| Fluphenazine | 1.1 | 0.1–2.2 | 0.4 (−0.7–1.5) |
| Non-drug controls | 0.8 | 0.1–1.6 | 1.3 (0.8–1.8) |
| Loxapine | 0.7 | −2.6–3.9 | – |
| Polypharmacy | 0.5 | 0.2–0.7 | 1.2 (0.4–2.1) |
| Haloperidol | 0.5 | 0.2–0.8 | 0.5 (0.1–1) |
| Ziprasidone | 0.3 | -0.3–0.8 | 0 (−0.5–0.6) |
| Trifluoperazine | 0.3 | -0.9–1.5 | – |
| Placebo | -1 | -1.8–0.1 | 0.4 (−1.3–0.5) |
| Pimozide | -2.7 | -9.3–3.9 | – |

*longer-term weight change in kg (random effects model)
[†]weight change at 10 weeks (fixed effects model)
Please bear in mind that this is aggregated data, so subject to error, weight was often measured at a different time and there may be a dose-relationship.

(n=123, Reynolds *et al, Lancet* 2002, **359**, 2086–87) and 5-HT$_{2A}$ receptor blockade (rats without a 5-HT$_{2C}$ receptor become obese), H1 or H2 receptor affinity (n=92, males, retrospective, Wirshing *et al, J Clin Psych* 1999, **60**, 358–63) and perhaps D2-blockade and polypeptides such as CCK (review by Stahl, *J Clin Psych* 1998, **59**, 500–1)

● Changes in leptin levels – leptin is a multifunctional polypeptide produced by fat cells to reduce appetite (by signalling the size of the adipose tissue to the brain) and increasing energy expenditure (Friedman and Halass, *Nature* 1998, **395**, 793–70). Weight gain induced by clozapine or olanzapine (n=44, Kraus *et al, Am J Psych* 1999, **156**, 312–14) and other antipsychotics (n=59 + 59, o/p, Herran *et al, B J Psych* 2001, **179**, 59–62) seems related to an increase in leptin levels. Other polypeptides, eg. reductin, may also be implicated

● Fluid retention – via peripheral oedema, a minor effect

● Endocrine effects – increased prolactin (which may promote adiposity and is related to weight gain in men; open, p/c, Baptista *et al, Pharmacopsychiatry* 1997, **30**, 250–55), variation in cortisol, altered insulin secretion.

Most weight is gained during the first 12–16 weeks of therapy, although can still continue for 6 months and maintained for at least 2 years. It can be more marked during in-patient stays, perhaps due to lower physical activity. A large US survey (schizophrenics n=570, non-schizophrenic comparators n=97,819) showed male schizophrenics to be as obese as the general population, but female schizophrenics to be as, or more, obese than the general population, suggesting that weight gain is a significant problem particularly for females taking antipsychotics (Allison *et al, J Clin Psych* 1999, **60**, 215–20).

**Reviews**:* general (Russell and Mackell, *CNS Drugs* 2001, **15**, 537–51; Taylor and McAskill, *Acta Psych Scand* 2000, **101**, 416–32, 94 refs; Baptista, *Acta Psych Scand* 1999, **100**, 3–16; 163 refs, Allison *et al, Am J Psych* 1999, **156**, 1686–96), comparative review (Wetterling, *Drug Safety* 2001, **24**, 59–73, 93 refs).

**Management***
(substantial review by Baptista, *Acta Psych Scand* 1999, **100**, 3–16, 163 refs)
Like all of us, people taking antipsychotics are increasingly aware of the harmful effects of sustained obesity:

1. Routinely take a baseline weight measurement, and warn the patient of the potential for change in weight, difficulty in predicting outcome, plateau effect after several months, need to optimise calorie intake etc.

2. Particularly counsel patients with a higher risk of weight gain, eg. being female, prone to overeat when under stress, narcissistic personality traits, family or personal history of obesity and a greater than 6.5kg difference between adult maximum and minimum weights (Kalucy, *Drugs* 1980, **19**, 268–78).

3. Most weight is gained in the first few months and since it is easier to prevent weight gain than lose it once gained, seek advice from a dietician. Moderate physical exercise may be helpful and carbohydrate craving and excessive intake of high calorie fluids avoided.

4. Adjust the dose. The relationship between dose and weight gain is complex, but generally only a major reduction is likely to help. A slower introduction of, eg. olanzapine may reduce final weight gain.

5.*Adjunctive therapy: appetite suppressants may exacerbate psychosis or fail to work. Fluoxetine augmentation is ineffective in counteracting olanzapine-induced weight gain (n=30, RCT, d/b, 8/52, Poyurovsky *et al, Am J Psych* 2002, **159**, 1058–60) and phenylpropanolamine ineffective in clozapine-induced weight gain (n=16, RCT, d/b, 12/52, Borovicka *et al, J Clin Psych* 2002, **63**, 345–48). Other drugs tried include orlistat (requires compliance with a low-fat diet), sibutramine (but not if taking a serotonergic drug), topiramate (has side effects) and H2-blockers (effectiveness unclear). Review by Werneke *et al, Int Clin Psychopharmacol* 2002, **17**, 145–60.

6. Intermittent and low-dose antipsychotics, although controversial, have been recommended (Buchanan and Carpenter, *CNS Drugs* 1996, **5**, 240–45). For clozapine, adjunctive quetiapine has been used. After 6 months on clozapine (200–800mg/d), patients had 25% dose converted to quetiapine (using ratio 1mg clozapine:2mg quetiapine) for 10 months. The average weight loss was 0.22–10.5kg after one month, and maintained, with 100% user satisfaction reported (n=65, open, 10/12, Reinstein *et al, Clin Drug Invest* 1999, **18**, 99–104).

7.* Metformin may have a role in (atypical) antipsychotic-induced weight gain (79% lost weight, n=19 adolescents, open, 12/52, Morrison *et al, Am J Psych* 2002, **159**, 655–57), although a smaller study had no significant benefit over placebo (n=5, 12/52, Baptista *et al, J Clin Psych* 2001, **62**, 653–55). Estrogen (which promotes weight loss by several mechanisms) and tamoxifen show a possible preventative role in animal studies (see Baptista, *Acta Psych Scand* 1999, **100**, 3–16).

## ANTIDEPRESSANTS

Weight change in depression is well known and weight loss or gain can be part of the presenting symptoms. Although weight gain with antidepressants may be reversal of a pre-treatment weight loss in some people (although heavier people are more likely to gain weight if they become depressed, n=68, *Psych Res* 1991, **38**, 197–200), the main cause with tricyc-

lics seems to be a decreased metabolic rate (Fernstein *et al, Biol Psych* 1985, **20**, 688–92) a little known but important and relevant effect. There is also an association with tricyclics of strong antihistaminic actions. Pooled data shows that more obese patients tend to lose more weight and weight loss is directly proportional to baseline weight. Underweight people may tend to gain weight (review in *Clin Pharm* 1989, **8**, 727–33).

### SSRIs *

Overall, there is a tendency with SSRIs for weight loss over the first 6 weeks, then gradually to regain this over 6 months, and then many may gain weight over the longer-term (reviewed by Sussman and Ginsberg, *Psych Ann* 1998, **28**, 89–97). In the short-term, SSRIs may increase metabolic rate, suppress appetite, and increase basal body temperature (n=20, RCT, p/c, Bross and Hoffer, *Am J Clin Nutrition* 1995, **61**, 1020–25). **Fluoxetine** acute therapy is associated with modest weight loss (n=839, Michelson *et al, Am J Psych* 1999, **156**, 1170–76) and a trial of obese patients, fluoxetine 60mg/d produced greater weight loss than placebo until 20 weeks, when this tended to wear off and the advantage of fluoxetine over placebo at 52 weeks was not clinically significant (n=458, RCT, Goldstein *et al, Int J Obesity* 1994, **18**, 129–35). **Paroxetine** has a slight clinically insignificant weight loss potential (*J Psychopharmacol* 1990, **4**, 300; n=71, Christiansen *et al, Acta Psych Scand* 1996, **93**, 158–63) although one study showed 30% of 61 patients gained 1–4kg (n=151, RCT, d/b, 6/52, Ohrberg *et al, Acta Psych Scand* 1992, **86**, 437–44). A 3-way clinical trial showed significant weight gain over 6 months with paroxetine, but not sertraline nor fluoxetine (n=284, RCT, 26–32/52, Fava *et al, J Clin Psych* 2000, **61**, 863–67). **Fluvoxamine** causes a non-significant weight loss (*J Psychopharmacol* 1990, **4**, 299) at 100–150mg/d over six months (Harris and Ashford, *B J Clin Res* 1991, **2**, 81–88). **Sertraline** may have a limited weight gain effect. No significant weight changes have been reported with **citalopram** (Milne & Goa, *Drugs* 1991, **41**, 450–77) although carbohydrate craving and weight gain has been reported, particularly early on in treatment (n=18, Bouwer and Harvey, *Int Clin Psychopharmacol* 1996, **11**, 273–78).

**Review**: role of serotonin in regulating food intake and food selection (Pijl and Meinders, *J Serotonin Res* 1994, **1**, 21–45).

## Tricyclics

Weight gain with tricyclics is well-documented but not as well known or appreciated as it should be. The two main causes are drug-induced carbohydrate craving (Paykel, *B J Psych* 1973, **123**, 501–7) **and** a decreased metabolic rate (Fernstein *et al, Biol Psych* 1985, **20**, 688–92), rather than improved mood. Little comparative data is available, but weight gain has been reported with **amitriptyline** (89% of patients; see also n=73, Christiansen *et al, Acta Psych Scand* 1996, **93**, 158–63) and nortriptyline (67%) in one of the few comparative studies (Fernstrom and Kupfer, *Psych Res* 1988, **26**, 256–71). It has also been reported with **imipramine** (n=128, Frank *et al, J Aff Dis* 1990, **20**, 165–72) and **clomipramine** (n=129, RCT, 6/52, Guelfi *et al, B J Psych* 1992, **160**, 519–24).

## MAOIs and RIMAs

With the MAOIs, weight gain may be related to reduced blood glucose concentrations stimulating hunger or through central mechanisms. Weight gain is very rare with **tranylcypromine** and weight loss is more likely (n=198, retrospective, Rabkin *et al, J Clin Psychopharmacol* 1985, **5**, 2–9). **Phenelzine** is the most widely implicated (45 reports, including 32 of over 15lbs added). 15% of 62 patients on **moclobemide** gained weight, although overall there was a mean 0.1kg weight loss in all patients (n=129, RCT, 6/52,

Guelfi *et al, B J Psych* 1992, **160**, 519–24).

## Other antidepressants *

**Venlafaxine** is usually associated with weight loss (eg. Anon, *J Clin Psych* 1993, **54**, 119–26). Unusual appetite and weight gain has been reported with **mianserin** (Harris and Harper, *Lancet* 1980, **i**, 590). There are only rare reports of weight changes with **trazodone** (Barnett *et al, J Clin Psychopharmacol* 1985, **5**, 161–64), but not **reboxetine** nor **nefazodone** (n=3500, Robinsons *et al, J Clin Psych* 1996, **57**(Suppl 2), 31–38). Increased appetite and weight gain has been reported in patients treated with **mirtazapine**. One study showed increased appetite but without significant weight changes (n=90, RCT, p/c, d/b, Claghorn and Lesem, *J Aff Dis* 1995, **34**, 165–71) and another showed a slightly higher incidence than with amitriptyline (n=150, RCT, d/b, p/c, Smith *et al, Psychopharmacol Bull* 1990, **26**, 191–96). Overall, the incidence of weight gain with mirtazapine in all trials combined seems to be about 12%, with weight loss in 3%.

## Management

It is always best to anticipate problems before they appear and suggest remedies beforehand. Switching antidepressants is probably the best strategy (see *2.2.5*) since reduced metabolism is the main mechanism. An open trial of naltrexone for tricyclic-induced weight gain (open, Zimmermann *et al, Biol Psych* 1997, **41**, 747–49) showed good improvement in continuous hunger and small weight loss at eight weeks. Anecdotally, ranitidine used at night has abolished the weight gain with mirtazapine, through reduction in 'midnight raids' on the fridge.

## MOOD STABILISERS *

There is a high prevalence of obesity in bipolar patients, especially with treatment (44% gain >5kg), so chose drugs unlikely to worsen this (n=50, Fagiolini *et al, J Clin Psych* 2002, **63**, 528–33), although many factors are involved eg. male gender, hypertension, arthritis (n=644, McElroy *et al, J Clin Psych* 2002, **63**, 207–13) and drug-induced changes in food preference, especially high-energy fluids and carbohydrates, and so dietary advice is essential (n=89, Elmslie *et al, J Clin Psych* 2001, **62**, 486–91).

**Lithium***

Weight gain, the second most common reason for non-compliance, is reported to occur in around 33% (up to 65%, n=70, open, Vendsborg *et al, Acta Psych Scand* 1976, **53**, 139–47), of which 25% are probably obese (review: Sachs and Guille, *J Clin Psych* 1999, **60** (Suppl 21), 16–19). Weight increase occurs predominantly during the first two years of treatment, more often in people already overweight and may be more common in women than men. Increased thirst has been noted in 89% and strongly correlates with weight gain. Increased hunger/food intake has not been directly shown (*J Psychopharmacol* 1990, **4**, 303) and so the predominant mechanism may be increased intake of high-calorie drinks. Thyroid status should also be assessed, as a possible contributory cause. Lithium also increases insulin secretion, which may lead to more adipose tissue being produced, contributing to BMI gain. Weight gain may positively correlate with increased leptin levels (n=15, 8/52, Atmaca *et al, Neuropsychobiology* 2002, **46**, 67–69).

Lithium-induced weight gain has been disputed by Armong (n=42, open, *B J Psych* 1996, **169**, 251–52) in a study that showed no significant weight gain, even if taken with concomitant antipsychotics and antidepressants, a surprising finding. One study showed a non-significant BMI increase, with 27% actually showing a reduced BMI (n=117, Mathew *et al, Acta Psych Scand* 1989, **80**, 538–40).

**Management**

Counselling, eg. use plain/low-calorie beverages, along with normal sodium intake, dietary advice and monitoring, particularly during the first year, may be adequate (Baptista *et al, Pharmacopsychiatry* 1995, **28**, 35–44).

**Reviews**: general (Baptista *et al, Pharmacopsychiatry* 1995, **28**, 35–44).

**Carbamazepine**

Studies have show that 43% may gain weight (n=70, Corman *et al, Can J Neurol Sci* 1997, **24**, 240–44) and 8% may gain over 5kg (n=490, RCT, p/c, d/b, Mattson *et al, NEJM* 1992, 327, 765–71), and may be due to increased appetite, reversed by discontinuation but not by dieting (n=4, Lampl *et al, Clin Neuropharmacol* 1991, **14**, 251–55).

**Valproate***

Weight gain is recognised as a common ADR and the UK SPC says that weight gain can be marked and progressive. In a study against lamotrigine, significant weight gain (mean 12lb) occurred by week 10 and was maintained (n=68, 32/52, Biton *et al, Neurology* 2001, **56**, 172–77). Insulin resistance/hyperinsulinaemia may be contributory, but leptin might not be involved independently (n=81, survey, Pylvanen *et al, Epilepsia* 2002, **43**, 514–17) although higher serum leptin and insulin levels were found in 15 patients becoming obese after one year of valproate, compared to the 25 who did not gain weight (n=40, Verrotti *et al, Neurology* 1999, **53**, 230–33; n=20, RCT, 3/12, Demir and Aysun, *Pediatr Neurol* 2000, **22**, 361–64).

## BENZODIAZEPINES

Alprazolam has been reported to cause increased appetite and weight gain in healthy male volunteers (n=17, Haney *et al, Psychopharmacology* 1997, **132**, 311–14). Weight gain has been reported with clobazam during one study (Ananth *et al, Curr Ther Res* 1979, 26, 119–26).

## ANTICONVULSANTS*

Review of mechanisms etc by Jallon and Picard, *Drug Saf* 2001, **24**, 969–78)

**Gabapentin**

In a study of high-dose gabapentin over at least 12 months, 10 patients gained more than 10% of their baseline weight, 15 gained 5% to 10%, 16 had no change and 3 lost 5% to 10%. Weight was gained in months 2 and 3 and tended to stabilise after 6–9 months, although the doses of gabapentin remained unchanged (n=44, DeToledo *et al, Ther Drug Monit* 1997, **19**, 394–96). Mean weight gain of 6.9kg (range 3.2–14.5kg) has been noted (n=11, open, Gidal *et al, Ann Pharmacother* 1995, **29**, 1048).

**Lamotrigine \***

In a study against valproate, weight gain with lamotrigine was low (1.3 +/− 11lb) at week 10 (n=68, 32/52, Biton *et al, Neurology* 2001, **56**, 172–77).

**Oxcarbazepine**

Weight gain has been reported as a relatively frequent side-effect.

**Tiagabine**

Adjunctive tiagabine may have no significant effect on body weight (n=349, Hogan *et al, Epilepsy Res* 2000, **41**, 23–28).

**Topiramate \***

Topiramate has been reported to produce weight loss eg. a dose-related weight loss occurred in 50% patients in a trial in bipolar disorder, with a mean 14.2lb weight loss (n=76, open, Ghaemi *et al, Ann Clin Psych* 2001, **13**, 185–89) and, compared to lithium and valproate, it produced an average of 1.2kg weight loss (n=214, open, chart, Chengappa *et al, Clin Ther* 2002, **24**, 1576–84). It has even been abused to try to increase weight loss (n=1, Colom *et al, J Clin Psych* 2001, **62**, 475–76). The effect appears dose-related, with average amounts lost ranging from 1.1kg/1.5% (up to 200mg/d) to 5.9kg/7% (800mg/d or above). The effect peaks at 12–15 months, is greater in people with higher starting weights and is at least partially reversible (MI).

**Vigabatrin**

Weight gain may occur in 5–40% patients prescribed vigabatrin long-term as add-on therapy (Grant and Heel, *Drugs* 1991, **41**, 889–926).

## OTHER DRUGS \*

No significant weight changes have been seen in clinical trials with **acamprosate**. A retrospective study showed weight loss with **methylphenidate** to occur more with heavier children and recommended that BMI percentile curves are used as the best measure of weight changes (study and review, Schertz *et al, Pediatrics* 1996, **98**, 763–69). Weight loss may occur with **bupropion**, with 28% treated losing greater than 5lb, but weight gain occurred in 9% patients (MI). Modest weight losses have been seen with long-term bupropion SR (n=423, p/c, 1yr, Croft *et al, Clin Ther* 2002, **24**, 662–72).

## 2.5 SEXUAL DYSFUNCTION WITH PSYCHOTROPICS \*

Dysfunction of the three phases of sexual activity (desire, excitement/erection and orgasm) is associated with some psychiatric illnesses, eg. reduced sexual desire/activity in schizophrenia, impotence and loss of libido in depression etc. Drug effects are thus difficult to identify accurately, but are usually rapidly reversible on discontinuing treatment.

Only recently has the literature treated this issue systematically, despite great clinical importance. Patients are often unwilling to volunteer or talk about sexual matters eg. in patients taking conventional antipsychotics, sexual dysfunction occurred in 45% (cf 17% normal controls and 61% at a sexual dysfunction clinic) with hyperprolactinaemia the largest single factor in males and females (n=101, Smith *et al, B J Psych* 2002, **181**, 49–55). Such side-effects (and fear thereof) will increase the risk of non-concordance/ compliance.

The incidence of sexual dysfunction with antidepressants is difficult to quantify, but one study put it at citalopram (73%), paroxetine (71%), venlafaxine (67%), sertraline (63%), fluvoxamine (62%), fluoxetine (58%), mirtazapine (24%), nefazodone (8%), amineptine (7%) and moclobemide (4%). Men had a higher frequency of sexual dysfunction (62%) than women (57%), although women had greater severity (n=1022, prospective, open, Montejo *et al, J Clin Psych* 2001, **62**(Suppl 3), 10–21).

**Reviews**:* general (Gregorian *et al, Ann Pharmacother* 2002, **36**, 1577–89), SSRI-related sexual dysfunction (Rosen *et al, J Clin Psychopharmacol* 1999, **19**, 67–85), effects of antidepressants on sexual function (Baldwin *et al, Int J Psych Clin Pract* 1997, **1**, 47–58, 67 refs; Seagraves, *J Clin Psych* 1998, **59**[Suppl 4], 48–54), sexual side-effects of new antidepressants (Mir and Taylor, *Psych Bull* 1998, **22**, 438–41), diagnosis, incidence and management (Clayton and Shen, *Drug Saf* 1998, **19**, 299–312), therapeutic options in female sexual dysfunction (Shepherd, *J Am Pharm Assoc (Wash)* 2002, **42**, 479–88; 54 refs), antipsychotics (mentioned in Wirshing *et al, Curr Opin Psych* 2000, **13**, 45–50; n=101, Smith *et al, B J Psych* 2002, **181**, 49–55), counselling advice (Gutierrez and Stimmel, *Pharmacotherapy* 1999, **19**, 823–31, 57 refs).

## Sexual functioning — stages, mechanisms and the effects of drug therapies

| Stage | Characteristics | Mechanisms | Drugs that enhance | Drugs that inhibit/cause problems | Management of problems |
|---|---|---|---|---|---|
| Libido | Desire — decreases in depression and schizophrenia and libido/disinhibition may increase in mania | Controlled by mesolimbic dopamine reward pathway, which may also mediate 'natural highs' and drug-induced highs.<br>Prolactin **may** be inhibitory on desire (unclear, but raised prolactin is the strongest predictor of sexual dysfunction).<br>Testosterone is essential for male, and estrogen and progesterone essential for female, sexual behaviour.<br>Facilitated by NA and 5-HT | Amphetamines and methylphenidate (through increased dopamine release in the mesolimbic reward pathway)<br>BDZs (indirectly, by reduced anxiety)<br>Bupropion (through dopamine reuptake inhibition in the mesolimbic)<br>Cannabis (some disinhibition, but is sedative)<br>Drugs enhancing noradrenaline, eg. TCAs, venlafaxine (may possibly raise arousal levels)<br>Lamotrigine ('Reawakening' reported)<br>Moclobemide (18% report improvement)<br>Mirtazapine (esp. in women)<br>SSRIs (rare increase in disinhibition of libido)<br>Trazodone (alpha-2 adrenoceptor antagonist but is a sedative — 60% may improve)<br>Yohimbine (alpha-2 adrenoceptor antagonist — may produce adrenergic activation and/or stimulate dopamine receptors) | Anticholinergics (may reduce arousal)<br>Anticonvulsants (esp. barbiturates and phenytoin)<br>Any drug increasing prolactin **may** be inhibitory<br>Any sedating drug (eg. TCAs, BDZs — by indirect effect)<br>Drugs blocking dopamine in the mesolimbic system (antipsychotics, but probably less with clozapine)<br>Lithium (reported in 20% males)<br>SSRIs/SNRIs (indirectly, via an enduring inhibition of arousal and orgasm). May occur in 45% of females | Switch drugs (eg. if antidepressant, then switch to bupropion, moclobemide or mirtazapine)<br>Adjunctive therapy |
| Arousal | Erection or lubrication and swelling of peripheral genitalia | Acetylcholine is one of the transmitters in the genitalia, and facilitates erection and swelling<br>Adrenergic fibres, through alpha1- adrenoceptors, produce smooth muscle contraction, hence detumescence<br>cAMP is also involved with smooth muscle relaxation<br>Dopamine — increased activity stimulates sexual arousal in human females<br>Nitric oxide (NO), activates the production of cGMP, which then relaxes the blood vessel muscles necessary for erection to occur. It is broken down by phosphodiesterases (PDEs), specifically PDE-5 in corpus cavernosum) | Alprostadil (injection only, stimulates cAMP formation)<br>Apomorphine (stimulates NOS to produce more NO, and hence more cGMP)<br>Moclobemide (some reports)<br>Papaverine (blocks all PDEs, but by injection only)<br>Pentoxifylline (may relax the blood vessels directly)<br>Prostaglandins (produced erection without stimulation)<br>Sildenafil/tadalafil (are orally active, and block PDE5, hence the breakdown of cGMP, allowing it to accumulate and maintaining an erection)<br>Yohimbine (partly through increased libido, and partly via blocking the alpha-1-adrenergic detumescence signals, plus alpha-2 effects) | Anticholinergic drugs, inc. tricyclics (dose-related, incidence 90% with clomipramine, 7% with venlafaxine) and typical antipsychotics (30% with thioridazine) by blocking acetylcholine, thus inhibiting its facilitatory effect and suppressing erection<br>Antipsychotics causing hyperprolactinaemia (may cause infertility, loss of libido in women; erectile dysfunction [failure, priapism, retrograde ejaculation, anorgasmia] in men, eg. thioridazine 60%)<br>Any drug causing hypotension (eg. typicals, tricyclics)<br>Any sedating drug, eg. higher-dose BDZs (indirect effect)<br>Lithium (minor effect in 30%)<br>MAOIs (40% incidence)<br>Reboxetine 5%<br>SSRIs (by inhibiting NO production, but only when sexual stimulation occurs.<br>Fluoxetine >paroxetine, see also orgasm) | Sildenafil/tadalafil<br>Switch drugs, eg. haloperidol-induced has been treated by switch to olanzapine (n=1, Tsai and Hong, *Gen/HospPsychiatry* 2000, **22**, 391–2)<br>Withdraw drug — problem seems rapidly reversible if the drug is withdrawn<br>Yohimbine and pentoxyfylline given 1–2 hours pre-intercourse have been shown to improve antidepressant-induced impotence.<br>Yohimbine PRN or 5.4–10.8mg tds have been used successfully |

| | Sexual functioning — stages, mechanisms and the effects of drug therapies continued. | | | |
|---|---|---|---|---|
| Stage | Characteristics | Mechanisms | Drugs that enhance | Drugs that inhibit/cause problems | Management of problems |
| Orgasm | Accompanied by ejaculation in men. Dysfunction probably grossly under-rated | Noradrenaline exerts an excitatory or facilitatory action. Serotonin fibres through the spine exert an inhibitory effect on orgasm via $5HT_{2A}$ receptors | Benzodiazepine withdrawal (rare reports). Cannabis (distorts perceptions of time). Clomipramine and fluoxetine (rare reports of spontaneous orgasm). Moclobemide (rare reports of hyperorgasmia) | Antipsychotics (thioridazine 30%, risperidone 8% at standard dose, haloperidol 7% at 10mg/d). Beta-blockers (through blockade of the excitatory action of noradrenaline). Bupropion (reports). Gabapentin (at 1200mg/d) in a male, resulting in non-compliance. SSRIs, TCAs, SNRIs, MAOIs, trazodone, nefazodone (through enhancing the inhibitory activity on $5HT_{2A}$ and NO) — dose/plasma-level dependent (paroxetine >sertraline >fluoxetine > citalopram >fluvoxamine, although 8% men/partners prefer effect) | Discontinue (gradually — beware anti-depressant discontinuation effects). Dose adjust (reduce, omitting selected doses, single daily dose, eg. at night to give trough levels). Switch (eg. bupropion, trazodone, nefazodone (=placebo on anorgasmia) or mirtazapine. Wait for spontaneous resolution (occurs in less than a third). Augment with amantadine, bethanechol, bupropion, buspirone, cyproheptadine, granisitron, nefazodone, sildenafil, stimulants (methylphenidate and dexamfetamine, trazodone, yohimbine — see next page). NB: ginkgo biloba has no effect |
| Priapism | Persistent painful penile turgidity in the absence of sexual arousal. May be high-flow (rare, not a true emergency, usually painless, favourable prognosis) or low-flow (majority, emergency, painful, poor prognosis if treatment delayed) | Mechanism is believe to be alpha1-adrenergic antagonism, which inhibits detumescence. Frequent prolonged erections before the onset of priapism may occur and so the reporting of these is essential. Duration greater than 4 hours is considered a urological emergency (up to 50% become impotent as a result) | **Antidepressants:** Trazodone: incidence estimated to be between 1 in 1000 and 1 in 10,000, majority occurring at 150mg/d or less (range 50–400mg/d) and within the first 28 days (range single dose through to 18 months). Isolated cases with nefazodone and some SSRIs. **Antipsychotics:** Phenothiazines, eg. chlorpromazine and thioridazine (both multiple reports), levomepromazine, mesoridazine, fluphenazine, perphenazine, pericyazine, promazine. Isolated reports for clozapine (could be reinstated), olanzapine (SPC <0.01%), quetiapine (SPC rare reports), risperidone, zuclopenthixol, molindone, haloperidol (rare) and thiothixine. Olanzapine, quetiapine and gabapenin overdoses. Few predictive indicators, eg. range after single dose to after 10 years. **Other drugs** implicated include diazepam, phenytoin and buspirone | Early treatment (within 4–6 hours before local hypoxemia) reduces morbidity, need for invasive procedures and impotence and may prevent or minimise long-term complications and need for surgical intervention. Immediate short-term treatment; conservative measures inc pain control, vigorous hydration, cold compress before urology consultation. Treatments include penile aspiration, irrigation, instillation of vasoactive agents, phenylephrine, and, if necessary, shunting procedures. (Review: Kalsi *et al, Hosp Med* 2002, **63**, 224–25) |
| Fertility | Release of fertile ova or sperm | Manufacture by gonads of sperm (6/12 store) or release of matured egg | Has been suggested that clozapine may improve male fertility | Reduced fertility is not thought to occur in males — some anticonvulsants implicated, high dose chlorpromazine reported to cause decreased fertility (diazepam, phenytoin and phenobarbital had no detectable effect). Lithium could possibly inhibit sperm motility in men. Amenorrhoea occurs with hyperprolactinaemia, esp with typical antipsychotics, where up to 50–90% may become amenorrhoeic | |

| Management of drug-induced anorgasmia: | |
|---|---|
| Counter-acting drugs (all these drug strategies are of highly variable reported efficacy): | |
| **Amantadine** | 100mg bd/tds can help treat fluoxetine-induced anorgasmia but was ineffective in the main study (RCT, p/c, 8/52, Michelson *et al, Am J Psych* 2000, **157**, 239–43) |
| **Bethanechol** | Taken 1–2 hrs prior to intercourse has been claimed to relieve tricyclic-induced sexual dysfunction but may only occasionally be successful. |
| **Bupropion** | 75–150mg, 1–2 hrs prior to sexual activity has successfully reversed a range of SSRI-induced sexual dysfunction in 66% of patients, with SR 300mg/d effective in 46% of women and 75% of men, most improvement occurring in the first two weeks (open, n=24, 7/52, Gitlin *et al, J Sex Marital Ther* 2002, **28**, 131–8), but an RCT failed to show an effect in SSRI-induced problems (n=30, RCT, p/c, Masand *et al, Am J Psych* 2001, **158**, 805–7). If switching to bupropion SR for SSRI-induced problems, 55% completing the change successfully (n=11, 8/52, Clayton *et al, J Clin Psych* 2001, **62**, 185–90). |
| **Buspirone** | 40% of patients taking either citalopram or paroxetine reported sexual problems, of whom 58% improved on buspirone 20–60mg/d, whereas only 30% improved on placebo. |
| **Cyproheptadine** | 2–4+ mg 30–60 minutes before sex (provided one can then stay awake) has been used to treat SSRI-induced anorgasmia, although relapse of depression has been reported (see *4.3.2.2*). Citalopram-induced anorgasmia has been treated with cyproheptadine 4mg (but not 2mg) the day before intercourse, this being referred to by the male patient as 'the catapult pills'. |
| **Ginkgo biloba** | A small study **failed** to show any significant reversal of SSRI-induced sexual dysfunction. |
| **Granisitron** | This 5-HT3 antagonist has been used to treat fluoxetine-induced anorgasmia, but 1–2mg was ineffective for SSRI-induced sexual dysfunction, with a significant placebo response noted (n=20, p/c, c/o, Nelson *et al, J Clin Psych* 2001, **62**, 469–73). |
| **Loratadine** * | 15mg/d may rapidly reverse SSRI-induced low libido and anorgasmia in men and women (n=10, case series, Brubaker, *J Clin Psych* 2002, **63**, 534). |
| **Mianserin** * | 7.5–15mg/d has been used (88% response) for SSRI-induced sexual dysfunction (n=17, open, 3/12, Dolberg *et al, Psychopharmacol (Berl)* 2002, **161**, 404–7). |
| **Sildenafil** | There are many reports of SSRI-induced anorgasmia responding to sildenafil 50–100mg 1 hour pre-sex in both men and women (n=98, d/b, p/c, Nurnberg *et al, Am J Psych* 2001, **158**, 1926–28). Onset is at about 30 minutes, peaking at 2 hours. |
| **Stimulants** | Methylphenidate and dexamfetamine (15–20mg/d) have been used, for antidepressant-induced anorgasmia. |
| **Tamsulosin** * | This has been used for painful ejaculation with reboxetine (n=2, Demyttenaere and Huygens, *Eur Neuropsychopharmacol* 2002, **12**, 337–41). |
| **Trazodone** * | This has reversed fluoxetine-induced dysfunction, but one study found no effect (positive or negative) on erectile function in men with erectile dysfunction (n=34, RCT, p/c, 4/52, Enzlin *et al, Int J Impot Res* 2000, **12**, 223–28). |
| **Yohimbine** | 5.5mg has been used to treat SSRI-induced anorgasmia but can cause insomnia, so rolling over and going to sleep afterwards is less of an option. In one trial, olanzapine, mirtazapine, yohimbine and placebo all improved function in premenopausal females with SSRI-induced sexual side-effects, but with no significant differences (n=148, RCT, p/c, 6/52, Michelson *et al, J Psych Res* 2002, **36**, 147–52). |

## 3.1 BREAST-FEEDING

| | Lower risk | Moderate risk | High risk |
|---|---|---|---|
| Antipsychotics | Sulpiride [5] | Amisulpride[5]<br>Flupentixol [4]<br>Haloperidol[6]<br>Loxapine?[8]<br>Phenothiazines (low dose only) [7]<br>Zuclopenthixol [4] | Aripiprazole [2]<br>Clozapine[2]<br>Olanzapine[2]<br>Phenothiazines [7]<br>Quetiapine [2]<br>Risperidone[1]<br>Sertindole [2]<br>Ziprasidone [2]<br>Zotepine[2] |
| Antidepressants | Flupentixol LD[4]<br>Moclobemide[16]<br>Tricyclics[12](most)<br>Tryptophan[16] | Amoxapine[16]<br>Mianserin[16]<br>Mirtazapine[11]<br>St John's wort[16]<br>SSRIs[9]<br>Trazodone[12] | Doxepin?[12]<br>MAOIs[15]<br>Maprotiline[12]<br>Nefazodone[13]<br>Reboxetine[14]<br>Venlafaxine[10] |
| Anxiolytics+ hypnotics | Benzodiazepines LD[17]<br>Chloral[21]<br>Temazepam LD[17]<br>Zolpidem[19] | Benzodiazepines[17]<br>Beta-blockers[20]<br>Clomethiazole[21] | Buspirone[18]<br>Zaleplon[19]<br>Zopiclone[19] |
| Anticonvulsants | Carbamazepine[22]<br>Phenytoin [24]<br>Valproate [23] | Acetazolamide [28]<br>Benzodiazepines[17]<br>Vigabatrin[27] | Barbituarates[25]<br>Gabapentin[26]<br>Lamotrigine?[26]<br>Levetiracetam [27]<br>Ethosuximide [28]<br>Oxcarbazepine [22]<br>Tiagabine[27]<br>Topiramate[27] |
| Others | | Anticholinergics[30]<br>Disulfiram[31]<br>Methadone[34] | Acamprosate [31]<br>Anticholinesterases [29]<br>Bupropion [36]<br>Lithium[34]<br>Memantine [29]<br>Methylphenidate[34]<br>Modafinil[33] |

**General Principals*** (adapted from *Maudsley Guidelines*)

1. All psychotropics pass into the milk, so no decision is risk-free. Breast milk is more acidic than plasma, so basic compounds may be retained and concentrations accumulate. Protein binding may also be a factor (in general, drug binding to milk proteins is less than to plasma proteins). The higher lipid content of the hind milk (second half of feed) makes it likely to have a higher drug concentration than the first half (fore milk).

2. Milk levels are usually around 1% of maternal plasma levels, but there have been few formal studies.

3. Drugs should be avoided if the infant is premature, or has renal, hepatic, cardiac or neurological impairment

4. Avoid drugs with long half-lives, sedating drugs etc.

5. Since nearly all psychotropics can be given as a once daily dose, this should be achieved, as a single daily dose just before the infants longest sleep period feed (eg. peak milk concentrations after oral administration: amitriptyline 1.5hrs, imipramine 1hr, moclobemide <3hrs, sertraline 7–11hrs, chlorpromazine 2hrs, fluvoxamine 4hrs), minimising actual concentration and maximising clearance before the next feed.

6. If a mother was taking a drug during pregnancy, it will not usually be necessary to switch drugs during breast feeding as the amount to which the infant is exposed will be less than that *in utero*.

7. Adverse effects will often be dose related so use the minimum effective maternal dose.

8. Polypharmacy may lead to enhanced adverse effects in the infant. Avoiding interacting drugs that raise plasma levels (even if asymptomatically) is essential.

9. Drug effects on the development of the infant's brain are not clear and so monitor biochemical and

behavioural parameters, especially if any infant shows signs of possible psychotropic side-effects (eg. sedation, tremulousness, colic etc.), take appropriate action, eg. dose reduction, drug change, etc.

**Reviews:*** pharmacokinetic overview and therapeutic implications (Spigset and Hagg, *CNS Drugs* 1998, **9**, 111–34), general (McElhatton, *Prescriber* 1999, **10**, 101–17), extensive (Burt *et al, Am J Psych* 2001, **158**, 1001–9; 124 refs).

### 3.1.1 Antipsychotics:

**Review**: general (Tenyi *et al, Paediatr Drugs* 2000, **2**, 23–28, recommending monotherapy at low dose has the lowest risk, polytherapy at higher doses not recommended).

1. The UK SPC for **risperidone** states that women should not breast-feed.

2.* **Olanzapine** is excreted in the milk. There is report with no human problems (n=3, Goldstein *et al, J Clin Psychopharmacol* 2000, **20**, 399–403). In another, the median relative infant dose was 1.6% (range 0–2.5%) with no reported adverse effects (n=5, Croke *et al, Int J Neuropsychopharmacol* 2002, **5**, 243–47). The UK SPC recommends not breast-feeding while taking this drug. No information is available for **quetiapine** and the SPC recommends avoiding. **Zotepine** and norzotepine may be secreted into breast milk (where milk levels can reach 50% of maternal plasma levels) and is incompatible with breast-feeding mothers (MI). There is no data on **ziprasidone** nor **aripiprazole**. **Sertindole** is excreted in the milk in rats but no human data exists so should not be used as it would be expected to be excreted in milk.

3. **Clozapine** is contraindicated as animal studies suggest it is excreted into milk and so risks agranulocytosis. In the close study of one mother, there was some accumulation of clozapine in breast milk (possibly due to higher lipid concentrations), and so doses must be kept low if breast-feeding is essential (Barnas, *Am J Psych* 1994, **151**, 945) and the infants plasma

monitored. There are reports indicating that babies experience sedation if mothers take clozapine and breast-feed (MI).

4. A study showed that 0.6mcg/kg or 1–2% of the maternal **flupentixol** dose might reach the infant and thus is probably safe at low dose (eg. <2mg/d) (n=6, *Eur J Clin Pharmacol* 1988, **35**, 217–20). Higher doses of **zuclopenthixol** (*Psychopharmacology* [Berlin] 1986, **90**, 417–18) and flupentixol can produce drowsiness in the child. More studies would be needed at higher doses to confirm safety.

5. A **sulpiride** dose of 100mg/d to the mother is likely to give the child less than 1mg/d. No adverse effects have been reported at higher doses (*BMJ* 1982, **285**, 249–51). There is no information available for **amisulpride**.

6. **Haloperidol** is excreted into breast milk but levels are probably low (eg. n=1, Whalley *et al, BMJ* 1981, **282**, 1746–47), although infant levels may be the same as adults. Some element of delayed development has been detected (n=5, Yoshida *et al, Psychol Med* 1998, **28**, 81–91) and so the infant must be monitored carefully.

7. High doses of **phenothiazines** can produce drowsiness in the infant. **Chlorpromazine** has an inconsistent milk/plasma ratio and drowsiness and lethargy are possible but not inevitable (*B J Clin Pharmacol* 1978, **5**, 272–73). With careful monitoring it should be safe. Some element of delayed development has been suggested (n=3, Yoshida *et al, Psychol Med* 1998, **28**, 81–91). In one case report the amount of **perphenazine** passed to an infant was about 0.1% of the adult dose in terms of mcg/kg body weight (Olesen *et al, Am J Psych* 1990, **10**, 1378–79) and this drug may become 'trapped' in milk due to its physio-chemical properties (*Clin Pharmacokin* 1980, **5**, 1–66).

8. **Loxapine** and its metabolites have been shown to appear in breast milk but no data on the potential effects is known.

### 3.1.2 Antidepressants:

The data on breast-feeding and antide-pressants is relatively limited, with few studies in which infant blood levels have been assessed. The collected data indicates that infants older than 10 weeks are at low risk of adverse events (review by Wisner *et al, Am J Psych* 1996, **153**, 1132).

9.* Treatment with the **SSRIs** seems to be compatible with breast-feeding, although fluoxetine should probably best be avoided during lactation, unless used during pregnancy. The limited data indicates that healthy full-term infants are unlikely to be harmed by SSRIs (McElhatton, *Prescriber* 1999, **10**, 101–17). One study suggests that paroxetine (n=16), flu-voxamine (n=4) and sertraline (n=30) produce minimal exposure to infants when taken by nursing mothers (Hendrick *et al, B J Psych* 2001, **179**, 163–66), although Angell (*B J Psych* 2002, **180**, 85–86) doesn't agree with this conclusion.

**Citalopram/escitalopram** and dem-ethylcitalopram are excreted into milk, with the mean combined dose (4.4–5.1% as citalopram equivalents) transmitted to infants below the 10% notional level of concern eg. infant levels appear low or undetectable (n=11, Heikkinen *et al, Clin Pharma-col Ther* 2002, **72**, 184–91). A prospec-tive, observational, cohort study was unable to show any significant clinical events in mothers who took citalo-pram and breastfed (n=43, Lee *et al, Clin Pharmacol Ther* 2002, **71**, P43) and another showed plasma concen-trations in the infants as very low or absent with no adverse effects (n=7, Rampono *et al, Br J Clin Pharmacol* 2000, **50**, 263–68). These data support the safety of the use of citalopram in breast feeding women, with care.

**Fluoxetine** (11 studies, n=190, Burt *et al, Am J Psych* 2001, **158**, 1001–9) plasma levels in the infant range from undetectable to one of 340ng/ml, but with no clear associations between dose, age and plasma levels. Plasma levels peak in breast milk at about 8hrs post-dose and are dose related, with 20mg/d or less producing low infant serum levels (n=19, Hendrick *et al, Biol Psych* 2001, **15**, 775–82), probably less than 10% of the adult therapeutic dose of fluoxetine (on a mg/kg basis) reaching the infant. This is considered low enough for women to continue breast-feeding (Nulman and Koren, *Teratology* 1996, **53**, 304-8; careful study, n=10 pairs, Suri *et al, Biol Psych* 2002, **52**, 446–51), with no developmental effects seen (n=4, Yoshida *et al, B J Psych* 1998, **172**, 175–79). Substantial levels of fluoxe-tine have, however, been detected in the serum of infants (n=1, Lester *et al, J Am Acad Child Adolesc Psych* 1993, **32**, 1253–55) and there is clearly some considerable interpatient variability and adverse effects have been observed in breast-fed infants eg. colic. Considering the potential for accumulation, careful monitoring of the infants is mandatory, especially in neonates exposed to these drugs *in utero* (n=14, Kristensen *et al, Br J Clin Pharmacol* 1999, **48**, 521–27).

**Fluvoxamine** levels in milk and infant plasma appear low in the few reported cases eg. the estimated daily intake by an infant was about 0.5% of the maternal dose (100 or 200mg/d), thought to be of little risk, with no concerns about development up to 21 months (n=1, Yoshida *et al, Br J Clin Pharmacol* 1997, **44**, 210–11). In another pair of infants, milk levels were low and none was detect-able in the infants plasma, so was con-sidered unlikely to cause harm (n=2, Kristensen *et al, J Hum Lact* 2002, **18**, 139–43). In a study using serial levels, milk fluvoxamine levels were found at higher levels than previously reported and roughly paralleled the serum levels, but that the absolute dose received by the infant was low, and that breast-feeding was at an accepta-ble risk (n=1, Hägg *et al, Br J Clin Pharmacol* 2000, **49**, 286–88).

**Paroxetine** has been well studied and 10–50mg/d is found in milk, but at highly variable levels (sample n=108, 2–101ng/ml). In 25 mother-infant sample sets, paroxetine was detected in all but one milk sample but undetectable (ie <0.1ng/ml) in the infants serum, with no adverse events reported (n=24, Misri *et al, J Clin Psych* 2000, **61**, 828–32). Hind-milk concentrations may be 78% higher than foremilk (also seen in 16 mother and infant pairs, Stowe *et al, Am J Psych* 2000, **257**, 185–89), and no adverse reactions were reported in another study (n=6, open, Ohman *et al, J Clin Psych* 1999, **60**, 519–23).

**Sertraline** and metabolite generally appear only in low levels in the infant, which are unlikely to cause any significant adverse effects (n=8, Kristensen *et al, Br J Clin Pharmacol* 1998, **45**, 453–57). Higher levels have been reported rarely (one of 9 had much higher levels) (Wisner *et al, Am J Psych* 1998, **155**, 690–92), as have withdrawal reactions in breast-fed children after the mother has abruptly stopped sertraline (Kent and Laidlaw, *B J Psych* 1995, **167**, 412–13), imply-ing that sertraline may appear in breast-milk at levels sufficient to sup-press withdrawal after birth. This does not seem to be a common pro-blem (Ratan and Friedman, *B J Psych* 1995, **167**, 824; Altshuler *et al, J Clin Psych* 1995, **56**, 243–45). Doses of up to 200mg/d may produce sertraline (and only just detectable desmethyl-sertraline) in the milk, peaking at 7–10 hours post-last dose, with no reported adverse effects (n=12, Stowe *et al, Am J Psych* 1997, **154**, 1255–60), less than 2% of the maternal dose per day, likely to be of minimal adverse effect (n=10, Dodd *et al, Hum Psychopharmacol* 2000, **15**, 161–64), especially as platelet 5HT uptake in the infants appears unaltered (n=14 mother-infant pairs, Epperson *et al, Am J Psych* 2001, **158**, 1631–37).

10.* The total dose of **venlafaxine** and O-desmethylvenlafaxine (OMV) ingested by breast-fed infants prob-ably usually around 6.4%, which is lower than the usual 10% notional level of concern but still needs moni-toring (n=6 mothers, 7 infants, Ilett *et al, B J Clin Pharmacol* 2002, **53**, 17–22). Other data suggests that venlafaxine can be metabolised by infants, with no detectable adverse effects nor apparent developmental issues (n=2, Hendrick *et al, Am J Psych* 2001, **158**, 2089–90).

11. **Mirtazapine** is excreted only in small amounts in breast milk, but use cannot yet be actually formally recommended.

12. **Tricyclic** antidepressants should be used with care, but it does not seem warranted to recommend that breast-feeding should be discontinued com-pletely, as significant tricyclic levels have not been detected in neonatal serum (except for doxepin and mapro-tiline). One study has indicated about 1% of maternal dose/kg reaching the infant, minute amounts in the infant serum, no acute toxic effects and no evidence of developmental delay (n=10, Yoshida *et al, J Aff Disord* 1997, **43**, 225–37). For **imipramine**, a milk/plasma ratio of 0.05–0.08, based on high dose samples, would lead to 0.1% of the maternal daily dose appearing in milk. **Amitriptyline**/nor-triptyline levels in the infant are prob-ably very low (Breyer-Pfaff, *Am J Psych* 1995, **152**, 812–13). Two stu-dies, including 12 mother-baby pairs, showed no detectable **nortriptyline** in the infant serum, despite some unu-sually high maternal plasma levels, although two infants had detectable levels of 10-hydroxy metabolites. None of the infants showed any adverse effects and so the risk could be considered very low (Wisner and Perel, *Am J Psych* 1996, **153**, 295). **Maprotiline** has a long half-life and is present in milk in significant amounts so should not be used (*Drug & Ther Bull* 1983, **21**, 48). In two studies of children who had received **dothiepin/dosulepin** via breast milk, no detect-able adverse effects on cognitive development were detected (com-pared to a variety of controls, Buist and Janson, *B J Psych* 1995, **167**, 370–

73) and the drug is unlikely to be a significant hazard for the infant (Ilett *et al, B J Clin Pharmacol* 1992, **33**, 635–39). Case reports suggest that the infant may receive only up to 3.7% of the mother's **clomipramine** dose (n=1, Pons *et al, Clin Pharmacokinetics* 1994, **27**, 270–89), with no adverse effects (n=4, Wisner *et al, J Clin Psych* 1995, **56**, 17–20). **Doxepin**, however, has a longer-acting metabolite N-desmethyldoxepin which may accumulate in breast-fed infants, causing severe drowsiness and respiratory depression (near fatal case at 75mg/d in 8-week-old baby: Matheson *et al, Lancet* 1985, **ii**, 1124; n=1, Frey *et al, Ann Pharmacother* 1999, **33**, 690–93). Another report failed to detect any effects in the infant with maternal doxepin doses of 150mg (Kemp *et al, Br J Clin Pharmacol* 1995, **20**, 497–99; Wisner *et al, Am J Psych* 1996, **153**, 1132) and so metabolic differences could explain these. If the former is accepted and extrapolated to other tricyclics, the general advice is to observe the child carefully for sedation and respiratory depression. A tricyclic with a short half-life for itself (and any active metabolites) would appear to be the better option.

It has been recommended that amitriptyline and imipramine are the preferred tricyclic antidepressants (review by Duncan and Taylor, *Psych Bull* 1995, **19**, 551–52).

13.* With **trazodone**, a 50mg single-dose study showed that 1% passed into the milk (n=6, *B J Clin Pharmacol* 1986, **22**, 367–70). More information on, eg. metabolites, is needed but it would appear to be of low risk. Drowsiness and poor feeding has been reported (n=1, Yapp *et al, Ann Pharmacother* 2000, **34**, 1269–72; n=2, Dodd *et al, Clin Psychopharmacol* 2000, **20**, 717–18). Caution is thus advised.

14. **Reboxetine** is excreted in milk in rats but no human data exists so the drug should be avoided (SPC).

15. Minimal data is available for the **MAOIs**. **Tranylcypromine** is excreted in breast milk but levels are not thought to be significant. Some sources state that MAOI levels in milk are too small to affect the child but this has not been supported by any studies other than with tranylcypromine.

16.* In 6 lactating women, 0.06% of a single dose of **moclobemide** was excreted unchanged in the milk. It would seem unlikely this amount would produce adverse effects in the baby (Pons *et al, B J Clin Pharmacol* 1990, **29**, 27–31). **Mianserin** 40–60mg/d may produce only low milk and infant plasma levels with no untoward effects (Buist *et al, B J Clin Pharmacol* 1993, **36**, 133–34). **Amoxapine** appears in human milk, probably at low levels (*J Nerv Mental Dis* 1979, **165**, 635). **St. John's wort** was excreted at a low (unquantifiable) level in one case, with no side effects seen (n=1, Klier *et al, Pharmacopsychiatry* 2002, **35**, 29–30), and so should best be avoided in breast-feeding until further information is available. There are no known problems with **tryptophan**.

### 3.1.3 Anxiolytics and hypnotics:

17.* The CSM has noted that since **benzodiazepines** are excreted in breast milk, they should not be given to lactating mothers (*Curr Prob* 1997, **23**, 10). Repeated doses of long-acting benzodiazepines can produce lethargy and weight loss but low and single doses are probably of low risk provided the infant is monitored for drowsiness. Oxazepam seems to be preferable to diazepam in lactating women, but with all anxiolytic benzodiazepines, infants should be observed for signs of sedation and poor suckling. **Diazepam, oxazepam, lorazepam, lormetazepam, nitrazepam** and **flunitrazepam** have all been shown in breast milk, and alprazolam withdrawal has been reported (n=1, Anderson and McGuire, *DICP* 1989, **23**, 614). **Temazepam** levels have been reported to be below detection levels at doses of 10–20mg/d and no adverse effects have been seen (Lebedevs *et al, B J Clin Pharmacol* 1992, **33**, 204–6).

18. **Buspirone** should be avoided, based on excretion studies in rats, although there is no specific human data to show adverse effects.

19. **Zaleplon** is excreted in breast milk, and should not be administered to breast-feeding mothers, although the actual amount likely to be transferred may be very low, eg. 0.017% of maternal dose (n=5, Darwish *et al, J Clin Pharmacol* 1999, **39**, 670–74). **Zopiclone** is contraindicated in breast-feeding as it is excreted in appreciable amounts (up to 50% of maternal levels: Matheson *et al, B J Clin Pharmacol* 1990, **30**, 267–71). Single occasional doses of 7.5mg are probably of low risk as accumulation is unlikely. The AAPCD considers **zolpidem** compatible with breast-feeding, as it is found only in minute amounts in milk due to its low lipophilic properties and rapid onset and excretion. In one study of women taking a (high) stat dose of 20mg, 0.76–3.88mg of zolpidem was excreted into breast milk, nearly all within 3 hours of a dose (n=5, Pons *et al, Eur J Clin Pharmacol* 1989, **37**, 245–48). A low dose at bedtime and avoiding breast-feeding for the next few hours would minimise the (unknown) potential effect on an infant.

20. The amounts of **beta-blockers** in milk are probably too small to effect the baby (less than 0.1% of maternal doses) but could produce bradycardia and hypoglycaemia in high doses.

21. **Clomethiazole** is excreted in insignificant amounts based on IV and oral studies in pre-eclampsia (*Acta Psych Scand* 1986, **73** [Suppl 329], 185–88). An infant might ingest active amounts and although the sedative effects of this could be relevant they are unlikely to be harmful. **Chloral** is excreted in breast milk and the sedation caused in the infant makes this a precaution, although only minimal sedation after large feeds has been reported (*Adv Drug React Bull* 1976[Dec] 212). The Amer-

ican Academy of Pediatrics recommends that it can safely be used in lactating mothers, as do the authorities in many European countries.

### 3.1.4 Anticonvulsants:

Breast-feeding should be encouraged as bonding is especially important in epileptic mothers (Brodie, *Lancet* 1990, **336**, 426–27). An extensive review (Hägg and Spigset, *Drug Safety* 2000, **22**, 425–40, 88 refs) of anticonvulsant use during lactation concluded that:

- Carbamazepine, valproate and phenytoin are compatible
- Ethosuximide, phenobarbital and primidone should be regarded as potentially unsafe and close clinical monitoring of the infant is recommended
- Data on the newer drugs is too sparse for reliable recommendations
- Occasional or short-term treatment with benzodiazepines could be considered as compatible with breast-feeding, although maternal diazepam treatment has caused sedation in suckling infants after short-term use. During long-term use of benzodiazepines, infants should be observed for signs of sedation and poor suckling.

**Review**: general (Bar-Oz *et al, Paediatr Drugs* 2000, **2**, 113–26).

22. **Carbamazepine** has been classified by the AAPCD as compatible with breast-feeding, as levels have been found to be relatively low but this is based on case reports in epilepsy, with only two so far when used as mood stabiliser. The half-life is longer in infants, with levels in milk ranging from 7% to 95% of the mother's serum, probably usually around 10%. There are cases of adverse effects in the infant (n=1, Merlob *et al, Ann Pharmacother* 1992, **26**, 1563–65; n=1, Frey *et al, Eur J Pediatr* 1990, **150**, 136–38) and several of poor feeding. Data is often from the first few days of life so the safety of carbamazepine is not well-proven and may need to be re-assessed. The

mother should be informed of the potential signs of hepatic dysfunction and CNS effects (review, Chaudron and Jefferson, *J Clin Psych* 2000, **161**, 79–90). **Oxcarbazepine** is excreted into breast milk, the breast milk/plasma ration for drug and metabolite being about 0.5, similar to carbamazepine (n=1, Bulau *et al, Eur J Clin Pharmacol* 1988, **34**, 311–13), and it is contraindicated in the UK.

23. **Valproate** has been classified by the AAPCD as compatible with breast-feeding, based on case reports in epilepsy. Infant serum levels range from undetectable (n=16, van Unruh *et al, Ther Drug Monit* 1984, **6**, 272–76) to 40% of the mother's serum level, 5–12% being common, with a wide variation mainly because of the low number of patients studied. In 6 mother-infant pairs where infant exposure was exclusively during breast-feeding, mothers had valproate levels in the usual range for bipolar (39–79 mcg/mL) but infants had low levels (0.7–1.5mcg/mL), thus presenting a relatively low risk compared to the risk of relapse in the mother (n=6, Piontek *et al, J Clin Psych* 2000, **61**, 170–72). There is a reported adverse (haematological) event (Stahl *et al, J Pediatr* 1997, **130**, 1001–3). Valproate appears relatively safe, but with the risk of haematological effects. Care and careful counselling is needed for higher doses (review, Chaudron and Jefferson, *J Clin Psych* 2000, **161**, 79–90).

24. Small quantities of **phenytoin** are excreted in breast milk, peaking at 3 hours, and have been considered clinically safe (*Adv Drug React Ac Pois Rev* 1982, **1**, 255–87).

25. Larger doses of **phenobarbital** and **primidone** may accumulate in breast milk. This may cause unacceptable drowsiness and lead to the need to stop or at least reduce breast-feeding.

26. Extensive passage of **lamotrigine** into breast milk occurs, and with a slow elimination in the newborn, concentrations in the infant may reach levels at which pharmacological

effects can be expected. In one report, the milk to maternal serum ratio was a consistent 0.6, with infant serum levels of 23–33% of the maternal serum levels. This is probably of low risk provided all remain alert to the potential for life-threatening rashes (n=3, Ohman *et al, Epilepsia* 1998, **39**[Suppl 2], 21; review, Chaudron and Jefferson, *J Clin Psych* 2000, **161**, 79–90). **Gabapentin** crosses into breast milk. The manufacturers have data on 6 cases, where gabapentin levels in milk were equal to plasma levels, with no reports of infant levels (review, Chaudron and Jefferson, *J Clin Psych* 2000, **161**, 79–90).

27. A small study suggested that the quantity of **vigabatrin** ingested through milk is small, at around 1–3% of the daily dose (n=2, Tran *et al, Br J Clin Pharmacol* 1998, **45**, 409–11), but other information is contradictory. **Topiramate** and **tiagabine** are not recommended as no human information is currently available. Animal studies indicate **levetiracetam** is excreted into breast milk and so breast-feeding is not recommended.

28. **Ethosuximide** is excreted in breast milk, with detectable infant levels. It might still be wise to monitor levels if possible. Very low doses of **acetazolamide** were transferred by breast-feeding in one reported case (Soderman *et al, Br J Clin Pharmacol* 1984, **17**, 599–600).

### 3.1.5 Others:

29.* There is no information available on **donepezil**, **galantamine** and **rivastigmine,** so should not be used in breast-feeding mothers (SPC). Human data is lacking but **memantine** is lipophilic and so is probably excreted into breast milk.

30. There is no data on **anticholinergics** in breast milk.

31. No information is available to date on **disulfiram** in breast milk and so use must be with great caution. There is the possibility of interactions with paediatric medicines (see *4.7.1*). Acamprosate is excreted in the milk

of lactating animals and so the UK SPC states that use in breast-feeding is a contraindication. No human data proving safety exists.

32. **Lithium** has been classified by the AAPCD as contraindicated in breast-feeding since 1989. Breast milk levels are approximately 40% (range 24–72%), with infant serum having levels 5–200% of the mother's serum concentrations, with 2 case reports of adverse events (eg. hypotonia and lethargy, possibly due to reduced renal clearance) attributed to lithium (n=1, Tunnessen and Hertz, *J Pediatr* 1972, **81**, 804-7; n=1, Skausig and Schou, *Ugeskr Laeger* 1977, **139**, 400–1), although the latter was probably multifactorial. The recommendation to contraindicate lithium in breast-feeding is thus based on limited evidence. Informed choice, with careful monitoring of the infant (considering poorer renal excretion and fluid balance/ electrolytes), use of low doses, may help if the risk of relapse is high if stopping.

**Reviews**: Chaudron and Jefferson, *J Clin Psych* 2000, **161**, 79–90; Amanth, *Lithium* 1993, **4**, 231–37; Llewellyn *et al*, *J Clin Psych* 1998, **59**[Suppl 6], 57–64.

33. **Modafinil** is contraindicated in breast-feeding (MI).

34. No information is available for **methylphenidate** (SPC) so do not use.

35.* **Methadone** at maintenance doses reduces the risk of poor quality street drugs being used and has been used successfully in breast-feeding. A 12-mother study showed that the amount of methadone in breast milk was measurable but low (insufficient to prevent the development of a neonatal absence syndrome in 7 infants), infant plasma levels were below the limit of detection in seven infants, and no adverse effects attributable to methadone were noted. The conclusion was that breast-feeding should not be discouraged in women on a methadone maintenance programme (Wojnar-Horton *et al*, *Br J Clin Pharmacol* 1997, **44**, 543). Stopping opiates is also dangerous as withdrawal reactions can damage the foetus more than methadone (for effect on the child in the first year, see *Arch Dis Childhood* 1989, **64**, 235–45), but the dose of methadone received via milk is unlikely to be sufficient to prevent the neonatal abstinence syndrome (n=8 pairs, Begg *et al*, *B J Clin Pharmacol* 2001, **52**, 681–85).

36*. **Bupropion** and metabolites accumulate in breast milk at higher levels than plasma, although reports indicate that these are not detectable in the infants plasma (n=1, Briggs *et al*, *Ann Pharmacother* 1993, **27**, 431–33; n=2 pairs, Baab *et al*, *J Clin Psych* 2002, **63**, 910–11).

## 3.2 CARDIOVASCULAR DISEASE

| | Lower risk | Moderate risk | Higher risk |
|---|---|---|---|
| Antipsychotics | Amisulpride [5]<br>Flupentixol [4]<br>Olanzapine [2]<br>Quetiapine [2]<br>Risperidone [1]<br>Sulpiride [5]<br>Zuclopenthixol [4] | Aripiprazole [2]<br>Haloperidol [6]<br>Loxapine [8]<br>Phenothiazines [7]<br>Risperidone [1] | Clozapine [3]<br>Pimozide [8]<br>Sertindole [2]<br>Thioridazine [7]<br>Ziprasidone [2]<br>Zotepine [2] |
| Antidepressants | Mianserin [16]<br>Mirtazapine [11]<br>SSRIs [9]<br>Trazodone [13]<br>Tryptophan [16] | MAOIs [15]<br>Moclobemide [16]<br>Nefazodone [13]<br>Reboxetine [14]<br>Venlafaxine [10] | Tricyclics (especially dothiepin) [12] |
| Anxiolytics + hypnotics | Benzodiazepines [17]<br>Buspirone [18]<br>Zaleplon [19]<br>Zolpidem [19]<br>Zopiclone [19] | Beta-blockers [20]<br>Chloral [21]<br>Clomethiazole [21] | |
| Anticonvulsants | Benzodiazepines [17]<br>Gabapentin [26]<br>Lamotrigine [26]<br>Tiagabine [27]<br>Topiramate [27]<br>Valproate [23]<br>Vigabatrin [27] | Barbiturates [25]<br>Carbamazepine [22]<br>Oxcarbazepine [22]<br>Paraldehyde [28]<br>Phenytoin [2] | Fosphenytoin [24] |
| Others | Acamprosate [31]<br>Memantine [29] | Anticholinergics [30]<br>Anticholinesterases [29]<br>Bupropion [36]<br>Dexamfetamine [34]<br>Lithium [32]<br>Modafinil [33] | Disulfiram [31] |

**General Principals** (adapted from *Maudsley Guidelines*)

1. Polypharmacy should be avoided where possible, particularly with drugs likely to effect cardiac rate and electrolyte balance.
2. Awareness of QT prolongation is increasing, and so care is essential. A QTc prolonged to about 450ms is considered of some concern, and above about 500ms to be of an unquantifiable risk of leading to Torsade de Pointes, which may be fatal.
3. Avoid drugs specifically contra-indicated eg. thioridazine etc.
4. Start low and go slow is, as ever, good advice. Rapid dose escalation should be avoided.

**Angina**

Avoid drugs causing orthostatic hypotension, which may exacerbate angina. Avoid drugs causing tachycardia, eg. phenothiazines, clozapine, risperidone etc. Trazodone and tricyclics are best avoided, although most other antidepressants are thought to be of relatively low risk.

**Arrhythmias**

SSRIs are first choice antidepressants for depression with arrhythmias, and are preferred to tricyclic antidepressants because of their lack of anti-arrhythmic/proarrhythmic potential (*Drugs & Ther Perspect* 1998, **11**, 11–13). Avoid phenothiazines, butyrophenones and pimozide. Sulpiride and olanzapine seem of low risk.

**Heart failure (HF)**

For chronic stable heart failure, avoid beta-blockers and take care with drugs causing orthostatic hypotension, eg. phenothiazines, clozapine, risperidone, tricyclics etc. For acute HF, the cause will indicate which drugs are safer to use. Remember that lithium and diuretics need extra care.

**Hypertension**

Drugs causing orthostatic hypotension should be monitored closely. Avoid MAOIs. Hypertension can occur with venlafaxine (high dose), clozapine and sometimes with tricyclics and antipsychotics.

**Myocardial infarction (MI)**
If essential, use SSRIs (except perhaps fluvoxamine), trazodone or mianserin. Avoid high-dose antipsychotics, phenothiazines and pimozide. Butyrophenones, thioxanthenes and benzamides are safer.
**Reviews:*** cardiac effects of psychotropics (Chong *et al, Ann Acad Med Singapore* 2001, **30**, 625–31).
**QTc prolongation:***
Many antipsychotics are known to affect cardiac conduction, with a class IA antiarrhythmic-like effect. One way this manifests itself is by lengthening of the QT interval. This may then lead onto torsades de pointes, which may be asymptomatic or in rare cases may lead on to ventricular fibrillation and sudden death. The QT interval shortens with increased heart rate, and so a rate-correct value QTc is usually used. The upper limit is arbitrary, but a QT interval of 500ms or more should prompt review and possibly action. QTc varies markedly throughout the day and so serial readings are necessary for accurate assessments.

**Risk factors for antipsychotic-induced QTc prolongation:***
- Recent introduction, dose increase or high doses (including overdose)
- Receiving other medicines associated with QT prolongation, including eg. some antiarrhythmic drugs, vasodilators, tricyclics, antipsychotics, macrolide and fluoroquinolone antibiotics, antimalarials, ketoconazole, antihistamines etc.
- Underlying cardiac disease eg. heart failure, angina, cardiac myopathy
- History of ventricular arrhythmias or Torsades de Pointes
- Bradycardia or 2nd or 3rd degree heart block
- Family history of QTc prolongation
- Severe renal or hepatic impairment
- Elderly or malnourished
- History of heavy alcohol consumption or substance misuse

- Electrolyte imbalance, especially hypokalaemia
- Undergoing restraint and/or severe stress
- Slow drug metabolisers
- Female (may occur more frequently)

If a prolonged QT interval is predictable, monitoring of electrolytes and ECG may be indicated, but interpretation is dependent upon the timing (since last dose, diurnal variation, postprandial state).

### 3.2.1 Antipsychotics: *

Antipsychotic use in schizophrenia is associated with increased rates of cardiac arrest, ventricular arrhythmia and death. One review has concluded that the greatest risk of prolonged QTc is from thioridazine, followed by pimozide, sertindole, droperidol and haloperidol, some with ziprasidone (but no evidence of leading on to torsades de pointes) and no association with olanzapine, quetiapine or risperidone (Glassman and Bigger, *Am J Psych* 2001, **158**, 1774–82), although interestingly thioridazine (except perhaps at high dose) was no greater risk than haloperidol in a Medicaid cohort study (n=95,632 + 29,086 controls, Hennessy *et al, BMJ* 2002, **325**, 1070–72).
**Reviews***: CV adverse effects of antipsychotics (Buckley and Sanders, *Drug Safety* 2000, **23**, 215–28; 80 refs), QTc prolongation (Vieweg, *J Clin Psych* 2002, **63**(Suppl 9), 18–24) and QTc, Torsade de Pointes and sudden death (Haddad and Anderson, *Drugs* 2002, **62**, 1649–71).
1.* **Risperidone** should be used with caution due to orthostatic hypotension, low doses slightly dropping bp and increasing heart rate. It is best to introduce it slowly over several weeks. In the study above (Medicaid cohort study, n=95,632 + 29,086 controls, Hennessy *et al, BMJ* 2002, **325**, 1070–72), risperidone was the only drug that had higher rates than haloperidol for cardiac arrest and ventricular arrhythmia, especially at lower dose, the authors concluding

that this was due to the frailest patients being given lowest doses.

2.* Postural hypotension has been seen infrequently with **olanzapine**. Blood pressure monitoring is recommended periodically in patients over 65. One study showed that olanzapine (mean 14mg/d) produced fasting triglyceride levels raised by a mean of 60mg/dL (37%) (n=25, 12/52, Osser *et al, J Clin Psych* 1999, **60**, 767–70), which, since triglycerides are a significant risk factor for exacerbation of CHD, needs care (Grundy, *Am J Cardiol* 1998, **81**(4A), 18B-25B). An increase in the QTc interval has only been seen rarely eg. data from four RCTs showed the risk of QTc > 450msec was approximately the same as at baseline, suggesting a minimal effect on QTc prolongation and hence fatal arrhythmias (n=2700, Czekalla *et al, J Clin Psych* 2001, **62**, 191–98). The SPC for **quetiapine** recommends caution with drugs known to prolong the QTc interval and in patients with cardiovascular disease or conditions predisposing to hypotension. Trials have not shown sustained changes in the QTc interval. Orthostatic hypotension is more common in the elderly, especially initially. **Zotepine** causes a dose-related QTc interval prolongation and caution is necessary in patients with CHD and with other drugs known to cause QTc prolongation. Increased heart rate can occur so care in angina pectoris is necessary, and orthostatic hypotension can occur initially in treatment, so bp measuring is recommended. Caution is necessary in severe hypertension. **Aripiprazole** may cause orthostatic hypotension and used with caution in known CV disease, cerebrovascular disease and hypotension (MI). Unlike other antipsychotics, it tends to cause a slight shortening of the QTc interval. **Ziprasidone** causes a well-publicised dose-related prolongation of QTc interval (mean 10msec), so should not be used in anyone with known prolonged inter-

val, recent MI or heart failure. It can cause a mean increase in heart rate of 1.4bpm. **Sertindole** also lengthens the QT interval and is thus contraindicated in people with a history of significant cardiovascular disease, congestive heart failure, cardiac hypertrophy, arrhythmia or bradycardia (<50bpm) and congential prolonged QT (>450msec in men, >470msec in women). Trials are underway to obtain naturalistic and comparative data.

3.* **Clozapine** has cardiac side-effects, eg. tachycardia and postural hypotension (particularly early in treatment). The CSM (*Curr Probs Pharmacovig* 2002, **28**, 8) has warned that with clozapine:

● Patients who develop clozapine-induced cardiomyopathy (data mining study, Coulter *et al, BMJ* 2001, **322**, 1207-9) should not be re-exposed to clozapine

● It should only be started if severe heart disease has been excluded through history, examination and possibly an ECG

● Myocarditis most commonly occurs in the first 2 months

● Persistent tachycardia at rest, especially during first 2 months, should be followed up and observed for other signs of cardiomyopathy/ myocarditis

● ECG changes should referred to a cardiologist for evaluation

● Clozapine should be discontinued in anyone for whom cardiomyopathy or myocarditis is suspected

One study showed that 13% had cardiac abnormalities before and 31% after starting clozapine. Risk factors included increased age (but less so if there was a normal ECG with other antipsychotics). Prolonged QTc was dose-dependent, often corrected itself with time, was mostly during the initial stages of treatment, mostly benign and pathological prolongation of QTc was rare (n=61, Kang *et al, J Clin Psych* 2000, **61**, 441–46). Case series in Australia have shown a strong association with potentially fatal myocarditis (n=15, 5 occurring within 5 weeks of starting) and cardiomyopathy (n=8) in physically healthy young adults (from Australian database of 8000, Kilian *et al, Lancet* 1999, **354**, 1841–45) and in USA myocarditis (n=28, 18 fatal) and cardiomyopathy (n=41, 10 fatal: Greande *et al, NEJM* 2001, **345**, 224–25). Regular ECG monitoring, especially at higher doses, may be very valuable.

4. Cardiac disease is a UK SPC precaution for **flupentixol** and **zuclopenthixol**.

5. No changes in ECG status have been reported in short and long-term studies of **amisulpride**. There are no specific problems reported with **sulpiride** (SPC).

6.* **Haloperidol** may have the risk of occasional arrhythmias and so the use of high dosage with non-responders is cautioned. Prolonged QT-interval has been reported with haloperidol (n=596, Reilly *et al, Lancet* 2000, **35**, 1048–52) although it appeared of no greater risk than thioridazine in a Medicaid cohort study (n=95,632 + 29,086 controls, Hennessy *et al, BMJ* 2002, **325**, 1070–72).

7. Some ECG abnormalities have been reported with **phenothiazines**, eg. tachycardia, T-wave abnormalities, ST depression, QT prolongation and right bundle branch block. **Thioridazine** is contraindicated in patients with a history of cardiac arrhythmias or at risk of problems. Dose-related increases in risk of lengthened QT-interval have been reported, detectable at doses as low as 10mg/d (n=596, Reilly *et al, Lancet* 2000, **355**, 1048–52). **Levomepromazine** (methotrimeprazine) causes orthostatic hypotension which can, on occasion, be prolonged and profound. Sudden death has also been reported.

8. **Loxapine** can increase pulse rate and produce transient hypotension. With **pimozide**, the UK CSM has had many reports of serious or fatal cardiac reactions to pimozide. They recommend:

i. Start at 2–4mg/d. Increase by 2–4mg/d weekly (max. 20mg/d).
ii. Perform ECG pre-treatment. C/I if a prolonged QT interval or a history of arrhythmia is noted.
iii. Repeat ECG annually. Review if QT interval is lengthened.
iv. Avoid concurrent treatment with other antipsychotics (including depots), tricyclics and other QT interval-prolonging drugs (eg. some anti-malarials, antiarrhythmics, terfenadine, astemizole and diuretics). For CSM advice, see *Curr Prob* 1995, **21**, 2.

## 3.2.2 Antidepressants:*

Depression is a risk factor for recurrence of cardiac problems and may be very poorly detected after MI (n=85, Luutonen *et al, Acta Psych Scand* 2002, **106**, 434–39). Depressed patients are at greater risk of myocardial infarction and vice versa, and, during the first six months post-infarction, patients who become depressed have a five-fold increase in mortality (Frazure-Smith *et al, JAMA* 1999, **270**, 1819–25). Depressed patients are less likely to follow recommendations to reduce cardiac risk during recovery from a myocardial infarction (n=204, survey, Ziegelstein *et al, Arch Int Med* 2000, **160**, 1818–23) and less likely to comply with antihypertensives (n=496, 1 yr, Wang *et al, J Gen Intern Med* 2002, **17**, 504–11). There is a strong association between the use of tricyclic antidepressants and cardiac events (especially IHD with dosulepin; n=933 + 5516 controls, Hippisley-Cox *et al,* BMJ 2001, **323**, 666–69; Cohen *et al, Am J Med* 2000, **108**, 2–8), but not with SSRIs, where the risk has actually been shown to be reduced by 65% compared to non-users (n=143, Kimmel *et al, J Am Heart Ass* 2001, **104**, 1894–98). Treatment of depression in this vulnerable group is thus of singular importance as, although the use of antidepressants in cardiac disease has risks, so does *not* using them (n=2847,

Penninx *et al, Arch Gen Psych* 2001, **58**, 221–27).

**Reviews**: general (Roose and Spatz, *Drug Safety* 1999, **20**, 459–65, 25 refs).

9.* Despite some reported cases of cardiac effects (eg. a plasma-level related potential for conduction problems eg. AV block, QTc prolongation etc; n=114, Rodriguez de la Torre *et al, Ther Drug Monit* 2001, **23**, 435–40), the SSRIs are generally considered safer to use in cardiac diseases (eg. n=456, Guy and Silke, *J Clin Psych* 1990, **51**[Suppl 13], 37–39; review by Glassman *et al, JAMA* 1993, **269**, 2673–75), with robust data accumulating to support this eg. in a recent major study, **sertraline** was shown not to increase cardiac events in depressed patients with unstable angina or recent MI and may even cut cardiac deaths post-MI by about 10% (n=369, RCT, Glassman *et al, JAMA* 2002, **288**, 701–9). Similarly, a naturalistic study in severely ill (subacute cardiac rehabilitation unit) elderly cardiac patients showed that **paroxetine**, **sertraline** and **fluoxetine** had little adverse effect on cardiac state and appeared relatively safe and effective, but care was needed with drug interactions (n=17, Askinazi, *Am J Psych* 1996, **153**, 135–36). Several open trials have indicated **fluoxetine** up to 60mg/day to have no significant adverse cardiac effects in patients with pre-existing CHF, conduction disease and/or ventricular arrhythmia (n=27, average age 73, open, 7/52, Roose *et al, Am J Psych* 1998, **155**, 660–66). In another, fluoxetine 20mg/d produced a modest reduction in bp, and patients with pre-existing, stable cardiovascular disease (including hypertension) showed no significant bp change (n=796, 12/52, Amsterdam *et al, J Clin Psychopharmacol* 1999, **19**, 9–14). Rare cases of, eg. atrial fibrillation, bradycardia and syncope have been reported. **Citalopram** (and presumably **escitalopram**) have no significant reported effect on blood pressure, cardiac conduction nor

heart rate (Milne and Goa, *Drugs* 1991, **41**, 450–77), but exacerbation of pre-existing bradycardia has been reported (eg. Nyth *et al, Acta Psych Scand* 1992, **86**, 138–45), as has occasional postural dizziness (review of citalopram cardiac safety: Rasmussen *et al, J Clin Psychopharmacol* 1999, **19**, 407–15).

10. **Venlafaxine** has a dose-dependent effect on supine diastolic blood pressure, clinically significant at high doses ( >200–300mg/d), probably as a result of noradrenergic potentiation (3% incidence at less than 100mg/d, 7% for 150–200mg/d and 13% above 300mg/d). Increased heart rate, serum lipids (eg. rises in cholesterol of 2-3mg/dL) and palpitations (Khan *et al, Psychopharmacol Bull* 1991, **27**, 141–44) have been reported and so caution is required for patients with pre-existing cardiovascular disease, recent myocardial infarction or hyperlipidaemia (Anon, *J Clin Psych* 1993, **54**, 119–26). It may not adversely effect control of blood pressure in people with pre-existing hypertension (meta-analysis, n=3744, Thase, *J Clin Psych* 1998, **59**, 502-8). People who get this effect may be CYP2D6 deficient, which might help predict future side-effects and drug responses (case and review, Blythe and Hackett, *Hum Exp Toxicol* 1999, **18**, 309–13). Blood pressure monitoring at doses above 200mg/d is recommended.

11. Although hypertension, hypotension and tachycardia have been reported with **mirtazapine**, the incidences of 6%, 4% and 2% respectively are the same as placebo (n=150, RCT, d/b, p/c, 6/52, Smith *et al, Psychopharmacol Bull* 1990, **26**, 191–6). No ECG changes have been observed in reported trials, nor bp and heart rate changes in a six-week depressed inpatient trial (n=251, RCT, Zivkov and Jongh, *Human Psychopharmacol* 1995, **10**, 173–80). Mild dizziness and vertigo was noted in two patients in one trial, although treatment continued (van Moffaert *et al, Int Clin Psychopharm* 1995, **10**, 3–9).

Mirtazapine would seem to be relatively safe.

12.* **Tricyclics** produce orthostatic hypotension (and hence occasional myocardial infarction), have anti-arrhythmic actions (quinidine-like) in high dose and antimuscarinic actions (raising heart rate). Thus, tricyclics should only be used with caution in patients with ischaemic heart disease, ventricular arrhythmia, angina, recent MI and hypertension. Indeed, a case-control primary care study indicated that the odds ratio for developing IHD was significantly raised for patients who had *ever* received a TCA (even adjusting for other factors), with a further specific, significant and dose-related association with dosulepin (n=922 with IHD, 5516 controls, Hippisley-Cox *et al, BMJ* 2001, **323**, 666–69). SSRIs are thus generally considered safer. In patients with recurrent chest pain but normal coronary angiograms, imipramine therapy over 9–33 months produced no symptoms of a pro-arrhythmic effect, a slightly prolonged corrected QT interval and reduced chest pain (n=58, Cannon *et al, NEJM* 1994, **330**, 1411–17). Conversely, in 24 patients with major depression compared with 24 controls, 150mg/d of amitriptyline increased heart rate from 78bpm to 93bpm and all other heart rate analysis parameters significantly worsened (Rechlin *et al, Psychopharmacology* 1994, **116**, 110–14). **Nortriptyline** has significant effects on cardiac vagal function and should only be used with care in IHD (n=44, Yeragani *et al, Neuropsychobiology* 2002, **46**, 125–35), especially in men, who may be more susceptible to its cardiac side effects (n=78, 6/52, Pomara *et al, PNBP* 2001, **25**, 1035–48). Doxepin-induced Torsade de Pointes tachycardia has been reported (Alter *et al, Ann Inter Med* 2001, **135**, 384–85).

13.* One case of reversible ventricular tachycardia (n=1, Vitullo *et al, Chest* 1990, **98**, 247–48) and QT prolongation has been reported with **trazodone** overdose (Levenson, *Am J Psych* 1999, **156**, 929–70) but is generally considered of low risk. **Nefazodone** should only be used with caution with recent infarction or unstable heart disease.

14. **Reboxetine** increased baseline heart rate in 20% of patients in short-term trials. Orthostatic hypotension occurs with increasing frequency at higher doses.

15. **Isocarboxazid**, **phenelzine** and **tranylcypromine** are contraindicated in severe cardiac disease.

16.* Many cases of hypertension have been reported with **moclobemide** (eg. Boyd, *Lancet* 1995, **346**, 1498) so monitoring bp may be useful. Occasional hypertension with tyramine in patients with pre-existing labile hypertension has also occurred (*Acta Psych Scand* 1990, **360**[Suppl], 69–70) and so caution in cardiac disease would be sensible. **St. John's wort** does not affect heart rate variability, unlike amitriptyline 75mg/d (n=12, RCT, d/b, c/o, 14/7 per arm, Siepmann *et al, B J Clin Pharmacol* 2002, **54**, 277–82). There are no apparent problems with **mianserin** and **tryptophan**.

### 3.2.3 Anxiolytics and hypnotics:

17. **Benzodiazepines** are relatively safe but contraindicated in acute pulmonary insufficiency. One study in elderly patients showed that temazepam (up to 30mg/d) caused a fall in systolic blood pressure and an increase in heart rate (n=12, Ford, *B J Clin Pharmacol* 1990, **29**, 61–67).

18. **Buspirone** may have some cardiac effects, eg. rare cases of hypertension and tachycardia.

19. There are no apparent problems with **zaleplon**, **zolpidem** and **zopiclone**.

20. The use of **beta-blockers** would depend upon the nature of the cardiac disease.

21. **Clomethiazole** is contraindicated in acute pulmonary insufficiency and should be used with care in chronic pulmonary insufficiency. **Chloral** is

contraindicated in severe cardiac disease.

### 3.2.4 Anticonvulsants:

22. Cardiovascular effects from **carbamazepine** are uncommon but cardiac conduction changes, hypertension and atrio-ventricular block (Labrecque *et al, Am J Psych* 1992, **149**, 572–73) have been reported. There is a case of a patient with a permanent dual-chamber pacemaker, where carbamazepine elevated ventricular and atrial thresholds, thus making the pacemaker ineffective (Ambrosi *et al, Lancet* 1993, **342**, 365). Patients on **oxcarbazepine** with cardiac insufficiency and secondary heart failure should have regular weight measurements to determine the occurrence of fluid retention (SPC).

23. There are some rare reports of cardiac effects with **valproate**, but no specific cautions.

24. **Phenytoin** has many cardiac effects and is a useful third-line treatment in cardiac arrhythmias. It is, however, contraindicated in sinus bradycardia, sino-atrial block, second and third degree A-V block and patients with Adams-Stokes syndrome. Severe cardiovascular ADRs have been reported with **fosphenytoin** IV, including asystole, VF and cardiac arrest, mostly within 30mins of an injection. The CSM thus recommend (*Curr Prob Pharmacovig* 2000, **26**[May], 1):

● Try to monitor heart rate, bp and respiration during the infusion

● Observe for at least 30 minutes after the infusion ends

● As hypotension may occur at recommended doses and rates, dose or rate reduction may be necessary

● Reduce the loading dose and/or infusion rate by 10–25% in elderly or those with hepatic or renal impairment

25. IV **barbiturates** can cause hypotension.

26. There is no evidence of any problems with **gabapentin** in cardiac disease. ECG monitoring is recommended in cases of **lamotrigine** overdose (Buckley *et al, Lancet* 1993, **342**, 1552–53).

27. There is no evidence to date of cardiac adverse effects from **vigabatrin**. No significant changes in ECG, blood pressure or heart rate have been noted in initial clinical trials with **topiramate** (MI) and **tiagabine** (MI).

28. There have been reports of hypotension and tachycardia in young children given IV **paraldehyde** (Sinal and Crowe, *Pediatrics* 1976,**57**, 158).

### 3.2.5 Others:

29.* **Anticholinesterases** may cause bradycardia so care is needed with the use of **donepezil** in patients with sick sinus syndrome or other conduction conditions (MI). Heart block has been reported with donepezil, and so the SPC has recommended to consider this before prescribing (*Curr Prob Pharmacovig* 1999, **25**, 7). Analysis of 4 studies indicated that **rivastigmine** appears not to cause adverse effects on ECG (n=2149, d/b, p/c, 26/52, Morganroth *et al, J Clin Pharmacol* 2002, **42**, 558–68), although rare cases of syncope and angina pectoris have been noted trials (MI). **Galantamine** would appear relatively safe but caution is advised in people with cardiovascular conditions, eg. sick sinus syndrome or other supraventricular cardiac conduction disturbances (SPC). There is little data on **memantine** in cardiac disease (hypertension, CHF, recent infarct) and use should be only with caution (SPC).

30. **Anticholinergics** should be used with caution, particularly in those with a tendency to tachycardia. Sinus bradycardia has been reported with **benzatropine** (*Am J Psych* 1992, **149**, 711) and **benzhexol**/trihexyphenidyl (*Drug Intell Clin Pharm* 1986, **20**, 786–87).

31. **Disulfiram** is contraindicated in the presence of cardiac failure, coronary artery disease, previous history of CVA and hypertension. The

Antabuse-alcohol reaction can cause cardiac arrest even in healthy adults. There are no known problems with **acamprosate**(MI).

32. **Lithium** rarely causes clinical problems although cardiac failure and sick sinus syndrome are contraindications Usually benign cardiovascular side-effects may occur in 20–30% patients. The main problems with lithium can be T-wave flattening (or possibly inversion), ventricular ectopics, congestive myopathy, bradycardia (Farag *et al, Lancet* 1994, **343**, 1371), ECG changes and conduction disturbances, eg. sinus node dysfunction (Terao *et al, Acta Psych Scand* 1996, **93**, 407–8). An analysis, however, of 827 patients by Ahrens *et al* (*J Aff Dis* 1995, **33**, 67–75) showed that deaths from cardiac-related causes are no different in people taking lithium than the general population and so, despite the above reported problems, lithium can be considered not to have a significant risk in this situation (reviewed by Ananth, *Lithium* 1993, **4**, 167–79). A pre-treatment ECG is very useful, especially in elderly people.

33. **Modafinil** is contraindicated in severe hypertension and arrhythmia and used with caution in patients with concurrent heart disease. Monitor heart rate and blood pressure if used in moderate hypertension (MI; discussion by Heitmann *et al, Clin Pharmacol & Therap* 1999, **65**, 328–35).

34. The manufacturers caution to monitor bp in hypertensive patients taking **methylphenidate**.

35. There is little evidence of developing hypertension with **dexamfetamine**, although regular bp testing has been recommended (ASDA, *Sleep* 1994, **17**, 348–51).

36. **Bupropion** may cause small rises in supine blood pressure (RCT, n=58, Kiev *et al, Ann Clin Psych* 1994, **6**, 107–15), but tends not to cause significant conduction complications, nor exacerbate ventricular arrhythmias and has a low rate of orthostatic hypotension (n=36, open trial in patients with depression and pre-existing heart disease, Roose *et al, Am J Psych* 1991, **148**, 512–16). Infrequent occurrences of orthostatic hypotension, tachycardia, stroke and vasodilation have been reported with bupropion. Significant cardiac conduction prolongation does not seem to occur (review: Roose, *Am Heart J* 2000, **140**[4 Suppl], 84–88).

## 3.3 DIABETES

| | Lower risk | Moderate risk | High risk |
|---|---|---|---|
| Antipsychotics | Amisulpride[5]<br>Aripiprazole [2]<br>Butyrophenones[6]<br>Loxapine[8]<br>Risperidone[1]<br>Sulpiride[5]<br>Thioxanthenes[4]<br>Ziprasidone [2] | Clozapine[3]<br>Phenothiazines[7]<br>Quetiapine [2]<br>Sertindole [2]<br>Zotepine[12] | Olanzapine?[2] |
| Antidepressants | Moclobemide[16]<br>Nefazodone[13]<br>Reboxetine[14]<br>SSRIs [9]<br>Trazodone[13]<br>Tryptophan[16]<br>Venlafaxine[10] | Fluoxetine[9]<br>Mianserin[16]<br>Mirtazapine[11]<br>Tricyclics[12] | MAOIs[15] |
| Anxiolytics and hypnotics | Benzodiazepines[17]<br>Buspirone[18]<br>Chloral[21]<br>Clomethiazole[21]<br>Zaleplon[19]<br>Zolpidem[19]<br>Zopiclone[19] | Beta-blockers[20] | |
| Anticonvulsants | Acetazolamide[28]<br>Barbiturates[25]<br>Benzodiazepines[17]<br>Carbamazepine[22]<br>Ethosuximide[28]<br>Gabapentin[26]<br>Oxcarbazepine[22]<br>Vigabatrin[27] | Phenytoin[24]<br>Tiagabine[27]<br>Topiramate?[27]<br>Valproate[23] | |
| Others | Acamprosate[31]<br>Anticholinergics[30]<br>Anticholinesterases[29]<br>Lithium[32]<br>Memantine [29]<br>Methylphenidate[22]<br>Modafinil[33] | Bupropion [34]<br>Disulfiram[31] | |

### 3.3.1 Antipsychotics: *

There is an increased risk of diabetes with all antipsychotics, but especially some "atypicals" eg. in a huge study of people taking antipsychotics (41% on typicals and 59% on atypicals [of which 48.4% were on olanzapine, 43.7% on risperidone, 5.3% on clozapine and 4.2% on quetiapine]), those on atypicals were 9% more likely to have diabetes than those on typicals. The prevalence was significantly increased for clozapine, olanzapine and quetiapine but not for risperidone (n=38,632, Veterans, Sernyak *et al*, *Am J Psych* 2002, **159**, 561–66). In another study in non-diabetic schizophrenics, glucose tolerance tests showed elevated plasma glucose (compared to placebo or typicals) at all time points for olanzapine, partly raised for clozapine and only raised with risperidone compared to untreated non-schizophrenics, indicating an adverse effect by some atypicals on glucose regulation (n=79, Newcomer *et al*, *Arch Gen Psych* 2002, **59**, 337–45).

1.* There appears to be only a clinically insignificant effect from **risperidone** on blood biochemistry (n=38,632, Veterans, Sernyak *et al*, *Am J Psych* 2002, **159**, 561–66) and is probably the least likely of the atypicals to exacerbate or cause diabetes (Gianfrancesco *et al*, *J Clin Psych* 2002, **63**, 920–30).

2.* The **olanzapine** UK SPC now states that in 5000 pts with baseline non-fasting glucose levels of <7.8/L, the incidence of raised glucose (<11mmol/L, suggestive of diabetes) was 1% (cf 0.9% placebo). Raised levels <11mmol/L (suggestive of hyperglycaemia) were 2% with olanzapine (cf 1.6% placebo) and so hyperglycaemia or exacerbation of pre-existing diabetes has been moved from common side effects (1–10%) to very rare (<0.01%). Post-marketing surveillance in the UK has shown the incidence of diabetes mellitus to be about 1 in 1000 (8 cases in sample of 8858, Biswasl *et al*, *J Psychopharmacol* 2001, **15**, 265–71). It is, however, clear that olanzapine is associated with a wide range of metabolic abnormalities eg. weight gain, elevated levels of insulin, leptin and blood lipids (triglycerides and cholesterol), as well as insulin resistance. There is a significantly increased diabetes risk (UK CSM warning: *Curr Probs* 2002, **28**, 3) eg. a population-based study showed that whilst there was a slight increase in risk with risperidone (odds ratio 2.2), the greatest risk was with olanzapine (OR of 5.8 cf. conventionals or non-antipsychotic treated) (n=19,637, Koro *et al*, *BMJ* 2002, **325**, 243–45). Olanzapine may precipitate or unmask diabetes in susceptible patients (n=237, Koller and Doraiswamy, *Pharmacotherapy* 2002, **22**, 841–52) and may severely exacerbate diabetic control (n=I, Ober *et al*, *Am J Psych* 1999, **156**, 970). One study showed that olanzapine (mean 14mg/d) produced fasting triglyceride levels raised by a mean of 60mg/dL (37%) (n=25, 12/52, Osser *et al*, *J Clin Psych* 1999, **60**, 767–70), which needs care since triglycerides are a risk factor for precipitation or exacerbation of diabetes (Grundy, *Am J Cardiol* 1998, **81**(4A), 18B-25B). There are of course numerous retrospective case reports as people improve their CVs eg. diabetes abruptly worsening after 3 years therapy (n=1, Bechara *et al*, *Pharmacother* 2001, **21**, 1444–47), individual cases (eg. n=1, Bonanno *et al*, *Ann Pharmacother* 2001, **35**, 563–65; n=2, Littrell *et al*, *J Clin Psych* 2001, **62**, 733–34, n=1, Van Meter *et al*, *J Clin Psych* 2001, **62**, 993–94), reversion on olanzapine discontinuation (n=1, Melkersson and Hulting, *Psychosomatics* 2002, **43**, 67–70) and hyperglycaemic non-ketonic coma (n=1, Roefaro and Mukherjee, *Ann Pharmacother* 2001, **35**, 300–2).

There is evidence for a slightly increased risk of diabetes with **quetiapine** (n=38,632, Veterans, Sernyak *et al*, *Am J Psych* 2002, **159**, 561–66). Occasional hypo- and hyperglycaemia has been reported with **zotepine** (MI). Short-term treatment with **ziprasidone** appears to have little effect on glucose levels, although it may actually lower serum cholesterol and triglyceride levels (n=37, 6/52, open, Kingsbury *et al*, *J Clin Psych* 2001, **62**, 347–49). **Aripiprazole** is not thought to have any problems in diabetes. **Sertindole** may modify insulin and glucose responses and may require adjustments to hypoglycaemic drug doses.

3.* Elevated insulin levels and diabetes have been shown with **clozapine** (Melkersson *et al*, *J Clin Psych* 1999, **60**, 783–91), and a dose-related effect noted, indicating a probable influence on insulin secretion and causal relationship (n=384, FDA MedWatch, Koller *et al*, *Am J Med* 2001, **111**, 716–23). There is also a study showing a non-significant increase in the number of people having or developing type 2 diabetes mellitus and/or impaired glucose tolerance on clozapine compared to depot antipsychotics (n=130, Hagg *et al*, *J Clin Psych* 1998, **59**, 294–99). Additional glucose monitoring is strongly recommended in diabetics on clozapine. In addition, a study has indicated that patients on clozapine experience significant weight gain and lipid abnormalities (eg. raised serum triglycerides) and have an increased risk (52% over 5 years) of hyperglycaemia and of diagnosed diabetes mellitus (37% over 5 years). Weight increase, surprisingly, was not a significant risk factor for developing diabetes (n=82, naturalistic, 5 years, Henderson *et al*, *Am J Psych* 2000, **157**, 975–81, including lengthy discussion of possible mechanisms, similar findings of raised triglycerides in a similar study: n=222, Gaulin *et al*, *Am J Psych* 1999, **156**, 1270–72). Addition of quetiapine has been suggested as a possible management option (n=65, open, 10/12, Reinstein *et al, Clin Drug Invest* 1999, **18**, 99–104). However, a case-control study of cases of newly treated diabetes indicated no increased risk of diabetes with clozapine but a modest and significant increased risk with chlorpromazine and perphenazine (n=7227 + 6780, Wang *et al, J Clin Psychopharmacol* 2002, **22**, 236–43).

4. Lack of relationship between serum levels of **zuclopenthixol** (n=9) and plasma insulin has been shown (Melkersson *et al, J Clin Psych* 1999, **60**, 783–91). The UK SPC for **flupenthixol** notes that control of diabetes may be impaired.

5. There are no apparent problems with **sulpiride** and **amisulpride**.

6. There are no apparent problems with **haloperidol**.

7. The 22 diabetics in a large study of **chlorpromazine** did not show any significant modifications to blood sugar levels. Five patients developed diabetes but all five appeared prone to diabetes, eg. overweight, family history etc (n=850, *Am J Psych* 1968, **125**, 253–55). Lack of relationship between serum levels of **perphenazine** (n=12) and plasma insulin has been shown (Melkersson *et al, J Clin Psych* 1999, **60**, 783–91).

8. There are no apparent problems with **pimozide** nor **loxapine**.

### 3.3.2 Antidepressants: *

Depression in diabetics may be as common as 27% and sertraline was recommended as the drug of choice and the SSRIs being generally preferred to tricyclics and MAOIs in a thorough review (Goodnick *et al, J Clin Psych* 1995, **56**, 128–36). SSRIs may decrease serum glucose levels by up to 30% and cause anorexia (reducing body weight), and may enable diabetics to control hunger and eating better, via their serotonergic effects, unlike the tricyclics, which often have an appetite-raising effect. Depression is independently associated with poor glycaemic control (meta-analysis, s=24, Lustman *et al, Diabetes Care* 2000, **23**, 934–42).

9.* No dose changes are recommended with **citalopram/escitalopram** and no changes in glycaemic control were seen in one trial (Sindrup *et al, Clin Pharmacol Ther* 1992, **52**, 547–52). Diabetics may become hypoglycaemic during **fluoxetine** treatment (*Drug & Ther Bull* 1990, **28**, 33) and its side-effects, eg. tremor, nausea, sweating and anxiety may be mistaken for hypoglycaemia. Most problems have been reported with the more common non-insulin dependent diabetes mellitus (NIDDM, type 2 disease, adult-onset) rather than the insulin dependent form (IDDM, type 1 disease, juvenile-onset). If fluoxetine is used, counsel about this effect, note a possible loss of hypoglycemic awareness (n=1, Sawka *et al, J Ped* 2000, **136**, 394–96) and regularly check serum glucose levels (review by Salmon, *Psych Bull* 1995, **19**, 553–54). Fluoxetine has been shown to effectively reduce the severity of depression in diabetics with a trend towards better glycaemic control, so it's not all bad news (n=60, RCT, p/c, 8/52, Lustman *et al, Diabetes Care* 2000, **23**, 618–23). Little is reported with **paroxetine**. There have been no major reports of problems with **sertraline**, including the 16 patients with diabetes mellitus receiving this drug in early clinical trials and it has been recommended sertraline as the drug of choice in diabetes (Goodnick *et al, J Clin Psych* 1995, **56**, 128–36). There are, however, cases of hypoglycemia associated with sertraline (eg. n=1, Takhar and Williamson, *Can J Clin Pharmacol* 1999, **6**, 12–14; n=1, Pollak *et al, Ann Pharmacother* 2001, **35**, 1371–74).

10. There is no published evidence of problems with **venlafaxine**.

11. The manufacturers of **mirtazapine** recommend care although there are no reports of problems and this is purely a 'class labelling' precaution.

12. **Tricyclics** may adversely affect diabetic control as they increase serum

glucose levels by up to 150%, increase carbohydrate craving and reduce metabolic rate but are generally considered safe unless the diabetes is very brittle. Hypoglycaemia has been associated with maprotiline (n=1, Isotani and Kameoka, *Diabetes Care* 1999, **22**, 862).

13. There is a single case of **nefazodone** producing rapid and wide fluctuations in blood sugar levels in a diabetic woman (Warnock, *Am J Psych* 1997, **154**, 288–89). There are no apparent problems with **trazodone**.

14. There are no apparent problems with **reboxetine**.

15. **MAOIs** may decrease serum glucose levels by up to 35% due to a direct influence on gluconeogenesis (Goodnick *et al, J Clin Psych* 1995, **56**, 128–36). Diabetes is a UK SPC precaution, eg. **isocarboxazid**.

16. There is a case of **mianserin** dose-related hyperglycaemia in a non-diabetic woman (Marley and Rohan, *Lancet* 1993, **342**, 1430–31). **Moclobemide** 600mg/d did not modify the effect of glibenclamide on plasma glucose and insulin levels in healthy individuals (Amrein *et al, Psychopharmacology* 1992, **106**, S24–S31).

### 3.3.4 Anxiolytics and hypnotics

17. There is a case of a diabetic presenting with a reduction in insulin requirements after discontinuing **clonazepam** (n=1, Wagner *et al, Diabetes Care* 1999, **22**, 2099).

18. There are no apparent problems with **buspirone**.

19. There are no apparent problems with **zaleplon, zolpidem** and **zopiclone**.

20. **Propranolol** may prolong the hypoglycaemic response to insulin and may effect hypoglycaemic episodes.

21. There are no apparent problems with **clomethiazole** or **chloral**.

### 3.3.4 Anticonvulsants:

22. There is an isolated report of **carbamazepine**-induced urinary retention in 2 diabetic patients, where withdrawal improved the condition

(Steiner and Birman, *Neurology* 1993, **43**, 1855–56). There are no apparent problems with **oxcarbazepine**.

23. **Valproate** may give false positives in urine tests for diabetes. Protein binding of valproate may be lower in diabetes (Doucet *et al, E J Clin Pharmacol* 1993, **45**, 577–79).

24. Hypoglycaemia has been reported with **phenytoin** and glucose metabolism can be affected. Protein binding of phenytoin may be lower in diabetes (Doucet *et al, E J Clin Pharmacol* 1993, **45**, 577–79).

25. There are no apparent problems with the **barbiturates**.

26. There are no apparent problems with **lamotrigine**. Blood glucose fluctuations have been reported with **gabapentin** (SPC).

27. No information is available on **topiramate** and **tiagabine**.

28. There are no apparent problems with **ethosuximide**. Hyperglycaemia has been reported with **acetazolamide** in diabetics and prediabetics, but probably not normal patients, so some care may be necessary.

### 3.3.5 Others:

29.* There are no apparent problems with **donepezil** nor **galantamine**, but diabetes mellitus is a precaution for **rivastigmine**. No effect with **memantine** has been reported.

30. There are no known problems with the **anticholinergic** agents.

31. The UK SPC for **disulfiram** recommends caution in diabetes mellitus. There are no apparent problems with **acamprosate**.

32.* There is no problem with **lithium** in diabetes, but many patients on lithium develop polyuria and polydipsia, a diabetes insipidus-like syndrome via an effect on cAMP and vasopressin. This can be controlled by ensuring an adequate fluid and salt intake. There is a case of increased clearance of lithium in a patient with persistent hyperglycaemia, probably due to the subsequent osmotic diuresis increasing renal clearance (n=1, Cyr *et al, Ann Pharmacother* 2002, **36**, 427–29). Lithium may also increase insulin secretion.

33. There are no apparent problems with **methylphenidate**. A transient loss of appetite may occur. There are no apparent problems with **modafinil**.

34. Animal studies suggest some risks with **bupropion**, and hyper- and hypoglycemia have been reported and so caution should be utilised with type II diabetics (El-Dakhakhny *et al, Arzneimittelforschung* 1996, **46**, 667–69).

## 3.4 EPILEPSY

|  | Lower risk | Moderate risk | High risk |
|---|---|---|---|
| Antipsychotics | Amisulpride [5]<br>Haloperidol [6]<br>Pimozide [8]<br>Quetiapine [2]<br>Risperidone? [1]<br>Sulpiride [5]<br>Zuclopenthixol [4] | Aripiprazole [2]<br>Olanzapine [2]<br>Phenothiazines (most) [7]<br>Sertindole [2]<br>Ziprasidone [2] | Chlorpromazine [7]<br>Clozapine [3]<br>Loxapine [8]<br>Zotepine [2] |
| Antidepressants | MAOIs [15]<br>Moclobemide? [16]<br>Reboxetine [14]<br>SSRIs [9]<br>Tryptophan [16] | Mianserin [16]<br>Mirtazapine [13]<br>Nefazodone [13]<br>Trazodone [13]<br>Tricyclics (most) [12]<br>Venlafaxine [10] | Amoxapine [12]<br>Maprotiline [12] |
| Anxiolytics and hypnotics | Benzodiazepines [17]<br>Beta-blockers [20]<br>Chloral [21]<br>Clomethiazole [21]<br>Zaleplon [19]<br>Zolpidem [19]<br>Zopiclone [19] | Buspirone [18] | |
| Others | Acamprosate [24]<br>Anticholinergics [23]<br>Modafinil [26] | Disulfiram [24]<br>Anticholinesterases [22]<br>Lithium [25]<br>Memantine [29]<br>Methylphenidate [26] | Bupropion [27] |

**Reviews\***: extensive reviews (Pisani *et al, Drug Safety* 2002, **25**, 91–110, 166 refs).

### 3.4.1 Antipsychotics:

#### General principals

1. Keep the daily dose as low as possible – the effect may be dose-related.
2. Take extra care with risk factors including head trauma, previous seizure history and concomitant drugs (especially other antipsychotics). The most susceptible patients are those with a history of epilepsy, a condition that predisposes to epilepsy and those withdrawing from central depressants, eg. benzodiazepines, alcohol etc.
3. Use lowest risk drugs unless essential.
4. Use a slow rate of introduction and withdrawal. Anticonvulsant cover may be appropriate.
5. Dose changes should be small and gentle.
6. Avoid antipsychotics having more antihistaminic, antiserotonergic, sedative and antiadrenergic effects, which may have a greater seizure threshold lowering effect

**Reviews**: antipsychotics in epilepsy (McConnell *et al, Psych Bull* 1997, **21**, 642–45; Ring, *Progress Neurol Psych* 1998, **2**, 29–32).

1. There is little information about **risperidone**. Pre-marketing trials showed a seizure incidence of 0.3% (n=2607).
2.\* The SPC for **olanzapine** states that it should be used cautiously in patients with a history of seizures. Unexplained (ie. patients without reported risk factors) seizures occurred in up to 0.88% patients during pre-marketing trials (n=2500). There may be a slightly higher risk of seizures in people over 65 (MI). The incidence of seizures during **quetiapine** trials has been equivalent to placebo (MI). **Zotepine** has an established dose-related proconvulsive effect. It should not be used in patients with a personal or family history of epilepsy. The risk of seizures is dose-related and rises above 300mg/d (open, n=129, Hori *et al, Jpn J Psychiatry Neurol* 1992, **46**, 161–67). In pre-marketing trials, seizures occurred in 0.1% patients taking **aripiprazole**, but should probably still be used with caution in epilepsy. Seizures occurred in 0.4% patients during pre-marketing trials with **ziprasidone** (many with

confounding factors) but it would be wise to use with caution in epilepsy. **Sertindole** should be used with caution in patients with a history of seizures as an incidence of 1% (n=2194) was shown in clinical studies (MI).

3. **Clozapine** can cause seizures, the risk rising from 1% (<300mg/d), through 2.7% (300–600mg/d) to 4.4% (>600mg/d). EEG changes occur in 75% people on clozapine, with up to 40% having paroxysmal discharges (reviewed by Pacia and Devinsky, *Neurology* 1994, **44**, 2247–49). A more rapid dose-titration increases the risk. Many centres use valproate as routine anticonvulsant cover at higher doses of clozapine. See also *4.2.2*.

4. **Zuclopenthixol** may have only mild to moderate effects, with few reports, and may be one of the drugs of choice.

5. There are no known problems with **amisulpride**, but a spontaneously resolving generalised convulsion occurred after a 3g overdose (Tracqui *et al, Hum Exp Toxicol* 1995, **14**, 294–98). **Sulpiride** may be a reasonable choice, with a few cases of convulsions reported and only minimal EEG effects, although care is recommended in unstable epilepsy.

6. **Haloperidol** may have only mild to moderate effects, and may be a lower risk drug.

7. **Thioridazine** may have a low effect as, although it may enhance spike activity at low dose, it may not do so at higher dose (Oliver *et al, Arch Gen Psych* 1982, **39**, 206–9). **Fluphenazine** may also be low (*JAMA* 1980, **244**, 1460–63). The incidence of seizures with **chlorpromazine** may be 9% at doses above 1g/d and 0.5% at less than 1g/d and is best avoided.

8. **Pimozide** may have a low effect as, although it may enhance spike activity at low dose, it may not do so at higher dose (Oliver *et al, Arch Gen Psych* 1982, **39**, 206–9). **Loxapine**, however, lowers the seizure threshold and can cause convulsions even at normal doses.

## 3.4.2 Antidepressants:

Unless a large scale trial is carried out (unlikely), the safest antidepressant in epilepsy will remain unknown. All patients require individual assessment of risk factors and recognition that there is a dose-dependent relationship between antidepressants and seizures. A **slow rate of introduction** reduces the risk.

**Reviews**: Duncan and Taylor *Psych Bull* 1995, **19**, 355–57 and correspondence; Curran and de Pauw, *Drug Safety* 1998, **18**, 125–33, 60 refs; Pisani *et al, Epilepsia* 1999, **40**[Suppl 10] S48–56.

9. Serotonin function is unlikely to be of major importance in the genesis of seizures and so **SSRIs** are likely to have a low pro-convulsive effect. **Fluvoxamine** probably has a low proconvulsive effect, although this has been disputed (*Lancet* 1990, **336**, 947) and there have been some CSM reports of fits. **Fluoxetine** has a probable seizure incidence of 0.2%, similar to other antidepressants (MI). In an open study of 17 patients with complex partial seizures (with and without secondary generalisation), the addition of fluoxetine in six resulted in disappearance of seizures and a 30% reduction in the other 11 (Favale *et al, Neurology* 1995, **45**, 1926–27). Paroxetine appears to have a minimal potential for producing seizures at clinically useful doses (*J Psychopharmacol* 1987, **1**, 31–34). Seizures have occurred rarely in trials and no cause-effect relationship has been proven (Milne and Goa, *Drugs* 1991, **41**, 450–77). With **sertraline**, seizures occurred in early clinical trials at a similar frequency to placebo and only in people with a history of seizures (MI). **Citalopram** has not been reported to interact with anticonvulsants nor have a proconvulsive effect.

10. Seizures have been reported in 0.26% of patients treated with **venlafaxine** during clinical trials and so a slow introduction and withdrawal is recommended.

11. One grand mal seizure has been reported in a patient with a history of seizures receiving **mirtazapine** at a high dose of 80mg/d during a trial. More definite information would be needed before a cause-effect link could be made. Care and monitoring would thus be standard.

12. All **tricyclics** seem to lower the seizure threshold, with **amitriptyline** reputed to be the most proconvulsive and **doxepin** possibly of lowest risk. TDM of tricyclics minimises the risk of toxicity (review by Preskorn and Fast, *J Clin Psych* 1992, **53**, 160–62). There is a high incidence of CSM reports of convulsions with **maprotiline** (*Lancet* 1979, **ii**, 1368) plus some EEG abnormalities (*Am J Med Genetics* 1988, **31**, 369–73) and should be avoided. A slow rate of introduction reduces the risk (*Psychol Med* 1977, **7**, 265–70).

13.* There have been only rare reports of seizures with **nefazodone** (cause not confirmed) and the SPC naturally recommends use only with caution. The SPC for **trazodone** was recently changed to include care in epilepsy, and to avoid abrupt changes in dose.

14. **Reboxetine** may be particularly useful in epilepsy as the spontaneous incidence of seizures is <0.2% (n=1500), with no seizures (even minor) in overdose and minimal interaction potential.

15. **MAOIs** are generally not considered epileptogenic at therapeutic doses (Rabkin *et al*, *J Clin Psychopharmacol* 1984, **4**, 270–78). The adverse reactions of myoclonic jerks (Lieberman *et al*, *J Clin Psychopharmacol* 1985, **5**, 221–28) and serotonin syndrome can occasionally be interpreted as seizures.

16. There have been no reports of problems with **moclobemide** nor **tryptophan** in epilepsy to date. **Mianserin** is often quoted as being relatively safe in epilepsy (*B J Clin Pharmacol* 1983, **15**, 290S–311S). One study of 84 overdoses of 1g or more showed no convulsions (*Curr Med Res Opin* 1980, **6**, 44). Seizures have been reported at therapeutic doses of **amoxapine** although the UK SPC states that this only occurs outside the recommended dosage range.

### 3.4.3 Anxiolytics and hypnotics:

17. For **benzodiazepines**, see *1.17*.

18. Animal studies show **buspirone** to have no anticonvulsant activity. The UK SPC states buspirone to be contraindicated in epilepsy but there is no evidence yet that it is actually epileptogenic.

19. A weak anticonvulsant activity for **zopiclone** has been shown (*Pharmacol Biochem Behav* 1985, **23**, 653–59). **Zolpidem** is not reported to have any anticonvulsant activity. There is no data on **zaleplon**.

20. There are no apparent problems with the **beta-blockers**.

21. For **chloral** and **clomethiazole**, see *1.17.1* and *1.17.2*.

### 3.4.4 Others:

22.* Cholinomimetics may have some potential for causing seizures so care is needed with **donepezil** in pre-existing seizure activity (MI). Care should be exercised with the use of **rivastigmine** in patients predisposed to seizures (MI). There has been no increase in the incidence of convulsions with **galantamine** in clinical trials (SPC). A single case report with **memantine** suggests it should only be used with caution (SPC).

23. There are no problems reported with the **anticholinergic** agents.

24. The UK SPC for **disulfiram** recommends caution in epilepsy. The manufacturers report no known problems with **acamprosate** in epilepsy.

25. **Lithium** has a marked epileptogenic activity in overdose, but probably has no effect at standard dose. **Carbamazepine** and **valproate** may be suitable alternatives.

26. **Methylphenidate** is not associated with significant risk at therapeutic doses (mentioned in Zaccara *et al*, *Drug Saf* 1990, **5**, 109–51), but the UK SPC suggests caution. There are no apparent problems with **modafinil**.

27.* **Bupropion** has some epileptogenic activity (CSM warning: *Curr Prob Pharmacovig* 2001, **27**, 5). Doses should not exceed 450mg/d (although new-onset seizures can occur at therapeutic doses up to 450mg/d eg. Pesola and Avasarala, *J Emerg Med* 2002, **22**, 235–39), no single dose should be above 200mg and doses should not be increased at more than 150mg/d (MI). The risk of seizures is about 4 in 1000 and there appears to be correlation between plasma concentration and the risk for seizures. It should be contraindicated in people with a history of seizures and concurrent eating disorder, known CNS tumour and abruptly withdrawing from benzodiazepines or alcohol. Other risk factors include concomitant use with any drug known to lower seizure threshold, alcohol abuse, history of head trauma, diabetes treated with hypoglycaemics or insulin, and use of stimulants or anorectics.

## 3.5 GLAUCOMA (angle-closure)

| | Lower risk | Moderate risk | Higher risk |
|---|---|---|---|
| Antipsychotics | Butyrophenones[2]<br>Risperidone[3]<br>Sertindole[2]<br>Sulpiride[3]<br>Thioxanthenes[2] | Aripiprazole[2]<br>Clozapine[2]<br>Loxapine[2]<br>Phenothiazines[1]<br>Ziprasidone[2]<br>Zotepine[3] | Olanzapine[3] |
| Antidepressants | Flupentixol[5]<br>MAOIs[5]<br>Mirtazapine[5]<br>Moclobemide[5]<br>Nefazodone[5]<br>Trazodone[5]<br>Tryptophan[5]<br>Venlafaxine[5] | SSRIs[5] | Tricyclics[4] |
| Others | Acamprosate[6]<br>Benzodiazepines[6]<br>Caffeine[8]<br>Clomethiazole[6]<br>Disulfiram[6]<br>Gabapentin[6]<br>Lithium[6]<br>Lofexidine[6]<br>Memantine[10]<br>Naltrexone[6]<br>Phenobarbital[6]<br>Phenytoin[6]<br>Tiagabine[6]<br>Valproate[6]<br>Vigabatrin[6] | Carbamazepine[6]<br>Topiramate[6] | Anticholinergics[10]<br>Dexamfetamine[7]<br>Methylphenidate[9] |

Angle-closure glaucoma (short review, Khaw, *Prescribers' J* 1997, **37**, 34–39) occurs in eyes with a narrow anterior chamber angle, where drainage of the aqueous fluid through the anterior chamber angle is reduced or blocked. Drugs with anticholinergic properties have the potential to either induce angle-closure glaucoma or to worsen it. Although the degree of anticholinergic effect of a drug is of relevance, the individual's susceptibility to those effects is of greater importance.

**General advice**: Patients with shallow anterior chamber and/or narrow angles or with previously diagnosed glaucoma may be treated with drugs with anticholinergic properties **provided** intraocular pressure is monitored, an ophthalmologist is involved and information given on the symptoms of acute-angle closure, with advice to stop the drug and seek medical attention immediately should those symptoms occur. In a patient with a shallow anterior chamber and narrow angles an ophthalmologist would normally perform an iridotomy or some type of drainage surgery to allow drug use. Treatment with miotic therapy,

eg. pilocarpine may not necessarily protect the patient with narrow angles against drug-induced angle closure. Indeed, pilocarpine itself has been reported to rarely cause pupillary block (Zimmerman *et al, Ophthalmology* 1981, **88**, 85–88).

The main symptoms of acute angle-closure glaucoma are blurred vision, 'coloured haloes' around bright lights, intense pain, lacrimation, lid oedema, red eye, nausea and vomiting (review by Oshika, *Drug Safety* 1995, **12**, 256–63). The incidence rises with age due to the aging process, eg. thickening of the lens. The peak effect from a drug on intraocular pressure can occur within 5–24 hours (or sooner) (Lieberman and Stoudemire, *Psychosomatics* 1987, **28**, 145–48).

### 3.5.1 Antipsychotics:

1. **Phenothiazines** are weak anticholinergics so some potential for problems exists. Screening for glaucoma has been recommended before initiating therapy (Reid *et al, Int Pharmacopsych* 1976, **11**, 163–74), although several studies have shown no detectable angle-closure glaucoma in, eg.

100 patients taking thioridazine, 98 on fluphenazine and 99 on chlorpromazine (Applebaum, *Arch Ophthalmol* 1963, **69**, 578–80). Thus, there is need for routine care (see introduction). There are a few case reports of stat high-dose iv or im chlorpromazine producing a transient decrease in intraocular pressure (mentioned in review by Bristow and Hirsch, *Drug Safety* 1993, **8**, 136–48, 76 refs).

2.* Other antipsychotics with similar anticholinergic effects would include **clozapine, loxapine, flupentixol, zotepine** and **zuclopenthixol**. No information is available on **ziprasidone, aripiprazole** or **sertindole**.

3. Antipsychotics with little or no anticholinergic effect must still be considered to have a potential for problems, albeit probably at a low level, eg. **sulpiride, haloperidol** and **risperidone. Olanzapine**, is, however, contraindicated in angle-closure glaucoma in the UK.

### 3.5.2 Antidepressants:

4. **Tricyclics** have a greater anti-cholinergic effect than phenothiazines. If patients are at risk of angle-closure glaucoma, pre-treatment examination by an ophthalmologist is recommended. Patients with a narrow anterior chamber angle who are receiving glaucoma treatment or who have had laser treatment should have few problems provided care (see introduction) is taken (Oshika, *Drug Safety* 1995, **12**, 256–63). There is a report of four patients with narrow angles all developing acute-angle closure glaucoma with imipramine (Ritch *et al, Arch Ophthalmol* 1994, **112**, 67–68), with clomipramine, exacerbated by postural hypotension (Schlingemann *et al, Lancet* 1996, **347**, 465) and acute exacerbation with maprotiline in a woman already being treated for angle-closure glaucoma (Yamada and Higashi, *Jpn J Clin Ophthalmol* 1991, **45**, 953–55). A survey by Reid & Blouin (*Psychosomatics* 1976, **17**, 83–85) showed no abnormal intraocular pressures in patients taking tricyclics, even in combination with phenothiazines, but a postal survey of ophthalmologists and psychiatrists indicated that occasional, probably drug-induced, cases had been seen, most frequently associated with amitriptyline (review by Lieberman and Stoudemire, *Psychosomatics* 1987, **28**, 145–48). See general advice.

5.* Antidepressants which can cause dilation of the pupil include the **SSRIs, mirtazapine, moclobemide, trazodone, nefazodone** and **MAOIs**. There is a possible case with **fluoxetine** in a patient sensitive to anticholinergic effects and with a positive family history (Ahmad, *DICP Ann Pharmacother* 1991, 25, 436). Acute angle-closure glaucoma associated with **paroxetine** has been reported (n=7, Eke and Bates, *BMJ* 1997, **314**, 1387), as has aggravation of narrow-angle glaucoma by fluvoxamine (n=1, Jimenez-Jimenez *et al, Ann Pharmacother* 2001, **35**, 1565–66). There is limited experience with **reboxetine** but the SPC recommends close supervision. Raised intraocular pressure or narrow-angle glaucoma is a **venlafaxine** UK SPC warning and bilateral acute angle-closure glaucoma developing rapidly with venlafaxine has been reported (n=1, Ng *et al, Med J Aust* 2002, **176**, 241).

### 3.5.3 Others:

6.* There are no reported problems with any of the **mood stabilisers, anxiolytics, hypnotics** or **anticonvulsants**, except topiramate, where secondary angle-closure glaucoma occurring within a month of treatment starting have led to a CSM warning, so care and advice needed (*Curr Probs* 2002, **28**, 4).

7. **Amfetamine** causes a transient rise in intraocular pressure but which is not associated with closure of the angle.

8.* **Caffeine** has been reported to cause a transient rise in intraocular pressure but which is not associated with closure of the angle. Average daily intakes of >180mg/d caffeine (not a lot) may cause a clinically significant elevation of intraocular pressure (n=28, Avisar *et al*, *Ann Pharmacother* 2002, **36**, 992–95).

9. **Methylphenidate** causes a transient rise in intraocular pressure but which is not associated with closure of the angle. There is a single case of uneventful use of methylphenidate in a 55-year-old male with ADHD and primary open-angle glaucoma well-controlled by pilocarpine and betaxolol (Bartlik *et al*, *Arch Gen Psych* 1997, **54**, 188–89).

10.* **Anticholinergics** are contraindicated in angle-closure glaucoma. Glaucoma is not mentioned in the SPC for **memantine**.

## 3.6 LIVER DISEASE

| | Lower risk | Moderate risk | Higher risk |
|---|---|---|---|
| Antipsychotics | Amisulpride[5]<br>Aripiprazole[2]<br>Flupentixol[4]<br>Haloperidol[6]<br>Pimozide[8]<br>Sulpiride[5]<br>Ziprasidone[2]<br>Zuclopenthixol[4] | Clozapine[3]<br>Loxapine[8]<br>Olanzapine[2]<br>Phenothiazines[7]<br>Quetiapine[2]<br>Risperidone[1]<br>Sertindole[2] | Zotepine[2] |
| Antidepressants | Mianserin[16]<br>Paroxetine[9]<br>Tryptophan[16] | Mirtazapine[11]<br>Moclobemide[16]<br>Reboxetine[14]<br>SSRIs[9]<br>St John's wort[16]<br>Trazodone[13]<br>Tricyclics[12]<br>Venlafaxine[10] | Lofepramine[12]<br>MAOIs[15]<br>Nefazodone[13] |
| Anxiolytics and hypnotics | Lorazepam LD[17]<br>Oxazepam LD[17]<br>Temazepam LD[17] | Buspirone[18]<br>Clomethiazole[21]<br>Propranolol LD[20]<br>Zaleplon[19]<br>Zolpidem[19]<br>Zopiclone[19] | Benzodiazepines (esp LA)[17]<br>Chloral[21]<br>Propranolol HD[20] |
| Anticonvulsants | Carbamazepine[22]<br>Ethosuximide[28]<br>Gabapentin[26]<br>Topiramate?[27]<br>Vigabatrin[27] | Acetazolamide[28]<br>Benzodiazepine[17]<br>Lamotrigine[27]<br>Levetiracetam[27]<br>Oxcarbazepine[22]<br>Paraldehyde[28]<br>Tiagabine[27] | Barbiturates[25]<br>Phenytoin[24]<br>Valproate[23] |
| Others | Donepezil[29]<br>Lithium[32]<br>Memantine[29] | Acamprosate[31]<br>Anticholinergics[30]<br>Bupropion[35]<br>Disulfiram[31]<br>Galantamine[29]<br>Methylphenidate[34]<br>Modafinil[33]<br>Rivastigmine[29] | |

LD = low dose.
HD = high dose.
SA = short-acting.
LA = long-acting.

**General Principals** (adapted from *Maudsley Guidelines*)

1. The greater the degree of hepatic impairment, the greater the degree of impaired drug metabolism, the greater the risk of drug toxicity, the lower should be the starting and final dose. People may be more sensitive to common or predictable side-effects.

2. Start low, go slow, monitor LFTs regularly (eg. weekly).

3. LFTs do not necessarily correlate well with metabolic impairment, although give a reasonable indication.

4. Care is needed with drugs with a high first-pass clearance effect.

5. In severe liver disease, avoid drugs with marked side-effects of sedation and constipation.

### 3.6.1 Antipsychotics:

1. Unbound **risperidone** increases in liver disease and so initial doses and dose increments should be halved in patients with liver impairment (SPC), and 4mg/d not exceeded. Risperidone-induced jaundice has been reported (n=1, Oyewole *et al, Int J Ger Psych* 1996. **11**, 179), as has rapid onset hepatotoxicity (Phillips *et al, Ann Pharmacother* 1998, **32**, 843).

2.* A lower **olanzapine** starting dose of 5mg/d may be appropriate (MI). Transient, asymptomatic elevations in ALT and AST have been noted and monitoring of these in patients with risk factors (eg. hepatic impairment, concomitant hepatotoxic drugs) may be appropriate. A single-dose study with **quetiapine** showed some reduced clearance so the starting dose should be 25mg/d, with dose increments of 25–50mg/d (eg. Thyrum *et al, PNBP* 2000, **24**, 521–33). **Zotepine** levels may be 2–3 times higher with liver impairment, so start at 25mg bd up to a maximum of 75mg bd and measure LFTs weekly for the first three months (MI). **Ziprasidone** is extensively metabolised and extended half-life has been shown in Child-Pugh Class A and B, but dose adjustment is not necessary in mild-to-moderate impairment (n=30, open, Everson *et al, B J Clin Pharmacol* 2000, **49**(S3), 21–26). No changes in dose with **aripiprazole** seem necessary with mild, moderate or severe hepatic impairment. Hepatic clearance of **sertindole** is reduced by a half in hepatic impairment so use slower titration and lower maintenance doses and monitor closely. Sertindole is contraindicated in severe hepatic failure.

3. Severe hepatic disease is a contraindication for **clozapine**, and so lower doses and regular plasma level monitoring would be necessary if used. There are reported cases of toxic hepatitis, with AST levels dramatically raised, an eosinophilia developing early and full LFT normalisation within 4–5 weeks of stopping (eg. Thatcher *et al, Am J Psych* 1995, **152**, 296–97).

4. No dosage adjustments are necessary for **flupentixol** nor **zuclopenthixol**, although both undergo hepatic metabolism and so some caution would be wise in significant hepatic impairment.

5. **Sulpiride** and **amisulpride** are virtually unmetabolised with little or no bilary excretion. There is a low incidence of liver toxicity reported, with a transient rise in serum transaminase the only reported effect. Dosage adjustments are thus unnecessary (SPC).

6. There are no apparent problems with **haloperidol**, although the UK SPC states liver disease to be a caution.

7. **Phenothiazines** may cause hepatocanalicular cholestasis and there have been suggestions of possible immunological liver damage. Onset is usually during the first month of therapy. Coma may be precipitated due to increased cerebral neurone sensitivity. **Chlorpromazine** is particularly hepatotoxic.

8. **Loxapine** is extensively metabolised so use in severe liver disease is likely to be a higher risk, although no specific problems have been reported.

### 3.6.2 Antidepressants:

9.* **Citalopram** and **escitalopram** are metabolised extensively by the liver, with three major metabolites. Doses at the lower end of the therapeutic range should be used (n=1000, Milne and Goa, *Drugs* 1991, **41**, 450–77), although no liver enzyme abnormalities were noted. In hepatic impairment, alternate day-dosing of **fluoxetine** is recommended. Cirrhotic patients show higher plasma levels of fluoxetine and norfluoxetine and lengthened half-lives, and a 50% reduction in dose is recommended, especially if a low albumin is present. **Fluvoxamine** should be started at

50mg/d and monitored carefully, as raised hepatic enzymes have been reported. **Paroxetine** appears to be the safest option, using doses at the lower end of the therapeutic range, although cases of hepatitis (Benbow and Gill, *BMJ* 1997, **314**, 1387) and hepatotoxicity have been reported (n=3, Azaz-Livshits *et al, Pharmacopsychiatry* 2002, **35**, 112–15). **Sertraline** is extensively metabolised by the liver and there is contraindicated in significant hepatic dysfunction. One study has shown a 2.5-fold increase in half-life and a 1.6-fold increase in sertraline/desmethylsertraline peak levels in 10 patients with stable chronic cirrhosis (cf 10 controls, Demolis *et al, Br J Clin Pharmacol* 1996, **42**, 394–97).

10. **Venlafaxine** clearance is reduced by about 35% in mild to moderate hepatic impairment and so doses should be reduced by about 25–50% respectively, although there is much inter-patient variability (Anon, *J Clin Psych* 1993, **54**, 119–26). It is not recommended in severe hepatic impairment.

11. **Mirtazapine** clearance was reduced by 33% in moderate hepatic impairment in a single dose study (n=16, Murdoch *et al, B J Clin Pharmacol* 1993, **35**, 76P) and so dosage reduction may be necessary. Transient asymptomatic raised liver enzymes (eg. SGTP) have been noted in a few patients in early clinical trials.

12. Most **tricyclics** have a high first-pass clearance by the liver, and so lower starting doses are necessary. Increased sedation with tricyclics is likely due to decreased metabolism eg. **amitriptyline** has been reported to have doubled or tripled plasma levels in patients with cirrhosis and should be avoided. Increased blood levels may also occur with reduced plasma protein binding if albumin levels are lower, as with many tricyclics protein binding is high. Particular care is obviously needed if albumin levels are low. SSRIs such as paroxetine would appear to be easier to use than tricyclics in liver disease. Cholestatic jaundice has occasionally been noted with tricyclics. **Lofepramine** is contraindicated.

13.* **Nefazodone** is associated with a high incidence of hepatic adverse reactions (Garcia-Pando *et al, J Clin Psych* 2002, **63**, 135–37) eg. severe liver failure (n=3, Aranda-Michel *et al, Ann Int Med* 1999, **130**, 285–88). The FDA have required a warning that "cases of life-threatening hepatic failure have been reported in patients", with an estimated incidence of 1 in 250 K to 300 K. Nefazodone has been discontinued in Europe, but remains in the USA. It should thus not be initiated in people with active liver disease or elevated baseline serum transaminases, and withdrawn if signs of liver injury occur. **Trazodone** should be used with care in severe hepatic impairment, as hepatoxicity has been reported (n=1, Rettman and McClintock, *Ann Pharmacother* 2001, **35**, 1559–61).

14. **Reboxetine** half-life and plasma levels appear to rise in severe hepatic insufficiency and dose adjustment may be necessary. A starting dose of 2mg bd is recommended (n=12, Tran *et al, Clin Drug Invest* 2000, **19**, 473–77).

15. **MAOIs** are hepatotoxic and may precipitate coma. Patients may also be more sensitive to side-effects. If essential, start with a low dose, increase gradually and observe carefully. **Isocarboxazid** is contraindicated with any degree of impaired hepatic function.

16.* **Moclobemide** clearance can be reduced and half-life increased in cirrhosis and so doses should be reduced by a half or third to avoid accumulation (Stoeckel *et al, Acta Psych Scand* 1990, **360**[Suppl], 94–97). There are no apparent problems with **mianserin** and **tryptophan**. **St John's wort** levels may rise in moderate liver cirrhosis and absorption is decreased in mild cirrhosis (n=16, Johne *et al, Clin Pharmacol Ther* 2002, **71**, P95).

### 3.6.4 Anxiolytics and hypnotics:

17. The metabolism of **diazepam** and **chlordiazepoxide** is impaired in liver disease. The half-lives of the metabolites desmethylchlordiazepoxide and demoxepam are reported to be prolonged to up to 346hrs and 150hrs respectively (n=1, Barton *et al, Med Tox Adv Drug Exp* 1989, **4**, 73–76) and may be detectable two months after stopping treatment in patients with hepatic encephalopathy (Meier *et al, Gastroenterology*, 1991, **101**, 274–75) and which may induce coma. Impaired metabolism has been reported with **alprazolam, clobazam** and **midazolam** (significantly impaired in cirrhosis, as it is metabolised by at least 3 different P450 enzymes, Wandel *et al, B J Anaesthesia* 1994, **73**, 658–61). The metabolism of **lorazepam, temazepam** and **oxazepam** is unchanged and in low dose are probably the benzodiazepines of choice (reviewed by Peppers, *Pharmacotherapy* 1996, **16**, 49–58).

18. **Buspirone** plasma levels are higher in patients with hepatic failure, with a good correlation between steady-state buspirone levels and serum albumin (open, Barbhaiya *et al, E J Clin Pharmacol* 1994, **46**, 41–47). Caution is recommended with a history of hepatic impairment and it should not used in severe hepatic disease.

19. Elimination of **zopiclone** can be reduced with hepatic dysfunction producing enhanced adverse effects (n=17, open, Parker and Roberts, *B J Clin Pharmac* 1983, **16**, 259). A lower dose of 3.75mg to 7.5mg (but no higher) can be used with caution in hepatic disease. Plasma protein binding of **zolpidem** is reduced in hepatic impairment (n=42, open, Pacifici, *Int J Clin Pharmacol Ther Toxicol* 1988, **26**, 439–43) and so is contraindicated in severe hepatic insufficiency. Reduced doses are recommended in cirrhosis and other hepatic impairment (where half-life may rise to 10 hours) and peak plasma concentra-

tions. Hepatoxicity has been reported (n=1, Karsenti *et al, BMJ* 1999, **318**, 1179). **Zaleplon** is contraindicated in severe hepatic insufficiency and the dose reduced to 5mg in mild to moderate hepatic impairment.

20. The metabolism of **propranolol** is impaired in decompensated liver disease and by portal systemic shunting. High doses are potentially toxic and so reduced oral doses are needed. Propranolol may increase the risk of developing hepatic encephalopathy.

21. Due to increased availability and reduced clearance, higher blood levels of **clomethiazole** occur in severe liver disease (perhaps a ten-fold increase) and so reduced oral doses are needed, eg. a third of normal and sedation can mask the onset of liver coma. **Chloral** is contraindicated in marked hepatic impairment.

### 3.6.4 Anticonvulsants:

22. Serious problems with **carbamazepine** are rare, but jaundice, hepatitis and liver function disorders have been reported, and so use should be with caution. Although **oxcarbazepine** is rapidly and extensively metabolised, no dose adjustments are generally needed in mild to moderate hepatic impairment it has not been studied in severe hepatic impairment (SPC).

23. **Valproate** is contraindicated in active liver disease, as it can be hepatotoxic and liver failure can occur in about 1 in 10,000 cases. The risk is higher early on in therapy and lessens after a couple of months (review by Eadie *et al, Med Tox* 1988, **3**, 85–106). Electron-microscopy shows lipid droplets and a scarcity of cytoplasmic cells and normal mitocondria (Caparros-Lefebvre *et al, Lancet* 1993, **341**, 1604). Hepatotoxicity occurs mostly in children and presents as worsening epilepsy, drowsiness and with biochemical and/or clinical evidence of liver failure. Some fatal cases have been reported. Care needs to be taken if valproate is used in children, especially if used with other anticonvulsants.

24. **Phenytoin** is highly protein bound and extensively metabolised and so accumulation and toxicity may occur in severe liver disease. Use reduced doses and monitor for toxicity. In uraemia, protein binding may be reduced but active/free levels remain unchanged so therapeutic control may be possible at plasma levels below the usual range. Severe cardio-vascular ADRs have been reported with **fosphenytoin** IV (see *3.2.4*) and a reduction in loading dose and/or infusion rate by 10–25% is recommended in hepatic impairment.

25. Increased cerebral sensitivity and the impaired metabolism of **barbiturates** may precipitate coma. Plasma albumin-binding may be reduced but this may have no clinical effect.

26.* **Gabapentin** is virtually unmetabolised and so dose adjustments are unnecessary. No adjustment to initial and maintenance doses of **lamotrigine** is necessary for Child-Pugh grade A cirrhosis but should be reduced by 50% in moderate (Child-Pugh grade B) hepatic impairment, and by 75% in severe (Child-Pugh grade C) impairment (n=36, Marcellin *et al, B J Clin Pharmacol* 2001, **51**, 410–14).

27. **Vigabatrin** can cause decreased LFT levels but there is no evidence of hepatic toxicity. **Topiramate** is not extensively metabolised and about 60% is excreted unchanged via the kidneys. In moderate-to-severe liver disease, clearance is reduced by about 26% although the resultant changes in plasma levels have been considered clinically insignificant by the manufacturers. **Tiagabine** is metabolised by the liver. Initial doses in mild to moderate hepatic impairment should be lower. Use in severe hepatic impairment is not recommended (n=13, open, 8/7, Lau *et al, Epilepsia* 1997, **38**, 445–51). No dose adjustment is needed with **levetiracetam** in mild to moderate hepatic impairment, but a 50% dose reduction is recommended in severe impairment due to concomitant renal impairment (see SPC).

28. There are no apparent problems with **ethosuximide**. **Acetazolamide** should be used with caution. **Paraldehyde** elimination is slowed in hepatic failure and so lower doses may be needed.

### 3.6.5 Others:

29.* No change in dose is necessary with **donepezil** in mild to moderate hepatic impairment (MI) and a 5mg single-dose study indicated that compromised hepatic function did not significantly alter the kinetics of donepezil (n=20, Tiseo *et al, B J Clin Pharmacol* 1998, **46**(Suppl 1), 51–55). **Rivastigmine** is contraindicated in severe liver impairment (MI). **Galantamine** is not affected by mild hepatic impairment (SPC) but clearance is reduced by 23% in moderate impairment and so care is necessary in moderate to severe impairment (n=25, open, Zhao *et al, J Clin Pharmacol* 2002, **42**, 428–36). Start with 4mg/d, increasing slowly to a maximum of 8mg bd. In severe (Child-Pugh >9) impairment, galantamine is contraindicated (due to current lack of safety data). There is no data for the use of **memantine** in hepatic impairment but since it is metabolised only to a minor extent to inactive metabolites, mild to moderate hepatic impairment is unlikely to have an significant effect.

30. The UK SPCs for the **anticholinergics** all urge some caution in hepatic disease.

31. The UK SPC for **disulfiram** recommends caution in liver disease. Although some evidence of further raised LFTs was noted, an open trial showed disulfiram was safe in patients with elevated LFTs and/or evidence of Hepatitis C virus, provided LFTs were monitored regularly (n=57, Saxon *et al, J Clin Psych* 1998, **59**, 313–16). The UK SPC for **acamprosate** states that use in severe hepatic failure (Child-Pugh grade C) is a contraindication but the pharmacokinetics are not altered by mild to moderate hepatic dysfunction.

32. There are no problems with **lithium** in liver disease.
33. The maximum **modafinil** dose of 400mg/d should only be used in the absence of hepatic impairment (MI).
34. There is no data on **methylphenidate**.
35. **Bupropion** is extensively metabolised and there are rare reports of abnormal LFTs, liver damage and hepatotoxicity, with some metabolite half-lives prolonged in cirrhosis. Reduced initial doses and close monitoring is required, as a prolonged half-life has been reported in hepatic failure (n=16, open, DeVane *et al*, *J Clin Psychopharmacol* 1990, **10**, 328–32).

## 3.7 OLD AGE

| | Lower risk | Moderate risk | Higher risk |
|---|---|---|---|
| Antipsychotics | Amisulpride[5]<br>Aripiprazole[2]<br>Risperidone?[1]<br>Sulpiride[5]<br>Ziprasidone[2] | Butyrophenones[6]<br>Loxapine[4]<br>Olanzapine?[2]<br>Phenothiazines[7]<br>Quetiapine[2]<br>Sertindole[2]<br>Thioxanthenes[4] | Clozapine[4]<br>Thioridazine[7]<br>Zotepine[2] |
| Antidepressants | Lofepramine[12]<br>Mirtazapine[11]<br>Moclobemide[16]<br>SSRIs[9]<br>Tryptophan[16]<br>Venlafaxine[10] | Flupentixol[4]<br>MAOIs[15]<br>Mianserin[16]<br>Nefazodone[13]<br>Nortriptyline[12]<br>Reboxetine[14]<br>Trazodone | Tricyclics (most)[12] |
| Anxiolytics & hypnotics | Alprazolam[17]<br>Buspirone[18]<br>Clobazam[17]<br>Lorazepam[17]<br>Oxazepam[17]<br>Oxprenolol[20]<br>Zaleplon[19]<br>Zopiclone[19] | Clomethiazole[21]<br>Flunitrazepam[17]<br>Flurazepam[17]<br>Propranolol[20]<br>Temazepam[17]<br>Zolpidem[19] | Benzodiazepines<br>long-acting[21] |
| Anticonvulsants[7] | Carbamazepine[22]<br>Clobazam[17]<br>Oxcarbazepine[22]<br>Tiagabine[27]<br>Topiramate?[27] | Barbiturates[25]<br>Clonazepam[17]<br>Gabapentin[26]<br>Lamotrigine[26]<br>Levetiracetam[27]<br>Piracetam?[27]<br>Valproate[23] | Acetazolamide[28]<br>Benzodiazepine (most)[17]<br>Fosphenytoin[24]<br>Paraldehyde[28]<br>Phenytoin[24]<br>Vigabatrin[27] |
| Others | Anticholinesterases[29]<br>Bupropion[35]<br>Memantine[29]<br>Modafinil[33] | Anticholinergics[29]<br>Lithium[32] | Acamprosate?[31]<br>Methylphenidate[34] |

In the elderly, drug absorption and distribution are altered, metabolism, cardiac output and renal perfusion are reduced and tissue sensitivity is usually increased.

**General Principals** (adapted from *Maudsley Guidelines*)

1. Increased sensitivity to drugs occurs due to age-related changes in pharmacokinetics (ADME and protein binding) and pharmacodynamics (neuronal changes, receptor binding etc). The over 70 s have about twice as many ADRs as under 50 s, eg. postural hypotension with antipsychotics, longer sedation with hypnotics, increased sensitivity to anticholinergic side-effects of drugs etc.

2. Hepatic changes (eg. reduced metabolism) and reduced renal clearance will affect many drugs.

3. The lowest effective dose should be used, so '**start low and go slow**', avoid polypharmacy (see below) and monitor effects (both positive and negative) regularly and frequently.

4. Avoid drugs with sedative and hypotensive effects, which can increase the under-rated risks of falls. A meta-analysis concluded that psychotropics are associated with a small increase in falls (Leipzig *et al*, *J Am Ger Soc* 1999, **47**, 30–39; reviewed by Shorr, *EBMH* 1999, **2**, 95).

5. Use drugs only when necessary, decide a treatment aim, keep therapy simple, use the smallest effective doses and discontinue gradually if no apparent benefit can be seen.

6. Most drugs are highly lipophilic and an increased fat to lean body mass ratio, in addition to decreased metabolism and excretion, means that half-lives usually increase.

7. Consider other factors, eg. potential poor compliance due to social

or physical reasons, or use of OTC medicines.

**Reviews**:* geriatric psychopharmacology (Zubenko and Sunderland, *Harvard Rev Psych* 2000, **7**, 311–33, 202 refs), anticholinergic side-effects (Mintzer and Burns, *J Royal Soc Med* 2000, **93**, 457–62, 37 refs).

### 3.7.1 Antipsychotics: *

Antipsychotics can relieve psychotic symptoms in older adults but pre-treatment assessment, repeated every 3–6 months, is recommended to detect common side effects such as postural hypotension, anticholinergic effects and Parkinsonism. Single daily doses are usually appropriate once stable (as indeed they are in younger adults). Doses should be reviewed regularly, and periodic reduction in dose (eg. by 10–25% every four weeks) for some patients may be indicated (Eimer, *Consult Pharm* 1992, **7**, 921–33). An article on atypicals in old age (Bouman and Pinner, *Adv Psych Treat* 2002, **8**, 49–58) reviewed clozapine (poorly tolerated, needs slow titration, may be an age-related increase in risk of agranulocytosis), risperidone (good evidence for treating behaviour and other symptoms of dementia, well tolerated, may cause EPS, but slow introduction and very low doses help), olanzapine (low incidence of EPS, some potential for anticholinergic effects) and quetiapine (lowest risk of EPS, so may be drug of choice in Parkinsons's disease and Lewy Body dementia).

**Reviews**: general (Sciolla and Jeste, *Int J Psych Clin Prac* 1998, **2**, S27–34, 55 refs), atypicals in elderly (Yiu-Chung *et al*, *Pharmacotherapy* 1999, **19**, 811–22; Jeste *et al*, *Am J Geriatr Psychiatry* 1999, **7**, 70–76; Bouman and Pinner, *Adv Psych Treat* 2002, **8**, 49–58).

1. **Risperidone** is partially metabolised to an active metabolite and so lower doses may be needed only if hepatic impairment is present (see *3.6.1*). Decreased clearance in the elderly may lengthen the half-life of risperidone, but the significance of this is not known (Cohen, *Pharma-*

*cotherapy* 1994, **14**, 253–65). The UK SPC now states that risperidone is well tolerated in the elderly when used with a starting dose of 0.5mg bd or lower and adjusted up to 2mg bd.

2.* Although not routinely recommended, a lower **olanzapine** starting dose of 5mg/d may be appropriate in some patients as the mean elimination half-life is 50% longer and clearance slightly reduced in healthy elderly patients. Blood pressure monitoring is recommended periodically and there may be a slightly higher risk of seizures in people over 65 (MI). Transient sedation and somnolence were more marked in the elderly in pre-marketing trials. A naturalistic study showed olanzapine well tolerated and superior to haloperidol for acute schizophrenia in elderly patients (n=20, RCT, open, Barak *et al*, *PNBP* 2002, **26**, 1199–202; review of use in psychosis in old age: Madhusoodanan *et al*, *Ann Clin Psych* 2001, **13**, 201–13). The mean clearance of **quetiapine** in elderly patients was 30–50% lower than healthy adults so the starting dose should be 25mg/d, with dose increments of 25–50mg/d and the final dose is likely to be less than in younger patients (Thyrum *et al*, *Psychopharmacol Bull* 1996, **32**, 524, abstract). Quetiapine may be well tolerated and clinically effective in elderly patients, with somnolence (32%), dizziness (13%) and postural hypotension (13%) the most common side-effects (n=151, open, 12/52, McManus *et al*, *J Clin Psych* 1999, **60**, 292–98). Orthostatic hypotension is more common in the elderly. **Zotepine** levels may be 2–3 times higher in elderly patients. Start at 25mg bd up to a maximum of 75mg bd for elderly patients. Age and gender does not influence the kinetics of **ziprasidone** (n=35, Wilner *et al*, *Br J Clin Pharmacol* 2000, **49**(Suppl.3), 15–20). No **aripiprazole** dose adjustments are necessary in the elderly. There is no difference in **sertindole** kinetics in young and elderly adults, but a slower dose titration and perhaps lower final doses may be needed if an increased sensitivity to alpha-blocking activity produces hypotension.

3. **Clozapine** may be safe, reasonably well-tolerated (with slower dose titration) and effective in the elderly (n=133, Barak *et al*, *Comp Psych* 1999, **40**, 320–25) at doses as low as 50–100mg, but as there may be an increased incidence of agranulocytosis, great care should be taken.

4. **Zuclopenthixol** and **flupentixol** should be used with caution in renal disease. Lower doses of flupentixol may be needed due to changed kinetics (review: Jann *et al*, *Clin Pharmacokinet* 1985, **10**, 315–33), and, as with other antipsychotics, the elderly suffer more side-effects (Balant-Gorgia and Balant, *Clin Pharmacokinet* 1987, **13**, 65–90).

5. Single doses of **amisulpride** are well tolerated and show a similar pharmacokinetic profile in healthy elderly and young subjects (n=20, open, Hamon-Vilcot *et al*, *Eur J Clin Pharmacol* 1998, **54**, 405–9).

6. For the **butyrophenones**, an increased severity of side-effects including oversedation, hypotension and respiratory depression may occur and so lower starting doses are indicated.

7. It is generally recommended that one half to one third the adult dose of **phenothiazines** should be used for elderly patients, who are more susceptible to Parkinsonian side-effects (n=120, open, Caligiuri *et al*, *J Clin Psychopharmacol* 1999, **19**, 322–28), and which are often then harder to manage. **Thioridazine** may cause orthostatic hypotension and QT prolongation and so should be avoided (open, Cohen and Sommer, *J Clin Psychopharmacol* 1988, **8**, 336–39). **Chlorpromazine**, except in very low dose, should be avoided **Levomepromazine** is not recommended for use in people over 50 unless the risk of hypotension has been assessed (MI).

8. Doses of **loxapine** of around 40mg/d have been used successfully in the elderly (n=26, open, 12/52, Branchey *et al*, *J Am Ger Soc* 1978, **26**, 263–67).

### 3.7.2 Antidepressants:

Depression increases mortality in the elderly with cardiac disease, so do not ignore, especially of long-standing and severe (n=652, Geerlings *et al*, *Psychol Med* 2002, **32**, 609–18). Heart failure is particularly marked in women with depression (n=2501, 14yrs, Williams *et al*, *Psychosom Med* 2002, **64**, 6–12). Drugs with anticholinergic side-effects may further harm an already compromised cholinergic system.

9.* SSRIs have obvious benefits in the elderly (fewer anticholinergic effects, a benign cardiovascular profile, ease of use and safety in overdose) but some unappreciated risks, including falls, hyponatraemia, weight loss, sexual dysfunction and drug interactions (review: Herrmann, *Can J Clin Pharmacol* 2000, **7**, 91–95). The half-life of **fluoxetine** appears not significantly different in the elderly (open, 7/7, Lemberger *et al*, *J Clin Psych* 1985, **46**, 14–19) and when compared to doxepin was as effective but produced less side-effects in the elderly (d/b, 6/52+open, 48/52, Feighner and Cohn, *J Clin Psych* 1985, **46**, 20–25). In an open study of 20 depressed and physically ill hospitalised elderly patients with multiple pathology and polypharmacy, fluoxetine was claimed to be a safe and effective antidepressant in this difficult to treat cohort (n=20, open, Evans and Lye, *J Clin Exp Gerontol* 1992, **14**, 297–307). No pharmacokinetic differences have been seen with **fluvoxamine** in the elderly and so no dose alterations are necessary (n=19, open, de Vries *et al*, *Ther Drug Monitor* 1992, **14**, 493–98). **Sertraline** clearance may be reduced by up to 40% and half-life increased by 40% in elderly volunteers, but this does not seem to warrant dosage adjustment (Warrington, *Int Clin Psychopharmacol* 1991,

6[Suppl 2], 11–21). A study of younger (18–45) and older (over 65) volunteers (n=22 for each group) showed a similar sertraline half-life (32–27 hours) in all groups except younger men, where the half-life was 22 hours (n=44, open, 30/7, Ronfeld *et al, Clin Pharmacokin* 1997, **32**[Suppl 1], 22–30). Initially, lower doses of 10mg are recommended for **paroxetine**, as blood levels with 20mg/d in the elderly can be similar to those of 30mg/d in younger people (n=21, open, 7/52, Lundmark *et al, Acta Psych Scand* 1989, **80**[Suppl 350], 76–80; review of paroxetine in old age Holliday and Plosker, *Drugs and Aging* 1993, **3**, 278–99). A prolonged **citalopram** half-life (up to 3.8 days) and raised steady-state plasma levels in the elderly may be due to reduced metabolism. Dose reduction (by up to 50%) has been suggested but normal adult doses have been used in some studies with no apparent problem (eg. n=96, d/b, 6/52, Bouchard *et al, Acta Psych Scand* 1987, **76**, 583–92). The manufacturers recommend a starting dose of 20mg/d in all patients. An initial dose of 5mg daily for the first two weeks of treatment is recommended for **escitalopram**. Depending on individual patient response, the dose may be increased to 10mg

10. **Venlafaxine** clearance is reduced by about 15% in the elderly, probably due to reduced renal function, but dosage adjustment is not generally considered necessary (Anon, *J Clin Psych* 1993, **54**, 119–26). Postural hypotension may be more common.

11.* **Mirtazapine** dosage is the same in the elderly as younger adults, although the manufacturers' recommend care with dosage increments eg. 15–45mg/d has equivalent efficacy to sub-therapeutic amitriptyline 30–90mg/d, but relatively fewer cardiac effects (n=115, d/b, Hoyberg *et al, Acta Psych Scand* 1996, **93**, 184–90). It is slightly quicker acting and better tolerated than paroxetine in elderly depressed patients (n=255, RCT,

d/b, 8 + 16/52, Schatzberg *et al, Am J Ger Psych* 2002, **10**, 541–50).

12.* Reduced initial doses of **tricyclics** are recommended, with perhaps slightly lower final doses, depending upon tolerance, as cognitive and central effects are enhanced in the elderly. Higher serum levels occur with standard doses (reviewed by Hicks *et al, J Clin Psych* 1981, **42**, 374–85) with reduced clearance and doubled half-life shown with **imipramine** (open, Benetello *et al, Int J Clin Pharmaco Res* 1990, **10**, 191–95). Single night-time doses of **dothiepin/ dosulepin** have been used in the elderly with no increase in side-effects (n=50, s/b, 4/52, Khan, *J Int Med Res* 1981, **9**, 108–12). Elderly patients may respond to lower doses of **lofepramine** but in depressed elderly in-patients, low dose lofepramine (70mg/d) appears no better than placebo, indicating that full, or at least higher, doses are necessary (n=63. 4/52, Tan *et al, B J Clin Pharmacol* 1994, **37**, 321–24). **Nortriptyline** kinetics appear the same in the elderly as the young (Katz *et al, Neuropsychopharmacology* 1989, **2**, 229–36) although individual variation is high and the elderly may respond to lower doses (Kanba *et al, PNBP* 1992, **16**, 301–9). ECG changes may occur so care is needed in cardiovascular disease. **Clomipramine** was as well-tolerated in patients 56–70 years as <56 yrs, although postural hypotension was more common (n=150, Stage *et al, Acta Psych Scand* 2002, **105**, 55–59). Anticholinergic side-effects are also more common. It has been noted that when tricyclic non-response has occurred in an elderly person, response to an alternative antidepressant, eg. MAOI etc may take up to 5–6 weeks, rather than the 3–4 weeks normally expected (Flint and Rifat, *J Aff Dis* 1996, **36**, 95–105) so do not give up too soon.

13. Single daily dosing of **trazodone** may not be appropriate in the elderly, and reduced doses may be appropriate, eg. one study showed 150mg/d to

be the optimum in the elderly (n=20, d/b, Mukherjee and Davey, *J Int Med Res* 1986, **14**, 279–84). Half-life is increased in elderly men, but not women (n=43, open, Greenblatt *et al*, *Clin Pharmacol Ther* 1987, **42**, 193–200). Increased plasma concentrations of **nefazodone** can occur, but may not have a significant effect (n=12, d/b, c/o, van Laar *et al*, *J Clin Psychopharmacol* 1995, **15**, 30–40).

14.* The incidence of side-effects with **reboxetine** is no greater in the elderly than in younger people, although the half-life is doubled in the elderly (Holm and Spencer, *CNS Drugs* 1999, **12**, 65–83) and so the starting dose should probably be 2mg bd as peak plasma levels are also over twice that in younger people (n=12, Bergmann *et al*, *Eur J Drug Metab Pharmacokinet* 2000, **25**, 195–98). A delayed lowering of potassium levels has been reported (SPC) and some treatment-emergent tachycardia (SPC). Frail elderly may need dose reductions. The UK SPC had the recommendation for use in the elderly removed in November 1997, for lack of positive information rather than the presence of negative information.

15. Although **MAOIs** are often considered as more toxic to the elderly, mainly due to postural hypotension and dizziness, they can be highly effective in resistant depression in the elderly (review by Volz and Gleiter, *Drugs & Aging* 1998, **13**, 341–55).

16. **Moclobemide** is considered to be safe, effective and having a seemingly beneficial effect on cognitive functions (use in the elderly reviewed by Nair *et al*, *Acta Psych Scand* 1995, **91** [Suppl 386], 28–35) and a trial in elderly depressed and/or demented patients showed it to cause no cognitive impairment, if not a slight improvement (n=694, d/b, p/c, Roth *et al*, *B J Psych* 1996, **168**, 149–57). **Mianserin** elimination is highly variable and often prolonged in the elderly (n=27, open, Begg *et al*, *B J*

*Clin Pharmacol* 1989, **27**, 445–51). Doses may need to be adjusted, although reduced receptor sensitivity may not necessarily lead to increased side-effects. There are no apparent problems with **tryptophan**.

### 3.7.3 Anxiolytics and hypnotics:

**Reviews**: hypnotics in the elderly (Woodward, *CNS Drugs* 1999, **11**, 263–79), sleep in the elderly (Asplund, *Drugs & Aging* 1999, **14**, 91–103).

17.* All **benzodiazepines** should be used with care in the elderly, as side-effects are likely to be enhanced. Half-lives are generally lengthened, sometimes only in men, although there is considerable interpatient variability. Enhanced side effects include sedation, disturbances in gait, daytime drowsiness, cognitive impairment, hypotension, memory impairment and reduced psychomotor performance. Prolonged half-lives in the elderly have been reported with **clonazepam** (Court and Kase, *J Neurol Neurosurg Psych* 1976, **39**, 297), **clobazam** and **alprazolam** (Greenblatt *et al*, *B J Clin Pharmac* 1981, **12**, 631–36), **flunitrazepam** (Davis and Cook, *Clin Pharmacokinet* 1986, **11**, 18–35), **nitrazepam**, **flurazepam**, **temazepam** (Ford, *B J Clin Pharmacol* 1990, **29**, 61–67), **chlordiazepoxide** and **clorazepate** (Ochs *et al*, *Clin Pharmacol Ther* 1987, **41**, 562–70), **diazepam** (Pomara *et al*, *J Clin Psych* 1985, **46**, 185–87) and **midazolam** (n=18, Albrecht *et al*, *Clin Pharmacol & Therap* 1999, **65**, 630–39). Normal adult doses of **oxazepam** can be used as there are apparently no clinically significant pharmacokinetic changes in the elderly (Dreyfuss *et al*, *J Clin Psych* 1986, **47**, 511–14; Salzman *et al*, *Arch Gen Psych* 1983, **40**, 293–97). If used as a hypnotic, **lorazepam** doses should probably be slightly reduced. **Loprazolam** appears well tolerated in the elderly, with a half-life similar to young adults, although peak levels are prolonged (n=12, Dorling and

Hindmarsh, *Drugs Exp Clin Res* 2001, **27**, 151–59).

18. There do not appear to be any significant changes in the pharmacokinetics of **buspirone** in the elderly and so dose adjustments are not considered necessary (n=48, open, Gammans *et al*, *J Clin Pharmacol* 1989, **29**, 72–78).

19.* Normal adult doses of **zopiclone** can be used (Goa and Heel, *Drugs* 1986, **32**, 48–65). In elderly people, **zolpidem** at 5mg is an effective hypnotic dose (n=40, Olubodun *et al*, *Clin Pharmacol Ther* 2002, **71**, P3) with no consistent memory or performance effects nor daytime drowsiness, with doses of 10mg or above reducing REM sleep slightly (n=30, Scharf *et al*, *J Clin Psych* 1991, **52**, 77–83). Another study showed similar efficacy and lack of adverse effects in an elderly population (n=221, Roger and Attali, *Clin Therap* 1993, **15**, 127–36). There appears to be no problem with **zaleplon** in the elderly.

20. Increased **propranolol** side-effects have been reported in the elderly and so reduced initial doses are generally recommended, unlike **oxprenolol** where dose reduction is not considered necessary.

21. **Clomethiazole** doses should be reduced, as the half-life can be at least doubled and plasma levels up to five times normal can occur (Dehlin, *Acta Psych Scand* 1986, **73**[Suppl 329], 112–15).

### 3.7.4 Anticonvulsants:

For **anticonvulsants**, it is best to avoid renally excreted drugs (eg. **vigabatrin** and **gabapentin**) as, for example, the renal excretion of vigabatrin may be reduced in the elderly to one sixth compared with younger people. Hepatically metabolised drugs, eg. **carbamazepine** and **lamotrigine** are not influenced by age, rather by genetic factors and are to be preferred.

**Reviews**:* management of epilepsy in old age (Stephen and Brodie, *Lancet* 2000, **355**, 1441–46; Bourdet *et al*, *J Am Pharm Assoc (Wash)* 2001, **41**,

421–36; Lackner, *Pharmacother* 2002, **22**, 329–64, 301 refs).

22. No significant changes have been shown with **carbamazepine** in the elderly (eg. n=10, Read *et al*, *Seizure* 1998, **7**, 159–62) and so doses are likely to be the same, although the elderly may be more susceptible to cardiac arrhythmias associated with carbamazepine (Richens, *Pharm J* 1993, **251**, 50). Although the AUC with **oxcarbazepine** may be 30–60% higher in the elderly, no dose recommendations exist, other than gradual dose titration (n=48, van Heiningen *et al*, *Clin Pharmacol Ther* 1991, **50**, 410–19), and any dose adjustment recommended if the patient has compromised renal function (SPC).

23. The half-life of **valproate** may be doubled in old age, possibly via reduced metabolism (n=13, open, Bryson *et al*, *B J Clin Pharmacol* 1983, **16**, 104–5) but total blood levels are similar to younger adults (n=12, open, 5/7, Bauer *et al*, *Clin Pharmacol Ther* 1985, **37**, 697–700). A naturalistic retrospective study of valproate in elderly patients showed a 62% response rate, no LFT abnormalities and was well tolerated (n=35, retrospective, Kando *et al*, *J Clin Psych* 1996, **57**, 238–40). The proportion of free drug may be increased via reduced protein binding but, overall, the effect is likely to be of low significance. Compared to younger adults, valproate for mania may have a different therapeutic window (65–90mcg/mL) in the elderly (n=59, retrospective, Chen *et al*, *J Clin Psych* 1999, **60**, 181–86).

24. Reduced doses of **phenytoin** may be needed with the elderly. Careful monitoring is necessary, especially in those with hypoalbuminaemia or renal disease as these may have an increased level of side-effects and toxicity (Hayes *et al*, *B J Clin Pharmacol* 1975, **2**, 73–79), including cardiac arrhythmias. In people aged from 60 to 80, doses 20% lower will maintain blood levels, compared to younger adults (n=92, open, Bauer

and Blouin, *Clin Pharmacol* 1982, **31**, 301–4). It may be that reduced doses are only needed with monotherapy, as opposed to anticonvulsant polypharmacy (review by Bachmann and Belloto, *Drugs & Aging* 1999, **15**, 235–50). Severe cardiovascular ADRs have been reported with **fosphenytoin** IV (see *3.2*), and a reduction in the loading dose and/or infusion rate by 10–25% in the elderly is recommended.

25. The half-lives of **phenobarbital** and **primidone** are longer in the elderly due to reduced metabolism and so reduced doses should be used (reviewed by Hicks *et al*, *J Clin Psych* 1981, **42**, 374–85).

26.* **Lamotrigine** is hepatically metabolised and this is influenced by genetic factors rather than by age. An increased volume of distribution in the elderly has been shown to increase the half-life of lamotrigine thus increasing the chance of side-effects, and so reduced doses may be needed. One study, however, showed that the half-life does not appear to be increased in the elderly (Betts, *Seizure* 1992, **1**, 3–6). **Gabapentin** clearance is reduced in old age, probably via reduced renal clearance (Boyd *et al*, *Pharm Res* 1990, **7**[Suppl], S215), although it seems to cause less cognitive impairment than carbamazepine in healthy senior adults (n=34, RCT, c/o, Martin *et al*, *Epilepsia* 2001, **42**, 764–71).

27. **Vigabatrin** is renally excreted and this may be reduced in the elderly to one sixth compared to younger people. Reduced doses have been recommended in people with a creatinine clearance of less than 60ml/min (Grant and Heel, *Drugs* 1991, **41**, 889–926) and some have recommended that it should be avoided in the elderly (eg. Richens, *Pharm J* 1993, **251**, 50). No age-related changes in pharmacokinetics have been detected with **topiramate**. The half-life of **piracetam** is extended in the elderly (n=10, open, Platt *et al*, *Arzneimittel Forschung* 1985, **35**, 533–

35). There is no need to adjust the dose of **tiagabine** on the basis of age, although slightly higher plasma levels may occur in the elderly (n=24, Snel *et al*, *J Clin Pharmacol* 1997, **37**, 1015–20). Since renal impairment may occur, reduced doses of **levetiracetam** are recommended (see renal), as the half-life may increase by about 40%.

28. Lower **acetazolamide** doses are indicated (n=12, open, Chapron *et al*, *J Clin Pharmacol* 1989, **29**, 348–53). Deaths have been reported in debilitated patients given only 8ml **paraldehyde** and so use should be with utmost caution (Baratham and Tinckler, *Med J Aust*, 1964, **51**, 877).

### 3.7.5 Others:

29.* There are no specific problems with **donepezil** and **rivastigmine**, provided the dose titration guidelines are followed. **Galantamine** levels are about 30–40% higher in elderly patients than healthy young individuals. **Memantine** has a usual maximum dose of 20mg/d.

30. Confusion can be induced in the elderly by further compromising brain cholinergic activity. An initial low dose is thus usually recommended for **benzhexol** (trihexyphenidyl) and **orphenadrine**. Clearance of **procyclidine** may be reduced in the elderly and so twice daily dosing may be more appropriate than thrice daily dosing (n=6, RCT, p/c, Whiteman *et al*, *Eur J Clin Pharmacol* 1985, **28**, 73–78).

31. The UK SPC for **acamprosate** states that it should not be used in the elderly, due more to lack of data rather than specific reported problems.

32.* Reduced **lithium** clearance occurs in the elderly through reduced renal function and increased volume of distribution (review by Sproule *et al*, *Drugs Aging* 2000, **16**, 165–77) so doses should be reduced by as much as 50% (Hardy *et al*, *J Clin Psychopharmacol* 1987, **7**, 153–58). The elderly may also develop symptoms of lithium toxicity at standard therapeutic blood levels (Nakra and Grossberg, *J Geriatr Drug Ther* 1987, **2**, 47–63). However, lithium can be safely used in the elderly if monitored closely and frequently and, just to prove it, a cross-sectional study in octogenarians showed that lithium can be well-tolerated provided serum levels, renal and thyroid function are monitored regularly (n=12, Fahy and Lawlor, *Int J Ger Psych* 2001, **16**, 1000–3). Hypothyroidism can also occur.

33. In the elderly, a **modafinil** starting dose of 100mg/d is recommended (MI).

34. There is no data for **methylphenidate**, but it has been used in depression in the elderly.

35. **Bupropion** appears well tolerated in the elderly, although some accumulation and greater side-effects might occur (Branconnier *et al*, *Psychopharmacol Bull* 1983, **19**, 658–62). There has been successful use for depression in elderly (n=100, RCT, Weihs *et al*, *J Clin Psych* 2000, **61**, 196–202).

## 3.8 PREGNANCY

| | Lower risk (FDA=A) | Moderate risk (FDA = B or C) | Higher risk (FDA = D or X) |
|---|---|---|---|
| Antipsychotics | | Aripiprazole[2]<br>Butyrophenones[6]<br>Clozapine[3]<br>Loxapine[8]<br>Olanzapine?[2]<br>Phenothiazines[7]<br>Quetiapine[2]<br>Risperidone[1]<br>Sertindole[2]<br>Sulpiride[5]<br>Thioxanthenes[4]<br>Ziprasdone[2] | Zotepine[2] |
| Antidepressants | Flupentixol?[4]<br>Tryptophan?[16] | MAOIs[15]<br>Mianserin[16]<br>Mirtazapine[11]<br>Moclobemide[16]<br>Nefazodone[13]<br>SSRIs[9]<br>St John's wort[16]<br>Trazodone[13]<br>Tricyclics[12]<br>Venlafaxine[10] | |
| Anxiolytics and hypnotics | | Beta-blockers[20]<br>Buspirone[18]<br>Chloral[21]<br>Clomethiazole[21]<br>Clonazepam[17]<br>Promethazine[21]<br>Zaleplon[19]<br>Zopiclone[19] | Alprazolam[17]<br>Chlordiazepoxide[17]<br>Lorazepam[17]<br>Oxazepam[17]<br>Temazepam[17]<br>Zolpidem[19] |
| Anticonvulsants[9] | | Acetazolamide[28]<br>Carbamazepine[22]<br>Clonazepam?[17]<br>Ethosuximide[28]<br>Gabapentin[25]<br>Lamotrigine[25]<br>Oxcarbazepine[22]<br>Paraldehyde[28]<br>Tiagabine[27] | Benzodiazepines[17]<br>Phenobarbital[25]<br>Phenytoin[24]<br>Topiramate[27]<br>Valproate[23]<br>Vigabatrin[27] |
| Others | | Anticholinergics[34]<br>Anticholinesterases[29]<br>Bupropion[35]<br>Dexamfetamine[42]<br>Disulfiram[38]<br>Lithium[36]<br>Memantine[2]<br>Methadone LD[35]<br>Methylphenidate[36] | Acamprosate[31]<br>Lithium[32]<br>Methadone HD[34]<br>Modafinil?[33] |

The FDA has established five categories to indicate a drugs potential for teratogenicity, and, where known, these classifications are noted in the text:

**A** – Controlled studies in women fail to show a risk in the first trimester and the risk of foetal harm seems remote.

**B** – *Either* animal tests do not show a risk but there are no human studies *or* animal studies show a risk but human studies have failed to show a risk to the fetus.

**C** – *Either* animal studies show teratogenic or embryocidal effects but there are no controlled studies in women *or* there are no studies in either animals or humans.

**D** – Definite evidence of a risk to the foetus exists but the benefits in certain circumstances (eg. life-threatening situations) may make use acceptable.

**X** – Foetal abnormalities have been shown in animals or humans or both and the risk outweighs any possible benefits.

Further information should be sought on individual drugs to balance the risk-benefit ratio in a particular individual patient. Such risk classification systems may not be a reliable source of information (Addis *et al*,

*Drug Safety* 2000, **23**, 245–53). For the record, spontaneous major or gross malformations (usually defined as incompatible with life or requiring surgical correction) occur in 2–3% of pregnancies and spontaneous abortions in about 10–20% of clinically recognised pregnancies. In the first trimester, teratogenicity is the main drug risk, in the 2–3rd, growth retardation and neurological damage may occur and after birth, drug withdrawal effects may occur. Although there are a few reports that pregnancy may protect against the risk of, eg. bipolar disorder, other papers show increased risk (reviewed by Viguera and Cohen, *Psychopharmacol Bull* 1998, **34**, 339–46).

In the UK, a National Teratology Information Service is available and would be delighted to give an answer your questions (0191–232–1525). NTIS carries out individual risk assessments for pregnant women exposed to drugs or chemicals and offers pre-conceptual advice, research and follow-up information.

**Reproductive toxicity** falls into five domains (Wisner *et al*, *Am J Psych* 2000, **157**, 1933–40, 44 refs):*

1. Intrauterine foetal death/miscarriage
2. Physical malformations
3. Growth impairment
4. Behavioural toxicity (post-birth)
5. Neonatal toxicity eg. withdrawal or direct adverse effects

**Assessing risk**: Recent retrospective studies are more useful pointers to risk than the length of time a drug has been on the market or anecdotal case reports.

**General Principals** (adapted from *Maudsley Guidelines*)

Planning for possible pregnancy provides time for informed decisions. In bipolar disorder, pregnancy and the postpartum periods can be considered as separate risk periods, and treatment plans may need to be different for each.

**Pre-conception:** *

1.* For planned conception, discuss the risks and benefits of discontinuing or continuing medication, eg. relapse, teratogenicity etc, the unpredictability of the pre-conceptual duration, and that no decision is risk-free. Avoiding all drugs during the first trimester is the ideal but risks relapse. Other options include continuing at the lowest possible dose (or switch to drug with shortest possible half-life) until a positive pregnancy test or to continue throughout pregnancy at lowest dose

2. Consider the risk of pregnancy even if not currently planned, eg. carry out a pregnancy test before starting teratogenic drugs in a woman of childbearing age. As up to 50% of pregnancies are unplanned, document the patient's birth control method, document potential risks for pregnancy exposure to drug(s), encourage proper nutrition, exercise and vitamin supplementation, note any other substances taken, eg. excess caffeine, alcohol, natural products etc and educate about the potential risks and inquire about any pregnancy plans and emphasise the need for pre-pregnancy consultation.

3. For drugs of known significant risk or where there is little data, consider switching to a lower-risk drug before conception.

**Pregnancy:**

1. Avoid all drugs during the first trimester if possible. The maximum teratogenic potential is from days 17–60 after conception, and decisions must balance the relative *vs* absolute risk.

2. Behavioural teratogenesis and subtle functional disturbances (eg. learning difficulties, neurological deficits, developmental delay etc), and an effect on labour and delivery may occur in the second and third trimesters.

3. Use the lowest possible (maintenance) dose and monitor effects (adverse and desired) carefully. Maintain a low threshold for reintroduction or dose increase.

4. In many cases, the risk of relapse (and subsequent higher dose drug use) will be higher than the risk of foetal damage.

5. Avoid polypharmacy, as synergistic teratogenicity can occur (up to 16% with multiple AEDs, n=172, Kaneko *et al*, *Epilepsia* 1988, **29**, 459–67).

6. The pharmacokinetics of drugs may change during pregnancy and so doses may need to be adjusted (see eg. lithium, tricyclics).

7. Discontinuation effects have been reported in the newborn (see benzodiazepines, tricyclics, SSRIs etc) and these psychotropics should, if possible, be gradually reduced or withdrawn over the weeks before delivery is due.

**Reviews:** * *Drugs in Pregnancy and Lactation: A Reference Guide to Fetal and Neonatal Risk*, by Briggs *et al*, Williams and Wilkins, Baltimore, MD; general (Koren *et al*, *NEJM* 1998, **338**, 1128–37, 95 refs; Craig and Sisodiya, *Prescriber* 2001, **12**, 30–36), mood stabilisers, atypicals and broad-spectrum psychotropics (Ernst and Goldberg, *J Clin Psych* 2002, **63**(Suppl 4), 42–55), pharmacokinetic changes during pregnancy and their clinical relevance to specific drugs (Loebstein *et al*, *Clin Pharmacokinet* 1997, **33**, 328–43), psychotropics in bipolar disorder (Viguera *et al*, *Can J Psych* 2002, **47**, 426–36).

---

### 3.8.1 Antipsychotics: *

Low folate intake and low serum folate levels have been shown in women taking atypicals, increasing the risk of neural tube defects (Koren *et al*, *Am J Psych* 2002, **159**, 136–37) and so dietary advice or folate supplements preconception would be useful.

**Reviews:** Trixler and Tenyi (*Drug Safety* 1997, **16**, 403–10, 67 refs) and Pinkofsky (*Ann Clin Psychiatry* 1997, **9**, 175–79).

1. **Risperidone** (FDA=C) has no reported teratogenicity in animal tests.

2.* From 23 documented pregnancies with **olanzapine** (FDC=C), 5% were premature, spontaneous abortion occurred in 13% and stillbirth in 5%, but with no major malformations. All these were reported as being within

normal ranges (n=23, Goldstein *et al*, *J Clin Psychopharmacol* 2000, **20**, 399–403). Use should only be when the potential benefit outweighs the potential risk (MI). No teratogenic effects have been seen in animal studies nor in anecdotal case reports (n=2, Malek-Ahmadi, *Ann Pharmacother* 2001, **35**, 1294–95; n=1, Mendhekar *et al*, *Pharmacopsychiatry* 2002, **35**, 122–23). The **quetiapine** (FDA=C) SPC recommends using only if the benefits justify the risk. One case of 400mg/d throughout pregancy was without complications and with normal development at 6/12 (n=1, Tényi *et al*, *Am J Psych* 2002, **159**, 674). **Zotepine** crosses the placenta and although there are no indications of teratogenicity (Fukuhara *et al*, *Arzneimittelforschung* 1979, **29**, 1600-6), there is insufficient data in humans and the drug is contraindicated in pregnancy. There are no adequate human studies during pregnancy with **ziprasidone** (FDA=C), nor during labour and delivery, nor on **aripiprazole** (FDA=C), although animal studies have been unremarkable. No teratogenic activity has been shown by **sertindole**, but some potential effects on weight gain and delayed development have been suggested. Sertindole is contraindicated in pregnancy.

3. Women are more likely to conceive on **clozapine** (FDA=B) than most other antipsychotics due to an absence of raised prolactin. In the close study of one patient, there was clear accumulation of clozapine in the infant, possibly due to higher albumin concentrations (Barnas, *Am J Psych* 1994, **151**, 945). Of 84 reports of pregnancy with clozapine with known outcomes, there were 51 births, 7 miscarriages and 14 elective terminations, of which one was due to known abnormalities (patient taking clozapine 25mg/d plus lithium). Of the 51 births, 43 were born healthy and normal and 8 had abnormalities, ranging from low glucose levels through to malformations. Clozapine

is known to pass the placental barrier in animals and is assumed to do so in humans. Novartis has full details and should be approached before decisions about use in pregnancy are taken. No clear conclusion can be drawn from this, although combined with animal studies it would appear clozapine is not a major teratogen, but not recommended as such.

4. **Thioxanthenes**: (no FDA classification as not available in US).
**Flupentixol** passes across the placenta and foetal levels are about a quarter of the mother's (n=5, open, Kirk and Jorgensen, *Psychopharmacology* 1980, **72**, 107–8). There is no positive evidence of teratogenicity although Lundbeck do not recommend its use. Studies in 3 species have not shown malformations. A number of variable birth defects have been reported but with no problem. With **zuclopenthixol**, few birth defects have been recorded, at a rate consistent with the spontaneous levels of malformations.

5. **Sulpiride** has been used as an antinauseant in pregnancy. There are no published reports of abnormalities in animals or humans (*Int J Res Preg* 1982, **3**, 173–77, + MI). (FDA N/A).

6. **Butyrophenones**:
The safety of **haloperidol** (FDA=C) in pregnancy has not been established although it was once used in hyperemesis gravidarum and the drug passes into the foetus (n=3, Uematsu *et al*, *Ther Drug Monit* 1991, **13**, 183–87). There are isolated cases of alleged teratogenicity with haloperidol (eg. unproven limb malformations) but no cause-effect relationship has been established and there are no reports of haloperidol alone causing abnormalities (MI).

7. **Phenothiazines**: (FDA: Chlorpromazine = C, levomepromazine = C, promazine = C, thioridazine = C, trifluoperazine = C, others N/A)
The teratogenicity of phenothiazines has been investigated in some studies, although most of the data is based on low doses and thus not necessarily applicable to higher dose use. The phenothiazines are considered by some as of low risk, although the potential for hypotension, sedation and anticholinergic effects means that any use must be with extreme care. Severe congenital abnormalities were not significantly different in the studies of 543 women taking low-dose phenothiazines, other than **prochlorperazine** (FDA=C) for nausea (Miklovich and van den Berg, *Am J Obstet Gynecol* 1976, **125**, 244–48) and in 1309 mothers, mostly taking prochlorperazine (prospective, Slone *et al*, *Am J Obstet Gynecol* 1977, **128**, 486–88). The largest study, of 315 pregnancies, where phenothiazines were taken in the first trimester, showed a statistically significant difference in malformation rate of 3.5% in the aliphatic (**chlorpromazine** and **promazine**) phenothiazine-treated group (11 malformed infants) compared with 1.6% in the control group. There was no apparent trend in the type of abnormality and the risk is still considered low. There was no difference with the other phenothiazines, which appear to have an incidence of malformations similar to the background incidence (*Teratology* 1977, **15**, 57–64). Although **levomepromazine** (methotrimeprazine) is an aliphatic phenothiazine, it has generally been considered safe for both mother and foetus if used occasionally in low dose, later in pregnancy. A follow-up of **trifluoperazine** pregnancies showed no teratogenic effects (Moriarity, *Can Med Assoc J* 1963, **88**, 97). In the neonate, lethargy and extrapyramidal symptoms have been reported, as has respiratory depression when given in high dose (above 500mg chlorpromazine equivalents) close to term. In the longer term, a lack of impaired mental or physical development has been shown at 2 and 7 years in a follow-up study (n=16, Ayd, *Int Drug Ther Newsletter* 1976, **11**, 5). See also a short comment about 'Is fluphenazine a teratogen?' (Merlob *et al*, *Am J Med Genet* 1994, **52**, 231–32).

8. The safety of **loxapine** (FDA=C) in pregnancy is unknown. There are two reports of gastrointestinal malformations in infants whose mothers took loxapine throughout pregnancy but no similar cases are reported elsewhere.

### 3.8.2 Antidepressants:

There is little data on the newer drugs so the lowest risk in the first trimester would appear to be to use either imipramine, amitriptyline or an SSRI, none of which have data suggesting a significant risk. A study (Nulman *et al*, *NEJM* 1997, **336**, 258–62) indicates that if women take antidepressant drugs during their pregnancy, there seems to be no effect on the neurological development or intelligence of their children (see 20 below).

**Review**: depression during pregnancy and postpartum (Dwight and Walker, *Curr Opin Psych* 1998, **11**, 85–88).

9.* **SSRIs**: (FDA: Citalopram = C, escitalopram = C, fluoxetine = B, fluvoxamine = C, paroxetine = B, sertraline = B).

In a prospective, multicentre cohort study of 267 women exposed to an SSRI (fluvoxamine, sertraline or paroxetine) during pregnancy and 267 controls, exposure to SSRIs at recommended doses did not appear to be associated with increased teratogenicity (relative risk 1.06, 95% CI, 0.43–2.62) or higher rates of miscarriage, stillbirth, or prematurity. Gestational ages and birth weights were similar amongst off-spring of both groups of women (prospective, Kulin *et al*, *JAMA* 1998, **279**, 609–10). There are reports of neonatal withdrawal symptoms (irritability, constant crying, shivering, increased tonus, eating and sleeping difficulties and convulsions) after in utero exposure to paroxetine (n=3), citalopram (n=1) and fluoxetine (n=1), four requiring calming with chlorpromazine (n=5, Nordeng *et al*, *Acta Paediatrica* 2001, **90**, 288–91).

The SPCs naturally state caution and use should only be if clearly needed. There is no information available for **sertraline, citalopram** nor **escitalopram**. Occasionally slightly increased doses of citalopram may be needed in pregnancy (n=11, Heikkinen *et al*, *Clin Pharmacol Ther* 2002, **72**, 184–91).

There is a mass of data on **fluoxetine**-exposed pregnancies, reported in 3 prospective cohort-controlled studies and 4 prospective surveys. Based on published studies, use in the first trimester is not associated with increased risk of major malformations (meta-analysis by Addis and Koren, *Psychol Med* 2000, **30**, 89–94; critical review by Gijsman, *EBMH* 2000, **3**, 122). There is an absence of perinatal sequelae and no evidence of increase in major malformations, spontaneous abortion, poor perinatal state or neuro-developmental delay. In a prospective study on first-trimester exposure involved 128 women taking fluoxetine, 110 taking no known teratogen and 74 taking a tricyclic, no statistical differences in pregnancy outcome, age or weight were shown, but a slight tendency to miscarriage with both drug groups (SSRI 14.8%, TCA 12.2%, no drug 7.8%). The authors concluded that fluoxetine was unlikely to be a major teratogen but further work on miscarriage and any potential developmental effects was needed (n=312, Pastuszak *et al*, *JAMA* 1993, **269**, 2246–48). Of 544 reported cases in the USA of fluoxetine taken during pregnancy, 91 were electively terminated and there were 72 (15.9%) spontaneous abortions, 13 (3.4%) perinatal major malformations and 7 postperinatal malformations reported. These rates have been concluded as being similar to the unexposed population (Goldstein and Marvel, *JAMA*, 1993, **270**, 2177–78) but this has been disputed, as the previous study (Pastuszak *et al*, *JAMA* 1993, **269**, 2246–48) showed similar miscarriage rates which were double that in the control group. Chambers *et al* (*NEJM* 1996, **335**, 1010–15, n=228) could not show increased miscarriage rates nor major foetal abnormalities or a consistent pattern of events suggesting teratogenicity, although there was a higher rate of having three or more minor anomalies and no account was taken of the severity of maternal depression (see Dwight and Walker, *Curr Opin Psych* 1998, **11**, 85–88). A careful prospective study of children (assessed between 18 and 86 months) whose mothers had taken either **fluoxetine** (n=55) or no drug (n=84) showed fluoxetine to have no effect on global IQ, language development or behavioural development (Nulman *et al*, *NEJM* 1997, **336**, 258–62). Further data on exposure to fluoxetine throughout pregnancy shows no adverse affect on cognition, language development nor temperament, whereas untreated depression was associated with poorer cognitive and language achievement in their children (TCA n=46, fluoxetine n=40, control n=36; open, Nulman *et al*, *Am J Psych* 2002, **159**, 1889–95).

No embryotoxic or teratogenic effects have been seen in animals with **paroxetine** (Baldwin *et al*, *Acta Psych Scand* 1989, **80** [Suppl 350], 37–39) and, in the limited human data available, no abnormalities have been seen yet. Third trimester exposure to paroxetine may cause neonatal complications due most likely to a withdrawal syndrome. 22% had neonatal complications (9=respiratory distress, 2=hypoglycaemia) all disappearing within 1–2 weeks (n=55 + controls; Costei *et al*, *Arch Ped Adolesc Med* 2002, **156**, 1129–32).

10.* Data on 150 **venlafaxine** (FDA= C) pregnancies showed 125 live births, 18 spontaneous abortions, 7 therapeutic abortions and 2 major malformations, suggesting that the base-rate of malformations does not rise above the spontaneous rate but, as with the SSRIs, the spontaneous abortion rate is slightly higher (n=150 compared to 150 SSRIs exposures and 150 non-teratogenic drug control exposures, Einarson *et al*, *Am*

*J Psych* 2001, **158**, 1728–30). It is contraindicated in the UK in pregnancy 11.* Animal tests do not show **mirtazapine** (FDA=C) to be teratogenic nor cause foetal harm. When used for depression, anxiety and hyperemesis gravidarum in seven pregnancies, all women improved and all babies were born healthy at term (n=7, Saks, *Arch Women's Ment Health* 2001, **3**, 165–170; see also n=2, Kesim *et al*, *Teratology* 2002, **66**, 204).

12.* **Tricyclic antidepressants:**

(FDA: amitriptyline = D, amoxapine = C, clomipramine = C, desipramine = C, doxepin = C, maprotiline = B, nortriptyline = D, protriptyline = C, trimipramine = C)

Evidence from studies shows no increase in spontaneous abortions, malformations nor pattern of defects from tricyclics (reviewed by Goldberg *et al*, *Int J Psych in Med* 1994, **24**, 129–47). A meta-analysis of the use of tricyclics in pregnancy, reviewing over 300,000 live births including 414 first trimester exposures, failed to show a significant association between tricyclics and congenital malformations, although withdrawal symptoms were noted (Altshuler *et al*, *Am J Psych* 1996, **153**, 592–605). The metabolism of tricyclics in the neonate is much slower, so anti-cholinergic and other side-effects are more marked. Amitriptyline and imipramine are considered the tricyclics of choice, based on cumulative data on their relative safety.

Discontinuation effects have been noted in the neonate, sometimes requiring active treatment, eg. clomipramine has caused jittery/twitchy infants which resolves upon introduction of the drug, either via a drip or via breast milk (n=1, Schimmel *et al*, *Clin Toxicol* 1991, **29**, 479–84), lethargic and cyanotic babies who had abnormal movements and feeding difficulties where symptomatic treatment was successful (n=2, Cowe *et al*, *Pediatrics* 1982, **69**, 233–34; Cowe *et al*, *BMJ* 1982, **284**, 1837–38) and foetal seizures unresponsive to phenobarbital and phenytoin, which settled with clomipramine, in a mother who took up to 150mg/d clomipramine and stopped abruptly (child was born prematurely 4 days later, Bromiker and Kaplan, *JAMA* 1994, **272**, 1722–23). In pregnancy, mild toxicity in the infant has been seen with imipramine, eg. respiratory distress, hypotonia, irritability, tremors, convulsions, jerky movements etc. (eg. Ware and DeVane, *J Clin Psych* 1990, **51**, 482–84). Phenobarbital can improve these symptoms, which can persist for a total duration of up to two weeks.

**Postnatal development:**
A careful study of children (assessed between 18 and 86 months) whose mothers had taken either a tricyclic (n=84) or no drug (n=80) showed tricyclics to have no effect on global IQ, language development or behavioural development compared to no drug (Nulman *et al*, *NEJM* 1997, **336**, 258–62). Further data on exposure to TCAs throughout pregnancy shows no adverse affect on cognition, language development nor temperament, whereas untreated depression was associated with poorer cognitive and language achievement in their children (TCA n=46, fluoxetine n=40, control n=36, open, Nulman *et al*, *Am J Psych* 2002, **159**, 1889–95).

13.* For **trazodone** (FDA=C) at very high doses (15+ times the maximum human dose), there appears to be some foetal resorption and congenital abnormalities but little human data exists to support this. There is no published evidence of problems with **nefazodone** (FDA=C).

14. No teratogenic effects have been noted with **reboxetine** in animal studies but little human data exists so the drug should be avoided in pregnancy (SPC).

15. **MAOIs:** (FDA: isocarboxazid = C, phenelzine = C, tranylcypromine = C).
There are no reports of human teratogenicity with **phenelzine** nor **tranylcypromine**, although it has been suggested that the risk of teratogenic

problems may be roughly doubled if tranylcypromine is taken in the first trimester (AAPCD, *Pediatrics* 1982, **69**, 241–43). (See also Briggs *et al*, *Drugs in Pregnancy and Lactation*, Williams and Wilkins). Growth retardation and foetal toxicity have been reported. MAOIs should be avoided if at all possible due to maternal toxicity and lack of published safety data. **MAOIs** may also interact with drugs used in labour (see pethidine under MAOIs in *4.3.4*).

16.* There is no evidence of teratogenicity with **mianserin** in animals except at toxic doses (Brogden *et al*, *Drugs* 1978, **16**, 273–301) but no human data is available (FDA=N/A). No firm data is available on the use of **moclobemide** in pregnancy, but there is a case of 300mg/d throughout pregnancy with no problems and normal development within the first 14 months (n=1, Rybakowski, *Pharmacopsychiatry* 2001, **34**, 82–83). No human data is available for **tryptophan**, but it is a naturally occurring substance in food. Slight in-vitro uterotonic activity has been reported and the lack of safety and toxicity data suggests that **St. John's wort** is currently best avoided in pregnancy.

### 3.8.3 Anxiolytics and hypnotics

For a review of the treatment of anxiety during pregnancy see McGrath *et al*, (*Drug Safety* 1999, **20**, 171–86).

17.* **Benzodiazepines:** (FDA: alprazolam = D, chlordiazepoxide = D, clonazepam = C, diazepam = D, lorazepam = D, oxazepam = D, temazepam = X, others not available)
Assessment of 104,000 births in the USA has shown a higher incidence of teratogenicity in women taking benzodiazepines but multiple alcohol and illicit substance exposure could account for this (Bergman *et al*, *Lancet* 1992, **340**, 694–96). A population-based case-control study indicated that **nitrazepam**, **medazepam**, **alprazolam** and **clonazepam** taken during pregnancy did not present a detectable teratogenic risk

(n=38,151, Eros *et al, Eur J Obstet Gynecol Reprod Biol* 2002, **101**, 147–54). With **chlordiazepoxide**, an increased risk of teratogenicity has been suggested if chlordiazepoxide is taken during the first 42 days of pregnancy (11.4 per 100 live births) compared to after 42 days (3.6 per 100 live births, 175 studied — Milkovich and van den Berg, *NEJM* 1974, **291**, 1268–71) although later Hartz *et al* (n=50,282 pregnancies, *NEJM* 1975, **292**, 726–28) were unable to find significant differences when 800 patients were studied. **Clobazam** is known to pass the placenta and benzodiazepine withdrawal symptoms in the neonate have been suggested. For **diazepam**, studies show a varying risk of oral clefts, with the worst case scenario bringing the risk to 7 in 1000. In late pregnancy, doses of 30mg or more of diazepam IM or IV during the last 15 hours of labour can induce neonatal respiratory depression and feeding problems. 10mg given IV within 10 minutes of birth has been shown not to affect Apgar scores (n=23, open, McAllister, *B J Anaesth* 1980, **52**, 423–27). As with other benzodiazepines, withdrawal symptoms in the neonate have been seen (n=3, Rementeria and Bhatt, *J Pediatr* 1977, **90**, 123–26). As **lorazepam** crosses the placenta, the floppy baby syndrome and respiratory depression can occur, especially if IV doses are used close to birth. Oral use during later pregnancy may show delayed feeding in full-term infants but premature infants may have lower Apgar scores and respiratory depression (n=53, open, Whitelaw *et al, BMJ* 1981, **282**, 1106–8). **Clorazepate** also passes the placenta. Animal studies have not shown teratogenicity although some cognitive impairment was indicated.

In 1997, the UK CSM restated the danger of benzodiazepine use during pregnancy or labour due to the effects on the neonate such as hypothermia, hypotonia, respiratory depression and withdrawal symptoms (*Curr Prob* 1997, **23**, 10). Shorter-acting benzodiazepines on a 'when required' basis may be acceptable later in pregnancy, but the first trimester should be avoided if possible.

After birth, benzodiazepine withdrawal symptoms have been noticed in the neonate with many benzodiazepines (Athinarayanan *et al, Am J Obstet Gynae* 1976, **124**, 212–13). The 'floppy baby' syndrome, as it is often termed, includes facial features and CNS dysfunction and can occur particularly with higher doses (eg. >30mg diazepam equivalent per day) of longer-acting benzodiazepines (n=8, Laegreid *et al, J Pediatrics* 1989, **114**, 126–31), eg. **nitrazepam** (Speight, *Lancet* 1977, **ii**, 878).

18. There is no evidence of a teratogenic effect from **buspirone** (FDA=B) but some effects on survival and weights has been noted in some, but not all, animal tests. This is a UK SPC contraindication.

19. **Zopiclone** has not been contraindicated in pregnancy. Animal tests have shown no abnormalities and the limited human data is unremarkable. Little information is currently available on **zolpidem** (FDA=B) and **zaleplon** (FDA=C). Until more is known, they should be avoided in pregnancy, especially during the first trimester. None of these three hypnotics are contraindicated in pregnacy in the UK SPCs.

20. **Beta-blockers:** (FDA: propranolol = C, oxprenolol = C)
**Beta-blockers** are not generally considered teratogens but a connection between **propranolol** use in pregnancy and tracheosophageal fistulas (Campbell, *NEJM* 1985, **313**, 518) and intrauterine growth retardation has been proposed but not substantiated. Direct effects of beta-blockade on the foetus would also occur, eg. bradycardia etc. (for reviews etc. see Livingstone *et al, Clin Exp Hypertens* 1983, **2**, 341–50; O'Connor *et al, Lancet* 1981, **2**, 1168). Use in the second and third trimesters may aggravate or produce neonatal hypoglycaemia.

Foetal and neonatal bradycardia may occur especially in pregnancies already complicated by placental insufficiency (eg. severe maternal hypertension). Due to direct cardiac effects, hypoglycaemia and apnoea, it may be prudent to discontinue treatment 1–2 weeks before delivery.

21. Maternally administered **chloral** (FDA=C) lowers bilirubin concentrations in the infant (Drew and Kitchen, *J Pediat* 1976, **89**, 657–61). No increase in congenital anomalies was seen in a study of 71 women who took chloral in the first 4 months of pregnancy or to 358 women who took chloral at some time in pregnancy (Heinonen *et al*, *Birth Defects and Drugs in Pregnancy*, Publishing Sciences Group 1977, 336–37). The UK manufacturers state that **clomethiazole** should not be used, particularly in the first and third trimesters, although it has been used widely for pre-eclampsia. Adverse effects of platelet aggregation in the neonate have been reported with **promethazine** (FDA=C) (Corby and Schulman, *J Pediatr* 1971, **79**, 307), although overall promethazine may be safe and appropriate as a hypnotic.

### 3.8.4 Anticonvulsants *

Pregnant women with epilepsy are at increased risk of seizures and complications, with increased seizures in about 25–33%. One of the main reasons for this increase is the marked alterations in plasma protein binding of drugs as pregnancy progresses, resulting in declining plasma levels.

A number of prospective and retrospective studies have shown that there are some risks associated with anticonvulsants (some used as mood stabilisers) used throughout pregnancy. Most have an uncomplicated pregnancy and normal healthy offspring (n=151 pregnancies, 124 women, retrospective, Sabers *et al*, *Acta Neurol Scand* 1998, **97**, 164–70), but the risk of abnormal outcomes (10.7%) may be three times that of controls (3.4%),

with phenobarbital showing the highest risk (n=211, prospective, Waters *et al*, *Arch Neurol* 1994, **51**, 250–53). There is an association with an increased risk of major congenital abnormalities with most AEDs, but in particular valproate, carbamazepine, benzodiazepines, caffeine and phenobarbital (n=1411, Samren *et al*, *Ann Neurol* 1999, **46**, 739–44). Polytherapy is associated with a (partly reversible) decline in body dimension (n=963, Swedish survey, Wide *et al*, *Epilepsia* 2000, **41**, 854–61), including risk of pre-term delivery, lower birthweight, length and head circumference (n=193, controls n=24,094, Hvas *et al*, *B J Obs Gynaecol* 2000, **107**, 896–902).

To balance this, one review of anticonvulsants in pregnancy (Malone and D'Alton, *Semin Perinatol* 1997, **21**, 114–23), concluded that the lowest dose of one of the major drugs probably has less risk than that of recurrent seizures.

### Postnatal development *

Three recent studies have suggested some specific effects on postnatal development of children exposed to anticonvulsants during pregnancy. One survey suggested a higher frequency of educational needs statements (10.3% drug exposed cf. 5.7% non-drug-exposed). The figure for valproate (30%), and possibly also polypharmacy, were much higher, supporting a drug effect (n=400 school-age children: 150 exposed to monotherapy, 74 to polytherapy and 176 to none, Adab *et al*, *J Neurol Neurosurg Psychiatry* 2001, **70**, 15–21). Another study concluded that while there were no global scores differences, phenytoin (n=16, but not CBZ n=35) caused a significant albeit subtle reduction in psychomotor development, which may be more obvious at school age (n=76 exposed, c/w 71 unexposed, Wide *et al*, *Acta Paediatrica* 2002, **91**, 409–14). Finally, in a review of the long-term health and neurodevelopment in children exposed to antiepileptic drugs before birth, developmental delay was seen in 24% exposed children (cf 11% non-exposed sibs) childhood medical problems in 31% (cf. 13% of non-exposed sibs) and behaviour disorders in 20% (cf. 5% of non-exposed) and concluded that prenatal antiepileptic drug exposure is associated with developmental delay and later childhood morbidity, in addition to congenital malformation (n=129 mothers, 293 children, Dean *et al*, *J Med Genet* 2002, **39**, 251–59).

**Summary of the risks of pregnancy in women with epilepsy:**
- 25–33% increase in maternal seizure frequency
- 10% risk of vaginal bleeding
- 7% risk of neonatal haemorrhage if no vitamin K is given
- 10% risk of infant facial dysmorphism
- 4–6% risk of major malformations (30% of which are oral facial defects)
- 1–2% risk of spina bifida with valproate
- 0.5–1% risk of spina bifida with carbamazepine.

(Yerby, *Epilepsia* 1992, **33**[Suppl 1], S23–27).

**Summary of risk minimisation strategies:**
Evidence suggests that recent literature has been slow to influence clinical practice (Wiebe, *BMJ* 2000, **320**, 3–4, editorial).

**1. Pre-conception:\***
- Education of the patient as to the risks and benefits of continued treatment
- Adequate Oral Contraceptive dosage (see interactions, *4.5*) until conception is planned, eg. 50–75mcg of ethinyloestradiol
- Regular multivitamins with folate before oral contraceptives are stopped, to reduce the chance of spina bifida. Folic acid antagonists (eg. carbamazepine, phenytoin, phenobarbital) during pregnancy increase the risk of cardiovascular birth defects and oral clefts, and oral folic acid (eg. in

multivitamins) may reduce the risks of these defects (n=6932, Hernandez-Diaz *et al*, *NEJM* 2000, **343**, 1608–14), although folic acid isn't always successful with valproate (n=2, Duncan *et al*, *Epilepsia* 2001, **42**, 750–53)
- Minimise exposure if possible to drugs with proven increases in risk eg. phenobarbital (n=211, prospective, Waters *et al*, *Arch Neurol* 1994, **51**, 250–53), phenytoin (n=151, retrospective, Sabers *et al*, *Acta Neurol Scand* 1998, **97**, 164–70), valproate, carbamazepine, benzodiazepines (n=1411, Samren *et al*, *Ann Neurol* 1999, **46**, 739–44).
- Seizure control with the lowest dose monotherapy targeted
- Diagnosis verified and the need for anticonvulsants confirmed.

**2. After conception:**
- Education of the patient about risk minimisation.

**3. Seizure control without toxicity:**
- Do not change drugs if the patient is stabilised
- Multivitamins with folate continued
- Frequent monitoring of free anticonvulsant concentrations and dose adjustment if necessary
- Monotherapy continued if possible
- Vitamin K given during last week of pregnancy if possible (Deblay *et al*, *Lancet* 1982, **1**, 1247)
- Ultrasound and AFPs carried out.

Facial dysmorphism has been described in uncontrolled seizure patients, as well as with phenytoin, phenobarbital, primidone, valproate, benzodiazepines and carbamazepine. All appear quite similar and not really drug-specific and some effects, especially digital, appear to resolve with age, although a review and multicentre study concluded that the distinctive pattern of physical abnormalities are associated with anticonvulsants rather than epilepsy itself (n=128,049, Holmes *et al*, *NEJM* 2001, **344**, 1132–38).

It is worth noting the study which showed that in female epileptics, only 38% recalled pre-pregnancy counseling, only 44% had planned the pregnancy (24% reported contraceptive failure) and only 11% took folate appropriately. Most advice is to neurologists, not the GPs by whom many patients are cared. The net result was malformation rates double the background rate and there was an excess of premature deliveries cf. controls (n=300, survey, Fairgrieve *et al*, *BMJ* 2000, **321**, 674–75).

**Reviews**: general (Leppik *et al*, *CNS Drugs* 1999, **11**, 191–206; Chang and McAuley, *Ann Pharmacother* 1998, **32**, 794–801, 63 refs; Nulman *et al*, *Drugs* 1999, **57**, 535–44, 75 refs; Simar, *CNS Drugs* 1999, **12**, 451–70), advice to patients (Yerby, *Epilepsia* 1997, **38**, 957–58), long-term outcomes (Koch *et al*, *Epilepsia* 1999, **40**, 1237–43).

22.* **Carbamazepine** (FDA=C) has been considered by many to be the anticonvulsant of choice in epilepsy, with some early studies showing no teratogenicity but an association has been made with malformations, particularly spina bifida (1% incidence, Rosa, *NEJM* 1991, **324**, 674–77), and a pattern of minor problems, such as craniofacial defects (11%), fingernail hypoplasia (27%) and developmental delay (20%) (n=72, retrospective, Jones *et al*, *NEJM* 1989, **320**, 1661–66, + correspondence in *NEJM*, 1989, **321**, 1480–81). All of these cases were in women on polytherapy and so a drug interaction effect is possible, and the effect of the epilepsy itself is not known (letters in *NEJM* 1991, **325**, 664–65). Population studies indicate a two-fold increase in major congenital malformations and a slight reduction in birth weight (n=210, 629 controls, Diav-Citrin *et al*, *Neurology* 2001, **57**, 321–24). In a pooled data study of 1255 exposures, carbamazepine increased the rate of congenital anomalies, mainly neural tube defects, cardiovascular and urinary tract anomalies, and cleft palate (a 'carbamazepine syndrome': Ornoy and Cohen, *Arch Dis Child* 1996, **75**, 517), plus some minor abnormalities and some reduced gestational age at delivery, with polytherapy increasing the risk (n=1255, Matalon *et al*, *Reprod Toxicol* 2002, **16**, 9–17). In monotherapy, carbamazepine may have a negative influence on body dimensions (n=963, Wide *et al*, *Epilepsia* 2000, **41**, 854–61). The CSM recommends the need for counselling and screening for neural tube defects (*Curr Problems* 1993, **19**, 8), which can detect 90–95% of neural tube defects if carried out with AFP levels at 16–18 weeks. In late pregnancy, routine vitamin K to mothers and the neonates is usually recommended.

In a controlled study of *in utero* exposure, 36 children born to mothers taking carbamazepine were compared to matched controls. Allowing for variables, the carbamazepine children had similar IQs and language abilities to controls (n=36, Scolnik *et al*, *JAMA* 1994, **271**, 767), suggesting the lack of a clinically important adverse effect on cognitive development.

**Oxcarbazepine** (FDA=C) is closely related to carbamazepine. The placenta may contribute to the metabolism of oxcarbazepine (Pienimaki *et al*, *Epilepsia* 1997, **38**, 309–16) and the UK SPC mentions that data indicates that oxcarbazepine may cause serious birth defects, and there is significant transfer through the placenta in humans (n=12, Myllynen *et al*, *Epilepsia* 2001, **42**, 1482–85).

23.* **Valproate** (FDA=D) crosses the placenta easily (Bailey *et al*, *BMJ* 1983, **286**, 190) and teratogenicity, especially spina bifida, has been strongly linked. UK rates with valproate are stated to be about 1%, which is 50 times the spontaneous rate. The CSM recommends counselling and screening for neural tube defects (*Curr Problems* 1993, **19**, 8).

This should take place in a specialist centre with high resolution ultrasound and experienced technicians. Amniocentesis should be carried out if plasma AFP levels are raised or ultrasound unclear (Orrell, *BMJ* 1991, **302**, 56–57; see also *Drug & Ther Bull* 1990, **28**, 59–60). In a small study of 17 infants born to 17 mothers on valproate during pregnancy, 11 were admitted to a neurological unit, 9 with neurological problems (including seizures) and 2 with major malformations. A 'foetal valproate syndrome' was proposed, presenting as congenital heart defects and a withdrawal syndrome of irritability, jitteriness, hypotonia and feeding problems. The authors related the former to valproate in the first trimester and the withdrawal syndrome to higher doses (Thisted and Ebbesen, *Arch Dis Child* 1993, **69**, 288–91). However, dysmorphic features, developmental delay and structural anomalies were found only in children exposed to maternal valproate doses above 1000mg/d (n=69, Mawer *et al*, *Seizure* 2002, **11**, 512–18), an important observation. The UK SPC now states that there have been rare reports of haemorrhagic syndrome in neonates whose mothers took valproate in pregnancy.

This has been a suggestion that *in utero* exposure to valproate may lead to a higher than expected incidence of education needs statements, although a prospective study would be needed to confirm this (n=400 school-age children: 150 exposed to monotherapy, 74 to polytherapy and 176 to none, Adab *et al*, *J Neurol Neurosurg Psychiatry* 2001, **70**, 15–21). Dividing daily doses and using SR preparations to reduce the peak levels may be wise. Folic acid supplementation at 4mg/d before and during pregnancy has also been recommended.

There is an association between valproate and polycystic ovary syndrome, which may have some effect on reproductive capacity (n=32, O'Donovan *et al*, *J Clin Psych* 2002,

**63**, 322–30; review by Genton *et al*, *Epilepsia* 2001, **42**, 295–304).

**Reviews**: valproate disposition in pregnancy (Omtzigt *et al*, *Eur J Clin Pharmacol* 1992, **43**, 381–88), valproate in women of reproductive age (Piontek and Wisner, *J Clin Psych* 2000, **61**, 161–63).

24. **Phenytoin** (FDA=D) crosses the placenta freely and teratogenicity is well established, particularly the 'foetal hydantoin syndrome'. This syndrome includes growth retardation, microcephaly, mental retardation, facial defects including cleft lip and/ or palate, digit and nail hypoplasia, rib anomalies, hirsuitism, low hairlines and inguinal hernia, plus cardiovascular gastro-intestinal or genitourinary anomalies (n=2 and review: Ozkinay *et al*, *Turk J Pediatr* 1998, **40**, 273–78). The full syndrome occurs in about 8–10% of children born to mothers who took phenytoin in the first trimester (Witter *et al*, *Obstet Gynecol* 1981, **58**, 100S-105S; n=88, Rodriguez-Palomares *et al*, *Arch Med Res* 1995, **26**, 371–77) and a part syndrome in a further 30% of children (n=3, Seeler *et al*, *Pediatrics* 1979, **63**, 524–27; see also controlled prospective study, n=34, Nulman *et al*, *Am J Med Genet* 1997, **68**, 18–24). It appears not to be dose-related (n=88, Rodriguez-Palomares *et al*, *Arch Med Res* 1995, **26**, 371–77). Prediction of the teratogenic risk may be possible by measuring microsomal epoxide hydrolase activity (n=19, Buehler *et al*, *NEJM* 1990, **332**, 1567–72). It has also been noted that epileptic fathers taking phenytoin have increased rates of malformed children (Friis, *Acta Neurol Scand* 1983, **94**[Suppl], 39–43).

The syndrome may be related to phenytoin-induced reduction in GSH levels, enhancing peroxidative damage to the foetus via the placental circulation (n=52, controlled, Lui *et al*, *Human Toxicol* 1997, **16**, 177–81). Phenytoin also inhibits the synthesis of Vitamin K-dependent clotting factors and neonatal haemorrhage may occur. Vitamin K deficiency may also be the cause of abnormal facial development, via abnormal development of the cartilaginous nasal septum. Early Vitamin K supplementation in at-risk pregnancies is thus recommended (n=10, Howe *et al, Am J Med Genet* 1995, **58**, 238–44) and to the neonate after birth (Yerby, *Epilepsia* 1987, **28**[Suppl 3], S29–S36).

The kinetics of phenytoin change in pregnancy, elimination increases (single dose study, n=5, Dickinson *et al, B J Clin Pharmacol* 1989, **28**, 17–27) and plasma levels fall steadily as the pregnancy progresses, with possible change in seizure frequency (45% increase: Knight and Rhind, *Epilepsia* 1975, **16**, 99–110; no significant change, Tomson *et al, Epilepsia* 1994, **35**, 122–30). Bound levels may be reduced with free (ie. active) levels unchanged in pregnancy and so care with plasma level interpretation is needed (review of phenytoin disposition and metabolism in pregnancy, Eadie *et al, Eur J Clin Pharmacol* 1992, **43**, 389–92; for 'Guidelines for the care of epileptic women of childbearing age' see *Epilepsia* 1989, **30**, 409–10).

**Risk reduction with phenytoin:**
The general consensus seems to be that where documented seizures are proven to be controlled by phenytoin, then the risks of withdrawal are probably greater than with the continued use of phenytoin, with the following precautions:

1. Use of minimal effective doses. At least monthly blood level monitoring both during pregnancy, and for up to six months after, are essential to avoid toxicity and an increased teratogenic risk (see above, noting relevance of free levels).

2. Use of folic acid 5mg/d from before conception. One study resulted in **no** birth defects in the 33 mothers who took folic acid from before conception or immediately upon becoming pregnant but there were 10 children with

malformations from the 66 born to mothers who did not take folic acid, a significant and **highly important** difference (n=66 retrospective, n=22 prospective, Biale and Lewenthal, *Eur J Obstet Gynecol Reprod Biol* 1984, **18**, 211). The neural tube closes around the time of the first missed period and so folic acid supplements need to be started before pregnancy is detected.

3. Vitamin K supplementation (see above).

After birth, a withdrawal syndrome, including irritability and haemorrhage has been reported (prospective, Hill *et al, Am J Dis Child* 1974, **127**, 645–53). One study has indicated a negative neurodevelopmental effect from phenytoin. In a controlled study of *in utero* exposure, 34 children born to mothers taking phenytoin and 36 children born to mothers taking carbamazepine were compared to matched controls. Allowing for other variables, the phenytoin children had a significantly lower mean IQ and language ability, the carbamazepine children being similar to controls (Scolnik *et al, JAMA* 1994, **271**, 767). This strongly suggests a clinically important adverse effect in the long-term. Developmental impairment and reduced growth and head circumference has been reported at 7 years (Gal and Sharpless, *Drug Intell Clin Pharm* 1984, **18**, 186–201). Reports of malignancies in the infant have probably been disproven (Koren *et al, Teratology* 1989, **40**, 157–62).

25.* **Phenobarbital** (FDA=D) has been implicated as a teratogen, although many cases that have occurred have been as part of combination therapy. Minor digital deformities (finger-like thumbs, rudimentary or missing nails) as well as hip and facial abnormalities have been reported. In the longer-term, a smaller head circumference and an impaired cognitive development was suggested in two studies (n=122, van der Pol *et al*, *Am J Obstet Gynecol* 1991, **164**, 121–28). Prenatal exposure to combined phenobarbital and phenytoin (n=172) compared to controls (n=168) produced smaller head size at birth and persistent learning problems (12%) compared to controls (1%) (Dessens *et al*, *Acta Paediatrica* 2000, **89**, 533–41). There is some evidence of a direct neurotoxic effect by phenobarbital on developing foetal neurones, which may be responsible for some cognitive or CNS abnormalities (Neale *et al*, *Pediatr Neurol* 1985, **1**, 143–50). Withdrawal symptoms, such as seizures and irritability have occurred in the neonate, some delayed by up to two weeks after birth. Neonatal bleeding in the first 24 hours has been reported, as has respiratory depression. However, antenatal phenobarbital exposure does not appear to affect the neurodevelopmental outcome of premature infants at 18–22 months of age (n=578, Shankaran *et al*, *Am J Obs Gyn* 2002, **187**, 171–77).

26.* The incidence of major malformations with first-trimester **lamotrigine** (FDA=C) has been reported to be 1.8%, but as high as 10% when taken with valproate (n=50). There was no specific pattern but although the sample size was small, levels are in line with other monotherapy studies in epilepsy so there is little at the moment to suggest a major problem (n=166, Tennis and Eldridge, *Epilepsia* 2002, **43**, 1161–67). Lamotrigine plasma levels may decrease significantly as pregnancy progresses, a 50% increased clearance of lamotrigine being noted (requiring increased doses in 11) which reverted rapidly after delivery (n=12, Tran *et al*, *Neurology* 2002, **59**, 251–55; n=1, Tomson *et al*, *Epilepsia* 1997, **38**, 1039–41). There were no congenital anomalies in the 11 babies born to mothers taking **gabapentin** (FDA=C) in the first trimester in the Southampton PMSS (n=3100, Wilton and Shakir, *Epilepsia* 2002, **43**, 983–92).

27.* **Vigabatrin** is contraindicated due to a slight increase in the incidence of cleft palate at high doses in one animal test as slow placental transfer of vigabatrin may occur (n=2, Tran *et al*, *Br J Clin Pharmacol* 1998, **45**, 409–11). No human data is available on **tiagabine** (FDA=C) in pregnancy and so use should only be where clearly indicated. **Topiramate** (FDA=C) appears to pass the placenta easily, with low but detectable levels in children, although no ADRs have been noticed (n=5 pairs, Ohman *et al*, *Epilepsia* 2002, **43**, 1157–60). It has shown some teratogenicity in animals and should not be used in pregnancy unless the benefit clearly outweighs the risk. Some animal studies show animal reproductive toxicity, and so **levetiracetam** (FDA=C) should not be used unless clearly necessary (MI).

28. For **acetazolamide** (FDA=C), animal tests indicate that it is teratogenic and can increase miscarriages at toxic doses, and two probable human cases exist (Worsham *et al*, *JAMA* 1978, **240**, 251–52). If use is essential, maternal electrolyte balance should be monitored. There are reported cases of malformations with **ethosuximide** (FDA=C) alone and about 35 when combined with other drugs but no cause-effect relationship has been proven. Although animal studies in rats have raised some concerns, no systematic human data is available. **Paraldehyde** FDA=C.

### 3.8.5 Others:

29.* Very high doses of **donepezil** (FDA=C) may have some minor effects in pregnancy but no teratogenicity has been detected (MI). The safety of **rivastigmine** (FDA=C) in pregnancy has not been established (MI). There is no data on **galantamine** in pregnancy, although animal studies show a slight delay in foetal and neonatal development (SPC). Human data is lacking with **memantine** but animal data suggests potentially reduced interuterine growth.

30. **Anticholinergics:** (FDA: benzhexol/ trihexyphenidyl = C, benzatropine = C, procyclidine = C)
There is little data available on these drugs. A 'small left colon syndrome' has been reported in two children born to mothers who took benzatropine and other psychotropic drugs late in pregnancy (Falterman and Richardson, *J Paediatr* 1980, **92**, 308–10) although a cause-effect relationship was not established.

31. For **disulfiram** (FDA=C) there have been isolated reports of congenital abnormalities (eg. Gardner and Clarkson, *NZ Med J* 1981, **93**, 184–86), although other drugs were often taken and the symptoms were similar to the foetal alcohol syndrome. In animals, disulfiram has been shown to be embryotoxic. The risk-benefit ratio for the risks of alcoholism against disulfiram for the foetus must be assessed carefully. The UK SPC for **acamprosate** states that use in pregnancy is a contraindication. Animal studies have not shown any evidence of teratogenicity.

32.* **Lithium** (FDA=D) readily crosses the placenta and cases of cardiac arrhythmia, hypotonia and hypothyroidism have been reported (full review by Schou, *J Clin Psych* 1990, **51**, 410–13). Studies show that congenital malformation rates with lithium (2.8%) are similar to control rates (2.4%) and suggest that lithium is not an important human teratogen, if used with adequate screening (including level II ultrasound and foetal echocardiography) to detect Ebstein's anomaly (n= 148, prospective Jacobson *et al*, *Lancet* 1992, **339**, 530–33). The malformation risk in the first trimester is of the order of 4–12% and hence still greater than the general population. The risk of Ebstein's anomaly (a rare congenital downward displacement of the tricuspid valve into the right ventricle) exists if the drug is taken during weeks 2 to 6 post-conception. Ebstein's anomaly is 20 times more common with lithium, but the risk rises from 1 in 20 K to 1 in 1 K, and must be weighed against the 50% chance of relapsing if the drug is stopped (Cohen *et al*, *JAMA* 1994, **271**, 146–50; *Pharm J* 1994, **252**, 119; review by Amanth, *Lithium* 1993, **4**, 231–37). The CSM has, however, stated lithium to be a 'commonly recognised' teratogen (*Curr Prob* 1997, **23**, 11).

A recent study (n=101, retrospective, Viguera *et al*, *Am J Psych* 2000, **157**, 179–84) has noted that:

- The heart is formed very early, so stopping lithium when pregnancy is confirmed is too late
- The relapse rates at 40 weeks after lithium discontinuation were similar for pregnant (52%) and non-pregnant (58%) women, but much higher than the year before discontinuation (21%), so pregnancy is relatively 'risk neutral'
- Women who remained stable over the first 40/52 since lithium discontinuation were 2.9 times more likely to relapse than non-pregnant women during weeks 41–62 (70% *vs* 24%)
- The rates are higher in rapid rather than gradual discontinuation
- The 50% relapse rate within 35 weeks is high, and the risk from consequentially needed drugs is high
- There were no major malformations in the children born to the women (n=9) who continued lithium throughout pregnancy
- An unstudied option might be to stop lithium gradually as soon as pregnancy is known, then reintroduce in the third trimester.

During pregnancy, thyroid suppression may also produce neonatal hypothyroidism (n=1, Frassetto *et al*, *Ann Pharmacother* 2002, **36**, 1745–48). Other reports exist of diabetes insipidus, cardiac arrhythmias and rarely polyhydramnios. Neonatal lithium toxicity is usually associated with poor maternal control, as renal clearance is increased during pregnancy and so higher doses are needed.

Lithium clearance changes markedly near end of term and the dose may need to be reduced by up to 30–50% in the last few weeks, so measure plasma levels carefully and frequently.

A study of 60 healthy children born to mothers who took lithium during the first trimester did not reveal any increased frequency of physical or mental anomalies among the lithium children compared to their non-lithium exposed siblings over 5–10 years (n=60, Schou, *Acta Psych Scand* 1976, **54**, 193–97; see also case and review by Pinelli *et al*, *Am J Obstet Gynecol* 2002, **187**, 245–49).

**Reviews**: Llewellyn *et al*, *J Clin Psych* 1998, **59**[Suppl 6], 57–64, Yonkers *et al CNS Drugs* 1998, **9**, 261–69.

33. **Modafinil** (FDA=C) is contra-indicated in pregnancy (MI). Pre-clinical studies have shown no teratogenicity but more information is required.

34. **Methadone** (FDA: B, or D if used in high dose or for prolonged periods) at maintenance doses has been used successfully, does not appear to be overtly teratogenic and reduces the risk of poor quality street drugs being used. With potential illicit drug-using mothers, teratogenicity with methadone will obviously be very difficult to ascertain but there does not appear to be a clear association with malformations (eg. study by Newman *et al*, *Am J Obstet Gynecol* 1975, **121**, 233–37; Newman, *NY J Med* 1974, **74**, 52). Predictably, a foetal withdrawal syndrome, occurring within the first 24 hours has been seen. Symptoms include tremor, irritability, hyperactivity, jitteriness, shrill cry, vomiting, diarrhoea and convulsions. Stopping opiates abruptly is dangerous as withdrawal reactions can damage the foetus more than methadone. Long-term developmental outcome seems unaffected (Kaltenbach and Finnegan, *Neurotoxicol Teratol* 1987, **9**, 311–13. For effect on child in first year see *Arch Dis Childhood* 1989, **64**, 235–45). There have also been numerous reports of sudden death, reduced body weight and head circumference etc. but these are virtually all in uncontrolled situations and so other effects can not be excluded. In a study of methadone maintenance in pregnancy, head circumference and birth weight were slightly lower with methadone compared to controls (n=32, Brown *et al*, *Am J Obs Gynecol* 1998, **179**, 459–63). Slow-release morphine is no better at reducing neonatal withdrawal symptoms than methadone (n=48, Fischer *et al*, *Addiction* 1999, **94**, 231–39).

35. No teratogenic effects have been reported in patients who took **dexamfetamine** (FDA=C) before knowing they were pregnant (Guilleminault, *Sleep* 1993, **16**, 199–201).

36. There is little information available for **methylphenidate** (FDA=C), and the few reported cases are unremarkable, but the UK SPC advises caution.

37. **Bupropion** (FDA=B). Animal studies have shown no definitive evidence of teratogenicity nor impaired fertility (Briggs *et al*, 1992).

## 3.9 RENAL IMPAIRMENT (see also BNF)

| | Lower risk | Moderate risk | Higher risk (greater care needed) |
|---|---|---|---|
| Antipsychotics | Loxapine[8]<br>Sertindole[2] | Aripiprazole [2]<br>Butyrophenones[6]<br>Clozapine[3]<br>Olanzapine[2]<br>Phenothiazines[7]<br>Quetiapine[2]<br>Thioxanthenes[4]<br>Ziprasidone [2] | Amisulpride[5]<br>Risperidone[1]<br>Sulpiride[5]<br>Zotepine[2] |
| Antidepressants | Mianserin[16]<br>Moclobemide[16]<br>Tricyclics[12]<br>Trazodone[13]<br>Tryptophan[16] | MAOIs[15]<br>Mirtazapine[11]<br>Nefazodone[13]<br>Reboxetine[14]<br>SSRIs[9] | Fluoxetine[9]<br>Venlafaxine[10] |
| Anxiolytics and hypnotics | Zaleplon[19]<br>Zopiclone[19] | Benzodiazepines[17]<br>Beta-blockers[20]<br>Clomethiazole[21]<br>Zolpidem[19] | Buspirone[18]<br>Chloral[21] |
| Anticonvulsants | Phenytoin[24]<br>Tiagabine[27] | Barbiturates[25]<br>Benzodiazepines[17]<br>Carbamazepine [22]<br>Ethosuximide[28]<br>Fosphenytoin[24]<br>Lamotrigine [26]<br>Piracetam[27]<br>Topiramate[27] | Gabapentin[26]<br>Levetiracetam[27]<br>Midazolam[17]<br>Oxcarbazepine[22]<br>Valproate[23]<br>Vigabatrin[27] |
| Others | Anticholinesterases[29] | Anticholinergics[30]<br>Bupropion[34]<br>Disulfiram[31]<br>Memantine [29]<br>Modafinil[33] | Acamprosate[31]<br>Lithium[32] |

| Grade | GFR<br>ml/min. | Serum Creatinine<br>micromol/L |
|---|---|---|
| Mild | 20–50 | 150–300 |
| Moderate | 10–20 | 300–700 |
| Severe | <10 | >700 |

**General Principals** (adapted from *Maudsley Guidelines*)

1. Renal impairment – the greater the impairment, the greater the potential for accumulation of drugs
2. Serum creatinine may not be raised in the elderly, although renal impairment may be present.
3. Care is needed with drugs or active metabolites predominantly cleared by the kidney, eg. antidepressants and antipsychotics (except substituted benzamides).
4. Start low and go slow, adjusting doses to tolerance.
5. Adverse effects such as postural hypotension, sedation and confusion may be more common.
6. Care is needed with drugs with marked anticholinergic activity, which may cause urinary retention and interfere with U&E measurements.

### 3.9.1 Antipsychotics:

Lower doses of all antipsychotics should be used as increased cerebral sensitivity and EPSEs may occur.

1. **Risperidone** elimination is reduced in renal disease and so initial doses and dose increments should be halved, up to about 4mg/d.
2.\* **Olanzapine** is excreted primarily (57%) via the renal pathway and 30% in faeces. A lower olanzapine starting dose of 5mg/d may be appropriate in renal impairment (review: Callaghan *et al*, *Clin Pharmacokinetics* 1999, **37**, 177–93). If creatinine clearance is <10ml/min, there is only a slight (11%) increase in half-life and 17% reduction in clearance. In severe renal impairment, **quetiapine** may have some reduced clearance compared to controls so the starting dose should be 25mg/d, with dose increments of 25–50mg/d (eg. n=8, Thyrum *et al*, *PNBP* 2000, **24**, 521–33). 17% of a dose of **zotepine** is excreted through the kidneys and levels may be 2–3 times higher in

patients with renal impairment. Start at 25mg bd up to a maximum of 75mg bd. Only 1% of **ziprasidone** is excreted unchanged via urine, 20% total via metabolites, and so dosage adjustment is not required in renal impairment (Aweeka *et al, Br J Clin Pharmacol* 2000, **49**(Suppl 3), 27–34). Dose adjustment with **aripiprazole** is not necessary even in severe renal impairment. **Sertindole** clearance is unchanged by deteriorating renal function and dialysis and usual doses can be used even in patients with severe renal impairment (MI). A 4mg single dose study showed that no dose adjustment was necessary in varying degrees of impairment (n=24, Wong *et al, Eur J Clin Pharmacol* 1997, **52**, 223–27). Only 4% of an oral dose is excreted via the kidneys.

3. **Clozapine** is contraindicated in severe renal disease. Start at 12.5mg/d and increase slowly in mild to moderate renal failure.

4. **Zuclopenthixol** and **flupentixol** should be used with caution in renal impairment (SPC), as some accumulation of metabolites has been reported. No dosage adjustment of flupentixol is usually necessary (review: Jann *et al, Clin Pharmacokinet* 1985, **10**, 315–33).

5. **Sulpiride** is mainly cleared by the kidneys and its half-life can range from 6–25hrs, depending upon renal function. Reduce the dose by 35–70% or extend the dosage interval by a factor of 1.5 to 3 if necessary (n=24, open, Bressolle *et al, Clin Pharmacokinet* 1989, **17**, 367–73). **Amisulpride** is principally cleared unchanged through the kidneys, so care is needed in moderate to severe renal insufficiency (GFR 10–30ml/min). It is not appreciably removed during haemodialysis.

6. There are no apparent problems with **haloperidol**, and it is less sedative and causes little postural hypotension. The UK SPC recommends caution as some accumulation might occur.

7. There is little information on phenothiazines, but excretion may be slower and accumulation may occur, causing sedation, postural hypotension etc. **Levomepromazine** (methotrimeprazine) should be used with care in renal disease, and **chlorpromazine** and **thioridazine** avoided.

8. **Loxapine** is 70% excreted via the kidneys and 30% via faeces. No specific problems in renal damage are known.

### 3.9.2 Antidepressants:

9.* Even severe renal failure did not affect the kinetics of **citalopram** in a single-dose study. Haemodialysis had an insignificant effect on plasma levels (n=12, open, Spigset *et al, Eur J Clin Pharmacol* 2000, **56**, 699–703). Renal clearance accounts for about 20% of the total citalopram elimination, and although half-life increases slightly, no reduction of citalopram dosage is warranted in patients with moderately impaired renal function but slight reduction in severe renal failure may be prudent (RCT, Joffe *et al, Eur J Clin Pharmacol* 1998, **54**, 237–42). Dosage adjustment with **escitalopram** is not necessary in patients with mild or moderate renal impairment. Caution is advised in patients with severely reduced renal. function (CLCR less than 30ml/min). If the GFR is less than 10ml/min do not use **fluoxetine**, unless the patient is on dialysis. If the GFR is 10–50ml/min. the manufacturers suggest alternate day dosing, with care. **Fluvoxamine** should be used with care, starting at 50mg/d and increasing only slowly. An unpublished report indicated that fluvoxamine does not accumulate at 100mg/d in renal impairment. In moderate renal impairment, reduce the initial dose of **paroxetine** to 10mg/d, and increase only if necessary. Use of **sertraline** is not recommended by the manufacturers although they have 'data on file' of a single dose study which showed no significant changes in sertraline kinetics in mild, moderate or severe renal failure.

10. About 1–10% of a **venlafaxine** dose is cleared unchanged by the kidney and 30% renally excreted as the major metabolite. Total clearance is reduced by about 35% in mild to moderate renal impairment (GFR 10–30ml/min) and so doses should be reduced by about 25–50% respectively, although there is much inter-patient variability in renal impairment (Anon, *J Clin Psych* 1993, **54**, 119–26). A study (12 with renal impairment, 8 on dialysis and 18 matched controls) showed that clearance was reduced by about 55% in moderate to severe renal disease, and the authors suggested a 50% reduction in venlafaxine dose, given once a day, where GFR was less than 30ml/min (n=36, open, Troy *et al*, *Clin Pharmacol Therapeut* 1994, **56**, 14–21). Single daily dosing is thus appropriate, with daily doses also reduced by 50% in dialysis and doses separated from dialysis itself. It is not recommended in severe renal failure but has been used in haemodialysis, with the dose reduced by 50% and withheld until after dialysis is complete.

11. **Mirtazapine** clearance is reduced by 33% in moderate and by 50% in severe renal failure, but not in mild renal impairment in a single dose study (n=40, Bengtsson *et al*, *Hum Psychopharmacol* 1998, **13**, 357–65), and so care with higher doses is recommended.

12. **Tricyclics** should be started at low dose and increased slowly, with divided doses. Avoid **lofepramine** in severe renal impairment, as 50% is renally excreted.

13. Accumulation of **nefazodone** metabolites could occur and so lower doses should be used in severe renal impairment. No dosage adjustment is necessary for **trazodone** (Catanese *et al*, *Boll Chim Farm* 1978, **117**, 424–27).

14. **Reboxetine's** half-life and plasma levels appear to rise (up to two-fold) in severe renal impairment where dose adjustment may be necessary. In a single-dose study, a reduction in starting dose to 2mg BD in patients with moderate to severe renal dysfunction has been suggested (n=18, open, Coulomb *et al*, *J Clin Pharmacol* 2000, **40**, 482–87).

15. No dosage adjustments are usually necessary for the **MAOIs**, although **isocarboxazid** should be used with caution with impaired renal function to prevent accumulation (SPC).

16. Dosage adjustments in renal disease are not necessary for **moclobemide** (n=12, open, Stoeckel *et al*, *Acta Psych Scand* 1990, **360**[Suppl], 94–97), **mianserin** nor **tryptophan**.

---

### 3.9.3 Anxiolytics and hypnotics:

17. Low dose anticonvulsant use of **benzodiazepines** may be acceptable as higher doses produce an increase in CNS side-effects. **Chlordiazepoxide** can be given in normal doses and is not affected by haemodialysis (review, Bennett *et al*, *Am J Kidney Dis* 1983, **3**, 155). In severe renal failure, doses of **oxazepam** should be reduced to 75%. In end stage renal failure and haemodialysis, **clobazam** and metabolite concentrations appeared no different to those with normal renal function and there may be no need to change doses in any degree of renal failure or in haemodialysis (n=1, Roberts and Zoanetti, *Ann Pharmacother* 1994, **28**, 966–67). Accumulation of metabolites of **midazolam** may be responsible for prolonged sedation (n=5, Bauer *et al*, *Lancet* 1995, **346**, 145–47) prolonged sedation with midazolam, not reversible by flumazenil (n=5, Bauer *et al*, *Lancet* 1995, **346**, 145–47).

18. **Buspirone** plasma levels have been shown to be higher in patients with renal failure, with a good correlation between steady-state buspirone levels and serum albumin (n=54, open, Barbhaiya *et al*, *E J Clin Pharmacol* 1994, **46**, 41–47). It is contraindicated in moderate or severe renal impairment.

19. Plasma protein binding of **zolpidem** is reduced in renal failure (Pacifici, *Int J Clin Pharmacol Ther Toxicol* 1988, **26**, 439–43). The half-life may be doubled but no dosage adjustments are recommended in mild renal dysfunction. The pharmacokinetics of **zaleplon** and **zopiclone** are not significantly different in renal insufficiency, and dose alteration is not required.

20. In severe renal disease plasma levels of **beta-blockers** may be higher and so starting doses should be lower. Beta-blockers may also reduce renal blood flow and adversely affect renal function.

21. Caution is needed with **clomethiazole** in chronic renal disease. **Chloral** is contraindicated in moderate to marked renal impairment.

### 3.9.4 Anticonvulsants:

22. **Carbamazepine** rarely causes renal disturbances although it has been suggested that doses should be reduced by 25% in severe renal failure (*Am J Kidney Dis* 1983, **3**, 155). For **oxcarbazepine** in renal impairment (creatinine clearance less than 30ml/min), start at half the usual dose (300mg/day), increasing at no more frequently than weekly intervals. In patients with pre-existing renal conditions associated with low sodium or in patients treated concomitantly with sodium-lowering drugs (eg, diuretics, desmopressin) as well as NSAIDs, serum sodium levels should be monitored (see SPC).

23. **Valproate** is eliminated mainly through the kidneys and the UK SPC states that it may be necessary to decrease dosage in renal insufficiency.

24. No specific dose adjustments are required, but **phenytoin** protein binding is altered in uraemia which can be problematic in accurately assessing serum levels. Severe cardiovascular ADRs have been reported with **fosphenytoin** IV (see *3.2*) and so a reduced loading dose and/or infusion rate by 10–25% in renal impairment is recommended.

25. **Phenobarbital** causes increased sedation and the dosage interval should be increased to at least 12–16 hours in severe renal failure. Large doses of **primidone** should be avoided. Active metabolites of **amylobarbital** accumulate in severe renal disease.

26. **Gabapentin** is mainly excreted unchanged in the urine (n=12, open, Hooper *et al*, *B J Clin Pharmacol* 1991, **31**, 171–74). The UK manufacturers recommend dose reductions as follows:

| Creatine clearance | Dosage and frequency |
| --- | --- |
| 60–90ml/min | 400mg tds |
| 30–60ml/min | 300mg bd |
| 15–30ml/min | 300mg/d |
| <15ml/min | 300mg alternate days |

Patients undergoing haemodialysis should receive a loading dose of 400mg and 200–300mg for every four hours of dialysis. Alternatively, a single-dose study of gabapentin 400mg in adults with varying degrees of renal function (but none on dialysis) showed that clearance correlated well with creatinine clearance, with increased half-life with poorer renal function. The authors suggested normal gabapentin doses for creatinine clearance of 60ml/min, 600mg/d for 30–59ml/min, 300mg/d for 15–29ml/min and 150mg/d for CLcr less than 15ml/min (n=60, open, Blum *et al*, *Clin Pharmacol Therapeut* 1994, **56**, 154–59). A reduced maintenance dose of **lamotrigine** is usually recommended in severe renal impairment, but the dose probably needs little adjustment in mild to moderate impairment (n=21, Wootton *et al*, *B J Clin Pharmacol* 1997, **43**, 23–27) and even in end stage renal failure (SPC), although the major glucuronide metabolite levels may increase eight-fold due to reduced renal clearance.

27. **Vigabatrin** is excreted by the kidneys and so reduced doses are recommended with a creatinine clearance of <60mL/min. About 60–70% of a **topiramate** dose is excreted unchanged via the kidneys. Time to steady state may be 10–15 days in

severe renal impairment instead of 4–8 days with normal renal function. Dose titration may thus need to be more careful. Supplemental doses of 50% of the daily dose should be given on haemodialysis days. There is an increased risk of renal stone formation, via its carbonic anhydrase inhibition, carbonic anhydrase being a known inhibitor of renal crystallisation. Care is needed to ensure adequate fluid throughput, especially in patients with known disposition to this problem (Wasserstein *et al, Epilepsia* 1995, **36**[Suppl 3], S153). **Piracetam** is excreted unchanged via the kidneys and dose adjustments may be needed in renal impairment (review: Tacconi and Wurtman, *Adv Neurol* 1986, **43**, 675–85). There are no apparent problems with **tiagabine** (n=25, Cato *et al, Epilepsia* 1998, **39**, 43–47). Since 66% of a dose of **levetiracetam** is excreted unchanged in the urine, dose reductions are necessary in impaired renal function:

| Renal function | Creatinine clearance | Dosage and frequency |
|---|---|---|
| Normal | >80ml/min | 500–1500mg bd |
| Mild | 50–79ml/min | 500–1000mg bd |
| Moderate 30–49ml/min | 250–750mg bd | |
| Severe | <30ml/min | 250–500mg bd |
| End-stage renal disease, undergoing dialysis | – | 50–100 bd |

Following dialysis, a 250–500mg supplemental dose is recommended.

28. **Ethosuximide** doses should be reduced by 25% in severe renal failure.

### 3.9.5 Others:

29.* No change in dose is necessary with **donepezil** in mild to moderate renal impairment (MI) and a 5mg single-dose study indicated that even moderate-to-severely impaired renal function did not significantly alter the kinetics of donepezil (open, n=22,

Tiseo *et al, B J Clin Pharmacol* 1998, **46**(Suppl 1), 56–60). There are no reported problems with **rivastigmine** (MI). No dosage reduction of **galantamine** is necessary for creatinine clearance greater than 9ml/min. In severe impairment (<9ml/min) galantamine is contraindicated (due current to lack of safety data) (SPC). No **memantine** dose reduction is necessary in mild impairment, but the maximum dose should be reduced to 10mg/d in moderate renal impairment. There is no data for severe renal impairment and use cannot be recommended.

30. The UK SPCs recommend some caution in renal disease with the **anticholinergics**.

31. The UK SPC for **disulfiram** recommends caution in renal disease. The UK SPC for **acamprosate** states that use in renal insufficiency (serum creatinine >120micromol/L) is a contraindication.

32. **Lithium** is contraindicated in severe renal impairment. If lithium use is unavoidable, use alternate day dosing, use very low doses (25–75% normal) and frequent level estimating. There is a case of lithium augmentation being used successfully in a 78-year-old woman with borderline impaired renal function, using 125mg on alternate days, with the above-mentioned close monitoring (Gash *et al, J Aff Dis* 1995, 51–53). For a review of lithium and the kidney, see Gitlin (*Drug Safety* 1999, **20**, 231–43, 77 refs).

33. The maximum **modafinil** dose of 400mg/d should only be used in the absence of renal impairment (MI).

34. **Bupropion** and metabolites are almost exclusively (85%) excreted through the kidneys and so, in renal failure, the initial dose should be reduced and close monitoring for toxicity carried out.

Full reviews, assessments and references for most of these interactions can be found in standard reference books. Resources include *Drug Interactions* by Ivan Stockley (Blackwell Scientific, Oxford), or *Drug Interactions in Psychiatry*, edited by Ciraulo, Shader, Greenblatt and Creelman (Williams & Wilkins, Maryland).

Absolute classification of interactions is impossible. Many factors, eg. age, concurrent illness, P450 status etc. are important. Single case reports merely suggest a possible interaction, and more structured formal studies may show the probable likelihood of an interaction. In order to give some guidance, interactions with the drugs in **CAPITAL LETTERS** are those which could be:

- Potentially hazardous
- Where a dosage adjustment is likely to have to be made
- Well-established and documented
- Of clinical significance
- Rare but important.

## How to use this section:

1. Look up the psychiatric drug or group.
2. Look up the drug group of the interacting drug.
3. If no entry there, look up the actual drug.
4. If still no entry, little or nothing has been reported to date.

## 4.1 ANXIOLYTICS & HYPNOTICS

### 4.1.1 BENZODIAZEPINES

Benzodiazepines are mainly metabolised by CYP2C and CYP3A3/4.
**Review:** Tanaka, *J Clin Pharm and Therapeut* 1999, **24**, 347.

### Acamprosate + benzodiazepines
See acamprosate (*4.6.1*).

### Acetazolamide + benzodiazepines
A theoretical interaction only.

### ALCOHOL + BENZODIAZEPINES
See alcohol (*4.7.1*).

### Alosetron + alprazolam*
Alosetron, a 5-HT3 receptor antagonist, has no effect on the kinetics of alprazolam (n=12, RCT, open, D'Souza *et al, J Clin Pharmacol* 2001, **41**, 452–54).

### Amfetamines + benzodiazepines
Animal studies have shown a clinically insignificant interaction.

### Amiodarone + clonazepam
Clonazepam toxicity at low dose caused by amiodarone has been reported (n=1, Witt *et al, Ann Pharmacother* 1993, **27**, 1463–64).

### Antacids + benzodiazepines
Benzodiazepine absorption is slightly delayed by antacids but total absorption remains the same.

### Anticholinergics + benzodiazepines
Benzodiazepine absorption may be delayed by anticholinergics, but the amount absorbed remains unchanged.

### Anticoagulants + benzodiazepines
Lack of an interaction has been demonstrated and benzodiazepines are a suitable alternative to chloral. Isolated cases of adverse reactions have been reported.

### Antihistamines + benzodiazepines
Enhanced sedation is possible.

### Antihypertensives + benzodiazepines
Enhanced hypotension is possible.

### Antipsychotics + benzodiazepines
See antipsychotics (*4.2.1*).

### Atropine + benzodiazepines
No interaction is thought to occur.

### Baclofen + benzodiazepines
Enhanced sedation can occur.

### Barbiturates + benzodiazepines
Enhanced sedation and increased benzodiazepine clearance may occur via CYP3A4 induction. Dose adjustment may be necessary.

### Beta-blockers + benzodiazepines
Propranolol and metoprolol produce a small but significant reduction in diazepam clearance and patients may become more 'accident-prone' on the combination. Propranolol and labetolol had no effect on oxazepam (n=6, Sonne *et al, B J Clin Pharmacol* 1990, **29**, 33–37), but some effect on

reaction times was seen. Metoprolol appears not to interact significantly with lorazepam (n=12, open, Scott *et al, Eur J Clin Pharmacol* 1991, **40**, 405–9).

### Buprenorphine + flunitrazepam

Buprenorphine does not inhibit the metabolism of flunitrazepam and so any interaction is likely to be pharmacodynamic rather than metabolic (microsome study, Kilicarslan and Sellers, *Am J Psych* 2000, **157**, 1164–66).

### Buspirone + benzodiazepines

See buspirone (*4.1.2*).

### CALCIUM-CHANNEL BLOCKERS + BENZODIAZEPINES*

Diltiazem significantly increases diazepam levels, probably via CYP3A4 inhibition (n=13, RCT, d/b, c/o, Kosuge *et al, Drug Metab Dispos* 2001, **29**, 1284–89). Both diltiazem and verapamil significantly raise midazolam levels and half-life, via 3A4 induction, increasing sedative side-effects. A 50% midazolam dose reduction has been suggested (n=9, RCT, d/b, c/o, 2/7, Backman *et al, B J Clin Pharmacol* 1994, **37**, 221–25).

### Cannabis + benzodiazepines

See cannabis (*4.7.2*).

### Carbamazepine + benzodiazepines*

See carbamazepine (*4.5.1*).

### Charcoal, activated + diazepam

25g activated charcoal given 30 minutes after diazepam 5mg reduced diazepam AUC by 27%, but not peak levels. Concurrent gastric lavage does not provide any additional reductions (n=9, RCT, Lapatto-Reiniluoto *et al, Br J Clin Pharmacol* 1999, **48**, 148–53).

### Citalopram + benzodiazepines

See citalopram/escitalopram (*4.3.2.1*).

### Clarithromycin + midazolam

Higher dose clarithromycin (2.5g/d) may increase the availability of midazolam, probably via CYP3A4 competition (n=16, open, 8/7, Gorski *et al, Clin Pharmacol Ther* 1998, **64**, 133–43).

### CLOZAPINE + BENZODIAZEPINES

See clozapine (*4.2.2*).

### Cyclophosphamide + benzodiazepines

Increased cyclophosphamide toxicity has been proposed.

### Dehydroepiandrosterone + alprazolam

Alprazolam rapidly and significantly increases dehydroepiandrosterone concentrations (n=38, Kroboth *et al, J Clin Psychopharmacol* 1999, **19**, 114–24).

### Dextropropoxyphene + alprazolam

Increased sedation can occur with alprazolam.

### Digoxin + benzodiazepines

Lack of interaction has been shown.

### Diflunisal + benzodiazepines

Diflunisal may reduce the effect of some benzodiazepines (lorazepam, temazepam and oxazepam) by increasing metabolism.

### Disulfiram + benzodiazepines

See disulfiram (*4.6.6*).

### Escitalopram + benzodiazepines

See citalopram/escitalopram (*4.3.2.1*).

### Ethambutol + diazepam

Lack of interaction has been shown.

### Fluoxetine + benzodiazepines

See fluoxetine (*4.3.2.2*).

### Fluvoxamine + benzodiazepines

See fluvoxamine (*4.3.2.3*).

### Food + benzodiazepines

Food delays the absorption of benzodiazepines, only significant if a rapid onset of action is needed.

### Gabapentin + benzodiazepines

See gabapentin (*4.5.3*).

### Grapefruit juice + triazolam

200ml normal-strength grapefruit juice increases plasma triazolam levels, and repeated consumption produces a greater increase (n=12, RCT, Lilja *et al, Eur J Clin Pharmacol* 2000, **56**, 411–15).

### H2-blockers + benzodiazepines*

Cimetidine inhibits the CYP3A4 metabolism of long-acting benzodiazepines but not lorazepam, oxazepam and temazepam. The clinical effect is probably negligible. The other H2-blockers do not interact this way (eg. ranitidine, n=9, RCT, d/b, c/o, 4/7, Klotz *et al, J Clin Pharmacol* 1987, **27**, 210–12), although ranitidine may slightly reduce the absorption of diazepam and increase the absorption of triazolam (n=30, RCT, open, 3/7, O'Connor-Semmes *et al, Clin Pharmacol Ther* 2001, **70**, 126–31).

### Heparin + benzodiazepines
A transient rise in benzodiazepine levels could occur (n=5, open, Routledge *et al, Clin Pharm Ther* 1980, **27**, 528–32).

### Indometacin + diazepam
Increased dizziness may occur (d/b, Nuotto and Saariolho, *Pharmacol Toxicol* 1988, **62**, 293–97).

### Isoniazid + benzodiazepines
Isoniazid reduces the clearance of diazepam but not of oxazepam (n=9, Ochs *et al, Clin Pharmacol Ther* 1981, **29**, 671–78).

### Itraconazole/ketoconazole + benzodiazepines
Increased chlordiazepoxide oral bioavailability and midazolam levels (up to 6-fold higher) occurs in patients on itraconazole and ketoconazole (n=9, RCT, d/b, 3×4/7, Olkkola *et al, Clin Pharmacol Ther* 1994, **55**, 481–85). Midazolam levels were significantly higher with itraconazole 200mg/d for 4 days, the effect being detectable up to four days after cessation of treatment (n=9, open, Backman *et al, Eur J Clin Pharmacol* 1998, **54**, 53–58).

### Lamotrigine + benzodiazepines
See lamotrigine (*4.5.4*).

### LEVODOPA + BENZODIAZEPINES
Levodopa can be antagonised by diazepam, nitrazepam and chlordiazepoxide (Yousselson *et al, Ann Int Med* 1982, **96**, 259–60), much reducing its effect, so observe for worsening symptoms.

### Lithium + benzodiazepines
See lithium (*4.4*).

### MAOIs + benzodiazepines
See MAOIs (*4.3.4*).

### Methadone + benzodiazepines
See methadone (*4.6.8*).

### Metronidazole + benzodiazepines
Lack of interaction has been reported.

### Mianserin + benzodiazepines
See mianserin (*4.3.3.1*).

### Mirtazapine + benzodiazepines
See mirtazapine (*4.3.3.2*).

### Moclobemide + benzodiazepines
See moclobemide (*4.3.3.3*).

### Modafinil + benzodiazepines *
See modafinil (*4.6.10*).

### Muscle relaxants + benzodiazepines
Variable relatively minor effects have been reported (n=113, Driessen *et al, Acta Anaesthesiol Scand* 1986, **30**, 642–46). Diazepam may hasten the onset and prolong the duration of action of vecuronium (n=20, RCT, Yuan *et al, Chung Hua I Hsueh Tsa Chih (Taipei)* 1994, **54**, 259–64), but midazolam appears not to do this (n=10, Husby *et al, Acta Anaesthesiol Scand* 1989, **33**, 280–82).

### Narcotic analgesics/opioids + benzodiazepines
Synergism (eg. n=95, RCT, d/b, Kissin *et al, Anesth Analg* 1990, **71**, 65–69) and changes in haemodynamic status (Heikkila *et al, Acta Anesthesiol Scand* 1984, **28**, 683–89) have been reported.

### NEFAZODONE + BENZODIAZEPINES
See nefazodone (*4.3.3.4*).

### Nimodipine + benzodiazepines
Lack of a clinically significant interaction during chronic oral administration has been reported (n=24, RCT, c/o, 3×5/7, Heine *et al, B J Clin Pharmacol* 1994, **38**, 39–43).

### Olanzapine + benzodiazepines
See olanzapine (*4.2.3*).

### Ondansetron + temazepam
Lack of interaction has been shown (n=24, RCT, d/b, c/o, 2/7, Preston *et al, Anaesthesia* 1996, **51**, 827–30).

### Oral contraceptives + benzodiazepines
OCs may increase the effects of longeracting benzodiazepines, not thought to be of clinical significance.

**Paraldehyde + benzodiazepines**
Enhanced sedation would be expected.

**Paroxetine + benzodiazepines**
See paroxetine (*4.3.2.4*).

**Phenytoin + benzodiazepines**
See phenytoin (*4.5.8*).

**Physostigmine + benzodiazepines**
Physostigmine may reverse diazepam-induced sleep (Speeg *et al, J Neurochem* 1980, **34**, 856–65) and midazolam-induced somnolence (Ho *et al, Ma Tsui Hsueh Tsa Chi* 1991, **29**, 643–47).

**Progabide + clonazepam**
Lack of interaction has been reported.

**Propofol + midazolam**
Propofol increases the half-life of midazolam by 61%, probably by inhibiting CYP3A4 (n=24, RCT, Hamaoka *et al, Clin Pharmacol & Ther* 1999, **66**, 110–17).

**Proton-pump inhibitors + benzodiazepines**
Omeprazole, but not pantoprazole (review: Steinijans *et al, Int J Clin Pharmacol Ther* 1996, **34**, S31–S50), can reduce diazepam clearance by up to 50% (n=12, 1/52, Andersson *et al, Eur J Clin Pharmacol* 1990, **39**, 51–54), probably by a P450 mechanism (microsome study, Zomorodi and Houston, *Br J Clin Pharmacol* 1996, **42**, 157–62).

**Quetiapine + benzodiazepines**
See quetiapine (*4.2.4*).

**Reboxetine + benzodiazepines**
See reboxetine (*4.3.3.5*).

**Rifampicin + benzodiazepines**
CYP3A4 induction by rifampicin can lead to increased diazepam clearance (n=21, 7/7, Ohnhaus, *Clin Pharmacol Ther* 1987, **42**, 148) and reduced midazolam levels (n=9, 9/7, Backman *et al, Eur J Clin Pharmacol* 1998, **54**, 53–58).

**Ritonavir + benzodiazepines**
Extensive impairment of triazolam and alprazolam clearance by short-term low-dose ritonavir may occur

(editorial: Greenblatt *et al, J Clin Psychopharmacol* 1999, **19**, 293–96).

**Rivastigmine + benzodiazepines**
See rivastigmine (*4.6.3.3*).

**Sertindole + benzodiazepines** *
See sertindole (*4.2.7.2*).

**Sertraline + benzodiazepines**
See sertraline (*4.3.2.5*).

**Smoking + benzodiazepines** *
See smoking (*4.7.4*).

**Tiagabine + benzodiazepines**
See tiagabine (*4.5.10*).

**Tricyclics + benzodiazepines**
Enhanced sedation has been reported and would be expected. Reduced hydroxylation of clomipramine has been reported and dose reduction may be necessary (*Pharmaceutisch Weekblad* 1992, **14**[4] Suppl D, D3).

**Valproate + benzodiazepines** *
Valproate displaces diazepam from plasma protein-binding sites and so doses may need to be reduced. Valproate increases lorazepam levels by up to 40% (n=16, RCT, Samara *et al, J Clin Pharmacol* 1997, **37**, 442–50) and coma has been reported with the combination, possibly via reduced lorazepam clearance (n=1, Lee *et al, Seizure* 2002, **11**, 124–25). Valproate and clonazepam have no apparent effect on each other (n=4, Wang and Wang, *Ther Drug Monit* 2002, **24**, 532–36) but clobazam may increase valproate levels.

**Venlafaxine + benzodiazepines**
See venlafaxine (*4.3.3.8*).

**Warfarin + benzodiazepines**
An interaction is unreported but theoretically possible (mentioned in Sayal *et al, Acta Psych Scand* 2000, **102**, 250–55).

**Xanthines + benzodiazepines**
Xanthines, eg. theophylline, aminophylline and caffeine antagonise the sedative (and possibly anxiolytic) effects of benzodiazepines (eg. midazolam 12mg is moderately antagonised by 250mg caffeine, n=114, Mattila *et al, Int J Clin Pharmacol Ther* 2000, **38**, 581–87). This can be very useful in the

treatment of benzodiazepine overdose but care must be taken if a patient on a benzodiazepine has theophylline stopped, as respiratory depression can then occur.

### Ziprasidone + benzodiazepines *
See ziprasidone (*4.2.7.3*).

### Zotepine + benzodiazepines
See zotepine (*4.2.6*).

---

### 4.1.2 BUSPIRONE
Buspirone may be metabolised by CYP3A4.

### Alcohol + buspirone
See alcohol (*4.7.1*).

### Benzodiazepines + buspirone
Two studies with diazepam have shown only a minimal enhanced sedation. Alprazolam appears not to interact with buspirone (n=24, 7/7, Buch *at el, J Clin Pharmacol* 1993, **33**, 1104–9).

### Calcium-channel blockers + buspirone
80mg verapamil or 60mg diltiazem increase buspirone plasma concentrations 3-fold and 5-fold respectively, peak plasma levels also being raised, probably by CYP3A4 inhibition, potentially enhancing the therapeutic and side-effects of buspirone (n=9, RCT, p/c, c/o, Lamberg *et al, Clin Pharmacol Ther* 1998, **63**, 640–45).

### Cimetidine + buspirone
Lack of interaction has been reported (n=10, open, Gammans *et al, Pharmacotherapy* 1987, **7**, 72–79).

### Citalopram + buspirone
See citalopram (*4.3.2.1*).

### Clozapine + buspirone
Near fatal gastrointestinal bleeding and hyperglycaemia occurring one month after buspirone was added to a stable clozapine regimen has been reported, but no firm explanation found (n=1, Good, *Am J Psych* 1997, **154**, 1473).

### Erythromycin + buspirone
Erythromycin and itraconazole may increase plasma buspirone levels dramatically, probably via CYP3A4 inhibition, with increased side-effects

noted (n=8, Kivisto *et al, Clin Pharmacol Ther* 1997, **62**, 348–54).

### Escitalopram + buspirone *
See citalopram/escitalopram (*4.3.2.1*).

### Fluvoxamine + buspirone
Fluvoxamine 100mg/d raises buspirone levels, probably via CYP3A4 inhibition but is probably of limited significance (n=10, RCT, Lamberg *et al, Eur J Clin Pharmacol* 1998, **54**, 761–66).

### Fluoxetine + buspirone
Reduced anxiolytic effect, dystonia, akathisia (n=1, Metz, *Can J Psych* 1990, **35**, 722–23) and anorgasmia (n=20, open, 8/52, Jenike *et al, J Clin Psych* 1991, **52**, 13–14) have been reported.

### Grapefruit juice + buspirone
200ml double-strength grapefruit juice raised peak buspirone plasma levels 4-fold, probably via CYP3A4 inhibition or delayed gastric emptying so avoid buspirone and at least large amounts of grapefruit juice, or adjust doses (n=10, RCT, Lilja *et al, Clin Pharmacol Ther* 1998, **64**, 655–60).

### Itraconazole + buspirone
See erythromycin + buspirone.

### MAOIs + BUSPIRONE
See MAOIs (*4.3.4*).

### NSAIDs + buspirone
GI side-effects and headache may be slightly more common with the combination (n=150, Kiev and Domantay, *Curr Ther Res* 1989, **46**, 1086–90).

### Phenytoin + buspirone
Buspirone does not appear to displace phenytoin from plasma binding sites (review: Gammans *et al, Am J Med* 1986, **80**[Suppl 3B], 41–51).

### Propranolol + buspirone
Buspirone appears not to displace propranolol from plasma binding sites (review: Gammans *et al, Am J Med* 1986, **80**[Suppl 3B], 41–51).

### Rifampicin + buspirone *
The buspirone SPC now states that rifampicin decreases buspirone plasma levels, probably via CYP3A4

induction. Significant changes in psychomotor tests have been noted and so dose adjustment may be necessary (n=10, Lamberg *et al, Br J Clin Pharmacol* 1998, **45**, 381–85).

### St John's wort + buspirone *
There is a possible case of serotonin syndrome (n=1, Dannawi, *J Psychopharmacol* 2002, **16**, 401).

### Trazodone + buspirone
There are some isolated reports of raised SGPT/ALT levels and a case of serotonin syndrome (n=1, Goldberg and Huk, *Psychosomatics* 1992, **3**, 235).

### Warfarin + buspirone
Buspirone does not appear to displace warfarin from plasma binding sites (review: Gammans *et al, Am J Med* 1986, **80**[Suppl 3B], 41–51).

### Zudovidine + buspirone
The combination has been used safely (n=2, Batki, *J Clin Psychopharmacol* 1990, **10**[Suppl 3], 111S–15S).

## 4.1.3 CHLORAL

### ALCOHOL + CHLORAL
See alcohol (*4.7.1*).

### Fluvoxamine + chloral
See fluvoxamine (*4.3.2.3*).

### Furosemide (frusemide) + chloral
Diaphoresis, facial flushing and agitation occurred with chloral and IV furosemide, which stopped when the chloral was discontinued (n=1, Dean *et al, Clin Pharm* 1991, **10**, 385–87).

### MAOIs + chloral
See MAOIs (*4.3.4*).

### Methadone + chloral *
See methadone (*4.6.8*).

### Phenytoin + chloral
See phenytoin (*4.5.8*).

### Nicoumalone + chloral
An enhanced anticoagulant effect can occur. See also warfarin + chloral.

### Warfarin + chloral
The anticoagulant effects of warfarin are increased slightly by chloral, probably by plasma protein displacement (BCDSP, *NEJM* 1972, **286**, 53–55). This can be important if chloral is given as a PRN hypnotic.

## 4.1.4 ZALEPLON
Zaleplon is primarily metabolised by aldehyde oxidase and a small amount by CYP3A4 to inactive metabolites. As with other such drugs, use with other CNS-depressants needs care.

### Alcohol + zaleplon *
See alcohol (*4.7.1*).

### Antipsychotics + zaleplon
Additive psychomotor effects may occur with combined zaleplon and thioridazine (n=12, RCT, Hetta *et al, Eur J Clin Pharmacol* 2000, **56**, 211–17).

### Carbamazepine + zaleplon
Co-administration may reduce zaleplon efficacy through CYP3A4 induction.

### Cimetidine + zaleplon
Raised zaleplon levels can occur with cimetidine, via aldehyde oxidase and CYP3A4 inhibition.

### Digoxin + zaleplon
Lack of interaction has been shown (n=20, Sanchez-Garcia *et al, Am J Health Syst Pharm* 2000, **57**, 2267–70).

### Erythromycin + zaleplon
Raised zaleplon levels can occur, via 3A4 inhibition.

### Ibuprofen + zaleplon
Lack of significant interaction has been shown (n=17, open, Sanchez-Garcia *et al, Am J Health Syst Pharm* 2000, **57**, 1137–41).

### Ketoconazole + zaleplon
Raised zaleplon levels can occur, via 3A4 inhibition.

### Narcotics + zaleplon
Enhanced euphoria is possible.

### Rifampicin + zaleplon
A four-fold reduction in zaleplon levels can occur, via CYP3A4 induction.

### Phenobarbital + zaleplon
Reduced zaleplon levels can occur, via CYP3A4 induction.

### Warfarin + zaleplon
No interaction occurs (MI).

## 4.1.5 ZOLPIDEM

Enhanced sedation would be expected with concurrent use of zolpidem with any CNS depressant. It is mainly metabolised by CYP3A4 but has no effect on 1A2, 2B6, 2C9, 2D6 and 3A4.

### Alcohol + zolpidem
See alcohol (*4.7.1*).

### Antipsychotics + zolpidem
Excessive sedation has been reported with chlorpromazine (n=6, d/b, single-dose, Desager *et al, Psychopharmacol* 1988, **96**, 63–66).

### Bupropion + zolpidem
See bupropion (*4.6.4*).

### Caffeine + zolpidem
In a parallel group study, 300mg caffeine did not antagonise the sedative effects of zolpidem given during the day (n=45+, d/b, p/c, Mattila *et al, Eur J Clin Pharmacol* 1998, **54**, 421–25).

### Fluconazole + zolpidem
See itraconazole + zolpidem.

### Food + zolpidem
The rate of absorption of zolpidem is slowed significantly by food.

### H2-blockers + zolpidem
Lack of a significant interaction has been shown with both cimetidine and ranitidine (n=6, c/o, 18/7, Hulhoven *et al, Int J Clin Pharmacol Res* 1988, **8**, 471–76).

### Itraconazole/ketoconazole/ fluconazole + zolpidem
Single doses of itraconazole or fluconazole slightly lengthen the half-life of zolpidem (n=12, RCT, Greenblatt *et al, Clin Pharmacol Ther* 1998, **64**, 661–71). Itraconazole 200mg/d for 4 days had no marked effect on the pharmacokinetics of zolpidem, although central effects were slightly increased (n=10, Luurila *et al, Eur J Clin Pharmacol* 1998, **54**, 163–66).

### Oral Contraceptives + zolpidem *
Zolpidem clearance is slightly higher and half-life slightly shorter in women using OCs (n=16, Olubodun *et al, J Clin Pharmacol* 2002, **42**, 1142–46).

### Rifampicin + zolpidem
Rifampicin significantly reduces zolpidem plasma levels and therapeutic effect, via CYP3A4 induction (n=8, RCT, Villikka *et al, Br J Clin Pharmacol* 1997, **43**, 629–34).

### Smoking + zolpidem *
Zolpidem half-life may be 30% shorter in smokers than non-smokers, probably of low clinical significance and due to minor CYP1A2 induction (n=16, Olubodun *et al, J Clin Pharmacol* 2002, **42**, 1142–46).

### SSRIs + zolpidem *
SSRIs may enhance zolpidem-associated hallucinations (n=5, Elko *et al, J Toxicol Clin Toxicol* 1998, **36**, 195–203). One study showed minimal pharmacokinetic interaction between **fluoxetine** and regular zolpidem in healthy women, with no significant psychomotor function changes, although zolpidem half-life increased slightly (n=29, 5/52, Allard *et al, Drug Metab Dispos* 1998, **26**, 617–22). The combination with **sertraline** may lead to a shorter onset of action and an increased effect from zolpidem (n=28, RCT, Allard *et al, J Clin Pharmacol* 1999, **39**, 184–91).

## 4.1.6 ZOPICLONE
Zopiclone is mainly metabolised by CYPA4.

### Alcohol + zopiclone
See alcohol (*4.7.1*).

### Aspirin + zopiclone
Lack of interaction has been shown (MI).

### Atropine + zopiclone
See metoclopramide + zopiclone below.

### Caffeine + zopiclone
Caffeine may moderately antagonise the psychomotor impairment caused by zopiclone (d/b, Mattila *et al, Pharmacol Toxicol* 1992, **70**, 286–89).

### Erythromycin + zopiclone
Erythromycin accelerates zopiclone absorption, leading to a more rapid onset, which could be clinically significant in the elderly (n=10, Aranko

*et al, B J Clin Pharmacol* 1994, **38**, 363–67).

### Itraconazole + zopiclone
Itraconazole significantly increased zopiclone plasma levels by 28% and half-life by 40% but had no clinical significance in the young volunteers (n=10, d/b, p/c, c/o, Jalava *et al, Eur J Clin Pharmacol* 1996, **51**, 331–34).

### Nefazodone + zopiclone *
Increased zopiclone levels, sedation and hangover has been reported with nefazodone (n=1, Alderman *et al, Ann Pharmacother* 2001, **35**, 1378–80).

### Ranitidine + zopiclone
Lack of interaction has been shown (MI).

### Rifampicin + zopiclone
Rifampicin significantly reduces zopiclone plasma levels and therapeutic effect, via CYP3A4 induction (n=8, RCT, Villikka *et al, Br J Clin Pharmacol* 1997, **43**, 471–74).

### Tricyclics + zopiclone
One study showed decreased levels of trimipramine and zopiclone, of doubtful significance (n=10, RCT, Caille *et al, Biopharm Drug Dispos* 1984, **5**, 117–25).

---

**4.2 ANTIPSYCHOTICS** — see also aripiprazole *(4.2.7.1)*, clozapine *(4.2.2)*, olanzapine *(4.2.3)*, risperidone *(4.2.4)*, quetiapine *(4.2.5)*, sertindole *(4.2.7.2)*, ziprasidone *(4.2.7.3)* and zotepine *(4.2.6)*.

---

### 4.2.1 ANTIPSYCHOTICS - GENERAL

---

There are few specific interactions reported for some antipsychotics, other than additive sedation.
**Reviews**: interactions with anti-hypertensive durgs (Markowitz *et al, Ann Pharmacother* 1995, **29**, 603–9).

### ACE inhibitors + antipsychotics
An enhanced hypotensive effect can occur, with severe postural hypotension with chlorpromazine and other antipsychotics, eg. captopril plus chlorpromazine (White, *Arch Int Med* 1986, **146**, 1833–34).

### Activated charcoal + phenothiazines
Decreased antipsychotic absorption is likely.

### ALCOHOL + ANTIPSYCHOTICS
See alcohol *(4.7.1)*.

### Amfetamines + antipsychotics
The antipsychotic effects of phenothiazines can be antagonised by amfetamines although haloperidol can be used to treat amfetamine-induced psychosis.

### Amiodarone + phenothiazines
The BNF notes an increased risk of ventricular arrhythmias with phenothiazines.

### Antacids + antipsychotics
Antacids may reduce chlorpromazine and possibly haloperidol serum levels. Sulpiride absorption may be reduced by sucralfate or aluminium containing antacids. Any problem can be minimised by separating doses by a couple of hours.

### Anticholinergics + antipsychotics *
Anticholinergics may reduce the improvement in positive symptoms produced by antipsychotics, probably by lowering the serum levels of oral and depot antipsychotics (n=25, Bamrah *et al, B J Psych* 1986, **149**, 726–33), but not by increased clearance (n=31, open, Chetty *et al, Eur J Clin Pharmacol* 1994, **46**, 523–26). Additive anticholinergic effects may also occur (see also *1.20.1*) eg. a case of acute intestinal pseudo-obstruction has been reported with benzatropine and haloperidol (n=1, Sheikh *et al, Am J Gastroenterol* 2001, **96**, 934–35).

### ANTICONVULSANTS + ANTIPSYCHOTICS
Antipsychotics lower the seizure threshold and may thus antagonise anticonvulsant actions. See also individual anticonvulsants *(4.5)*.

## ANTIHISTAMINES + ANTIPSYCHOTICS

There is an increased risk of cardio-vascular side-effects (such as syncope, prolonged QT interval and ventricular arrhythmias) with terfenadine and astemizole, and it should not be used with other potentially arrhythmogenic drugs such as antipsychotics, a 1993 CSM warning. Loratadine is metabolised by CYP2D6 and CYP3A4, allowing alternate pathways to be used if one is inhibited. Loratadine and chlorphenamine are currently considered suitable, although there are three unproven reports of arrhythmia with loratadine.

### Antihypertensives + phenothiazines

A combined hypotensive effect can cause dizziness etc.

### Antimalarials + chlorpromazine

One study showed markedly increased chlorpromazine levels with anti-malarials, eg. chloroquine and 'Fansidar' (open, Makanjuola *et al*, *Trop Geogr Med* 1988, **40**, 31–33).

### Ascorbic acid + fluphenazine

An isolated case exists of reduced fluphenazine levels (Dysken *et al*, *JAMA* 1979, **241**, 2008) with 1g/d of ascorbic acid.

## BARBITURATES + ANTIPSYCHOTICS

Additive sedative effects can occur acutely with this combination, eg. death following IM injection of haloperidol and phenobarbital has been recorded (n=1, Greenblatt *et al*, *J Clin Psych* 1978, **39**, 673). Phenobarbital administration may lower the plasma levels of some antipsychotics, eg. haloperidol by 40–75% (Gay and Madsen, *Neurology* 1983, **33**, 1631–32). Antagonism of the anticonvulsant effects may also occur.

### Benzodiazepines + antipsychotics

Enhanced sedation and impaired psychomotor function can occur (see *1.1*).

### Beta-blockers + antipsychotics

Generally, raised antipsychotic plasma levels of the occur, of possible clinical significance, eg. chlorpromazine levels may rise by up to 100–500% with propranolol (Peet *et al*, *Lancet* 1980, **ii**, 978), although pindolol has no significant effect on haloperidol levels (n=26, open, Greendyke and Gulya, *J Clin Psych* 1988, **49**, 105–7). See also review by Markowitz *et al (Ann Pharmacother* 1995, **29**, 603–9). Thioridazine is contraindicated with propranolol due to QTc prolongation.

### Betel nut + antipsychotics

Betel nut (Areca catechu), which contains the cholinergic alkaloid arecoline, has been reported to cause EPSE, bradykinesia, stiffness and akathisia with flupentixol and fluphenazine (n=1, Deahl, *Mov Disord* 1998, **4**, 330–33).

### Bromocriptine + antipsychotics

A predictable reversal of the antipsychotic effect may occur. Antipsychotics may also antagonise the hypoprolactinaemic and anti-parkinsonian effects of bromocriptine.

### Calcium-channel blockers + antipsychotics

An increased antipsychotic concentration or enhanced hypotension could be predicted (review by Markowitz *et al*, *Ann Pharmacother* 1995, **29**, 603–9).

### Cannabis + antipsychotics

See cannabis (*4.7.2*).

## CARBAMAZEPINE + ANTIPSYCHOTICS

See carbamazepine (*4.5.1*).

### Citalopram + antipsychotics

See citalopram/escitalopram (*4.3.2.1*).

## CLARITHROMYCIN + ANTIPSYCHOTICS

The BNF notes an increased risk of arrhythmias with phenothiazines and recommends avoiding the combination. Death has been reported when clarithromycin was added to pimozide in a man with a documented prolonged QT interval (n=1, Flockhart *et al*, *J Clin Psychopharmacol* 2000, **20**, 317–24).

## Clonidine + antipsychotics
Animal studies have shown phenothiazines and haloperidol (but not pimozide) to antagonise the hypotensive effect of clonidine. Case reports exist of severe hypotension (Fruncillo *et al, Am J Psych* 1985, **142**, 274) and of delirium (review by Markowitz *et al, Ann Pharmacother* 1995, **29**, 603–9).

## Clozapine + antipsychotics
See clozapine (*4.2.2*).

## Cocaine + antipsychotics
See cocaine (*4.7.3*).

## Desferrioxamine + prochlorperazine
Prolonged unconsciousness may occur (MI).

## Diazoxide + chlorpromazine
Enhanced hypoglycaemia has been reported (n=1, Aynsley-Green and Illig, *Lancet* 1975, **2**, 658).

## Disopyramide + antipsychotics
Increased anticholinergic effects may occur.

## Disulfiram + antipsychotics
See disulfiram (*4.6.6*).

## Domperidone + antipsychotics
There is an enhanced risk of EPSEs.

## Donepezil + antipsychotics *
See donepezil (*4.6.3.1*).

## Erythromycin + antipsychotics
See clarithromycin + antipsychotics.

## Escitalopram + antipsychotics
See citalopram/escitalopram (*4.3.2.1*).

## FLUOXETINE + ANTIPSYCHOTICS
Severe EPSEs have been reported with fluoxetine and haloperidol (n=1, Tate, *Am J Psych* 1989, **146**, 399–400), dystonia with fluphenazine 2.5mg (n=1, Katai, *Am J Psych* 1993, **150**, 836–37), stupor and confusion with pimozide 8mg/d (n=1, Hansen-Grant *et al, Am J Psych* 1993, **150**, 1750–51), and of severe bradycardia and drowsiness (n=1, Friedman, *Can J Psych* 1994, **39**, 634). The probable mechanism is CYP2D6 inhibition leading to raised levels. The combination should thus be avoided if possible (Ahmed *et al, Can J Psych* 1993, **38**, 62–63). Citalopram, escitalopram

and sertraline would be suitable alternatives.

## Fluvoxamine + antipsychotics *
See fluvoxamine (*4.3.2.3*).

## Ginseng + haloperidol
Ginseng may potentiate the general effects of haloperidol (Mitra *et al, Indian J Exp Biol* 1996, **34**, 41–47).

## GUANETHIDINE + ANTIPSYCHOTICS
Reduced hypotensive effects may occur.

## H2-blockers + antipsychotics
Chlorpromazine levels may be reduced by 30% by cimetidine (Howes *et al, Eur J Clin Pharmacol* 1983, **24**, 99–102). Ranitidine is a suitable alternative.

## Haloperidol + chlorpromazine *
Chlorpromazine may significantly increase haloperidol levels, probably via CYP2D6 inhibition (n=43, Suzuki *et al, Ther Drug Monit* 2001, **23**, 363–68).

## Hydroxyzine + phenothiazines
The antipsychotic effect of phenothiazines may be decreased (Ross and Priest, *Dis Nerv Syst* 1970, **31**, 412).

## Hypoglycaemics + chlorpromazine
Chlorpromazine 100mg or more can induce hyperglycaemia and upset the control of diabetes with oral hypoglycaemics (Schwarz and Munoz, *Am J Psych* 1968, **125**, 253).

## Indometacin + haloperidol
One study showed profound drowsiness and confusion on the combination (Bird *et al, Lancet* 1983, **i**, 830–31).

## Itraconazole + haloperidol
Itraconazole 200mg/d for 7 days significantly increases haloperidol and metabolite levels, leading to increased side effects, presumably due to CYP3A4 inhibition (n=13, Yasui *et al, J Clin Psychopharmacol* 1999, **19**, 149–54).

## LEVODOPA + ANTIPSYCHOTICS
The therapeutic effect of levodopa is antagonised by antipsychotics and

vice versa. Levodopa may worsen antipsychotic-induced EPSEs.

**Lithium + antipsychotics**
See lithium (*4.4*).

**MAOIs + antipsychotics**
See MAOIs (*4.3.4*).

**Memantine + antipsychotics** *
See memantine (*4.6.7*).

**Methyldopa + haloperidol**
Pseudo-dementia with haloperidol and methyldopa has been reported (n=3, Nadel and Wallach, *B J Psych* 1979, **135**, 484). There is also an enhanced risk of EPSEs and postural hypotension.

**Metirosine + antipsychotics**
An enhanced risk of EPSEs exists.

**Metoclopramide + antipsychotics**
An enhanced risk of EPSEs exists.

**Minocycline + phenothiazines**
There is a case of pigmented galactorrhoea with the combination (n=1, Basler and Lynch, *Arch Dermatol* 1985, **121**, 417).

**Naltrexone + phenothiazines**
Severe drowsiness may occur with thioridazine (Maany *et al, Am J Psych* 1987, **144**, 966) or chlorpromazine.

**Nefazodone + antipsychotics**
See nefazodone (*4.3.3.4*).

**Olanzapine + antipsychotics (other)***
See olanzapine (*4.2.3*).

**Oral contraceptives + chlorpromazine***
There is report of a combined oral contraceptive raising chlorpromazine levels six-fold (n=1, Chetty and Miller, *Ther Drug Monit* 2001, **23**, 556–58).

**Orlistat + haloperidol** *
A small trial suggested lack of interaction (n=8, open, 8/52, Hilger *et al, J Clin Psychopharmacol* 2002, **22**, 68–70).

**Oxcarbazepine + antipsychotics**
See oxcarbazepine (*4.5.6*).

**Paroxetine + antipsychotics**
See paroxetine (*4.3.2.4*).

**Pethidine + phenothiazines**
Increased CNS toxicity and hypotension can occur (n=10, open, c/o, Stambaugh and Wainer, *J Clin Pharmacol* 1981, **21**, 140–46).

**Phenylpropanolamine + thioridazine**
A single fatal case of ventricular arrhythmia exists (n=1, Chouinard *et al, Can Med Ass J* 1978, **119**, 729).

**PHENYTOIN + ANTIPSYCHOTICS**
Phenytoin may reduce haloperidol levels by 40–75%, probably via enzyme induction (n=30, open, Linnoila *et al, Am J Psych* 1980, **137**, 819). Chlorpromazine may increase phenytoin levels by up to 50% (n=27, open, Sands *et al, Drug Intell Clin Pharm* 1987, **21**, 267–72) although other studies show a nil or opposite effect. Antipsychotics lower the seizure threshold and may antagonise the anticonvulsant effect of phenytoin.

**Piperazine + chlorpromazine**
The validity of a single case of convulsions with the combination has been queried by a small study (Sturman, *B J Pharmacol* 1974, **50**, 153–55).

**Polymyxin + phenothiazines**
The neuromuscular blocking effects of polypeptide antibiotics may be increased by phenothiazines with prolonged respiratory depression possible (Pohlmann, *JAMA* 1966, **196**, 181).

**Procarbazine + antipsychotics**
Enhanced sedation is possible (MI).

**Quetiapine + antipsychotics (other)**
See quetiapine (*4.2.4*).

**Reboxetine + antipsychotics** *
See reboxetine (*4.3.3.5*).

**RIFAMPICIN + HALOPERIDOL**
Rifampicin may reduce haloperidol serum levels by a third (n=17, Kim *et al, J Clin Psychopharmacol* 1996, **16**, 247–52), a clinically significant effect. Care would also be needed if rifampicin were stopped.

**Sertindole + antipsychotics (other)** *
See sertindole (*4.2.7.2*).

**Smoking + antipsychotics**
See smoking (*4.7.4*).

## Suxamethonium + promazine

Prolonged apnoea has been reported (n=1, Regan and Aldrete, *Anesth Analg* 1967, **46**, 315–18).

## Sucralfate + antipsychotics

See antacids + antipsychotics.

## Tea or coffee + antipsychotics

Typical antipsychotics precipitate out of solution to form a tannin complex with tea and coffee (*Lancet* 1979, ii, 1130–31). The clinical significance is thought to be minimal (*Lancet* 1981, i, 1217–18).

## Tetrabenazine + antipsychotics

Only a single case of enhanced EPSEs in a Huntington's patient exists (Moss and Stewart, *Can J Psych* 1986, **31**, 865–66) although it would be a predictable effect.

## Thiazide diuretics + antipsychotics

Although no case reports exist, enhanced thioridazine cardiotoxicity has been suggested (Thornton and Pray, *Am J Nurs* 1976, **76**, 245–46).

## Trazodone + antipsychotics

See trazodone (*4.3.3.6*).

## Tricyclics + antipsychotics *

See tricyclics (*4.3.1*).

## Valproate + antipsychotics

**Chlorpromazine** may inhibit the metabolism of valproate and so monitoring of valproate levels may be appropriate (open, Ishizaki *et al, J Clin Psychopharmacol* 1984, **4**, 254–61). Valproate has no significant effect on either plasma levels of haloperidol or on psychopathology (n=27, 4/52, Hesslinger *et al, J Clin Psychopharmacol* 1999, **19**, 310–15). There are cases of dose-related generalised oedema with **risperidone** and valproate (n=2, Sanders and Lehrer, *J Clin Psych* 1998, **59**, 689–90), although valproate has no significant effect on plasma levels of risperidone and 9-hydroxyrisperidone (n=33, Spina et al, *Ther Drug Monit* 2000, **22**, 481–85). Two studies have shown that valproate produces a non-clinically significant rise in **clozapine**, but lower norclozapine, levels (n=37 + 6, Facciola *et al, Ther Drug Monit*

1999, **21**, 341–45). Antipsychotics lower the seizure threshold and may antagonise the anticonvulsant effect of valproate.

## Venlafaxine + antipsychotics

See venlafaxine (*4.3.3.8*).

## Warfarin + antipsychotics

An interaction is theoretically possible (mentioned in Sayal *et al, Acta Psych Scand* 2000, **102**, 250–55).

## Zaleplon + antipsychotics

See zaleplon (*4.1.4*).

## Zolpidem + antipsychotics

See zolpidem (*4.1.5*).

## Zotepine + antipsychotics (other)

See zotepine (*4.2.6*).

---

## ANTIPSYCHOTICS — ARIPIPRAZOLE (see *4.2.7.1*)

---

## 4.2.2. ANTIPSYCHOTICS — CLOZAPINE (see also *4.2.1* for other, more general, interactions)

---

The major metabolic route of clozapine is to norclozapine, which is more stable but more toxic to stem cells (Gerson *et al, B J Haematology* 1994, **86**, 555–61). CYP1A2 is the major metabolising enzyme, with 2D6 and 3A4 possibly having an effect, as well as many other P450 and FMO enzymes involved.

**Reviews:** clozapine interactions (Taylor, *B J Psych* 1997, **171**, 109–12, 46 refs), general (Linnet *et al, Drug Metab Dispos* 1997, **25**, 1379–82; Chang *et al, PNBP* 1998, **22**, 723–39).

## ACE inhibitors + clozapine *

Clozapine plus diltiazem or enalapril (Aronowitz *et al, J Clin Psychopharmacol* 1994, **14**, 429–30) has been reported to produce additional hypotension. There is also a well-documented case of a clinically important rise in clozapine and norclozapine levels with lisinopril, via an unknown mechanism (n=1, Abraham *et al, Am J Psych* 2001, **158**, 969).

## Alcohol + clozapine

See antipsychotics + alcohol (*4.7.1*).

## ANTIBIOTICS + CLOZAPINE

Antibiotics reported to cause leucopenia/neutropenia may enhance the likelihood of clozapine-induced neutropenia and should be avoided if possible.

1. **LESS likely to cause neutropenia (safer to use)**: penicillins (all except benzylpenicillin G), all tetracyclines, aminoglycosides, macrolides, clarithromycin, some anti-TBs (ethambutol, pyrazinamide, streptomycin), clofazimide, hexamine, sodium fusidate, spectinomycin, colistin, polymixin B and cycloserine.

2. **MORE likely/CAN cause leucopenia and/or neutropenia (less safe to use)**: cephalosporins and cephamycins, clindamycin, lincomycin, sulphonamides and trimethoprim, some anti-TBs (capreomycin, isoniazid, rifampicin), dapsone, metronidazole, tinidazole, the 4-Quinolones (ciprofloxacin, nalidixic acid etc), nitrofurantoin, chloramphenicol, vancomycin and telcoplanin.

Chose antibiotics from the *first list as first choice* where possible and be aware of the potential for problems if drugs from the second list must be used (full details in *Clozaril newsletter*, Spring 1994, 5). See also individual drugs for other interactions.

### Anticholinergics + clozapine

See antipsychotics (*4.2.1*).

### Antihypertensives + clozapine

Potentiation of the antihypertensive effects may occur. This can be particularly important during the upward dose titration period.

## ANTIPSYCHOTICS (other) + CLOZAPINE *

There is an enhanced risk of agranulocytosis (MI) which would additionally be complicated by the long-term nature of any drug given as a depot eg. a case of thrombocytopenia associated with **fluphenazine** and clozapine has been reported (n=1, Mihaljevic-Peles *et al, Nord J Psychiatry* 2001, **55**, 449–50). Elevated **haloperidol** levels have been reported in combination with clozapine (n=1, Allen, *J Clin Pharmacol* 2000, **40**, 1296–97), as has myoclonic and GTC seizures (n=1, Haberfellner, *Eur Psych* 2002, **17**, 55–56). Although one study has shown that **risperidone** 2–4mg/d does not affect serum clozapine (250–650mg/d) levels to any significant degree (n=18, Raaska *et al, Eur J Clin Pharmacol* 2002, **58**, 587–91), there are many cases of raised clozapine levels with this combination, eg. clozapine levels 73% higher with risperidone 2mg/d (Tyson *et al, Am J Psych* 1995, **152**, 1401–2), a sudden agranulocytosis six weeks after risperidone 6mg/d was added to a stable clozapine regimen (Godleski and Sernyak, *Am J Psych* 1996, **153**, 735), and a neurotoxic reaction or mild NMS (n=1, Kontaxakis *et al, PBNP* 2002, **26**, 407–9). The mechanism cannot be explained by inhibition of 1A2, 2D6 nor 2C19 (n=8, Eap *et al, Ther Drug Monit* 2001, **23**, 228–31).

## BENZODIAZEPINES + CLOZAPINE *

There are rare cases of severe hypotension and respiratory depression (eg. n=3, Finkel *et al, NEJM* 1991, **325**, 518), sudden death after IV lorazepam (n=1, Klimke & Klieser, *Am J Psych* 1994, **151**, 780), and sedation (n=2, Cobb *et al, Am J Psych* 1991, **148**, 1606–7) and delirium (n=3, Jackson *et al, Ann Clin Psych* 1995, **7**, 139–41) with lorazepam and clozapine. Monitor for enhanced sedation and take particular care when a clozapine dose is being increased.

### Buspirone + clozapine

See buspirone (*4.1.2*).

### Caffeine + clozapine

Caffeine and clozapine are both metabolised by CYP1A2 and so some competitive inhibition of metabolism may occur. Caffeine in doses of 400–1000mg inhibits the metabolism of clozapine to an extent that might be significant in some people (n=12, RCT, open, Hagg *et al, Br J Clin Pharmacol* 2000, **49**, 59–63). Drowsiness and sialorrhoea occurred with the combination, with clozapine levels halving when caffeine was stopped (n=1, Odom-White and de Leon, *J Clin Psych* 1996, **57**, 175–76).

## CARBAMAZEPINE + CLOZAPINE

See antipsychotics + carbamazepine (*4.5.1*).

### Chloramphenicol + clozapine

There is an enhanced risk of agranulocytosis.

### Ciprofloxacin + clozapine

There is a case of clozapine levels falling by nearly 50% when ciprofloxacin was stopped, probably due to CYP1A2 inhibition (Markowitz *et al*, *Am J Psych* 1997, **153**, 881).

### Clonidine + clozapine

See clonidine + antipsychotics (*4.2.1*).

### Cocaine + clozapine

See antipsychotics + cocaine (*4.7.3*).

### Co-trimoxazole + clozapine

There is an enhanced risk of agranulocytosis (mandatory precaution in the UK SPC).

### Cytotoxic agents + clozapine

There is an enhanced risk of agranulocytosis (mandatory precaution in the UK SPC).

### Digoxin + clozapine

The UK SPC for clozapine advises caution with highly bound drugs, which would include digoxin. Monitor for adverse effects and adjust doses as necessary.

### Erythromycin + clozapine

Raised clozapine levels have been reported, with seizures seven days after erythromycin 250mg/d was added to clozapine 800mg/d, with levels falling by 50% when the erythromycin was stopped (Funderburg *et al*, *Am J Psych* 1994, **151**, 1840) and increased toxicity, eg. somnolence and leukocytosis (n=1, Cohen *et al*, *Arch Int Med* 1996, **156**, 675–77). Reduced clozapine metabolism via CYP1A2 is the probable mechanism

## FLUOXETINE + CLOZAPINE

Fluoxetine produces significant increases in plasma clozapine and norclozapine levels, with some interindividual variation (n=80, open, Centorrino *et al*, *Am J Psych* 1996, **153**, 820–22), with several case reports (eg. n=6, Centorrino *et al*, *Am J Psych* 1994, **151**, 123–25), including death (n=1, Ferslew *et al*, *J Forensic Sci* 1998, **43**, 1082–85). Uncontrollable myoclonic jerks have been reported (n=1, Kingsbury and Puckett, *Am J Psych* 1995, **152**, 473–72). The mechanism is possibly CYP2D6 inhibition. The risk of clozapine toxicity must be considered and measuring clozapine levels may be useful.

## FLUVOXAMINE + CLOZAPINE *

Clozapine plasma levels may rise up to 9-fold with the addition of fluvoxamine 100–200mg/d (eg. n=2, Dequardo and Roberts, *Am J Psych* 1996, **153**, 840–41; n=1, Armstrong and Stephans, *J Clin Psych* 1997, **58**, 499), probably by CYP1A2 inhibition. So predictable is the effect that fluvoxamine has been used to counteract CYP1A2 induction by smoking which can lead to clozapine nonresponse (n=3, Bender and Eap, *Arch Gen Psych* 1998, **55**, 1048–50) in CYP1A2 rapid metabolisers. In a study in Chinese male in-patients, 50mg/d fluvoxamine increased clozapine levels by a mean of 130% (137 to 327ng/ml) and norclozapine levels by 78% (from 65 to 116ng/ml) within 2 weeks. Clozapine levels rose further (to 440–480ng/ml) with 100mg/d (n=12, Lu *et al*, *J Clin Psychopharmacol* 2002, **22**, 626–28). Close pharmacokinetic monitoring is thus necessary as the effect can be dramatic over a few days in some patients even with very low doses eg. 10–20mg/d fluvoxamine.

### Grapefruit juice + clozapine *

GFJ has no effect on clozapine levels (n=15, open, 12/52, Lane *et al*, *Drug Metabol Drug Interact* 2001, **18**, 263–78).

### H2-blockers + clozapine

Clozapine levels may rise by over 50% with cimetidine (n=1, Czymanski *et al*, *J Clin Psych* 1991, **52**, 21). Ranitidine is a safer alternative.

### Influenza vaccine + clozapine *

Influenza vaccine has no effect on clozapine levels (n=14, Raaska *et al, Eur J Clin Pharmacol* 2001, **57**, 705–8).

### Itraconazole/ketoconazole + clozapine *

Itraconazole 200mg/d over 7 days had no effect on plasma clozapine and norclozapine levels (RCT, n=7, Raaska and Neuvonen, *Eur J Clin Pharmacol* 1998, **54**, 167–70) and ketoconazole also has no effect on clozapine (Lane *et al, Drug Metabol Drug Interact* 2001, **18**, 263–78).

### Lamotrigine + clozapine *

An unexplained three-fold increase in clozapine levels was seen two weeks after lamotrigine 100mg/d was added to a stable clozapine 400mg/d regimen (n=1, Kossen *et al, Am J Psych* 2001, **158**, 1930).

### Lithium + clozapine

See antipsychotics + lithium (*4.4*).

### MAOIs + clozapine

Enhanced sedation may occur with all CNS depressants (MI).

### Nefazodone + clozapine *

Nefazodone may raise clozapine and norclozapine levels, probably via CYP3A4 inhibition (n=1, Khan and Preskorn, *J Clin Psych* 2001, **62**, 375–76).

### Oral Contraceptive's + clozapine *

Elevated plasma clozapine levels and address have been reported with norethindrone, resolving on OC discontinuation (n=1, Gabbay *et al, J Clin Psychopharmacol* 2002, **22**, 621–22).

### Orlistat + clozapine *

A small trial suggested lack of interaction (8/52, Hilger *et al, J Clin Psychopharmacol* 2002, **22**, 68–70).

### PAROXETINE + CLOZAPINE

Paroxetine produces significant increases in plasma clozapine and norclozapine levels (n=60, open, Centorrino *et al, Am J Psych* 1996, **153**, 820–22) and so the risk of clozapine toxicity must be considered carefully.

### Penicillamine + clozapine

There is an enhanced risk of agranulocytosis (mandatory precaution in the UK SPC).

### Phenobarbital + clozapine

Elevated plasma clozapine levels (requiring dose reduction) have been reported after discontinuation of phenobarbital, presumably from removal of CYP1A2 induction (n=1, Lane *et al, J Clin Psych* 1998, **59**, 131–33).

### Phenylbutazone + clozapine

There is an enhanced risk of agranulocytosis (mandatory precaution in the UK SPC).

### PHENYTOIN + CLOZAPINE

Serum concentrations of clozapine may be markedly reduced by phenytoin (n=2, Miller *et al, J Clin Psych* 1991, **52**, 23) via CYP1A2 induction, so monitor for reduced effect.

### PPIs + clozapine *

A switch from omeprazole to pantoprazole does not alter average clozapine plasma levels, although some individual increases may be seen (n=13, Mookhoek and Loonen, *Br J Clin Pharmacol* 2002, **53**, 545P).

### Pyrazolone analgesics + clozapine

There is an enhanced risk of agranulocytosis (mandatory precaution in UK SPC).

### Reboxetine + clozapine *

See reboxetine (*4.3.3.5*).

### Rifampicin + clozapine

There is a case of a 600% reduction in clozapine levels 2–3 weeks after rifampicin was started, probably via 1A2 and 3A4 induction (n=1, Joos *et al, J Clin Psychopharmacol* 1998, **18**, 83–85).

### Sertraline + clozapine *

Sertraline produces significant increases in plasma clozapine and norclozapine levels, with some inter-individual variation (n=80, Centorrino *et al, Am J Psych* 1996, **153**, 820–22). There is a case of sudden death with the combination, probably as a result of cardiac arrhythmia (n=1, Hoehns *et al, Ann Pharmacother*

2001, **35**, 826–66). The risk of clozapine toxicity must be considered carefully.

### Smoking + clozapine
See antipsychotics + smoking (*4.7.4*).

### Sulphonamides + clozapine
There is an enhanced risk of agranulocytosis (MI).

### Tricyclics + clozapine
See antipsychotics + tricyclics (*4.3.1*)

### Valproate + clozapine
Although valproate is often used as anticonvulsant cover for higher dose clozapine, a careful study showed valproate to produce a 15% drop in clozapine levels and a 65% drop in norclozapine levels (n=7, Longo and Salzman, *Am J Psych* 1995, **152**, 650), although raised clozapine levels have been reported (n=1, Costello and Suppes, *J Clin Psychopharmacol* 1995, **15**, 139–41). Clozapine may of course also lower the seizure threshold and antagonise the anticonvulsant effect of valproate.

### Venlafaxine + clozapine
See venlafaxine (*4.3.3.8*).

### Warfarin + clozapine
The UK SPC for clozapine advises caution with highly bound drugs, which would include warfarin. There are no case reports, although caution is still needed (mentioned in Sayal *et al, Acta Psych Scand* 2000, **102**, 250–55). Monitor carefully for an enhanced warfarin effect and adjust doses as necessary.

---

### 4.2.3 ANTIPSYCHOTICS — OLANZAPINE (see also *4.2.1* for other, more general, interactions)

---

Olanzapine is metabolised by CYP1A2 and CYP2D6, with little or no effect on CYP1A2, 2D6, 2C19, 2C9 and 3A at normal doses. It is highly bound to albumin (90%) and alpha 1-acid glycoprotein (77%) and interactions may be possible through this mechanism. The metabolic pathways of olanzapine also include N-glucuronidation, reducing its overall sensitivity to drugs that might induce or inhibit its own metabolism via CYP or flavin-containing mono-oxygenase (FMO) systems. Olanzapine is approximately 60% excreted in urine and 30% in faeces. Fixed doses appear to give higher levels in women.

**Review:** extensive, of pharmacokinetics and pharmacodynamics (Callaghan *et al, Clin Pharmacokinetics* 1999, **37**, 177–93, 56 refs).

### Alcohol + olanzapine
See antipsychotics + alcohol (*4.7.1*).

### Antacids + olanzapine
Antacids have no effect on olanzapine bioavailability (MI).

### Antipsychotics(other) + olanzapine *
An interaction has been suggested (Gomberg, *J Clin Psychopharmacol* 1999, **19**, 272–73) and there is a case of NMS in combination with haloperidol (n=1, Mujica and Weiden, *Am J Psych* 2001, **158**, 650–51). Seizures have been reported with **quetiapine** and **olanzapine** (n=1, Hedges and Jeppson, *Ann Pharmacother* 2002, **36**, 437–39).

### Benzodiazepines + olanzapine
Single dose studies showed no effect of olanzapine on the metabolism of diazepam. Mild increases in heart rate, sedation and dry mouth were noted with the combination, but no dose adjustment deemed necessary (MI).

### Biperiden + olanzapine
Lack of interaction has been reported (MI).

### Carbamazepine + olanzapine
See carbamazepine (*4.5.1*).

### Charcoal (activated) + olanzapine
Activated charcoal reduces olanzapine bioavailability by 50–60% (MI).

### Cimetidine + olanzapine
There is no effect on olanzapine bioavailability (MI).

### Ciprofloxacin + olanzapine
Raised olanzapine levels have been reported, possibly caused by ciprofloxacin (n=1, Markowitz and DeVane, *J Clin Psychophamacol* 1999, **19**, 289–91).

### Lithium + olanzapine
See antipsychotics + lithium (*4.4*).

### Probenecid + olanzapine *
Probenecid appears to decrease olanzapine glucuronidation (n=12, RCT, d/b, c/o, Markowitz *et al, Clin Pharmacol Ther* 2002, **71**, 30–38).

### Smoking + olanzapine
See antipsychotics + smoking (*4.7.4*).

### SSRIs + olanzapine*
**Fluvoxamine** (but not **sertraline**) inhibits the metabolism of olanzapine, probably through CYP1A2 inhibition (n=165, Weigmann *et al, Ther Drug Monit* 2001, **23**, 410–13), with 100mg/d raising steady-state olanzapine levels by 12–112%, and although well tolerated care is needed (n=8, open, Hiemke *et al, J Clin Psychopharmacol* 2002, **22**, 502–6). Could be a useful trick for keeping olanzapine doses within BNF limits with the MHA commissioners around. Higher doses of **fluoxetine** may slightly increase olanzapine levels, probably via CYP2D6 inhibition (n=15, Gossen *et al, AAPS PharmSci* 2002, **4**, E11) and melancholic depression has been reported with the combination (n=1, Nelson and Swartz, *Ann Clin Psych* 2000, **12**, 167–70).

### Tricyclics + olanzapine
Single dose studies show no effect of olanzapine on the metabolism of imipramine (n=9, open, Callaghan *et al, J Clin Pharmacol* 1997, **37**, 971–78) and desipramine (MI). Seizures have been reported with olanzapine and clomipramine (Deshauer *et al, J Clin Psychopharmacol* 2000, **20**, 283–84).

### Warfarin + olanzapine
Single dose studies show no effect of olanzapine on the metabolism of warfarin (MI) although it could be possible (mentioned in Sayal *et al, Acta Psych Scand* 2000, **102**, 250–55).

### Xanthines + olanzapine
Lack of interaction has been shown with aminophylline and theophylline (n=19, RCT, Macias *et al, Pharmacotherapy* 1998, **18**, 1237–48).

## 4.2.4 ANTIPSYCHOTICS — QUETIAPINE (see also *4.2.1* for other, more general, interactions)

Quetiapine is metabolised primarily by the CYP3A4 enzyme.

### Alcohol + quetiapine
See alcohol (*4.7.1*).

### Antipsychotics (other) + quetiapine*
Thioridazine 400mg/d significantly decreased quetiapine 600mg/d by up to 68%, but haloperidol 15mg/d and risperidone 6mg/d had no effect (n=36, RCT, 9/7, Potkin *et al, J Clin Psychopharmacol* 2002, **22**, 121–30). See also olanzapine (*4.2.3*).

### Barbiturates + quetiapine
Lower levels of quetiapine would be expected, due to CYP3A4 induction by barbiturates.

### Benzodiazepines + quetiapine
Single doses of lorazepam and diazepam are unaffected by quetiapine.

### Carbamazepine + quetiapine
See antipsychotics + carbamazepine (*4.5.1*).

### Cimetidine + quetiapine *
No interaction occurs (n=13, open, Strakowski *et al, J Clin Psychopharmacol* 2002, **22**, 201–5).

### Erythromycin + quetiapine
Raised quetiapine levels are likely via CYP3A4 inhibition.

### Ketoconazole + quetiapine
Raised quetiapine levels are likely via CYP3A4 inhibition.

### Lovastatin + quetiapine *
A prolonged QTc interval has been reported with the combination (n=1, Furst *et al, Biol Psych* 2002, **51**, 264–65).

### Lithium + quetiapine
Slightly increased lithium levels may occur.

### Phenytoin + quetiapine
Lower levels of quetiapine would be expected, due to CYP3A4 induction by phenytoin.

### Rifampicin + quetiapine
Lower levels of quetiapine would be expected, due to CYP3A4 induction by rifampicin.

## SSRIs + quetiapine *
Fluoxetine 60mg/d has no significant effect on quetiapine kinetics (n=26, RCT, Potkin *et al, J Clin Psychopharmacol* 2002, **22**, 174–82).

## Tricyclics + quetiapine *
Imipramine 150mg/d has no significant effect on quetiapine (n=26, RCT, Potkin *et al, J Clin Psychopharmacol* 2002, **22**, 174–82).

## Warfarin + quetiapine
No interaction is likely to occur (mentioned in Sayal *et al, Acta Psych Scand* 2000, **102**, 250–55), but an isolated case has been reported (n=1, Rogers *et al, J Clin Psychopharmacol* 1999, **19**, 382–83).

## 4.2.5 ANTIPSYCHOTICS — RISPERIDONE (see also *4.2.1* for other, more general, interactions)

**Review**: DeVane and Nemeroff, *J Clin Psychopharmacol* 2001, **21**, 408–16.

## CARBAMAZEPINE + RISPERIDONE
See antipsychotics + carbamazepine (*4.5.1*).

## CLOZAPINE + RISPERIDONE *
See antipsychotics + clozapine (*4.2.2*).

## Donepezil + risperidone
See antipsychotics + donepezil (*4.6.3.1*).

## FLUOXETINE + RISPERIDONE *
Fluoxetine 20mg/d has caused a 75% increase in risperidone levels over 4 weeks, resulting in side effects in 30% (n=10, Spina *et al, J Clin Psychopharmacol* 2002, **22**, 419–23) and severe EPSE and urinary retention has been reported (n=1, Bozikas *et al, J Psychopharmacol* 2001, **15**, 142–43).

## Fluvoxamine + risperidone *
Neurotoxicity (confusion, diaphoresis, myoclonus etc) has been reported within 2 days when fluvoxamine was added to risperidone (n=1, Reeves *et al, Ann Pharmacother* 2002, **36**, 440–43).

## Galantamine + risperidone *
See antipsychotics + galantamine (*4.6.3.2*).

## Lithium + risperidone
See antipsychotics + lithium (*4.4*).

## Methadone + risperidone *
See methadone (*4.6.8*).

## Mirtazapine + risperidone
See mirtazapine (*4.3.3.2*).

## Paroxetine + risperidone *
Paroxetine 20mg/d for 4 weeks can raise risperidone levels by 45–62% and so a risperidone dose might need to be adjusted should side effects occur (n=10, open, 4/52, Spina *et al, Ther Drug Monit* 2001, **23**, 223–27).

## Phenytoin + risperidone
Severe EPSEs have been reported (n=1, Sanderson, *J Clin Psych* 1996, **57**, 177).

## Probenecid + risperidone *
Probenecid has no effect on risperidone kinetics (n=12, RCT, d/b, c/o, Markowitz *et al, Clin Pharmacol Ther* 2002, **71**, 30–38).

## Reboxetine + risperidone *
See reboxetine (*4.3.3.5*).

## Ritonavir/indinavir + risperidone *
Addition of ritonavir/indinavir to risperidone has led to severe EPSE, dystonia (n=1, Kelly *et al, Ann Pharmacother* 2002, **36**, 827–30) and reversible coma (n=1, Jover *et al, Clin Neuropharmacol* 2002, **25**, 251–53), probably due to risperidone toxicity.

## Tricyclics + risperidone *
See antipsychotics + tricyclics (*4.3.1*).

## Valproate + risperidone
See antipsychotics (*4.2.1*).

## Venlafaxine + risperidone *
Steady-state venlafaxine had no significant effect on the kinetics of a single 1mg dose of risperidone, although some enzyme inhibition led to slightly raised risperidone plasma levels (n=30, open, Amchin *et al, J Clin Pharmacol* 1999, **39**, 297–309).

## ANTIPSYCHOTICS — ZIPRASIDONE (see *4.2.7.3*)

## 4.2.6 ANTIPSYCHOTICS — ZOTEPINE (see also 4.2.1 for other, more general, interactions)

Zotepine is metabolised by CYP1A2 and CYP3A4 to norzotepine and both have a plasma protein binding of 97%, making protein-displacement interactions unlikely. Zotepine has no significant effect on CYP2D6.

### Alcohol + zotepine
Zotepine should not be used in people with alcohol intoxication (MI).

### Anticonvulsants + zotepine
Zotepine lowers the seizure threshold.

### Anticholinergics + zotepine
Biperiden had no effect on zotepine kinetics, side-effects or efficacy in one study (n=21, Otani *et al, B J Psych* 1990, **157**, 128–30).

### Anticoagulants + zotepine
The Japanese SPC notes that zotepine has been reported to enhance the risk of bleeding when given with anti-coagulants, eg. with nicoumalone, dicoumarol and warfarin, possibly via a change in protein binding.

### Antipsychotics (other) + zotepine
Co-prescribing other antipsychotics with zotepine can raise the incidence of seizures.

### Benzodiazepines + zotepine
Diazepam increases zotepine levels by 10% (higher in Japanese patients) and doubles norzotepine levels (n=17, open, Kondo *et al, Psychopharmacol (Berl)* 1996, **127**, 311–14), possibly via CYP3A4 inhibition.

### Carbamazepine + zotepine
See antipsychotics + carbamazepine (*4.5.1*).

### Clonidine + zotepine
The Japanese SPC notes that zotepine has alpha-1-adrenergic antagonistic properties which may decrease the hypotensive actions of clonidine and other hypotensive agents.

### Hypotensive drugs + zotepine
See clonidine.

### Phenytoin + zotepine
The Japanese SPC notes that zotepine may increase phenytoin plasma levels, so more frequent monitoring is required.

### Smoking + zotepine
See antipsychotics + smoking (*4.7.4*).

### SSRIs + zotepine
Fluoxetine increases zotepine levels by 10% and doubles norzotepine levels (MI). Deep vein thrombosis possibly linked to concurrent paroxetine and zotepine has been reported (n=2, Pantel *et al, Pharmacopsychiatry* 1997, **30**, 109–11).

### Tricyclics + zotepine
Desipramine does not seem to affect zotepine levels (MI).

## 4.2.7 OTHER ANTIPSYCHOTICS*

Aripiprazole and ziprasidone are available in some countries and may become available in others during the life of this book.

## 4.2.7.1 ARIPIPRAZOLE *

Aripiprazole is metabolised by many enzyme systems eg. mainly CYP2D6 and 3A4, but not CYP1A1, 1A2, 2C9/19. It has no effect on CYP2D6, 2C9, 2C19 and 3A4.

### Alcohol + aripiprazole *
No significant difference in performance or gross motor skills has been shown with this combination.

### Carbamazepine + aripiprazole *
See antipsychotics + carbamazepine (*4.5.1*).

### Dextromethorphan + aripiprazole *
Lack of interaction has been shown (MI).

### H2-blockers + aripiprazole *
Lack of significant interaction has been shown famotidine (MI).

### Ketoconazole + aripiprazole *
Ketoconazole decreases aripiprazole metabolism and so an aripiprazole dose should be decreased by a half during co-administration.

### Lithium + aripiprazole *
No interaction (Citrome *et al, Int J Neuropsychopharmacol* 2002, **5**(Suppl 1), S187).

### Omeprazole + aripiprazole *
Lack of interaction has been shown (MI).

### Quinidine + aripiprazole *
Quinidine decreases aripiprazole metabolism and so aripiprazole doses should be halved.

### Smoking + aripiprazole *
See smoking (*4.7.4*)

### Valproate + aripiprazole *
No interaction occurs (Citrome *et al, Int J Neuropsychopharmacol* 2002, **5**(Suppl 1), S187).

### Warfarin + aripiprazole *
Lack of interaction has been shown (MI).

---

### 4.2.7.2 SERTINDOLE

Sertindole is extensively metabolised by CYP2D6 and 3A4 and is a weak 2D6 and 3A4 inhibitor. It is contraindicated in patients also receiving drugs known to prolong the QT interval.

### Aluminium-magnesium antacids + sertindole *
There is no effect on sertindole absorption (MI).

### ANTIPSYCHOTICS (other) + SERTINDOLE *
The UK SPC for sertindole states that it is contraindicated with drugs known to prolong the QT interval eg. thioridazine, ziprasidone.

### ASTEMIZOLE + SERTINDOLE *
The UK SPC for sertindole states that it is contraindicated with drugs known to prolong the QT interval eg. astemizole.

### ANTI-ARRHYTHMICS + SERTINDOLE *
The UK SPC for sertindole states that it is contraindicated with drugs known to prolong the QT interval eg. class Ia and III antiarrhythmics eg. quinidine, amiodarone, sotalol, dofetilide etc.

### Benzodiazepines + sertindole *
Sertindole has no significant on alprazolam (n=14, open, Wong *et al, Psychopharmacol (Berl)* 1998, **135**, 236–41).

### Calcium-channel blockers + sertindole *
Minor, non-significant increases in sertindole levels have been detected with calcium-channel antagonists via CYP3A4 inhibition.

### CARBAMAZEPINE + SERTINDOLE *
Carbamazepine can reduce sertindole levels 2–3-fold by CYP3A4 induction, so higher maintenance doses might be needed.

### CIMETIDINE + SERTINDOLE *
The UK SPC for sertindole states that it is contraindicated for use with cimetidine due to CYP3A4 inhibition. Ranitidine would be a suitable alternative.

### Citalopram + sertindole *
No interaction via CYP2D6 appears to occur.

### Escitalopram + sertindole *
See citalopram above.

### MACROLIDES + SERTINDOLE *
QT prolongation potential makes this combination a contraindication. Minor, non-significant increases in sertindole levels have been detected with erythromycin and other macrolides, via CYP3A4 inhibition.

### FLUOXETINE + SERTINDOLE *
Plasma levels of sertindole are increased 2–3-fold via CYP2D6 inhibition, so lower maintenance doses might be needed or use of a non-2D6 inhibiting antidepressant.

### HIV PROTEASE INIBITORS + SERTINDOLE *
The UK SPC for sertindole states that it is contraindicated with drugs such as indinavir due to 3A4 inhibition.

### ITRACONAZOLE/KETOCONAZOLE + SERTINDOLE *
The UK SPC for sertindole states that it is contraindicated for use with systemic itraconazole and ketoconazole due to CYP3A4 inhibition.

### LITHIUM + SERTINDOLE *
The QT prolongation potential makes this combination a contraindication.

### PAROXETINE + SERTINDOLE *
Plasma levels of sertindole are increased 2-3-fold via CYP2D6 inhibition, so lower maintenance doses might be needed or use a non-2D6

inhibiting antidepressant. There is a case of sertindole enhancing paroxetine withdrawal symptoms (Walker-Kinnear and McNaughton, *B J Psych* 1997, **170**, 389).

### PHENYTOIN + SERTINDOLE *

Phenytoin can reduce sertindole levels 2-3-fold by 3A4 induction, so higher maintenance doses might be needed.

### Propranolol + sertindole *

No interaction via 2D6 seems to occur (MI).

### QUINIDINE + SERTINDOLE *

Plasma levels of sertindole are thought to be increased 2-3-fold via 2D6 inhibition, so use is contraindicated. The UK SPC for sertindole also states that it is contraindicated with drugs known to prolong the QT interval eg. quinidine.

### QUINOLONE ANTIBIOTICS + SERTINDOLE *

QT prolongation potential makes the combination with eg. gatifloxacin a contraindication.

### Sertraline + sertindole *

No interaction via CYP2D6 appears occur.

### TRICYCLICS + SERTINDOLE *

The UK SPC for sertindole states that it is contraindicated with drugs known to prolong the QT interval eg. some tricyclics. No interaction via CYP2D6 appears to occur with the tricyclics (MI).

---

### 4.2.7.3 ZIPRASIDONE*

Ziprasidone is partly metabolised by CYP3A4 (with a minor amount from 1A2), plus about 2/3rds via aldehyde reductase. It has no effect on CYP1A2, 2C9/19, 2D6 nor 3A4. It is 99% plasma bound. Due to the QTc prolonging effect, ziprasidone should not be used with drugs also likely to prolong the QTc eg. sotalol, quinidine, other Class Ia and III anti-arrhythmics, phenothiazines, tricyclics, pimozide, mefloquine, dolasetron etc (see SPC).

### Antacids + ziprasidone *

Lack of interaction has been shown with 30ml Maalox (n=11, RCT, Wilner *et al, B J Clin Pharmacol* 2000, **49**(S3), 57–60).

### Anticholinergics + ziprasidone *

Lack of interaction has been shown with benzatropine.

### Benzodiazepines + ziprasidone *

Lack of interaction with lorazepam has been shown.

### Beta-blockers + ziprasidone *

Lack of interaction has been shown with propranolol.

### Carbamazepine + ziprasidone *

Carbamazepine decreases ziprasidone AUC by about 35%, which may require slightly raised doses (n=25, RCT, 4/52, Miceli *et al, B J Clin Pharmacol* 2000, **49**(S3), 65–70).

### Cimetidine + ziprasidone *

Lack of interaction has been shown (n=11, RCT, Wilner *et al, B J Clin Pharmacol* 2000, **49**(S3), 57–60).

### Dextromethorphan + ziprasidone*

Lack of interaction has been shown (Wilner *et al, B J Clin Pharmacol* 2000, **49**(S3), 43–48).

### Ketoconazole + ziprasidone *

Ketoconazole decreases ziprasidone AUC by about 35%, which may require slightly raised doses.

### Levodopa + ziprasidone *

Ziprasidone may antagonise the effects of levodopa and other dopaminergic agents.

### Lithium + ziprasidone *

Lack of interaction has been shown (n=25, RCT, Apseloff *et al, B J Clin Pharmacol* 2000, **49**(S3), 61–64).

### Oral contraceptive + ziprasidone *

Lack of interaction has been shown with a combined oral contraceptive (n=19, d/b, p/c, c/o, Muirhead *et al, B J Clin Pharmacol* 2000, **49**(S3), 49–56).

### QT-prolonging drugs + ziprasidone*

See introduction.

## Smoking + ziprasidone *

See antipsychotics + smoking (*4.7.4*)

## Warfarin + ziprasidone *

Lack of interaction has been shown.

## 4.3 ANTIDEPRESSANTS

**Reviews:**\* significant drug interactions with antidepressants in the elderly (Spina and Scordo, *Drugs & Aging* 2002, **19**, 299–320, 95 refs).

## 4.3.1 TRICYCLIC ANTIDEPRESSANTS

Tricyclics are metabolised by a range of P450 enzymes, eg. CYP1A2, CYP2D6 and CYP3A3/4. Some tricyclics have several metabolic routes, which may vary with concentration and where another might take over should one be inhibited.

## Acamprosate + tricyclics

See acamprosate (*4.6.1*).

## Acetazolamide + tricyclics

An interaction is unlikely to occur.

## ALCOHOL + TRICYCLICS

See alcohol (*4.7.1*).

## Amiodarone + tricyclics

The BNF notes an increased risk of ventricular arrhythmias with tricyclics.

## Anaesthetics + tricyclics

Halothane and pancuronium (or gallamine) should be used with care with tricyclics with strong anticholinergic actions. Enflurane may be a safer alternative.

## Anticholinergics + tricyclics

Enhanced anticholinergic effects may occur, especially in the elderly.

## Antihistamines + tricyclics

Enhanced sedation and anticholinergic effects are possible.

## Antipsychotics + tricyclics *

Tricyclic levels may be up to twice as high if **haloperidol** is taken concurrently, eg. with desipramine (n=30, open, Nelson *et al, Am J Psych* 1980, **137**, 1232–34), nortriptyline and imipramine. Tricyclic levels may also rise with phenothiazines (eg. Siris *et al, Am J Psych* 1982, **143**, 104–6) giving enhanced side-effects, eg. **perphenazine** increases nortriptyline levels by about 25%, probably by CYP2D6 inhibition (n=25, Mulsant *et al, J Clin Psychopharmacol* 1997, **17**, 318–21). **Thioridazine** may increase imipramine levels (n=1, Maynard and Soni, *Ther Drug Monit* 1996, **18**, 728–31). No significant interaction has been reported with the **thioxanthenes**, although raised imipramine levels with flupentixol have occurred (n=1, Cook *et al, Can J Psychiatry* 1986, **31**, 235–37). Up to 100mg/d amitriptyline had no effect on **risperidone** (n=12, open, Sommers *et al, Int Clin Psychopharmacol* 1997, **12**, 141–45) but risperidone may raise maprotiline levels, not a thing you'd want to do accidentally (Normann *et al, J Clin Psychopharmacol* 2002, **22**, 92–94). Some antidepressants may also be counter-productive in psychosis (mentioned in *Drug Dev Res* 1988, **12**, 259–66).

## Aspirin + imipramine *

Imipramine plasma levels may rise and ADRs increase when aspirin is added to imipramine (n=20, Juarez-Olguin *et al, Clin Neuropharmacol* 2002, **25**, 32–36).

## Baclofen + tricyclics

A patient with multiple sclerosis lost muscle tone when nortriptyline and imipramine were added to baclofen (n=1, Silverglat, *JAMA* 1981, **246**, 1659).

## BARBITURATES + TRICYCLICS

Barbiturates can reduce the serum levels of amitriptyline, desipramine, protriptyline (n=30, Moody *et al, Eur J Clin Pharmacol* 1977, **11**, 51–56) and nortriptyline by 14–60%, via CYP3A4 induction. Pentobarbital may affect nortriptyline metabolism within 2 days, both when starting (induction) and on discontinuation (n=6, von Bahr *et al, Clin Pharmacol Ther* 1998, **64**, 18–26). Use an alternative to barbiturates or monitor tricyclic levels.

### Benzodiazepines + tricyclics
See benzodiazepines (*4.1.1*).

### Beta-blockers + tricyclics
Enhanced maprotiline toxicity has been reported, labetolol increases imipramine plasma levels by 28% (n=12, RCT, p/c, c/o, Hermann *et al*, *J Clin Pharmacol* 1992, **32**, 176–83) and there are two uncertain cases of propranolol possibly raising imipramine levels in children (n=2, Gillette and Tannery, *J Am Acad Child Adolesc Psych* 1994, **33**, 223–4), possibly via 2D6 inhibition. This would appear to be a rare but possible interaction.

### Buprenorphine + amitriptyline
No enhanced CNS depressant or respiratory effects have been seen (n=12, d/b, p/c, c/o, Saarialho-Kere *et al*, *Eur J Clin Pharmacol* 1987, **33**, 139–46).

### Bupropion + tricyclics *
See bupropion (*4.6.4*).

### Cannabis + tricyclics
See antidepressants + cannabis (*4.7.2*).

### Calcium-channel blockers + tricyclics
Amitriptyline clearance was reduced by diltiazem and verapamil one study, with adverse effects increased (n=32, Hermann *et al*, *J Clin Pharmacol* 1992, **32**, 176–83). Diltiazem may increase nortriptyline concentrations (n=1, Krahenbuhl *et al*, *Eur J Clin Pharmacol* 1996, **49**, 417–19). Enhanced cardiac side-effects are also possible.

### CARBAMAZEPINE + TRICYCLICS *
See carbamazepine (*4.5.1*).

### Charcoal, activated + tricyclics
5–10g may reduce absorption of tricyclics by up to 75% if given within 30 minutes and may be an effective treatment for overdose even up to two hours after the overdose was taken (open, Dawling *et al*, *Eur J Clin Pharmacol* 1978, **14**, 445–47).

### Cholestyramine + doxepin
Plasma levels of doxepin may be reduced to a third by cholestyramine (n=1, Geeze *et al*, *Psychosomatics* 1988, **29**, 233–35).

### CLONIDINE + TRICYCLICS
Tricyclics can be expected to antagonise the hypotensive effects of clonidine (eg. Hui, *J Am Ger Soc* 1983, **31**, 164–65).

### Cocaine + tricyclics
See antidepressants + cocaine (*4.7.3*).

### Co-trimoxazole + tricyclics
Five cases of relapse when co-trimoxazole was added to antidepressant therapy have been reported (*L'Encephale* 1987, **8**, 123–26).

### Dextropropoxyphene + doxepin
There are reports of doxepin plasma levels raised by up to 150% with dextropropoxyphene, via 2D6 inhibition.

### Dicoumarol + tricyclics
An enhanced dicoumarol half-life is possible (Veseil *et al*, *NEJM* 1970, **283**, 1484–88), shown with amitriptyline and nortriptyline (Pond *et al*, *Clin Pharmacol Ther* 1975, **18**, 191).

### Disopyramide + tricyclics
Increased anticholinergic effects may be seen (Hartel *et al*, *Clin Pharmacol Ther* 1974, **15**, 551–55) and the BNF notes an increased risk of ventricular arrhythmias.

### Disulfiram + tricyclics
Amitriptyline may enhance the effects of disulfiram (MacCallum, *Lancet* 1969, **i**, 313) and tricyclic levels may be increased by about 30% by enzyme inhibition (n=2, Ciraulo *et al*, *Am J Psych* 1985, **142**, 1373–74).

### Fibre + tricyclics
There are several cases of a high fibre diet reducing tricyclic levels by up to a third (and hence to inactive levels), eg. with doxepin. This might explain non-response in some patients.

### Fluconazole + nortriptyline *
A case of inhibition of CYP3A4 by fluconazole has resulted in elevated, toxic nortriptyline levels (n=1, Gannon, *Ann Pharmacother* 1992, **26**, 1456–57) and syncope has been associated with concurrent amitriptyline

and fluconazole therapy (Robinson *et al, Ann Pharmacother* 2000, **34**, 1406–9).

**Glyceryl trinitrate + tricyclics**
See nitrates + tricyclics.

**GUANETHIDINE + TRICYCLICS**
The hypotensive effects of guanethidine and similar drugs are antagonised by tricyclics.

**H2-blockers + tricyclics**
CYP1A2 inhibition by cimetidine may decrease the metabolism and increase half-life and blood levels of tricyclics, eg. amitriptyline (by 37–80%, Curry *et al, Eur J Clin Pharmacol* 1985, **29**, 429–33), doxepin (by 30%, n=10, RCT, Abernethy and Todd, *J Clin Psychopharmacol* 1986, **6**, 8–12), imipramine (by over 100%, n=12, RCT, d/b, p/c, c/o, Wells *et al, Eur J Clin Pharmacol* 1986, **31**, 285–90) and nortriptyline (by 20%, Henauer and Hollister, *Clin Pharmacol Ther* 1984, **35**, 183–87). Other H2-blockers, eg. ranitidine, do not appear to interact this way (n=6, open, Sutherland *et al, Eur J Clin Pharmacol* 1987, **32**, 159–64).

**Hypoglycaemics + tricyclics**
There are two isolated cases of enhanced hypoglycaemia with doxepin and nortriptyline (n=2, True *et al, Am J Psych* 1987, **144**, 1220–21) so monitor blood glucose regularly.

**Levodopa + tricyclics**
A small reduction in the effect of levodopa may be seen (open, Morgan *et al, Neurology* 1975, **25**, 1029) but is of low clinical significance.

**Levothyroxine + tricyclics**
This is usually a synergistic interaction (see depression, *1.14*) but a few isolated cases of tachycardia and hypothyroidism have been reported.

**Lithium + tricyclics \***
The combination is well used (see depression, *1.14*) but some adverse reactions have been reported, eg. myoclonus (Devanand *et al, J Clin Psychopharmacol* 1988, **8**, 446) and neurotoxicity with motor symptoms and seizures (eg. Austin *et al, J Clin*

*Psych* 1990, **51**, 344). NMS has been reported with amoxapine and lithium (n=1, Gupta and Racaniello, *Ann Clin Psych* 2000, **12**, 107–9).

**MAOIs + TRICYCLICS**
See MAOIs (*4.3.4*).

**Methadone + tricyclics \***
See methadone (*4.6.8*).

**Methyldopa + desipramine**
The hypotensive effect of methyldopa may be decreased, with possible tachycardia and CNS stimulation (Van Spanning *et al, Int J Clin Pharmacol Biopharm* 1975, **11**, 65–67).

**Methylphenidate + tricyclics \***
See methylphenidate (*4.6.9*).

**Mirtazapine + tricyclics \***
See mirtazapine (*4.3.3.2*)

**Moclobemide + tricyclics**
See moclobemide (*4.3.3.3*).

**Modafinil + tricyclics**
See modafinil (*4.6.10*).

**Morphine + tricyclics**
Tricyclics such as amitriptyline and clomipramine increase the bioavailability of morphine and potentiate the analgesic effect, a usually beneficial effect (Ventafridda *et al, Lancet* 1987, **i**, 1204).

**Nefazodone + tricyclics**
See nefazodone (*4.3.3.4*).

**Nitrates (sublingual) + tricyclics**
Dry mouth may reduce the dissolution of sublingual nitrates.

**Olanzapine + tricyclics**
See olanzapine (*4.2.3*).

**Oral Contraceptives/estrogens + tricyclics**
Akathisia (n=3, Krishnan *et al, Am J Psych* 1984, **141**, 696–97), reduced tricyclic effectiveness and enhanced tricyclic toxicity have been reported. Best to monitor the tricyclic closely.

**Orlistat + tricyclics \***
A small trial suggested lack of interaction with clomipramine (n=8, 8/52, Hilger *et al, J Clin Psychopharmacol* 2002, **22**, 68–70).

**Phenindione + tricyclics**
An enhanced risk of bleeding may occur with this combination.

**Phenylbutazone + tricyclics**

Tricyclic absorption may get delayed or reduced by phenylbutazone (Consolo *et al, Eur J Pharmacol* 1970, **10**, 239–42).

**PHENYTOIN + TRICYCLICS** *

See phenytoin (*4.5.8*).

**Quetiapine + tricyclics** *

See quetiapine (*4.2.4*).

**Quinine and quinidine + tricyclics**

Studies have shown a much reduced clearance of nortriptyline with quinidine and quinine (n=10, Steiner *et al, Clin Pharmacol Ther* 1988, **43**, 577–81), via 2D6 inhibition. Best to monitor tricyclic levels.

**Reboxetine + tricyclics**

See reboxetine (*4.3.3.5*).

**SERTINDOLE + TRICYCLICS** *

See sertindole (*4.2.7.2*).

**Smoking + tricyclics**

See smoking (*4.7.4*).

**SSRIs + TRICYCLICS** *

The SSRIs inhibit CYP2D6 in a dose-related way, but fluoxetine, paroxetine and fluvoxamine all cause significant inhibition at therapeutic doses, whereas citalopram/escitalopram and sertraline cause little clinically significant 2D6 inhibition at standard doses. **Citalopram** (and presumably escitalopram) has no effect on some tricyclic levels (n=5, Baettig *et al, Eur J Clin Pharmacol* 1993, **44**, 403–5), although desipramine (but not imipramine) levels may rise slightly (Gram *et al, Ther Drug Monit* 1993, **15**, 18–24; n=1, Ashton, *J Clin Psych* 2000, **61**, 144). **Fluoxetine** may double or triple tricyclic levels eg. with **amitriptyline** (eg. fatality reported by Preskorn and Baker, *JAMA* 1997, **277**, 1682; n=29, open, Vandel *et al, Pharmacol Res* 1995, **31**, 347–53), **clomipramine** (n=4, Vandel *et al, Neuropsychobiology* 1992, **25**, 202–7), **desipramine** (peak plasma levels may rise by 100% and AUC by 480%, persisting for up to three weeks after the fluoxetine was stopped: n=18, RCT, Preskorn *et al, J Clin Psychopharmacol* 1994, **14**, 90–98), imipramine (Leroj and

Walentynowicz, *Can J Psychiatry* 1996, **41**, 318–19) and **nortriptyline** (eg. n=5, case series, Aranow *et al, Am J Psych* 1989, **146**, 911–13). Potentiation may occur even if the tricyclic is used after an interval (Extein, *Am J Psych* 1991, **148**, 1601–2). It has been suggested that tricyclic dosage should be reduced by 75% when fluoxetine is added (n=3, Westermeyer, *J Clin Pharmacol* 1991, **31**, 388–92). **Fluvoxamine** has been shown to increase amitriptyline, clomipramine (Bertschy *et al, Eur J Clin Pharmacol* 1991, **40**, 119–20) and imipramine levels (Maskall and Lam, *Am J Psych* 1993, **150**, 1566), but not with desipramine (n=12, open, Spina *et al Ther Drug Monit* 1993, **15**, 243–46). Fluvoxamine may inhibit both hydroxylation and N-demethylation, indicating a dual effect on tricyclic metabolism (Hartter *et al, Psychopharmacology* 1993, **110**, 302–8). **Paroxetine** significantly reduces the metabolism of amitriptyline, imipramine (eg. Skjelbo and Brosen, *B J Clin Pharmacol* 1992, **34**, 256–61) and desipramine (n=17, open, Brosen *et al, Eur J Clin Pharmacol* 1993, **44**, 349–55), resulting in enhanced tricyclic toxicity. **Sertraline** 50mg/d produced only a 60% increase in desipramine levels (Lydiard *et al, Am J Psych* 1993, **150**, 1125–26) and 50mg/d increased desipramine 50mg/d peak plasma levels by 31% and AUC by 23% (cf. 400% and 480% for fluoxetine 20mg/d, n=18, RCT, 7/52, Preskorn *et al, J Clin Psychopharmacol* 1994, **14**, 90–98). However, sertraline 150mg/d increased desipramine levels by 70%, with a 200–300% increase in 4 patients (Zussman *et al, Br J Clin Pharmacol* 1995, **39**, S530–S551; see also n=12, RCT, open, Kurtz *et al, Clin Pharmacol Ther* 1997, **62**, 145–56). A serotonin syndrome has been reported with may SSRI-tricyclic combinations (see *5.14*).

**St. John's wort + tricyclics** *

See St. John's wort (*4.3.3.9*).

### Sucralfate + amitriptyline
One small study showed a marked reduction in amitriptyline absorption (*Fed Proc* 1986, **45**, 205).

### Tea or coffee + tricyclics
Studies have shown that some tricyclics (eg. amitriptyline and imipramine) precipitate out of solution to form a tannin complex with tea and coffee (*J Pharm Sci* 1984, **73**, 1056–58). The clinical significance is thought to be minimal (Bowen *et al*, *Lancet* 1981, **i**, 1217–18).

### Terbinafine + tricyclics *
Terbinafine may triple desipramine plasma levels (n=1, O'Reardon *et al*, *Am J Psych* 2002, **159**, 492) and induce imipramine (eg. n=1, Teitelbaum and Pearson, *Am J Psych* 2001, **158**, 2086) and nortriptyline toxicity (n=1, van der Kuy *et al*, *Ann Pharmacother* 2002, **36**, 1712–14).

### Valproate + tricyclics
See antidepressants + valproate (*4.5.12*).

### VASOCONSTRICTOR SYMPATHO-MIMETICS + TRICYCLICS
A greatly enhanced response, eg. hypertension and arrhythmias, to norepinephrine and phenylephrine in patients taking tricyclics has been shown in many reports. Doxepin and maprotiline may have a lesser effect. Local anaesthetics with epinephrine appear safe. Moderate doses of cold cures containing sympathomimetics should present little risk in healthy patients.

### Venlafaxine + tricyclics *
Venlafaxine increases imipramine levels, showing a consistent but probably clinically modest effect (n=8, Albers *et al*, *Psych Res* 2000, **96**, 235–43). Serotonin syndrome has been reported with venlafaxine and amitriptyline (n=1, *Postgrad Med J* 2000, **76**, 254–56) and a GTC fit with venlafaxine 150mg/d and trimipramine 100mg/d (n=1, Schlienger *et al*, *Ann Pharmacother* 2000, **34**, 1402–5).

### Warfarin + tricyclics
Normally there is no problem but occasional control problems have been reported with lofepramine (mentioned in Sayal *et al*, *Acta Psych Scand* 2000, **102**, 250–55 and Duncan *et al*, *Int Clin Psychopharmacol* 1998, **13**, 87–94).

### Yohimbine + tricyclics
Tricyclics can potentiate the blood pressure changes caused by yohimbine, especially if blood pressure is already raised (mentioned in Fugh-Berman, *Lancet* 2000, **355**, 134–38).

### Zopiclone + tricyclics
See zopiclone (*4.1.6*).

### Zotepine + tricyclics
See zotepine (*4.2.6*).

---

### 4.3.2 SSRIs (Selective Serotonin Reuptake Inhibitors)
Drug interactions involving the P450 system have been described for all SSRIs but there are significant differences in the isoenzymes inhibited and the degree of inhibition (review by van Harten, *Clin Pharmacokinet* 1993, **24**, 203–20).

The most well-known is CYP2D6. *In vitro* inhibition on a molar basis is: paroxetine (most potent), norfluoxetine, fluoxetine, sertraline, fluvoxamine, citalopram (least potent). *In vivo* is probably broadly similar. Fluoxetine and paroxetine are probably similar in 2D6 inhibition, but with some variation (n=31, RCT, using multiple-dose fluoxetine 60mg/d, fluvoxamine 100mg/d, paroxetine 20mg/d, or sertraline 100mg/d, Alfaro *et al*, *J Clin Psychopharmacol* 1999, 19, 155–63). There are few other controlled trials; evidence is mainly from case studies and so firm conclusions on the relative merits of the SSRIs for interactions with, eg. tricyclics are difficult to make.

**Reviews***: overview and review of SSRI interactions and P450 effects (Preskorn, *Clin Pharmacokinet* 1997, [Suppl 1], 1–21, 143 refs, *Prescrire International* 2001, **10**, 25–31), clinically significant SSRI interactions (Mitchell, *Drug Safety* 1997, **17**, 390–406, 163 refs) and clinically significant SSRI-CNS interactions (Sproule *et al*, *Clin Pharmacokinet* 1997, **33**, 454–71, 106 refs).

### 4.3.2.1 CITALOPRAM AND ESCITALOPRAM*

Citalopram is a weak inhibitor of CYP2D6 (Baettig *et al, Eur J Clin Pharmacol* 1993, **44**, 403–5) and metabolised by CYP3A4. A review (Brosen and Naranjo, *Eur Neuropsychopharmacol* 2001, **11**, 275–83) concludes that citalopram is neither a source nor a cause of clinically important drugdrug interactions. Escitalopram would be expected to have similar characteristics.

### Alcohol + citalopram/escitalopram
See alcohol (*4.7.1*).

### Alimemazine (trimeprazine) + citalopram/escitalopram
See antipsychotics + citalopram/ escitalopram in this section.

### Acenocoumarol + citalopram/escitalopram *
There is a reported case of interaction (n=1, Borras-Blasco *et al, Ann Pharmacother* 2002, **36**, 345).

### Antipsychotics + citalopram/escitalopram
Levomepromazine and alimemazine may both increase plasma levels of citalopram by about a third (Milne and Goa, *Drugs* 1991, **41**, 450–77), possibly via enzyme inhibition and of minimal clinical significance. There has been no detectable effect from citalopram on the plasma levels of other antipsychotics (n=90, d/b, Syvalahti *et al, J Int Med Res* 1997, **25**, 24–32), eg. citalopram 40mg/d had no effect over 8 weeks on the plasma levels of clozapine (n=8, 200–400mg/d), risperidone (n=7, 4–6mg/d) and their active metabolites in patients with chronic schizophrenia (Avenoso *et al, Clin Drug Investigation* 1998, **16**, 393–98).

### Benzodiazepines + citalopram/escitalopram
No pharmacokinetic interaction could be demonstrated between citalopram and the CYP3A4 substrate triazolam (n=18, open, Nolting and Abramowitz, *Pharmacother* 2000, **20**, 750–55).

### Buspirone + citalopram/escitalopram
Hyponatraemia and serotonin syndrome has been reported with the combination (Spigset and Adielsson, *Int Clin Psychopharmacol* 1997, **12**, 61–63).

### Carbamazepine + citalopram/escitalopram *
Carbamazepine may reduce the proportion and concentration of the active S-citalopram isomer (n=6, Steinacher *et al, Eur Neuropsychopharmacol* 2002, **12**, 255–60). Citalopram had no effect on carbamazepine kinetics in another study (n=12, open, Moller *et al, J Clin Psychopharmacol* 2001, **21**, 493–99).

### Charcoal, activated + citalopram/escitalopram
25g activated charcoal given 30 minutes after citalopram reduced citalopram AUC by 51%, and peak levels by over 50%. Concurrent gastric lavage did not provide any additional reductions (n=9, RCT, Lapatto-Reiniluoto *et al, Br J Clin Pharmacol* 1999, **48**, 148–53).

### Ciclosporin + citalopram/escitalopram *
Citalopram had no effect on ciclosporin kinetics in one report (Liston *et al, Psychosomatics* 2001, **42**, 370–72).

### Digoxin + citalopram/escitalopram *
Steady state citalopram 40mg/d had no effect on the kinetics of single doses of digoxin 1mg (n=11, open, c/o, 50/7, Larsen *et al, J Clin Pharmacol* 2001, **41**, 340).

### Donepezil + citalopram/escitalopram
See SSRIs + donepezil (*4.6.3.1*).

### Fluvoxamine + citalopram/escitalopram *
Fluvoxamine may increase the ratio of S-citalopram to R-citalopram, enhancing it's action (n=7, open, Bondolfi *et al, Psychopharmacol (Berl)* 1996, **128**, 421–25).

### Ketoconazole + citalopram/escitalopram *
Single doses of ketoconazole have no effect on the kinetics of citalopram (n=18, RCT, d/b, c/o, Gutierrez and Abramowitz, *Pharmacotherapy* 2001, **21**, 163–68).

### Lithium + citalopram/escitalopram
No pharmacokinetic interaction was noted in one study (n=24, open, Gram *et al, Ther Drug Monit* 1993, **15**, 18–24).

### MAOIs + citalopram/escitalopram
See MAOIs (*4.3.4*).

### Moclobemide + citalopram/escitalopram *
See SSRIs + moclobemide (*4.3.3.3*).

### Oxcarbazepine + citalopram/escitalopram
See oxcarbazepine (*4.5.6*).

### Perhexiline + citalopram/escitalopram *
Perhexiline toxicity with citalopram has been reported (n=1, Nyfort-Hansen, *Med J Aust* 2002, **176**, 560–61).

### Selegiline + citalopram/escitalopram
A study showed the lack of a clinically significant interaction (n=18, RCT, Laine *et al, Clin Neuropharmacol* 1997, **20**, 419–33).

### Sertindole + citalopram/escitalopram*
See sertindole (*4.2.7.2*).

### Silbutramine + citalopram/escitalopram *
A case of hypomania has been reported with this combination (n=1, Benazzi, *J Clin Psych* 2002, **63**, 165).

### St. John's wort + citalopram/escitalopram
See SSRIs + St. John's wort (*4.3.3.9*).

### Sympathomimetics + citalopram/escitalopram
Augmentation of amfetamines is theoretically possible (see also sympathomimetics + fluoxetine).

### Triptans + citalopram/escitalopram
The BNF notes an increased risk of CNS toxicity with sumatriptan and recommends avoiding the combination. See also triptans + fluoxetine (*4.3.2.2*).

### Tricyclics + citalopram/escitalopram*
See SSRIs + tricyclics (*4.3.1*).

### Warfarin + citalopram/escitalopram
Citalopram 40mg/d may produce a small increase in prothrombin time (n=12, Preskorn *et al, Br J Clin Pharmacol* 1997, **44**, 199), but this is probably clinically insignificant (Sayal *et al, Acta Psych Scand* 2000, **102**, 250–55).

### Zolpidem + citalopram/escitalopram
See SSRIs + zolpidem (*4.1.5*).

## 4.3.2.2  FLUOXETINE
Fluoxetine substantially inhibits CYP2D6 and probably CYP2C9/10, moderately inhibits CYP2C19 and weakly inhibits CYP3A3/4 and may have a higher incidence of interactions with drugs metabolised by these enzymes. Norfluoxetine is a potent CYP3A4 inhibitor and appears a moderately potent inhibitor of CYP2D6.
**Review**: Preskorn, *Int Clin Psychopharmacol* 1994, **9**(Suppl 3), 13–19.

### Alcohol + fluoxetine
See alcohol (*4.7.1*).

### Alosetron + fluoxetine *
There is no significant effect from the 5-HT3 antagonist alosetron on fluoxetine kinetics (n=12, D'Souza *et al, J Clin Pharmacol* 2001, **41**, 455–58).

### Amfetamines + fluoxetine
See sympathomimetics + fluoxetine.

### ANTIPSYCHOTICS + FLUOXETINE
See antipsychotics (*4.2.1*), clozapine (*4.2.2*), quetiapine (*4.2.4*), risperidone (*4.2.5*) and olanzapine (*4.2.3*).

### Beta-blockers + fluoxetine *
Bradycardia may occur in people taking fluoxetine and metoprolol, possibly due to CYP2D6 inhibition. Atenolol or sotalol may be suitable

alternatives (n=2, Proudlove, *Lancet* 1993, **341**, 967). Fluoxetine may inhibit the metabolism of R-carvedilol (rather than S-carvedilol) but this appears to have little clinical significance (n=10, RCT, d/b, c/o, 28/7, Graff *et al, J Clin Pharmacol* 2001, **41**, 97–106).

### Benzodiazepines + fluoxetine
Fluoxetine may slightly increase the plasma levels of some benzodiazepines (eg. diazepam: n=10, Lemberger *et al, Clin Pharmacol Ther* 1988, **43**, 412–19). Desmethyldiazepam levels may be lower, which may explain the lack of additive psychomotor impairment (review: Ciraulo and Shader, *J Clin Psychopharmacol* 1990, **10**, 213–17). Increased alprazolam levels with fluoxetine are due to decreased clearance (RCT, p/c, Greenblatt *et al, Clin Pharmacol Ther* 1992, **52**, 479–86) but this does not seem to occur with clonazepam. The clinical significance is minor.

### Bupropion + fluoxetine *
See bupropion (*4.6.4*).

### Buspirone + fluoxetine
See buspirone (*4.1.2*).

### Calcium-channel blockers + fluoxetine
Oedema, weight gain and headache have occurred with verapamil and fluoxetine (n=2, Sternbach, *J Clin Psychopharmacol* 1991, **11**, 390). Lowering doses is recommended if an interaction is suspected.

### Cannabis + fluoxetine
See antidepressants + cannabis (*4.7.2*).

### Carbamazepine + fluoxetine
Two studies have shown that fluoxetine and norfluoxetine inhibit carbamazepine metabolism, increasing levels by up to 25% (n=14, Gidal *et al, Ther Drug Monit* 1993, **15**, 405–9). One small study, however, showed fluoxetine 20mg/d to have no effect on carbamazepine levels (n=8, open, Spina *et al, Ther Drug Monit* 1993, **15**, 247–50). A toxic serotonin syndrome has also been reported (n=1, Dursun *et al, Lancet* 1993, **342**, 442–43).

### Ciclosporin + fluoxetine
Ciclosporin plasma concentrations were nearly doubled by fluoxetine 20mg/d in one case, probably by CYP3A4 inhibition (Holton and Bonser, *BMJ* 1995, **311**, 422).

### Clarithromycin + fluoxetine
Acute delirium has been reported when clarithromycin was added to fluoxetine (eg. n=1, Tracy and Johns Cupp, *Ann Pharmacother* 1996, **30**, 1199–200), probably via CYP3A4 inhibition.

### Cocaine + fluoxetine
See antidepressants + cocaine (*4.7.3*).

### Cyproheptadine + fluoxetine
Patients treated with cyproheptadine for fluoxetine-induced anorgasmia may relapse (n=3, Feder, *J Clin Psych* 1991, **52**, 163–64) and interaction has been reported in a bulimic patient (n=2, Goldbloom and Kennedy, *J Clin Psych* 1991, **52**, 261–62).

### Dextromethorphan + fluoxetine
Visual hallucinations lasting 6–8hrs occurred in one patient taking fluoxetine 20mg/d who also took a cough mixture containing dextromethorphan (Achamallah, *Am J Psych* 1992, **149**, 1406).

### Donepezil + fluoxetine
See SSRIs + donepezil (*4.6.3.1*).

### Lithium + fluoxetine
See lithium (*4.4*).

### LSD + fluoxetine
GTC convulsions occurred in one patient who took a double dose of LSD while on fluoxetine 20mg/d, having previously taken single doses of LSD uneventfully (n=1, Achamallah, *Am J Psych* 1992, **149**, 843–44).

### MAOIs + FLUOXETINE
See MAOIs (*4.3.4*).

### Methadone + fluoxetine *
See methadone (*4.6.8*).

### Mirtazapine + fluoxetine *
See mirtazapine (*4.3.3.2*).

### Moclobemide + fluoxetine
See SSRIs + moclobemide (*4.3.3.3*).

### Morphine + fluoxetine *
Fluoxetine may mildly enhance the analgesic effects of morphine and reduce it's side effects (n=15, d/b, Erjavec et al, J Clin Pharmacol 2000, **40**, 1286–95).

### Nefazodone + fluoxetine
Fluoxetine may increase the plasma levels of nefazodone (BNF).

### Olanzapine + fluoxetine
See SSRIs + olanzapine (4.2.3).

### Oral contraceptives + fluoxetine *
Lack of interaction has been shown (n=1698, Koke et al, Am J Obs Gynecol 2002, **187**, 551–55).

### Pentazocine + fluoxetine
Rapid toxicity has been reported, although an interaction was not proven (n=1, Hansen et al, Am J Psych 1990, **147**, 949–50).

### PHENYTOIN + FLUOXETINE
See phenytoin (4.5.8).

### Quetlapine + fluoxetine
See SSRIs + quetiapine (4.2.4).

### Reboxetine + fluoxetine *
See reboxetine (4.3.3.5).

### RISPERIDONE + FLUOXETINE *
See risperidone (4.2.5).

### Rivastigmine + fluoxetine
See rivastigmine (4.6.3.3).

### Selegiline + fluoxetine
Three cases exist of toxic reactions, eg. hypomania, hypertension and shivering (Suchowersky and de Vries, Can J Neurol Sci 1990, **17**, 352), ataxia in a complex regimen (n=1, Jermain et al, Ann Pharmacother 1992, **26**, 1300) and hypertension (Montastruc et al, Lancet 1993, **341**, 555). Discontinue one or both drugs if an adverse reaction occurs.

### SERTINDOLE + FLUOXETINE *
See sertindole (4.2.7.2).

### Sertraline + fluoxetine
See sertraline (4.3.2.5).

### St. John's wort + fluoxetine
See SSRIs + St. John's wort (4.3.3.9).

### Sympathomimetics + fluoxetine
An interaction has been suggested by reports of extreme restlessness, agitation and psychotic symptoms, apparently caused by fluoxetine-augmentation of amfetamines (n=2, Barrett et al, B J Psych 1996, **168**, 253).

### Tolterodine + fluoxetine
Fluoxetine has been shown to inhibit the metabolism of tolterodine (n=13, open, Brynne et al, B J Clin Pharmacology 1999, **48**, 553–63).

### Tramadol + fluoxetine *
Serotonin syndrome has been reported with fluoxetine and tramadol (n=1, Kesavan and Sobala, J Roy Soc Med 1999, **92**, 474–75), as has mania and serotonin syndrome (n=1, Gonzalez-Pinto et al, Am J Psych 2001, **158**, 964–65).

### Trazodone + fluoxetine *
Trazodone toxicity may occur with the combination (eg. Neirenberg et al, J Clin Psych 1992, **53**, 83). Myoclonus has been reported within a few days of fluoxctine being added to trazodone (n=1, Darko et al, Vet Hum Toxicol 2001, **43**, 214–15).

### TRICYCLICS + FLUOXETINE
See SSRIs + tricyclics (4.3.1).

### Triptans + fluoxetine *
Lack of significant interaction has been reported with **sumatriptan** (n=14, open, Blier and Bergeron, J Clin Psychopharmacol 1995, **15**, 106–9) although post-marketing surveillance in Canada indicated that a serotonin-like syndrome may occur rarely with the combination (n=22, Joffe and Sokolov, Acta Psych Scand 1997, **95**, 551–52). The BNF notes an increased risk of CNS toxicity and recommends avoiding the combination. Fluoxetine 60mg/d has only a modest effect on **alotriptan** peak levels, with no clinically significant side effects or changes in vital signs or ECGs (n=14, RCT, c/o, 8/7, Fleishaker et al, J Clin Pharmacol 2001, **41**, 217–23).

### Tryptophan + fluoxetine
Central toxicity has been reported (n=5, Steiner and Fontaine, Biol Psych 1986, **21**, 1067–71).

### Valproate + fluoxetine
Valproate levels may rise by up to 50% if fluoxetine is added, although the mechanism is not established (eg. Lucena *et al, Am J Psych* 1998, **155**, 575) and reduced valproate levels have been reported (Droulers *et al, J Clin Psychopharmacol* 1997, **17**, 139–40).

### Venlafaxine + fluoxetine
Serotonin syndrome has been reported when venlafaxine was started immediately after fluoxetine was discontinued (n=1, Bhatara *et al, Ann Pharmacother* 1998, **32**, 432–36) and severe anticholinergic side-effects may occur during combined fluoxetine 20mg/d and venlafaxine 37.5mg/d (n=4, Benazzi, *J Clin Psychopharmacol* 1999, **19**, 96–98, letter).

### WARFARIN + FLUOXETINE
An *in vitro* study indicated fluoxetine has a potentially potent effect on warfarin (Schmider *et al, B J Clin Pharmacol* 1997, **44**, 495–98). Raised INR has been reported, within ten days of starting fluoxetine (n=2, Woolfrey *et al, BMJ* 1993, **307**, 241) and in patients on warfarin with stable INRs who experienced dramatic increases in INR when fluoxetine 20mg/d was added (n=2, Hanger and Thomas, *NZ Med J* 1995, **108**, 157). There is also a case report of an elderly man prescribed warfarin, diazepam and fluoxetine who developed an elevated INR and died from a cerebral haemorrhage (Dent and Orrock, *Pharmacotherapy* 1997, **17**, 170–72).

### Zolpidem + fluoxetine
See SSRIs + zolpidem (*4.1.5*).

### Zotepine + fluoxetine
See SSRIs + zotepine (*4.2.6*).

---

### 4.3.2.3 FLUVOXAMINE
Fluvoxamine strongly inhibits CYP1A2, CYP2D6, CYP3A and CYP2C19 activity and may have a high incidence of interactions with drugs metabolised by these enzymes, which may have serious implications for a variety of drugs (n=20, *Clin Pharmacol Ther* 1998, **64**, 257–68).

### Alcohol + fluvoxamine
See alcohol (*4.7.1*).

### Antipsychotics + fluvoxamine *
Seizures have been reported with levomepromazine and fluvoxamine (n=1, Grinshpoon *et al, Int Clin Psychopharmacol* 1993, **8**, 61–62), although levomepromazine does not appear to increase fluvoxamine levels (n=15, Yoshimura *et al, Int Clin Psychopharmacol* 2000, **15**, 233–35). Thioridazine is contraindicated with fluvoxamine due to QTc prolongation. See also clozapine (*4.2.2*).

### Astemizole + fluvoxamine
This is a possible contraindication because of the risk of fatal ventricular arrhythmias via inhibition of CYP3A4.

### Benzodiazepines + fluvoxamine
Plasma concentrations of bromazepam are doubled by fluvoxamine, but lorazepam is unaffected (van Harten *et al*, mentioned in *Clin Pharmacokinet* 1993, **24**, 203–20). A study showed that fluvoxamine 100mg/d increased alprazolam plasma levels by 100% and so reduced doses of alprazolam should be used (n=60, Fleishaker and Hulst, *E J Clin Pharmacol* 1994, **46**, 35–39).

### Beta-blockers + fluvoxamine
Lack of significant interaction has been shown with atenolol. Propranolol plasma levels can be raised by fluvoxamine by up to 500% but without major clinical effect (reviewed by Benfield and Ward, *Drugs* 1988, **32**, 313–34).

### Buspirone + fluvoxamine
See buspirone (*4.1.2*).

### Caffeine + fluvoxamine *
Even low-dose fluvoxamine (10–20mg/d) inhibits the metabolism of caffeine, presumably via 1A2 inhibition (n=10, Christensen *et al, Clin Pharmacol Ther* 2002, **71**, 141–52), and half-life may rise from 5hrs to 22hrs (Slaughter and Edwards, *Ann Pharmacother* 1995, **29**, 619–24), so an enhanced effect is possible. One study indicated that the effect was likely to be minimal (n=10, Spigset,

*Eur J Clin Pharmacol* 1998, **54**, 665–66).

## Carbamazepine + fluvoxamine
One small study showed no effect on carbamazepine levels from fluvoxamine 100mg/d (n=15, RCT, Spina *et al, Ther Drug Monit* 1993, **15**, 247–50) although several cases exist of fluvoxamine increasing carbamazepine levels and toxicity (eg. Martinelli *et al, B J Clin Pharmacol* 1993, **36**, 615–16).

## Ciclosporin + fluvoxamine
There is a case report of ciclosporin levels elevated by the introduction of fluvoxamine to a ciclosporin-treated allograft recipient, probably via CYP3A4 inhibition. Intensive monitoring of the serum creatinine and ciclosporin level was indicated, along with appropriate dose reductions (Vella and Sayegh, *Am J Kidney Dis* 1998, **31**, 320–23).

## Chloral + fluvoxamine
Lack of interaction has been reported (Wagner *et al, Adv Pharmacother* 1986, **2**, 34–56).

## CLOZAPINE + FLUVOXAMINE
See clozapine (*4.2.2*).

## Digoxin + fluvoxamine
Lack of interaction has been reported (d/b, Ochs *et al, J Clin Pharmacol* 1989, **29**, 91–95).

## Donepezil + fluvoxamine
See SSRIs + donepezil (*4.6.3.1*).

## Glimepiride + fluvoxamine *
Fluvoxamine may produce a modest increase in glimepiride plasma concentrations (n=12, RCT, d/b, c/o, 4/7, Niemi *et al, Clin Pharmacol Ther* 2001, **69**, 194–200).

## Lithium + fluvoxamine
Although lack of interaction has been reported (Hendrickx and Floris, *Curr Ther Res* 1991, **49**, 106–10), case reports exist of serotonin syndrome (n=1, Ohman and Spigset, *Pharmacopsychiatry* 1993, **26**, 263–64) and irresistible somnolence (n=1, Evans and Marwick, *B J Psych* 1990, **156**, 286).

## MAOIs + FLUVOXAMINE
See MAOIs (*4.3.4*).

## Melatonin + fluvoxamine
Fluvoxamine 50mg inhibits the metabolism of oral melatonin 5mg, increasing plasma levels (n=5, open, Hartter *et al, Clin Pharmacol Ther* 2000, **67**, 1–6), supported by a further case, where combining the treatments improved sleep (n=1, Grozinger *et al, Arch Gen Psych* 2000, **57**, 812–13).

## Methadone + fluvoxamine *
See methadone (*4.6.8*).

## Metoclopramide + fluvoxamine
Acute dystonia has been associated with the combination (n=1, Palop *et al, Ann Pharmacother* 1999, **33**, 382).

## Mirtazapine + fluvoxamine *
See mirtazapine (*4.3.3.1*).

## Moclobemide + fluvoxamine *
See SSRIs + moclobemide (*4.3.3.3*).

## NICOUMALONE + FLUVOXAMINE
The anticoagulant effects may be enhanced by fluvoxamine.

## Olanzapine + fluvoxamine *
See olanzapine (*4.2.2*).

## PHENYTOIN + FLUVOXAMINE *
See phenytoin (*4.5.8*).

## Pipamperone + fluvoxamine
ECG changes have occurred as a result of acute overdose with this combination (Gallerani *et al, Clin Drug Investigat* 1998, **15**, 64–68).

## Quinidine + fluvoxamine
Fluvoxamine significantly inhibits the clearance of quinidine, probably by 3A4 inhibition (n=6, open, Damkier *et al, Eur J Clin Pharmacol* 1999, **55**, 451–56).

## Reboxetine + fluvoxamine
See reboxetine (*4.3.3.5*).

## Risperidone + fluvoxamine *
See risperidone (*4.2.5*).

## Smoking + fluvoxamine *
See smoking (*4.7.4*).

## St. John's wort + fluvoxamine
See SSRIs + St. John's wort (*4.3.3.9*).

## Sympathomimetics + fluvoxamine
Augmentation of amfetamines is theoretically possible (see also fluoxetine, *4.3.2.2*).

### Tacrine + fluvoxamine

Fluvoxamine is a potent inhibitor of tacrine metabolism *in vivo* (n=18, RCT, open, Teilmann-Larsen *et al, Eur J Clin Pharmacol* 1999, **55**, 375–82).

### THEOPHYLLINE + FLUVOXAMINE

Several cases of theophylline toxicity have been reported (eg. Devane *et al, Am J Psych* 1997, **154**, 1317–18), probably via CYP1A2 inhibition. The UK CSM recommends avoiding the combination (*Curr Prob* 1994, **20**, 12).

### Tolbutamide + fluvoxamine *

Fluvoxamine 150mg/d may increase tolbutamide levels by about 20% (n=14, RCT, Madsen *et al, Clin Pharmacol Ther* 2001, **69**, 41–47).

### TRICYCLICS + FLUVOXAMINE

See SSRIs + tricyclics (*4.3.1*).

### Triptans + fluvoxamine

The BNF notes an increased risk of CNS toxicity with sumatriptan and recommends avoiding the combination. See also fluoxetine (*4.3.2.2*).

### Tryptophan + fluvoxamine

Central toxicity has been suggested with fluvoxamine (n=5, Steiner and Fontaine, *Biol Psych* 1986, **21**, 1067–71).

### Valproate + fluvoxamine

Augmentation of fluvoxamine has been seen with valproate (Corrigan, *Biol Psych* 1992, **31**, 1178–79).

### WARFARIN + FLUVOXAMINE *

An *in vitro* study indicated fluvoxamine has the most potent effect on warfarin of the SSRIs (Schmider *et al, B J Clin Pharmacol* 1997, **44**, 495–98). Fluvoxamine can increase warfarin levels by up to 65%, increasing prothrombin time (Benfield and Ward, *Drugs* 1986, **32**, 313–34; n=1, Limke *et al, Ann Pharmacother* 2002, **36**, 1890–92), and elevated INR has occurred up to two weeks after fluvoxamine was stopped, a prolonged effect (n=1, Yap and Low, *Singapore Med J* 1999, **40**, 480–82).

### Zolpidem + fluvoxamine

See zolpidem (*4.1.5*).

### Zotepine + fluvoxamine

See SSRIs + zotepine (*4.2.6*).

---

### 4.3.2.4  PAROXETINE

Paroxetine is probably the most potent SSRI inhibitor of CYP2D6 but does not appear to inhibit any other CYP enzyme. It may thus have a higher incidence of interactions with drugs metabolised by this enzyme. The main metabolite has approximately one third the CYP2D6 inhibition potency of paroxetine.

### Alcohol + paroxetine

See alcohol (*4.7.1*).

### Anticholinergics + paroxetine

See SSRIs + anticholinergics (*4.6.2*).

### Antipsychotics + paroxetine

Lack of interaction between haloperidol and paroxetine has been shown (Cooper *et al, Acta Psych Scand* 1989, **80**[Suppl 350], 53–55). Paroxetine (3-day course) had no detectable effect on thiothixene (a thioxanthene) pharmacokinetics in a small study (n=10, Guthrie *et al, J Clin Pharm Ther* 1997, **22**, 221–16).

### Benzodiazepines + paroxetine

Lack of interaction has been shown (Boyer and Blumhardt, *J Clin Psych* 1992, **53**[Suppl 2], 132–24), eg. with oxazepam (Cooper *et al, Acta Psych Scand* 1989, **80**[Suppl 350], 53–55). A case of serotonin syndrome has been reported in a person taking maintenance paroxetine after a single dose clonazepam (Rella and Hoffman, *J Toxicol Clin Toxicol* 1998, **36**, 257–58).

### Beta-blockers + paroxetine

CYP2D6 inhibition by paroxetine 20mg/d leads to accumulation of S-metoprolol, and so reduced metoprolol levels might be needed (n=8, open, Hemeryck *et al, Clin Pharmacol Ther* 2000, **67**, 283–91). Raised paroxetine levels after the addition of pindolol has been reported, probably via 2D6 inhibition (n=1, Olver and Burrows, *Int J Psych Clin Pract* 1998, **2**, 225–27).

### Bupropion + paroxetine *

See bupropion (*4.6.4*).

## Carbamazepine + paroxetine
No significant interaction has been found (n=20, s/b, p/c, c/o, 23/7, Andersen *et al, Epilepsy Res* 1991, **10**, 201–4).

## Cimetidine + paroxetine
Cimetidine may inhibit the first-pass metabolism of paroxetine, increasing bioavailability by up to 50% (Bannister *et al, Acta Psych Scand* 1989, **80**[Suppl 350], 102–6) so use ranitidine instead.

## CLOZAPINE + PAROXETINE
See clozapine (*4.2.2*).

## Dextromethorphan + paroxetine
Paroxetine would be expected to increase dextromethorphan levels by CYP2D6 inhibition (see reported case with fluoxetine, *4.3.2.2*).

## Digoxin + paroxetine
Lack of interaction has been shown (Boyer & Blumhardt, *J Clin Psych* 1992, **53**[Suppl 2], 132–34).

## Donepezil + paroxetine
See SSRIs + donepezil (*4.6.3.1*).

## Galantamine + paroxetine
See galantamine (*4.6.3.2*).

## Interferon alpha + paroxetine
Previous good response to paroxetine and trazodone was reversed by interferon alpha, which has anti-serotonergic actions (n=1, McAllister-Williams *et al, B J Psych* 2000, **176**, 93).

## Lithium + paroxetine *
There are some cases (n=4) of a possible serotonin syndrome with paroxetine and lithium (n=17, Fagiolini *et al, J Clin Psychopharmacol* 2001, **21**, 474–78).

## Methadone + paroxetine *
Steady-state plasma methadone levels may rise with paroxetine, but only in poor 2D6 metabolisers (n=10, 12/7, Begre *et al, J Clin Psychopharmacol* 2002, **22**, 211–15).

## Mirtazapine + paroxetine *
See mirtazapine (*4.3.3.2*).

## Moclobemide + paroxetine
See SSRIs + moclobemide (*4.3.3.3*).

## MAOIs + PAROXETINE
See MAOIs (*4.3.4*).

## Oral contraceptives + paroxetine
Lack of interaction has been shown (Boyer and Blumhardt, *J Clin Psych* 1992, **53**[Suppl 2], 132–34).

## Phenytoin + paroxetine
Paroxetine bioavailability may be decreased slightly (Andersen *et al, Epilepsy Res* 1991, **10**, 201–4).

## Phenobarbital + paroxetine
Paroxetine bioavailability may be decreased slightly, resulting in a 25% decrease in plasma concentrations (Bannister *et al, Acta Psych Scand* 1989, **80**[Suppl 350], 102–6). No interaction occurs with **amylobarbital** (Cooper *et al, Acta Psych Scand* 1989, **80**[Suppl 350], 53–55).

## Risperidone + paroxetine *
See risperidone (*4.2.5*).

## SERTINDOLE + PAROXETINE *
See sertindole (*4.2.7.2*).

## St. John's wort + paroxetine
See SSRIs + St. John's wort (*4.3.3.9*).

## Sympathomimetics + paroxetine
Augmentation of amfetamines is theoretically possible (see sympathomimetics + fluoxetine *4.3.2.2*).

## TRICYCLICS + PAROXETINE
See SSRIs + tricyclics (*4.3.1*).

## Triptans + paroxetine *
The BNF notes an increased risk of CNS toxicity and recommends avoiding sumatriptan and paroxetine although almost complete lack of interaction has been shown with rizatriptan and paroxetine (n=12, RCT, 14/7, Goldberg *et al, J Clin Pharmacol* 1999, **39**, 192–99). See also fluoxetine (*4.3.2.2*).

## Valproate + paroxetine
No significant interaction occurs (n=20, s/b, p/c, c/o, 23/7, Andersen *et al, Epilepsy Res* 1991, **10**, 201–4).

## Warfarin + paroxetine
An *in vitro* study indicated that all SSRIs have an effect on warfarin (Schmider *et al, B J Clin Pharmacol* 1997, **44**, 495–98), eg. an up to a 3 point rise in INR has been reported in

several patients (mentioned by Aski-nazi, *Am J Psych* 1996, **153**, 135–36).

## Zolpidem + paroxetine
See SSRIs + zolpidem (*4.1.5*).

## Zotepine + paroxetine
See SSRIs + zotepine (*4.2.6*).

---

### 4.3.2.5 SERTRALINE
Sertraline produces a dose-related inhibition of CYP2D6 but has little, if any, effect on CYP1A2, CYP2C9/10, CYP2C19 or CYP3A3/4. It appears less potent in inhibiting CYP2D6 than most other SSRIs (Baettig *et al, Eur J Clin Pharmacol* 1993, **44**, 403–5) and has, at 50–100mg/d, a low incidence of interactions with drugs metabolised by 2D6.

## Alcohol + sertraline
See alcohol (*4.7.1*).

## Anticholinergics + sertraline
See SSRIs + anticholinergics (*4.6.2*).

## Benzodiazepines + sertraline
A study in male volunteers showed no sertraline effect on diazepam and suggested no effect on the CYP2C and CYP3A4 enzymes (n=20, RCT, d/b, p/c, c/o, Gardner *et al, Clin Pharmacokinetics* 1997 [Suppl 1], 43–49), but a slight decrease in plasma levels by 13% may occur (review: Warrington, *Int Clin Psychopharmacol* 1991, **6**[Suppl 2], 11–21).

## Beta-blockers + sertraline
No pharmacodynamic interaction has been found with atenolol (eg. n=10, RCT, Ziegler and Wilner, *J Clin Psych* 1996, **57**[Suppl 1], 12–15).

## Carbamazepine + sertraline
Lack of significant interaction has been reported, but there are cases where sertraline 100mg/d increased carbamazepine (600mg/d) plasma levels, probably via 3A4 inhibition (d/b, p/c, Joblin, *N Z Med J* 1994, **107**, 43; Lane, *N Z Med J* 1994, **107**, 209), and where non-response to ser-traline was due to low plasma levels associated with carbamazepine use, possibly via CYP3A4 induction (n=2, Khan *et al, J Clin Psych* 2000, **61**, 526–27).

## Clozapine + sertraline *
See clozapine (*4.2.2*).

## Digoxin + sertraline
No interaction has been noted (For-ster *et al, Biol Psych* 1991, **29**, 355S).

## Dolasetron + sertraline *
A serotonin syndrome has been reported with the combination (n=1, Sorscher, *J Psychopharmacol* 2002, **16**, 191).

## Donepezil + sertraline
See SSRIs + donepezil (*4.6.3.1*).

## Erythromycin + sertraline
Serotonin syndrome has been reported with the combination, possi-bly via CYP3A4 inhibition (n=1, Lee and Lee, *Pharmacother* 1999, **19**, 894–96).

## Fluoxetine + sertraline
A possible serotonin syndrome has been reported (see switching anti-depressants in *2.2.5*).

## Lamotrigine + sertraline
See lamotrigine (*4.5.4*).

## Lithium + sertraline
See SSRIs + lithium (*4.4*).

## MAOIs + SERTRALINE
See MAOIs (*4.3.4*).

## Mirtazapine + sertraline
See SSRIs + mirtazapine (*4.3.3.2*).

## Moclobemide + sertraline *
See SSRIs + moclobemide (*4.3.3.3*).

## Olanzapine + sertraline *
See SSRIs + olanzapine (*4.2.2*).

## Oxycodone + sertraline *
Visual hallucination and tremor induced by sertraline and oxycodone in a bone marrow transplant patient has been reported (n=1, Rosebraugh *et al, J Clin Pharmacol* 2001, **41**, 224).

## Phenytoin + sertraline *
Lack of significant interaction has been shown (n=30, RCT, Rapeport *et al, J Clin Psych* 1996, **57**[Suppl 1], 24–28), but dramatically raised phe-nytoin levels have been reported after the addition of sertraline (n=2, Haselberger *et al, J Clin Psychophar-macol* 1997, **17**, 107–9), as has signifi-cant reduction in sertraline levels by phenytoin (Pihlsgard and Eliasson,

*Eur J Clin Pharmacol* 2002, **57**, 915–16), so monitoring levels would seem sensible.

### Sertindole + sertraline *
See sertindole (*4.2.7.2*).

### St. John's wort + sertraline
See SSRIs + St. John's wort (*4.3.3.9*).

### Sumatriptan + sertraline
The BNF notes an increased risk of CNS toxicity and recommends avoiding the combination. See also fluoxetine (*4.3.2.2*).

### Sympathomimetics + sertraline
Augmentation of amfetamines is theoretically possible (see sympathomimetics + fluoxetine, *4.3.2.2*).

### Tolbutamide + sertraline
In a parallel-group study, 200mg/d sertraline produced a 16% decrease in tolbutamide clearance, possibly via inhibition of CYP2C9 (n=25, RCT, Tremaine *et al, Clin Pharmacokinet* 1997, [Suppl 1], 31–36). A 16% decrease in plasma levels has been reported (n=25, RCT, Warrington, *Int Clin Psychopharmacol* 1991, **6**[Suppl 2], 11–21).

### Tramadol + sertraline
Serotonin syndrome has been reported when a tramadol dose was increased with concomitant sertraline (n=1, Mason and Blackburn, *Ann Pharmacother* 1997, **31**, 175–77).

### Tricyclics + sertraline
See SSRIs + tricyclics (*4.3.1*).

### Venlafaxine + sertraline
Acute liver damage possibly related to sertraline and venlafaxine ingestion has been reported (Kim *et al, Ann Pharmacother* 1999, **33**, 381–82, letter).

### Warfarin + sertraline
An *in vitro* study indicated that, of the SSRIs, sertraline had the least potent effect on warfarin (Schmider *et al, B J Clin Pharmacol* 1997, **44**, 495–98). It may produce only a modest increase in prothrombin time, considered clinically insignificant (n=12, RCT, 22/7, Apseloff *et al, Clin Pharmacokinet* 1997, [Suppl 1], 37–42). However, prothrombin time can be increased by 9% (Wilner *et al, Biol Psych* 1991, **29**, 354S–355S) and up to a 3 point rise in INR has been reported in several patients (mentioned by Askinazi, *Am J Psych* 1996, **153**, 135–36).

### Zolpidem + sertraline *
See SSRIs + zolpidem (*4.1.5*).

### Zotepine + sertraline
See zotepine (*4.2.6*).

## 4.3.3 OTHER ANTIDEPRESSANTS

### 4.3.3.1 MIANSERIN

### ALCOHOL + MIANSERIN
See alcohol (*4.7.1*).

### Benzodiazepines + mianserin
Enhanced sedation may occur.

### Carbamazepine + mianserin
Plasma levels of mianserin and enantiomers may be halved by carbamazepine, probably via 3A4 induction (n=12, Eap *et al, Ther Drug Monit* 1999, **21**, 166–70).

### Warfarin + mianserin
There is normally no problem but occasional control problems have been reported (Warwick and Mindham, *B J Psych* 1983, **143**, 308).

### 4.3.3.2 MIRTAZAPINE
Mirtazapine does not inhibit CYP2D6, CYP1A2 and CYP3A and so interactions via these enzymes are unlikely. Mirtazapine appears mainly metabolised by CYP2D6 and CYP1A2 (Montgomery, *Int Clin Psychopharmacol* 1995, **10**[Suppl 4], 37–45) and if one enzyme is inhibited, the other takes over, so mirtazapine appears less susceptible to P450 interactions. It has linear kinetics from 15–75mg/d, with 100% excreted via the urine and faeces.

**Review**: Clinical pharmacokinetics (Timmer *et al, Clin Pharmacokinet* 2000, **38**, 461–74).

### Alcohol + mirtazapine
See alcohol (*4.7.1*).

### Benzodiazepines + mirtazapine
The combination of diazepam and mirtazapine, not surprisingly, produces an additive sedative effect (n=12, RCT, d/b, c/o, Mattila *et al, Pharmacol Toxicol* 1989, **65**, 81–88) and so anyone on the combination should be warned about driving etc.

### Carbamazepine + mirtazapine *
Mirtazapine does not significantly effect carbamazepine levels but carbamazepine produces a 60% decrease in mirtazapine levels, probably by CYP3A4 induction, and mirtazapine levels may need to be increased (RCT, 4/52, Sitsen *et al, Eur J Drug Metab Pharmacokinet* 2001, **26**, 109–21).

### Cimetidine + mirtazapine
Mirtazapine had no effect on cimetidine but mirtazapine levels were higher (probably by CYP3A4 inhibition by cimetidine), but not enough to require dose reduction (n=12, d/b, p/c, c/o, Sitsen *et al, Eur J Clin Pharmacol* 2000, **56**, 389–94).

### Fluoxetine + mirtazapine *
Fluoxetine 20–40mg/d caused a clinically insignificant 32% increase in mirtazapine (15mg/d) plasma levels after an abrupt switch (n=40, Preskorn *et al, Biol Psych* 1997, **41**, 96S), although mania associated with mirtazapine augmentation of fluoxetine has been reported (n=1, Ng, *Depress Anxiety* 2002, **15**, 46–47)

### Fluvoxamine + mirtazapine *
Fluvoxamine 50–100mg/d may increase mirtazapine serum levels 3–4 fold, a significant effect (n=2, Anttila *et al, Ann Pharmacother* 2001, **35**, 1221–23) and a serotonin syndrome has been reported with the combination (n=1, Demers and Malone, *Ann Pharmacother* 2001, **35**, 1217–20).

### Levodopa + mirtazapine *
Psychosis has been reported when mirtazapine was added to a stable levodopa regimen (n=1, *Pharmacopsychiatry* 1997, **30**, 263–65).

### Lithium + mirtazapine
There was no pharmacokinetic interaction detected between lithium 600mg/d and mirtazapine 30mg (n=12, 10/7, Sitsen *et al, J Clin Psychopharmacol* 2000, **14**, 172–76).

### MAOIs + mirtazapine
The manufacturers cautiously recommend a two-week gap between stopping an MAOI and starting mirtazapine.

### Paroxetine + mirtazapine *
Mirtazapine had no effect on the kinetics of paroxetine and the combination was better tolerated than either alone, suggesting a lack of clinically relevant interaction (n=24, RCT, c/o, 6/7 per arm, Ruwe *et al, Hum Psychopharmacol* 2001, **16**, 449–59).

### Phenytoin + mirtazapine *
A multiple dose study showed that mirtazapine had no effect on the steady-state kinetics of phenytoin but that phenytoin reduced mirtazapine levels by a mean of 46%, probably clinically significant (n=17, RCT, open, Spaans *et al, Eur J Clin Pharmacol* 2002, **58**, 423–29).

### Risperidone + mirtazapine
Mirtazapine 30mg/d had no effect on risperidone 2–6mg/d kinetics in a trial (n=6, open, 8/52, Loonen *et al, Eur Neuropsychopharmacol* 1999, **10**, 51–57).

### Sertraline + mirtazapine
Hypomania associated with mirtazapine 15mg/d augmentation of sertraline 250mg/d has been reported (n=1, Soutullo *et al, J Clin Psych* 1998, **59**, 320).

### Tricyclics + mirtazapine *
Amitriptyline caused clinically irrelevant increases in mirtazapine plasma levels and *vice versa* (n=24, Sennef *et al, Hum Psychopharmacol* 2003, **38**, 91–101).

### Venlafaxine + mirtazapine *
Serotonin syndrome has been reported during a cross-over (n=1, Dimellis, *World J Biol Psych* 2002, **3**, 167).

## Warfarin + mirtazapine

No interaction is known or suspected, but there is insufficient information to confirm this at present (Sayal *et al, Acta Psych Scand* 2000, **102**, 250–55).

### 4.3.3.3 MOCLOBEMIDE

Moclobemide is metabolised by 2C19, and inhibits 2D6, 2C19 and 1A2.

**Reviews:** general (Livingstone, *Lancet* 1995, **345**, 533–34; Berlin and Lecrubier, *CNS Drugs* 1996, **5**, 403–13).

## Alcohol + moclobemide

See alcohol (*4.7.1*).

## Benzodiazepines + moclobemide

No significant interaction occurs (Zimmer *et al, Acta Psych Scand* 1990, **360**, 84–86).

## Bupropion + moclobemide

See MAOIs + bupropion (*4.6.4*).

## CIMETIDINE + MOCLOBEMIDE

Cimetidine may reduce the clearance and prolong the half-life of moclobemide so start with lower doses and monitor closely (n=8, open, Schoerlin *et al, Clin Pharmacol Ther* 1991, **49**, 32–38).

## Digoxin + moclobemide

Lack of interaction has been reported (Berlin and Lecrubier, *CNS Drugs* 1996, **5**, 403–13).

## Ibuprofen + moclobemide

Moclobemide is alleged to potentiate the effect of ibuprofen (MI), but lack of interaction has been reported (Berlin and Lecrubier, *CNS Drugs* 1996, **5**, 403–13).

## Metoprolol + moclobemide

Concurrent metoprolol and moclobemide results in further lowering of blood pressure although postural hypotension was not reported (Zimmer *et al, Acta Psych Scand* 1990, **360**, 84–86).

## Nifedipine + moclobemide

No significant interaction occurs, apart from some slight reduction in blood pressure (Zimmer *et al, Acta Psych Scand* 1990, **360**, 84–86).

## Opiates + moclobemide

Moclobemide is alleged to potentiate the effect of opiates (MI) and dose reductions of morphine and fentanyl may be considered necessary.

## Oral contraceptives + moclobemide

No significant interaction has been detected (Zimmer *et al, Acta Psych Scand* 1990, **360**, 84–86).

## SELEGILINE + MOCLOBEMIDE

Selegiline is an MAO-B inhibitor and if combined with an MAO-A inhibitor, such as moclobemide, could produce full MAO inhibition (albeit reversible). The combination is not recommended but if the two need to be used together then full MAOI dietary precautions might be required.

## SSRIs + moclobemide *

Excitation, insomnia and dysphoria have been reported with **fluvoxamine** and moclobemide in refractory depression (n=36, open, 6/52, Ebert, *Psychopharmacology* 1995, **119**, 342–44), as have headaches and fatigue (review, Dingemanse, *Int Clin Psychopharmacol* 1993, **7**, 167–80). The serotonin syndrome would also be a possibility with the combination and the UK SPC for moclobemide contraindicates the combination. A fatal case, following overdose of **paroxetine** and moclobemide and subsequent serotonin syndrome, has been reported (Singer and Jones, *J Anal Toxicol* 1997, **21**, 518–20). However, in a study where up to 600mg/d moclobemide was added to established **fluoxetine** therapy, there was no change in the number, intensity, or type of adverse events. Fluoxetine markedly inhibited the metabolism of moclobemide but did not lead to excessive accumulation nor any indication of development of a serotonin syndrome (n=18, RCT, open, Dingemanse *et al, Clin Pharmacol Ther* 1998, **63**, 403–13). A case of serotonin syndrome has been reported with **sertraline** and metoclopramide (n=1, *Ann Pharmacother* 2002, **36**, 67–71). A fatal serotonin syndrome has been reported with moclobemide and citalopram (n=1, Dams *et al, J Anal Toxicol* 2001, **25**, 147–151) and disputed

(Isbister *et al*, *J Anal Toxicol* 2001, **25**, 716–17).

### Sympathomimetics + moclobemide

The UK SPC recommends avoiding this combination. Phenylephrine may slightly raise blood pressure in people taking high dose (600mg/d) moclobemide (Amrein *et al*, *Psychopharmacology* 1992, **106**, S24–S31) and ephedrine produces a greater rise in bp (Dingemanse, *Int Clin Psychopharmacol* 1993, **7**, 167–80). Another study noted no clinically significant interaction, although the pressor effect may be slightly enhanced (Zimmer *et al*, *Acta Psych Scand* 1990, **360**, 84–86).

### Tricyclics + moclobemide

A rapid and fatal serotonin syndrome has been caused by moclobemide-clomipramine overdose (n=1, Ferrer-Dufol *et al*, *J Toxicol Clin Toxicol* 1998, **36**, 31–32).

### Triptans + moclobemide *

The BNF notes an increased risk of CNS toxicity with sumatriptan or zolmitriptan and moclobemide (review by Rolan, *Cephalalgia* 1997, **17**[Suppl 18], 21–27; Morales Asin, *Neurologia* 1998, **13**[Suppl 2], 25–30), and that lower doses should be used, although a small study suggested combined use with sumatriptan was safe with care (n=14, open, Blier and Bergeron, *J Clin Psychopharmacol*, 1995, **15**, 106–9). Moclobemide increases the plasma concentration of almotriptan but the combination appears well tolerated (n=12, RCT, open, c/o, Fleishaker *et al*, *B J Clin Pharmacol* 2001, **51**, 437–41) and moclobemide may significantly potentiate the effects of rizatriptan and the combination is not recommended (n=12, RCT, Van Haarst *et al*, *B J Clin Pharmacol* 1999, **48**, 190–96).

### Tyramine + moclobemide

Moclobemide does not appear to significantly potentiate the pressor effects of tyramine. Dietary restrictions are generally not required but patients should avoid eating excessive amounts of tyramine containing foods, especially if they have pre-existing hypertension. Minor pressor effects are not seen until about 100mg tyramine (Zimmer *et al*, *Acta Psych Scand* 1990, **360**, 84–86). Even 150mg tyramine is suggested by some as being safe (*Acta Psych Scand* 1990, **360**[Suppl], 78–80). The use of this combination has, however, been used to treat severe postural hypotension (eg. n=1, Karet *et al*, *Lancet* 1994, **344**, 1263–65) and in counteracting clozapine-induced hypotension, allowing dose increases to an active therapeutic level (n=1, Taylor *et al*, *B J Psych* 1995, **167**, 409–10).

### Tricyclics + moclobemide

The UK SPC contraindicates the combination if the tricyclic (or metabolite) is a serotonin reuptake inhibitor, eg. clomipramine, amitriptyline or imipramine. Serotonin syndrome has been reported with moclobemide and clomipramine, imipramine (Brodribb *et al*, *Lancet* 1994, **343**, 475–76) or an SSRI (eg. Spigest *et al*, *BMJ* 1993, **306**, 248), and after moclobemide plus either citalopram or clomipramine overdoses (n=5, fatal, Neuvonen *et al*, *Lancet* 1993, **342**, 1419). Aggressive therapy is needed if taken in overdose with serotonergic agents (Neuvonen *et al*, *Lancet* 1993, **342**, 1419). Lack of interaction has been noted with desipramine (Zimmer *et al*, *Acta Psych Scand* 1990, **360**, 84–86) and amitriptyline 150mg/d (eg. n=21, Amrein *et al*, *Psychopharmacology* 1992, **106**, S24–S31).

### Venlafaxine + moclobemide *

See venlafaxine (*4.3.3.8*).

### Warfarin + moclobemide

No interaction is reported, but moclobemide inhibits CYP1A2 and 2C19 and so some potential exists (Sayal *et al*, *Acta Psych Scand* 2000, **102**, 250–55).

---

### 4.3.3.4 NEFAZODONE

Nefazodone is 99% protein bound and metabolised by CYP3A4 to mCPP, which is metabolised by

CYP2D6. It is a potent inhibitor of CYP3A4 and weak CYP1A2 inhibitor.

### Alcohol + nefazodone
See alcohol (*4.7.1*).

### Antihypertensives + nefazodone *
Nefazodone doses may be needed to be reduced.

### Antipsychotics + nefazodone
Caution is recommended as haloperidol bioavailability may be increased.

### Astemizole + nefazodone
This is a possible contraindication.

### BENZODIAZEPINES + NEFAZODONE
Combined psychomotor impairment can occur.

### CARBAMAZEPINE + NEFAZODONE *
An increase in carbamazepine dose may be needed if nefazodone is stopped (n=3, Roth and Bertschy, *Eur Psych* 2001, **16**, 320–21), probably via CYP3A4 inhibition.

### Ciclosporin + nefazodone
Ciclosporin levels may be elevated by nefazodone, probably via CYP3A4 inhibition. Monitor with great care.

### Cimetidine + nefazodone
Lack of interaction has been shown.

### Clozapine + nefazodone *
See clozapine (*4.2.2*).

### Digoxin + nefazodone
Nefazodone may increase digoxin levels by up to 29%.

### Fluoxetine + nefazodone *
See fluoxetine (*4.3.2.2*).

### Lithium + nefazodone
The nefazodone UK SPC recommends caution with the combination.

### Lidocaine (lignocaine) + nefazodone
Lidocaine protein binding is unaffected *in vitro* by nefazodone.

### Loratadine + nefazodone *
High-dose loratadine at 20mg/d combined with nefazodone has been reported to result in QTc prolongation.

### MAOIs + nefazodone
See MAOIs (*4.3.4*).

### Oral contraceptives + nefazodone *
Toxicity (from a low-dose OC) has been reported within a week of starting nefazodone 500mg/d, probably through CYP3A4 inhibition.

### Phenytoin + nefazodone
See phenytoin (*4.5.8*).

### Prazosin + nefazodone
Prazosin protein binding is unaffected *in vitro* by nefazodone.

### Propranolol + nefazodone
Propranolol protein binding is unaffected *in vitro* by nefazodone.

### Sildenafil + nefazodone
Raised sildenafil levels could enhance the cardiovascular risk and other ADRs.

### SSRIs + nefazodone *
See individual drugs.

### Statins + nefazodone
Asymptomatic CK elevation has been reported with pravastatin (but strongly disputed) and rhabdomyolysis with simvastatin.

### Trazodone + nefazodone *
Serotonin syndrome has been reported with the combination.

### Tricyclics + nefazodone
Desipramine protein binding is unaffected *in vitro* by nefazodone.

### Warfarin + nefazodone
Warfarin protein binding is unaffected *in vitro* by nefazodone.

### Verapamil + nefazodone
Verapamil protein binding is unaffected *in vitro* by nefazodone.

### Zopiclone + nefazodone *
See zopiclone (*4.1.6*).

---

### 4.3.3.5 REBOXETINE *

Reboxetine is extensively (97%) bound to plasma proteins (particularly the alpha-1 acid glycoprotein fraction) and may interact with drugs with a high affinity for this fraction, eg. dipyridamole, propranolol, methadone, imipramine, chlorpromazine (see antipsychotics below) and local anaesthetics. Concomitant tricyclics, SSRIs, MAOIs and lithium have not been assessed. The UK SPC states that in high doses reboxetine inhibits

CYP3A4 and CYP2D6 in vitro and is metabolised by CYP3A4, but there is a wide safety margin.

### Alcohol + reboxetine
See alcohol (*4.7.1*).

### Antipsychotics + reboxetine *
An interaction is possible (see above). Reboxetine has no effect on clozapine or risperidone plasma levels, (n=7, Spina *et al, Ther Drug Monit* 2001, **23**, 675–78).

### Benzodiazepines + reboxetine
Lack of interaction has been reported (SPC), although some mild to moderate drowsiness and transient increases in heart rate were noted.

### Dipyridamole + reboxetine
An interaction is possible (see above).

### Disopyramide + reboxetine
The BNF advises caution with the combination.

### Diuretics + reboxetine
There may be an increased risk of hypokalaemia with loop diuretics or thiazides (BNF).

### Erythromycin + reboxetine
The BNF advises caution with the combination.

### Flecainide + reboxetine
The BNF advises caution with the combination.

### Fluoxetine + reboxetine *
There are no statistically significant effects of reboxetine on fluoxetine or norfluoxetine pharmacokinetics, and a minimal clinical impact is suggested (n=30, RCT, d/b, p/c, 8/7, Fleishaker *et al, Clin Drug Investigat* 1999, **18**, 141–50), although urinary retention has been reported with the combination (n=1, Benazzi, *Can J Psych* 2000, **45**, 936).

### Fluvoxamine + reboxetine
The BNF advises caution with the combination.

### Ketoconazole + reboxetine
Ketoconazole decreases the clearance of the two enantiomers of reboxetine, with no adverse effects, but some caution may be advisable (n=11, open, Herman *et al, Clin Pharmacol Therapeut* 1999, **66**, 374–79).

### Lidocaine + reboxetine
An interaction is possible (see above), and with other local anaesthetics. The BNF advises caution with the combination.

### MAOIs + reboxetine
This has not been evaluated so avoid until further notice, and leave a 2-week gap after an MAOI and one week after reboxetine before switching to the other.

### Methadone + reboxetine
An interaction is possible (see above).

### Potassium-losing diuretics + reboxetine
See diuretics (above).

### Propafenone + reboxetine
The BNF advises caution with the combination.

### Propranolol + reboxetine
An interaction is possible (see above).

### Tricyclics + reboxetine
An interaction is possible (see above).

### Warfarin + reboxetine
No interaction is known or suspected, but there is insufficient information to confirm this at present (Sayal *et al, Acta Psych Scand* 2000, **102**, 250–55).

## 4.3.3.6 TRAZODONE
Trazodone is metabolised by CYP2D6 and inhibits CYP3A4.

### ALCOHOL + TRAZODONE
See alcohol (*4.7.1*).

### Antipsychotics + trazodone
Enhanced hypotension may occur when trazodone was added to either chlorpromazine or trifluoperazine (n=2, Asayesh, *Can J Psych* 1986, **31**, 857–58). Thioridazine may raise trazodone levels by about 25% (n=11, Yasui *et al, Ther Drug Monit* 1995, **17**, 333–35).

### Buspirone + trazodone
See buspirone (*4.1.2*).

### Carbamazepine + trazodone *
See carbamazepine (*4.5.1*).

### Cocaine + trazodone
See antidepressants + cocaine (*4.7.3*).

### Digoxin + trazodone
Cases of digoxin toxicity exist with trazodone (n=2, Rauch and Jenike, *Psychosomatics* 1984, **25**, 334–35).

### Fluoxetine + trazodone *
See fluoxetine (*4.3.2.2*).

### Gingko biloba + trazodone *
Coma has been reported with concomitant use in an Alheimer's patient (n=1, Galluzzi *et al, J Neurol Neurosurg Psych* 2000, **68**, 679–80).

### Interferon alpha + trazodone
See interferon alpha + paroxetine (*4.3.2.4*).

### MAOIs + trazodone
See MAOIs (*4.3.4*).

### Nefazodone + trazodone *
See nefazodone (*4.3.3.4*).

### Phenytoin + trazodone
See phenytoin (*4.5.8*).

### Venlafaxine + trazodone *
See venlafaxine (*4.3.3.7*).

### Warfarin + trazodone
INR and PT fell when trazodone was added to warfarin, and rose when trazodone was stopped, and so caution is necessary (adjust doses and/or monitor) if trazodone is used, especially if as a PRN (eg, n=1, Small and Giamonna, *Ann Pharmacother* 2000, **34**, 734–36).

## 4.3.3.7 TRYPTOPHAN

### Fluoxetine + tryptophan
See fluoxetine (*4.3.2.2*).

### Fluvoxamine + tryptophan
See fluvoxamine (*4.3.2.3*).

### MAOIs + tryptophan
See MAOIs (*4.3.4*).

## 4.3.3.8 VENLAFAXINE

Venlafaxine is metabolised by CYP2D6 to O-desmethylvenlafaxine, a major active metabolite. Other, minor, metabolic pathways exist. Venlafaxine has low potential for CYP2D6 and 3A4 inhibition (Ball *et al, Br J Clin Pharmacol* 1997, **43**, 619–26) and does not appear to have a significant effect on other P450 enzymes.

### Alcohol + venlafaxine
See alcohol (*4.7.1*).

### Antipsychotics + venlafaxine
Urinary retention has been reported with **haloperidol** (Benazzi, *Pharmacopsychiatry* 1997, **30**, 27) and the UK SPC notes that venlafaxine causes a 70% increase in haloperidol AUC and 88% increase in peak levels, so care is needed. Increased **clozapine** levels and adverse effects have also been reported.

### Benzodiazepines + venlafaxine
A study showed that diazepam 10mg had no significant effect on venlafaxine or metabolite kinetics, but venlafaxine slightly increased diazepam clearance. No clinically significant interaction thus seems likely (n=17, Troy *et al, J Clin Pharmacol* 1995, **35**, 410–19).

### Bupropion + venlafaxine *
See bupropion (*4.6.4*).

### Carbamazepine + venlafaxine
Lack of interaction has been shown in a (Wyeth) study (n=17, Wiklander *et al*, poster at ECNP, Venice 1995).

### Cimetidine + venlafaxine
A 45% reduction in venlafaxine clearance via reduced first-pass metabolism, can result in increased venlafaxine levels and patients should be monitored for dose-related side-effects, eg. nausea, bp changes. The major metabolite, O-desmethylvenlafaxine, is unaffected.

### Fluoxetine + venlafaxine
See fluoxetine (*4.3.2.2*).

### Indinavir + venlafaxine *
A study has shown that venlafaxine reduced indinavir peak plasma levels by 36% and AUC by 28%, a potentially clinically significant effect (n=9, Levin *et al, Psychopharmacol Bull* 2001, **35**, 62–71).

### Lithium + venlafaxine
Venlafaxine has been shown to have no significant effect on lithium kinetics in a single dose study (open, Troy *et al, J Clin Pharmacol* 1996, **36**, 175–81) but there are cases of raised lithium levels and of serotonin syndrome (eg. Mekler and Woggon,

*Pharmacopsychiatry* 1997, **30**, 272–73). Lithium reduces the renal clearance of venlafaxine but without apparent clinical significance.

## MAOIs + VENLAFAXINE

Wyeth state that venlafaxine and MAOIs should not be used together and recommend a 14-day gap after stopping an MAOI before starting venlafaxine, and a 7-day gap after venlafaxine before an MAOI is used. There are many reported cases of severe reactions, eg. extreme agitation, diaphoresis, rapid respiration and raised CPK levels (n=1, Phillips and Ringo, *Am J Psych* 1995, **152**, 1400–1), hypomania, heavy perspiration, shivering and dilated pupils (n=1, Klysner *et al, Lancet* 1995, **346**, 1298–99) and several of serotonin syndrome (eg. n=1, Weiner *et al, Pharmacother* 1998, **18**, 399–403). The manufacturers' recommendations should thus be followed carefully.

## Mirtazapine + venlafaxine *

See mirtazapine (*4.3.3.2*).

## Moclobemide + venlafaxine *

The UK SPC for venlafaxine states very cautiously that venlafaxine and moclobemide should not be used together and that serious adverse reactions may occur. It recommends a 14-day gap after stopping moclobemide before starting venlafaxine, and a 7-day gap after venlafaxine before moclobemide is used. This seems overcautious, although a serotonin syndrome has been reported (n=1, *Ann Pharmacother* 2002, **36**, 67–71).

## Propafenone + venlafaxine *

An organic psychosis has been reported, with raised venlafaxine levels (n=1, Pfeffer and Grube, *Int J Psych Med* 2001, **31**, 427–32).

## Risperidone + venlafaxine *

See risperidone (*4.2.5*).

## Selegiline + venlafaxine

The UK SPC for venlafaxine state that the combination should not be used and that serious adverse reactions may occur. It recommends a 14-day gap after stopping selegiline

before starting venlafaxine, and a 7-day gap after venlafaxine before selegiline is used.

## Sertraline + venlafaxine

See sertraline (*4.2.5*).

## Trazodone + venlafaxine *

A serotonin syndrome has been reported (n=1, McCue and Joseph, *Am J Psych* 2001, **158**, 2088–89).

## Tricyclics + venlafaxine *

See tricyclics (*4.3.1*).

## Verapamil + venlafaxine

A fatality has been reported (n=1, Kusman *et al, J Forensic Sci* 2000, **45**, 926–28).

## Warfarin + venlafaxine

The UK SPC states that potentiation of anticoagulant effects of warfarin has been reported, including increased PT or INR.

---

## 4.3.3.9 ST. JOHN'S WORT *

Although not licensed for depression in the UK, this section has been included because concerns about its interactions are frequently raised. Minor serotonin, noradrenaline and dopamine reuptake inhibition activity has been detected from St. John's wort (SJW) and might thus potentiate any antidepressants, and so should in theory best be avoided, particularly at high dose. SJW, when taken at recommended doses for depression, is unlikely to inhibit CYP2D6 or 3A4 activity (n=7, open, Markowitz *et al, Life Sci* 2000, **66**, 133–39). It may induce CYP3A (n=2, Ruschitzka *et al, Lancet* 2000, **355**, 548). SJW increases the expression of P-glycoprotein (a liver enzyme), which may have implications for drug interactions (n=22, Hennessy *et al, B J Clin Pharmacol* 2002, **53**, 75–82). There are reports of serotonin syndrome with SJW and antidepressants in elderly patients (n=5, Lantz *et al, J Ger Psychiatry Neurol* 1999, **12**, 7–10). The UK CSM issued advice about potential interactions in February 2000 (*Pharm J* 2000, **264**, 358). SJW is widely used as self-medication so remember to ask about it (up to 15% have used it recently, and

7% may be taking it at any one time; n=101, Redvers *et al, Psych Bull* 2001, **25**, 254–56).

**Reviews:** herbal medicine interactions (Cupp, *Am Fam Physician* 1999, **59**, 1239–45), general (Henney, *JAMA* 2000, **283**, 1679; *Curr Prob Pharmacovig* 2000, **26**, 6–7).

### Anticonvulsants + St. John's wort

SJW may induce the metabolism of carbamazepine, phenobarbital and phenytoin, increasing the risk of seizures, and so should not be taken together (CSM warning, 2000), although suddenly stopping SJW may require dose adjustment of any anticonvulsant. Check anticonvulsant levels before and after stopping SJW.

### Anti-HIV drugs + St. John's wort

SJW may induce the metabolism of anti-HIV drugs, reducing efficacy, and so should not be taken together (CSM warning, 2000), although suddenly stopping SJW may require dose adjustment of any anti-HIV drug.

### Buspirone + St. John's wort *

See buspirone (*4.1.2*).

### Carbamazepine + St. John's wort *

SJW seems to have no effect on carbamazepine clearance (n=8, 5/52, Burstein *et al, Clin Pharmacol Ther* 2000, **68**, 605–12).

### Ciclosporin + St. John's wort *

SJW may induce the metabolism of ciclosporin, reducing plasma levels significantly, and so should not be taken together (CSM warning, 2000; n=1, Barone *et al, Ann Pharmacother* 2000, **34**, 1013–16; Moschella and Jaber, *Am J Kid Dis* 2001, **38**, 1105–7). Heart transplant rejection due to SJW has been reported (n=2, Ruschitzka *et al, Lancet* 2000, **355**, 548).

### Digoxin + St. John's wort

SJW may induce the metabolism of digoxin, reducing AUC by up to 25%, and so should not be taken together (n=25, 10/7, s/b, p/c, Johne *et al, Clin Pharmacol Ther* 1999, **66**, 338–45; Cheng, *Arch Int Med* 2000, **160**, 2548). Suddenly stopping SJW may also require dose adjustment of digoxin.

### Fexofenadine + St John's wort *

SJW may inhibit the metabolism of fexofenadine (open, c/o, Wang *et al, Clin Pharmacol & Therapeutics* 2002, **71**, 414–20).

### Indinavir + St. John's wort

SJW may reduce the levels of indinavir (AUC reduced by 57%), reducing efficacy, and so should not be taken together (n=8, Piscitelli *et al, Lancet* 2000, **355**, 547). The same would probably be true for other protease inhibitors, eg. ritonavir and saquinavir.

### MAOIs + St. John's wort

Minor MAOI activity has been detected from SJW and might thus potentiate existing MAOI therapy, and should be avoided, particularly at high dose.

### Oral contraceptives + St. John's wort *

The UK CSM has recommended that, since SJW reduces the effectiveness of oral contraceptives, the two should not be taken together (2 cases of pregnancy mentioned in *Pharm J* 2002, **268**, 198) and reduced efficacy of combined OC's has been discussed (n=12, Gorski *et al, Clin Pharmacol Ther* 2002, **71**, P25).

### SSRIs + St. John's wort

Minor serotonin reuptake inhibition activity has been detected from SJW and might thus potentiate existing SSRI therapy and so should, in theory, be avoided, particularly at high dose.

### Statins + St. John's wort *

SJW may decrease simvastatin (but not pravastatin) plasma levels (n=16, d/b, c/o, 14/7, Fujimura *et al, Clin Pharmacol Ther* 2002, **71**, P63).

### Theophylline + St. John's wort

SJW may induce the metabolism of theophylline, reducing efficacy, and so should not be taken together (CSM warning, 2000), although suddenly stopping SJW may require dose adjustment of theophylline (Nebel et al, *Ann Pharmacother* 1999, **33**, 502, letter). Check theophylline levels before and after stopping SJW.

### Tricyclics + St. John's wort *

Minor serotonin and noradrenaline reuptake inhibition activity has been detected from SJW and might thus potentiate existing tricyclic therapy, and so should, in theory, be avoided, particularly at high dose. Amitriptyline and nortriptyline levels reduced by 22% have been reported (n=12, Johne *et al, J Clin Psychopharmacol* 2002, **22**, 46–54).

### Triptans + St. John's wort

The CSM has warned that SJW may increase the serotonergic effects of sumatriptan, naratriptan, rizatriptan and zolmitriptan, with increased adverse effects and so the two should not be used together.

### Tyramine + St. John's wort

There is not thought to be an interaction (mentioned by Cupp, *Am Fam Physician* 1999, **59**, 1239–45).

### Warfarin + St. John's wort

SJW may induce the metabolism of warfarin, reducing efficacy, and so should not be taken together (CSM warning, 2000). Suddenly stopping SJW may require dose adjustment of warfarin so check INR before and after stopping SJW and adjust doses as necessary.

---

## 4.3.4 MONO-AMINE OXIDASE INHIBITORS (MAOIS)

Review of MAOI interactions; Berlin and Lecrubier, *CNS Drugs* 1996, **5**, 403–13.

### Adrenaline + MAOIs

See noradrenaline + MAOIs.

### ALCOHOL + MAOIs

See alcohol (*4.7.1*).

### Amantadine + MAOIs

Hypertension occurred in one patient taking amantadine, 48 hours after starting phenelzine (Jack and Daniel, *Arch Gen Psych* 1984, **41**, 726) with one case of safe use of both (Greenberg and Meyers, *Am J Psych* 1985, **142**, 273).

### AMFETAMINE + MAOIs

See dexamfetamine + MAOIs.

### Anaesthetics + MAOIs

With proper monitoring, general and local anaesthesia can be given safely with MAOIs (n=27, el-Ganzouri *et al, Anesth Analg* 1985, **64**, 592–96) although occasional cases of reactions have been reported (eg. *Anaesthesia* 1987, **42**, 633–35). Generally considered safe although care with analgesics and sympathomimetics is needed.

### Anticholinergics + MAOIs

Enhanced anticholinergic effects have been postulated.

### Anticoagulants + MAOIs

An enhanced anticoagulant effect has been shown in animals.

### Antipsychotics + MAOIs

Unexplained deaths with levomepromazine exist, but are probably are not related to a drug interaction. The combination is a risk factor for NMS and may enhance anticholinergic and EPSEs. See also clozapine (*4.2.2*).

### Aspartane + MAOIs

Recurrent headaches following aspartane ingestion have been reported (n=1, Ferguson, *Am J Psych* 1985, **142**, 271).

### Atracurium + MAOIs

A single case report of atracurium-induced hypertension exists (n=1, Sides, *Anaesthesia* 1987, **42**, 633).

### Barbiturates + MAOIs

Barbiturate sedation may be prolonged. Although little human data exists, be aware of the potential toxicity as one fatality has been reported.

### Benzodiazepines + MAOIs

Although there are isolated cases of MAOI toxicity, oedema and hepatotoxicity (eg. Young and Walpole, *Med J Aust* 1986, **144**, 166–67), this is normally considered a safe combination.

### Beta-blockers + MAOIs

Propranolol used with MAOIs has caused severe hypertension (Risch *et al, J Clin Psych* 1982, **43**, 16) and slight bradycardia (*Psychosomatics*

1989, **30**, 106–8) although not invariably so (review: Davidson *et al, J Clin Psych* 1984, **45**, 81–84). Best to monitor bp carefully, especially in the elderly.

### Bretylium + MAOIs
Bretylium may increase the heart rate with MAOIs but it is only dangerous if other sympathomimetics are present. There are no case reports.

### Bupropion + MAOIs
See bupropion (*4.6.4*).

### BUSPIRONE + MAOIs
There are four unpublished reports of increased bp and possible CVA although the combination has been used safely.

### Caffeine + MAOIs
Case reports exist of increased jitteriness with caffeine taken while on MAOIs (Berkowitz *et al, Eur J Pharmacol* 1971, **16**, 315).

### Carbamazepine + MAOIs
Carbamazepine is structurally related to the tricyclics and so an interaction is postulated with case reports of raised carbamazepine levels but a lack of interaction with tranylcypromine (Lydiard *et al, J Clin Psychopharmacol* 1987, **7**, 360) and phenelzine (Yatham *et al, Am J Psych* 1990, **147**, 367).

### Chloral + MAOIs
There are two poorly documented case reports of fatal hyperpyrexia and hypertension with chloral and phenelzine. Not thought to be important.

### Citalopram + MAOIs
There are many reported cases of serotonin syndrome (see *1.32*) with other SSRIs and MAOIs and so care is needed if this combination is used (review: Graber *et al, Ann Pharmacother* 1994, **28**, 732–35).

### Clozapine + MAOIs
See clozapine (*4.2.2*).

### Cyproheptadine + MAOIs
An isolated case of hallucinations with cyproheptadine and phenelzine exists (Hahn, *Am J Psych* 1987, **144**, 1242–43).

### DEXAMFETAMINE + MAOIs
There is a case report of a death with phenelzine and dexamfetamine (*BMJ* 1965, **ii**, 168) and one with amfetamine.

### Dextromethorphan + MAOIs
Although this is mainly extrapolation from pethidine, case reports exist with cough mixtures containing dextromethorphan but since all also contained sympathomimetics, these are questionable. Two were fatal so care is advised. Dizziness and muscle spasms with dextromethorphan have been reported (Harrison *et al, J Clin Psych* 1989, **50**, 64–65), as has a serotonin syndrome (Nierenberg *et al, Clin Pharmacol Ther* 1993, **53**, 84–88).

### Dextropropoxyphene + MAOIs
Dextropropoxyphene sedation has been enhanced by phenelzine (n=1, Garbutt, *Am J Psych* 1987, **144**, 251–52) as has severe hypotension, ataxia and impaired coordination when propoxyphene was added to phenelzine (n=1, Zornberg & Hegarty, *Am J Psych* 1993, **150**, 1270).

### Disulfiram + MAOIs
See disulfiram (*4.6.6*).

### DOPAMINE/DOXAPRAM + MAOIs
Animal studies show a clear interaction, with side-effects enhanced by MAOIs. The manufacturers recommend that dopamine or doxapram can be used if their initial dose is reduced to one tenth the normal dose and great care is taken.

### Droperidol/hyoscine + MAOIs
There is an isolated questionable case of hypotension when droperidol and hyoscine were given as a pre-med.

### Ecstasy/MDMA + MAOIs
There is a case of a hypertensive crisis with MDMA/Ecstasy and phenelzine (n=1, Smilkstein *et al, J Toxicol Clin Toxicol* 1987, **25**, 149–59) and two of muscle tension, coma and delirium with raised blood pressure (Kaskey *Am J Psych* 1992, **192**, 411–12).

### Escitalopram + MAOIs *
See citalopram + MAOIs above.

## FLUOXETINE + MAOIs

There are several reported interactions (eg. Sternbach, *Lancet* 1988, **ii**, 850–51), including 4 deaths. A gap must be also be left when switching from one to the other (see *2.2.5*).

## FLUVOXAMINE + MAOIs

There is an SPC recommendation to allow a 2-week gap between therapies. There are many reported cases of serotonin syndrome with other SSRIs and MAOIs and so care is needed with this combination.

## Ginseng + MAOIs

There are cases of headache, tremor (Shader and Greenblatt, *J Clin Psychopharmacol* 1985, **5**, 65) and mania (Jones and Runikis, *J Clin Psychopharmacol* 1987, **7**, 201–2) with Ginseng and phenelzine.

## GUANETHIDINE + MAOIs

MAOI reversal of hypotension has been seen in a single-dose study (n=5, *Clin Pharmacol Ther* 1966, **7**, 510).

## Hypoglycaemics + MAOIs

An enhanced hypoglycaemic effect with insulin and sulphonylureas has been noted.

## Indoramin + MAOIs

The SPC for indoramin states this to be a contraindication, as indoramin antagonises alpha-receptors, thus competing with noradrenaline for post-synaptic alpha-receptors, which could cause vaso-constriction and raised blood pressure. No case reports are known.

## Isoprenaline + MAOIs

This is a postulated interaction with some evidence that no interaction occurs. No case reports exist.

## LEVODOPA + MAOIs

Low dose levodopa with carbidopa or benserazide seems safe but higher doses should be avoided, as should levodopa on its own (*Clin Pharmacol Ther* 1975, **18**, 273).

## Lithium + MAOIs

Lack of an interaction has been reported (*Am J Psych* 1988, **145**, 249–50).

## MAOIs + MAOIs

There is some evidence that different MAOIs may interact with each other especially if abruptly changed, eg. isocarboxazid to tranylcypromine (n=1, Bazire, *Drug Intell Clin Pharm* 1986, **20**, 954–55) and phenelzine to isocarboxazid (*Ann Pharmacother* 1992, **26**, 337–38). Tranylcypromine is metabolised to an amfetamine and an internal autoreaction (ie. interacts with itself) has been postulated (*BMJ* 1989, **298**, 964).

## Methadone + MAOIs

Lack of an interaction has been reported (*Med J Aust* 1979, **1**, 400).

## METHOXAMINE + MAOIs

There is evidence of enhanced bp with methoxamine and MAOIs (*J Lab Clin Med* 1960, **56**, 747).

## Methyldopa + MAOIs

There is a single-case report of hallucinations with methyldopa and pargyline.

## METHYLPHENIDATE + MAOIs

A less severe interaction than with amfetamines would be expected. A single case of headaches and hyperventilation has been reported.

## Mirtazapine + MAOIs

See mirtazapine (*4.3.3.2*).

## Morphine + MAOIs

This is mainly extrapolation from pethidine. Two cases exist of hypotension and loss of consciousness with IV morphine (Barry, *Anaesth Intens Care* 1979, **7**, 194), responsive to naloxone. Low dose morphine and other narcotics, eg. codeine and fentanyl are probably safe. Methadone may be a suitable alternative. If opiates are used, it is best to start at a third or half the normal dose of opiate and titrate carefully, noting blood pressure and levels of consciousness. See also pethidine.

## Nefazodone + MAOIs

The BNF recommends a 2-week gap between stopping an MAOI and starting nefazodone, and a 1-week gap vice versa.

## NEFOPAM + MAOIs

The manufacturers of nefopam recommend avoiding this combination.

## Noradrenaline + MAOIs

Noradrenaline is potentially dangerous by injection and/or if other sympathomimetics are present is unlikely to cause problems if used with care.

## Orciprenaline + MAOIs

The manufacturers recommend caution if the two are used together.

## Oxcarbazepine + MAOIs

See oxcarbazepine (*4.5.6*).

## Oxymetazoline/xylometazoline + MAOIs

There is thought to be little systemic effect when these drugs are used nasally, but use in nose drops and sprays has not been studied.

## OXYPERTINE + MAOIs

CNS excitation and hypertension can occur (MI).

## Paraldehyde + MAOIs

Enhanced CNS sedation and respiratory depression have been suggested.

## Paroxetine + MAOIs

Nothing has been reported but see other SSRIs in this MAOI section.

## PETHIDINE + MAOIs

A well-documented, rapid, severe and potentially fatal interaction, although not inevitable (*Br J Anest* 1968, **40**, 279).

## Reboxetine + MAOIs

See reboxetine (*4.3.3.5*).

## Salbutamol + MAOIs

No interaction occurs.

## SERTRALINE + MAOIs

The manufacturers suggest a one-week washout period after sertraline before an MAOI is used. Several cases of suspected serotonergic syndrome have been reported, so care is essential (eg. cases and review, Graber *et al, Ann Pharmacother* 1994, **28**, 732–35).

## St. John's wort + MAOIs

See St. John's wort (*4.3.3.9*).

## Sulphonamides + MAOIs

An isolated case exists of adverse effects with sulphafurazole and phenelzine (Boyer and Lake, *Am J Psych* 1983, **140**, 264–65).

## Suxamethonium + MAOIs

There are three cases of enhancement of suxamethonium by phenelzine (Bodley *et al, BMJ* 1969, **3**, 510–12).

## SYMPATHOMIMETICS + MAOIs

Hypertension has been reported with many indirectly acting sympathomimetic amines, eg. ephedrine, metaraminol, pseudoephedrine and phenylpropanolamine. Phenylephrine is found in many O-T-C cough and cold remedies and can cause a massive rise in blood pressure with MAOIs. Use in nasal sprays and drops is not recommended although there are no case reports.

## Tetrabenazine + MAOIs

Reports exist of a central excitation and hypertension with tetrabenazine.

## Trazodone + MAOIs

There are many reported cases of serotonin syndrome with SSRIs and MAOIs and so care may be needed if this combination is used (n=1, Graber *et al, Ann Pharmacother* 1994, **28**, 732–35).

## TRICYCLICS + MAOIs

The combination of tranylcypromine and clomipramine has caused death in four cases but other MAOI/tricyclic combinations have been used with extreme care (Graham *et al, Lancet* 1982, **ii**, 440). There are cases of excitation, seizures and hyperpyrexia and a serotonin syndrome after a clomipramine overdose (325–750mg) with phenelzine (Nierenberg *et al, Clin Pharmacol and Ther* 1993, **53**, 84–88). The dangers could have been exaggerated and the combination may be relatively event-free if the following precautions are taken:

● Avoid imipramine, desipramine, clomipramine and tranylcypromine.

- Prefer amitriptyline, trimipramine and nortriptyline.
- Use oral doses only.
- Monitor patient closely.
- Start both drugs simultaneously at low dose.
- Keep doses in check.

See also combinations in depression (*1.14*) for a review of the potentially beneficial effects.

### TRIPTANS + MAOIs

The SPC recommends sumatriptan is not used with MAOIs, or for two weeks after an MAOI has stopped. The SPC contraindicates MAOIs with rizatriptan.

### Tryptophan + MAOIs

There are cases of behavioural and neurological toxicity with high doses of tryptophan, mostly with tranylcypromine (n=8, Pope *et al, Am J Psych* 1985, **142**, 491–92), which may respond to propranolol (Guze and Baxter, *J Clin Psychopharmacol* 1986, **6**, 119–20). Potentiation of the therapeutic effect is well known. So monitor carefully.

### TYRAMINE + MAOIs

Ingestion of dietary tyramine, levodopa or a sympathomimetic drug by a patient on an MAOI can produce a hypertensive crisis, eg. headache, rapid and prolonged rise in blood pressure, intracranial haemorrhage, acute cardiac failure and death. The effect is probably only seen with slow acetylators, as fast acetylators seem able to handle tyramine and other monoamines better (60% of the UK population are slow acetylators). The effect is hugely variable, but 8mg tyramine can produce a 30mm Hg rise in bp in 50% people, and 25mg and above is potentially dangerous (Blackwell and Mabbitt, *Lancet* 1965, **1**, 938–40). 20–50mg tyramine produces hypertension with tranylcypromine (Berlin *et al, Clin Pharmacol Ther* 1989, **46**, 344–51). In a normal person, BP rises within 10–20 minutes (range 0–60) of tyramine ingestion, peaking at 20–110 minutes, prolonged if an MAOI is taken. For advice on dietary tyramine see the following section.

### VENLAFAXINE + MAOIs

See venlafaxine (*4.3.3.8*).

### Warfarin + MAOIs

No interaction is known, although tranylcypromine is known to inhibit 2C19 and so some potential exists (Sayal *et al, Acta Psych Scand* 2000, **102**, 250–55).

### Xanthines + MAOIs

There is report of possible hypertension with phenelzine and oxtriphylline, a theophylline derivative (*J Clin Psychopharmacol* 1985, **5**, A17).

### Xylometazoline + MAOIs

See oxymetazoline + MAOIs.

**Treatments for MAOI hypertensive crisis:**

1. Phentolamine 2–10 mg by slow IV infusion (adults), repeated if necessary.
2. If not phentolamine, chlorpromazine 50–100 mg IM can be used, as can diazoxide (50–100 mg by IV injection). Repeat after 10 minutes if necessary.
3. Alternative advice might be to bite open a 10 mg capsule of nifedipine, swallow the contents with water (*Am J Psych* 1991, **148**, 1616) then go immediately to a hospital casualty department. This produces a consistent and prompt fall in arterial blood pressure but due to serious adverse events (stroke, hypotension etc), s/l nifedipine should only be used with care (Marwick, (*JAMA* 1996, **275**, 423–4; Grossman *et al, JAMA* 1996, **276**, 1328–31). **NB**. nifedipine is light-sensitive and should not be left in bright light. Safer alternatives include sublingual captopril, clonidine and labetolol (review Matuschka, (*J Pharm Tech* 1999, **15**, 199–203)
4. Cool any fever with external cooling.
   - **Blood pressure should be monitored frequently.**

## PATIENT INFORMATION: WARNING SIGNS OF A REACTION

If a patient experiences any of the following symptoms, especially after eating, taking drugs of any type or if unexpected or severe, a reaction should be suspected and appropriate medical attention sought immediately: *Headache (especially at the back of the head), lightheadedness or dizziness, flushing of the face, pounding of the heart, numbness or stiffness in the neck, photophobia, chest pain or nausea and vomiting. It usually occurs about two hours after ingestion of the compound.*

## FOODS

Compliance with the MAOI diet is often very poor (Neil *et al, J Clin Psych* 1979, **40**, 3–37).
**Reviews**: Cheese and drink tyramine contents (Berlin and Lecrubier, *CNS Drugs* 1996, **5**, 403–13), 'The making of a user-friendly MAOI diet' (Gardner *et al, J Clin Psych* 1996, **57**, 99–104).

### 1. General Principles
Freshness of food is vital. If there is any sign of spoilage then omit. Avoid foods which are matured or might be 'spoiling'. Avoid tyramine-containing foods. Generally, the more 'convenience' the food, the safer it is, eg. packet soups are generally safe. Although many foods have only small amounts of tyramine, it is possible to have local concentrations which might give a reaction.

### 2. Tyramine-containing foods to avoid
The following may be of use as general guidelines:

● **Dairy products:**
Hard cheeses, soft cheeses and cheese spreads (eg. Philadelphia) must be avoided. Special care is needed with salty, bitter tasting, refrigerated cheese. Foods containing cheese (eg. pizzas, pies, etc, see below) must also be avoided and are a known cause of inadvertent ingestion and death. Cottage cheese, 'Dairylea' cream cheese, Ricotta and processed cheese contain only minute amounts of tyramine and large quantities would be needed to produce a reaction.

● **Fruit and vegetables:**
Broad bean pods (but not the beans) and banana skins (occasionally cooked as part of whole unripe bananas in a stew) must be avoided. Avocado has been reported to produce a reaction and should be avoided if possible.

● **Game, meat and fish:**
Pickled or salted dried herrings and any hung or badly stored game, poultry or other meat which might be 'spoiling' must be avoided. NB. The original reports with pickled herrings may have been due to spoilage in the brine surrounding the fish, and are probably safe.

● **Meat products:**
Avoid chicken liver pâté, liver pâté and any other liver which is not fresh. Avoid aged and cured meats (eg. salami, mortadella, pastrami). **Fresh** chicken liver, **fresh** beef liver and **fresh** pâté, should be safe.

● **Pizzas:**
Commercially available pizzas from large chain outlets seem safe (analysis by Shulman and Walker, *J Clin Psych* 1999, **60**, 191–93; comment by Feinberg and Holzer, reply by Shulman and Walker, *J Clin Psych* 2000, **61**, 145–46), and even those with double orders of cheese appeared safe. Gourmet pizzas from smaller outlets had higher tyramine contents, especially if mature cheeses were used.

● **Soy and Soybean:**
Some samples of Soy sauce and soybean preparations may have very high tyramine levels. Either avoid entirely or a 10ml maximum is recommended.
**Soy sauce** (Pearl River etc) — some have high quantities, ie. up to 3.4mg/15ml, and so double or triple helpings could be well above the threshold for a reaction (Shulman

and Walker, *J Clin Psych* 1999, **60**, 191–93)

**Soybean curd** (eg. Tofu) — some have high quantities, especially if kept refrigerated for 7 days or longer, ie. up to 5mg/300mg helping, and so double or triple helpings could be well above thresholds for reactions (Shulman and Walker, *J Clin Psych* 1999, **60**, 191–93).

● **Yeast and meat extracts:**

'Oxo', 'Marmite', 'Bovril' and other meat or yeast extracts must be avoided. Gravy made with UK 'Bisto' is safe (all contain less than 0.0022mg/g tyramine and a full half pint of gravy would contain less than 0.05mg tyramine). Gravy made from juices of the roast or fresh meat should be safe. Brewers yeast (Shulman *et al*, *J Clin Psychopharmacol* 1989, **9**, 397–402) and bread are safe.

**3. Foods known to contain some tyramine where excessive consumption is not advisable, albeit unlikely:**

Plums, matured pork, sauerkraut, spinach.

**4. Foods thought to contain only minute amounts of tyramine:**

Banana pulp (skins unsafe), chocolate (one anecdotal report of headache), cottage cheese, cream cheese, Dairylea cheese, aubergine, fruit juices, octopus, peanuts, raspberries (minor reports of raised tyramine), sausages, soy milk, tomato, vinegar, yoghurt (commercial), Worcester sauce, eg. Lee and Perrins and others (very low, Shulman and Walker, *J Clin Psych* 1999, **60**, 191–93).

**5. Other foods with isolated reports:**

Chicken nuggets, chapatti, protein dietary supplement, sea kale.

**6. Alcoholic drinks:**

Patient instructions usually state that all alcoholic and some non-alcoholic drinks must be avoided. Real ales may contain up to 110mg/L, with reports of hypertensive crisis after 0.6 pint (79 brand study, Tailor *et al*, *J Clin Psychopharmacol* 1994, **14**, 5–14). There is some evidence that low or non-alcoholic beers contain significant amounts of tyramine (Murray

*et al*, *Lancet* 1988, **i**, 1167–68), shown by three reactions to less than 2/3 pint of alcohol-free and 'de-alcoholised' beer (n=3, Thakore *et al*, *Int Clin Psychopharmacol* 1992, **7**, 59–60). There is a large variation in other beers, so take in moderation (ie. 1–2 bottles a day maximum), prefer canned beers from major brewers and take care with dealcoholised beers. The maximum reported level in Chianti wine is 12mg/l, likely to be dangerous only in overdose.

The following may, however, be of use where a particular patient wishes to drink:

| 1. | **Avoid:** |
|---|---|
| | Chianti |
| | Home-made beers and wines |
| | Real ales |
| | Red wines |
| **2.** | **True moderation** (eg. 1 unit): |
| | White wines |
| | Non-alcoholic beers and lagers |
| **3.** | **Safest**: |
| | Gin, vodka |
| | Other clear spirits |

Red wines contain phenolic flavanoids which inhibit the enzymes which metabolise catecholamines, including tyramine (*BMJ* 1990, **301**, 544).

## OVER THE COUNTER MEDICINES

Each patient should be warned about the possibility of interactions with over-the-counter medicines. The general advice for patients is:

**1. Only buy medicines from a Pharmacy.**

Do not use supermarket shelves, drug stores, newsagents etc. Do not take medicines given to you by friends or relatives. Do not take medicines taken before the MAOI was prescribed until advice has been sought.

**2. Carry an MAOI card and show it to any doctor, dentist or pharmacist who may treat you.**

**3. Take special care over any medicines for coughs, colds, flu, hay fever, asthma and catarrh.**

## 4.4 LITHIUM

Lithium may interact with other drugs, particularly via changes in renal excretion.

**Review**: clinical relevance of lithium interactions (Finley *et al, Clin Pharmacokinetics* 1995, **29**, 172–91, 147 refs).

### ACE INHIBITORS + LITHIUM

There are many cases of lithium toxicity with ACE inhibitors (n=9, open, DasGupta *et al, J Clin Psych* 1992, **53**, 398–400), especially in the elderly (n=20, Finley *et al, J Clin Psychopharmacol* 1996, **16**, 68–71), so either monitor very carefully (review: Lehmann and Ritz, *Am J Kidney Dis* 1995, **25**, 82–87) or use, eg. beta-blockers.

### Acetazolamide + lithium

Lithium excretion may be increased or, less likely, possibly decreased by acetazolamide (n=2, Gay *et al, Encephale* 1985, **11**, 261–62). This is inadequately studied and probably of minimal importance.

### Alcohol + lithium

See alcohol (*4.7.1*).

### AMINOPHYLLINE + LITHIUM

See theophylline + lithium.

### Amiodarone + lithium

The BNF notes an increased risk of hypothyroidism with the combination.

### Amfetamines + lithium

Lithium may suppress amfetamine 'highs' (n=3, Flemenbaum, *Am J Psych* 1974, **131**, 820–21).

### Antacids + lithium

See sodium + lithium.

### Antipsychotics + lithium

This is generally considered a useful combination but cases of mostly reversible neurotoxicity have been reported, particularly with haloperidol (although these may have been undiagnosed NMS). Reports of encephalopathy, enhanced EPSE, neurotoxicity or irreversible brain damage have been reviewed (*Human Psychopharmacol* 1990, **5**, 263–97) but without being able to demonstrate the interaction. The main risk factors seem to be if high doses of both drugs are used and signs of impending toxicity are ignored. There are a number of reports for individual drugs. **Chlorpromazine** levels may be lowered by up to 40% by lithium, with enhanced EPSEs and rarely neurotoxicity. With **risperidone**, reports include delirium (n=1, Chen and Cardasis, *Am J Psych* 1996, **153**, 1233–34), and possible NMS (n=1, Swanson *et al, Am J Psych* 1995, **152**, 1096). No interaction has been noted with **olanzapine** (MI). With **clozapine** there is an increased risk of developing NMS (SPC) and reversible neurotoxicity (n=1, Blake *et al, J Clin Psychopharmacol* 1992, **12**, 297–99), and one despite lithium levels below 0.5mEq/l (n=1, Lee and Yang, *Chung Hua I Hsueh Tsa Chih (Taipei)* 1999, **62**, 184–87). Cases of diabetic ketoacidosis have been reported (eg. n=1, Peterson and Byrd, *Am J Psych* 1996, **153**, 737–38), and so glucose monitoring might be indicated with this particular combination. For a review of reported cases, with the suggestion that all symptoms are consistent with lithium toxicity alone, with the antipsychotic affecting fluid balance mechanisms and intracellular concentrations, see Knorring (*Hum Psychopharmacol* 1990, **5**, 287–92).

### Aripiprazole + lithium *

See aripiprazole (*4.2.7.1*).

### Baclofen + lithium

Two cases of aggravation of movement disorder in Huntington's disease exist (Anden *et al, Lancet* 1973, **ii**, 93).

### Beta-blockers + lithium

A case of bradycardia with propranolol and lithium has been reported (Becker, *J Clin Psych* 1989, **50**, 473), although propranolol and nadolol (n=1, Dave and Langbart, *Ann Clin Psych* 1994, **6**, 51–52) have been used uneventfully for lithium-induced tremor.

### Benzodiazepines + lithium
There have been several anecdotal reports of reactions, eg. hypothermia (Naylor *et al, BMJ* 1977, **2**, 22) and, although a neurotoxic syndrome in combination with lithium has been reported (n=5, Koczerginski *et al, Int Clin Psychopharm* 1989, **4**, 195–99), extensive use of this usually beneficial combination suggests it to be safe.

### Bumetanide + lithium
Although studies have shown a minimal effect, bumetanide may cause lithium toxicity (Kerry *et al, BMJ* 1980, **281**, 371).

### Calcium-channel blockers + lithium
Cases of enhanced effect and toxicity with unchanged plasma levels have been reported with verapamil (Price and Giannini, *J Clin Pharmacol* 1986, **26**, 717–19), as have reduced lithium levels (Weinrauch *et al, Am Heart J* 1984, **108**, 1378–80). Acute EPSEs and bradycardia have been reported with diltiazem (n=1, Binder *et al, Arch Int Med* 1991, **151**, 373–74).

### Candesartan + lithium *
There is a case of a patient prescribed 16mg/d candesartan (an Angiotensin II antagonist) who developed severe lithium eight weeks later (n=1, Zwanzger *et al, J Clin Psych* 2001, **62**, 208–9).

### Cannabis + lithium
See cannabis (*4.7.2*).

### Carbamazepine + lithium *
See carbamazepine (*4.5.1*), plus 'combinations' in bipolar disorder (*1.10*) for a review of some beneficial effects.

### Cisplatin + lithium
Reports exist of lithium levels decreased by up to 64% (eg. Vincent *et al, Cancer Chemother Pharmacol* 1995, **35**, 533–34).

### Citalopram + lithium
See citalopram (*4.3.2.1*).

### Clonidine + lithium
Lithium may reduce the hypotensive effect of clonidine (Goodnick and Meltzer, *Biol Psych* 1984, **19**, 883–89). Monitor carefully.

### Cocaine + lithium
See cocaine (*4.7.3*).

### Corticosteroids + lithium
An isolated case of lithium reducing the effect of corticosteroids on the kidneys exists (Stewart *et al, Clin Endocrinol* 1987, **27**, 63).

### Co-trimoxazole + lithium
Two cases exist of enhanced toxicity with reduced levels (*NZ Med J* 1984, **97**, 729–32).

### Digoxin + lithium
Lack of interaction has been shown (n=6, open, Cooper *et al, Br J Clin Pharmac* 1984, **18**, 21–25).

### Dipyridamole + lithium
Lack of interaction has been shown (Wood *et al, B J Clin Pharmacol* 1989, **27**, 749–56).

### Disulfiram + lithium
See disulfiram (*4.6.6*).

### Domperidone + lithium
An enhanced risk of EPSEs exists.

### Escitalopram + lithium
See citalopram/escitalopram (*4.3.2.1*).

### Fluoxetine + lithium
The incidence of problems may be low (n=110, open, Bauer *et al, J Clin Psychopharmacol* 1996, **16**, 130–34) and lack of significant pharmacokinetic interaction shown (n=10, open, Breuel *et al, Int J Clin Pharmacol Ther* 1995, **33**, 415–19). The combination may, however, be poorly tolerated (n=14, open, Hawley *et al, Int Clin Psychopharmacol* 1994, **9**, 31–33), with reports of serotonin syndrome (n=1, Muly *et al, Am J Psych* 1993, **150**, 1565), absence seizures (Sacristan *et al, Am J Psych* 1991, **148**, 146–47) and acute confusion or lithium toxicity reported (*Int J Ger Psych* 1992, **7**, 687–88, reviewed by Levinson *et al, DICP Ann Pharmacother* 1991, **25**, 657–61).

### Fluvoxamine + lithium
See fluvoxamine (*4.3.2.3*).

### Furosemide (frusemide) + lithium
Studies have shown a minimal effect and furosemide to be the safest diuretic with lithium (eg. n=13, RCT,

Crabtree *et al, Am J Psych* 1991, **148**, 1060–63).

### Gabapentin + lithium

Although both are exclusively eliminated by renal excretion, a single-dose study showed that the pharmacokinetics of lithium are not altered by gabapentin (n=13, Frye *et al, J Clin Psychopharmacol* 1998, **18**, 461–64).

### Herbal diuretics + lithium *

A clear case of life-threatening lithium toxicity (4.5mmol/L) induced by a herbal diuretic preparation has been reported (n=1, Pyevich and Bogenschutz, *Am J Psych* 2001, **158**, 1329).

### Hypoglycaemics + lithium

Lithium has been used to improve glucose metabolism and assist the effects of oral hypoglycaemics and insulin (n=38, Hu *et al, Biol Trace Elem Res* 1997, **60**, 131–37).

### Iodides + lithium

Enhanced antithyroid and goitre effects of lithium have been reported.

### Ispaghula husk + lithium

A single case exists of reduced lithium levels (Perlman, *Lancet* 1990, **335**, 416).

### Lamotrigine + lithium *

Lamotrigine does not cause significant change in the pharmacokinetics of lithium (n=20, RCT, 6/7, Chen *et al, Br J Clin Pharmacol* 2000, **50**, 193–96).

### Levodopa + lithium

Lithium has been used to treat levodopa-induced psychiatric side-effects, eg. psychosis, mania etc (n=1, Braden, *Am J Psych* 1977, **134**, 808). Reversible Creutzfeldt-Jakob like syndrome has been reported (n=1, Broussolle *et al, J Neurol Neurosurg Psychiatry* 1989, **52**, 686–87).

### Levofloxacin + lithium *

A case has been reported of severe lithium toxicity (with plasma levels more than doubled) two days after starting levofloxacin in a stable bipolar patient (n=1, Takahashi *et al, J Clin Psych* 2000, **61**, 949–50).

### Losartan + lithium

A case has been reported of marked lithium toxicity five weeks after losartan 50mg/d was added to stable therapy (n=1, Blanche *et al, Eur J Clin Pharmacol* 1999, **52**, 501).

### MAOIs + lithium

See MAOIs (*4.3.4*).

### METHYLDOPA + LITHIUM

Many cases of rapidly appearing lithium toxicity with normal plasma levels have been reported (eg. Yassa, *CSAJ* 1986, **134**, 141–42).

### Metoclopramide + lithium

An enhanced risk of EPSEs and of neurotoxicity exists.

### Metronidazole + lithium

Cases of toxic lithium levels induced by metronidazole exist (Teicher *et al, JAMA* 1987, **257**, 3365–66).

### Mirtazapine + lithium

See mirtazapine (*4.3.3.2*).

### Nefazodone + lithium

See nefazodone (*4.3.3.4*).

### Neuromuscular blocking agents + lithium

A few cases of enhanced blockade have been reported with neostigmine (eg. Martin and Kramer, *Am J Psych* 1982, **139**, 1326–28). Animal studies indicate the possibility of an interaction and so the last dose or two of lithium before the use of an NMBA could be omitted.

### NON-STEROIDAL ANTI-INFLAMMATORY DRUGS + LITHIUM *

This is a well known interaction, probably due to inhibition of renal prostaglandin PGE2 and reduced blood flow. Lithium levels should be monitored frequently if the combination is to be used. For a review, see Brouwers and de Smet, *Clin Pharmacokinet* 1994, **27**, 462–85.

**Avoid:**

**Indometacin:** 61% increases in lithium levels have been reported (eg. n=10, open, Reimann *et al, Arch Gen Psych* 1983, **40**, 283–86).

**Extra care:**

**Ibuprofen:** Studies show a variable effect, with a 25% increase in lithium levels possible (eg. n=9, open, Ragheb, *J Clin Psych* 1987, **48**, 161–63; Bailey *et al, South Med J* 1989, **82**, 1197). As ibuprofen is available over the counter this interaction should be considered carefully.

**Diclofenac:** Lithium levels may rise by up to 23% (n=5, Reimann and Frolich, *Clin Pharmacol Ther* 1981, **30**, 348–52).

**Piroxicam:** Several cases exist of a slow-onset (eg. several months) lithium toxicity (eg. Walbridge and Bazire, *B J Psych* 1985, **147**, 206–4).

**Care:**

**Azapropazone:** The BNF notes the possibility of raised lithium levels.

**Celecoxib:** * A potential interaction has been reported (Gunja *et al, Int Med J* 2002, **32**, 494).

**Ketoprofen:** raised lithium levels have been reported (n=1, Singer *et al, Therapie* 1981, **36**, 323–26).

**Ketorolac:** lithium levels nearly doubled by ketorolac have been reported (n=1, Langlois and Paquette, *Can Med Ass J* 1994, **150**, 1455–56; n=5, Cold *et al, J Clin Psychopharmacol* 1998, **18**, 33–37).

**Mefenamic acid:** acute lithium toxicity, possibly with renal damage, has been reported (n=2, MacDonald and Neale, *BMJ* 1988, **297**, 1339).

**Meloxicam:** * Meloxicam 15mg moderately increases plasma lithium, so plasma levels should be closely monitored (n=16, Turck *et al, Br J Clin Pharmacol* 2000, **50**, 197–204).

**Naproxen:** short-term naproxen has little effect on lithium levels (n=12, Levin *et al, J Clin Psychophamacol* 1998, **18**, 237–40) although one study showed some increased lithium levels (n=7, Ragheb and Powell, *J Clin Psychopharmacol* 1986, **6**, 150–54).

**Phenylbutazone:** doubled lithium levels have been reported (n=1, Singer et al, *L'Encephale* 1978, **4**, 33–40; see also Ragheb, *J Clin Psychopharmacol* 1990, **10**, 149–50).

**Rofecoxib:** * 50mg/d can increase lithium levels, particularly with higher starting lithium levels (n=10, Sajbel *et al, Pharmacotherapy* 2001, **21**, 380; abstract; n=1, Lundmark *et al, B J Clin Pharmacol* 2002, **53**, 403–4).

**Tiaprofenic acid**: increased serum lithium levels (requiring a dose reduction) occurred in a woman taking fosinopril and lithium to which tiaprofenic acid was added (Alderman and Lindsay, *Ann Pharmacother* 1996, **30**, 1411–13).

**Least risk:**

**Aspirin:** 4g/d for seven days had no effect on lithium levels in one study (n=10, open, Reimann *et al, Arch Gen Psych* 1983, **40**, 283–86), and other studies have shown a mildly variable effect (eg. Ragheb, *J Clin Psych* 1987, **48**, 425; Bendz and Feinberg, *Arch Gen Psych* 1984, **41**, 310–11).

**Sulindac:** Reports show either a slightly reduced level of lithium (n=2, Furnell and Davies, *Drug Intell Clin Pharm* 1986, **19**, 374–76), no effect (n=4, Ragheb and Powell, *J Clin Psych* 1986, **47**, 33–34) or raised levels (n=2, Jones and Stoner, *J Clin Psych* 2000, **61**, 527–28).

**Oxcarbazepine + lithium**
See oxcarbazepine (*4.5.6*).

**Phenytoin + lithium**
There are several reports of lithium neurotoxicity, without increased lithium levels (eg. Raskin, *J Clin Psychopharmacol* 1984, **4**, 120).

**Potassium iodide + lithium**
An additive effect may cause hypothyroidism.

**Psyllium + lithium**
See Ispaghula husk + lithium.

**Quetiapine + lithium**
See quetiapine (*4.2.4*).

**SERTINDOLE + LITHIUM** *
See sertindole (*4.2.7.2*).

**Smoking + lithium**
See smoking (*4.7.4*).

**Sodium + lithium**
Excess sodium (eg. as bicarbonate in antacids) can reduce lithium levels (eg. McSwiggan, *Med J Aust* 1978, **1**, 38–39) and sodium restriction can lead to lithium intoxication (eg. Baer *et al, J Psych Res* 1971, **8**, 91–105).

**Spironolactone + lithium**
A rise in lithium levels has been reported (Baer *et al, J Psych Res* 1971, **8**, 91–105), as has synergism (see combinations, *1.10*).

**SSRIs + lithium** *
See citalopram/escitalopram (*4.3.2.1*), fluoxetine (*4.3.2.2*), fluvoxamine (*4.3.2.3*) and paroxetine (*4.3.2.4*). No interaction has been seen yet with sertraline.

**Tetracyclines + lithium**
Cases of lithium intoxication (eg. McGennis, *BMJ* 1978, **2**, 1183) have been reported so monitor lithium regularly.

**THEOPHYLLINE + LITHIUM**
Theophylline may reduce lithium levels by 20–30% (Cook *et al, J Clin Psych* 1985, **46**, 278–79) as may aminophylline, probably by increased excretion. An increased lithium dose can counteract this so monitoring of levels is essential, especially if theophylline is then stopped. The interaction has been made use of to treat lithium toxicity.

**THIAZIDE DIURETICS + LITHIUM**
Thiazides reduce the renal clearance of lithium and levels rise within a few days, with potentially serious consequences. Thiazides should only be used where unavoidable and where strict monitoring is used. The combination has occasionally been used in patients where large doses of lithium do not produce therapeutic levels.
**Chlorothiazide**: A 50% rise in lithium levels has been reported (Levy *et al, Am J Psych* 1973, **130**, 1014–18).

**Bendroflumethiazide (bendrofluazide)**: a 24% reduction in lithium excretion has been shown, (Petersen *et al, BMJ* 1974, **2**, 143–45), as has lithium toxicity (n=1, Vipond *et al, Anaesthesia* 1996, **51**, 1156–58).
**Co-amilozide**: Single case report (Dorevitch and Baruch, *Am J Psych* 1986, **143**, 257–58).
**Hydroflumethiazide**: One study showed a 24% reduction in lithium excretion (Petersen *et al, BMJ* 1974, **2**, 143–45).
**Hydrochlorthiazide**: The effect may only be minor (n=13, RCT, Crabtree *et al, Am J Psych* 1991, **148**, 1060–63).
**Triamterene**; increased lithium clearance may occur (n=8, open, Wetzels *et al, Nephrol Dial Transplant* 1989, **4**, 939–42).

**Topiramate + lithium** *
Elevated and toxic lithium levels have been reported with higher (800mg/d) doses of topiramate, but not with 500mg/d (Pinninti and Zelinsji, *J Clin Psychopharmacol* 2002, **22**, 340).

**Tricyclics + lithium** *
See tricyclics (*4.3.1*).

**Trimethoprim + lithium** *
Lithium toxicity has been reported following addition of trimethoprim (n=1, de Vries, *Ned Tijdschr Geneeskd* 2001, **145**, 539–40).

**Triptans + lithium**
The BNF notes an increased risk of CNS toxicity with sumatriptan.

**Venlafaxine + lithium**
See venlafaxine (*4.3.3.8*).

**Warfarin + lithium**
No interaction is suspected nor reported (mentioned in Sayal *et al, Acta Psych Scand* 2000, **102**, 250–55).

**Ziprasidone + lithium** *
See ziprasidone (*4.2.7.2*).

## 4.5 ANTICONVULSANTS

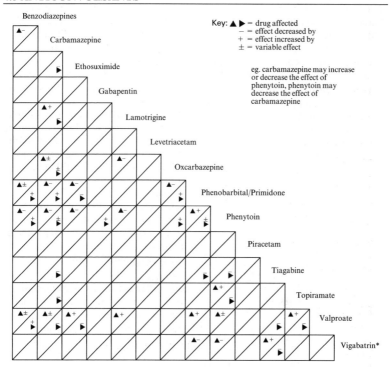

Key: ▲ ▶ = drug affected
  − = effect decreased by
  + = effect increased by
  ± = variable effect

eg. carbamazepine may increase or decrease the effect of phenytoin, phenytoin may decrease the effect of carbamazepine

The above table shows the effect of adding one anticonvulsant to a therapy including another. The opposite effect to the above will usually occur when a drug is discontinued from a regimen.

**Reviews\***: detailed reviews of pharmacokinetic interactions between anticonvulsants (Tanaka, *J Clin Pharm & Ther* 1999, **24**, 87; Hachad *et al, Ther Drug Monit* 2002, **24**, 91–103), AED-OC interactions (Crawford, *CNS Drugs* 2002, **16**, 263–72, which concludes that if on CBZ, oxcarbazepine, phenobarbital, phenytoin or topiramate, one needs an OC with at least 50mcg ethinylestradiol or Depot Provera given every 10 weeks rather than 12).

### 4.5.1 CARBAMAZEPINE

Carbamazepine is principally metabolised by the CYP3A4 enzyme but is also a potent inducer of CYP3A4 and other oxidative mechanisms in the liver. This auto-induction takes 1–4 weeks to occur, although is virtually complete after a week. Carbamazepine (CBZ) is metabolised to carbamazepine-epoxide (CBZ-E), which may be more toxic than carbamazepine itself and so alteration of the CBZ:CBZ-E ratio by another drug would alter toxicity. Carbamazepine is extensively plasma protein-bound. Major diurnal variations in plasma levels occur, which can be as much as 90% during polytherapy compared to monotherapy (Hoppener *et al, Epilepsia* 1980, **21**, 341–50).

**Review**: significant interactions (Spina *et al, Clin Pharmacokinet* 1996, **31**, 198–214).

### Acetazolamide + carbamazepine

CYP3A4 inhibition may raise carbamazepine levels (mentioned in Spina *et al, Clin Pharmacokinet* 1996, **31**, 198–214).

**Alcohol + carbamazepine**
See alcohol (*4.7.1*).

**ANTIPSYCHOTICS + CARBAMAZEPINE \***
There are a variety of well documented interactions. Carbamazepine very significantly reduces **haloperidol** levels, resulting in worsening symptoms and worsening outcome (eg. n=27, 4/52, Hesslinger *et al, J Clin Psychopharmacol* 1999, **19**, 310–15). More importantly, a significantly extended QT interval has been shown, probably by increased haloperidol metabolite concentrations. Care is thus needed (n=2, Iwahashi *et al, Am J Psych* 1996, **153**, 135). **Loxapine** may induce CBZ metabolism to CBZ-E or inhibit CBZ-E metabolism (n=1 + review: Collins *et al, Ann Pharmacother* 1993, **27**, 1180–83), which may enhance toxicity, even with normal carbamazepine levels (n=1, Collins *et al, Ann Pharmacother* 1993, **27**, 1180–83). There are cases of **clozapine** levels increasing by up to 100% after carbamazepine was stopped (Raitasuo *et al, Am J Psych* 1993, **150**, 169) and of neurotoxicity (n=1, Yerevanian and Hodgman, *Am J Psych* 1985, **142**, 785–86). There is also the very real enhanced risk of agranulocytosis (mandatory precaution in UK SPC), so carbamazepine and clozapine should not be used together (n=1, Gerson, *Lancet* 1991, **338**, 262–63). Carbamazepine may halve plasma levels of **risperidone** and 9-hydroxyrisperidone, probably via 2D6 and 3A4 induction (n=34, Spina *et al, Ther Drug Monit* 2000, **22**, 481–85; n=11, Ono *et al, Psychopharmacol (Berl)* 2002, **162**, 50–54), and there are cases of EPS after carbamazepine was discontinued from a combination with risperidone (n=2, Takahashi *et al, Clin Neuropharmacol* 2001, **24**, 358–60). Alternatively risperidone 1mg/d may increase steady-state carbamazepine levels by 10% over 24 hrs and 20% over 2 weeks (n=8, Mula and Monaco, *Clin Neuropharmacol* 2002, **25**, 97–100). Carbamazepine

increases **olanzapine** clearance by 44% and reduces half-life by 20% (n=31+16, Linnet and Olesen, *Ther Drug Monit* 2002, **24**, 512–17), probably by CYP1A2 induction, but dose adjustment is not needed as olanzapine has a wide therapeutic index (n=11, Lucas et al, *Eur J Clin Pharmacol* 1998, **54**, 639–43). Toxic levels of CBZ-E (the toxic CBZ metabolite) raised 3–4 fold have been reported with concurrent quetiapine (n=2, Fitzgerald and Okos, *Pharmacother* 2002, **22**, 1500–3). The Japanese SPC notes that carbamazepine may reduce **zotepine** levels, via CYP3A4 induction. Antipsychotics lower the seizure threshold, antagonising the anticonvulsant effects. Increased **aripiprazole** metabolism occurs through 3A4 induction and the aripiprazole dose should be doubled.

**Benzodiazepines + carbamazepine \***
A large study concluded that concomitant clonazepam and carbamazepine results in a 22% increase in clonazepam clearance and a 20% decrease in carbamazepine clearance (n=183, Yukawa *et al, J Clin Psychopharmacol* 2001, **21**, 588–93). Slightly higher benzodiazepine doses may be needed (Baba *et al, B J Clin Pharmacol* 1990, **29**, 766–69). Carbamazepine toxicity has occurred after the addition of clobazam (Genton *et al, Epilepsia* 1998, **39**, 1115–18), probably related to progressive increases in norclobazam.

**Bupropion + carbamazepine**
See bupropion (*4.6.4*).

**Caffeine + carbamazepine**
Carbamazepine induces the CYP1A2 metabolism of caffeine (n=5, Parker *et al, Br J Clin Pharmacol* 1998, **45**, 176–78).

**CALCIUM-CHANNEL BLOCKERS + CARBAMAZEPINE \***
One study showed that verapamil increases carbamazepine plasma levels by 50%, via CYP3A4 inhibition (n=6, open, McPhee *et al, Lancet* 1986, **i**, 700–3; n=43, open, Bahls *et al, Neurology* 1991, **41**, 740–42).

Other evidence, eg. cases with diltiazem (n=1, Eimer and Carter, *Drug Intell Clin Pharm* 1987, **21**, 340–42), and verapamil suggests a substantial risk of toxicity. Since no interaction occurs with nifedipine (n=43, open, Bahls *et al, Neurology* 1991, **41**, 740–42; n=1, Brodie and MacPhee, *BMJ* 1986, **292**, 1170–71), it is the calcium-channel blocker of choice with carbamazepine, although the BNF notes the efficacy of nifedipine may be reduced, so care is needed. The antihypertensive effect of nilvadipine (n=1, Yasui-Furukori and Tateishi, *J Clin Pharmacol* 2002, **42**, 100–3) and isradipine may be reduced.

### Charcoal, activated + carbamazepine

Carbamazepine absorption may be almost completely stopped if activated charcoal is given five minutes after ingestion, with a lesser affect if given after an hour (Neuvonen and Elonen, *Eur J Clin Pharmacol* 1980, **17**, 51–57).

### Chinese medicine + carbamazepine *

Paeoniae Radix, a traditional Chinese medicine, may increase carbamazepine absorption (in rats, Chen *et al, Biol Pharm Bull* 2002, **25**, 532–35).

### CICLOSPORIN + CARBAMAZEPINE

Ciclosporin metabolism is accelerated by carbamazepine, to give reduced plasma levels.

### Citalopram + carbamazepine *

See citalopram (*4.3.2.1*).

### Cocaine + carbamazepine

See cocaine (*4.7.3*).

### CORTICOSTEROIDS + CARBAMAZEPINE

Corticosteroid CYP3A4 metabolism is accelerated by carbamazepine, giving a reduced effect (n=15, open, Bartoszek *et al, Clin Pharmacol Ther* 1987, **42**, 424–32).

### Clarithromycin + carbamazepine

See erythromycin + carbamazepine.

### DANAZOL + CARBAMAZEPINE

Danazol inhibits carbamazepine metabolism to give an increased effect (n=6, open, Zielinski *et al, Ther Drug Monit* 1987, **9**, 24–27) so monitor levels and observe for side-effects.

### DEXTROPROPOXYPHENE + CARBAMAZEPINE *

Dextropropoxyphene enhances carbamazepine toxicity via CYP3A4 inhibition (eg. *Neurology* 1987, **37** [Suppl 1], 87) and levels may rise by 44–77%. In one case, carbamazepine levels increased 4-fold over 24 hours and led to cerebellar dysfunction, which resolved over 48 hours (n=1, Allen, *Postgrad Med J* 1994, **70**, 764). Monitor closely if used together, especially in the elderly (n=84, open, Bergendal *et al, Eur J Clin Pharmacol* 1997, **53**, 103–6).

### Digoxin + carbamazepine

An isolated case exists of bradycardia with digitalis and carbamazepine but not with digoxin.

### Disulfiram + carbamazepine

See disulfiram (*4.6.6*).

### Diuretics + carbamazepine

Hyponatraemia may uncommonly occur with furosemide or hydrochlorothiazide (n=2, Yassa *et al, J Clin Psych* 1987, **48**, 281–83).

### DOXYCYCLINE + CARBAMAZEPINE

Doxycycline metabolism is accelerated by carbamazepine, reducing efficacy and halving half-life (Penttila *et al, BMJ*, 1974, **2**, 470–72). Other tetracyclines appear not to interact.

### Enteral feeds + carbamazepine

Carbamazepine suspension absorption has been shown to be slightly slowed and reduced during nasogastric feeding (n=8, RCT, c/o, Bass *et al, Epilepsia* 1989, **30**, 364–69) so take care with dosing after enteral feeding is stopped.

### Escitalopram + carbamazepine

See citalopram/escitalopram (*4.3.2.1*).

### Ethosuximide + carbamazepine

See ethosuximide (*4.5.2*).

### Etretinate + carbamazepine

A girl treated with the combination only responded to etretinate when carbamazepine was withdrawn (n=1,

Mohammed, *Dermatology* 1992, **185**, 79).

## ERYTHROMYCIN + CARBAMAZEPINE *

A rapid 100–200% rise in carbamazepine levels has been reported (n=4, Wroblewski *et al, JAMA* 1986, **255**, 1165–67; n=1, Tatum and Gonzalez, *Hosp Pharm* 1994, **29**, 45) and with IV erythromycin use (Mitsch, *Drug Intell Clin Pharm* 1989, **23**, 878–79), probably via CYP3A4 inhibition. Monitor levels or use an alternative antibiotic. A review of the interaction concluded that highest risk is with high doses and least with clarithromycin (Pauwels, *Pharmacol Res* 2002, **45**, 291–98).

### Fluconazole + carbamazepine *
Potential fluconazole-induced carbamazepine toxicity has been reported (n=1, Nair and Morris, *Ann Pharmacother* 1999, **33**, 790–92), with elevated CBZ levels (n=1, Finch *et al, South Med J* 2002, **95**, 1099–100).

### Fluoxetine + carbamazepine
See fluoxetine (*4.3.2.2*).

### Fluvoxamine + carbamazepine
See fluvoxamine (*4.3.2.3*).

### Gabapentin + carbamazepine
See gabapentin (*4.5.3*).

### Gestrinone + carbamazepine *
The UK SPC states that carbamazepine may reduce the activity of gestrinone.

### Grapefruit juice + carbamazepine
300ml grapefruit juice increased carbamazepine levels by 40% and AUC by 41%, probably by CYP3A4 inhibition in the gut wall and liver (n=10, RCT, Garg *et al, Clin Pharmacol Ther* 1998, **64**, 286–88).

### Griseofulvin + carbamazepine
A reduced griseofulvin level by enzyme induction (*Am J Hosp Pharm* 1986, **16**, 52) has been postulated.

## H2-BLOCKERS + CARBAMAZEPINE
Studies have shown a transient 20% rise in carbamazepine levels with cimetidine (n=8, open, 7/7, Dalton *et al, Epilepsia* 1986, **27**, 553–58), reduced clearance, prolonged half-life (n=12, open, 8/52, Webster *et al, Eur J Clin Pharmacol* 1984, **27**, 341–43) and inhibition of non-renal elimination (n=8, RCT, c/o, Dalton *et al, Epilepsia* 1985, **26**, 127–30) via CYP3A4 inhibition. Studies show no interaction with ranitidine (eg. n=8, RCT, Dalton *et al, Drug Intell Clin Pharm* 1985, **19**, 941–44), which would thus appear a safer option.

### Indinavir + carbamazepine
See protease inhibitors + carbamazepine.

### Influenza vaccine + carbamazepine *
A transient 10% increase in carbamazepine levels occurred in one study (n=55, open, Jann and Fidone, *Clin Pharm* 1986, **5**, 817–20) and there is a report of carbamazepine toxicity after influenza vaccination (Robertson, *Pediatr Neurol* 2002, **26**, 61–63).

## ISONIAZID + CARBAMAZEPINE
Rapid carbamazepine toxicity may occur via 3A4 inhibition by isoniazid, in this potentially serious interaction (Valsalan and Cooper, *BMJ* 1982, **285**, 261–62). It may be potentiated by cimetidine (n=1, Garcia *et al, Ann Pharmacother* 1992, **26**, 841–42). Monitor carefully for toxicity.

### Isotretinoin + carbamazepine
Isotretinoin may slightly reduce carbamazepine plasma levels and alter the CBZ:CBZ-E ratio (n=1, Marsden *et al, Br J Derm* 1988, **119**, 403).

### Itraconazole + carbamazepine
Sub-therapeutic itraconazole levels may occur with carbamazepine so monitor for lack of efficacy (n=12, open, Tucker *et al, Clin Infect Dis* 1992, **14**, 165–74).

### Lamotrigine + carbamazepine
See lamotrigine (*4.5.4*).

### Levetiracetam + carbamazepine *
See levetiracetam (*4.5.5*).

### Levothyroxine (thyroxine) + carbamazepine
Levothyroxine metabolism is accelerated by carbamazepine, increasing the thyroxine requirements in hypothyroidism.

### Lithium + carbamazepine *
Although this combination is often used in rapid-cycling bipolar disorder, neurotoxicity may rarely occur without increased plasma levels (n=5, Shukla *et al, Am J Psych* 1984, **141**, 1604–6; Marcoux, *Ann Pharmacother* 1996, **30**, 547), but mostly in patients with pre-existing brain damage (n=5, Shukla *et al, Am J Psych* 1984, **141**, 1604–6), although there is some evidence of minor cognitive impairment on the combination (*Human Psychopharmacology* 1990, **5**, 41–45). An additive antithyroid effect can occur, lowering T4 and free T4 levels (n=23, open, Post *et al, Am J Psych* 1990, **147**, 615–20) and there is a case of lithium intoxication due to carbamazepine-induced renal failure (n=1, Mayan *et al, Ann Pharmacother* 2001, **35**, 560–62). Monitor carefully and regularly for signs of toxicity.

### MAOIs + carbamazepine
See MAOIs (*4.3.4*).

### Mefloquine + carbamazepine *
The UK SPC now states that mefloquine may antagonise the anticonvulsant effect of carbamazepine.

### Methadone + carbamazepine *
See methadone (*4.6.7*).

### Methylphenidate + carbamazepine *
See methylphenidate (*4.6.8*).

### Metoclopramide + carbamazepine
There is a single case of apparent carbamazepine neurotoxicity occurring after metoclopramide 30mg/d was added, which resolved when metoclopramide was stopped (Sandyk, *BMJ* 1984, **288**, 830).

### Metronidazole + carbamazepine
Plasma carbamazepine levels rose by 60% in a woman when metronidazole was added, resulting in symptoms of toxicity (Patterson, *Ann Pharmacother* 1994, **28**, 1304).

### Mianserin + carbamazepine
See mianserin (*4.3.3.1*).

### Miconazole + carbamazepine
An isolated case report of an adverse response has appeared (n=1, *Therapie* 1982, **37**, 437–41).

### Mirtazapine + carbamazepine *
See mirtazapine (*4.3.3.2*).

### NEFAZODONE + CARBAMAZEPINE *
See nefazodone (*4.3.3.4*).

### Neuromuscular blocking agents + carbamazepine
Studies show reduced responses and recovery times to NMBAs (*Anaesthesiology* 1989, **71**, A784), eg. vecuronium doses need to be significantly higher in patients on maintenance carbamazepine (n=8, open, Whalley and Ebrahim, *Br J Anaesth* 1994, **72**, 125–26) and recovery times can be 40–60% faster with atracurium and pancuronium (n=53, open, Tempelhoff *et al, Anesth Analg* 1990, **71**, 665–69).

### NICOUMALONE + CARBAMAZEPINE
The metabolism of nicoumalone is accelerated by carbamazepine to give a reduced effect.

### ORAL CONTRACEPTIVES + CARBAMAZEPINE *
The CYP3A4 metabolism of OCs is accelerated by carbamazepine to give a **reduced contraceptive effect** (n=10, open, Crawford *et al, B J Clin Pharmacol* 1990, **30**, 892–96). Any OC needs to contain at least 50mcg ethinylestradiol or Depot Provera given every 10 rather than 12 weeks (review by Crawford, *CNS Drugs* 2002, **16**, 263–72) or alternative methods used.

### Orlistat + carbamazepine *
A small trial suggested lack of interaction (n=8, open, 8/52, Hilger *et al, J Clin Psychopharmacol* 2002, **22**, 68–70).

### Oxcarbazepine + carbamazepine
See oxcarbazepine (*4.5.6*).

### Paracetamol + carbamazepine *
Co-administration with carbamazepine may reduce the bioavailability of paracetamol (UK SPC).

### Paroxetine + carbamazepine
See paroxetine (*4.3.2.4*).

## Phenobarbital + carbamazepine

Phenobarbital induces carbamazepine CYP3A4 metabolism, slightly reducing plasma levels (Christianssen and Dam, *Acta Neurol Scand* 1973, **49**, 543–46). Carbamazepine may raise phenobarbital levels but not to a clinically significant amount (d/b, c/o, 4×21/7, Cereghino *et al Clin Pharmacol Ther* 1975, **18**, 733–41).

## PHENYTOIN + CARBAMAZEPINE *

Phenytoin induces carbamazepine CYP3A4 metabolism, reducing levels, often dramatically (eg. n=2, Chapron *et al, Drug Intell Clin Pharm* 1993, **27**, 708–11) but with some evidence of increased carbamazepine metabolites in the CSF (discussion by Morris *et al, Neurology* 1987, **37**, 1111–18). Monitoring of CBZ levels is useful, although seizure control may not be affected. Raised carbamazepine levels may result from withdrawal of phenytoin via removal of enzyme induction (n=2, Chapron *et al, Ann Pharmacother* 1993, **27**, 708–11) so carbamazepine levels must be monitored during the deinduction stage to prevent toxicity developing. Raised phenytoin concentrations may occur due to CYP2C19 inhibition (Lakehal *et al, Epilepsy Res* 2002, **52**, 79–83) and mean serum levels have increased by 35% (some studies by up to 100%), producing neurotoxicity (Browne *et al, Neurology* 1988, **38**, 1146–50). The clinical effect may be limited but best to monitor the levels of both drugs.

## Progabide + carbamazepine

Progabide has no effect on carbamazepine levels (n=24, open, Bianchett *et al, Epilepsia* 1987, **28**, 68–73) but may slightly increase CBZ-E levels.

## Protease inhibitors + carbamazepine *

The UK SPC notes the possibility of reduced plasma indinavir and saquinavir levels with the carbamazepine. Raised carbamazepine levels and toxicity (including hepatic) have been reported with ritonavir, a protease inhibitor, probably by CYP3A4 inhibition and a recent SPC addition (n=1, Kato *et al, Pharmacother* 2000, **20**, 851–54; Antonio *et al, Ann Pharmacother* 2001, **35**, 125–26).

## PROTON-PUMP INHIBITORS + CARBAMAZEPINE

Carbamazepine induces the CYP3A4 metabolism of **omeprazole**, but has little or no effect on hydroxylation via CYP2C19 (n=5, open, Bertilsson *et al, Br J Clin Pharmacol* 1997, **44**, 186–89). Multiple dose omeprazole may decrease carbamazepine clearance by 40% and thus increase levels (Naidu *et al, Drug Invest* 1994, **7**, 8–12). **Pantoprazole** appears to have no effect on carbamazepine (n=20, RCT, Huber *et al, Int J Clin Pharmacol Ther* 1998, **36**, 521–24).

## Rifampicin + carbamazepine *

Rapid CYP3A4 induction may lower carbamazepine levels (n=1, Zolezzi, *Am J Psych* 2002, **159**, 874).

## Ritonavir + carbamazepine *

See protease inhibitors + phenytoin.

## Saquinavir + carbamazepine *

See protease inhibitors + phenytoin.

## SERTINDOLE + CARBAMAZEPINE *

See sertindole (*4.2.7.2*).

## Sertraline + carbamazepine

See sertraline (*4.3.2.5*).

## Smoking + carbamazepine *

See smoking (*4.7.4*).

## St. John's wort + carbamazepine *

See anticonvulsants + St. John's wort (*4.3.3.8*).

## Stiripentol + carbamazepine *

Stiripentol appears to be a potent inhibitor of CBZ-E formation (n=14, Tran *et al, Clin Pharmacol Ther* 2002, **71**, P33).

## Theophylline + carbamazepine

Theophylline metabolism is accelerated by carbamazepine to give a reduced effect (Mitchell *et al, NZ Med J* 1986, **99**, 69–70).

## Tiagabine + carbamazepine

See tiagabine (*4.5.10*).

### Tibolone + carbamazepine*
The UK SPC states that carbamazepine may reduce the activity of tibolone.

### Topiramate + carbamazepine
See topiramate (*4.5.11*).

### Tramadol + carbamazepine*
The UK SPC states that carbamazepine may reduce the activity of tramadol.

### Trazodone + carbamazepine*
Raised carbamazepine levels have been reported with 100mg/d trazodone (n=1, Romero *et al, Ann Pharmacother* 1999, **33**, 1370).

### TRICYCLICS + CARBAMAZEPINE*
The CYP3A4 metabolism of imipramine, doxepin and amitriptyline may be accelerated by carbamazepine to give plasma levels reduced by 42–50% (eg. n=29 + 22, Leinonen *et al, J Clin Psychopharmacol* 1991, **11**, 313–18). This is a common combination and other evidence supports this to be a clinically significant interaction but not well recognised, although one study concluded that while the total blood concentration of imipramine drops with carbamazepine, the free fraction remains unchanged so dose increases may not be necessary (n=13, Szymura-Oleksiak *et al, Psychopharmacology (Berl)* 2001, **154**, 38–42).

### VALPROATE + CARBAMAZEPINE
Valproate seems to inhibit several carbamazepine metabolic pathways, resulting in raised CBZ-10,11-epoxide concentrations (which has led to CBZ-E-induced psychosis, n=1, McKee *et al, Lancet* 1989, **i**, 167, and so watch closely for toxicity) but sometimes with unchanged carbamazepine levels (n=27, Bernus *et al, Br J Clin Pharmacol* 1997, **44**, 21). In one study, carbamazepine levels fell by about 25% when valproate was added (n=7, open, Levy *et al, Epilepsia* 1984, **25**, 338–45). Valproate may also displace carbamazepine from binding sites on plasma proteins (n=8, open, Macphee, *B J Clin Pharmacol* 1988, **25**, 59–66). Conversely, carbamazepine induces valproate metabolism, reducing plasma levels by about 20% (n=8, RCT, d/b, c/o, Larkin *et al, B J Clin Pharmacol* 1989, **27**, 313–22). This is probably minor **but** a mean 59% increase in valproate levels can occur on carbamazepine withdrawal (n=6, open, Jann *et al, Epilepsia* 1988, **29**, 578–81). Overall, no adjustments in carbamazepine doses are generally necessary but beware of the altered metabolite ratio and monitor if clinical symptoms change.

### Venlafaxine + carbamazepine
See venlafaxine (*4.3.3.8*).

### Vigabatrin + carbamazepine*
See vigabatrin (*4.5.13*).

### Vincristine + carbamazepine
Carbamazepine significantly increases the clearance of vincristine, probably by CYP3A4 induction (n=15, open, Villikka *et al, Clin Pharmacol & Therapeut* 1999, **66**, 589–93).

### WARFARIN + CARBAMAZEPINE
The metabolism of warfarin is accelerated by carbamazepine, reducing efficacy. Warfarin doses may need to be increased by up to 100% (Kendall and Boivin, *Ann Int Med* 1981, **94**, 280) and then reduced carefully if carbamazepine is discontinued (n=1, Denbow and Fraser, *South Med J* 1990, **83**, 981).

### Zaleplon + carbamazepine
See zaleplon (*4.1.4*).

### Ziprasidone + carbamazepine*
See ziprasidone (*4.2.7.2*).

---

## 4.5.2 ETHOSUXIMIDE

### Barbiturates + ethosuximide
See phenobarbital (*4.5.7*).

### Carbamazepine + ethosuximide
Carbamazepine induces ethosuximide metabolism, reducing plasma levels by about 17% (n=6, open, 55/7, Warren *et al, Clin Pharmacol Ther* 1980, **28**, 646–51), although this is probably of minor significance.

## Phenytoin + ethosuximide
A study showed that phenytoin reduces ethosuximide plasma levels (n=198, retrospective, Battion *et al, Clin Pharmacokinet* 1982, **7**, 176–80).

## Valproate + ethosuximide
Valproate may increase ethosuximide plasma levels by up to 50% via enzyme inhibition, although this may only be a transient effect (n=6, Pisani *et al, Epilepsia* 1984, **25**, 229–33), and standard regular monitoring will probably suffice especially if the patient becomes sedated. Conversely, adding ethosuximide to valproate may reduce valproate levels by 28% (n=4) and stopping ethosuximide from an ethosuximide/valproate combination has led to valproate levels rising by 36% (n=9). The mechanism is unknown (open, Salke-Kellermann *et al, Epilepsy Res* 1997, **26**, 345–49).

## Zotepine + ethosuximide
See anticonvulsants + zotepine (*4.2.6*).

---

## 4.5.3 GABAPENTIN

Gabapentin is not protein bound so there is little chance of an interaction via this mechanism. Excretion is almost completely via the kidney.

## Antacids + gabapentin
The antacid 'Maalox' reduces gabapentin levels by 20% when given concurrently. Separating the doses by 2 hours resulted in only a 5% reduction in levels (Busch *et al, Epilepsia* 1993, **34**[Suppl 2], 158), although nothing is reported with other antacids.

## Benzodiazepines + gabapentin
No significant interaction has been noted with clonazepam (n=127, d/b, p/c, UKGSG, *Lancet* 1990, **335**, 1114–17).

## Carbamazepine + gabapentin
No significant interaction has been noted (eg. n=26, open, Radulovic *et al, Epilepsia* 1994, **35**, 155–61).

## Cimetidine + gabapentin
1200mg/d of cimetidine reduces gabapentin clearance by about 10%, which requires no dosage adjustment (Busch *et al, Epilepsia* 1993, **34**[Suppl 2], 158).

## Levetiracetam + gabapentin
See levetiracetam (*4.5.5*).

## Lithium + gabapentin
See lithium (*4.4*).

## Oral contraceptives + gabapentin
No change in the kinetics of norethisterone and ethinyloestradiol were seen with gabapentin (Busch *et al, Epilepsia* 1993, **34**[Suppl 2], 158).

## Phenobarbital + gabapentin
One study showed no significant interaction (n=12, open, 52/7, Hooper *et al, B J Clin Pharmacol* 1991, **31**, 171–74).

## Phenytoin + gabapentin *
Only a slight trend towards an increase in phenytoin levels has been observed (eg. Graves *et al, Pharmacotherapy* 1989, **9**, 196) although toxic phenytoin levels have occurred with gabapentin 600mg/d (eg. n=1, Sanchez-Romero *et al, Rev Neurol* 2002, **34**, 952–53).

## Valproate + gabapentin
No significant interaction has been noted n=127, d/b, p/c, UKGSG, *Lancet* 1990, **335**, 1114–17).

## Zotepine + gabapentin
See anticonvulsants + zotepine (*4.2.6*).

---

## 4.5.4 LAMOTRIGINE

## Barbiturates + lamotrigine
Lamotrigine has no significant effect on primidone and phenobarbital (*Epilepsia* 1991, **32**[Suppl 1], 96).

## Benzodiazepines + lamotrigine
Lamotrigine has no significant effect on clonazepam (*Epilepsia* 1991, **32**[Suppl 1], 96).

## Bupropion + lamotrigine *
In a small study, steady-state bupropion 300mg/d had no effect on a single 100mg dose of lamotrigine (n=12, RCT, Odishaw and Chen, *Pharmacotherapy* 2000, **20**, 1448–53).

## Carbamazepine + lamotrigine
A higher incidence of CNS side-effects with the combination has been noted (Gilman, *Ann Pharmac-*

*other* 1995, **29**, 144–51). Toxicity appears more likely to occur when lamotrigine is added to CBZ if the initial CBZ level is high, eg. greater than 8mg/L, probably via a pharmacodynamic interaction (n=47, open, Besag *et al, Epilepsia* 1998, **39**, 183–87). However, lamotrigine does not seem to raise the levels of CBZ-E and, in fact, may reduce the levels of this active but toxic metabolite (n=14, open, Eriksson and Boreus, *Ther Drug Monit* 1997, **19**, 499–501). Carbamazepine reduces the half-life of lamotrigine from 29 hours to about 15 hours via enzyme induction (n=23, open, 4/52, Jawad *et al, Epilepsia Res* 1987, **1**, 194–201).

### Clozapine + lamotrigine *
See clozapine (*4.2.2*).

### Fosphenytoin + lamotrigine
See phenytoin + lamotrigine.

### Levetiracetam + lamotrigine
See levetiracetam (*4.5.5*).

### Lithium + lamotrigine *
See lithium (*4.4*).

### Oral contraceptives + lamotrigine*
No loss of contraceptive effect has been reported (*Epilepsia* 1991, **32**[Suppl 1], 96) but a mean 47% (range 41-64%) reduction in lamotrigine levels (leading to increased seizures) has been reported when OC's were added to lamotrigine (n=7, Sabers *et al, Epilepsy Res* 2001, **47**, 151–54).

### Oxcarbazepine + lamotrigine
See oxcarbazepine (*4.5.6*).

### Phenytoin + lamotrigine
Lamotrigine has no effect on phenytoin but phenytoin reduces the half-life of lamotrigine from 29 hours to about 15 hours via enzyme induction (*Epilepsia Res* 1987, **1**, 194–201).

### Sertraline + lamotrigine
Sertraline may increase lamotrigine levels eg. sertraline 25mg/d doubled lamotrigine levels in one case and, in another, a 25mg/d dose reduction halved lamotrigine levels, despite a 33% lamotrigine dose increase (n=2, Kaufman and Gerner, *Seizure* 1998, **7**, 163–65).

### Topiramate + lamotrigine *
Topiramate does not cause a significant change in lamotrigine levels (n=24, Berry *et al, Epilepsia* 2002, **43**, 818–23).

## VALPROATE + LAMOTRIGINE *
Lamotrigine has no significant effect *on* valproate levels (n=372, open, Mataringa *et al, Ther Drug Monit* 2002, **24**, 631–36) but valproate inhibits lamotrigine glucuronidation resulting in reduced clearance (by 21%), and half-life lengthening from 29 hours to about 59 hours (eg. Panay *et al, Lancet* 1993, **341**, 445), probably a dose-dependent (n=28, open, Kanner and Frey, *Neurology* 2000, **55**, 588–91) rather than concentration-dependent effect (n=62, open, Gidal *et al, Epilepsy Res* 2000, **42**, 23–31). Lamotrigine should start at half the usual dose when used with valproate. The interaction has been used to enhance the effect of both drugs with striking responses in adults and children with intractable epilepsy (Pisani *et al, Lancet* 1993, **341**, 1224), although disabling postural and action tremor has been reported (n=3, Reutens *et al, Lancet* 1993, **342**, 185–86), as has a raised incidence of rash. In one study, adding lamotrigine to valproate was without incident in 76%, but with an increased incidence of rash and other adverse effects in the remainder (n=112, open, Faught *et al, Epilepsia* 1999, **40**, 1135–40). There is a case of lupus induced by valproate and lamotrigine (n=1, Echaniz-Laguna *et al, Epilepsia* 1999, **40**, 1661–63).

### Zotepine + lamotrigine
See anticonvulsants + zotepine (*4.2.6*).

---

### 4.5.5 LEVETIRACETAM
Levetiracetam has, as yet, no demonstrable drug interactions. It is not bound to plasma proteins, is not extensively metabolised and does not inhibit nor induce CYP1A2, 2A6, 2C8/9/10, 2C19, 2D6, 2E1 and 3A4, nor UGT enzymes.

**Alcohol + levetiracetam**
No data is available (MI).

**Carbamazepine + levetiracetam** *
Lack of pharmacokinetic interaction has been demonstrated (MI), although disabling symptoms consistent with carbamazepine toxicity (but with unchanged levels) have been reported with the addition of levetiracetam (n=4, Sisodiya *et al, Epilepsy Res* 2002, **48**, 217–19).

**Digoxin + levetiracetam** *
Lack of pharmacokinetic interaction has been demonstrated (n=11, RCT, Levy *et al, Epilepsy Res* 2001, **46**, 93–99).

**Food + levetiracetam**
Levetiracetam absorption is slightly slowed by food, but total absorption remains unchanged.

**Gabapentin + levetiracetam**
Lack of pharmacokinetic interaction has been demonstrated (MI).

**Lamotrigine + levetiracetam**
Lack of pharmacokinetic interaction has been demonstrated (MI).

**Oral contraceptives + levetiracetam** *
Lack of pharmacokinetic interaction has been demonstrated (n=18, RCT, d/b, c/o, Ragueneau *et al, Epilepsia* 2002, **43**, 697–702).

**Phenobarbital + levetiracetam**
Lack of pharmacokinetic interaction has been demonstrated (MI). Lack of pharmacokinetic interaction has been demonstrated with primidone (MI).

**Phenytoin + levetiracetam**
Levetiracetam has no effect on the kinetics of phenytoin (n=6, open, Browne *et al, J Clin Pharmacol* 2000, **40**, 590–95).

**Probenecid + levetiracetam**
Probenecid may inhibit the clearance of the primary (inactive) metabolite of levetiracetam, but not of the parent drug (MI).

**Valproate + levetiracetam** *
Lack of pharmacokinetic interaction has been demonstrated (n=16, open, c/o, Coupez *et al, Epilepsia* 2003, **44**, 171–78).

**Warfarin + levetiracetam** *
Lack of pharmacokinetic interaction has been demonstrated (n=42, RCT, Ragueneau-Majlessi *et al, Epilepsy Res* 2001, **47**, 55–63).

**Zotepine + levetiracetam**
See anticonvulsants + zotepine (*4.2.6*).

### 4.5.6 OXCARBAZEPINE

Oxcarbazepine and MHD inhibit cytochrome CYP2C19, and induce 3A4 and 3A5 at higher doses (n=4, open, Patsalos *et al, Eur J Clin Pharmacol* 1990, **39**, 187–88), but probably not lower doses (n=8, Larkin *et al, Br J Clin Pharmacol* 1991, **31**, 65–71).

**Alcohol + oxcarbazepine**
Caution should be exercised if alcohol is taken (SPC) as additive sedation can occur.

**Antipsychotics + oxcarbazepine**
It should be well known that carbamazepine reduces the plasma levels of many antipsychotics. As oxcarbazepine seems to have little enzymeinducing activity, when substituted for carbamazepine, it can lead to plasma levels of antipsychotics (haloperidol, chlorpromazine and clozapine) increasing by 50–200% over 2–4 weeks (n=6, Raitasuo *et al, Psychopharmacology* [*Berl*] 1994, **116**, 115–16).

**Carbamazepine + oxcarbazepine**
Addition of oxcarbazepine to carbamazepine has resulted in a less than 10% change in carbamazepine plasma levels (US SPC).

**Ciclosporin + oxcarbazepine** *
Trough ciclosporin levels may fall slightly with oxcarbazepine (n=1, Rosche *et al, Clin Neuropharmacol* 2001, **24**, 113–16).

**Cimetidine + oxcarbazepine**
Cimetidine has no effect on the kinetics of oxcarbazepine (n=8, c/o, Keranen *et al, Acta Neurol Scand* 1992, **85**, 239–42).

**Citalopram + oxcarbazepine**
Carbamazepine may induce the plasma levels of citalopram, and when oxcarbazepine is substituted, citalopram plasma levels may rise

(n=2, Leinonen *et al, Pharmacopsychiatry* 1996, **29**, 156–58).

### Erythromycin + oxcarbazepine
Erythromycin has no effect on the kinetics of oxcarbazepine (n=8, c/o, Keranen *et al, Acta Neurol Scand* 1992, **86**, 120–23).

### Escitalopram + oxcarbazepine
See citalopram above.

### Felodipine + oxcarbazepine
Repeated doses of oxcarbazepine reduce felodipine AUC and plasma levels by 28% and 34% respectively, which might slightly reduce its clinical effect (n=8, open, Zaccara *et al, Ther Drug Monit* 1993, **15**, 39–42).

### Fosphenytoin + oxcarbazepine
See phenytoin + oxcarbazepine.

### Lamotrigine + oxcarbazepine
Oxcarbazepine induces the metabolism of lamotrigine, and so plasma levels fall by 29%. Reduced doses may be necessary if oxcarbazepine is discontinued (n=222, retrospective, May *et al, Therap Drug Monit* 1999, **21**, 175–81).

### Lithium + oxcarbazepine
The combination of lithium and oxcarbazepine might theoretically cause enhanced neurotoxicity (SPC).

### MAOIs + oxcarbazepine
A theoretical risk of interaction exists (SPC).

## ORAL CONTRACEPTIVES + OXCARBAZEPINE *
Oxcarbazepine can produce significant reductions in some OC plasma levels, with some breakthrough bleeding (n=13, Klosterskov-Jensen *et al, Epilepsia* 1992, **33**, 1149–52; n=16, RCT, Fattore *et al, Epilepsia* 1999, **40**, 783–87). Any OC needs to contain at least 50mcg ethinylestradiol or Depot Provera given every 10 rather than 12 weeks (review by Crawford, *CNS Drugs* 2002, **16**, 263–72) or alternative methods used.

### Phenobarbital + oxcarbazepine
Phenobarbital levels raised by 14% and reduced oxcarbazepine/MHD levels by 25% have been observed with the combination (US SPC). The

clinical significance has not been quantified.

### Phenytoin + oxcarbazepine
Doses of oxcarbazepine above 1200mg/d have been reported to increase phenytoin levels by up to 40% (less than 10% for doses below 1200mg/d), probably due to CYP2C19 inhibition (microsomes, Lakehal *et al, Epilepsy Res* 2002, **52**, 79–83) and so close monitoring of phenytoin is essential, especially at higher doses (n=4, Patsalos *et al, Eur J Clin Pharmacol* 1990, **39**, 187–88).

### Propoxyphene + oxcarbazepine
Unlike carbamazepine, propoxyphene has no significant effect on oxcarbazepine kinetics (n=8, open, Mogensen *et al, Acta Neurol Scand* 1992, **85**, 14–17).

### Valproate + oxcarbazepine
Valproate levels may rise if oxcarbazepine replaces carbamazepine (n=4, Patsalos *et al, Eur J Clin Pharmacol* 1990, **39**, 187–88). There is also a theoretical increase in the risk of teratogenicity, due to the presence of increased levels of metabolites.

### Verapamil + oxcarbazepine
Verapamil can produce a 20% reduction in MHD levels, which could be clinically significant (US SPC).

### Warfarin + oxcarbazepine
Oxcarbazepine does not appear to affect the anticoagulant activity of warfarin (n=10, 1/52, Kramer *et al, Epilepsia* 1992, **33**, 1145–48).

### Zotepine + oxcarbazepine
See anticonvulsants + zotepine (*4.2.6*).

## 4.5.7 PHENOBARBITAL (phenobarbitone) AND PRIMIDONE

### ALCOHOL + BARBITURATES
See alcohol (*4.7.1*).

### ANTICOAGULANTS + BARBITURATES
A well-documented and clinically significant reduction in anticoagulant levels and effects with barbiturates occurs. Doses of the anticoagulant may need to be raised by up to 60% if a barbiturate is started.

## ANTIPSYCHOTICS + BARBITURATES
See antipsychotics (*4.2.1*) and quetiapine (*4.2.4*).

### Benzodiazepines + barbiturates
See benzodiazepines (*4.1.1*).

### Beta-blockers + barbiturates
Blood levels of metoprolol and propranolol are reduced by barbiturates (open, Seideman *et al, B J Clin Pharmacol* 1987, **23**, 267–71). Those of timolol (n=12, RCT, c/o, Mantyla *et al, Eur J Clin Pharmacol* 1983, **24**, 227–30), atenolol and nadolol do not appear to be altered.

### Bupropion + phenobarbital
See bupropion (*4.6.4*).

## CALCIUM-CHANNEL BLOCKERS + BARBITURATES
Phenobarbital may induce the CYP3A4 metabolism of verapamil (open, Rutledge *et al, J Pharmacol Exp Therap* 1988, **246**, 7–13), diltiazem, isradipine, nicardipine and nifedipine, reducing efficacy and so some care may be needed.

### Carbamazepine + phenobarbital
See carbamazepine (*4.5.1*).

### Charcoal, activated + barbiturates
If given within 5 minutes, activated charcoal can almost completely prevent barbiturate absorption and can be an effective adjunct in overdose treatment (Neuvonen and Elonen, *Eur J Clin Pharmacol* 1980, **17**, 51–57).

### Chloramphenicol + barbiturates
Chloramphenicol metabolism is accelerated by barbiturates to reduce oral chloramphenicol efficacy (n=1, Koup *et al, Clin Pharmacol Ther* 1978, **24**, 571–75).

## CICLOSPORIN + PHENOBARBITAL
Even low dose phenobarbital induces the CYP3A4 metabolism of ciclosporin (Carstensen, *et al, B J Clin Pharmacol* 1986, **21**, 550–51).

### Cimetidine + phenobarbital
Reduced actions of both can occur but this is of very limited significance (n=8, open, 6/52, Somogyi *et al, Eur J Clin Pharmacol* 1981, **19**, 343).

### Clozapine + phenobarbital
See clozapine (*4.2.2*).

## CORTICOSTEROIDS + PHENOBARBITAL
CYP3A4 induction reduces the effect of some corticosteroids (Brooks *et al, NEJM* 1972, **286**, 1125–28).

### Digoxin + phenobarbital
Digitoxin (but not digoxin) levels can be reduced by up to 50% by phenobarbital, probably via enzyme induction and of little significance (Kaldor *et al, Int J Clin Pharmacol Biopharm* 1975, **12**, 403–7).

### Disopyramide + phenobarbital
Barbiturates induce the CYP3A4 metabolism of disopyramide, reducing plasma levels (n=14, open, Kapil *et al, Br J Clin Pharmacol* 1987, **24**, 781–91).

### Doxorubicin + phenobarbital
Indirect results from one study showed that doxorubicin clearance may be increased by barbiturates and so doses may need to be increased (Riggs *et al, Clin Pharmacol Ther* 1982, **31**, 263).

### Doxycycline + phenobarbital
Doxycycline levels are reduced by CYP3A4 induction by barbiturates, reducing its effect, with a halved half-life (Neuvonen and Penttila, *BMJ* 1974, **2**, 535–36). Other tetracyclines appear not to interact.

### Ethosuximide + phenobarbital
A possible interaction may lead to reduced phenobarbital effectiveness. A study showed that ethosuximide levels may fall if primidone is used (n=198, Battino *et al, Clin Pharmacokinet* 1982, **7**, 176–80).

### Fenoprofen + phenobarbital
Phenobarbital may slightly increase fenoprofen metabolism and reduce its efficacy (Helleberg *et al, B J Clin Pharmacol* 1974, **1**, 371).

### Furosemide (frusemide) + phenobarbital
One study showed no effect of barbiturates on furosemide diuresis (n=10, open, Lambert *et al, Clin Pharmacol Ther* 1983, **34**, 170–75).

**Gabapentin + phenobarbital**
See gabapentin (*4.5.3*).

**Glyceryl trinitrate + phenobarbital**
A reduced nitrate effect via enzyme induction may occur.

**Griseofulvin + phenobarbital**
Cases have been reported of griseofulvin levels reduced by up to 45% by phenobarbital, either by enzyme induction, eg. (*Am J Hosp Pharm* 1986, **16**, 52) or reduced absorption.

**Indinavir + barbiturates**
The BNF notes that the plasma levels of indinavir may be reduced by barbiturates via CYP3A4 induction.

**Influenza vaccine + phenobarbital**
A transient 20% rise in barbiturate levels has been reported (n=35, open, Jann and Fidone, *Clin Pharm* 1986, **5**, 817–20).

**Isoniazid + primidone**
Steady state primidone levels rose by 80% in a patient given isoniazid 300mg/d (n=1, Sutton and Kupferberg, *Neurology* 1975, **25**, 1179–81). Blood levels should be monitored.

**Ketoconazole + phenobarbital**
A case exists of reduced ketoconazole levels in a man taking phenobarbital (n=1, *Antimicrob Ag Chemother* 1982, **21**, 151–58).

**Lamotrigine + barbiturates**
See lamotrigine (*4.5.4*).

**Levetiracetam + phenobarbital**
See levetiracetam (*4.5.5*).

**Levonorgestrel + phenobarbital**
There is a case of levonorgestrel implant (Norplant) failing twice in a woman also taking phenobarbital (Shane-McWhorter *et al*, *Pharmacotherapy* 1998, **18**, 1360–64).

**Levothyroxine (thyroxine) + barbiturates**
Levothyroxine metabolism is accelerated by barbiturates to give a reduced effect and this may increase requirements in hypothyroidism.

**Lidocaine + barbiturates**
Serum lidocaine levels may be lower in people taking barbiturates than in those not (LeLorier, *Toxicol Appl Pharmacol* 1978, **44**, 657), via CYP3A4 induction.

**MAOIs + barbiturates**
See MAOIs (*4.3.4*).

**Memantine + barbiturates** *
See memantine (*4.6.7*).

**Methadone + barbiturates** *
See methadone (*4.6.8*).

**Methyldopa + phenobarbital**
Methyldopa levels are not reduced by phenobarbital (eg. Kristensen *et al*, *BMJ* 1973, **1**, 49).

**Metronidazole + phenobarbital**
One study showed metronidazole metabolism to be accelerated by barbiturates, reducing levels by a third (*Clin Pharmacol Ther* 1987, **41**, 235).

**Nicotinamide + primidone**
There are report of reduced conversion from primidone to phenobarbital (n=1, Bourgeois *et al*, *Neurology* 1982, **32**, 1122).

**NICOUMALONE + BARBITURATES**
Nicoumalone metabolism is accelerated by barbiturates, giving a reduced anticoagulant effect.

**ORAL CONTRACEPTIVES + PHENOBARBITAL** *
Contraceptive failure via CYP3A4 enzyme induction has been reported many times (eg. n=5, Back *et al*, *Contraception* 1980, **22**, 495–503). Use higher dose OC (equivalent to 50–100mcg ethinylestradiol, eg. Eugynon-50) or Depot Provera given every 10 rather than 12 weeks (Crawford, *CNS Drugs* 2002, **16**, 263–72) and adjust the dose if necessary or use alternative contraceptive methods. See also levonorgestrel.

**Oxcarbazepine + phenobarbital**
See oxcarbazepine (*4.5.6*).

**Paracetamol + phenobarbital**
An isolated case of enhanced hepatotoxicity exists (Pirotte, *Ann Int Med* 1984, **101**, 403).

**Paroxetine + phenobarbital**
See paroxetine (*4.3.2.4*).

**Pethidine + phenobarbital**
A single case of severe CNS sedation on the combination has been reported (n=12, open, c/o, Stambaugh *et al*, *J Clin Pharmacol* 1978, **18**, 482–90).

**Phenylbutazone + phenobarbital**
Reduced levels of phenylbutazone may occur (Levi *et al*, *Lancet* 1968, **i**, 1275).

**Phenytoin + phenobarbital**
See barbiturates + phenytoin (*4.5.8*).

**Pyridoxine + phenobarbital**
Large doses of pyridoxine (eg. 200mg/d) can reduce phenobarbital levels by up to 40–50% (Hansson and Sillanpaa, *Lancet* 1976, **i**, 256).

**Quetiapine + barbiturates**
See quetiapine (*4.2.4*).

**Quinidine + phenobarbital**
CYP3A4 induction may reduce quinidine levels by up to 50% (Rogers and Blackman, *Drug Intell Clin Pharm* 1983, **17**, 819–20).

**Rifampicin + barbiturates**
Rifampicin has been shown to induce barbiturate metabolism and so a decreased efficacy might be predicted (for effect on hexobarbital: n=40, open, see Richter *et al*, *Eur J Clin Pharmacol* 1980, **17**, 197–202).

**Smoking + phenobarbital** *
See smoking (*4.7.3*).

**St. John's wort + phenobarbital** *
See anticonvulsants + St John's wort (*4.7.3*).

**Sulphonamides + barbiturates**
No reports of interaction exist.

**Testosterone + phenobarbital**
A reduced steroid effect via CYP3A4 induction can occur.

**THEOPHYLLINE + BARBITURATES**
Theophylline metabolism is accelerated by barbiturates in premature neonates, giving a reduced effect (n=24, Kandrokas *et al*, *Ther Drug Monit* 1990, **12**, 139–43).

**Tiagabine + phenobarbital**
See tiagabine (*4.5.10*).

**Topiramate + phenobarbital**
See topiramate (*4.5.11*).

**TRICYCLICS + BARBITURATES**
See tricyclics (*4.3.1*).

**Tropisetron + barbiturates**
Phenobarbital reduces the plasma levels of tropisetron (BNF).

**WARFARIN + PHENOBARBITAL**
See anticoagulants + barbiturates in this section.

**VALPROATE + PHENOBARBITAL**
Valproate may reduce glucuronidation and increase phenobarbital plasma concentrations by up to 25% (mean of 5.87mg/L, n=20, Bernus *et al*, *B J Clin Pharmacol* 1994, **38**, 411–16), increasing sedation and other side-effects (eg. Kapetanovic *et al*, *Clin Pharmacol Ther* 1981, **99**, 314), although this may only be transient (review by Keys, *Drug Intell Clin Pharm* 1982, **16**, 737–39). Thus, reduce the phenobarbital dosage if sedation occurs and monitor blood levels regularly.

**Vigabatrin + phenobarbital**
See vigabatrin (*4.5.13*).

**Zaleplon + phenobarbital**
See zaleplon (*4.1.6*).

**Zotepine + phenobarbital**
See anticonvulsants + zotepine (*4.2.6*).

## 4.5.8 PHENYTOIN

**Phenytoin** has a narrow therapeutic index and is prone to drug-drug interactions via several mechanisms, eg. extensive binding to plasma proteins, CYP3A4 induction and saturable metabolism. It can be displaced, giving an increased proportion of free active phenytoin, significant where TDM just measures **total** phenytoin rather than the proportion of free (hence active) phenytoin. Measuring free phenytoin levels may be more appropriate in certain circumstances, eg. interaction with drugs displacing it from binding sites, as well as hypoalbuminaemia and renal failure, eg. total plasma levels may be within the alleged therapeutic range. Decreased protein binding produces a decline in total concentration, but no change in free levels (Wilkinson, *Pharmacol Rev* 1987, **39**, 1–47).

Thus, low concentrations may appear below the normal therapeutic range, but free (active) levels are appropriate, prompting inappropriately increased doses or discontinuation. More usual concentrations could have toxic (seizure-inducing) free levels, which might then provoke an increase in dosage to bring it into the 'optimum' range (see Toler, *Ann Pharmacother* 1994, **28**, 808–9).

**Review:** pharmacokinetic interactions (Nation *et al, Clin Pharmacokinet* 1990, **18**, 37–60).

### Acetazolamide + phenytoin

Case reports indicate that acetazolamide may enhance the osteomalacia secondary to phenytoin use in a few patients (n=2, Mallette, *Arch Int Med* 1977, **137**, 1013).

### ALCOHOL + PHENYTOIN

See alcohol (*4.7.1*).

### Allopurinol + phenytoin

Phenytoin toxicity may occur with repeated high-dose allopurinol (Ogiso et al, *et al, J Pharmacobiodyn* 1990, **13**, 36–43).

### AMIODARONE + PHENYTOIN

Amiodarone reduces phenytoin metabolism, toxicity developing over 2 weeks (n=7, open, 8/52, Nolan *et al, Am J Cardiol* 1990, **65**, 1252–57). Reduce the phenytoin dose by at least 25%.

### Anaesthetics + phenytoin

Documentation of an interaction is limited but case reports of phenytoin toxicity following halothane exist (Karlin and Kutt, *J Pediat* 1970, **76**, 941–44) and so caution should be used.

### Antacids + phenytoin

Antacids probably reduce phenytoin levels, shown in several studies (eg. n=6, McElnay *et al, Br J Clin Pharmacol* 1982, **13**, 501) and seizure control could be impaired. It is thus best to separate doses by about three hours or use ranitidine (see also cimetidine).

### ANTIPSYCHOTICS + PHENYTOIN

See antipsychotics (*4.2.1*), clozapine (*4.2.2*), quetiapine (*4.2.4*), risperidone (*4.2.5*) and zotepine (*4.2.6*).

### Ayurvedic herbal mixtures + phenytoin

See shankhapushpi + phenytoin.

### Barbiturates + phenytoin

At normal doses it is thought that phenobarbital enhances the metabolism of phenytoin, reducing levels but the clinical effect may be minimal (n=6, open, Browne *et al, Neurology* 1988, **38**, 639–42). Phenytoin serum levels are increased by very high dose barbiturates and the effect may be dose-dependent with a curvilinear relationship (n=1, Kuranari *et al, Ann Pharmacother* 1995, **29**, 83–84). Care is also be needed if phenobarbital is stopped, as phenytoin levels may change. Vice versa, phenytoin may raise phenobarbital levels by up to 100%, producing increased sedation, probably of minor clinical significance (n=1, Porro *et al, B J Clin Pharmacol* 1982, **14**, 294–97) but regular monitoring should still be done, especially as a case of fatal agranulocytosis has been reported with the combination (n=1, Laurenson *et al, Lancet* 1994, **344**, 332–33).

### Benzodiazepines + phenytoin

Diazepam, clonazepam and chlordiazepoxide have been reported to potentiate phenytoin leading to possible intoxication although some studies have not shown this effect. It is best to monitor phenytoin plasma levels regularly. Conversely, phenytoin induces the metabolism of clonazepam, reducing levels by up to 50% (n=27, open, Sjo *et al, Eur J Clin Pharmacol* 1975, **8**, 249–54).

### Bupropion + phenytoin

See bupropion (*4.6.4*).

### Buspirone + phenytoin

See buspirone (*4.1.2*).

### Calcium-channel blockers + phenytoin *

High dose **diltiazem** (240mg 8hourly) increases phenytoin levels and toxicity and in one patient a 40% reduction in phenytoin dose was needed to stabilise levels (n=2, Clarke *et al, Pharmacotherapy* 1993, **13**, 402–5; n=43, Bahls *et al, Neurology* 1991, **41**, 740–42). **Isradipine** can raise phenytoin levels producing toxicity, probably by P450 inhibition (n=1, Cachat and Tufro, *Ann Pharmacother* 2002, **36**, 1399–402). Lack of interaction between **nifedipine** and phenytoin has been noted in several studies (eg. n=8, open, Schellens *et al, B J Clin Pharmacol* 1991, **31**, 175–78), although tremor, headache and restlessness with phenytoin levels tripled has been reported, which fell to normal after the nifedipine was discontinued (n=1, Ahmad *et al, J Am Coll Cardiol* 1984, **3**, 1581). **Verapamil** may inhibit phenytoin metabolism (*Neurology* 1991, **41**, 740–42). Almost complete lack of verapamil absorption (at up to 400mg/d) has been reported (n=1, Woodcock *et al, NEJM* 1991, **325**, 1179). The effects of isradipine and **nicardipine** may be reduced by phenytoin.

### CARBAMAZEPINE + PHENYTOIN *
See carbamazepine (*4.5.1*).

### Charcoal, activated + phenytoin
Phenytoin absorption is almost completely (98%) prevented if activated charcoal is taken within 5 minutes and reduced by about 80% if given after one hour (n=6, open, c/o, Neuvonen *et al, Eur J Clin Pharmacol* 1978, **13**, 213–18). Multiple-dose activated charcoal has been used successfully over several days for phenytoin toxicity secondary to hepatitis and thus, extraordinarily, may have some use even up to a week after phenytoin ingestion (n=1, Howard *et al, Ann Pharmacother* 1994, **28**, 201–3).

### Chinese medicines + phenytoin
Phenytoin poisoning after using Chinese proprietary medicines has been reported (n=1, Lau *et al, Hum & Experimental Toxicol* 2000, **19**, 385–86).

### Chloral + phenytoin
Dichloralphenazone has been shown to decrease phenytoin levels (n=5, Riddell *et al, B J Clin Pharmacol* 1980, **9**, 118P), although whether the chloral part of the molecule was responsible for this is not known.

### CHLORAMPHENICOL + PHENYTOIN
Phenytoin toxicity may occur with oral chloramphenicol via enzyme inhibition (*Aust J Hosp Pharm* 1987, **17**, 51–53). This is an uncommon combination but a well-documented and serious interaction. Monitor very carefully if the combination has to be used.

### Chlorphenamine (chlorpheniramine) + phenytoin
Two isolated cases exist of phenytoin intoxication (Pugh *et al, Br J Clin Pharmac* 1975, **2**, 173–75) and so care may be needed.

### CICLOSPORIN + PHENYTOIN
Ciclosporin levels can be reduced by 80% by phenytoin, via increased metabolism (n=6, Freeman *et al, B J Clin Pharmacol* 1984, **18**, 887–93).

### Ciprofloxacin + phenytoin
Phenytoin toxicity would be expected to occur via P450 enzyme inhibition, and raised phenytoin levels from oral ciprofloxacin has been reported (n=1, Hull, *Ann Pharmacother* 1993, **27**, 1283) and IV ciprofloxacin has led to halved phenytoin levels (n=1, *Int Pharm J* 1992, **6**, 109), and resulting in sub-therapeutic levels, seizures and increased phenytoin dose requirements with IV ciprofloxacin (Dillard *et al, Ann Pharmacother* 1992, **26**, 263; n=1, Brouwers and de Boer, *Ann Pharmacother* 1997, **31**, 498). There is a case of a phenytoin dose increased during ciprofloxacin therapy, only for toxic levels to appear when the antibiotic course was completed (n=1, Pollak and Slayter, *Ann Pharmacother* 1997, **31**, 61–64). More frequent phenytoin plasma level monitoring would be wise. Higher steady state phenytoin levels have also been reported with clinafloxacin

(Randinitis *et al, Drugs* 1999, **58**[Suppl 2], 254–55).

## CLOZAPINE + PHENYTOIN

See clozapine (*4.2.2*).

## CORTICOSTEROIDS + PHENYTOIN

Steroid metabolism is accelerated by phenytoin to give a reduced effect (McLelland and Jack, *Lancet* 1978, **i**, 1096–97) and so higher doses may be needed. Hydrocortisone may be less affected than other steroids. Phenytoin levels may also be changed.

### Co-trimoxazole + phenytoin

A single case exists of phenytoin intoxication caused by increased plasma phenytoin levels and an enhanced antifolate effect (Gillman and Sandyk, *Arch Int Med* 1985, **102**, 559).

## DEXAMETHASONE + PHENYTOIN

Phenytoin levels may be halved by dexamethasone (eg. n=1, Lackner, *Pharmacother* 1991, **11**, 344–47; n=1, Griffiths and Taylor, *Can J Hosp Pharm* 1999, **52**, 96–98) and very high doses of phenytoin may be necessary (eg. 900mg/d) to maintain levels (case and review by Recueno *et al, Ann Pharmacother* 1995, **29**, 935). Regular and frequent monitoring of phenytoin levels is thus essential.

### Dextropropoxyphene + phenytoin

See propoxyphene + phenytoin.

## DIAZOXIDE + PHENYTOIN

Reduced phenytoin levels occur via increased metabolism (Turck *et al, Presse Med* 1986, **15**, 31) so monitor carefully.

## DICOUMAROL + PHENYTOIN

Phenytoin levels may rise rapidly by over 100% (Hansen *et al, Acta Med Scand* 1971, **189**, 15–19) via enzyme inhibition. Avoid the combination if at all possible or monitor very carefully.

### Digoxin + phenytoin

Phenytoin reduces digoxin half-life by 30% (n=6, RCT, open, c/o, Rameis *et al, Eur J Clin Pharmacol* 1985, **29**, 49–53) so monitor both carefully.

## DISOPYRAMIDE + PHENYTOIN

Phenytoin reduces the plasma levels of disopyramide, possibly to below therapeutic levels (Kessler *et al, Clin Pharm* 1982, **1**, 263–64).

### Disulfiram + phenytoin

Phenytoin toxicity and delirium may occur via enzyme inhibition (eg. n=1, Brown *et al, Ann Emerg Med* 1983, **12**, 310–13).

### Dopamine + phenytoin

Hypotension may occur in patients on dopamine if phenytoin is added (n=5, Bivins *et al, Arch Surg* 1978, **113**, 245–49) although lack of interaction has been reported in a well studied case (n=1, Torres *et al, Ann Pharmacother* 1995, **29**, 1300–1).

### Doxifluridine + phenytoin *

Elevated phenytoin levels have been reported (n=1, Konishi *et al, Ann Pharmacother* 2002, **36**, 831–34).

## DOXYCYCLINE + PHENYTOIN

Doxycycline metabolism is accelerated by phenytoin to give a reduced effect, with a halved half-life (Penttila *et al, BMJ* 1974, **ii**, 470). Other tetracyclines appear not to interact, so make dosage adjustments or use an alternative.

### Enteral feeds + phenytoin

See nasogastric feeds + phenytoin.

### Ethosuximide + phenytoin

See ethosuximide (*4.5.2*).

## FLUCONAZOLE + PHENYTOIN

Oral fluconazole inhibits phenytoin metabolism producing rapid and severe toxicity (Mitchell and Holland, *BMJ* 1989, **298**, 1315; reviewed by Cadle *et al, Ann Pharmacother* 1994, **28**, 191–95). Continuous phenytoin plasma monitoring is recommended with doses of fluconazole at 200mg/d or above (n=20, RCT, p/c, Blum *et al, Clin Pharmacol & Ther* 1991, **49**, 420–5).

### Fluorouracil + phenytoin *

Cases exist of elevated phenytoin levels 11 weeks after starting fluorouracil and leucovorin, possibly via CYP2C9 inhibition (n=1, Gilbar and Brodribb, *Ann Pharmacother* 2001,

**35**, 1367–70; n=1, Rosemergy and Findlay, *NZ Med J* 2002, **115**, U124).

## FLUVOXAMINE + PHENYTOIN *

Fluvoxamine may triple phenytoin levels with associated toxicity, probably by 2C9/19 inhibition (n=1, Mamiya *et al, Ther Drug Monit* 2001, **23**, 75–77).

## FLUOXETINE + PHENYTOIN

Phenytoin levels raised by 66% have been reported two weeks after fluoxetine was added, with levels falling back to nearly normal within a week of stopping fluoxetine (n=1, Woods *et al, N Z Med J* 1994, **107**, 19). Conversely, loss of phenytoin efficacy as a result of fluoxetine discontinuation has been reported (n=1, Shad and Preskorn, *J Clin Psychopharmacol* 1999, **19**, 471).

## Folic acid + phenytoin

Serum folate decreases when phenytoin is started and folic acid supplementation is usually used to counteract this folate deficiency. However, folic acid supplementation in folate-deficient patients changes the kinetics of phenytoin and plasma phenytoin levels are then reduced (n=4, open, Berg *et al, Ther Drug Monit* 1983, **5**, 389–99). Folate supplementation should thus be started with phenytoin. If started later, phenytoin levels should be monitored and changes in seizure activity looked for (extensive review by Lewis *et al, Ann Pharmacother* 1995, **29**, 726–35).

## Furosemide (frusemide) + phenytoin

The diuretic effect may be reduced by up to 50% by phenytoin (eg. Bissoli *et al, Recenti Prog Med* 1996, **87**, 227–28) so larger doses may be needed.

## Gabapentin + phenytoin *

See gabapentin (*4.5.3*).

## Glucagon + phenytoin

Patients on phenytoin may get false negatives with glucagon stimulation tests (*Ann Int Med* 1974, **80**, 697).

## Glucocorticoids + phenytoin

A reduced steroid effect via enzyme induction is possible.

## Griseofulvin + phenytoin

It is postulated that reduced griseofulvin levels may occur, via enzyme induction (*Am J Hosp Pharm* 1986, **16**, 52).

## H2-blockers + phenytoin

Phenytoin toxicity has occurred with **cimetidine** (n=1, Phillips and Hansky, *Med J Aus* 1984, **141**, 602), with a 30% increase in phenytoin levels in other reports (*Pharm International* 1985, **6**, 223–24; n=9, open, Salem *et al, Epilepsia* 1983, **24**, 284–88) and so toxicity may occur, even with OTC cimetidine (n=9, Rafi *et al, Ann Pharmacother* 1999, **33**, 769–74). The effect is rapid and can occur within two days. An alternative is **ranitidine**, where lack of interaction has been shown (eg. Watts *et al, B J Clin Pharmacol* 1983, **15**, 499–500). There have, however, been several cases of elevated phenytoin levels (eg. Tse *et al, Ann Pharmacother* 1993, **27**, 1448–51), including where oral ranitidine induced toxic phenytoin levels, remaining high for a week even though the phenytoin was stopped, and only dropping when the ranitidine was also stopped (Tse and Iagmin, *Ann Int Med* 1994, **120**, 892–93). Best to monitor phenytoin levels. No significant interaction occurs with **famotidine** (n=10, RCT, open, c/o, Sambol *et al, Br J Clin Pharmacol* 1989, **27**, 83–87) nor **nizatidine** (Bachmann *et al, Br J Clin Pharmacol* 1993, **36**, 380–82).

## Indinavir + phenytoin

Plasma indinavir levels may be reduced by phenytoin (BNF).

## Influenza vaccine + phenytoin

This is reported to reduce total and free phenytoin levels (Smith *et al, Clin Pharm,* 1988, **7**, 828–32), although one study showed a transient 60% increase in levels (Jann and Fidone, *Clin Pharm* 1986, **5**, 817–20).

### Irinotecan + phenytoin *
Phenytoin appears to decrease plasma levels of irinotecan (Murry et al, J Pediatr Hematol Oncol 2002, **24**, 130–33).

### ISONIAZID + PHENYTOIN
Phenytoin toxicity may occur via enzyme induction (n=1, Witmer and Ritschel, *Drug Intell Clin Pharm* 1984, **18**, 483–86) so observe for toxicity and reduce phenytoin doses if necessary.

### KETOCONAZOLE + PHENYTOIN
Phenytoin toxicity may occur via enzyme inhibition. Ketoconazole may also have a reduced effect.

### Lamotrigine + phenytoin
See lamotrigine (*4.5.4*).

### Levetiracetam + phenytoin
See levetiracetam (*4.5.5*).

### Levodopa + phenytoin
Levodopa can be completely antagonised by phenytoin (Mendez et al, *Arch Neurol* 1975, **32**, 44–46) and so increased levodopa doses may be necessary.

### Levothyroxine (thyroxine) + phenytoin
Levothyroxine metabolism is accelerated by phenytoin, increasing requirements (Blackshear et al, *Ann Int Med* 1983, **99**, 341–42).

### Lidocaine (lignocaine) + phenytoin
CNS effects may be enhanced if used concurrently (Karlsson et al, *Eur J Clin Pharmacol* 1974, **7**, 455–59). Sinoatrial arrest has been reported (Wood, *BMJ* 1971, **i**, 645) which was reversed by isoproterenol. The mechanism is probably enhanced cardiac depression.

### Lithium + phenytoin
See lithium (*4.4*).

### Losartan + phenytoin *
Losartan has no effect on phenytoin but losartan levels may rise via 2C9 inhibition (n=16, RCT, c/o, Fischer et al, *Clin Pharmacol Ther* 2002, **72**, 238–46).

### Memantine + phenytoin *
See memantine (*4.6.7*).

### Methadone + phenytoin *
See methadone (*4.6.8*).

### Methotrexate + phenytoin
An increased antifolate effect with phenytoin may occur.

### Methylphenidate + phenytoin
See methylphenidate (*4.6.9*).

### METRONIDAZOLE + PHENYTOIN
Mild phenytoin toxicity via enzyme inhibition is possible (Blyden et al, *J Clin Pharmacol Ther* 1988, **28**, 240–45).

### MEXILITINE + PHENYTOIN
Mexilitine levels are reduced by up to 50% via enzyme induction and adjust dosage as necessary (n=6, open, Begg et al, *Br J Clin Pharmac* 1982, **14**, 219–23).

### MICONAZOLE + PHENYTOIN
Phenytoin toxicity via enzyme inhibition has been reported (n=2, Rolan et al, *BMJ* 1983, **287**, 1760).

### Mirtazapine + phenytoin *
See mirtazapine (*4.3.3.2*).

### Nasogastric feeds + phenytoin
Reduced phenytoin levels have been reported with nasogastric feeds (eg. Osmolite, Ensure) and other enteral feeds (*Pharm J* 1989, **243**, 181; *Hosp Pharm* 1989, **24**, 562). One study showed that the absolute bioavailability of phenytoin was unaffected by enteral feeds but that the absorption patterns were significantly different, with phenytoin sodium more rapidly absorbed (n=10, RCT, Doak et al, *Pharmacother* 1998, **18**, 637–45). Phenytoin dosage should be spaced to one hour before feeding or two hours after feeding (tube may need to be clamped). Monitor plasma levels frequently (see comment by Au Yeung and Ensom, *Ann Pharmacother* 2000, **34**, 896–905, 32 refs).

### Nefazodone + phenytoin
Single doses of nefazodone have no effect on phenytoin kinetics (n=18, Marino et al, *J Clin Psychopharmacol* 1997, **17**, 27–33).

### Neuromuscular blocking agents + phenytoin
Phenytoin reduces the effects of most NMBAs, eg. pancuronium (n=1, Hickey et al, *Anaesthesia* 1988, **43**,

757–59; n=1, Liberman *et al, Int J Clin Pharmacol Ther Toxicol* 1988, **26**, 371–74) and vecuronium (n=100, Ornstein *et al, Anesthesiology* 1987, **67**, 191–96), although atracurium appears unaffected.

### NICOUMALONE + PHENYTOIN

Nicoumalone metabolism is induced by phenytoin, reducing its effect, although enhancement has also been reported.

### Nitrofurantoin + phenytoin

There is a report of a stable epileptic developing seizures when nitrofurantoin was added, requiring increased phenytoin dosage (n=1, Heipertz and Pilz, *J Neurol* 1978, **218**, 297–301).

### NSAIDs + phenytoin

One study shows no interaction to occur with **ibuprofen** (n=10, open, Bachmann, *B J Clin Pharmacol* 1986, **21**, 165–69) but toxicity has been reported (n=1, Sandyk, *S Afr Med J* 1982, **62**, 592). Phenytoin levels may be increased by **aspirin** via binding displacement (n=10, open, 11/7, Leonard *et al, Clin Pharmacol Ther* 1981, **29**, 56–60), free levels seeming to remain constant. Transient toxicity may be the only effect and then only at high (900mg 4hrly) aspirin doses. Plasma phenytoin levels may be increased by **azapropazone** via enzyme inhibition (n=5, open, Geaney *et al, Br J Clin Pharmac* 1983, **15**, 727–34).

### ORAL CONTRACEPTIVES + PHENYTOIN *

Contraceptive failure via enzyme induction has been reported many times (eg. *JAMA* 1986, **256**, 238–40). Any OC needs to contain at least 50mcg ethinylestradiol, Depot Provera given every 10 rather than 12 weeks (Crawford, *CNS Drugs* 2002, **16**, 263–72), or alternative contraceptive methods used.

### Oxcarbazepine + phenytoin

See oxcarbazepine (*4.5.6*).

### Paroxetine + phenytoin

See paroxetine (*4.3.2.4*).

### Pethidine + phenytoin

Attenuation of pethidine's effect via enzyme induction, with increased metabolite levels, is possible (n=4, open, Pond and Kretschzmar, *Clin Pharmacol Ther* 1981, **29**, 273).

### Phenindione + phenytoin

No interaction is thought to occur (n=54, open, Skovsted *et al, Acta Med Scand* 1976, **199**, 513).

### PHENYLBUTAZONE + PHENYTOIN

Phenytoin toxicity may occur via enzyme inhibition and plasma protein displacement (n=6, open, Neuvonen *et al, Eur J Clin Pharmacol* 1979, **15**, 263–68). Dosage adjustment may be necessary.

### PROGABIDE + PHENYTOIN

Phenytoin levels may rise by up to 40% (n=6, open, Bianchetti, *Epilepsia* 1987, **28**, 68–73).

### Propoxyphene + phenytoin

Large doses of propoxyphene may raise phenytoin levels (Kutt *et al, Ann NY Acad Sci* 1971, **179**, 704) but normal doses have little or no effect (n=16, open, Hansen *et al, Acta Neurol Scand* 1980, **61**, 357).

### Proton pump inhibitors + phenytoin

A lack of effect of **omeprazole** on phenytoin kinetics has been reported, as has a mild rise in phenytoin levels (n=10, RCT, d/b, c/o, 9/7, Prichard *et al, Br J Clin Pharmac* 1987, **24**, 543–45). The SPC for omeprazole states that patients should be monitored on this combination and doses adjusted if necessary. Lack of interaction has been reported with **pantoprazole** (n=23, RCT, d/b, p/c, c/o, Middle *et al, Int J Clin Pharmacol Ther* 1996, **34**, S72–S75).

### Pyrimethamine + phenytoin

There is an increased risk of an antifolate effect.

### Pyridoxine + phenytoin

Large doses of pyridoxine (eg. 200mg/d) can reduce phenytoin levels by up to 40–50% (Hansson and Sillanpaa, *Lancet* 1976, **i**, 256). Monitoring levels would thus be wise.

## Quetiapine + phenytoin
See quetiapine (*4.2.4*).

## QUINIDINE + PHENYTOIN
A reduced quinidine effect may occur via enzyme induction (Anon, *NEJM* 1983, **308**, 724–25) so monitoring of quinidine levels or effect may be necessary.

## RIFAMPICIN + PHENYTOIN
Significant reductions in phenytoin levels may occur via enzyme induction (Abajo, *BMJ* 1988, **297**, 1048).

## Sertindole + phenytoin *
See sertindole (*4.2.7.2*).

## Sertraline + phenytoin
See sertraline (*4.3.2.5*).

## Shankhapushpi + phenytoin
It has been recommended to avoid the Ayurvedic herbal mixture shank hapushpi, as decreased plasma phenytoin levels may occur (mentioned by Fugh-Berman, *Lancet* 2000, **355**, 134–38).

## Statins + phenytoin
There is a case of phenytoin reducing the therapeutic effect of simvastatin and atorvastatin, probably via 3A4 induction (n=1, Murphy and Dominiczak, *Postgrad Med J* 1999, **75**, 359–60).

## St. John's wort + phenytoin *
See anticonvulsants + St John's wort (*4.3.3.9*).

## SUCRALFATE + PHENYTOIN
One study showed a small reduction in phenytoin bioavailability (n=9, open, Hall *et al, Drug Intell Clin Pharm* 1986, **20**, 607–11) by decreased absorption. This can be avoided by giving phenytoin two hours or more after sucralfate.

## Sulphonamides + phenytoin
Phenytoin toxicity is known to be possible via P450 inhibition with cotrimoxazole (Gillman and Sandyk, *Ann Int Med* 1985, **102**, 559) and other sulphonamides so monitor plasma levels and reduce phenytoin doses if necessary.

## Theophylline + phenytoin
Phenytoin produces a 45% increase in clearance of theophylline so higher doses may be needed (n=8, open, Adebayo, *Clin Exp Pharmacol Physiol* 1988, **15**, 883–87). Phenytoin absorption may also be reduced (*Int Pharm J* 1989, **3**, 98–101). Separating the doses by 1–2 hours may reduce the effect.

## Tiagabine + phenytoin
See tiagabine (*4.5.10*).

## Ticlopidine + phenytoin *
Ticlopidine 500mg/d inhibits phenytoin clearance so dose adjustment and careful monitoring should be considered (n=6, Donahue *et al, Clin Pharmacol & Therapeut* 1999, **66**, 563–68; n=1, Privitera and Welty, *Arch Neurology* 1996, **53**, 1191–92), especially since the onset of phenytoin toxicity may be delayed by several weeks (n=1, Dahm and Brors, *Tidsskr Nor Laegeforen* 2002, **122**, 278–80).

## Tolbutamide + phenytoin
Mild phenytoin toxicity may occur via increased free levels (n=18, Tassaneeyakul *et al, B J Clin Pharmacol* 1992, **34**, 494–98).

## Topiramate + phenytoin
See topiramate (*4.5.11*).

## Trazodone + phenytoin
There is a report phenytoin toxicity developing when relatively high dose trazodone was added to therapy (n=1, Dorn, *J Clin Psych* 1986, **47**, 89).

## TRIMETHOPRIM + PHENYTOIN
Plasma phenytoin levels and the antifolate effect may be increased by trimethoprim.

## TRICYCLICS + PHENYTOIN *
Phenytoin levels may be raised by imipramine (Perucca & Richens, *Br J Clin Pharmac* 1977, **4**, 485–86), but not nortriptyline (Houghton and Richens, *Int J Clin Pharmacol* 1975, **12**, 210–16) nor amitriptyline (*Clin Pharmacol Ther* 1975, **18**, 191–99), probably due to CYP2C19 inhibition (Shin *et al, Drug Metab Dispos* 2002, **30**, 1102–7). Phenytoin levels may need to be monitored frequently.

Tricyclics may lower the seizure threshold.

## VALPROATE + PHENYTOIN *

Valproate inhibits phenytoin metabolism and competes for its binding sites. If enzyme saturation has not occurred then this displacement of phenytoin leads to decreased bound but increased free phenytoin (n=12, Lai and Huang, *Biopharm Drug Dispos* 1993, **14**, 365–70). More phenytoin is then metabolised so the net result is reduced total and bound concentrations. The free concentration will remain about the same and **lower** plasma levels will still contain about the same amount of active/free drug. Thus, beware of raising the dose of phenytoin to bring the total plasma concentration into the 'therapeutic range' as it would then be toxic (Keys, *Drug Intell Clin Pharm* 1982, **16**, 737–39). If the enzyme is saturated, then displacement may lead to a stable total concentration but decreased bound and increased free phenytoin (n=6, open, Johnson *et al, B J Clin Pharmacol* 1989, **27**, 843–49). This could lead to toxic effects within the therapeutic range. In practice, phenytoin levels tend to fall initially by up to 50%, then return to normal over about five weeks. Toxicity is possible if levels were higher at the start. Reports of a toxic interaction are not common but monitoring is essential. Finally, changing valproate from a standard tablet to a slow-release tablet has been shown to result in a 30% rise in phenytoin levels and toxicity (n=11, Suzuki *et al, Eur J Clin Pharmacol* 1995, **48**, 61–63).

## VIGABATRIN + PHENYTOIN

Vigabatrin produces a mean 20–30% reduction in phenytoin levels (n=8, open, Rimmer and Richens, *B J Clin Pharmacol* 1989, **27**, 27S–33S) and may compromise seizure control (eg. n=89, s/b, Browne *et al, Neurology* 1987, **37**, 184–89).

## Vincristine + phenytoin

Phenytoin significantly increases the clearance of vincristine, probably by CYP3A4 induction (n=15, open, Villikka *et al, Clin Pharmacol & Therapeut* 1999, **66**, 589–93).

## WARFARIN + PHENYTOIN

Warfarin metabolism is accelerated by phenytoin, reducing its effect, although enhanced levels of both and death have been reported (n=1, Panegyres and Rischbieth, *Postgrad Med J* 1991, 67, **98**; Meisheri, *J Ass Physicians India* 1996, **44**, 661–62).

## Zinc + phenytoin

One case exists of reduced phenytoin levels probably caused by zinc (*Am J Hosp Pharm* 1988, **18**, 297–98).

## Zotepine + phenytoin

See anticonvulsants + zotepine (*4.2.6*).

## 4.5.9 PIRACETAM

## Warfarin + piracetam

Significantly prolonged prothrombin time has been reported with piracetam and warfarin (n=1, Pan and Ng, *Eur J Clin Pharmacol* 1983, **24**, 711).

## 4.5.10 TIAGABINE

Tiagabine appears to be metabolised by CYP3A4.

## Alcohol + tiagabine

Lack of interaction has been shown (n=20, RCT, d/b, p/c, c/o, Kastberg *et al, Drug Metabol Drug Interact* 1998, **14**, 259–73), although some caution is still advised.

## Benzodiazepines + tiagabine

No interaction with triazolam has been detected (n=12, RCT, Richens *et al, Drug Metabol Drug Interact* 1998, **14**, 159–77).

## Carbamazepine + tiagabine

Tiagabine clearance is 60% greater with carbamazepine, with plasma levels reduced by a factor of 1.5–3, probably by CYP3A4 induction (MI). There is no effect on carbamazepine.

## Cimetidine + tiagabine

No interaction has been detected (MI).

### Digoxin + tiagabine
Lack of interaction has been shown (n=13, open, Snel *et al, Eur J Clin Pharmacol* 1998, **54**, 355–57).

### Erythromycin + tiagabine
Lack of significant interaction has been shown (n=13, open, c/o, Thomsen *et al, J Clin Pharmacol* 1998, **38**, 1051–56).

### Fosphenytoin + tiagabine
See phenytoin + tiagabine.

### Oral contraceptives + tiagabine
No interaction has been detected (MI).

### Phenobarbitone + tiagabine
Tiagabine clearance is 60% greater in people also taking phenobarbital, with plasma levels reduced by a factor of 1.5–3, probably by CYP3A4 induction (MI). There is no effect on phenobarbital.

### Phenytoin + tiagabine
Tiagabine clearance is 60% greater in people also taking phenytoin and plasma levels are reduced by a factor of 1.5–3, probably by CYP3A4 induction (MI). There is no effect on phenytoin.

### Theophylline + tiagabine
No interaction has been detected (MI).

### Valproate + tiagabine
Tiagabine causes a 10–12% reduction in steady-state valproate levels whilst valproate increases free tiagabine levels by about 40% (n=12, open, Gustavson *et al, Am J Ther* 1998, **5**, 73–79).

### Warfarin + tiagabine
No interaction has been detected (MI).

### Zotepine + tiagabine
See anticonvulsants + zotepine *(4.2.6)*.

---

## 4.5.11 TOPIRAMATE

Topiramate is 13-17% bound to plasma proteins (and thus unlikely to interact with highly bound drugs) and not extensively metabolised. Excretion is mainly via the kidneys. *In vitro* data suggests that effects on hepatic enzyme metabolism are small and interactions with antipsychotics, tricyclics, antide-pressants, caffeine, xanthines and coumarin are unlikely via this mechanism.

Concomitant use with drugs predisposing to nephrolithiasis (renal stone formation) is not recommended eg. allopurinol, megadose ascorbic acid, furosemide (frusemide), methyldopa, phenolphthalein abuse, steroids and Worcester Sauce overdose.

**Reviews**: Johannessen, *Epilepsia* 1997, **38**[Suppl 1], S18–S23; Bourgeois, *Epilepsia* 1996, **37**[Suppl 2], S14–S17).

### Acetazolamide + topiramate
There may be an increased risk of renal stone formation in susceptible patients.

### Barbiturates + topiramate
Topiramate has been shown to have no effect on the plasma levels of phenobarbital or primidone (Floren *et al, Epilepsia* 1989, **30**, 646). The effect of the barbiturates on topiramate has not been studied.

### Carbamazepine + topiramate *
Topiramate has been shown to have no effect on the plasma levels of CBZ or CBZ-E, although there is a suggestion that it may increase CBZ levels (n=2 + 23, Mack *et al, Seizure* 2002, **11**, 464–67) but topiramate levels may need to be lowered if CBZ is reduced or discontinued (n=12, open, Sachdeo *et al, Epilepsia* 1996, **37**, 774–80).

### Digoxin + topiramate
Topiramate may decrease the plasma concentration of digoxin, with peak levels reduced by 16%, possibly by reduced bioavailability. Dose reduction or routine digoxin blood levels might be considered.

### Lamotrigine + topiramate *
See lamotrigine *(4.5.4)*.

### Lithium + topiramate *
See lithium *(4.4)*.

### ORAL CONTRACEPTIVES + TOPIRAMATE *
Serum estrogen levels are reduced by topiramate in patients taking combined estrogen/progesterone oral contraceptives. An oral contraceptive containing not less than 35–50mcg of

estrogen or Depot Provera given every 10 rather than 12 weeks is recommended, or the use of alternative methods (n=12, Rosenfeld *et al, Epilepsia* 1997, **38**, 317–23; review by Crawford, *CNS Drugs* 2002, **16**, 263–72). Any changes in bleeding patterns should be reported. There were no contraceptive failures reported in 52 patients in early clinical trials.

### Phenytoin + topiramate
Decreases in phenytoin clearance may occur in a few patients with topiramate, probably via CYP2C19 inhibition (n=12, Sachdeo *et al, Epilepsia* 2002, **43**, 691–96). Conversely, topiramate plasma levels are reduced by about 40% by phenytoin, which could be important if phenytoin is withdrawn (Floren *et al, Epilepsia* 1989, **30**, 646).

### Triamterene + topiramate
There may be an increased risk of renal stone formation in susceptible patients.

### Valproate + topiramate *
Topiramate has been shown to produce a small but significant increase in valproate clearance, reducing plasma levels, although *enhanced* valproate side effects eg. apathy, hypothermia and raised LFTs have been reported (n=3, Longin *et al, Epilepsia* 2002, **43**, 451–54). Topiramate plasma levels are increased by about 15% by valproate, which could be important if valproate is withdrawn (MI).

### Zotepine + topiramate
See anticonvulsants + zotepine (*4.2.6*).

### 4.5.12 VALPROATE (sodium valproate, valproic acid, valproate semisodium, divalproex sodium etc)
### Antacids + valproate
A slight decrease in valproate absorption with antacids has been noted (n=7, open, May *et al, Clin Pharm* 1982, **1**, 244–47).

### ANTIDEPRESSANTS + VALPROATE
Antidepressants lower the seizure threshold and may antagonise valproate's anticonvulsant effect. Tri-

cyclic levels may be raised by 19% by valproate (n=15, open, amitriptyline and nortriptyline, Wong *et al, Clin Pharmacol Ther* 1996, **60**, 48–53) and status epilepticus has been reported, with valproate possibly elevating clomipramine to toxic levels (n=1, DeToledo *et al, Ther Drug Monit* 1997, **19**, 71–73; see also Fehr *et al, J Clin Psychopharmacol* 2000, **20**, 493–94).

### Antipsychotics + valproate *
See antipsychotics (*4.2.1*), aripiprazole (*4.2.7.1*) and risperidone (*4.2.5*).

### Aspirin + valproate
Valproate's effect and toxicity may be enhanced by repeated high-dose aspirin (n=3, Goulden *et al, Neurology* 1987, **37**, 1392–94), and levels may rise by 12–43% (n=6, open, Orr *et al, Clin Pharmacol Ther* 1982, **31**, 642–49), so the potential for interaction should be noted.

### Benzodiazepines + valproate *
See benzodiazepines (*4.1.1*).

### Bupropion + valproate
See bupropion (*4.6.4*).

### CARBAMAZEPINE + VALPROATE
See carbamazepine (*4.5.1*).

### Charcoal, activated + valproate
Activated charcoal reduces the absorption of sodium valproate by 65% (n=6, Neuvonen *et al, Eur J Clin Pharmacol* 1983, **24**, 243–46) but has no effect on valproate elimination (n=8, Al-Shareef *et al, Br J Clin Pharmacol* 1997, **43**, 109–11).

### Clozapine + valproate
See clozapine (*4.2.2*).

### Erythromycin + valproate
Valproate levels may rise three-fold when erythromycin is started, resulting in CNS toxicity (n=1, Redington *et al, Ann Int Med* 1992, **116**, 877–78).

### Ethosuximide + valproate
See ethosuximide (*4.5.2*).

### Fluoxetine + valproate
See fluoxetine (*4.3.2.2*).

### Fluvoxamine + valproate
See fluvoxamine (*4.3.2.3*).

**Gabapentin + valproate**
See gabapentin (*4.5.3*).

**H2-blockers + valproate**
One study showed that **cimetidine** reduces the clearance and prolongs the half-life of valproate but **ranitidine** does not interact (n=12, RCT, Webster *et al, Eur J Clin Pharmacol* 1984, **27**, 341–43).

**Isoniazid + valproate**
Enhanced hepatotoxicity has been reported (n=1, Dockweiler, *Lancet* 1987, **2**, 152).

**LAMOTRIGINE + VALPROATE** *
See lamotrigine (*4.5.4*).

**Levetiracetam + valproate** *
See levetiracetam (*4.5.5*).

**Methylphenidate + valproate** *
See methylphenidate (*4.6.8*).

**Oral contraceptives + valproate**
A reduced contraceptive effect has not been reported with valproate (Mattson *et al, JAMA* 1986, **256**, 238–40; n=6, Crawford *et al, Contraception* 1986, **33**, 23–29).

**Oxcarbazepine + valproate**
See oxcarbazepine (*4.5.6*).

**Paroxetine + valproate**
See paroxetine (*4.3.2.4*).

**PHENOBARBITAL + VALPROATE**
See phenobarbital (*4.5.7*).

**PHENYTOIN + VALPROATE**
See phenytoin (*4.5.8*).

**Thiopental + valproate**
An animal study suggested that the effects of thiopental may be slightly enhanced (Aguilera *et al, Br J Anaesth* 1986, **58**, 1380–83).

**Tiagabine + valproate**
See tiagabine (*4.5.10*).

**Topiramate + valproate** *
See topiramate (*4.5.11*).

**Tricyclics + valproate** *
See antidepressants above.

**Vigabatrin + valproate**
See vigabatrin (*4.5.13*).

**Warfarin + valproate**
Rapidly raised INR (to 3.9) has been reported after a single dose of valproate (Guthrie *et al, J Clin Psychopharmacol* 1995, **15**, 138–39). Care is thus needed.

**Zidovudine + valproate**
Valproate produces a dose-dependent inhibition of AZT glucuronidation, leading to raised zidovudine levels (Trapnell *et al, Antimicrob Agents Chemother* 1998, **42**, 1592–96), possibly by up to 3-fold (n=1, Akula *et al, Am J Med Sci* 1997, **31**, 244–46). This is a new UK SPC warning.

## 4.5.13 VIGABATRIN

Vigabatrin is not metabolised, does not induce enzymes and is not protein bound. It is renally excreted.

**Carbamazepine + vigabatrin** *
A 10% rise in carbamazepine levels has been reported with vigabatrin (n=66, Jedrzejczak *et al, Epilepsy Res* 2000, **39**, 115–20), as has an 18% reduction in steady-state carbamazepine plasma levels (n=15, Sanchez-Alcaraz *et al, J Clin Pharm Ther* 2002, **27**, 427–30).

**Oral contraceptives + vigabatrin**
Vigabatrin is unlikely to consistently affect the efficacy of oral contraceptives, although in one study two women showed reduced ethinylestradiol levels (n=113, Bartoli *et al, Epilepsia* 1997, **38**, 702–7).

**Phenobarbital + vigabatrin**
One study reported non-clinically significant 7–11% reductions in barbiturate levels (*Neurology* 1987, **37**, 184–89).

**PHENYTOIN + VIGABATRIN**
See phenytoin (*4.5.8*).

**Valproate + vigabatrin**
Lack of interaction has been shown (eg. McKee *et al, Epilepsia* 1993, **34**, 937–43) but a small rise in levels may occur (Lisart *et al, Eur Hosp Pharm* 1996, **2**, 33–36; disputed by Mumford, *Eur Hosp Pharm* 1996, **2**, 190–91).

**Zotepine + vigabatrin**
See anticonvulsants + zotepine (*4.2.6*).

## 4.6 OTHER DRUGS

### 4.6.1 ACAMPROSATE

Acamprosate is not protein bound, is excreted in the urine and is not significantly metabolised and so probably has a low liability for drug-drug interactions by these mechanisms.

**Alcohol + acamprosate**

See alcohol (*4.7.1*).

**Benzodiazepines + acamprosate**

Lack of interaction with diazepam has been shown (MI).

**Disulfiram + acamprosate**

Lack of interaction has been shown (n=118, RCT, p/c, 2yrs, Besson *et al, Alcohol Clin Exp Res* 1998, **22**, 573–79).

**Food + acamprosate**

Food reduces the oral absorption of acamprosate.

**Naltrexone + acamprosate** *

Naltrexone causes a clinically insignificant increase in acamprosate absorption (n=24, RCT, d/b, 7/7, Mason *et al, Neuropsychopharmacol* 2002, **27**, 596–606).

**Tricyclics + acamprosate**

Lack of interaction with imipramine has been shown (MI).

### 4.6.2 ANTICHOLINERGIC OR ANTIMUSCARINIC AGENTS

**Anticholinesterases + anticholinergics**

Some antagonism would be expected.

**Antipsychotics + anticholinergics**

See antipsychotics (*4.2.1*).

**Benzodiazepines + anticholinergics**

See benzodiazepines (*4.1.1*).

**Beta-blockers + anticholinergics**

Propantheline increased atenolol bioavailability by 36%, increasing its effect (open, Regardh *et al, Biopharm Drug Dispos* 1981, **2**, 79–87) but not metoprolol (n=15, open, Briant *et al, Eur J Clin Pharmacol* 1983, **25**, 353).

**Betel nut + anticholinergics**

Heavy betel nut consumption has resulted in severe EPSEs, possibly by antagonising the effect of procycli-

dine (n=1, Deahl, *Mov Disord* 1989, **4**, 330–32).

**H2-blockers + anticholinergics**

A single-dose study showed possible reduced cimetidine absorption (Kanto *et al, Br J Clin Pharmacol* 1981, **11**, 629–31) but not with ranitidine (n=12, open, Donn *et al, Pharmacother* 1984, **4**, 89–92) nor nizatidine (Knadler *et al, Clin Pharmac Ther* 1987, **42**, 514–20).

**Levodopa + anticholinergics**

Anticholinergics may reduce the peak blood levels of levodopa and reduce total absorption (Algeri *et al, Eur J Pharmacol* 1976, **35**, 293–99), possibly by slowed gut motility and increased gut metabolism.

**MAOIs + anticholinergics**

See MAOIs (*4.3.4*).

**Memantine + anticholinergics** *

See memantine (*4.6.7*).

**Nitrofurantoin + anticholinergics**

Nitrofurantoin bioavailability may be increased by anticholinergics (n=10, Mannisto, *Int J Clin Pharmacol Biopharm* 1978, **16**, 223–28).

**Olanzapine + biperiden**

See olanzapine (*4.2.3*).

**Paracetamol + anticholinergics**

Propantheline delays the absorption of paracetamol (Nimmo *et al, BMJ* 1973, **i**, 587–89).

**Procarbazine + anticholinergics**

Increased sedation could occur.

**SSRIs + anticholinergics**

There are several cases of the combination probably causing delirium, eg. **sertraline** and benzatropine (n=1, Byerly *et al, Am J Psych* 1996, **153**, 965–66), **paroxetine** and benzatropine (Armstrong and Schweitzer, *Am J Psych* 1997, **154**, 581–82, where paroxetine definitely raised benzatropine levels) and a variety (n=5, Roth *et al, J Clin Psych* 1994, **55**, 491–95). CYP2D6 inhibition seems the likely mechanism.

**Thiazide diuretics + anticholinergics**

Thiazide bioavailability may be enhanced (open, Beermann *et al, Eur J Clin Pharmacol* 1978, **13**, 385–87).

**Tricyclics + anticholinergics**
See tricyclics (*4.3.1*).

**Ziprasidone + anticholinergics** *
See ziprasidone (*4.2.7.2*).

**Zotepine + anticholinergics**
See zotepine (*4.2.6*).

## 4.6.3 ANTICHOLINESTERASES

### 4.6.3.1 DONEPEZIL

Donepezil is metabolised slowly by CYP2D6 and 3A4 to multiple metabolites, only one of which appears to be pharmacologically active.

**Anticholinergics + donepezil**
See anticholinesterases + anticholinergics (*4.6.2*).

**Antipsychotics + donepezil** *
Lack of interaction has been reported (MI) although there is a case of NMS with bromperidol (n=1, Ueki *et al, Nippon Ronen Igakkai Zasshi* 2001, **38**, 822–24) and severe EPSEs with risperidone (n=1, Magnuson *et al, Am J Psych* 1998, **155**, 1459).

**Cimetidine + donepezil**
Lack of significant pharmacokinetic interaction has been reported (n=19, open, Tiseo *et al, B J Clin Pharmacol* 1998, **46**[Suppl 1], 25–29).

**Digoxin + donepezil**
Lack of significant pharmacokinetic interaction has been reported (n=12, open, Tiseo *et al, B J Clin Pharmacol* 1998, **46**[Suppl 1], 40–44).

**Ketoconazole + donepezil**
Donepezil levels may rise by around 25% over a week (n=21, open, Tiseo *et al, B J Clin Pharmacol* 1998, **46**[Suppl 1], 30–34).

**Memantine + donepezil** *
See anticholinesterases + memantine (*4.6.7*).

**NMBAs + donepezil**
A synergistic effect could be predicted (MI).

**NSAIDs + donepezil**
The manufacturers of donepezil recommend additional monitoring of patients at risk of developing ulcers, eg. if taking concomitant NSAIDs.

**SSRIs + donepezil**
Lack of interaction has been reported, although case reports exist with paroxetine (Carrier, *J Am Geriatr Soc* 1999, **47**, 1037).

**Suxamethonium + donepezil** *
Donepezil is a cholinesterase inhibitor and would be likely to enhance the effect of suxamethonium-type muscle relaxants (n=1, Crowe and Collins, *Anesthiology* 2003, **98**, 574–75) eg. during ECT (letter: Walker and Perks, *Anaesthesia* 2002, **57**, 1041).

**Theophylline + donepezil**
Lack of significant pharmacokinetic interaction has been reported (n=12, open, Tiseo *et al, B J Clin Pharmacol* 1998, **46**[Suppl 1], 35–39).

**Warfarin + donepezil**
Lack of significant pharmacokinetic interaction has been reported (n=12, open, Tiseo *et al, B J Clin Pharmacol* 1998, **46**[Suppl 1], 45–50).

### 4.6.3.2 GALANTAMINE

Galantamine is metabolised by CYP2D6 and CYP3A4, and any interaction with potent inhibitors may result in increased side-effects initially, eg. nausea and vomiting. Reduced maintenance doses might be appropriate (SPC). Galantamine has minimal effect on P450 enzymes.

**Anticholinergics + galantamine**
See anticholinesterases + anticholinergics (*4.6.2*).

**Antipsychotics + galantamine** *
Lack of interaction has been reported with risperidone (n=16, RCT, open, c/o, Huang *et al, J Clin Pharmacol* 2002, **42**, 1341–51).

**Beta-blockers + galantamine**
As galantamine may cause bradycardia, the UK SPC recommends care with drugs that significantly reduce heart rate, eg. beta-blockers.

**Digoxin + galantamine**
As galantamine may cause bradycardia, the UK SPC recommends care with drugs that significantly reduce heart rate, eg. digoxin. Galantamine

has been shown to have no effect on the kinetics of digoxin (SPC).

### Erythromycin + galantamine
A 12% increase in galantamine plasma levels has been reported (SPC), probably by CYP3A4 inhibition.

### Ketoconazole + galantamine
A 30% increase in galantamine plasma levels has been reported (SPC), probably by CYP3A4 inhibition, and so a reduced maintenance dosage might be appropriate.

### Memantine + galantamine *
See memantine (4.6.7).

### Paroxetine + galantamine
A 40% increase in galantamine plasma levels has been reported (SPC), probably by CYP2D6 inhibition, and so a reduced maintenance dosage might be appropriate.

### Suxamethonium + galantamine
Galantamine is likely to enhance the effect of suxamethonium-type muscle relaxants (SPC).

### Warfarin + galantamine
Galantamine has been shown to have no effect on the kinetics of warfarin (SPC).

---

### 4.6.3.3 RIVASTIGMINE

Rivastigmine has minimal protein binding, a short half-life and little effect on P450 enzymes and lack of significant interaction has been shown with 22 different therapeutic classes (Grossberg *et al, Int J Ger Psychiatry* 2000, **15**, 242–47).

### Anticholinergics + rivastigmine
See anticholinesterases + anticholinergics (4.6.2).

### Benzodiazepines + rivastigmine
No interaction in healthy volunteers has been seen (MI).

### Digoxin + rivastigmine
No interaction in healthy volunteers has been seen (MI).

### Fluoxetine + rivastigmine
No interaction in healthy volunteers has been seen (MI).

### Memantine + rivastigmine *
See anticholinesterases + memantine (4.6.7).

### Suxamethonium + rivastigmine
Rivastigmine may enhance the effect of suxamethonium-type muscle relaxants during anaesthesia (MI).

### Warfarin + rivastigmine
No interaction in healthy volunteers has been seen (MI).

---

### 4.6.4 BUPROPION

Bupropion is primarily metabolised by CYP2B6, with a significant first-pass metabolism, although poor metabolisers may accumulate hydroxybupropion, leading to reduced efficacy (n=12, Pollock *et al, Ther Drug Monit* 1996, **18**, 581–85).

**Review:** interactions with anticonvulsants (Popli *et al, Ann Clin Psychiatry* 1995, **7**, 99–101).

### Alcohol + bupropion
There is an increased risk of seizures, so alcohol should be avoided or minimised. Extreme care is needed in overdose, chronic use and in alcohol withdrawal states.

### Antipsychotics + bupropion *
The CSM recommends caution due to the possible increased risk of seizures.

### Carbamazepine + bupropion
Carbamazepine induces bupropion metabolism, markedly decreasing bupropion plasma levels (n=17, RCT, Ketter *et al, J Clin Psychopharmacol* 1995, **15**, 327–33).

### Ciclosporin + bupropion *
A life-threatening decrease in ciclosporin levels has been reported with bupropion (n=1, Lewis *et al, J Child Adolesc Psychopharmacol* 2001, **11**, 193–98).

### Cimetidine + bupropion
Cimetidine may inhibit the metabolism of bupropion, and increase adverse effects, although no effect on bupropion SR was seen in one study (n=24, RCT, open, Kustra *et al, J Clin Pharmacol* 1999, **39**, 1184–88).

### Clonidine + bupropion
Lack of interaction has been reported (n=8, RCT, d/b, c/o, Cubeddu *et al, Clin Pharmacol Ther* 1984, **35**, 576–84).

## Fluoxetine + bupropion *

Bupropion produces no significant changes in fluoxetine levels (open, 8/52, Kennedy *et al, J Clin Psych* 2002, **63**, 181–86). Panic disorder has been reported with the combination (Young, *J Clin Psych* 1996, **57**, 177–78).

## Fosphenytoin + bupropion

See phenytoin + bupropion.

## Guanfacine + bupropion

There is a report of a grand mal seizure with the combination (n=1, Tilton, *J Am Acad Child Adolesc Psych* 1998, **37**, 682–83).

## MAOIs + bupropion

Animal studies have indicated that acute bupropion toxicity might occur, and the combination is contra-indicated.

## Lamotrigine + bupropion *

See lamotrigine (*4.5.4*).

## Levodopa + bupropion

An increased incidence of side-effects has been reported with the combination.

## Moclobemide + bupropion

See MAOIs + bupropion.

## Paroxetine + bupropion *

Bupropion produces no significant changes in paroxetine levels (open, 8/52, Kennedy *et al, J Clin Psych* 2002, **63**, 181–86) but the CSM recommends caution.

## Phenobarbital + bupropion

Phenobarbital may induce the metabolism of bupropion, which would reduce bupropion efficacy.

## Phenytoin + bupropion

Phenytoin may induce the metabolism of bupropion, which would reduce bupropion efficacy.

## Pseudoephedrine + bupropion *

There is a report of acute myocardial ischaemia with the combination (n=1, Pederson *et al, Can J Cardiol* 2001, **17**, 599–601).

## Ritonavir + bupropion

Ritonavir may decrease the metabolism of bupropion, which would increase side-effects.

## Selegiline + bupropion

See MAOIs + bupropion.

## Smoking + bupropion

In a single-dose study, cigarettes had no detectable effect on bupropion kinetics (open, Hsyu *et al, J Clin Pharmacol* 1997, **37**, 737–43).

## Tricyclics + bupropion *

Bupropion has been reported to increase imipramine and desipramine levels, through decreased clearance (n=1, Shad and Preskorn, *J Clin Psychopharmacol* 1997, **17**, 118–19). Seizures have been reported with bupropion and trimipramine (n=1, Enns, *J Clin Psych* 2001, **62**, 478–77) as has nortriptyline toxicity secondary to bupropion SR (n=1, Weintraub, *Depress Anxiety* 2001, **13**, 50–52).

## Valproate + bupropion

Valproate does not seem to induce bupropion metabolism, but raised metabolite levels are possible (n=17, RCT, Ketter *et al, J Clin Psychopharmacol* 1995, **15**, 327–33).

## Venlafaxine + bupropion *

Bupropion has been shown to produce a significant increase in venlafaxine but decrease O-desmethylvenlafaxine levels (open, 8/52, Kennedy *et al, J Clin Psych* 2002, **63**, 181–86).

## Zolpidem + bupropion

There are some reported cases of anti-depressants and zolpidem causing short-lived hallucinations (eg. Elko *et al, Clin Toxicol* 1998, **36**, 195–203).

## 4.6.5 CLOMETHIAZOLE
### (chlormethiazole)

Clomethiazole inhibits CYP2E1.

## Alcohol + clomethiazole

See alcohol (*4.7.1*).

## Cimetidine + clomethiazole

Cimetidine inhibits the metabolism of clomethiazole, raising plasma levels.

## Methadone + clomethiazole *

See methadone (*4.6.7*).

## 4.6.6 DISULFIRAM *

Disulfiram is a potent inhibitor of CYP1A2 and CYP2E1 (the enzyme that metabolises ethanol), but chronic use could affect other enzymes too (n=7, Frye and Branch, *B J Clin Pharmacol* 2002, **53**, 155–62).
Review of disulfiram interactions: *Acta Psych Scand* 1992, **86**[Suppl 369], 59–66.

### Acamprosate + disulfiram
See acamprosate (*4.6.1*).

### ALCOHOL + DISULFIRAM *
See disulfiram under 'Alcohol abuse and dependence' treatment options (*1.4*) and alcohol (*4.7.1*).

### Antipsychotics + disulfiram
There is a report of psychotic symptoms reappearing when disulfiram was started and an increased first-pass metabolism of perphenazine has been noted (n=1, Hansen *et al*, *Lancet* 1982, **2**, 1472).

### Benzodiazepines + disulfiram
Disulfiram may inhibit the metabolism of diazepam, chlordiazepoxide and temazepam (n=1, Hardman *et al*, *Lancet* 1994, **344**, 1231–32), leading to lengthened half-lives but not with oxazepam (open, MacLeod, *Clin Pharmacol Ther* 1978, **24**, 583–89) nor alprazolam (n=11, 2/52, Diquet *et al*, *Eur J Clin Pharmacol* 1990, **38**, 157–60).

### Caffeine + disulfiram
Disulfiram may reduce caffeine clearance from the body by a half (n=21, open, Beach *et al*, *Clin Pharmacol Ther* 1986, **39**, 265–70).

### Cannabis + disulfiram
See cannabis (*4.7.2*).

### Carbamazepine + disulfiram
Lack of significant interaction has been shown (n=7, open, Krag *et al*, *Acta Neurol* 1981, **63**, 395–98).

### Isoniazid + disulfiram
CNS toxicity has been reported in patients taking isoniazid who then took disulfiram (Rothstein, *JAMA* 1972, **219**, 1216).

### Lithium + disulfiram
These appear compatible, with no theoretical or clinical reasons why an interaction should occur.

### MAOIs + disulfiram
Delirium has been reported with the combination (n=1, Blansjaar and Egberts, *Am J Psych* 1995, **152**, 296; n=1, Circulo, *J Clin Psychopharmacol* 1989, **9**, 315–16).

### Methadone + disulfiram *
See methadone (*4.6.8*).

### Metronidazole + disulfiram
Psychotic reactions have been reported (n=2, Hotson and Langston, *Arch Neurol* 1976, **33**, 141–42).

### NICOUMALONE + DISULFIRAM
An enhanced anticoagulant effect is possible.

### Omeprazole + disulfiram
There is a report of confusion, disorientation and catatonia on the combination (n=1, Hajela *et al*, *Can Med Assoc J* 1990, **143**, 1207).

### Paraldehyde + disulfiram
An enhanced disulfiram-reaction is possible (mentioned in Hadden and Metzner, *Am J Med* 1969, **47**, 642).

### Phenytoin + disulfiram
See phenytoin (*4.5.8*).

### Theophylline + disulfiram
Theophylline levels may be increased via enzyme inhibition. Monitor and reduce the theophylline dose if necessary (n=20, RCT, Loi *et al*, *Clin Pharmacol Ther* 1989, **45**, 476–86).

### Tricyclics + disulfiram
See tricyclics (*4.3.1*).

### WARFARIN + DISULFIRAM
Prothrombin time can fall by about 10% (Rothstein, *JAMA* 1972, **221**, 1051–52), with one study showing a marked effect with reduced warfarin doses sometimes necessary (n=7, open, O'Reilly, *Clin Pharmacol Ther* 1981, **29**, 332). The BNF notes this to be a significant effect.

## 4.6.7 MEMANTINE *

Memantine is only minimally metabolised, does not inhibit CYP1A2, 2A6, 2C9, 2D6, 2E1 nor 3A, nor the FMO system, nor epoxide hydrolase or sulphation, and so metabolic interactions are unlikely. Raised urinary pH (eg. infections, diet change, excessive alkalising gastric buffers etc) may significantly reduce excretion. Plasma protein binding is 45%.

### Amantadine + memantine *
Both are NMDA-antagonists and the combination should be avoided as CNS ADRs may be more frequent (SPC). The same may be true of ketamine and dextromethorphan (SPC).

### Anticholinergics + memantine *
Anticholinergic's effects may be enhanced by memantine (SPC).

### Anticholinesterases + memantine *
Lack of interaction has been suggested, along with a possible synergistic effect (Wenk *et al, Life Sci* 2000, **66**, 1079–83).

### Antipsychotics + memantine *
Antipsychotic effects may be reduced by memantine (SPC).

### Antispasmodic agents + memantine *
The effects may be modified by memantine and dose adjustment may be necessary (SPC).

### Baclofen + memantine *
The effects may be modified by memantine and dose adjustment may be necessary (SPC).

### Barbiturates + memantine *
Barbiturate effects may be reduced by memantine (SPC).

### Dantrolene + memantine *
The effects may be modified by memantine and dose adjustment may be necessary (SPC).

### Dextromethorphan + memantine *
See amantadine.

### Dopamine agonists + memantine *
Dopamine antagonists such as bromocriptine may be enhanced by memantine (SPC).

### H2-blockers + memantine *
A theoretical interaction via competition for cationic transport system exists and there is the potential for increased plasma levels (SPC).

### Hydrochlorthiazine + memantine *
There is a theoretical possibility of reduced diuretic effect (SPC).

### Ketamine + memantine *
See amantadine.

### Levodopa + memantine *
The effects of levodopa may be enhanced by memantine (SPC).

### Phenytoin + memantine *
There is one case report of interaction.

### Procainamide + memantine *
A theoretical interaction via competition for cationic transport system exists and there is the potential for increased plasma levels (SPC).

### Quinidine/quinine + memantine *
A theoretical interaction via competition for cationic transport system exists and there is the potential for increased plasma levels (SPC).

### Smoking + memantine *
A theoretical interaction via competition for cationic transport system exists and there is the potential for increased plasma levels (SPC).

---

### 4.6.8 METHADONE *

Methadone is metabolised mainly by CYP3A4, partly by 2D6 and inhibits CYP2D6 and 3A4.

### Alcohol + methadone *
See alcohol (*4.7.1*).

### Ascorbic acid + methadone *
Vitamin C and other urine acidifiers (e.g. ammonium chloride) can decrease plasma levels via increased renal excretion if the pH is less than 6. Half-life can be halved to around 19–20hrs.

### Barbiturates + methadone *
Enhanced sedation and respiratory depression may occur. Reduced methadone levels have been reported with phenobarbital (eg. n=43, Bell *et al, Clin Pharmacol Ther* 1988, **43**, 623–29; n=1, Liu and Wang, *Am J Psych* 1984, **141**, 1287–88).

### Benzodiazepines + methadone *
There is no pharmacokinetic interaction but additive sedation can occur

(eg. n=5, RCT, Preston *et al, Drug Alc Dep* 1986, **18**, 195–202).

**Buprenorphine + methadone** *

An antagonistic effect would be predicted. Enhanced sedation and respiratory depression may occur.

**Carbamazepine + methadone** *

Reduced methadone levels can occur through CYP3A4 induction (Ketter *et al, J Clin Psychopharmacol* 1991, **11**, 198–203; n=43, Bell *et al, Clin Pharmacol Ther* 1988, **43**, 623–29).

**Chloral + methadone** *

Additive sedation can occur.

**Cimetidine + methadone** *

Raised methadone levels can occur.

**Clomethiazole + methadone** *

Additive sedation can occur.

**Cyclizine + methadone** *

There are rare reports of hallucinations with the combination.

**Didanosone + methadone** *

Serum levels of didanosone can be reduced by about 40% (n=27, open, Rainer *et al, JAIDS* 2000, **24**, 241–48).

**Diphenhydramine + methadone** *

There are rare reports of additional CNS effects with the combination.

**Disulfiram + methadone** *

Lack of kinetic interaction has been shown (n=7, Tong *et al, J Clin Pharmacol* 1980, **20**, 506–13).

**Domperidone + methadone** *

Increased absorption has been reported.

**Efavirenz + methadone** *

Efavirez can induce CYP3A4 and produce withdrawal symptoms from reduced methadone levels (n=1, Pinzani *et al, Ann Pharmacother* 2000, **34**, 405–7; n=1, Marzolini *et al, AIDS* 2000, **14**, 1291–92).

**Erythromycin + methadone** *

Raised methadone levels through CYP3A4 inhibition could occur.

**Fluconazole/ketoconazole + methadone** *

Methadone levels can rise by a mean of 27% through CYP3A4 inhibition, although one study did not detect any signs of toxicity (n=25, RCT, d/b, p/c, 14/7, Cobb *et al, Clin Pharmacol Ther* 1998, **63**, 655–62).

**Fluoxetine + methadone** *

Lack of significant interaction has been shown (n=16, open, 9/52, Batki *et al, J Clin Psychopharmacol* 1993, **13**, 243–50).

**Fluvoxamine + methadone** *

Fluvoxamine may inhibit methadone metabolism leading to raised levels (n=1, DeMaria and Serota, *J Addict Dis* 1999, **18**, 5–12; Perucca *et al, Clin Pharmacokinet* 1994, **27**, 175–90) and severe hypoventilation has been reported (n=1, Alderman and Frith, *Aust NZ J Psych* 1999, **33**, 99–101).

**Fosphenytoin + methadone** *

See phenytoin.

**Grapefruit juice + methadone** *

Raised methadone levels through CYP3A4 inhibition could theoretically occur.

**Hypnotics + methadone** *

Enhanced sedation.

**Indinavir + methadone** *

Slightly raised methadone levels have been reported (MI).

**MAOIs + methadone** *

See MAOIs (*4.3.4*).

**Metapyrone + methadone** *

Metapyrone can cause a withdrawal-like syndrome with methadone (n=15, open, Kennedy *et al, B J Addict* 1990, **85**, 1133–40).

**Naltrexone + methadone** *

This opiate antagonist would block the effect of methadone.

**Naloxone + methadone** *

This opiate antagonist would block the effect of methadone, an effect that can occur within 5–10 minutes (Tornabene, *Ann Int Med* 1974, **81**, 349–51).

**Nevirapine + methadone** *

Reduced methadone levels through CYP3A4 induction can occur, producing a withdrawal state (n=4, Otero *et al, AIDS* 1999, **13**, 1004–5; n=7, Altice *et al, AIDS* 1999, **13**, 957–62).

## Phenytoin + methadone *

Reduced methadone levels through CYP3A4 induction can occur, with withdrawal symptoms occurring within 4 days (open, Tong *et al, Ann Int Med* 1981, **94**, 349–51; n=43, Bell *et al, Clin Pharmacol Ther* 1988, **43**, 623–29). Dosage adjustment may be needed.

## Paroxetine + methadone *

See paroxetine (*4.3.2.4*).

## Reboxetine + methadone *

See reboxetine (*4.3.3.5*).

## Rifampicin + methadone *

Methadone levels reduce by 30–65% within 4–5 days in 70% patients given rifampicin, through CYP3A4 induction (n=30, Kreek *et al, NEJM* 1976, **294**, 1104–6).

## Risperidone + methadone *

There is a report of possible interaction, resulting in irritability and aches (n=1, Wines and Weiss, *J Clin Psychopharmacol* 1999, **19**, 265–67).

## Ritonavir + methadone *

Ritonavir may decrease methadone levels slightly (n=1, Geletko and Erickson, *Pharmacother* 2000, **20**, 93–94), although ritonavir/saquinavir has been used without dose adjustment in AIDS patients (n=12, Gerber *et al, JAIDS* 2001, **27**, 153–60).

## Sodium bicarbonate + methadone *

Sodium bicarbonate and other urinary alkalinisers can increase plasma levels via decreased renal excretion.

## Tricyclics + methadone *

Additive sedation might occur. A small study showed desipramine blood levels can double with methadone (n=5, Maany *et al, Am J Psych* 1989, **146**, 1611–13).

## Zidovudine + methadone *

Raised zidovudine levels have been reported (AUC increased by 41%) (n=8, McCance-Katz *et al, J Acquir Immune Defic Synd Hum Retrivirol* 1998, **18**, 435–43).

## 4.6.9 METHYLPHENIDATE *

**Review:** interactions with psychostimulants (Markowitz *et al, Int Clin Psychopharmacol* 1999, **14**, 1–18).

## Carbamazepine + methylphenidate *

Carbamazepine has been reported to cause an extreme reduction of methylphenidate levels (n=1, Behar *et al, J Am Acad Child Adolesc Psych* 1998, **37**, 1128–29).

## Ciclosporin + methylphenidate *

A rise in ciclosporin levels has been reported with methylphenidate (n=1, Lewis *et al, J Child Adolesc Psychopharmacol* 2001, **11**, 193–98).

## MAOIs + methylphenidate *

See MAOIs (*4.3.4*).

## Modafinil + methylphenidate *

See modafinil (*4.6.10*).

## Phenytoin + methylphenidate *

Phenytoin toxicity has been reported (n=3, Ghofrani, *Dev Med Child Neurol* 1988, **30**, 267–68).

## Tricyclics + methylphenidate *

Mood and cognitive deterioration has been reported with imipramine and methylphenidate (n=2, Grob and Coyle, *J Dev Behav Pediatr* 1986, **7**, 265–67). Methylphenidate may inhibit the metabolism of tricyclics producing up to a four-fold increase in levels (eg. n=2, Grob and Coyle, *J Dev Behav Pediatrics* 1986, **7**, 265–67).

## Valproate + methylphenidate *

Rapid onset and severe dyskinesia and bruxism has been reported with the combination (n=2, Gara and Roberts, *J Child Adolesc Psychopharmacol* 2000, **10**, 39–43).

## 4.6.10 MODAFINIL

Modafinil is moderately bound to plasma proteins (62%), essentially to albumin. Renal excretion is the main route of elimination.

## Amfetamines + modafinil *

Low dose amfetamines appear to have no significant effects on steady state modafinil (n=32, RCT, open,

Hellriegel *et al, J Clin Pharmacol* 2002, **42**, 450–60).

### Benzodiazepines + modafinil *

Triazolam levels may be significantly reduced by modafinil, probably via 3A4 induction (n=41, RCT, 4/52, Robertson, *Clin Pharmacol Ther* 2002, **71**, 46–56).

### Dexamphetamine + modafinil *

Dexamphetamine has no apparent effect on steady state modafinil levels (n=32, RCT, open, *J Clin Pharmacol* 2002, **42**, 450–60).

### Ethinylestradiol + modafinil *

Ethinylestradiol levels may be reduced by modafinil, probably via 3A4 induction (n=41, RCT, 4/52, Robertson, *Clin Pharmacol Ther* 2002, **71**, 46–56).

### Methylphenidate + modafinil *

Low-dose methylphenidate does not appear to interact with modafinil (n=32, RCT, open, Hellriegel *et al, J Clin Pharmacol* 2002, **41**, 895–904), although methylphenidate may slightly slow the absorption of modafinil (RCT, Wong *et al, J Clin Pharmacol* 1998, **38**, 276–82).

### Oral contraceptives + modafinil

Higher dose oral contraceptives containing 50mcg ethinylestradiol should be used (MI).

### Tricyclics + modafinil

A single dose study showed a clinically important interaction with clomipramine 50mg/d (n=1, Grozinger *et al, Clin Neuropharmacol* 1998, **21**, 127–29).

### Warfarin + modafinil *

A single-dose study suggested no interaction (n=28, Robertson *et al, J Clin Pharmacol* 2002, **42**, 205–14).

---

## 4.7 NON-PRESCRIBED DRUGS
### and VICES (alcohol, cannabis, cocaine and smoking)

---

### 4.7.1 ALCOHOL

Alcohol/ethanol-psychotropic drug interactions can occur frequently and with varied outcome, depending upon:

- **Alcohol usage** (eg. chronic and/or acute, leading to altered enzymes etc)
- **Consumption** (amount, time span)
- **Type of interaction** (eg. additive sedation, antagonism or cross-tolerance)
- **What the individual then tries to do** (eg. sleep, drive etc.)
- **Comorbidity** (eg. asthma etc).

These variables need to be taken into consideration when assessing the effect or potential effect of the interaction.

Alcohol distribution is wide, with the direct central depressant effect impairing all central functions (eg. cognition, respiration etc), and contributing to many of the drug-drug interactions. Alcohol also promotes the action of GABA and may release other amines such as dopamine and endorphins.

**Reviews**: pharmacokinetic interactions (Fraser, *Clin Pharmacokinet* 1997, **33**, 79–90, 151 refs), drug-alcohol interactions (Ferner, *Adv Drug React Bull* 1998, **189**, 719–22, 40 refs).

### Acamprosate + alcohol

Continued alcohol consumption may negate the therapeutic effect of acamprosate. There is no detectable pharmacokinetic interaction (review by Nalpas *et al, Encephale* 1990, **16**, 175–79).

## ANTIPSYCHOTICS + ALCOHOL

Enhanced CNS depression is well-documented, particularly with the phenothiazines, resulting in impaired concentration, co-ordination and judgement, drowsiness and lethargy, as well as hypotension and respiratory depression. Alcohol-related drowsiness is significant with **phenothiazines** and **flupentixol**. EPSEs may also be enhanced (Freed, *Med J Aust* 1981, **2**, 44–45), as can hepatotoxicity with, eg. chlorpromazine (Strubelt, *Biochem Pharmacol* 1980, **29**, 1445–49). Single oral doses of **amisulpride** do not seem to enhance the effects of alcohol on the performance and memory of healthy subjects (n=18, RCT, Mattila *et al, Eur J Clin Pharmacol* 1996, **51**, 161).

There is no published evidence that alcohol reduces antipsychotic efficacy (n=31, open, Chetty *et al, Eur J Clin Pharmacol* 1994, **46**, 523–26). Overall, this is a potentially important interaction, especially in the community. Accidental alcohol overdosage, especially in people with asthma, respiratory depression or chest infections, could prove fatal if combined with antipsychotics.

## Aripiprazole + alcohol *
See aripiprazole (*4.2.7.1*).

## BARBITURATES + ALCOHOL
Enhanced or prolonged CNS and respiratory depression can occur, seriously impairing concentration and performance. *Acute* alcohol ingestion may increase barbiturate levels but *chronic* alcohol use may *decrease* barbiturate levels (Mezey and Robles, *Gastroenterology* 1974, **66**, 248–53). The lethal dose of barbiturates is up to 50% lower when alcohol is also present (Bogan and Smith, *J Forensic Sci* 1967, **7**, 37–45), mainly due to additive respiratory depression.

## BENZODIAZEPINES + ALCOHOL
Alcohol can enhance the sedation caused by benzodiazepines by 20–30%, well established, documented and predictable interaction. Synergistic sedation has been reported with lorazepam (d/b, c/o, Lister and File, *J Clin Psychopharmacol* 1983, **3**, 66–71), clorazepate and diazepam. Larger quantities of alcohol may inhibit benzodiazepine metabolism, especially in those with impaired or borderline hepatic function (review by Guthrie and Lane, *Alcoholism* 1986, **10**, 686–90), and diazepam, where acute ethanol decreases diazepam clearance by up to 50%, (Laisi *et al, Eur J Clin Pharmacol* 1979, **16**, 263–70).

## Beta-blockers + alcohol
Alcohol may slightly reduce propranolol absorption and increase excretion (n=5, open, Grabowski *et al, Int J Clin Pharmacol Ther Toxicol* 1980, **18**, 317–19; Sotaniemi *et al, Clin Pharmacol Ther* 1981, **29**, 705–10).

## Bupropion + alcohol
See bupropion (*4.6.4*).

## Buspirone + alcohol
A minimal interaction and slightly increased sedation has been reported (n=24, RCT, Erwin *et al, J Clin Psychopharmacol* 1986, **6**, 199–209).

## Cannabis + alcohol
See cannabis (*4.7.2*).

## Carbamazepine + alcohol
There is virtually nothing published but additive sedation would be expected.

## CHLORAL + ALCOHOL
Additive (or more) CNS depressant effects occur when alcohol is taken with chloral. Tachycardia, impaired concentration, disulfiram-like effects and profound vasodilation may also occur (Owen and Taberner, *B J Pharmacol* 1978, **64**, 400).

## Clomethiazole + alcohol
Alcohol increases the bioavailability of oral clomethiazole, probably via inhibition of first pass metabolism (Neuvonen *et al, Int J Clin Pharmacol Ther Toxicol* 1981, **19**, 552–60).

## Citalopram + alcohol
There is little published at present on this. The manufacturers state that citalopram does not enhance the sedation caused by alcohol.

## Cocaine + alcohol
See cocaine (*4.7.3*).

## DISULFIRAM + ALCOHOL
Disulfiram inhibits the aldehyde dehydrogenase enzyme, leading to accumulation of acetaldehyde from incomplete alcohol metabolism. The main symptoms of the 'Antabuse reaction' are flushing, sweating, palpitations, hyperventilation, increased pulse, hypotension, nausea and vomiting (often in that order). Arrhythmias and shock can follow. The reaction occurs within 5–15minutes and can be fatal. Factors affecting the severity of the reaction include the dose of disulfiram, rate and dose of alcohol ingestion, sensitivity, individual aldehyde dehydrogenase activity, concurrent

medication (see disulfiram interactions, *4.6.4*) and coexisting pulmonary or cardiac disease. Patients should be warned that reactions can occur with disguised sources of alcohol, eg. 'Listerine' mouthwash, sauces, pharmaceuticals (eg. cough mixtures), topical preparations (eg. shampoo; Stoll and King, *JAMA* 1980, **244**, 2045) etc. Delirium has been reported with the combination (Park and Riggio, *Ann Pharmacother* 2001, **35**, 32–35).

### Escitalopram + alcohol
See citalopram + alcohol.

### Fluoxetine + alcohol
Alcohol has no additional significant effect on drowsiness, sedation or task performance tests with fluoxetine 40mg/d, compared with fluoxetine alone (eg. Shaw *et al, Human Psychopharmacol* 1989, **4**, 113–20).

### Fluvoxamine + alcohol
Moderately enhanced sedation has been reported (*J Clin Pharmacol* 1989, **29**, 91–95), but a later study showed no significant potentiation of the cognitive effects of 40g IV alcohol by single and multiple doses of 50mg fluvoxamine (n=24, van Harten *et al, Clin Pharmacol Ther* 1992, **52**, 427–35).

### Levetiracetam + alcohol
See levetiracetam (*4.5.5*).

### Lithium + alcohol
Impaired driving skills have been reported (Linnoila *et al, Eur J Clin Pharmacol* 1974, **7**, 337), although no clinically significant adverse interactions have actually been reported. Alcohol may produce a slight (12%) increase in peak lithium levels (n=10, RCT, d/b, p/c, c/o, Anton *et al, Clin Pharmacol Ther* 1985, **38**, 52–55).

### MAOIs + ALCOHOL
As well as an interaction occurring with alcoholic and low alcoholic drinks (see MAOIs, *4.3.4*), alcohol may increase central catecholamine synthesis and release, and MAOIs may inhibit alcohol dehydrogenase, potentiating alcohol (comprehensive

review by Weller *et al, Psychosomatics* 1984, **25**, 301–9).

### Methadone + alcohol
Predictably, increased sedation and respiratory depression may occur with the combination (Bellville *et al, Clin Pharmacol Ther* 1971, **12**, 607–12), as could hepatotoxicity.

### MIANSERIN + ALCOHOL
Mianserin causes drowsiness, which is enhanced considerably by alcohol (n=13, RCT, Seppala *et al, Eur J Clin Pharmacol* 1984, **27**, 181–89).

### Mirtazapine + alcohol
Lack of pharmacokinetic interaction has been shown, but additive sedation was noted (Mercer, mentioned in Timmer *et al, Clin Pharmacokinet* 2000, **38**, 461–74).

### Moclobemide + alcohol
Some degree of potentiation of the effects of alcohol has been noted, albeit less than with trazodone and clomipramine (Zimmer *et al, Acta Psych Scand* 1990, **360**[Suppl], 84–86).

### Nefazodone + alcohol *
The SPC advises caution but the effect may be minimal (n=12, RCT, 8/7, Frewer and Lader, *Int Clin Psychopharmacol* 1993, **8**, 13–20).

### Olanzapine + alcohol
Enhanced CNS sedation would be expected. Raised heart rate and increased postural hypotension have been reported (MI).

### Oxcarbazepine + alcohol
See oxcarbazepine (*4.5.6*).

### Paraldehyde + alcohol
An enhanced sedative effect can be expected (BNF).

### Paroxetine + alcohol
Lack of interaction has been shown (review by Boyer and Blumhardt, *J Clin Psych* 1992, **53**[Suppl 2], 132–34).

### PHENYTOIN + ALCOHOL
Alcohol usually decreases phenytoin levels but increases them via enzyme induction if alcohol intake is heavy, and so higher doses may be needed initially in alcoholics. The half-life of

phenytoin can be up to 50% shorter in an abstaining alcoholic than in a non-drinker (Kater *et al, Gastroenterology* 1969, **56**, 412; see also n=1, Bellibas and Tuglular, *Therapie* 1995, **50**, 487–88).

### Quetiapine + alcohol
Additive sedation would be expected.

### Reboxetine + alcohol
No potentiation of alcohol's cognitive effects has been reported (UK SPC), and up to 4mg/d showed no interaction with alcohol in one trial (n=10, d/b, Kerr *et al, B J Clin Pharmacol* 1996, **42**, 239–41).

### Sertraline + alcohol
The evidence for a lack of interaction has been reviewed by Warrington (*Int Clin Psychopharmacol* 1991, **6**[Suppl 2], 11–21).

### Tiagabine + alcohol
See tiagabine (*4.5.10*).

### TRAZODONE + ALCOHOL
Additive sedation has been reported (n=26, d/b, c/o, Warrington *et al, Neuropsychobiology* 1986, **15**[Suppl 1], 31–37).

### TRICYCLICS + ALCOHOL
Enhanced sedation with most tricyclics is known, but surprisingly little has actually been published and most studies refer to the effect on driving performance. Sedation caused by amitriptyline (Shaw *et al, Human Psychopharmacol* 1989, **4**, 113–20), maprotiline and doxepin is enhanced by alcohol, but less, or minimally so, with nortriptyline, clomipramine, desipramine and amoxapine, which are less sedating. Both alcohol and tricyclics lower the seizure threshold and care is needed in patients susceptible to seizures. Concurrent alcohol may also increase the oral bioavailability of tricyclics by reducing the first pass effect (n=5, open, Dorian *et al, Eur J Clin Pharmacol* 1983, **25**, 325–31).

### Venlafaxine + alcohol
There appears to be no significant additive effect between alcohol and venlafaxine (n=16, RCT, d/b, p/c,

c/o, Troy *et al, J Clin Pharmacol* 1997, **37**, 1073–81).

### Zaleplon + alcohol *
Whilst zaleplon enhances alcohol performance impairment, the effect appears short-lived and less than triazolam (n=18, c/o, Roehrs *et al, Sleep Med* 2001, **2**, 323–32) and zolpidem, albeit less potent on a mg for mg basis (n=10, RCT, c/o, Drover *et al, Clin Ther* 2000, **22**, 1443–61).

### Zolpidem + alcohol
There is no published information available indicating an interaction.

### Zopiclone + alcohol
There appears to be no significant interaction (n=9, RCT, Hindmarch, *Int Clin Psychopharmacol* 1990, **5**[Suppl 2], 105–13).

### Zotepine + alcohol
See zotepine (*4.2.6*).

---

## 4.7.2 CANNABIS
### (Tetrahydrocannabinol)

Cannabis/marijuana is a frequently (and usually secretively) used drug but with the exception of perhaps tricyclics, has few known important adverse drug interactions.

### Alcohol + cannabis
Decreased ethanol metabolism may occur, with enhanced CNS depression (n=10, RCT, p/c, d/b, c/o, Consroe *et al, Psychopharmacol* 1979, **66**, 45–50). Cannabis may also reduce peak alcohol levels (n=15, RCT, p/c, Lukas *et al, Neuropsychopharmacology* 1992, **7**, 77–81).

### Antidepressants + cannabis
Mental state changes consistent with delirium and tachycardia and other clinically significant adverse events have been reported following use of marijuana and **tricyclics** (n=4, Wilens *et al, J Am Acad Child Adolesc Psychiatry* 1997, **36**, 45–48; *Lancet* 1997, **349**, 106). Increased heart rate has been reported, eg. marked sinus tachycardia, possibly via a combined beta-adrenergic effect (eg. n=2, Hillard and Vieweg, *Am J Psych* 1983, **140**, 626–27). Mania has been

reported with **fluoxetine** (n=1, Stoll *et al, J Clin Psych* 1991, **52**, 280–81).

### Antipsychotics + cannabis *

Chlorpromazine clearance has been shown to be increased by cannabis smoking, although the clinical significance is not known (n=31, Chetty *et al, Eur J Clin Pharmacol* 1994, **46**, 523–26). Cessation of cannabis smoking can lead to **clozapine** intoxication through removal of CYP1A2 induction (n=1, Zullino *et al, Int Clin Psychopharmacol* 2002, **17**, 141–43). Additive drowsiness has been reported (review by Benowitz and Jones, *Clin Pharmacol Ther* 1977, **22**, 259–68).

### Benzodiazepines + cannabis

Additive drowsiness with benzodiazepines and hypnotics has been reported (review by Benowitz and Jones, *Clin Pharmacol Ther* 1977, **22**, 259–68).

### Cocaine + cannabis

See cocaine (*4.7.3*).

### CNS depressants + cannabis

The combination has resulted in additive drowsiness (review by Benowitz and Jones, *Clin Pharmacol Ther* 1977, **22**, 259–68), eg. anticholinergics, barbiturates etc.

### Disulfiram + cannabis

There have been two reported reactions; a hypomanic episode in an alcoholic on disulfiram taking marijuana (n=1, Lacoursiere and Swatek, *Am J Psych* 1983, **140**, 242–44) and an acute confusional state (Mackie and Clark, *B J Psych* 1994, **164**, 421).

### Lithium + cannabis

There is a case of lithium levels raised into the toxic range by secretive use of cannabis (n=1, Ratey *et al, J Clin Psychopharmcol* 1981, **1**, 32) and additive drowsiness has been reported (review by Benowitz and Jones, *Clin Pharmacol Ther* 1977, **22**, 259–68).

### 4.7.3 COCAINE

**Review**: Ciraulo, *J Clin Psychopharmacol* 1992, **12**, 49–55 (73 refs).

### Alcohol + cocaine

Simultaneous cocaine and alcohol may produce changes in heart rate and blood pressure, increasing the risk of cardiovascular toxicity (Farre *et al, J Pharmacol Exp Ther* 1993, **166**, 1364–73). Combined use has led to enhanced cocaine-induced hepatotoxicity.

### Antidepressants + cocaine

In combination with cocaine, desipramine may reduce the effect, fluoxetine has no significant effect (n=5, Walsh *et al, J Clin Psychopharmacol* 1994, **14**, 396–407), trazodone has minor physiological effects and MAOIs probably augment the pressor effect.

### Antipsychotics + cocaine

Flupentixol may reduce cocaine craving and haloperidol may moderate the stimulant effects. Clozapine increases cocaine levels but reduced cocaine 'high', and some cardiac events (near-syncopal episode) have been reported, so caution is necessary (n=8, Farren *et al, Drug Alcohol Depend* 2000, **59**, 153–63).

### Cannabis + cocaine

Enhanced cardiotoxicity (eg. increased heart rate) may occur.

### Carbamazepine + cocaine

Cocaine may enhance the cardiac effects of carbamazepine.

### Lithium + cocaine

Lithium probably has little effect on cocaine.

### 4.7.4 SMOKING

Many people with mental health problems smoke. There are over 3000 different known chemicals in cigarette smoke, but which ones are significant is not fully known. Only a few smoking drug interactions are significant, and only brief details of the more significant psychotropic ones are included here (review by Schein, *Ann Pharmacother* 1995, **29**, 1139–48). The major enzyme metabolising nicotine is probably CYP2A6, with CYP2B6 and CYP2D6 playing lesser, but still substantial, roles. Cigarette smoke contains polycyclic aromatic hydrocarbons, which are potent inducers of CYP1A2.

**Reviews\***: general (Zevin and Benowitz, *Clin Pharmacokinet* 1999, **36**, 425–38, 128 refs; Desai *et al, CNS Drugs* 2001, **15**, 469–94, 100 refs).

### Antipsychotics + smoking *

Evidence supporting a significant interaction is that schizophrenics who smoke tend to receive higher doses of antipsychotics than non-smokers (n=78, open, Goff *et al, Am J Psych* 1992, **149**, 1189–94), possibly via increased hepatic metabolism and renal excretion (n=90, RCT, d/b, p/c, Salokangas *et al, Schizophren Res* 1997, **23**, 55–60). Plasma levels of **haloperidol** are around 23% lower in smoking than in non-smoking schizophrenic patients (n=66, open, Shimoda *et al, Ther Drug Monit* 1999, **21**, 293–96; confirmed by another study, n=63, Pan *et al, Ther Drug Monit* 1999, **21**, 489). **Chlorpromazine** clearance may be increased by cigarette smoking, but the clinical significance is unclear (n=31, Chetty *et al, Eur J Clin Pharmacol* 1994, **46**, 523–26). **Clozapine** levels are lowered by smoking (n=148, open, Haring *et al, Am J Psych* 1990, **147**, 1471–75), the 1A2 induction leading to clozapine non-response, with fluvoxamine occasionally used to inhibit CYP1A2 to raise clozapine levels (n=3, Bender and Eap, *Arch Gen Psych* 1998, **55**, 1048–50), so stopping smoking could be dangerous for someone taking clozapine (n=1, Skogh *et al, Ther Drug Monit* 1999, **21**, 580). In fact, one study showed a mean 72% increase in stable clozapine levels on smoking cessation, with one case so extreme it caused a significant ADR (n=11, open, Meyer, *J Clin Psychopharmacol* 2001, **21**, 569–74). The change in plasma clozapine levels can, in 80% cases, be predicted by using the formula:

*Non-smoking level = 45.3 + (1.474 x smoking level).*

**Olanzapine** clearance may be higher and half-life 21% shorter in smokers compared to non-smokers (MI), probably via CYP1A2 induction. Smoking cessation can lead to olanzapine intoxication through removal of CYP1A2 induction (n=1, Zullino *et al, Int Clin Psychopharmacol* 2002, **17**, 141–43). Smoking seems to have no effect on **zotepine** plasma levels (n=14, Kondo *et al, Psychopharmacol [Berl]* 1996, **127**, 311–14). Lack of interaction has been shown with **ziprasidone** and **aripiprazole**. Many schizophrenics may smoke to relieve subjective distress from the illness and treatment (review, McEvoy, *Curr Opin Psych* 2000, **113**, 115–19).

### Benzodiazepines + smoking *

Early studies suggested an increased clearance of benzodiazepines in smokers (review by Schein, *Ann Pharmacother* 1995, **29**, 1139–48). One review noted increased clearance by smoking of alprazolam, lorazepam, oxazepam, diazepam but not chlordiazepoxide (mentioned in Desai *et al, CNS Drugs* 2001, **15**, 469–94).

### Bupropion + smoking

See bupropion (*4.6.4*).

### Carbamazepine + smoking *

There appears to be no interaction (mentioned in Desai *et al, CNS Drugs* 2001, **15**, 469–94).

### Fluvoxamine + smoking *

Fluvoxamine levels are significantly lower in smokers, probably due to CYP1A2 induction (n=30, open, Yoshimura *et al, Neuropsychobiology* 2002, **45**, 32–35).

### Lithium + smoking

Smoking induces CYP1A2 and caffeine is metabolised by CYP1A2. Theoretically, ceasing smoking could raise xanthine levels, which could increase lithium excretion (as with theophylline), lowering levels.

### Memantine + smoking *

See memantine (*4.6.7*).

## Phenobarbital + smoking *

Smoking has been shown not to effect the drowsiness caused by phenobarbital (n=12, d/b, Mirfazaelian *et al, Biopharm Drug Dispos* 2001, **22**, 403–6).

## Propranolol + smoking

Steady-state propranolol levels may be reduced in smokers, via 1A2 induction.

## Tricyclics + smoking

Although serum levels of tricyclics fall in smokers, free levels rise, minimising the clinical significance (n=24, open, Perry *et al, Ther Drug Monit* 1986, **8**, 279–84).

## Zolpidem + smoking *

See zolpidem (*4.1.5*).

## Cytochrome P450 Drug Metabolism/Inhibition

Knowledge of the role of the P450 enzyme system is rapidly developing. These tables may be of use in determining actual or potential interactions. There are, however, many discrepancies in the published literature and so these tables may inadvertently perpetuate some inaccuracies or incomplete knowledge.

**Some points about P450 interactions include:**

1. Some drugs are metabolised by several enzymes, so if one enzyme is inhibited, another may compensate. There are over 40 known human P450 enzymes.
2. A drug may inhibit or induce an enzyme, but be metabolised by another.
3. Onset and offset of inhibition is dependent on the half-life and time to steady state of the inhibitory drug (may be 24 hours or several months) and the drug to be metabolised, but is frequently rapid.
4. Onset and offset of induction may take hours or several weeks to become apparent, dependent on the inducing drugs half-life, enzyme turnover, age (induction reduces with age) and concurrent liver disease (reduced induction ability).
5. Also important are the **UGT** (uridine diphosphate glucuronosyltransferase) enzymes (de Wildt *et al, Clin Pharmacokinet* 1999, **36**, 439–52). Phenytoin, valproate, phenobarbital and CBZ are UGT inducers, lamotrigine a weak UGT inducer. The Flavin Mono-oxygenase (FMO) system is also important. Humans have FMO1, FMO3, FM04 and FM05 enzymes in the liver, intestine and kidney. Imipramine, chlorpromazine and orphenadrine are known to be metabolised by this enzyme system.

**The general rules for avoiding P450 interactions are:**

1. Avoid reported and predictable interactions.
2. With potential interactions, use reduced doses where possible (ie. start low and go slow).
3. Measure plasma levels of drugs with narrow therapeutic indices.

## CYP1A2*

| Substrates, ie. drugs metabolised by this enzyme | Significant enzyme inducers | Significant enzyme inhibitors |
|---|---|---|
| Caffeine | Cabbage | Celery |
| Clozapine (most) | Caffeine | Cimetidine |
| Diazepam | Charcoal-broiled food | Ciprofloxacin |
| Fluvoxamine (partly) | Cigarette smoke (inc. cannabis) | Clarithromycin |
| Haloperidol (partly) | Omeprazole | Diet (low protein/ |
| Mexiletine | Phenobarbital (weak) | high carbohydrate) |
| Mirtazapine (partly) | Phenytoin (weak) | Disulfiram (strong) |
| Olanzapine (partly) | Rifampicin | Enoxacin |
| Ondansetron | Ritonavir | Erythromycin |
| Paracetamol | | Fluoroquinolones (eg. ciprofloxacin |
| Perphenazine | | and norfloxacin) (strong) |
| Pimozide (possibly) | | Fluvoxamine (potent — other |
| Propafenone | | SSRIs only very weakly) |
| Propranolol? | | Grapefruit juice |
| Tacrine | | Griseofulvin? |
| Tamoxifen | | Isoniazid |
| Theophylline | | Ketoconazole |
| Tricyclics—tertiary (eg. | | Mirtazapine (very weak) |
| amitriptyline, clomipramine, | | Moclobemide |
| desipramine, imipramine) | | Nefazodone (very weak/nil) |
| Verapamil | | Norfloxacin |
| Warfarin-R (major) | | Omeprazole |
| Zotepine | | Parsley |
| Ziprasidone (minor) | | Parsnip |
| | | Sertraline (weak) |

## CYP2C9/10/19 *

2C is a sub-family, containing many closely related enzymes, eg. 2C9, 2C10, 2C19 etc. About 20% Asians and 3–5% Caucasians are poor CYP2C19 metabolisers.

| Substrates, ie. drugs metabolised by this enzyme | Significant enzyme inducers | Significant enzyme inhibitors |
|---|---|---|
| Alosetron (9) | Carbamazepine (weak) | Amiodarone (9) |
| Barbiturates (19) | Phenobarbital (weak) | Carbamazepine (9, 19) |
| Bupropion (8/9) | Phenyton (weak) | Chloramphenicol (9) |
| Citalopram (19, major 60%) | Rifampicin (9) | Cimetidine (9, 19) |
| Diazepam (19) | | Cyclizine (9) |
| Fluoxetine (9) | | Fluconazole |
| Flunitrazepam (19) | | Fluorouracil (9) |
| Irbesartan (9) | | Fluoxetine (9,weak: 19, moderate) |
| Losartan (9) | | Fluvastatin (9) |
| Mephenytoin (19) | | Fluvoxamine (9/19) |
| Moclobemide (19-major) | | Gingko biloba (9, weak) |
| NSAIDs (8/9) | | Ginseng (9, weak) |
| Omeprazole (19) | | Isoniazid (19, potent) |
| Perphenazine (19) | | Ketoconazole (19) |
| Phenytoin (8/9/19) | | Moclobemide (19) |
| Propranolol (part) (19) | | Modafinil (9) |
| Sildenafil (9, partly) | | Omeprazole (9/19) |
| Tricyclics — tertiary (eg. | | Oxcarbazepine (19) |
|   amitriptyline, clomipramine, | | Paroxetine (9/19, weak) |
|   trimipramine, imipramine) (19) | | Phenylbutazone (9) |
| Tolbutamide (8/9) | | Promethazine (9) |
| Topiramate (19) | | Sertraline (9, moderate: 19, weak) |
| Valsartan (9) | | Ticlopidine (19) |
| Warfarin (part) (8/9) | | Topiramate |
| R-Warfarin (19) (minor) | | Tranylcypromine (19) |
| S-Warfarin (9) (major) | | Tricyclics (19) |
| | | Valproate (919) |
| | | Venlafaxine (weak) |

## CYP2D6 *

CYP2D6 metabolism occurs both in the liver and in the brain. An individual's CYP2D6 status can be determined by giving the probes debrisoquine or dextromethorphan and measuring the ratios of drug and metabolite. 5–8% whites, 8.5% African-Americans and 2–10% Asians are slow metabolisers. All CYP2D6 inhibition is probably concentration-dependent and so inclusion in this list only predicts that an interaction could occur, not that it will occur.

| Substrates, ie. drugs metabolised by this enzyme | Significant enzyme inducers | Significant enzyme inhibitors |
|---|---|---|
| Amfetamines | Carbamazepine (weak) | Amiodarone |
| Antiarrhythmics Type 1c (encainide, flecainide etc.) | Phenobarbital (weak) | Bupropion |
| | Phenytoin (weak) | Chloroquine |
| Beta-blockers (especially lipophilic) | Rifampicin (weak) | Chlorphenamine |
| Carvedilol | Ritonavir (weak) | Chlorpromazine |
| Chlorphenamine | | Cimetidine |
| Citalopram (minor) | | Citalopram (very weak/nil) |
| Clozapine (minor and unproven) | | Cocaine |
| Codeine (to morphine) | | Cyclizine |
| Dexfenfluramine | | Dextromethorphan |
| Dextromethorphan | | Dextropropoxyphene |
| Donepezil | | Diltiazem (weak) |
| Fenfluramine | | Diphenhydramine |
| Fluoxetine (partly) | | Fenfluramine? |
| Fluvoxamine (partly) | | Flecainide |
| Galantamine | | Fluoxetine (strong) |
| Haloperidol | | Fluphenazine |
| Hydrocodone | | Fluvoxamine (very weak) |
| Loratadine | | Haloperidol |
| Maprotiline (possibly) | | Indinavir |
| m-CPP | | Levomepromazine |
| Methadone (part) | | Methadone (weak?) |
| Methamphetamine | | Metoclopramide |
| Metoprolol | | Metoprolol |
| Mexiletine | | Mexiletine |
| Mianserin | | Mibefradil |
| Mirtazapine (minor) | | Mirtazapine (very weak/nil) |
| Morphine derivatives | | Moclobemide |
| Nefazodone | | Nefazodone (very weak/nil) |
| Nicotine (partly) | | Nicardipine |
| Olanzapine (partly) | | Norfluoxetine (strong) |
| Oxycodone | | Paroxetine (strong, dose-related) |
| Paroxetine | | Perphenazine |
| Perphenazine | | Pindolol |
| Phenothiazines (eg chlorpromazine, fluphenazine, thioridazine) | | Primaquine |
| | | Promethazine |
| | | Propafenone |
| Propafenone | | Propranolol |
| Propranolol | | Quinine |
| Risperidone | | Ritonavir |
| Sertindole (partly) | | Sertraline (weak, dose-related, moderate at 150 mg/d) |
| Timolol | | Terbinafine (weak to moderate) |
| Tramadol | | Thioridazine |
| Trazodone | | Timolol |
| Tricyclics — secondary and tertiary tricyclics (eg. nortriptyline, imipramine, maprotiline, trimipramine, amitriptyline, clomipramine and desipramine (weak)) | | Tricyclics (all, strong) |
| | | Venlafaxine (very weak/nil) |
| | | Yohimbine |
| Venlafaxine (partly) | | |
| Zuclopenthixol | | |

References used include: Meyer *et al, Acta Psych Scand* 1996, **93**, 71–79; Nemeroff *et al, Am J Psych* 1996, **153**, 311–20; Callahan *et al, Harvard Rev Psych* 1996, **4**, 153–58; Centorinno *et al, Am J Psych* 1996, **153**, 820–82; Cohen and De Vane, *Ann Pharmacother* 1996, **30**, 1471–80.

## CYP3A3/4 (Very similar structures, so one of the grouped together) *

CYP3A4 is an important P450 enzyme, and may account for up to 50–60% of the total liver P450. There is little genetic polymorphism so little inter-individual variation exists. CYP3A4 occurs in the liver, gut and, possibly, the brain. Ultra-rapid metabolisers have not yet been identified.

| Substrates, ie. drugs metabolised by this enzyme | |
| --- | --- |
| Alfentanil | Methadone (main) |
| Alosetron | Mianserin |
| Amiodarone | Mibefradil |
| Antihistamines (eg. astemizole) | Miconazole |
| Astemizole | Mirtazapine (partly) |
| Benzodiazepines (eg. alprazolam, clonazepam, diazepam, flunitrazepam, midazolam, temazepam, triazolam, but not lorazepam) | Nefazodone |
| | Omeprazole |
| | Ondansetron |
| Buspirone | Orphenadrine |
| Busulfan | Paclitaxol |
| Calcium-channel Blockers (eg amlodipine, diltiazem, felodipine, isradipine, nicardipine, nifedipine, verapamil) | Paracetamol |
| | Perphenazine |
| | Pimozide (mostly) |
| Cannabinoids | Prednisone |
| Carbamazepine | Progesterone |
| Cisapride | Propafenone |
| Citalopram (minor, 30%) | Quetiapine |
| Clindamycin | Quinidine |
| Clozapine (partly) | Quinine |
| Cocaine | Reboxetine |
| Codeine | Rifampicin |
| Cortisol | Risperidone |
| Cyclophosphamide | Ritonavir |
| Cyclosporin | Saquinavir |
| Dapsone | Sertindole (partly) |
| Desamethasone | Sertraline |
| Dextromethorphan | Sildenafil (partly) |
| Disopyramide | Sodium valproate |
| Donepezil | Statins (eg. atorvastatin, lovastatin, pravastatin) |
| Doxorubicin | Steroids, eg. dexamethasone |
| Estradiol (oestradiol) | Tacrolimus |
| Ethosuximide | Tamoxifen |
| Ethinylestradiol | Terfenadine |
| Fentanyl | Testosterone |
| Fexofenadine | Tiagabine |
| Fluoxetine | Tricyclics – tertiary (eg. imipramine, amitriptyline, clomipramine) |
| Galantamine | |
| Glyburide | Topiramate (possibly) |
| Indinavir | Valproate |
| Irinotecan | Venlafaxine |
| Itraconazole | Vinblastine |
| Ketoconazole | Vincristine |
| Lansoprazole (weak) | R-Warfarin (minor) |
| Lidocaine (lignocaine) | Zaleplon (secondary route) |
| Loratadine | Ziprasidone |
| Losartan | Zolpidem (mainly) |
| Macrolides (eg. erythromycin and clarithromycin) | Zotepine |
| | Zopiclone (mostly) |

| Significant enzyme inducers (decrease levels of substrates) | Significant enzyme inhibitors (increase levels of substrates) | |
| --- | --- | --- |
| Barbiturates (all) | Acetazolamide | Mibofradil |
| Carbamazepine | Amiodarone | Miconazole (strong) |
| Cortisol | Cannabinoids | Mirtazapine (very weak/nil) |
| Dexamethasone | Cimetidine (moderate) | Nefazodone (strong) |
| Efavirez (?) | Citalopram (weak) | Nelfinavir |
| Ethosuximide | Clotrimazole | Norfluoxetine moderate) |
| Modafinil? | Danazol | Omeprazole (weak) |
| Nevirapine (?) | Diltiazem (weaker) | Orange juice (weak) |
| Omeprazole | Fluconazole (strong) | Paroxetine (weak) |
| Oxcarbazepine | Fluoxetine (weak) | Quinine |
| Phenobarbital | Fluvoxamine (moderate) | Ritonavir (moderate) |
| Phenytoin | Grapefruit juice (weaker) | Sertindole (weak) |
| Prednisone | Indinavir (moderate) | Sertraline (minor/mod) |
| Primidone | Itraconazole (strong) | Stiripentol (variable) |
| Rifampicin (rapid) | Isoniazid (potent) | Terbinafine |
| Troglitazone | Ketoconazole (strong) | Trazodone |
| | Macrolides (some, eg. clarithromycin, erythromycin) (strong) | Tricyclics (moderate) |
| | | Troleandomycin (strong) |
| | | Venlafaxine (weak) |
| | Methadone (weak?) | Verapamil (weak) |
| | Metronidazole | Zafirlukast |

The drugs listed in each section have been reported to cause that condition in some context (eg. standard dose, high dose, prolonged courses etc). The main references at the end of this section and others (where known or where they exist) next to the drug should be consulted to ascertain the circumstances of reports. The references are offered without qualification and no indication of frequency or status of reports can be given as this information is not really available, except where a side-effect is well-recognised. The UK CSM requests reports of all side-effects of new drugs and severe reactions to established drugs.

**Review**: psychiatric adverse effects of anticonvulsant drugs (Wong *et al, CNS Drugs* 1997, **8**, 492–509), general (Bishop and Lee, *Pharm J* 1998, **261**, 935–39).

---

## 5.1 AGITATION, ANXIETY and NERVOUSNESS

---

● **Psychotropics etc**

Benzodiazepine withdrawal (eg. *Am J Psych* 1984, **141**, 848–52)

Bromocriptine

Bupropion (9.7%, MI)

Carbamazepine (*J Am Acad Child Adolesc Psych* 1988, **27**, 500–3)

Clomethiazole

Citalopram (cases in *Eur J Clin Pharmacol* 1986, **31**, 18–22)

Dexamfetamine (*Curr Ther Res* 1973, **15**, 358–66)

Fluoxetine (9% incidence? eg. *J Clin Psych* 1985, **46** (3 Pt 2), 32–37)

Moclobemide (5–10% incidence, eg. *J Neural Transm* 1989, **28** [Suppl], 77–89)

Olanzapine (*Can J Psych* 1998, **43**, 1054)

Paroxetine (11%? incidence, *Acta Psych Scand* 1989, **80**[Suppl 350], 117–37)

Phenobarbital and other barbiturates

Risperidone (n=1, *Am J Psych* 1995, **152**, 1096–97)

Rivastigmine (<5%, MI)

Temazepam

Tricyclics (eg. amitriptyline, lofepramine at <2%, review in *Drugs* 1989, **37**, 123–40)

● **Anticonvulsants** *

Carbamazepine

Clonazepam

Ethosuximide

Gabapentin

Gabapentin withdrawal (n=1, *J Clin Psych* 1998, **59**, 131)

Lamotrigine

Valproate (n=1, *J Neuropsych Clin Neurosci* 2001, **13**, 528–30)

Vigabatrin

● **Anti-Parkinsonian drugs**

Atropine eye drops (n=1, *J Ped Ophthal Strabis* 1985, **22**, 38–39)

Levodopa (common)

● **Gastrointestinal**

Famotidine (mentioned in *Digestion* 1985, **32**[Suppl 1] 24–31)

Mesalazine (MI)

Nizatadine (MI)

Omeprazole (MI)

● **Cardiovascular**

Doxazosin (2.4% incidence)

Hydralazine

Methyldopa (rare)

Nicardipine (rare)

● **NSAIDs and analgesics**

Ibuprofen (several cases3)

Indometacin (n=1, *South Med J* 1983, **76**, 679–80)

Mefenamic Acid

Naproxen

Naproxen + chloroquine (*Ann Pharmacother* 1993, **27**, 1058–59)

Nefopam

Pentazocine (eg. *BMJ* 1974, **2**, 224)

● **Miscellaneous** *

Amantadine (MI)

Aminophylline

Baclofen (n=2, *Lancet* 1977, **2**, 44)

Bismuth Intoxication (*Postgrad Med J* 1988, **64**, 308–10)

Botulinum toxin A injection (*South Med J* 1999, **92**, 738)

Caffeine OD

Co-trimoxazole (n=1, *J Clin Psychopharmacol* 1991, **11**, 144–5)

Dexamethasone and other gluco-corticoids (eg. *Arch Gen Psych* 1981, **38**, 471–77)

Fentanyl transdermal

Flumazenil (MI)

Flunisolide (MI)

Gancyclovir (*NEJM* 1990, **322**, 933–34)

Ginseng (see *Arch Gen Psych* 1998, **55**, 1033–44)

Granisetron (unconfirmed, eg. *Eur J Cancer* 1990, **26** (Supp 1), S19–23)

Isoniazid (*Lancet* 1989, **ii**, 735–36)

Levamisole (rare, *NEJM* 1990, **322**, 352–58)

Levothyroxine

Mefloquine (*Pharm J* 1989, **243**, 561)

Methoxamine (MI)

Methyltestosterone

Misoprostol (MI)

Morphine

Naltrexone

Neostigmine (cases in *Deutsch Med Wschr* 1966, **91**, 699)

Octreotide (MI)

Phenylephrine (rare)

Phenylpropanolamine OD (*Lancet* 1979, **ii**, 1367)

Piperazine (see *Trans Roy Soc Trop Med Hyg* 1976, **70**, 358)

Prednisone (esp. in children, cases in *Clin Paediatr* 1990, **29**, 382–88)

Pseudoephedrine (n=1, *Eur J Clin Pharmacol* 1978, **14**, 253–59)

Pyridostigmine (rare)

Salbutamol

Sibutramine (SPC)

Streptokinase (see *Drugs* 1973, **5**, 357)

Theophylline

Yohimbine (see *Arch Gen Psych* 1998, **55**, 1033–44)

## 5.2 AGGRESSION * including hostility and violence

**Review**: Shaw and Fletcher, *Adv Drug React & Toxicolog Rev* 2000, **19**, 35–45, 64 refs.

Alcohol withdrawal

Amantadine (cases in *BMJ* 1972, **3**, 50)

Amphetamine withdrawal

Anabolic steroid withdrawal

Barbiturate withdrawal

Benzodiazepines (alprazolam study, *J Aff Dis* 1995, **35**, 117–23; during prolonged benzodiazepine use: *Can J Psych* 2000, **45**, 89–90; aggressogenic effect from diazepam, n=60 male, *Addict Behav* 2002, **27**, 167–77; review *CNS Drugs* 1998, **9**, 41–57; flunitrazepam: *J Am Acad Psych Law* 1999, **27**, 83–99)

Carbamazepine

Dapsone (*BMJ* 1991, **4**, 300)

Donepezil (eg. *Am J Psych* 1998, **155**, 1632–33)

Gabapentin (n=1, *J Neuropsychiatry Clin Neurosci* 2001, **13**, 424)

Lamotrigine (survey, n=19, *Epilepsia* 1998, **39**, 280–82)

Naloxone IV (n=2, *Ann Pharmacother* 1992, **26**, 196–98)

Omeprazole (MI)

Olanzapine (*Can J Psych* 1998, **43**, 1054)

Oxandrolone (and other anabolic steroids)

Paroxetine withdrawal (*Lancet* 1995, **346**, 57)

Tricyclics (rare)

Vigabatrin (eg. *Drugs* 1991, **41**, 889–926)

## 5.3 BEHAVIOURAL CHANGES

Anabolic steroids (*Am J Psych* 1992, **149**, 271–72)

Barbiturates

Benzodiazepines

Clonazepam (*Develop Med & Child Neurol* 1991, **33**, 362–65)

Bismuth (*Acta Neurologica Belgica* 1979, **79**, 73)

Carbamazepine (*J Paediatrics* 1982, **101**, 785–87)

Donepezil (eg. n=7, *Am J Psych* 1998, **155**, 1632–33)

Levodopa

Levodopa + carbidopa

Lithium + antipsychotics

Methyldopa + haloperidol
Prednisone withdrawal (*JAMA* 1989, **261**, 1731)
Theophylline (disputed—not in children, *JAMA* 1992, **267**, 2621–24)

## 5.4 DELIRIUM (*acute organic psychosis*) and CONFUSION

Drug-induced delirium is usually an acute reaction and always with fluctuating levels of awareness of self and environment. It is most frequent in frail or dementing elderly, drug misusers and with pre-existing organic brain disease and strongly associated with anticholinergic activity:

- High risk drug groups are TCAs and typical antipsychotics
- Medium risk drugs include benzodiazepines, sedatives, dopamine-activating drugs, anti-epileptics, histamine H2 receptor blockers, digoxin, beta-blockers and analgesics. Most of these do not have direct anticholinergic effects but *in vitro* have shown to bind to muscarinic receptors.

**Reviews**: drug-induced delirium, including management (Francis, *CNS Drugs* 1995, **5**, 103–14), short review (Jacoby, *Pres J* 1998, **38**, 242–48), general review (Karlsson, *Dement Geriatr Cogn Disord* 1999, **10**, 412–15; Brown, *Semin Clin Neuropsychiatry* 2000, **5**, 113–24), in the elderly (Moore and O'Keeffe, *Drugs & Aging* 1999, **15**, 15–28; Inouye, *Demen & Geri Cog Disord* 1999, **10**, 393–400).

- **Psychotropics etc** *
Alcohol + disulfiram (n=1, *Ann Pharmacother* 2001, **35**, 32–35)
Amfetamines
Anticholinergic drugs (particular association, *J Am Geriatr Soc* 1988, **36**, 525; n=278, *Arch Int Med* 2001, **161**, 1099–1105)
Barbiturates
Benzodiazepines (commonest cause)
Bromides
Bupropion (cases, eg. *J Clin Psych* 1990, **51**, 307–8)

Butyrophenones
Cannabis
Chloral and derivatives
Clomethiazole
Clozapine withdrawal (n=3, *J Clin Psych* 1997, **58**, 252–55)
Cocaine (*Am J Forensic Med Pathol* 1999, **20**, 120–27)
Disulfiram (*Am J Psych* 1974, **131**, 1281)
Disulfiram + alcohol (n=1, *Ann Pharmacother* 2001, **35**, 32–35)
Donepezil (n=1, *J Clin Psych* 2002, **63**, 250–51)
Fluoxetine (n=1, *Am J Psych* 1995, **152**, 295–96)
Lithium (eg. *Am J Psych* 1983, **140**, 1612)
MAOIs eg. phenelzine (*J Clin Psych* 1987, **48**, 340–41)
Meprobamate
Mianserin (*BMJ* 1988, **296**, 137)
Mirtazapine (n=3, *Int Clin Psychopharmacol* 2000, **15**, 239–43)
Paroxetine and benztropine (*Am J Psych* 1997, **154**, 581–82)
Phenothiazines (esp. sedative ones)
Risperidone (n=1, *Can J Psych* 1998, **43**, 194)
Rivastigmine (<5%, MI)
Solvent intoxication
Trazodone (n=3, *Int Clin Psychopharmacol* 1998, **13**, 225–28)
Tricyclics (*J Clin Psych* 1983, **44**, 173–76)
Zolpidem (several cases e.g. *J Clin Psych* 2000, **61**, 449–50; n=1, *Ann Pharmacother* 2001, **35**, 1562–64)

- **Drug withdrawal/cessation etc** *
Alcohol (*Am J Psych* 1997, **154**, 846–51)
Baclofen (*BMJ* 2001, **323**, 870, letter)
Barbiturates
Benzodiazepines
Clomethiazole
Dextropropoxyphene
Nicotine (*J Pain & Symptom Manage* 1998, **15**, S18; n=5, *Neurology* 2001, **57**, 551–53)

- **Anticonvulsants** *
Barbiturates (dose-related)

Carbamazepine (especially early in therapy)

Ethosuximide

Phenytoin (dose-related)

Primidone

Topiramate (n=1, *Bipolar Disord* 2001, **3**, 211–12)

Valproate (high dose)

● **Anti-parkinsonian drugs**

Amantadine (case in *Am J Psych* 1980, **137**, 240–42)

Anticholinergics (esp. longer-acting ones, eg. benzhexol)

Bromocriptine

Levodopa (*Lancet* 1973, **ii**, 929)

Lysuride

Methixene

Pergolide withdrawal (*Clin Neuro-pharmacology* 1988, **11**, 545–48)

Selegiline

● **Cardiovascular drugs**

Amiodarone (n=1, *Am J Psych* 1999, **156**, 1119)

Amiloride

Beta-blockers (eg. *Postgrad Med J* 1990, **66**, 1050–52; atenolol n=1, *BMJ* 1988, **297**, 1048)

Clonidine (*Curr Med Res Opin* 1977, **4**, 630)

Digoxin (*Am Heart J* 1983, **106**, 419; *J Clin Pharmac* 1979, **19**, 747)

Disopyramide

Diuretics (via severe K + loss)

Hydralazine

Lidocaine

Methyldopa

Mexilitine

Procainamide

Spironolactone

● **NSAIDs and analgesics**

Aspirin toxicity (*Lancet* 1971, **2**, 242)

Fenoprofen

Ibuprofen (*Arthritis Rheumat* 1982, **25**, 1013)

Indometacin, inc. OD (*Drugs* 1980, **19**, 220–42)

Nalbuphine

Naproxen (cases)

Narcotics

Papaveretum

Salicylate OD (rare cases)

Sulindac (*JAMA* 1980, **243**, 1630)

Tramadol (n=11, *Curr Problems* 1995, **21**, 2)

● **Anticholinergics**

Anti-parkinsonian drugs (separate section)

Atropine and homatropine eye drops

Scopolamine (transdermal) (*JAMA* 1988, **260**, 478)

● **Anti-infection**

These may indirectly cause delirium if inducing diarrhoea and dehydration.

Acyclovir (eg. *Nervenarzt* 1998, **69**, 1015–18)

Cephalosporins (*BMJ* 1989, **299**, 393)

Chloramphenicol (*Clin Pharmac Therap* 1970, **11**, 194)

Chloroquine

Ciprofloxacin (eg. n=1, *Ann Pharmacother* 1997, **31**, 252, letter)

Clarithromycin (*Psychosomatics* 1998, **39**, 540–42)

Cycloserine

Isoniazid (*BMJ* 1969, **i**, 461)

Mefloquine (*Pharm J* 1989, **243**, 561)

Penicillin

Rifampicin

Streptomycin

Sulphadiazine

Sulphonamides

● **Miscellaneous** *

Adrenocorticotrophin

Aminophylline

Anaesthetic agents (56% incidence, *B J Psych* 2001, **178**, 360–66)

Baclofen

Caffeine (*Am J Psych* 1978, **135**, 855–56)

Cimetidine (eg. *Ann Int Med* 1992, **115**, 658–59)

Corticosteroids (11% incidence? review by Ismail and Wessely, *B J Hosp Pharm* 1995, **53**, 495–99)

Cycloserine

Doxapram

Ergotamine-caffeine (n=1, *Pharmacother* 2002, **22**, 126–29)

Famotidine (n=1, *Pharmacother* 1998, **18**, 404–7)

Gancyclovir (*NEJM* 1990, **322**, 933–34)

Hydroxychloroquine
Hypoglycaemics (oral)
Iodoform gauze (n=1, *Lancet* 1997, **350**, 1294)
Interferon Alfa (*Arch Int Med* 1987, **147**, 1557–80)
Mentholatum (n=1, *Am J Psych* 2000, **157**, 483–84)
Methylprednisolone
Misoprostol (*Drug Intell Clin Pharm* 1991, **25**, 133–44)
Nabilone
Nalbuphine
Phenylpropanolamine O/D (*Br Heart J* 1982, **47**, 51–54)
Piperazine
Ranitidine (*Ann Int Med* 1992, **115**, 658–59; *BMJ* 1987, **294**, 1616)
Theophylline (*BMJ* 1982, **284**, 939)
Triamcinolone

## 5.5 DEPRESSION

Occurs mainly in patients with a history of depression.

**Reviews**: general (Patten and Love, *Psychother Psychosom* 1997, **66**, 63–73), in elderly (Dhondt *et al*, *Int J Ger Psych* 1996, **11**, 141–48).

### ● Psychotropics etc *

Benzodiazepines (especially resistant depression):
  Alprazolam (*Am J Psych* 1987, **144**, 664–65)
  Bromazepam (*Acta Psych Scand* 1989, **74**, 451–58)
  Clorazepate
  Lorazepam (*Am J Psych* 1989, **146**, 1230)
Benzodiazepine withdrawal (*Psychol Med* 1984, **14**, 937–40)
Buspirone (3% incidence? *J Clin Psych* 1982, **43**[sect 2], 100–2)
Disulfiram (case in *Arch Neurol* 1976, **33**, 141)
Flumazenil (<1% incidence, MI)
Fluoxetine (intense suicidal ideation) (*Am J Psych* 1990, **147**, 570–72 etc), disproven (*BMJ* 1991, **303**, 685–92), as fluoxetine shows a slight reduction in suicidal behaviour (n=185, *Am J Psych* 1999, **156**, 195–201)

Fluphenazine depot (n=1, *BMJ* 1969, **3**, 564–67)
MDMA ('Ecstasy') (case in *Lancet* 1991, **338**, 1520; letter, *Lancet* 1996, **347**, 833; former chronic users report higher levels of depression than matched controls – n=29, *J Psychopharmacol* 2001, **15**, 181–86)
Nortriptyline (n=2, *BMJ* 1964, **2**, 1593)
SSRIs (no association with risk of suicide: *Curr Prob* 2000, **26**, 11–12)
Smoking cessation, especially if previous MDD (n=1, *Acta Psych Scand* 1998, **98**, 507–8; n=304, *Am J Psych* 2000, **157**, 368–74; n=100 with history of MDD, 2/12, *Lancet* 2001, **357**, 1929–32; see also *Lancet* 2001, **357**, 1900–1)
Tetrabenazine
Zuclopenthixol

### ● Anticonvulsants *

Carbamazepine
Clobazam (n=1, *BMJ* 1983, **286**, 1246–47)
Clonazepam
Ethosuximide
Lamotrigine (rare, *Epilepsia* 1991, **32** [Suppl 2], S17–21)
Levetiracetam (MI)
Phenobarbital (*Pediatrics* 1990, **85**, 1086–91)
Topiramate (n=1, *Am J Psych* 2001, **158**, 1736)
Vigabatrin (<10%, *Neurology* 1991, **41**, 363–64; *Lancet* 1990, **335**, 970)

### ● Anti-parkinsonian drugs *

Amantadine (mentioned in *JAMA* 1972, **222**, 792–95)
Alpha-adrenoceptor blockers (case-control study concluding no association, *Pharmacoepidemiology & Drug Safety* 2002, **11**, 55–61)
Anticholinergics
Levodopa (well known, review in *NEJM* 1976, **295**, 814–18)

- **Cardiovascular drugs** *

One review has shown that users of medium and high lipid-soluble beta-blockers may have an increased risk of suicide, but there is no greater risk with calcium-channel blockers and ACE inhibitors (n=58,529, *B J Clin Pharmacol* 2001, **52**, 313–18).

Amiodarone (n=1, *B J Psych* 1999, **174;** 366–67; n=1, *J Pharm Tech* 1999, **15**, 50–53)

Beta-blockers (*Drug Intell Clin Pharm* 1984, **18**, 741–42). Lipophilic drugs may be more likely: atenolol, nadolol (low lipid solubility), labetalol, oxprenolol, timolol, acebutol (low/moderate), pindolol (moderate), metoprolol (moderate/high), propranolol (high). Theory disputed in *JAMA* 1992, **267**, 1783–87;1826–27).

Acebutol (mentioned in *Am J Med* 1987, **83**, 223–26)

Atenolol (*J Hum Hypertens* 1987, **1**, 87–93)

Metoprolol (5% incidence? review in *Drugs* 1977, **14**, 321–48)

Nadolol (*Lancet* 1982, **i**, 1286)

Propranolol (*Am J Psych* 1982, **139**, 1187–88)

Timolol

Calcium-channel blockers (no increased risk of suicide with use of calcium channel blockers compared to other antihypertensives, n=153, 458, Gasse *et al*, *BMJ* 2000, **320**, 1251)

Felodipine (cases in *Br Heart J* 1987, **58**, 122–28)

Nicardipine (cases mentioned in *B J Clin Pharmacol* 1985, **20**[Suppl], 178–86)

Nifedipine (*B J Psych* 1991, **159**, 447–48)

Clonidine (1% incidence, case study in *Postgrad Med J* 1993, **150**, 1750)

Diltiazem (*BMJ* 1989, **299**, 796)

Enalapril (n=1, *South Med J* 1989, **82**, 402–3)

Hydralazine

Inositol (n=3, *Am J Psych* 1996, **153**, 839)

Lisinopril (rare, MI)

Methyldopa (review in *Am J Psych* 1983, **140**, 534–38)

Procainamide

Quinapril (n=1, *Am J Psych* 1999, **156**, 1115)

Quinidine (several cases eg. *J Am Geriatr Soc* 1985, **33**, 504–6)

Streptokinase (cases, eg. *Drugs* 1973, **5**, 357–445)

- **Gastrointestinal**

Cimetidine (several cases, eg. *Can J Psych* 1981, **26**, 260–61; *Am J Psych* 1979, **136**, 346)

Famotidine (rare reports, MI)

Metoclopramide (cases, eg. *Am J Gastroenterology* 1989, **84**, 1589–90)

Omeprazole (unproven reports)

Ranitidine (n=3, *Am J Psych* 1986, **143**, 915–16)

Sulphasalazine (MI)

- **NSAIDs and analgesics**

Diflunisal (<1% incidence, MI)

Etodolac (rare, MI)

Flurbiprofen (>1% incidence? MI)

Ibuprofen (uncommon, *Arthritis Rheumat* 1982, **25**, 1013)

Indometacin (4% incidence? *BMJ* 1972, **4**, 398)

Nabilone

Nalbuphine

Naproxen (rare)

Pentazocine (*Southern Med J* 1975, **68**, 808)

Sulindac

Tramadol (n=1, *Am J Psych* 1996, **153**, 843–44)

- **Anti-infection** *

Anti-TB drugs (*Lancet* 1989, **ii**, 735–36)

Cephradine (n=1, *Med J Aus* 1973, **2**, 742)

Chloramphenicol (rare mild cases)

Ciprofloxacin (very rare)

Clotrimazole – oral (review in *Drugs* 1975, **9**, 424)

Co-trimoxazole (rare, but severe cases, eg. *Drug Intell Clin Pharm* 1988, **22**, 267)

Dapsone (*BMJ* 1989, **298**, 1524)

Griseofulvin (as part of psychosis, case in *JAMA* 1974, **229**, 1420)

Interferon alpha (appears relatively common with Hep C; n=39, 33% incidence, *Mol Psychiatry* 2002, **7**, 942–47; n=1, *Am J Psych* 1999, **156**, 1120; n=1, *J Clin Psych* 2002, **63**, 166–67; review *Am J Psych* 2000, **157**, 867–76; can be treated with paroxetine [*NEJM* 2001, **344**, 961–66] or sertraline [*Med J Aus* 2000, **173**, 359-61])

Mefloquine (*Am J Psych* 1992, **149**, 712; CSM warning, *Curr Prob Pharmacovig* 1999, **25**, 15)

Metronidazole (n=1, *Am J Psych* 1977, **134**, 329–30)

Piperazine (cases, eg. *J Indian Med Assoc* 1976, **66**, 33)

Primaquine (n=1, *Ann Int Med* 1980, **92**, 435)

Sulphonamides/sulfonamides

● **Respiratory**

Aminophylline (*BMJ* 1980, **281**, 1322)

Ephedrine (as part of a psychosis, *BMJ* 1968, **2**, 160)

Flunisolide (inhaled, 1–3% incidence, MI)

Theophylline (*BMJ* 1980, **281**, 1322)

● **Cytotoxics etc**

Mesna

Mithramycin

Octreotide (rare, MI)

Plicamycin

Tamoxifen (n=1, *Ann Int Med* 1984, **101**, 652)

Triamcinolone (up to 8%, see *BMJ* 1969, **i**, 682)

● **Steroids**

Review: Ismail and Wessely, *B J Hosp Med* 1995, **53**, 495–99.

Dexamethasone (up to 40% incidence, *Arch Gen Psych* 1981, **38**, 471–77)

Methyltestosterone (rare)

Prednisolone (*J Ass Physicians India* 1973, **21**, 909)

Prednisone (review in *Clin Paediatr* 1990, **29**, 382–88)

Stanozolol

● **Miscellaneous** *

Allopurinol

Anaesthetic agents (in elderly, n=140, *B J Psych* 2001, **178**, 360–66)

Astemizole (debatable – *Drugs* 1984, **28**, 38–61)

Baclofen (rare cases eg. *Arch Int Med* 1985, **145**, 1717–18)

Botulinum toxin A injection (*South Med J* 1999, **92**, 738)

Caffeine withdrawal (review in *NEJM* 1992, **327**, 1160–61)

Cholesterol-lowering drugs? (higher incidence of low cholesterol in parasuicide [n=100, *B J Psych* 2000, **177**, 77–83] and suicide [n=783, Bocchetta *et al, Acta Psych Scand* 2001, **104**, 37–41]; but high risk of violent suicide with high cholesterol, n=37,635, *Am J Psych* 2000, **157**, 648–50). Low cholesterol seems to be connected with higher suicide rates.

Cinnarizine (*BMJ* 1988, **297**, 722)

Clomiphene

Codeine – long-term use (community survey, *J Clin Psychopharmacol* 1999, **19**, 373–76)

Danazol (rare cases, *Am J Obstet* 1977, **127**, 130)

Diphenoxylate (MI)

Etretinate (*BMJ* 1989, **298**, 964)

Fentanyl (transdermal)

Hydroxyzine (some reports)

Isotretinoin (v. rare, *J Am Dermatol* 1988, **18**, 543–52; summary—*Pharm J* 1998, **260**, 547; case of suicide – *JAMA* 1998, **279**, 1057; n=1 and discussion, *World J Biol Psych* 2001, **2**, 159–61)

Ondansetron (n=1, *Am J Psych* 1995, **152**, 1101)

Oral contraceptives combined (16–56% incidence, review in *J Adolescent Health Care* 1981, **2**, 53–64)

Organophosphates (n=761, *Ann Epidemiol* 2002, **12**, 389–94)

Phenylpropanolamine (*Am J Psych* 1990, **147**, 367–68)

Pravastatin (n=4, *Lancet* 1993, **341**, 910)

Progestogens (*Drug Treatment Psych* 1982, **12**, 234–35)
Roaccutane (SPC)
Simvastatin (*Curr Prob* 1992, **33**, n=4, *Lancet* 1993, **341**, 14. Low cholesterol is a high risk factor for attempted suicide – *Am J Psych* 1995, **152**, 419–23)
Tamoxifen (**no** increased risk, n=11,064, *J Natl Cancer Inst* 2001, **93**, 1615–23)
Trimeprazine/alimemazine
Xylometazoline (case in child in *JAMA* 1970, **211**, 123–24)

## 5.6 HALLUCINATIONS (including visual disturbances, see also psychosis)

- **Psychotropics etc** *

Alcohol
Amfetamines (*Biol Psych* 1980, **15**, 749)
Benzodiazepines
Fluoxetine (case in *Am J Psych* 1993, **150**, 1750)
Imipramine
LSD (*J Nerv Mental Dis* 1991, **179**, 173–74)
Maprotiline (n=1, *Acta Psych Scand* 2000, **101**, 476–77)
Methadone (*J Am Acad Child Adolesc Psych* 1999, **38**, 355–56)
Midazolam IV (*Drug Intell Clin Pharm* 1989, **23**, 671–72)
Nefazodone (visual field shimmering, n=2, *J Clin Psych* 1999, **60**, 124)
Phenelzine (n=1, *Am J Psych* 1994, **151**, 450)
Sertraline + oxycodone (n=1, *J Clin Pharmacol* 2001, **41**, 224)
Tricyclics
Zolpidem (n=5, *J Toxicol Clin Toxicol* 1998, **36**, 195–203)
Zopiclone (*Pharm J* 1990, **245**, 210)

- **Anti-convulsants** *

Carbamazepine
Gabapentin
Valproate

- **Anti-parkinson drugs** *

Amantadine (n=1, *Med J Aus* 1973, **1**, 444)

Anticholinergics
Bromocriptine (<1% incidence – *Ann Int Med* 1984, **101**, 149)
Levodopa (<26% incidence in elderly, eg. *Postgrad Med J* 1989, **65**, 358–61)
Levodopa-carbidopa + paroxetine (n=1, *Ned Tijdschr Geneeskd* 2002, **146**, 1056–57).
Pergolide (in up to 13% eg. *Neurology* 1982, **32**, 1181–84)
Pergolide withdrawal (*Clin Neuropharmacology* 1988, **11**, 545–48)

- **Cardiovascular drugs**

Beta-blockers (*Postgrad Med J* 1987, **63**, 57–58)
Clonidine (n=3, *Ann Int Med* 1980, **93**, 456)
Digoxin (*Ann Int Med* 1979, **91**, 865).
Diltiazem (*Psychiatr Prax* 1998, **25**, 91–92)
Disopyramide
Procainamide
Streptokinase (reported in *Drugs* 1973, **5**, 357–445)
Timolol (*JAMA* 1980, **244**, 768)

- **NSAIDs and analgesics** *

Buprenorphine (rare <1%, eg. *BMJ* 1988, **296**, 214)
Buprenorphine–epidural (*BMJ* 1989, **298**, 928)
Celecoxib (auditory n=1, *Am J Psych* 2000, **157**, 1022–23)
Fenbufen (*BMJ* 1985, **290**, 822)
Indometacin (rare, eg. *BMJ* 1966, **1**, 80; OD in *Drugs* 1980, **19**, 220–42)
Nefopam (*Curr Problems*, **24**, 1.89)
Oxycodone + sertraline (n=1, *J Clin Pharmacol* 2001, **41**, 224)
Pentazocine
Salicylates
Tramadol (n=6, *Curr Probs* 1995, **21**, 2)

- **Anti-infections** *

Amoxycillin/amoxicillin (*Practitioner* 1984, **228**, 884)
Ciprofloxacin (*Arch Int Med* 1989, **110**, 170–71)
Gentamicin (*JAMA* 1977, **238**, 53)
Itraconazole, oral (n=1, *Clin Infect Dis* 1995, **21**, 456)

● **Miscellaneous** *

Cimetidine
(*Arch Int Med* 1983, **98**, 677)

Corticosteroids

Decongestants (*BMJ* 1984, **288**, 1688)

Dextromethorphan (n=1,
*Psychosomatics* 1996, **37**, 71–74)

Erythropoetin (n=5, *NEJM* 1991, **325**,
285; *J Neurol* 1999, **246**, 614–16)

Famotidine (n=1, *Pharmacother* 1998,
**18**, 404–7)

Ginseng (n=1, *Acta Psych Scand* 2002,
**105**, 76–78)

Hydroxyurea

Khat chewing (n=4, *B J Hosp Med*
1995, **54**, 322–26)

Ketamine (*Anaesthesia* 1990, **45**, 422)

Mefloquine (*NEJM* 1990, **322**,
1752–53)

Phenylephrine (*JAMA* 1982, **247**, 1859)

Phenylpropanolamine (*JAMA* 1981,
**245**, 601–2)

Promethazine (*Acta Paediatrica Scand*
1989, **78**, 131–32)

Pseudoephedrine

Radiocontrast media (n=2, review, *Br
J Clin Pharmacol* 1999, **47**, 226–27)

Ranitidine (*E J Clin Pharm* 1985, **29**,
375–76)

Salbutamol (nebulised) (*BMJ* 1986,
**292**, 1430)

Steroid-induced mania (case, review,
risk factors; *Can J Clin Pharmacol*
2001, **8**, 109–12)

Sulphasalazine

Tolterodine (n=1, *B J Urol* 1999, **84**,
1109)

## 5.7 MANIA, HYPOMANIA or EUPHORIA

Antidepressant-induced mania may be a marker for increased vulnerability to antidepressant-induced cycle acceleration. The most common symptoms of drug-induced mania are increased activity, rapid speech, elevated mood and insomnia. The main risk factors are prior history, family history or concurrent mood disorder. Steroids, levodopa, triazolo-benzodiazepines and hallucinogens are most commonly associated. A sudden switch to mania or hypomania may be indicative of the diagnosis of Bipolar III.

**Reviews**: antidepressant-induced mania (Altshuler *et al, Am J Psych* 1995, **152**, 1130–38), drug induced mania (Peet and Peters, *Drug Safety* 1995, **12**, 146–53).

● **Hallucinogens**

LSD (*Am J Psych* 1981, **138**, 1508–9)

● **CNS stimulants**

Amfetamine withdrawal (*J Clin Psych* 1980, **41**, 33–34)

Dexamfetamine (*Am J Psych* 1976, **133**, 1177–80)

Ephedrine (*J Clin Psychopharmacol* 1983, **3**, 97–100; and in a Herbal Diet Supplement, case in *Am J Psych* 1995, **152**, 647)

Methylphenidate (*J Clin Psych* 1986, **47**, 566–67)

Pemoline (possible case in *Biol Psych* 1981, **16**, 987–89)

Phenylephrine (*Am J Psych* 1981, **138**, 837–38)

Phenylpropanolamine (*Am J Psych* 1981, **138**, 392)

Pseudoephedrine (*Psych J of Uni Ottawa* 1987, **12**, 47–48)

● **Antidepressants** *

Antidepressant-induced switching to mania is well known (especially in Bipolar III), as is the spontaneous swing to hypomania from depression in bipolars. SSRIs and bupropion are generally considered less likely to switch. The incidence of switch from depression to mania is in the order of 25% with placebo and 50% with tricyclics (Post *et al, CNS Drugs* 1997, **8**, 352–65, 80 refs). Risk factors include increased antidepressant trials and substance misuse (n=53, Goldberg and Whiteside, *J Clin Psych* 2002, **62**, 792–95). Switching can be reduced by using adjunctive lithium (n=44, review by Henry *et al, J Clin Psych* 2001, **62**, 249–55). SSRI-induced hypomania may be dose-related (n=2, Ramasubbu, *Acta Psych Scand* 2001, **104**, 236–39) and

may be similar with SSRIs and bupropion (retrospective, Joffe *et al, Acta Psych Scand* 2002, **105**, 427–30).
**Reviews**: Peet, *B J Psych* 1995, **164**, 549–50; Benazzi, *J Aff Dis* 1997, **46**, 73–77.

Amitriptyline (*BMJ* 1991, **303**, 331–32, 720, 1200; *Neurology* 1989, **39**, 305)

Amitriptyline withdrawal (*J Clin Psych* 1980, **41**, 33–34)

Amoxapine (*Compr Psych* 1982, **23**, 590–92)

Bupropion (n=1, within a week, *Bipolar Disorders* 2001, **3**, 159–60)

Clomipramine (*Arch Gen Psych* 1979, **36**, 560–65)

Citalopram + silbutramine (n=1, *J Clin Psych* 2002, **63**, 165)

Desipramine (*Am J Psych* 1985, **142**, 386)

Desipramine withdrawal (*Am J Psych* 1983, **140**, 624–25)

Fluoxetine (cases in *Ann Pharmacother* 1991, **25**, 1395–96; *Am J Psych* 1991, **148**, 1403–4; n=3, *J Child Adolesc Psychopharmacol* 1998, **8**, 73–80)

Flupentixol (n=6, *Eur Psych* 2002, **17**, 349–52)

Fluvoxamine (*Am J Psych* 1991, **148**, 1263–64; case series in *Ann Pharmacother* 1993, **27**, 1455–57; n=1, *World J Biol Psych* 2001, **2**, 201–4)

Imipramine (eg. *J Clin Psychopharmacol* 1985, **5**, 342–43)

Imipramine withdrawal (*Am J Psych* 1986, **143**, 260)

Isocarboxazid (n=3, *J Clin Psych* 1986, **47**, 40–41)

Isocarboxazid withdrawal (n=2, *J Clin Psychopharmacol* 1985, **5**, 340–42)

Maprotiline (cases in *Curr Ther Res* 1976, **19**, 463–68)

Mianserin

Mirtazapine (n=1, *J Neuropsychiatry Clin Neurosci* 1999, **11**, 115–16; n=1, *B J Psych* 1999, **175**, 390; n=1 + review, *Int Clin Psychopharmacol* 2002, **17**, 319–22)

Mirtazapine withdrawal (n=1, *B J Psych* 1999, **175**, 390)

Mirtazapine + sertraline (n=1, *J Clin Psychiatry* 1998, **59**, 320)

Mirtazapine + fluoxetine (n=1, *Depress Anxiety* 2002, **15**, 46–47)

Nefazodone (several cases eg. n=1, *Am J Psych* 1997, **154**, 578–79)

Paroxetine (case of psychotic mania, *Am J Psych* 1995, **152**, 1399–440)

Phenelzine (eg. *Biol Psych* 1985, **20**, 1009–14)

Quetiapine (n=1, *Eur Psych* 2002, **17**, 292–93)

Reboxetine (n=3, *Am J Psych* 2001, **62**, 655–56)

Sertraline (cases in *Am J Psych* 1987, **144**, 1513–14; *Am J Psych* 1994, **343**, 606–7)

St. John's wort (n=1, *J Clin Psych* 1998, **59**, 689; n=2, *Biol Psych* 1999, **46**, 1707–8; n=1, *World J Biol Psych* 2002, **3**, 58–59; n=1, *Ned Tijdschr Geneeskd* 2001, **145**, 1943–45)

Trazodone (eg. *B J Psych* 1991, **158**, 275–78)

Trazodone withdrawal (*B J Psych* 1987, **151**, 274)

Tryptophan + MAOI (*Am J Psych* 1985, **142**, 1487–88)

Venlafaxine (SPC; *J Clin Psychopharmacol* 1999, **19**, 184–85)

● **Other Psychotropics etc \***

Alprazolam (*J Clin Psych* 1987, **48**, 117–18)

Benzodiazepine withdrawal (*Acta Psych Scand* 1989, **79**, 406–7)

Bupropion (rare, *Am J Psych* 1991, **148**, 541)

Buspirone (*B J Psych* 1991, **158**, 136–37)

Disulfiram (*J Clin Psychopharmacol* 1986, **6**, 178–80; *J Am Acad Child Adolesc Psych* 1988, **27**, 500–3)

Fenfluramine (eg. *Med J Aus* 1976, **2**, 537; *Am J Psych* 1997, **154**, 711)

Lithium + TCA (*B J Psych* 1988, **153**, 828–30)

Lithium toxicity (*Drug Intell Clin Pharm* 1987, **21**, 979)

Lorazepam withdrawal (*J Aff Dis* 1989, **17**, 93–95)

Midazolam (euphoria possible)

Olanzapine (review, concludes half of reports are poorly documented but in the others mood elevating effects were prominent, n=26, *J Clin Psych* 2000, **61**, 649–55).

Risperidone (review, concludes half of reports are poorly documented but in the others mood elevating effects were prominent, n=26, *J Clin Psych* 2000, **61**, 649–55; eg. *Ann Pharmacother* 1999, **33**, 380–81).

Risperidone withdrawal (n=1, *J Clin Psych* 1998, **59**, 620–21)

Ziprasidone (n=3, *Am J Psych* 2002, **159**, 673–74)

● **Anticonvulsants** *

Carbamazepine (*J Clin Psych* 1984, **45**, 272–74)

Carbamazepine withdrawal (n=1, *B J Psych* 1995, **167**, 698)

Clonazepam (*Drug Intell Clin Pharm* 1991, **25**, 938–39)

Ethosuximide (MI)

Gabapentin (n=1, *B J Psych* 1995, **166**, 679–80; review in *B J Psych* 1995, **167**, 549–54; n=1, *B J Psych* 1999, **175**, 291)

Phenobarbital (*Paediatrics* 1984, **74**, 1133)

Topiramate (n=1, *J Neurol Neurosurg Psych* 2002, **73**, 208–9)

Valproate

Vigabatrin (n=1, *Lancet* 1994, **343**, 606–7)

● **Anti-Parkinsonian drugs**

Amantadine (n=1, *J Clin Psych* 1989, **50**, 143–44)

Bromocriptine (*BMJ* 1984, **289**, 1101–3)

Levodopa (cases in, eg. *NEJM* 1971, **285**, 1326)

Levodopa + carbidopa (*J Clin Psychopharmacol* 1985, **5**, 338–39)

Procyclidine (eg. *B J Psych* 1982, **141**, 81–84)

● **Cardiovascular drugs**

Captopril (*Am J Psych* 1985, **142**, 759–60; case in *Am J Psych* 1993, **150**, 1429–30)

Clonidine (*Am J Psych* 1982, **139**, 1083)

Clonidine withdrawal (*J Clin Psychopharmacol* 1981, **1**, 93–95)

Digoxin (*Medical Journal & Record* 1929, **130**, 381–82)

Diltiazem (*Clin Cardiology* 1984, **7**, 611–12)

Hydralazine

Methyldopa withdrawal (*Am J Psych* 1989, **146**, 1075–76)

Procainamide (*Am J Psych* 1988, **145**, 129–30)

Propranolol (*Southern Med J* 1984, **77**, 1603)

Propranolol withdrawal (*Am J Psych* 1986, **143**, 1633)

● **NSAIDs and analgesics**

Buprenorphine (up to 1%, *B J Clin Pract* 1980, **34**, 144–46)

Codeine + paracetamol (n=1, *Aust N Z J Psych* 1998, **32**, 586–88)

Indometacin (*J Clin Psychopharmacol* 1987, **7**, 203–4)

Nefopam IM (euphoria reported—*B J Anaesth* 1979, **51**, 691–95)

Pentazocine (*Southern Med J* 1975, **68**, 808)

● **Gastrointestinal**

Cimetidine (*J Clin Psych* 1983, **44**, 267–68)

Metoclopramide (case in *J Clin Psych* 1984, **45**, 180)

Ranitidine IV (case in *Southern Med J* 1987, **80**, 1467)

● **Steroids** *

Steroid-induced mania (case, review, risk factors; *Can J Clin Pharmacol* 2001, **8**, 109–12)

ACTH (*Psychosomatic Med* 1953, **15**, 280–91)

Beclometasone/beclomethasone aerosol (*Am J Psych* 1989, **146**, 1076–77)

Beclometasone/beclomethasone nasal spray (*B J Psych* 1989, **155**, 871–72)

Corticosteroids (*Clin Pharm* 1987, **6**, 186; n=1, *Anesthesiology* 1996, **85**, 1194–96)

Cortisone (*Psychosomat Med* 1953, **15**, 589–97)

Dexamethasone (up to 31% incidence, *Arch Gen Psych* 1981, **38**, 471–77)

Hydrocortisone (*J Nerv Mental Dis* 1979, **167**, 229–36; *Postgrad Med J* 1992, **68**, 41–43)

Prednisone (*J Aff Dis* 1983, **5**, 319–24)

Testosterone-patches (n=1, *Am J Psych* 1999, **156**, 969)

Triamcinolone (rare cases)

● **Anti-infection** *

Anti-TB drugs (*Lancet* 1989, **ii**, 735–36)

Chloroquine (*B J Psych* 1991, **159**, 164–65 + 735)

Clarithromycin (n=1, *Am J Psych* 1998, **155**, 1626)

Dapsone (*BMJ* 1989, **298**, 1524)

Efavirenz overdose (n=1, *Clin Infect Dis* 2001, **33**, 270–71)

Isoniazid (*BMJ* 1957, **ii**, 743–46)

Mepacrine (*Mayo Clin Proceed* 1989, **64**, 129)

Zidovudine (*JAMA* 1988, **259**, 3406)

● **Miscellaneous** *

Alimemazine/trimeprazine (rare cases)

Aminophylline

Baclofen (eg. *Biol Psych* 1982, **17**, 757–59)

Baclofen withdrawal (*Am J Psych* 1980, **137**, 1466–67)

Bromide (*Am J Psych* 1976, **133**, 228–29)

Calcium IV (*J Nerv Mental Dis* 1980, **168**, 562–63)

Cyclizine (MI)

Cyclosporin (*Biol Psych* 1984, **19**, 1161–62)

Cyproheptadine (rare, eg. *Am J Psych* 1980, **137**, 378–79)

Decongestants

Dextromethorphan (n=1, *Psychosomatics* 1996, **37**, 71–74)

Dextromethorphan abuse (cases in *BMJ* 1986, **293**, 597; *BMJ* 1993, **306**, 896)

Dihydroepiandrosterone (*Biol Psych* 1999, **45**, 241–42)

Ginseng (n=1, *Acta Psych Scand* 2002, **105**, 76–78)

Herbal remedies (n=1, *Am J Psych* 1998, **155**, 1627)

Interferon-alpha (n=1, *Postgrad Med J* 1997, **73**, 834–35)

Mazindol (not reported — *B J Addict* 1972, **67**, 39–44)

Nicotine withdrawal (*Am J Psych* 1990, **147**, 1254–55; *Am J Psych* 1992, **149**, 708)

Omega-3 fatty acids (n=1, *Arch Gen Psych* 2000, **57**, 715–16)

Procarbazine (*BMJ* 1982, **284**, 82)

Salbutamol

Silbutramine + citalopram (n=1, *J Clin Psych* 2002, **63**, 165).

Thyroid (*Am J Psych* 1970, **126**, 1667–69)

Tramadol (n=1, *Am J Psych* 1997, **154**, 1624)

Triptorelin (n=1, *B J Psych* 1999, **175**, 290–91),

Triiodothyronine (*J Clin Psych* 1986, **47**, 521–32)

Yohimbine? (see *Arch Gen Psych* 1998, **55**, 1033–44)

## 5.8 MOVEMENT DISORDERS

### EXTRA-PYRAMIDAL DISORDERS

Four distinct types of drug-induced extra-pyramidal or movement disorders are common, especially by anti-psychotics. These are dystonia, akathisia, pseudoparkinsonism and dyskinesia. All can occur acutely or be delayed (tardive). Acute reactions are usually at the start of treatment or after a dose increase and are usually reversible. The tardive forms are not invariably reversible on discontinuation of the drug or on dose reduction and can be aggravated by anticholinergics.

**Reviews**: calcium channel blockers as cause of EPSEs (*Ann Pharmacother* 1995, **29**, 73–75), general (Jimenez-Jimenez *et al*, *Drug Safety* 1997, **16**, 180–204, 643 refs; n=1559, Muscettola *et al*, *J Clin Psychopharmacol* 1999, **19**, 203–8), SSRI-induced movement disorders (Gerber and Lynd, *Ann Pharmacother* 1998, **32**, 692–98), management of acute antipsychotic-induced EPSEs (Remington and Bezchlibnyk-Butler, *CNS Drugs* 1996,

5[Suppl 1], 21–35), tardive EPSEs (Marsalek, *Pharmacopsychiatry* 2000, **33**[Suppl 1], 14–33).

### 5.8.1 Pseudoparkinsonism
This is characterised by akinesia, tremor and rigidity, and generally occurs within a month of the start of treatment.

● **Psychotropics etc** *

Amoxapine (*Am J Psych* 1983, **140**, 1233–35)

Antipsychotics (see *2.1.5*).

Bromocriptine

Bupropion (n=1, *J Clin Psych* 1992, **53**, 157–59)

Clozapine (n=1, *Ann Pharmacother* 2000, **34**, 615–18)

Cocaine abuse (*Arch Int Med* 1997, **157**, 241)

Dexamfetamine

Donepezil (n=1, *Ann Pharmacother* 1998, **32**, 610–11)

Fluoxetine (*Am J Psych* 1989, **146**, 1352–53; case in *Neurology* 1993, **43**, 211–13; review of n=21, *Parkinsonism Relat Disord* 2002, **8**, 325–27)

Fluoxetine withdrawal (*Am J Psych* 1991, **148**, 1263)

Fluvoxamine (*Am J Psych* 1989, **146**, 1352–53)

Lithium - long-term (eg. *B J Psych* 1980, **136**, 191) and short-term (*J Neurol Sci* 2000, **176**, 78–79)

MAOIs

Olanzapine overdose (n=1, *Am J Psych* 1998, **155**, 1630–31)

Paroxetine (cases reported in *Current Problems* 1993, **19**, 1; incidence as with other SSRIs-*Lancet* 1993, **341**, 624)

Prochlorperazine

Risperidone (case with 2mg/d, *Lancet* 1995, **346**, 1226; probable case, *Am J Psych* 1996, **153**, 843)

Sertraline (n=1, *Am J Psych* 1994, **151**, 288)

Sertraline and oxycodone (n=1, *J Clin Pharmacol* 2001, **41**, 224)

SSRIs (review, *Prescrire Internat* 2001, **10**, 118–19; concluding annual

incidence around 1 or 2 cases per 1000 patients)

Trazodone (*Clin Neuropharmacol* 1988, **11**, 180–82; n=1, *Nephron* 2002, **90**, 222–23)

Tricyclics

● **Anticonvulsants** *

Carbamazepine (tremor may occur in 22% of pts, *NEJM* 1992, **327**, 765–71)

Lamotrigine (SPC)

Valproate (n=1, elderly, demented patient, *J Clin Psych* 2002, **63**, 75)

● **NSAIDs and analgesics**

Fenoprofen

Flurbiprofen (*BMJ* 1990, **300**, 549)

Ibuprofen (case in *Postgrad Med J* 1987, **63**, 593–94)

Indometacin

Mefenamic acid (n=1, *J Roy Soc Med* 1983, **76**, 435)

Nabilone

Pethidine and other opioids

Sulindac (single case in *Ann Neurol* 1985, **17**, 104–5)

● **Cardiovascular drugs**

Amiodarone (*Annals Neurol* 1989, **25**, 630–32)

Diazoxide (n=6, *BMJ* 1973, **3**, 474–75)

Diltiazem (*Am J Med* 1989, **87**, 95–96)

Methyldopa (cases in *Can Med Assoc J* 1966, **95**, 928)

Metirosine

Mexilitine

Nifedipine (*BMJ* 1978, **i**, 1619)

Tocainide

● **Gastrointestinal**

Cimetidine (possible case in *Postgrad Med J* 1982, **58**, 527–28)

Domperidone (rare, case in *Helv Paediat Acta* 1984, **39**, 285–88)

Metoclopramide (2–30% incidence, cases in, eg. *Ann Int Med* 1989, **149**, 2486–92)

Prochlorperazine (common, eg. *Lancet* 1984, **2**, 1082–83)

● **Anti-infection**

Acyclovir

Cephaloridine

Chloroquine
- **Respiratory drugs**
Antihistamines
Brompheniramine (*NEJM* 1975, **293**, 486)
Cinnarizine (*Lancet* 1987, **i**, 1324)
Diphenhydramine (*NEJM* 1977, **296**, 111)
Orciprenaline
Promethazine (*Clin Pharm* 1984, **3**, 83)
Salbutamol
Terbutaline
- **Hormones**
Medroxyprogesterone
- **Cytotoxics**
Cyclosporin
Interferons
- **Miscellaneous**
Cyclizine
Levodopa
Ondansetron (cases in *Ann Pharmacother* 1994, **28**, 280 and *Ann Pharmacother* 1996, **30**, 196)
Prednisolone (increases incidence with neuroleptics, review in *JAMA* 1973, **224**, 889)
Tetrabenazine

### 5.8.2 Akathisia

Characterised by motor restlessness, with an inability to stay still. Onset is around 6–60 days and has been implicated with all antipsychotics, but especially with the high potency ones.
**Review**: symptoms, classification, drug effects, treatment etc (Gattera *et al*, *Aus J Hosp Pharm* 1994, **24**, 480–89).
- **Psychotropics etc** *
Alimemazine /trimeprazine (MI)
Alprazolam (MI)
Amoxapine (*Curr Ther Res* 1972, **14**, 381–89)
Antipsychotics (*Psychopharmacol* 1989, **97**, 1–11. Trifluoperazine and haloperidol more likely than less potent drugs, eg. chlorpromazine or thioridazine)
Buspirone (n=1, *Ann Int Med* 1983, **99**, 794–95).
Citalopram (n=1, *J Clin Psych* 1988, **49**[Suppl], 18–22)

Clozapine (6% incidence claimed: *Psychopharmacology* 1995, **118**, 52–56; but may be rarer, see *Biol Psych* 1991, **29**, 1215–19)
Fluoxetine (*J Clin Psych* 1991, **52**, 491–93; *J Clin Psych* 1989, **50**, 339–42)
Fluvoxamine (n=1, resulting in suicide attempt, *J Clin Psych* 1999, **60**, 869)
Haloperidol (review in *Psychopharmacol* 1985, **21**, 69–72)
Imipramine (n=1, *J Clin Psychopharmacol* 1987, **7**, 254–57)
Lithium (*J Neurol Sci* 2000, **176**, 78–79)
Lorazepam (n=1, *Oncology* 1990, **47**, 415–17)
Mianserin (*B J Psych* 1989, **155**, 415–17)
Mirtazapine (*Med J Aust* 2002, **176**, 242)
Olanzapine (6% incidence)
Paroxetine (*Can J Psych* 2000, **45**, 398)
Pipothiazine (study in *Curr Ther Res* 1981, **29**, 903–14)
Prochlorperazine (44% incidence with IV, n=140, *Ann Emerg Med* 1999, **34**, 469–75)
Promazine (MI)
Risperidone (*Neurology* 1995, **45**, 1419)
Risperidone withdrawal (*Am J Psych* 1997, **154**, 437–38; n=2, *Actas Esp Psiquiatr* 2002, **30**, 195–97)
Risperidone + levomepromazine (n=1, *Eur Psych* 2002, **17**, 294–95)
Sertraline (n=1, *Am J Psych* 1993, **150**, 986–87; *J Clin Psych* 1993, **54**, 321; mistaken for panic attack, n=1, *Psychiatr Serv* 2002, **53**, 1477–78)
Tricyclics (*BMJ* 1986, **282**, 1529)
Venlafaxine withdrawal (n=1, *Am Fam Physician* 1997, **56**, 455–62)
Zuclopenthixol (study in *Pharmatherapeutica* 1989, **5**, 380–86)
- **Others** *
Diltiazem (n=1, *Ann Int Med* 1983, **99**, 794)
Interferon-alpha (*Gen Hosp Psychiatry* 1999, **21**, 134–35)
Levodopa (review in *Neurology* 1990, **40**, 340–45)

Melotonin withdrawal (*Mov Disord* 1999, **14**, 381–82)

Metoclopramide (n=1, *Milit Med* 1987, **152**, 585–86)

Ondansetron (n=1, *Cancer* 1992, **69**, 1275)

Prochlorperazine (n=1, *JAMA* 1985, **253**, 635)

Verapamil (*Lancet* 1991, **338**, 893)

### 5.8.3 Dystonias

Includes oculogyric crisis, trismus and torticollis. May occur within 72 hours of start of therapy. Occurs more frequently with high-potency antipsychotics, where the incidence may be as high as 10% (*Applied Therapeutics*, Koda-Kimble, 1988).

**Review**: van Harten *et al, BMJ* 1999, **319**, 623–26, 34 refs.

● **Psychotropics etc** *

Amoxapine (*Psychosomatics* 1984, **25**, 66–69)

Benzatropine (case in child in *Ann Emerg Med* 1986, **15**, 594–96)

Bupropion (n=1, *J Clin Psych* 1997, **58**, 218; n=1, *Ann Pharmacother* 2002, **36**, 251–54)

Buspirone (possible case in *Neurology* 1990, **40**, 1904; discussion in *Neurology* 1991, **41**, 1850)

Carbamazepine (n=1, *Postgrad Med J* 1994, **70**, 54; n=1, *NZ Med J* 1994, **107**, 360–61)

Clozapine (rare, n=1, *Am J Psych* 1995, **152**, 647–48)

Clozapine withdrawal, abrupt (cases, *J Clin Psych* 1998, **59**, 472–77)

Cocaine (risk factor for neuroleptic-induced acute dystonia, *J Clin Psych* 1998, **59**, 128–30)

Cocaine withdrawal (*Neurology* 1989, **39**, 996)

Disulfiram (n=1, *Mov Disord* 1991, **6**, 166–70)

Fluoxetine (*Am J Psych* 1994, **151**, 149; n=1, *Mov Disorder* 2001, **16**, 767–69)

Flupentixol decanoate (n=1, *BMJ* 1981, **282**, 1756)

Loxapine (MI)

Midazolam (*BMJ* 1990, **300**, 614)

Mirtazapine (n=1, *J Clin Psych* 2002, **63**, 452–53)

Olanzapine (n=1, *Am J Psych* 1999, **156**, 1662; tardive n=1, *Neurol Sci* 2001, **22**, 331–32)

Paroxetine (cases reviewed in *Current Problems* 1993, **19**, 1)

Phenelzine (n=1, *J Clin Psychopharmacol* 1990, **10**, 144–45)

Prochlorperazine

Risperidone (n=1, *Am J Psych* 1996, **153**, 577; *Can J Psych* 1999, **44**, 507–8; n=1, *Lancet* 1999, **353**, 981, letter)

Sertraline (n=1, *J Clin Psychopharmacol* 1999, **19**, 98–100; mistaken for panic attack, n=1, *Psychiatr Serv* 2002, **53**, 1477–78)

Tiagabine (n=3, *Epilepsia* 2001, **42**, 944–46)

Tricyclics

Venlafaxine (SPC)

Zuclopenthixol (study in *Acta Psych Scand* 1991, **84**, 14–16)

● **Others** *

Alimemazine/trimeprazine (MI).

Amiodarone (isolated case in *Lancet* 1979, **1**, 981–82)

Azapropazone (n=1, *J Neurol Neurosurg Psych* 1988, **51**, 731–32)

Diphenhydramine oral (*Clin Pharm* 1989, **8**, 471)

Diphenhydramine IV (*Ann Int Med* 1989, **111**, 92–93)

Domperidone

Ergotamine (*Mov Disord* 1991, **6**, 263–64)

Indometacin (n=1, *J Neurol Neurosurg Psych* 1988, **51**, 731–32)

Metoclopramide (3% incidence, see *NEJM* 1983, **309**, 433; cases in, eg. *Ann Int Med* 1989, **149**, 2486–92)

Nifedipine (*Ann Int Med* 1985, **104**, 125)

Penicillamine (review in *Arch Neurol* 1987, **44**, 490–93)

Prochlorperazine (many cases)

Promethazine (n=1, *Clin Pharm* 1984, **3**, 83–85)

Propofol (n=45, *Anesth Analg* 2002, **94**, 1237–40)

Propranolol

Sumatriptan (possible case in *Ann Pharmacother* 1994, **28**, 1199)

Verapamil (n=1, *J Clin Pharmacy Ther* 1998, **23**, 79–80)

## 5.8.4 Dyskinesia (eg. Tardive)*

If of late onset, TD can be a potentially irreversible movement disorder with possible relationship to drug, dose and duration (see *1.20.3*).

Amoxapine (mentioned in *J Clin Psychopharmacol* 1987, **7**, 243–46)

Benztropine (study showed worsening TD—*Neuropsychobiology* 1980, **6**, 109)

Bupropion (*J Clin Psych* 1997, **58**, 218)

Buspirone? (*Pharm J* 1989, **243**, 480)

Clomipramine (*Am J Psych* 1993, **150**, 165–66)

Clozapine (n=1, *Biol Psych* 1994, **35**, 886–87; n=1, *J Clin Psych* 2002, **63**, 167–68)

Clozapine withdrawal, abrupt (cases, *J Clin Psychiatry* 1998, **59**, 472–77)

Cocaine (n=1, *Neurology* 2001, **56**, 964–65)

Donepezil (*Ann Pharmacother* 2000, **34**, 1347, letter)

Doxepin (10% incidence in study in *J Clin Psychopharmacol* 1987, **7**, 243–46)

Diphenhydramine (n=1, *Can J Psych* 1985, **30**, 370–71)

Fluoxetine (*Am J Psych* 1991, **148**, 1403; *Am J Psych* 1995, **152**, 122–25)

Fluvoxamine (n=1, *J Clin Psychopharmacol* 1993, **13**, 365–66)

Fluoxetine + low dose neuroleptics (*Am J Psych* 1991, **148**, 683)

Flupentixol decanoate (*Psychopharmacol* 1983, **81**, 359–62)

Gabapentin (n=1, *J Clin Psychopharmacol* 2001, **21**, 623–24)

Haloperidol (many cases)

Lithium (*Am J Psych* 1979, **136**, 1229–30; *B J Psych* 1990, **156**, 128–29)

Loxapine (MI)

Metoclopramide (BNF, many cases, eg. *Neurology* 1984, **34**, 238–39)

Olanzapine (n=2, *Ann Int Med* 1999, **131**, 72; n=1, *J Clin Psych* 1999, **60**, 870)

Phenytoin (n=1, *NEJM* 1978, **298**, 457)

Pimozide (35% incidence reported, probably rarer – see *Neurology* 1982, **32**, 1335–46)

Quetiapine (n=1, *Am J Psych* 1999, **156**, 796–97; n=1, *Am J Psych* 2001, **158**, 1737)

Risperidone (n=1, *Pharmacopsychiatry* 1998, **31**, 68–69; n=1, *Ann Pharmacother* 2000, **34**, 1487–88; clear case, *Am J Psych* 1999, *156*, 1290; n=1, *J Clin Psych* 1999, **60**, 485–87; although a lower incidence in the elderly with low-dose has been reported, n=330, open, 12/52, RCT, *Am J Psych* 2000, **157**, 1150–55)

Risperidone/citalopram abrupt withdrawal (n=1, *Ann Pharmacother* 2000, **34**, 269)

Sulpiride (*Clin Neuropharmacology* 1990, **13**, 248–52)

Venlafaxine (SPC)

Ziprasidone (n=1, *Am J Psych* 2002, **159**, 1436

## 5.8.5 OTHER MOVEMENT DISORDERS

### 5.8.5.1 Catatonia *

**Review**: in young people (*J Am Acad Child Adolesc Psych* 1999, **38**, 1040–46)

Allopurinol (n=1, *BMJ* 1991, **302**, 970)

Baclofen (cases, *Clin Neuropharmacol* 1992, **15**, 56–62)

Benzodiazepine withdrawal (n=5, *J Clin Psychopharmacol* 1996, **16**, 315–19)

Bupropion (n=1, *J Clin Psych* 1992, **53**, 210)

Clozapine (*Can J Psych* 2001, **46**, 458)

Cycloserine

Cocaine (n=1, *Am J Psych* 1998, **155**, 1629)

Disulfiram (n=1, *Arch Neurol* 1989, **46**, 798–804; possible case in *Am J Psych* 1992, **149**, 1279–80)

Fluphenazine (n=1, *B J Psych* 1973, **122**, 240)

Loxapine (n=1, *J Clin Psych* 1983, **44**, 310–12)

Morphine epidural (n=1, *Lancet* 1980, **2**, 984)

Phenelzine + haloperidol (n=1, *Can J Psych* 1988, **33**, 633–34)

Piperazine (mentioned in *Trans Roy Soc Trop Med Hyg* 1976, **70**, 358)

Prochlorperazine (n=1, *Postgrad Med* 1976, **60**, 171–73)

### 5.8.5.2 Choreas

● **Psychotropics etc** *

Amoxapine

Amfetamines/amphetamines (chronic abuse, eg. *J Clin Psychopharmacol* 1988, **8**, 146)

Benzhexol/trihexyphenidyl

Chlorpromazine (n=1, *Postgrad Med J* 1970, **540**, 633–34)

Cocaine (cases in *Am J Emerg Med* 1991, **9**, 618–20)

Donepezil? (n=1, *Ann Pharmacother* 2000, **34**, 1347)

Fluoxetine (n=1, *J Clin Psych* 1999, **60**, 868–69)

Haloperidol (many cases)

Lamotrigine + phenytoin (n=3, *Seizure* 2001, **10**, 596–99)

Methadone

Methylphenidate

Mianserin (case in *B J Psych* 1989, **154**, 113–14)

Oral contraceptives (n=2, *Rev Med Chil* 1999, **127**, 468–71)

Paroxetine (n=1, after a single dose, *B J Psych* 1997, **170**, 193–94)

Phenytoin (review in *Pediatr* 1983, **72**, 831–34)

Risperidone (n=1, *J Clin Psych* 1999, **60**, 485–87)

Sulpiride (n=1, *J Psychopharmacol* 1993, **7**, 290–92; n=6, *Clin Neuropharmacol* 1990, **13**, 248–52)

Valproate (n=3, *Arch Neurol* 1994, **51**, 702–4; n=1, *Seizure* 2002, **11**, 205-6)

● **Others**

Anabolic steroids

Cimetidine (pos. case in *Ann Int Med* 1982, **96**, 531)

Cyclizine (n=1, *J Neurol Sci* 1977, **31**, 237–44)

Dienoestrol/dienestrol (MI)

Metoclopramide (n=1, *Lancet* 1982, **2**, 1153)

Oral Contraceptives (cases in *Drugs* 1983, **26**, 124)

Ranitidine (n=1, *Lancet* 1988, **2**, 158)

### 5.8.5.3 Tics (inc. Tourette's Syndrome)

Amfetamines (*JAMA* 1982, **247**, 1729–31)

Androgenic steroids (eg. stanozolol, methandrostenolol, testosterone) (*NEJM* 1990, **322**, 1674)

Carbamazepine (*Clin Neuropharmacol* 1989, **12**, 298–302)

Clozapine (n=1, *Am J Psych* 1995, **152**, 649)

Cocaine (*NEJM* 1986, **315**, 398; n=1, *Am J Psych* 1996, **153**, 965)

Dexamfetamine (see amfetamine)

Fluoxetine (cases in *Drug Intell & Clin Pharm* 1993, **27**, 725–26; *Am J Psych* 1994, **151**, 946–47)

Haloperidol (*Am J Psych* 1986, **143**, 1176–77)

Lamotrigine (n=3, *Neurology* 1999, **52**, 1191–94; n=5, *Epilepsia* 2000, **41**, 862–67)

Methylphenidate (*JAMA* 1982, **247**, 1729–31)

Ofloxacin (n=1, *Ann Pharmacother* 1996, **30**, 138–41)

Pemoline (*JAMA* 1982, **247**, 1729–31)

Risperidone withdrawal (n=1, *J Am Acad Child Adolesc Psych* 1997, **36**, 162–63)

Thioridazine + methylphenidate (n=1, *J Clin Psych* 1986, **47**, 44–45)

### 5.9 NEUROLEPTIC MALIGNANT SYNDROME

NMS is mostly related to the use of therapeutic or high doses of neuro-leptics, particularly phenothiazines and high potency drugs. It frequently occurs within 4–11 days of initiation, or alteration of dosages, of neuroleptic therapy (*Am J Psych* 1989, **146**, 717–25). NMS may be due to a sudden and profound reduction in dopaminergic function, caused by dopamine blocking drugs. See *Chapter 1.22* for treatments.

**Review**: NMS with risperidone, clozapine and other novel antipsychotics (Hasan and Buckley, *Am J Psych* 1998, **155**, 1113–16).

● **Antidepressants** *

Amoxapine (pos. cases in *B J Psych* 1991, **159**, 889; *Drug Intell Clin Pharm* 1989, **23**, 50–51)

Amoxapine + lithium (n=1, *Ann Clin Psychiatry* 2000, **12**, 107–9)

Clomipramine (MI)

Desipramine (n=1, *Neurology* 1990, **40**, 1797–98)

Phenelzine (many cases, eg. *Can Med Assoc J* 1991, **145**, 817–19)

Trimipramine (n=1, *J Clin Psych* 1989, **50**, 144–45)

Venlafaxine + trifluoperazine (n=1, *Lancet* 2000, **354**, 289–90)

● **Antipsychotics** *

Bromperidol + donepezil (n=1, *Nippon Ronen Igakkai Zasshi* 2001, **38**, 822–24)

Clozapine + risperidone (n=1, *Prog Neuropsychopharmacol Biol Psych* 2002, **26**, 407–9)

Clozapine (rare, but cases exist, eg. n=2 and review, *Ann Pharmacother* 1999, **33**, 623–30; long-term n=1, *Chang Gung Med J* 2001, **24**, 522–25; n=1, *Ann Int Med* 2002, **137**, 374)

Chlorpromazine (eg. n=2, *Biol Psych* 1983, **18**, 1441–46)

Flupentixol (pos. case in *B J Psych* 1988, **152**, 558–59)

Fluphenazine (reviewed in *Compr Psych* 1985, **26**, 63–70)

Haloperidol (many cases, eg. *J Trauma* 1989, **29**, 1595–97; in pregnancy, n=1, *Obstet Gynecol* 2001, **98**, 906–8)

Haloperidol + olanzapine (n=1, *Am J Psych* 2001, **158**, 650–51)

Lithium + amoxapine (n=1, *Ann Clin Psychiatry* 2000, **12**, 107–9)

Lithium + risperidone (possible case in *Am J Psych* 1995, **152**, 1096)

Loxapine (*B J Psych* 1991, **159**, 572–73)

Olanzapine (n=1, *Arch Gen Psych* 1999, **56**, 101–2; n=1, *Am J Psych* 1999, **156**, 1115–16; n=1, *Am J Psych* 1999, **156**, 1836; atypical syndrome, n=1, *Pharmacotherapy* 2002, **22**, 641–44; n=1, with severe hypernatraemia, *Hum Psychopharmacol* 2001, **16**, 279–81)

Olanzapine + levomepromazine (n=1, *Acta Psych Scand* 2000, **102**, 231–22)

Promazine

Quetiapine (n=1, Stanley and Hunter, *B J Psych* 2000, **176**, 497; n=1, *J Neuropsych Clin Neurosci* 2002, **14**, 87; n=1, *Am J Psych* 2002, **159**, 149–50)

Risperidone (many cases, eg. *Pharmacotherapy* 1997, **17**, 617–21; *Hosp Pharm* 1997, **32**, 42 and 512–18)

Risperidone + haloperidol (during switch, *Ann Pharmacother* 2001, **35**, 698–701)

Thioridazine (several cases, eg. *Biol Psych* 1987, **22**, 1293–97)

Zuclopenthixol (n=1, *B J Psych* 1989, **154**, 562–63)

● **Others** *

Alimemazine (n=1, *Eur J Pediatr* 2002, **161**, 259–61)

Amantadine

Amantadine, abrupt withdrawal (n=1, *Am J Psych* 1994, **151**, 451–52)

Anticholinergic withdrawal (n=1, *Int Clin Psychopharmacol* 1996, **11**, 207–9

Carbamazepine (may also complicate symptoms, *B J Psych* 1990, **157**, 437–38; n=1, *B J Psych* 1994, **164**, 270)

Carbamazepine withdrawal (*Am J Psych* 1990, **147**, 1687)

Ganciclovir (n=1, *Pharmacother* 2000, **20**, 479–83)

Iron (low levels? *Am J Psych* 1991, **148**, 148–49)

Levodopa

Levodopa withdrawal (n=3, *JAMA* 1985, **254**, 2792–95)

Lithium (pos. cases in *J Clin Psychopharmacol* 1987, **7**, 339–41)

Methylphenidate (n=1, *Pediatr Neurol* 1998, **19**, 299–301)

Metoclopramide (several cases eg. *Arch Int Med* 1987, **147**, 1495–97; *Ann Pharmacother* 1999, **33**, 644–45)

Oral contraceptives (possible case in *Drug Intell Clin Pharm* 1989, **23**, 811)

## 5.10 OBSESSIVE-COMPULSIVE SYMPTOMS *

Clozapine (n=1, *Am J Psych* 1998, **155**, 1629–30; especially early in schizophrenia, n=121, *J Clin Psych* 1999, **60**, 364–65)

Gabapentin withdrawal (n=1, *J Clin Psych* 1998, **59**, 131)

Methamphetamine (*J Clin Psych* 1999, **60**, 337–38; n=1, *J Am Acad Child Adolesc Psych* 1998, **37**, 135)

Olanzapine (n=2, *Am J Psych* 1999, **156**, 799–800; severity associated with duration of treatment: n=113, *J Clin Psych* 2002, **63**, 104–7)

Risperidone (dose dependent case, *Aust NZ J Psychiatry* 1998, **32**, 299–301; n=1, *B J Psych* 1999, **174**, 559; see also *J Clin Psych* 1999, **60**, 261–63 for an obsessive discussion)

*Risperidone and olanzapine – no differences in incidence but severity associated with longer duration of olanzapine (n=113, *J Clin Psych* 2002, **63**, 104–7)

Stimulants (n=1, *Biol Psych* 1985, **20**, 1332–37)

## 5.11 PANIC DISORDER

### ● Psychotropics etc *

Alprazolam (*J Am Board Fam Pract* 2002, **15**, 69–72; *J Am Board Fam Pract* 2002, **15**, 69–72)

Amfetamines (n=3, *Biol Psych* 1992, **32**, 91–95)

Buspirone (case + correspondence in *Lancet* 1989, **2**, 46–47, 615, 682–83)

Citalopram (n=1, *South Med J* 2002, **95**, 1088–89)

Clobazam (withdrawal, eg. *BMJ* 1981, **282**, 1931)

Clozapine (n=1, *Am J Psych* 2000, **157**, 2056)

Cocaine (review in *J Addict Dis* 1992, **11**, 47–58)

Flumazenil (mentioned in *Psych Res* 1991, **36**, 115)

Fluoxetine (unless initial doses kept very low, eg. *J Clin Psychopharmacol* 1987, **7**, 329–32)

Fluoxetine + bupropion (*J Clin Psych* 1996, **57**, 177–78)

Marijuana (n=1, *Acta Psych Scand* 1998, **98**, 254–55)

Naltrexone (*Am J Psych* 1998, **155**, 447)

Olanzapine (ie. hyperventilation, n=1, *J Psych Neurosci* 2002, **27**, 360–63)

Topiramate (n=1, *J Clin Psychopharmacol* 2001, **21**, 461–62)

Trazodone

### ● Others *

Aspartame (unproven case with high doses in *Lancet* 1986, **12**, 631)

Carvedilol (n=1, *Ann Pharmacother* 2002, **36**, 1736–40)

Co-trimoxazole (n=1, *J Clin Psychopharmacol* 1991, **11**, 144–45)

Lactate oral (eg. in calcium lactate tablets, case in *Ann Pharmacother* 1995, **29**, 539–40)

Oxymetazoline (case in abuse, *J Clin Psych* 1987, **48**, 293)

Phenylephrine (n=1, *B J Psych* 1980, **136**, 297–99)

Sibutramine (n=1, *Am J Psych* 2002, **159**, 1793–94)

Smoking cessation (n=2, *J Clin Psych* 2002, **63**, 594–95)

Sodium lactate (study in *Arch Gen Psych* 1989, **46**, 135–40)

Steroids (mentioned in *J Psychiatry Neurosci* 1997, **22**, 346–47)

Sumatriptan (7%, panic being interpretation of side-effects such as chest pain, palpitations etc, *Am J Psych* 1996, **153**, 1505)

Yohimbine (see *Arch Gen Psych* 1998, **55**, 1033–44)

## 5.12 PARANOID or SCHIZOPHRENIC-LIKE PSYCHOSES *( See also hallucinations 5.6 )*

Characterised by paranoid delusions and hallucinations in a person with little clouding of consciousness.

The literature on drug-induced psychosis is extensive but mainly case reports and short uncontrolled studies. A classification has been proposed:

**Intoxication mimicking functional**: (ie. drug-induced), eg. stimulants and cannabis. Persists for several days until the drug has cleared.

**Psychoactive drugs altering the clinical presentation of an existing psychosis**: eg. cannabis or amphetamines etc. creating a more aggressive and disturbed schizophrenic patient (Davison and Roth, *B J Psych* 1996, **168**, 651).

**Chronic hallucinations induced by substance abuse**: insight usually present, no clouding of consciousness, continue despite long-term abstinence, eg. alcoholic hallucinosis, LSD or cannabis flashbacks.

**Drug-induced relapse of functional psychosis**: eg. schizophrenia.

**Withdrawal states**: eg. delirium tremens, benzodiazepine or barbiturate withdrawal.

**Others**: acute intoxication/confusion with clouding of consciousness, post-intoxication depression, eg. post-amphetamine crash, panic/anxiety attacks, eg. from hallucinogens such as LSD.

**True drug-induced psychosis**: any psychotic symptoms which occur with drug intoxication and then persist after elimination of the causing drug, ie. one to two drug-free weeks.

There is surprisingly little, if any, proof that such causal link can be made firmly between drug use and later psychosis, eg. there is no direct proof that cannabis causes schizophrenia rather than schizophrenics trying to self-medicate before symptoms become clear to others.

● **Hallucinogens etc** *(Major cause)

Cannabis (at higher doses is a **risk factor** for the development or relapse of schizophrenia: *B J Psych* 2001, **178**, 116–22; acute onset, usually resolves in 2–7 days, *Acta Psych Scand* 1991, **83**, 34–36)

Dimethoxy-methylamphetamine (DOM)

Lysergic acid diethylamide (LSD)

Khat chewing (n=4, *B J Hosp Med* 1995, **54**, 322–26)

Mescaline

MDMA/Ecstasy (*BMJ* 1991, **302**, 1150, *B J Psych* 1991, **159**, 713–15; *Arch Gen Psych* 1993, **50**, 75)

Petrol (*Am J Psych* 1964, **126**, 757)

Phencyclidine (angel dust)

Psilocybin (magic mushrooms) (*B J Psych* 1978, **132**, 602)

Volatiles (*BMJ* 1962, **ii**, 1448)

● **CNS stimulants** * (Major cause)

Amfetamines/amphetamines (eg. *Biol Psych* 1980, **15**, 749; treatment/review in *Topic Emerg Med* 1985, **7**, 18–32)

Cocaine (*Am J Psych*, 1991, **148**, 495–98)

Ephedrine (review in *B J Psych* 1987, **150**, 252–55)

Methamphetamine (n=1, *Am J Psych* 1999, **4**, 662)

Phenylephrine (eg. *JAMA* 1982, **247**, 1859–60)

Phenylpropanolamine (*Am J Psych* 1990, **147**, 367–68; n=1, *Am J Psych* 2000, **157**, 1021–22)

Pseudoephedrine (many cases, eg. *South Med J* 1990, **83**, 64–65)

Solvent abuse (*B J Psych* 1989, **152**, 132)

- **Other CNS drugs** *
Alcohol (*Schizophrenia Today*, 1976, Pergamon Press, Oxford)
Alcohol, caffeine and "vigueue fit" (n=1, *Med Sci & Law* 2001, **41**, 331–36)
Antihistamines
Barbiturates
Benzodiazepines:
  Alprazolam
  Lorazepam (*B J Psych* 1985, **147**, 211)
  Midazolam (pos. case in *Drug Intell Clin Pharm* 1989, **23**, 671–72)
  Triazolam (eg. *Pharmacopsychiat* 1989, **22**, 115–19)
Benzodiazepine withdrawal (*Int J Ger Psych* 1995, **10**, 901–2)
Buspirone (*Am J Psych* 1991, **148**, 1606; *J Psychopharmacol* 1993, **7**, 295–300)
Chloral
Chlorpromazine (n=1, *Can Med Assoc J* 1970, **102**, 642; n=1, *Brain Inj* 1993, **7**, 77–83)
Clozapine withdrawal (ie. rebound psychosis, study in *Psychopharmacol* 1988, **24**, 260–63; n=3, *J Clin Psych* 1997, **58**, 252–55)
Codeine OD (n=1, *Neurobehavioral Toxicol Teratol* 1985, **7**, 193–94)
Disulfiram (n=1, *BMJ* 1992, **305**, 763; n=1, *Ned Tijdschr Geneeskd* 2002, **146**, 965)
Haloperidol (*Drug Intell Clin Pharm* 1981, **15**, 209)
Methadone withdrawal (eg. *J Clin Psych* 1995, **56**, 73–76)
Modafinil (may exacerbate: n=1, *Arch Gen Psych* 2002, **59**, 292–93)
Morphine (rare, *B J Psych* 1990, **157**, 758–59)
Promethazine (rare but possible, eg. *NEJM* 1960, **263**, 747)
Zolpidem (*Lancet* 1992, **339**, 813)
Zopiclone (some cases reported— *WHO Drug Information*, 1990, **4**, 179)

- **Antidepressants** *
Bupropion (many cases, eg. n=1, *Am J Psych* 1999, **156**, 2017–18)

Fluoxetine (*J Nerv Mental Dis* 1990, **178**, 55–58)
Fluvoxamine (n=1, *Can J Psych* 2000, **45**, 762)
Imipramine (eg. *Am J Psych* 1974, **131**, 21)
Mirtazapine + levodopa (n=1, *Pharmacopsychiatry* 1997, **30**, 263–65)
Paroxetine (case of psychotic mania, *Am J Psych* 1995, **152**, 1399–440)
Phenelzine – eg. *B J Psych* 1991, **159**, 716–17)
Venlafaxine + propafenone (*Int J Psych Med* 2001, **31**, 427–32)

- **Anticonvulsants** *
Psychosis induced by anticonvulsants may be the result of 'forced normalisation'. Risk factors include TLE, treatment resistance, past history of psychosis or affective disorder, and becoming suddenly seizure-free (best to do this gradually). Drug regimens should be changed gradually and compliance should be maintained to prevent epileptic psychoses (n=44, Matsuura, *J Neurol, Neurosurg & Psych* 1999, **67**, 231–33).
Carbamazepine toxicity (*Lancet* 1989, **i**, 167)
Clonazepam (n=1, *J Nerv Ment Dis* 1982, **170**, 117)
Ethosuximide
Gabapentin
Phenytoin (*Drug Intell Clin Pharm* 1988, **22**, 1003–5)
Tiagabine (RCT shows no significant risk; n=554, *Epilepsia* 2002, **43**, 394–98)
Topiramate (n=5 and review, *Seizure* 1999, **8**, 235–37; n=1, *J Clin Psych* 2001, **62**, 653)
Valproate (isolated cases, eg. *Clin Electroencephalography* 1982, **13**, 50–53)
Vigabatrin (2% incidence, eg. *J Neurol Neurosurgery & Psychiatry* 1989, **52**, 467–71; cases in *Lancet* 1994, **343**, 606–7; *Ann Pharmacother* 1995, **29**, 1115–17)

Vigabatrin withdrawal (letter in *Lancet* 1990, **335**, 1279)

● **Anti-parkinsonian drugs** (excess DA)

Amantadine (mentioned in *Drugs* 1981, **21**, 341–53)

Anticholinergic withdrawal (*Am J Psych* 1980, **137**, 1613)

Benzhexol/trihexyphenidyl (see benzatropine)

Benzatropine (many cases, review in *J Psychoactive Drug* 1983, **15**, 319–21)

Bromocriptine (<1% chance, review in *Biol Psych* 1985 , **20**, 326–28)

Levodopa (esp. hallucinations—*Arch Neurol* 1970, **23**, 193–200)

Lisuride/lysuride (a few cases, eg. *Lancet* 1986, **2**, 510)

Pergolide (esp. hallucinations, in up to 13%, eg. *Neurology* 1982, **32**, 1181–84)

Selegiline (a few cases, eg. *Neurology* 1981, **31**, 19–23)

● **NSAIDs and analgesics**

Aspirin (*JAMA* 1965, **193**, 555–58)

Ibuprofen (*J Clin Psych* 1982, **43**, 499–500)

Indometacin (rare, eg. *South Med J* 1983, **76**, 679–80; *BMJ* 1977, **2**, 994)

Pentazocine (esp. hallucinations, eg. *BMJ* 1974, **2**, 224)

Sulindac (*JAMA* 1980, **243**, 1420)

● **Cardiovascular drugs**

Amyl nitrate (Martindale 1993)

Beta-blockers (see under depression for differentials) eg:

Atenolol (rare, n=1, *Am J Psych* 1983, **140**, 1382)

Propranolol (well known, eg. *Biol Psych* 1989, **25**, 351–54)

Clonidine (n=1, *Prog NeuroPsychopharmacol* 1980, **4**, 21)

Clonidine withdrawal (*Am J Psych* 1982, **139**, 110–11)

Digoxin toxicity (rare, *J Nerv Mental Dis* 1978, **166**, 817)

Diltiazem (n=1, *Arch Int Med* 1991, **151**, 373–74)

Disopyramide (isolated cases, eg. *Lancet* 1978, **1**, 858 + 1152)

Doxazosin (n=1, *BMJ* 1997, **314**, 1869; n=1, *BMJ* 1997, **314**, 1869)

Enalapril (n=1, *Drug Intell Clin Pharm* 1991, **25**, 558–59)

Hydralazine

Lidocaine/lignocaine IV (n=6, *Ann Int Med* 1982, **97**, 149–50)

Methyldopa

Mexilitine (n=1, *Am Heart J* 1984, **107**, 1091–98)

Nifedipine (pos. case in *J Am Geriat Soc* 1984, **32**, 408)

Procainamide

Tocainide (*BMJ* 1984, **288**, 606–7)

● **Anti-infection** *

Amphotericin B IV (n=1, *Ariz Med* 1972, **29**, 322)

Antituberculous drugs (*Lancet* 1989, **ii**, 105 + 735–36)

Cefuroxime (*Lancet* 1984, **i**, 965)

Cephalexin (n=1, *Med J Aust* 1973, **i**, 497)

Cephalothin (*Drug Intell Clin Pharm* 1974, **8**, 71)

Chloroquine (cases in *Lancet* 1985, **2**, 37)

Ciprofloxacin (n=1, *Ann Pharmacother* 1992, **26**, 930–31; n=1, *Postgrad Med J* 1998, **74**, 189–90)

Clarithromycin (*Eur J Clin Microbiol Infect Dis* 1999, **18**, 70–71)

Colistin (esp. with large doses)

Dapsone (*BMJ* 1989, **299**, 324)

Erythromycin (*Arch Int Med* 1986, **146**, 897)

Ganciclovir (n=1, *Pharmacother* 2000, **20**, 479–83)

Isoniazid (rare—*Am J Psych* 1991, **148**, 1402; *Ann Pharmacother* 1998, **32**, 889–91)

Ketoconazole (*Am J Psych* 1990, **147**, 677)

Mefloquine (n=179, more common in females and first-time users; *Eur J Clin Pharmacol* 2002, **58**, 441–45)

Metronidazole (case in *Am J Psych* 1997, **154**, 1170–71)

Nalidixic acid (many cases, eg. *BMJ* 1965, **2**, 590)

Primaquine (n=1, *Ann Int Med* 1980, **92**, 435)

Procaine Penicillin G (several cases, eg. *B J Psych* 1990, **156**, 554)

Sulphonamides

Tobramycin (a few cases, eg. *Pediatr Pulmonol* 1988, **4**, 201–4)

● **Steroids** (*Postgrad Med J* 1984, **60**, 467–70)

Adrenocorticotrophin

Clomiphene (n=2, *Am J Psych* 1997, **154**, 1169–70)

Corticosteroids (11% incidence? Review by Ismail and Wessely, *B J Hosp Pharm* 1995, **53**, 495–99)

Cortisone

Methylprednisolone

Methyltestosterone (*Lancet* 1987, **i**, 863)

Prednisone (usually >40mg/d, eg. *J Clin Psych* 1982, **43**, 75–76 inc. brief overview; case and discussion in *B J Psych* 1993, **162**, 549–53)

Triamcinolone (possible but no specific reports)

● **Miscellaneous** *

Anti-diarrhoeals (OTC) (*B J Psych* 1990, **157**, 758–59)

Atropine (oral, IV, eye drops. Many cases, eg. *DICP Ann Pharmacother* 1990, **24**, 708–9)

Baclofen

Carbaryl (n=1, *Am J Psych* 1995, **152**, 646–47)

Carbimazole

Chlorphenamine OD (case in child in *Med J Aust* 1973, **1**, 382–86)

Cimetidine (*Am J Psych* 1980, **137**, 1112)

Desmopressin (n=1, *Lancet* 1981, **2**, 808)

Dextromethorphan (n=1, *Am J Psych* 2000, **157**, 304)

Dicyclomine (MI)

Diphenhydramine (n=1, *JAMA* 1968, **203**, 301)

Disulfiram

Hyoscine-transdermal (*Postgrad Med* 1988, **84**, 73–76)

Interferon alpha (n=1, *Addiction* 2000, **95**, 1101–4)

Isotretoin (possible case, *J Clin Psych* 1999, **60**, 407–8)

Lactate oral (eg. in calcium lactate tablets, case in *Ann Pharmacother* 1995, **29**, 539–40)

Oxymetazoline (several cases, eg. *Scott Med J* 1982, **27**, 175–76)

Viloxazine

Estrogen withdrawal (review, n=26, *J Acta Psych Scand* 2001, **104**, 323)

Insulin abuse (*BMJ* 1971, **4**, 792–93)

Lariam (severe is extremely low, eg. 1 in 6000, *Pharm J* 1996, **256**, 184)

Yohimbine (unproven, see *Arch Gen Psych* 1998, **55**, 1033–44)

Ketamine (discussion, *Am J Psych* 1997, **154**, 805–11)

Melatonin (n=1, *Ann Pharmacother* 1997, **31**, 1408)

Nabilone

Nicotine, abrupt withdrawal of (*Am J Psych* 1994, **150**, 452)

Phenylephrine (*JAMA* 1982, **247**, 1859)

Phenylpropanolamine (n=1, *Am J Psych* 2000, **157**, 1021–22)

Pyridostigmine (case in German in *Deutsch Med Wschr* 1966, **9**, 699)

Quinine (*B J Psych* 1988, **153**, 575)

Quinidine (*BMJ* 1987, **294**, 1001–2; *Med J Aus* 1990, **153**, 47–49)

Salbutamol (*Biol Psych* 1989, **26**, 631–33)

Scopolamine (transient to transdermal, n=3, *Can J Hosp Pharm* 1994, **47**, 67–69)

Silbutramine (*Am J Psych* 2000, **157**, 2057–58)

## 5.13 SEIZURES

These are rare at normal doses and occur mostly where seizure threshold is reduced, in at-risk patients or in overdose. The list of drugs which could induce seizures is enormous and so a literature search would be needed to clarify the current situation for any one drug.

**Reviews:**\* drug-induced seizures: controversies in their identification and management (Alldredge, *Pharmacotherapy* 1997, **17**, 857–60, editorial, 26 refs), general review (*Drug Safety* 2002, **25**, 91–110, 166 refs), assessment, management and prevention, (Murphy and Delanty, *CNS Drugs* 2000, **14**, 135–46).

● **Psychotropics etc** *
Alcohol (*NEJM* 1989, **320**, 596–97)
Amitriptyline (*Am J Psych* 1980, **137**, 1461–62)
Amoxapine (*J Clin Psych* 1981, **42**, 238–42)
Antipsychotics (esp phenothiazines)
Bupropion (see *3.4* , eg. n=1, *Clin Neuropharmacol* 2001, **24**, 304–6)
Bupropion overdose (n=1, *Lancet* 2001, **357**, 1624, letter)
Bupropion + trimipramine (n=1, *J Clin Psych* 2001, **62**, 478–77)
Citalopram (n=1, non-CSE, *Eur J Neurol* 2002, **9**, 319-20)
Clozapine (*Neurology* 1991, **41**, 369–71; *CSM Current Problems* 1991, No 31; *Am J Psych* 1993, **150**, 1128. Higher incidence with rapid upward titration, recent ECT, head trauma with loss of consciousness and concurrent use of seizure threshold-lowering drugs. They may be due to hyponatremia: *Lancet* 1992, **340**, 672)
Donepezil (*Curr Prob Pharmacovig* 1999, **25**, 7; *J Neurol, Neurosurg & Psych* 1999, **66**, 410)
Fluoxetine (*Clin Pharm* 1989, **8**, 296–98; *Am J Psych* 1992, **149**, 273; prolonged seizure reported in *Postgrad Med J* 1994, **70**, 383–84)
Fluvoxamine (n=1, *Ann Pharmacother* 2000, **34**, 1276–78)
Imipramine
Levomepromazine + fluvoxamine (*Int Clin Psychopharmacol* 1993, **8**, 61–62)
Lithium (*Biol Psych* 1987, **22**, 1184–90)
MAOIs
Maprotiline (*J Clin Psych* 1982, **43**, 117–18)
Mianserin
Olanzapine (fatal case, *Ann Pharmacother* 1999, **33**, 787–89; non-fatal case *Ann Pharmacother* 1999, **33**, 554–56)

Quetiapine + olanzapine (n=1, *Ann Pharmacother* 2002, **36**, 437–39).
Sertraline (n=1, *Am J Psych* 1996, **153**, 732)
Tacrine (n=6, *Lancet* 1996, **347**, 1339–40)
Venlafaxine OD (*Ann Pharmacother* 1997, **31**, 178–80)
Venlafaxine + trimipramine (n=1, *Ann Pharmacother* 2000, **34**, 1402–5)
Zolpidem (review, *Lancet* 1998, **352**, 383–90)

● **Drug withdrawal**
Alcohol (*NEJM* 1989, **320**, 596–97)
Anticonvulsants (ie. *non-compliance*)
Barbiturates
Benzodiazepines: Alprazolam (*J Nerv Mental Dis* 1990, **178**, 208–9)
Carbamazepine (*J Clin Psych* 1988, **49**[Suppl], 410)
Zolpidem (abrupt high dose withdrawal, case report *JAMA* 1994, **272**, 1721–22)

● **CNS stimulants**
Cocaine (*Neurology* 1990, **40**, 404–7)
Ephedrine (*Lancet* 1977, **1**, 587–88)

● **Anticonvulsants** *
**Reviews:*** general (Perucca *et al*, *Epilepsia* 1998, **39**, 5–17; 155 refs, editorial by Loiseau, *Epilepsia* 1998, **39**, 2–4, 43 refs), partial seizures (*Neurology* 2002, **59**, 79–83)
Carbamazepine (n=1, *Clin Electroencephalogr* 2002, **33**, 174–77)
Carbamazepine OD (n=2, *J Toxicol Clin Toxicol* 2002, **40**, 81–90)
Carbamazepine withdrawal (*Ther Drug Monit* 2000, **22**, 753–56)
Ethosuximide
Phenobarbital
Phenytoin (*Epilepsia* 1989, **30**, 230–34)
Tiagabine (n=2, *Epilepsia* 1999, **40**, 1159–62; n=3 non-CSE, and review, *Seizure* 2002, **11**, 57–59 and 243–49)
Tiagabine OD (status; *Epilepsia* 2002, **43**, 773–74)
Valproate

● **NSAIDs and analgesics**
Dextroproxyphene (*Arch Inn Med* 1973, **132**, 191–94)

Fentanyl (*Anesth Anal* [*Cleve*] 1982, **61**, 1020–21)

Indometacin (rare, eg. *BMJ* 1966, **1**, 80)

Mefenamic Acid (*Drug Intell Clin Pharm* 1983, **17**, 204–5)

Penicillamine

Pentazocine (eg. *Ann Emerg Med* 1983, **12**, 28–31)

Pethidine (*Ann Neurol* 1983, **13**, 180–85)

Propoxyphene (*Arch Intern Med* 1973, **132**, 191–94)

Salicylates OD (*Lancet* 1998, **352**, 383–90)

Sulindac

Tramadol (reviews in *JAMA* 1997, **278**, 1661 and *Pharmacother* 1998, **18**, 607–11; the latter concluding that seizures seem rarely attributable to tramadol)

● **Cardiovascular drugs**

**Beta-blockers**, eg:

Oxprenolol (*Lancet* 1972, **i**, 587–88)

Propranolol (*Lancet* 1972, **i**, 587–88)

Digoxin toxicity (rare eg. *BMJ* 1982, **284**, 162–63)

Disopyramide

Enoximone Inf (*BMJ* 1990, **300**, 613)

Lidocaine (*Eur J Clin Pharmacol* 1989, **36**, 583–86)

—s/c (*Clin Pharm* 1989, **8**, 767–68)

Metolazone (*BMJ* 1976, **i**, 1381)

Mexilitine

Thiazide diuretics (review, *Lancet* 1998, **352**, 383–90)

Tocainide

● **Anti-infection**

Ampicillin? (*Lancet* 1982, **ii**, 617)

Benzylpenicillin (*Lancet* 1977, **i**, 587)

Carbenicillin (*JAMA* 1971, **218**, 1942)

Cefazolin (*Am J Hosp Pharm* 1980, **37**, 271)

Ceftazidime (editorial in *Lancet* 1990, **340**, 400–1)

Cephalexin (n=1, *Med J Aust* 1973, **1**, 497)

Cephalosporins (high dose in renal failure)

Chloroquine (*BMJ* 1989, **299**, 1524)

Ciprofloxacin (*Pharm J* 1989, **242**, 340)

Cycloserine

Gentamicin (*J Neurol Orthop Med & Surg* 1985, **6**, 123)

Imipenem (*Ann Int Med* 1989, **149**, 1881–83)

Isoniazid (review in *J Clin Pharm Ther Toxicol* 1987, **25**, 259–61)

Mefloquine (*Pharm J* 1989, **243**, 561; CSM warning, *Curr Prob Pharmacovig* 1999, **25**, 15)

Metronidazole (*Drug Intell Clin Pharm* 1982, **16**, 409)

Nalidixic Acid (*BMJ* 1977, **2**, 1518)

Niridazole

Ofloxacin (n=1, *Ann Pharmacother* 1997, **31**, 1475–77; *J Pharm Technol* 1997, **13**, 174)

Penicillins (reviewed in *Ann Pharmacother* 1992, **26**, 26–29, 30–31)

Piperazine

Piperacillin (*Clin Pediatr* 1997, **36**, 475–76)

Pyrimethamine

Zudovidine (case in *Lancet* 1995, **346**, 452)

● **Respiratory drugs**

Aminophylline (*Lancet* 1977, **i**, 587)

Doxapram

Phenylpropanolamine (*J Med Soc New Jersey* 1979, **76**, 591–92)

Terbutaline (*Am J Dis Child* 1982, **136**, 1091–92)

Theophylline (*Ann Int Med* 1975, **82**, 784)

Theophylline toxicity (*J Toxicol Clin Toxicol* 1999, **37**, 99–101)

● **Hormones**

Glucocorticoids

Insulin

Oral contraceptives (exacerbate pre-existing)

Oxytocin

Prostaglandins

● **Cytotoxics**

Alprostadil

Busulphan (*Ann Int Med* 1989, **111**, 543–44; *Ann Pharmacother* 1992, **26**, 30–31)

Chlorambucil (*Postgrad Med J* 1979, **55**, 806–7)

Ciclosporin (*J Neurol Neurosurg Psych* 1989, **55**, 1068–71; *Psychosomatics* 1991, **32**, 94–102)

Cisplatin (*BMJ* 1991, **302**, 416)

Methotrexate

Vinblastine

Vincristine

● **Anaesthetics** *

Alfentanil (*Anaesthesia & Analgesia* 1989, **68**, 692–93)

Enflurane (*Anaesthesia* 1992, **47**, 79–80)

Ether

Etomidate (pre-ECT, n=1, *B J Psych* 2000, **177**, 373).

Halothane

Ketamine

Local Anesthetics:
Bupivacaine (*Anesthesiology* 1979, **50**, 454–56)
Lidocaine (mentioned in *Drugs Aging* 1995, **7**, 38–48)
Etidocaine (*Anesthesiology* 1979, **50**, 51–53)
Procaine

Methohexital

Propofol (*Anaesthesia* 1990, **45**, 255–56, can be delayed by up to 6 days – *CSM Curr Prob* 1992, **35**, 2; systematic review concluding that rapid changes in cerebral concentration may be causal; n=81, *Neurology* 2002, **58**, 1327–32)

Propofol withdrawal (*Anaesthesia* 1990, **45**, 741–42)

● **Miscellaneous** *

Allopurinol withdrawal (*Ann Neurology* 1990, **27**, 691)

Aluminium toxicity (unproven, *Ann Int Med* 1989, **111**, 543–44)

Amantadine (unproven, *Ann Int Med* 1989, **110**, 323–24; *Drugs Aging* 1995, **7**, 38–48)

Baclofen IT (*Lancet* 1992, **339**, 373–74)

Baclofen withdrawal (*Neurology* 1992, **42**, 447–49)

Brompheniramine

Bupivacaine epidural (case in 4yo: *Anaesthesia* 1995, **50**, 563–77)

Caffeine (*Acta Psych Scand* 1959, **15**, 331–34)

Camphor (*Clin Pediatr [Phila]* 1977, **16**, 901–2)

Clomiphene (n=1, *BMJ* 1994, **309**, 512)

Colchicine OD

Cyclopentolate eye drops (*J Paed & Child Health* 1990, **26**, 106–7)

Diphenhydramine (*J Pediat* 1977, **90**, 1017–18)

Diptheria-tetanus-pertussis vaccine (*JAMA* 1990, **263**, 1641–45)

Flumazenil (n=49, *Epilepsia* 2000, **41**, 186–92)

Fluorescin IV (*Annals Opthal* 1989, **21**, 89–90; *Acta Neurol Scand* 1999, **100**, 278–80)

Ginkgo biloba (review of anecdotal reports: *Ann Int Med* 2001, **134**, 344)

Hepatitis B vaccine (*J Paed & Child Health* 1990, **26**, 65)

Interferon (n=1, *Pediatrics* 1994, **93**, 511–12)

Ketamine

Ketotifen (n=19, *Epilepsia* 1998, **39**[Suppl 5], 64)

Levodopa (mentioned in *Drugs Aging* 1995, **7**, 38–48)

Levothyroxine (n=1, *Ann Pharmacother* 1993, **27**, 1139)

Lindane, topical (*B J Dermatol* 1995, **133**, 1013)

Measles/Mumps/Rubella vaccine (review in *Pediatrics* 1991, **88**, 881–85)

Naftidrofuryl

Naloxone (rare)

Ondansetron (*Clin Pharm* 1993, **12**, 613–15)

Pertussis vaccine

Phenylpropanolamine (n=1, *J Pediatr* 1983, **102**, 143–45)

Pyridoxine (n=1 and review, *J Paed Child Health* 2001, **37**, 592-96).

Pyrimethamine

Radiographic Contrast Media (eg. metrizamide)

Sodium bicarbonate (*JAMA* 1989, **262**, 1328–39)

Steroids, eg.
Dexamethasone
Hydrocortisone
Prednisolone

Prednisone (with hypocalcaemia)
(mentioned in *Lancet* 1977, **1**, 587–88)

Sulphasalazine

Sulphonylureas

Terfenadine (*BMJ* 1993, **307**, 241)

Terfenadine OD (*BMJ* 1989, **298**, 325)

Yohimbe (unproven, see *Arch Gen
Psych* 1998, **55**, 1033–44)

## 5.14 SEROTONIN SYNDROME

Serotonin syndrome has been
reported with a variety of antidepressants, buspirone, carbamazepine,
pethidine, dextromethorphan and
levodopa, usually in combination but
can be single drugs or in overdose.

**Reviews**: Mir and Taylor, *Psych Bull*
1999, **23**, 742–47; Chan *et al, Med J
Aust* 1998, **169**, 523–25; Lane and
Baldwin, *J Clin Psychopharmacol*
1997, **17**, 208–21.

- **Individual drugs** *

Amitriptyline (n=1, *Postgrad Med J*
2000, **76**, 254–56)

Clomipramine (*J Clin Psychopharmacol* 1999, **19**, 285–87; possible case
after withdrawal of clozapine: *Ann
Pharmacother* 2001, **35**, 180–82)

Citalopram low dose (*J Clin
Psychopharmacol* 2000, **20**, 713–14)

Dexfenfluramine (n=1, *JAMA* 1996,
**276**, 1220–21)

Dothiepin overdose (*J Child Adolesc
Psychopharmacol* 1998, **8**, 201–4)

Ecstasy (*JAMA* 1993, **269**, 869–70;
review *Clin Neuropharmacol* 1996,
**19**, 157–64)

Fluoxetine (n=1, *Psychiatr Pol* 1995,
**29**, 529–38)

Fluvoxamine (*Ann Emerg Med* 1999,
**33**, 457–59; after single dose n=1,
*Ann Emerg Med* 1999, **34**, 806–7;
mild syndrome may occur in 43%
people on fluvoxamine alone, n=37,
*Int J Neurosci* 2001, **109**, 165–72)

Mirtazapine (n=1, *Ann Pharmacother*
2002, **36**, 641–43)

Nefazodone (n=8, *B J Gen Pract* 1999,
**49**, 871–74)

Paroxetine (*Am J Emerg Med* 1995, **13**,
606–7)

Sertraline low dose (*J Clin
Psychopharmacol* 2000, **20**, 713–14)

Sertraline overdose (n=1, *Arch Pediatr
Adolesc Med* 1997, **151**, 1064–67)

Trazodone (*Int J Ger Psychiatry* 1997,
**12**, 129–30)

Venlafaxine (n=1, *J Emerg Med* 1997,
**15**, 491–93; n=1, *Postgrad Med J*
2000, **76**, 254–56)

Venlafaxine overdose (*J Accid Emerg
Med* 1998, **15**, 333–34)

- **Combinations including SSRIs** *

SSRIs + MAOIs (overview, Henry,
*Lancet* 1994, **343**, 607)

Citalpram + buspirone (n=1, *Int Clin
Psychopharmacol* 1997, **12**, 61–63)

Citalopram + moclobemide (*Med Clin
[Barc]* 1999, **113**, 677–78)

Citalopram overdose + moclobemide
(*Lancet* 1993, **342**, 1419)

Citalopram + moclobemide overdose
(fatal, *J Anal Toxicol* 2001, **25**,
147–51)

Fluoxetine/moclobemide/clomipramine
overdose (fatal case in *Anaesth
Intensive Care* 1995, **23**, 499–502)

Fluoxetine + buspirone (*Ann
Pharmacother* 2000, **34**, 871–74)

Fluoxetine + carbamazepine (n=1,
*Lancet* 1993, **342**, 442–43)

Fluoxetine + lithium (n=1, *Ugeskrift
for Laeger* 1995, **157**, 1204–5)

Fluoxetine + mirtazapine (*Int J Geriatr
Psychiatry* 1998, **13**, 495–96; n=1,
*Ann Pharmacother* 2001, **35**,
1217–20)

Fluoxetine + moclobemide (eg.
Benazzi, *Pharmacopsychiatry* 1996,
**29**, 162; n=1, *Can J Anaesth* 2000,
**47**, 246–50)

Fluoxetine + nefazodone (n=1, *J Clin
Psych* 2000, **61**, 146)

Fluoxetine + paroxetine (n=1, *Am
Fam Physician* 1995, **52**, 1475–82)

Fluoxetine + Parstelin (n=1,
*Anaesthesia* 1991, **46**, 507–8)

Fluoxetine + sertraline (n=1, *Clin
Pharmacol Ther* 1993, **1**, 84–88)

Fluoxetine + tramadol (n=1, *J Royal
Soc Med* 1999, **92**, 474–75)

Fluoxetine + trazodone (*Biol Psych* 1996, **39**, 384–85)

Fluoxetine + venlafaxine (*Ann Pharmacother* 1998, **32**, 432–36)

Paroxetine + lithium (n=1, *Pharmacopsychiatry* 1997, **30**, 106–7)

Paroxetine + moclobemide (fatal case, *J Anal Toxicol* 1997, **21**, 518–20; *J Accid Emerg Med* 1999, **16**, 293–95)

Paroxetine + nefazodone (n=1, *Ann Emerg Med* 1997, **29**, 113–19)

Paroxetine + OTC cold remedy (*Am J Emerg Med* 1994, **12**, 642–44)

Paroxetine + risperidone (*J Clin Psychopharmacol* 2000, **20**, 103–5)

Paroxetine + tramadol (n=11, *Int Clin Psychopharmacol* 1997, **12**, 181–82)

Paroxetine + trazodone (*Psychosomatics* 1995, **36**, 159–60)

Sertraline + amitriptyline (*Ann Pharmacother* 1996, **30**, 1499–500)

Sertraline + dolasetron (n=1, *J Psychopharmacol* 2002, **16**, 191)

Sertraline + erythromycin (*Pharmacotherapy* 1999, **19**, 894–96)

Sertraline + linezolid (n=1, *Clin Infect Dis* 2002, **34**, 1651–52)

Sertraline + metoclopramide (n=1, *Ann Pharmacother* 2002, **36**, 67–71)

Sertraline + phenelzine (n=1, *Ann Pharmacother* 1994, **28**, 732–35)

Sertraline + tramadol (n=1, *Ann Pharmacother* 1997, **31**, 175–77; n=1, *Aust Pres* 2002, **25**, 19)

Sertraline + tranylcypromine (n=1, *Clin Pharm* 1993, **12**, 222–25)

Sertraline + buspirone + loxapine (n=1, *Therapie* 1999, **54**, 269–71)

● **Combinations including MAOIs** (see also above)

MAOIs + TCAs (overview, Henry, *Lancet* 1994, **343**, 607)

Phenelzine + clomipramine (n=1, *Clin Pharmacol Therap* 1993, **53**, 84–88)

Phenelzine + dextromethorphan (n=1, *Clin Pharmacol Therap* 1993, **53**, 84–88)

Phenelzine + venlafaxine (n=1, *Pharmacother* 1998, **18**, 399–403; n=1, *Ann Pharmacother* 1996, **30**, 84)

Tranylcypromine + venlafaxine (cases in *Vet Hum Toxicol* 1996, **38**, 358–61 and *Hum Exp Toxicol* 1997, **16**, 14–17)

● **Other combinations** * (see also above)

Mirtazapine + tramadol + olanzapine (n=1, *Am J Psych* 2002, **159**, 672–73)

Moclobemide + clomipramine overdose (*Intensive Care Med* 1997, **23**, 122–24; *J Toxicol Clin Toxicol* 1998, **36**, 31–32)

Moclobemide + clomipramine (n=1, *BMJ* 1993, **306**, 248)

Moclobemide + pethidine (possible case, *Med J Aust* 1995, **162**, 554)

Nortriptyline + selegiline (n=1, *J Neurol* 2000, **247**, 811)

St John's wort + buspirone (n=1, *J Psychopharmacol* 2002, **16**, 401)

Trazodone + amitriptyline (n=1, *Int Clin Psychopharmacol* 1996, **11**, 289–90)

Trazodone + nefazodone (n=1, *Am J Psych* 2000, **157**, 1022)

Venlafaxine + amitriptyline (n=1, *Postgrad Med J* 2000, **76**, 254–56)

Venlafaxine + dexamphetamine (n=1, *Med J Aust* 2002, **176**, 240–41)

Venlafaxine + metoclopramide (n=1, *Ann Pharmacother* 2002, **36**, 67–71)

Venlafaxine + mirtazapine (n=1, *World J Biol Psych* 2002, **3**, 167)

Venlafaxine + trazodone (n=1, *Am J Psych* 2001, **158**, 2088–89).

Venlafaxine + selegiline (n=1, *J Clin Psychopharmacol* 1997, **17**, 66–67)

Venlafaxine + St John's wort? (*Presse Med* 2000, **29**, 1285–86)

## 5.15 SLEEP PROBLEMS

### 5.15.1 Sleep disturbances

Review of non-psychotropic causes: Novak and Shapiro, *Drug Safety* 1997, 16, 133–49.

● **Psychotropics etc** *

Benperidol

Biperiden withdrawal (n=2, *Int Clin Psychopharmacol* 2000, **15**, 357–59)

Bupropion (11%, MI)

Chlorpromazine

Donepezil (n=2, *J Am Geriatr Soc*
1998, **46**, 119–20)
Fluoxetine
Fluspirilene
Lamotrigine (dose dependent, n=7,
*Epilepsia* 1999, **40**, 322–25)
Levetiracetam (MI)
Lorazepam
MAOIs (*Am J Psych* 1989, **146**, 1078)
Methysergide
Nicotine (n=252, *J Clin Psych* 2001,
**62**, 319–24)
Olanzapine (somnambulism, n=2, *Am
J Psych* 2001, **158**, 1158)
Phentermine (*Practitioner* 1970, **24**,
423–25)
Phenytoin
Rivastigmine (<5%, MI)
SSRIs (somnambulism, n=1,
*J Pharm Tech* 1999, **15**, 204–7;
paroxetine and fluvoxamine disrupt
sleep architecture, RCT, n=14,
*J Clin Psych* 2001, **62**, 642–52)
Sulpiride
Stimulants (methylphenidate)
Trazodone
Tricyclics
● **Anti-parkinsonian drugs** *
Amantadine (4% incidence, see
*J Clin Psych* 1981, **42**, 9)
Bromocriptine
Pramipexole (n=6, *Mov Disord* 2000,
**15**, 658–63)
Ropinirole and/or pramipexole (n=2,
*Pharmacother* 2000, **20**, 724–26)
● **Cardiovascular drugs** *
Amiodarone (frequent eg.
*Am J Cardiol* 1983, **52**, 975–79)
Beta-blockers (very common,
especially with propranolol)
Atenolol (see *Adv Psych Treat* 1999,
**5**, 30–38)
Carvedilol (n=1, *Ann Pharmacother*
2002, **36**, 1736–40)
Clonidine
Digoxin (see *Adv Psych Treat* 1999, **5**,
30–38)
Diltiazem (see *Adv Psych Treat* 1999,
**5**, 30–38)
Isradipine (up to 3%, *Am J Med* 1989,
**86**[Suppl 4A], 98–102)

Methyldopa
Nifedipine (see *Adv Psych Treat* 1999,
**5**, 30–38)
● **NSAIDs and analgesics**
Diclofenac
Diflunisal
Fenoprofen
Indometacin
Naproxen (*Eur J Rheumatol Inflamm*
1981, **4**, 87–92)
Nefopam
Sulindac
● **Respiratory drugs**
Aminophylline
Brompheniramine
Clomiphene
Pseudoephedrine
Theophylline
● **Anti-infection**
Cinoxacin
Ciprofloxacin (n=1, *Lancet* 1986, **1**,
819–22)
● **Miscellaneous** *
Bismuth toxicity
(*Postgrad Med J* 1988, **64**, 308–10)
Dexamethasone
Ginseng (see *Arch Gen Psych* 1998, **55**,
1033–44)
Lovastatin (*Lancet* 1994, **343**, 973)
Nicotine (n=252, *J Clin Psych* 2001,
**62**, 319–24)
Propantheline
Ranitidine (see *Adv Psych Treat* 1999,
**5**, 30–38)
Sibutramine (SPC)
Simvastatin (*Curr Prob* 1992, 33)
Sulphasalazine
Tolazamide
Triamcinolone

## 5.15.2 Vivid dreams and nightmares

**Review**: Thompson and Pierce, *Ann
Pharmacother* 1999, **33**, 93–98
Baclofen
Beta-blockers:
Atenolol (*Clin Pharm Ther* 1979,
**25**, 8)
Propranolol (*Adv Drug React Bull*
1983, **99**, 364)
Clonidine (*Adv Drug React Bull* 1983,
**99**, 364)

Digoxin toxicity (*Ann Int Med* 1980, **93**, 639)

Famotidine (n=1, *Pharmacother* 1998, **18**, 404–7)

Indometacin (rare eg. *BMJ* 1965, **2**, 1281)

Methyldopa (*Adv Drug React Bull* 1983, **99**, 364)

Nalbumetone (*Pharm J* 1990, **244**, 764)

Pergolide (eg. *Clin Neuropharmacol* 1986, **9**, 160–64)

Nicotine patches (*Pharm J* 1992, **249**, 384)

Stanozolol (MI)

Verapamil (*NEJM* 1988, **318**, 929–30)

Withdrawal from barbiturates, benzodiazepines, narcotics etc.

## 6.1 SECTIONS OF THE MENTAL HEALTH ACT 1983

The England and Wales Mental Health Act came into effect on 30 September 1983 and comprises a series of 149 sections which modify, supplement and extend the 1959 Act. It is principally concerned with the grounds for detaining patients in hospital, aiming to improve patients' rights and protect staff, in a variety of ways. It is currently (2003) being reviewed. The new Scottish MHA will be enacted in 2004.

### 6.1.1 COMPULSORY DETENTION ORDERS (non-offenders)

#### Section 2

- Admission for assessment, or assessment followed by treatment. It can include treatment as part of the assessment.
- Maximum of 28 days as you can be discharged before the end. Not renewable.
- Application made by nearest relative or Approved Social Worker, endorsed by two doctors (one a psychiatrist and the other, eg. a GP) and goes to a hospital manager.
- Can be appealed against or reviewed within 14 days.

#### Section 3

- Admission for treatment, but only where the patient's health or safety, or other's safety, is threatened.
- Maximum of six months, renewable after six months, then annually.
- Application made by a nearest relative or Approved Social Worker and endorsed by two medical recommendations.
- Can be appealed against or reviewed once every six months.
- Consent to treatment regulations refer to a professional person, other than a doctor or a nurse, who is involved with the case, so this can include a pharmacist (Branford, *Pharm J* 1988, **240**, 220–1).

#### Section 4 – Emergency admission

- Admission for assessment in cases of emergency. Used where the patient is incapable of giving consent, eg. unconscious, under age etc, and in areas where psychiatric resources are thinly spread.
- Maximum 72-hour holding order
- Application made by a relative or Approved Social Worker and endorsed by one doctor (often the GP).

#### Section 5(2) – Emergency holding power by a doctor

- Detention of an informal patient already in hospital, on grounds of danger to self or others. Assessment should start as soon as possible. Usually proceeds to a Section 2.
- Maximum 72 hours.
- Application made by a doctor or a single nominated deputy.

#### Section 5(4) – Emergency holding power by a nurse

- Detention of an informal patient already in hospital and receiving psychiatric treatment, on grounds of danger to self or others.
- Nurses holding powers.
- Maximum six hours.
- Applied by a Registered Mental Nurse.

#### Section 57 – Consent to treatment

- For treatments which require consent AND a second opinion, ie. irreversible treatments, such as psychosurgery or hormonal implants.
- Informal or detained patients.

#### Section 58 – Consent to treatment

- For any treatment which requires consent OR a second opinion, eg. ECT or prolonged (more than three months) medication.
- There is no time limit but should be renewed annually.
- Detained patients only.

**Section 59**
- As for Section 58, but the person does not consent and thus requires a doctor appointed by the MHA Commission.

**Section 117**
- After-care co-ordination for long-term patients (post Sections 3, 37, 47, 48). Sets a planned programme, with a named responsible person. May include in-patients.

**Section 136**
- Removal from a public place to a place of safety by a police constable. Must then be assessed by an ASW and Doctor.
- Maximum 72 hours.

## COMPULSORY DETENTION ORDERS (mentally abnormal offenders)

**Section 35**
- Remand to hospital for a medical report (on grounds of mental disorder).
- Made by Magistrates or Crown Court.
- 28 days duration, renewable every 28 days up to a maximum of 12 weeks.

**Section 36**
- Remand to hospital for treatment of a defendent awaiting trial, made by Crown Court.
- 28 days duration, renewable up to a maximum of 12 weeks.

**Section 37 – Hospital treatment Order**
- Hospital and guardianship order for convicted persons (Court equivalent of Section 3).
- Made by Crown (or exceptionally by Magistrates) Court.
- Six-month treatment order, renewable for 6 months, then yearly.
- Appeal allowed during the second 6 months, then yearly.

**Section 38**
- Interim Hospital order for assessment, allowing treatment for

a convicted person (Hospitalisation appropriate).
- Made by Magistrates or Crown Court – no appeal allowed.
- 12 weeks duration, renewable at 28 day intervals up to a maximum of 6 months.

**Section 41**
- Restriction order for a convicted person (to protect public from serious harm).
- Imposed by Crown Court. Only dischargable by the Home Secretary.
- Not usually time limited.

**Mental Health Review Tribunal:**
Patients, or their nearest relatives, may appeal to the M.H.R.T., which has the power to grant leave and transfer or discharge patients.

## 6.2 NEW PSYCHOTROPIC DRUGS EXPECTED

This is a list of drugs which are known to have a product license application lodged in the UK or where it is thought to be planned soon. The time between application and approval can be as short as six months or as long as two or more years, depending upon the data presented and perceived risks. Accurate marketing dates are thus not available.

The author would be grateful for any additional information or corrections to help with this section, which relies to a large extent on 'randomly acquired' information.

**Drugs or preparations possible in 2003–2004**
**Adderall \***

Adderall is a racemic mixture of d- and l-amphetamine, approved in USA for ADHD and possibly to be licensed in UK/Europe. In one study, 54% responded 'in a positive fashion' to Adderall. 38% were poor or non-responders but acute anxiety occurred in 4 of 7 with co-morbid anxiety (n=24, open, Horrigan and Barnhill, *J Clin Psych* 2000, **61**, 414–17). It appears effective as a once-a-day preparation (n=584, RCT, p/c, d/b, Biederman *et al, Pediatrics* 2002, **110**, 258–66; Pelham *et al, Pediatrics* 1999, **104**, 1300–11).

## Aripiprazole ('Abilify', BMS, 2003?)

See chapter one. This drug is available in US and several other countries, and may be available in Europe during 2003.

## Atomoxetine (Lilly, 2003/4)

This is a desipramine analogue and non-stimulant NARI for ADHD, with low side effects, especially insomnia and weight loss. It has been compared favourably with methylphenidate (n=228, RCT, open, Kratochvil *et al, J Am Acad Child Adolesc Psychiatry* 2002, **41**, 776–84) and placebo (n=291, RCT, d/b, p/c, Biederman *et al, Pediatrics* 2002, **110**, e75; n=297, RCT, p/c, 8/52, Michelson *et al, Pediatrics* 2001, **108**, E83).

## Duloxetine ('Cymbalta', Lilly, 2004?) *

An SNRI antidepressant, duloxetine was superior to placebo and with a trend to superiority over fluoxetine (n=173, d/b, p/c, Goldstein *et al, J Clin Psych* 2002, **63**, 225–31) and 60mg/d was superior to placebo in MDD, with nausea, dry mouth and somnolence the main ADRs (n=245, RCT, d/b, 9/52, Detke *et al, J Clin Psych* 2002, **63**, 308–15). Submitted in USA 2001.

## Fluoxetine (Prozac once-weekly) *

A 90mg once weekly oral form (slow-release to reduce peak levels) has been marketed in USA. Since fluoxetine and norfluoxetine have long half-lives and 5mg/d is the lowest effective dose, 90mg a week should be therapeutically active. In an abrupt switch study from daily and established sertraline, citalopram or paroxetine, 79% completed successfully and 9.3% discontinued due to lack of efficacy. It was well tolerated in all groups (n=246, Miner *et al, J Clin Psych* 2002, **63**, 232–40). After a 13/52 open trial of 20mg/d fluoxetine, responders allocated to once-weekly enteric-coated fluoxetine 90mg had similar relapse rates to 20mg/d, significantly lower than placebo (n=501, 25/52, RCT, Schmidt *et al, J Clin Psych* 2000, **61**, 851–57). Slightly higher compliance has been shown over daily fluoxetine (86% vs 79%) (Lilly study, n=117, 3/12, Claxton *et al, J Clin Psych* 2000, **61**, 928–32).

## Gepirone ('Ariza', Organon) *

Gepirone is a $5HT_{1A}$ partial agonist, with some alpha-2 activity, being developed as an antidepressant, with a launch planned 2003 in USA. Gepirone needs an SR form to reduce g/i upset. The main ADR is lightheadedness (Leslie, *Curr Opin Investig Drugs* 2001, **2**, 1120–27) and needs care in poor renal function (n=37, Dogterom *et al, Clin Drug Invest* 2002, **22**, 513–22).

## Iloperidone (Novartis)

Iloperidone is a D2 and 5HT2 antagonist, with some alpha-1 blocking activity, currrently undergoing phase III trials for schizophrenia.

## Melotonin (Genzyme)

This may be licensed for insomnia, as it produces a significant improvement in sleep (n=24, Dolberg *et al, Am J Psych* 1998, **155**, 1119–21), following 5–10mg at 9pm ('interesting, but not miraculous' review, Anon, *Prescrire Internat* 1998, **7**, 180–87, 83 refs).

## Milnacipran (Ixel) (Fabre)

SNRI, license currently on hold in UK, available in France (Peuch *et al, Int Clin Psychopharmacol* 1997, **12**, 99–108; study by Leinonen *et al, Acta Psych Scand* 1997, **96**, 497–504). Reviews by Lecrubier (*Hum Psychopharmacol* 1997, **12**, S127–S134) and Kasper (*Hum Psychopharmacol* 1997, **12**, S135–S141, Spencer and Wilde, *Drugs* 1998, **56**, 405–27), pharmacodynamics in young and elderly (Hindmarch *et al, B J Clin Pharmacology* 2000, **49**, 118–25).

## Pregabalin (Pfizer, 2003?) *

Pregabalin is a gabapentenoid, being trialled for GAD, epilepsy and neuropathic pain.

**Tianeptine ('Stablon', Servier)** *

'Novel tricyclic' (*B J Psych* 1992, **160** Suppl 15) which apparently works as a selective serotonin re-uptake enhancing properties, but decreases both serotonin transporter mRNA and binding sites, just like other SSRIs (Kuroda *et al, Eur J Pharmacol* 1993, **268**, R3–5). It may also increase extracellular dopamine (Sacchetti *et al, Eur J Pharmacol* 1993, **236**, 171–75), like bupropion. Available in France. Phase III trials in UK. Review (Wagstaff *et al, CNS Drugs* 2001, **15**, 231–59).

**Ziprasidone ('Zeldox', Pfizer, 2004?)**

See chapter one. This drug is available in several European countries and in the US, but not to be licensed in the UK in the immediate future.

---

Other drugs or preparations known to be under study and for which UK license applications may be made in due course:

**Eptastigmine**

Anticholinesterase for Alzheimer's disease (RCT, n=491, Imbimbo *et al, Neurology* 1999, **52**, 700–9), with good efficacy (6/12, d/b, p/c, n=349, Imbimbo *et al, Demen & Ger Cog Disord* 2000, **11**, 17–24) but potential adverse haematological effects.

**Nalmefene (Schering Plough)**

More potent and longer-acting version of naloxone. Launched USA 1996.

**Pramipexole (Mirapex, Pharmacia)**

D2 agonist being investigated for depression and schizophrenia.

**Rufinamide (Novartis)**

GABA reuptake inhibitor for epilepsy.

---

**6.3 LABORATORY TEST INTERPRETATIONS**

A guide to normal ranges, variations, causes and drug influences. Local ranges may differ slightly from these here.

---

**UREA AND ELECTROLYTES (U&ES)**

**Bicarbonate** 22–30mmol/l

**Calcium** 2.25–2.6mmol/l
↑ malignancy (55%), hyperparathyroidism (35%), hyperthyroidism, Vit D excess.
↓ hypoparathyroidism, Vit D deficiency.
▲ OCs, lithium, thiazides.
▼ barbiturates, cimetidine, corticosteroids, phenytoin.

**Chloride** 9–105mmol/l

**Glucose** 3.3–5.6mmol/l
↑ >6.7 overnight=diabetes mellitus?
▲ cimetidine, OCs, furosemide, lithium, phenothiazines, thiazides, phenytoin, some atypicals
(▲) ascorbic acid, levodopa, metronidazole.
▼ dextropropoxyphene.
(▼) ascorbic acid.

**Magnesium** 0.7–1.2mmol/l
↑ renal failure
↓ severe diarrhoea

**Phosphate** 0.8–1.4mmol/l (Adversely affects calcium metabolism)
↓ malnutrition (esp in alcoholics)

**Potassium 3.5–5.3mmol/l**
↑ dangerous. Treat as emergency.
↓ produces muscle weakness.
▼ salbutamol, insulin.

**Protein** Total 50–70 g/l
Albumin 35–55 g/l
↑ =haemoconcentration
↓ =haemodilution, neuropathy, cirrhosis, catabolism.

**Sodium 133–149mmol/l (Rate of change is as important as the actual level)**
↑ excess fluid loss/poor intake, renal failure.
↓ cardiac or renal failure, D&V, chest disorders (infections or carcinoma), hypoalbuminaemia, bulimia?
▲ high dose sodium salt antibiotics, lithium.
▼ diuretics (esp thiazides), steroids, carbamazepine, oxcarbazepine, tricyclics, SSRIs, chlorpropamide, clofibrate.

## Urea (2.5–8.0mmol/l)
↑ renal failure, catabolism, haemorrhage
▲ salicylates, tetracyclines.

## RENAL FUNCTION

### Creatinine clearance
M 97–140ml/min,
F 85–125ml/min
(Best measure of GFR if collection of the 24-hour samples is accurate).

### Creatinine conc
M 50–120mol/l
F 40–100mol/l
↑ Catabolism, pregnancy. Should decrease with age.
(▲) ascorbic acid, methyldopa.
▲ salicylates, captopril, cimetidine, co-trimoxazole.

### Urea (BUN) 1–5mmol/l
↑ renal failure, high protein food, catabolism.

## LIVER FUNCTION TESTS (LFTS)

Ranges quoted by laboratories vary with the method and conditions of the assay.

### ALT (SGPT) 5–30 iu/l
↑ hepatocellular damage, cholestasis, occasionally cirrhosis.
▲ alcohol, OCs, levodopa, phenothiazines, phenytoin, valproate, antibiotics.
▼ vigabatrin.
(▼) metronidazole.

### Albumin 35–55 g/l
↓ oedema, neuropathy, cirrhosis
(▲) penicillins.
▼ alcohol, phenytoin.

### Alkaline Phosphatase (ALP) 20–100 iu/l
↑ cholestasis, hepatocellular damage, bone disease (eg. Pagets, carcinoma), pregnancy.
▲ alcohol, carbamazepine, disulfiram, phenothiazines, phenytoin.
(▼) nitrofurantoin, zinc.

### Aspartate transaminase (AST or SGOT) 5–40 iu/l
↑ hepatocellular damage, cholestasis, cirrhosis, infarction, muscle trauma, respiratory failure.
▼ vigabatrin.

## Bilirubin 2–20mmol/l
↑ liver cell damage, cholestasis, haemolytic states.
(▲) beta-blockers, valproate, isulfiram, phenothiazines, alcohol, antibiotics.
(▼) ascorbic acid.

### Gamma-Glutamyl transferase (GGT) 5–45 iu/l
↑ cholestasis, hepatitis, cirrhosis, cellular damage (eg. paracetamol or disulfiram OD), enzyme inducers (especially phenobarbital and phenytoin), excess alcohol, metastatic carcinoma
▲ alcohol, barbiturates, OCs, phenytoin, oxcarbazepine, simvastatin.

### Prothrombin ratio 1–1.2
### Prothrombin time 10–135
↑ severe, usually chronic, liver damage.

## BLOOD

### Blood pH 7.35–7.45
Outside range metabolic function is impaired.

### WBC/WCC 4.0–11.0×10⁹/l
$$WBC/WCC\ 4.0–11.0\times10^9/l$$
↑↑ malignancy.
↑ infection.
↓ many drugs, some infections.
**RBC** M $4.5–6\times10^{12}$/l
F $4.3–5.5\times10^{12}$/l
↑ fluid loss, polycythaemia.
↓ fluid overload, anaemia, marrow aplasia.
**Hb** M 13–18 g/dl
F 12–16 g/dl
↓ haemorrhage, iron deficiency, marrow depression.

### MCV (Mean Cell Volume) 80–95 fl
↑ folate or B12 deficiency, liver disease, alcohol.
↓ iron deficiency.
**ESR** M 0–9mm/h
F 0–20mm/h
(viscosities now more usually used).
↑ infections, inflammatory diseases.

### Lymphocytes 1–4×10⁹/l
↑ (lymphocytosis) mononucleosis, viral infections, TB, some leukemias, auto-immune diseases, toxoplasmosis.

↓ (lymphopenia) in marrow failure, plus treatment with corticosteroids and azathioprine.

**Platelets 100–450×10⁹/l**

↓ marrow failure or toxicity, leukaemia, splenomegaly.

**Neutrophils 1.8–8×10⁹/l (45–75% of WBCs)**

↑ infection, inflammation, carcinoma, leukaemia, gout.

↓ viral infections, autoimmune disease, marrow failure drugs

▼ chlorpromazine, phenytoin, chloramphenicol etc.

**Monocytes 0.1–1.1×10⁹/l**

↑ (monocytosis) in TB, endocarditis, typhoid, leukaemia.

**Eosinophils 0.04–0.8×10⁹/l (1–4% of WBCs)**

↑ (eosinophilia) in atopic asthma, hay fever, worm infestations, lymphomas, skin disease.

**Basophils 0.01–0.4×10⁹/l**

↑ (basophil leucocytosis) leukaemia, ulcerative colitis.

## MISCELLANEOUS

**Amylase (serum) 60–300 μ/l**

↑ acute pancreatitis, abdominal trauma, renal failure.

▲ furosemide, morphine, valproate.

**Blood pressure (Adult) ≤ 140/90**

Systolic/Diastolic, the latter more important. Possibly higher limit allowed in elderly.

**Cortisol/Dexamethasone Suppression Test** 200nmol/l

↑ adrenal hyperplasia or tumour (or depression?)

**CSF Protein 0.2–0.5 g/l**

↑ infection, haemorrhage.

**CSF glucose 2.8–4mmol/l**

↑ haemorrhage.

↓ infection.

**Folate Serum 2.5–15 μg/l**

↓ best guide to folate deficiency.

**Folate RBC 150–750 μg/l**

↓ guide to long term folate deficiency.

▼ chloramphenicol, erythromycin, penicillins

(▼) barbiturates, OCs, phenytoin, alcohol.

**Iron Serum** M 10–30 μmol/l
        F 7–25 μmol/l

↑ inflammation.

↓ iron deficiency, rheumatoid arthritis.

**Iron Binding Capacity (serum) 45–72 μmol/l**

↑ iron deficiency.

↓ rheumatoid arthritis.

**Lipids:**

— **cholesterol** 4–7mmol/l

↑ hyperlipidaemia, diabetes, nephrotic syndrome, biliary obstruction.

▲ disulfiram, levodopa, OCs, phenytoin, oxcarbazepine.

▼ metronidazole, tetracyclines.

— **triglyceride** 0.6–1.8mmol/l
(post 12hr fasting)

↑ diabetes, nephrotic syndrome pancreatitis, alcohol abuse.

▲ alcohol, beta-blockers, clozapine, OCs, olanzapine, quetiapine.

**Osmolality 285–295mOsm/kg**

↑ fluid depletion

↓ fluid excess.

**pCO₂ 4.5–6 kPa or 34–45mmHg**

Measure of respiratory function

**Thyroxine-total 60–140nmol/l**

↑ hyperthyroidism (Grave's Disease—confirm by TRH)—varies with age

↓ hypothyroidism

▲ beta-blockers, OCs.

▼ carbamazepine, lithium, phenytoin, salicylates.

**T4/Thyroxine-Free 10–25pmol/l**

↑ hypothyroidism (Myxodema)

↓ hyperthyroidism

**T3 1.1–2.3nmol/l**

↑ hypothyroidism

↓ hyperthyroidism

**TSH 0.15–3.20mIU/l**

↑ hypothyroidism

↓ hyperthyroidism

**Urate 150–500 umol/l**

↑ purine metabolic defect, carcinoma, diminished excretion (eg. acidosis, renal failure, diuretics)

▲ alcohol, furosemide, salicylates, thiazides.

**Vitamin B12 160–900 ng/l**

↓ diet deficiency, pernicious anaemia, ileitis or short bowel syndrome. May lead to macrocytic anaemia and peripheral neuropathy.

---

**KEY**

---

↑ increased level mainly caused by:
↓ decreased level mainly caused by:
▲ drugs which raise level include:
▼ drugs which lower level include:
(▲) drugs which appear to raise levels by test interference:
(▼) drugs which appear to lower levels by test interference:

# INDEX

All the main psychotropic drugs are indexed according to their BNF or other main indications in chapter one, but obviously may appear elsewhere. In order to keep the index down to a manageable size, you are then referred to the index listing for that drugs chemical or therapeutic group. Individual drugs should be looked up under their drug group.

## Abbreviations used

\* = new data added to the text since the 2001/02 edition

**For details of studies:**
n = number of patients
RCT = Randomised controlled trial
d/b = double-blind
c/0 = cross-over
o/p = out-patient
s/b = Single blind (trial)
p/c = placebo-controlled

**Other abbreviations:**
AAPCD = American Academy of Pediatrics Committee on Drugs
ACh = Acetylcholine
ADHD = Attention deficit hyperactivity disorder
ADD = Attention deficit disorder
ADME = Absorption, distribution, metabolism and excretion
ADR = Adverse drug reaction
AED = Anti-epileptic drug
AFP = Alpha-fetoprotein
AIMS = Abnormal involuntary movement scale
APE = Acute psychiatric emergency
APA = American Psychiatric Association
AWS = Alcohol withdrawal syndrome

BAP = British Association for Psychopharmacology
BDI = Beck Depression Inventory
BDZ = Benzodiazepine(s)
BMA = British Medical Association
BMI = Body mass index
BNF = British National Formulary
BPD = Borderline psychiatric disorder
BPRS = Brief Psychiatric Rating Scale
bp = blood pressure
BP = British Pharmacopoeia

CBT = Cognitive behavioural therapy
CBZ = Carbamazepine
CBZ-E = Carbamazepine-epoxide
CCK = Cholecystokinin

CDSR = Cochrane Database Systematic Reviews
CGI = Clinical global impression
CHD = coronary heart disease
CNS = Central nervous system
CPK = Creatinine phosphokinase
CSE = Convulsive Status Epilepticus
CSM = Committee on the Saftey of Medicines

D1 = Dopamine-1 (receptor)
D2 = Dopamine-2 (receptor)
DA = Dopamine
DSM-IV = Diagnostic Statistical Manual IV

e/c = enteric-coated
ECG = Electrocardiogram
ECT = Electroconvulsive therapy
EBMH = Evidence-Based Mental Health (Journal)
EEG = Electro-encephalogram
EPO = Evening primrose oil
EPSE = Extra-pyramidal side-effects

FBC = Full blood count

GABA = Gamma-aminobutyric acid
GFR = Glomerular filtration rate
GTC = Generalised tonic-clonic (seizure)

5-HT = 5-hydroxy-tryptamine
HF = heart failure

IV = Intra-venous
IM = Intra-muscular
INR = International normalized ratio
ISE = Ion-selective electrode

L/A = Long-acting
LD = Low dose
LFT = Liver function tests
LTG = Lamotrigine

MAOI = Mono-amine oxidase inhibitor
MHA = Mental Health Act (1983)
MI = Manufacturers'

information
MMSE = Mini-Mental State Examination

NA = Noradrenaline
NE = Norepinephrine
N/K = Not known
NMDA = N-methyl-D-aspartate receptor
NMS = Neuroleptic malignant syndrome
NNT = Numbers needed to treat

OCD = Obsessive-compulsive disorder
O/C = Oral contraceptive
OD = Overdose
OTC = Over-the-counter (medicine)

PBNP = Prog Neuropsychopharmacol Biol Psych
PD = Personality disorder, Pro-drug
PMH = Previous medical history
PMS = Pre-menstrual syndrome
PT = Prothrombin time
PTSD = Post-traumtic stress disorder
REM = Rapid eye movement
RIMA = Reversible Inhibitor of Monoamine-A
RPSGB = Royal Pharmaceutical Society of Great Britain
RT = Rapid tranquillisation

SA = Short-acting
s/c = sub-cutaneous
SF = Sugar-free
SIB = Self-injurious behaviour
SJW = St. John's wort
SPC = Summary of product characteristics
SSRI = Serotonin-selective reuptake inhibitor

$t_{1/2}$ = half-life
TCA = Tricyclic antidepressant
TD = Tardive dyskinesia
TDM = Therapeutic drug monitoring

U&E = Urea and electrolytes
USP = United States Pharmacopoeia